PRINCIPLES OF

MICROECONOMICS

FOURTH EDITION

RYAN C. AMACHER
Professor of Economics, Clemson University

HOLLEY H. ULBRICH
Alumni Professor of Economics, Clemson University

HB67DA1
PUBLISHED BY
SOUTH-WESTERN PUBLISHING CO.
CINCINNATI   WEST CHICAGO, IL   CARROLLTON, TX   LIVERMORE, CA

1 2 3 4 5 6 7 8 9 0 Ki 7 6 5 4 3 2 1 0 9 8

Printed in the United States of America

Amacher, Ryan C.
    Principles of economics.

    Includes index.
    1. Economics.   I. Ulbrich, Holley H.
II. Title.
HB171.5.A397   1988   330   88-26391
ISBN 0-538-80074-7

PREFACE

The fourth edition of a textbook is a challenge—we fully realize the need to keep what users like, to identify those things that need to be changed, and to make the textbook up-to-date and responsive to changing ideas, methods, and interests. In putting together this fourth edition, we have been fortunate to have feedback not only from users of earlier editions but also from over 200 teachers of principles of economics.

We reiterate our goal from earlier editions. We do not want to make professional economists out of students. A common complaint is that instructors and textbook authors treat the principles of economics course as the first step in work toward the Ph.D. This text is not intended to train professional economists but to provide the analytical tools that economic theory offers the policy analyst or adviser to governments or business firms. This book is intended to teach enough theory to enable students to understand policy, and to present enough policy situations to give them an understanding of how to apply the theory.

CHANGES IN THE FOURTH EDITION

A major change that has been incorporated into this fourth edition has been the development of a truly international approach for every chapter. The need to teach introductory economics from the standpoint of its importance as a global phenomenon was one of the real concerns that surfaced during three seminars held by South-Western Publishing for instructors in the field of introductory economics. Thus, we have created International Perspective "boxes" for each chapter that extend the material presented from the purely domestic scene to its worldwide implications and focus on related concrete international issues. The chapter that deals with the Great Depression also shows the effects of the Depression in Europe. In like manner, the chapter on poverty and income distribution looks at how income redistribution is handled in other countries; and even the introductory supply and demand presentation illustrates market supply and demand curves by including foreign sellers (our imports) among suppliers and foreign buyers (our exports) among demanders.

We have attempted to address the needs of the student in a much more direct fashion by including frequent summaries and study materials. Key terms and their definitions in the margins have been retained, as have the numbered chapter summaries, but the number of end-of-chapter questions has been greatly increased, and "list boxes"—concise summaries of main points—are now featured within the chapters.

Our retention of the marginal definitions and the single column format should not mislead anyone with regard to our concern about length—the need to keep this book from becoming encyclopedic, as textbooks do tend to become in subsequent editions. In person and in a telephone survey, instructors kept telling us that sixteen chapters were all they could handle in one semester. The first sixteen chapters of this edition cover the four introductory chapters and all of the macro chapters. If micro is taught in the second semester, a brief reprise of the introductory chapters should make it possible for the instructor to cover all of the micro chapters. We have eliminated the introductory microeconomics chapter and made the chapter on indifference curves into a briefer appendix, while splitting resource markets into two chapters. We have also been more selective in drawing and locating the graphs, reducing their number by substituting intuitive explanations in some places.

Chapter 1 features a new emphasis on methodology and a much-enhanced appendix on the use and interpretation of graphs. Chapter 2 has been reorganized to link specialization and comparative advantage more closely to the production possibilities curve. It uses circular flow as a capstone to tie the chapter's concepts together and provide an overview of macro and micro. Chapter 3 has a new section that gives examples of allocative mechanisms that have been used to replace the market. The material on the interaction of law and economics that appeared at the end of the third edition has been moved to Chapter 4, which also contains a new section on privatization of governmental functions.

Chapter 5 reintroduces and reviews the concepts of supply and demand with new examples and material brought together from several chapters of the previous edition. Chapter 6 (elasticity) and Chapter 7 (utility) are much the same as they were, except that the chapter on the indifference curve has been condensed and placed at the end of Chapter 7 as an appendix.

Chapter 8, which introduces the student to the theory of the firm, has new material on households as firms and on nonprofit firms. There is a new appendix covering isoquant and isocost curves at the end of Chapter 8, which is intended to parallel the development of indifference curves in the appendix to Chapter 7. The chapters on pure competition, monopoly, monopolistic competition, and oligopoly are much the same as in the third edition, but with updated examples and problems. There is new material concerning competition on the buyers' side of the market, a section on "what's so great about pure competition," and a discussion of monopoly rent seeking. The final chapter of this section updates antitrust and regulatory changes that have occurred since the last edition.

The long chapter on factor markets has been split. We begin in Chapter 14 with a discussion of marginal productivity and relate it to labor. Chapter 15 follows the labor productivity theory with a discussion of U.S. labor history. All the material on rent, interest, and profit appears in a new Chapter 16. The section ends with the chapter on poverty and income distribution. It has been reorganized to emphasize the market determination of income distribution and its relationship to poverty, and to give more background on recent debates about the role of government in income redistribution.

Chapters 18 and 19 in turn discuss market failure and governmental failure. There is new material and additional examples on both sides of the argument. The appendix to Chapter 19 presents case studies in two areas of market and government failure: the farm problem and urban problems.

The international section comprises four chapters. The chapter on international trade now contains a longer discussion of nontariff barriers and the new immigration law. The section on cartels has been deleted since they are covered in the oligopoly chapter. The international monetary chapter has added a box on the gold buffs in the light of current discussions about revamping the international monetary system. The development chapter has been updated and the comparative chapter has been revised to reflect the reform movements in the Peoples' Republic of China and the Soviet Union.

Finally, the concluding chapter, on becoming an economist, has been thoroughly rewritten and expanded while retaining the features that have made it popular. It looks at what economists do, how much they are paid, how they are educated, and why students might major in economics. This chapter answers a host of questions that potential majors might have about economics as a career option. The various branches of the total field of economics are discussed, and a new final section provides suggestions for regular reading for those students who might wish to keep abreast of current economic issues. No other textbook on the market touches upon so many career-related aspects of economic studies.

IMPORTANT FEATURES OF THE FOURTH EDITION

The following features make this introductory text a useful and unique teaching and learning tool:

Organization

This book allows the student to see the power of economic analysis very quickly. As soon as elementary tools are discussed, they are applied to a wide range of social policy questions.

The length and content of the fourth edition represent a very careful weighing of thoroughness against brevity. While we did not go quite so far as to apply "zero-based editing" by requiring each item to justify its inclusion, we did carefully rethink what to include and did some pruning to make room for new material and ideas.

Important Economists, Economic Issues, and International Perspectives

Each chapter includes boxed insets. One inset is always an international perspective, extending the material in the chapter to a global view. Some are extensions of the theory, others historical events or current issues. Other insets may deal with an important economist, an important institution, a relevant historical event, another international issue, or a pressing current issue. The insets are placed close to the relevant chapter material and highlight the development of theory or its application to current domestic or global problems.

List Boxes, Questions, and Reading Suggestions

A new feature of the fourth edition is the "list box"—a capsule summary of the preceding section or sections placed at strategic points in each chapter. There is a much longer selection of end-of-chapter questions for use as review, homework, or class discussion. Suggested answers are provided in the instructor's manual. The carefully annotated "Suggestions for Further Reading" in each chapter have been updated and expanded to include current material.

Glossary

All terms that appear in boldface type and in the margins of the book are defined in the Glossary.

TEACHING AND STUDY AIDS

In addition to the teaching and study aids that make up part of the textbook—the list boxes, chapter questions, and summaries—there is also a *Study Guide*, and *Instructor's Manual*, and a *Test Bank*. All of these materials were prepared by Patricia Pando of Albany State College, who prepared the *Test Bank* for the third edition. The revised and expanded *Test Bank* for the fourth edition uses a new test generator, MicroSWAT II, for the disk version. The *Study Guide* has been completely rewritten to meet the students' needs, and the *Instructor's Manual* has been enlarged and reworked to assist the instructor in planning, organizing, and opening up the material in the text for class discussion.

The Study Guide

The *Study Guide* is completely new for the fourth edition. A useful new feature is an exercise page for each chapter which can be used for homework or quizzes. (Answers are provided in the *Instructor's Manual*.) We think that this greatly improved *Study Guide* will be a real asset for your students. Each chapter in the *Study Guide* corresponds to a chapter in the textbook and includes a chapter overview; matching questions based on the important terms and concepts; true/false questions, review problems requiring numerical and/or graphical solutions (where appropriate), and multiple choice questions for review; a review of the learning objectives for the chapter; complete answers to all questions in the *Study Guide*; and the chapter exercise.

The Instructor's Manual

The *Instructor's Manual* also contains a chapter corresponding to each chapter in the text. Each chapter of the *Manual* includes a short discussion of the purposes of the chapter, an outline corresponding to the headings in the text chapter, learning objectives for the chapter, a summary of the chapter, key terms from the chapter with their definitions, suggestions for lectures, extensions, and applications, suggested answers to all end-of-chapter questions, and answers to the *Study Guide* exercises. Transparency masters are also included in the *Instructor's Manual*.

The Test Bank

An extensive *Test Bank* is available to adopters. It consists of over 2,000 multiple-choice questions, none of which duplicate those in the *Study Guide*. The *Test Bank* received a major overhaul with the third edition and response has been very positive. The fourth edition updates and refines the good work that went into the previous edition. To facilitate preparation of multiple-choice examinations, the *Test Bank* is available both in written form and on disks with the test generator program already mentioned, MicroSWAT II. MicroSWAT II allows the instructor to create new questions, edit questions, and delete questions.

Transparencies

A set of color acetate transparencies that reproduces important illustrations from *Principles of Economics* is available to adoptors.

The Microcomputer Tutorials

The microcomputer tutorials were first introduced with the third edition. These disks, available for IBM® or IBM®-compatible machines[1], contain eight segments—four in micro, four in macro—designed for either individual or group use when reviewing basic concepts. These tutorials have been thoroughly revised in response to suggestions from users and are available to adopters. Copies may be made for student use.

The Video Tapes

New with the fourth edition is a set of six video segments featuring the authors. These are suitable for classroom use, often as a way of introducing the topic. The videos, available for adopters, are accompanied by a user's guide with suggested follow-up questions for classroom discussion.

ACKNOWLEDGEMENTS

We are grateful to the following individuals who made specific comments that were incorporated into the fourth edition or reviewed drafts of this fourth edition:

Greg Brown, Lincoln Memorial University
Bernard Feigenbaum, California State University, Northridge
Stephen Happel, Arizona State University
Dannie E. Harrison, Murray State University
David Jobson, Keystone Junior College
Andrew Larkin, St. Cloud State University
Anton D. Lowenberg, California State University, Northridge
Robert Main, Butler University
Robert McAuliffe, Babson College
Rob Roy McGregor, University of South Carolina
Gary Quinlivin, St. Vincent College
Malcolm Russell, Andrews University
Fred A. Tarpley, Jr., Georgia Institute of Technology
John and Mellie Warner, Clemson University
William F. Watson, Jr., Brunswick Junior College
Bernard J. Widera, University of Wisconsin, Madison

We are most appreciative of a group of senior undergraduate students enrolled in the international economics course at Clemson University who came up with suggestions for the international perspectives: Sandy Claghorn, Scott Jackson, Katie Mahon, Henrik Skov, Dave Thrams, Stefanie Weber, and Ricky Wright. Stephen Silver and Ross Newman, both of Bentley College, prepared detailed reviews of the tutorial software. Russell Shannon of Clemson University provided much valued assistance both as a reviewer and in developing the videos.

In addition, we owe a significant debt of gratitude to users and reviewers of the earlier editions of the textbook. In particular, we would like to thank the following individuals who took the time to write or to

---

1. IBM® is a registered trademark of International Business Machines Corporation. Any reference to IBM equipment refers to this footnote.

make suggestions to South-Western representatives regarding the first three editions of this book:

Ogden Allsbrook, University of Georgia
Lari Arjomand, Clayton State College
Mohsen Bahmani-Oskooee, University of Wisconsin, Milwaukee
Ted Ball, Consumnes River College
Allen Bergland, Northern Arizona University
Jack Blicksilver, Georgia State University
Robert Bray, California State Polytechnic University
Paul Burgess, Arizona State University
Doris Cash, Clayton State College
David Crary, Eastern Michigan University
Larry Davis, East Texas State University
Paul DePippo, Glendale Community College
Larry Ellis, Appalachian State University
Keith Evans, California State University, Northridge
Mark Evans, California State College, Bakersfield
Gregory Falls, Central Michigan University
Lois Fenske, South Puget Sound Community College
Rudy Fichtenbaum, Wright State University
Gordon Galbraith, Portland Community College
Brother Edward Grinder, St. Vincent College
Amyra Grossbard-Shechtman, San Diego State University
William Gunther, University of Alabama
W. W. Hall, University of North Carolina, Wilmington
Bruce Harger, Lake Superior State College
Pershing Hill, University of Alaska
Ken Howard, East Texas Baptist College
Jo Ann Jones, Georgia College
David Klingaman, Ohio University
Michael Knedler, Iowa Western Community College
Lubomyr M. Kowal, University of Michigan, Flint
Michael Lawson, Boston University
Dale Lehman, Fort Lewis College
C. Mather Lindsay, Emory University
Albert Link, University of North Carolina, Greensboro
Adolph Mark, DePaul University
Nolin Masih, St. Cloud State University
Paul McGouldrick, SUNY Binghamton
Pat McMurry, Missouri Western State College
Michael Melvin, Arizona State University
Clark Nardinelli, Clemson University
Narayan Nargund, Allegheny College
Gerald Nickelsburg, University of Southern California
Tilton Prater, Meridian Junior College
Abu Selimuddin, Berkshire Community College
Teresa Sherrouse, Augusta College
Edwin Stecher, University of San Diego
Donald Swanson, Indiana University Southeast
Dana Thompson, Loma Linda University
Lloyd Valentine, University of Cincinnati
Myles Wallace, Clemson University
Norman Walzer, Western Illinois University
Frank Wert, Central State University

Larry Wilson, Sandhills Community College
Charles Wishart, Indiana State University
N. Keith Womer, University of Mississippi
Joesph Zoric, University of Steubenville

Finally, we want to thank our spouses, Susan and Carl, who continue to help with many of the technical aspects of revision, and are constant sources of encouragement and inspiration.

Ryan C. Amacher
Holley H. Ulbrich

BRIEF CONTENTS

xi

PART 5 MARKET FAILURE, GOVERNMENT FAILURE, PUBLIC CHOICE

PART 6 THE WORLD ECONOMY

PART 7 BEING AN ECONOMIST

CONTENTS

xiii

PART 2   DEMAND AND CONSUMER CHOICE

PART 3   MARKETS

PART 7   BEING AN ECONOMIST

PART ONE

INTRODUCTION
TO ECONOMICS

CHAPTER 1

ECONOMICS, ECONOMIC ISSUES, AND ECONOMIC METHODS

INTRODUCTION

In this introductory chapter, we explore what economics is, the kinds of problems and issues that economists deal with, the methods that economists use, and some basic assumptions of the economic view of the world. We particularly want you to develop an economic way of thinking. The chapter ends with an introduction to some typical issues studied by economists.

WHY STUDY ECONOMICS?

Before we proceed, it is appropriate to address the question of why you should study economics. Many, perhaps most, of you are in an economics course and are therefore reading this textbook because you are required to do so. It's very likely that economics is a required course, whether you are majoring in liberal arts, business, engineering, or other fields. The initial response to the question Why study economics? could be that professors in many fields believe that training in economics is a good foundation for almost all students. But this really doesn't answer the question; it simply avoids it. Therefore, we will offer you some better answers.

The fact that professors from many different disciplines think economics belongs in your curriculum offers a clue to why you should study economics. Economics interacts with almost all other academic disciplines. It is intimately intertwined with current events, and it has a significant effect on political events, both domestic and international. One possible answer, then, is quite straightforward: You should study economics to understand better the profound effect that economics has on the world.

A second reason for studying economics is based on the impact that economic ideas and theories have on world leaders. Much of what political decision makers do is based on economic theory. As John Maynard Keynes, one of the most influential economists of all time, wrote:

The ideas of economists and political philosophers, both when they are right and when they are wrong, are more powerful than is commonly understood. Indeed, the world is ruled by little else. Practical men, who believe themselves to be quite exempt from any intellectual influences, are usually the slaves of some defunct economist. Madmen in authority, who hear voices in the air, are distilling their frenzy from some academic scribbler of a few years back. [1]

Keynes was saying that if we want to understand what politicians are advocating, be they great or be they mad, we must understand the economic theories upon which they are acting.

A third, and perhaps most important, reason for studying economics is that it provides a better understanding of how the world and its people function. Economic theory is very useful in understanding behavior because it allows the person who understands it to develop models with predictive power. As Alfred Marshall, another noted economist, wrote, "Economics is the study of mankind in the ordinary business of life." [2]

Finally, economics is fun, and people who are trained in economics find rewarding jobs and careers. The last chapter in this textbook describes the many career paths open to those with economics training. If you like to think in a logical fashion, you will enjoy studying economics.

WHAT IS ECONOMICS?

For most of you, this is your first course in economics. **Economics** is the scientific study of how people and institutions make decisions about producing and consuming goods and services and how they face the problem of scarcity.

The study of economics is often divided into microeconomics and macroeconomics. **Microeconomics** looks at the interactions of producers and consumers in individual markets—say, the market for shoes. It also examines the interactions between different markets—say, changes in the demand for steel on the market for aluminum. *Micro* is a Greek prefix meaning small. This is in contrast to the Greek prefix *macro*, which means large.

Macroeconomics, the study of the economy as a whole, is concerned with *aggregates*, or numbers that are determined by adding across many markets. Macroeconomics studies the behavior of economy-wide measures, such as the value of the final output that the economy produces in a given time period. It also studies measures derived from many individual markets taken together, such as the price level or total employment and unemployment.

ECONOMICS
The scientific study of how people and institutions make decisions about producing and consuming goods and services and how they face the problem of scarcity.

MICROECONOMICS
The study of individual market interactions. Microeconomics concentrates on production and consumption by the individual consumer, the firm, and the industry.

MACROECONOMICS
The study of the economy as a whole, or economic aggregates, such as the level of employment and the growth of total output.

1. J.M. Keynes, *The General Theory of Employment, Interest, and Money* (London: Macmillan Publishing Co., Inc., 1936), 383.

2. Alfred Marshall, *Principles of Economics*, 8th ed. (Don Mills, Ontario: The Macmillan Co. of Canada, Ltd., 1920), 323.

In both microeconomics and macroeconomics, the most important tools are demand and supply. The study of demand and supply helps to explain prices and outputs in individual markets. They also explain how prices and outputs in different markets are related. In microeconomics, you may look at the demand for the output of a single industry, such as bicycles. In macroeconomics, economists look at the overall level of prices and output for the economy as a whole, using aggregate demand and aggregate supply as the principal tools. Even though they are often studied separately, microeconomics and macroeconomics are very much related.

ECONOMICS IN RELATION TO OTHER FIELDS

Economics usually is classified as a **social science**. This label makes economics an academic relative of political science, sociology, psychology, and anthropology. All of these disciplines study the behavior of human beings, individually and in groups. They study different subsets of the actions and interactions of human beings. (For this reason they also are sometimes termed *behavioral sciences*.)

SOCIAL SCIENCE
A discipline that studies the behavior of human beings, individually and in groups, and examines their interactions.

Economics is particularly concerned with consumption, production, and resource use by individuals and groups. Economics is also concerned with the processes by which households and firms make decisions about the use of scarce resources. Inevitably, this definition of the "territory" of economics leads to some overlap with the other disciplines. Psychologists and economists share an interest in what motivates people to take certain actions. However, economists are primarily interested in those actions that are reflected in market activity or in economic decisions made through government. While sociologists are interested in all facets of organized human activity, economists are interested mainly in organized activities that relate to the production and consumption of goods and services. In general, economists assume that individuals pursue their own self-interest and respond to various signals or incentives in the light of that self-interest. Although that may seem obvious, it is a somewhat different viewpoint on human behavior from that of psychologists and sociologists. This perspective often leads economists to draw different conclusions. As you learn more about economics, you will better understand how it overlaps with, and how it differs from, other social sciences.

Economics is also part of a group of disciplines called **decision sciences**, which includes some branches of applied mathematics, operations research, and some areas of management and engineering. All of these disciplines deal with how individuals and groups make decisions. Economists are specifically interested in those decisions relating to production, consumption, and resource use. As a decision science, economics is closely allied to business and management courses.

DECISION SCIENCE
A discipline that deals with the processes by which decisions are made.

ECONOMIC THEORY AND METHOD

Economic theory often suffers from bad press. It is sometimes viewed as abstract and irrelevant, maybe even too difficult. In part, the

THE INTERNATIONAL PERSPECTIVE
THE NOBEL PRIZE FOR ECONOMICS

The Nobel Committee, set up by the Swedish Royal Academy of Sciences, awarded the first Nobel Prize in 1901. It wasn't until 1969, however, that the first *Nobel Prize for Economics* was awarded. The Bank of Sweden funded the 1969 prize to celebrate its 300th anniversary.

The emergence of economics into the Nobel Prize family, which includes chemistry, physics, and medicine, suggests that economics has surpassed most other social sciences in the eyes of the world's scientific community.

Receipt of a Nobel Prize is a high and monetarily rewarding honor for an economist.

More than half the recipients have been Americans. The following have been winners of the prize since 1969:

1969	Ragnar Frisch, Norway
	Jan Tinbergen, Netherlands
1970	Paul A. Samuelson, United States
1971	Simon Kuznets, United States
1972	Kenneth J. Arrow, United States
	Sir John R. Hicks, Great Britain
1973	Wassily Leontief, United States
1974	Gunnar Myrdal, Sweden
	Friedrich A. von Hayek, Great Britain
1975	Leonid V. Kantorovich, Soviet Union
	Tjalling C. Koopmans, United States
1976	Milton Friedman, United States
1977	James E. Meade, Great Britain
	Bertil Ohlin, Sweden
1978	Herbert A. Simon, United States
1979	Sir Arthur Lewis, Great Britain
	Theodore Schultz, United States
1980	Lawrence R. Klein, United States
1981	James Tobin, United States
1982	George Stigler, United States
1983	Gerard Debreu, United States
1984	Sir Richard Stone, Great Britain
1985	Franco Modigliani, United States
1986	James M. Buchanan, United States
1987	Robert Solow, United States

THEORY
A set of principles that can be used to make inferences about the world.

complaints are justified. Theory for theory's sake is a waste of time for most people. **Theory** is valuable, however, because it allows the development of a set of principles that can be used to untangle the web of different forces involved in social problems. These principles provide a framework for thinking. We call this way of thinking the *economic approach*. This approach will allow you to analyze and understand a wide range of social interactions.

Economists approach a variety of problems with a fairly standard toolkit of principles and theories to explain a variety of situations. Because they use the same tools, economists tend to approach problems in very similar ways, even if they arrive at different conclusions or policy recommendations. The major purpose of this textbook is to introduce you to the basic tools in that kit and to give you some practice in using those tools on real problems and policy issues.

The following chapters will develop and use theoretical economic models. You in turn can use these models to understand and explain the workings of markets, the behavior of producers and consumers, and the effects of various policies on a wide range of social problems. Scientists of all kinds differ from nonscientists in that scientists appeal to facts in a systematic manner. Early scientists in all fields did little more than systematize and classify the facts that they uncovered. This approach has limited value, however. Unless your mind works like a giant filing cabinet, it is very easy to get lost and to become bogged down with facts. As an alternative, economic theorists, like other scientists, make assumptions that simplify a problem and then develop a theoretical model that will yield a testable hypothesis. A **testable hypothesis** is an inference from economic theory that can be verified by empirical testing. This hypothesis then can be tested by comparing it with the facts and seeing if they are consistent.

TESTABLE HYPOTHESIS
An inference from economic theory that can be subjected to empirical testing.

Theories

The role of theory is an important one in everything we do. Any interpretation about the environment around us is based on an implicit theory. Small children, for example, very quickly develop testable hypotheses based on experience; my finger will hurt if I touch the hot stove, or the kitty will scratch me if I pull its tail. Our senses receive information, and we interpret that information on the basis of some theory we have developed over time about the world. These theories are, for most people, constantly being revised and improved. The only difference with the theory in this textbook and the various kinds of theories that you use in your daily life is that we will make economic theory explicit and examine its implications in detail.

Models

Economists and other theorists embody their theories in formal models. A **model** is a formal statement of a theory. It includes one or more assumptions that generate one or more "if-then" hypotheses about what will happen in the real world. Often these hypotheses are expressed in simple mathematical terms in the model. These hypotheses are then tested in real situations or experiments. As an example, consider the theory of how prices and quantities are determined. The model that expresses that theory is usually shown in the form of a supply and demand graph or sometimes a set of equations with price and quantity terms. One hypothesis of that model is that if supply is held constant while demand increases, then price will rise. We could then examine actual situations in which supply remained constant while demand increased and determine if the price did indeed rise.

MODEL
A set of assumptions and hypotheses that is a simplified description of reality.

Unlike physical scientists, economists rarely have the chance to conduct controlled experiments to validate their models. Instead, eco-

CETERIS PARIBUS
A Latin term that means "holding everything else constant."

nomic models are tested by looking at actual experience in markets. Such experiments often are referred to by economists as *ceteris paribus* experiments. The economist changes one variable in the theoretical model (demand, in this example) and then hypothesizes what would happen *ceteris paribus*, or "holding everything else constant." In this example, if demand rises *ceteris paribus*, the model predicts that price will rise. The economist must then disentangle the effects of the change in demand from anything else that changed in the real world in the market or time period being used to test the model.

The way that economists develop theories and construct models of those theories is often a point of disagreement among economists. Specifically, there has been a long and heated debate over the role of assumptions between two American Nobel Prize winners in economics. They are Paul Samuelson, of Massachusetts Institute of Technology (MIT), and Milton Friedman, who was at the University of Chicago for many years. The traditional view, taken by Samuelson, is that once a theory is demonstrated to be logically correct, its usefulness then depends on whether its assumptions are realistic. Friedman disputes this view, arguing that the purpose of theory is to abstract from the unimportant aspects of reality. The only important test of the usefulness of the theory is: Does it work? Does it accurately describe and predict what happens to the important aspects of reality?

Although the debate has never been resolved, it raises some important concerns about theorizing and model building. Assumptions can fulfill very different roles. Some assumptions are fundamental to the analysis; others are not. Some assumptions are helpful in simplifying the problem and reducing it to manageable proportions. In other cases, simplifying assumptions can take the model too far from the real world to be useful in describing and predicting economic events.

▪ Assumptions

You have already been introduced to the broad class of *ceteris paribus* assumptions that lie behind most economic models. There is one other fundamental assumption that is incorporated in most economic models. The assumption is that most people behave in a self-interested manner. In general, **self-interested behavior** means trying to get the most of (or maximize) some goal out of available resources. For consumers, self-interested behavior is *utility maximization*; for resource owners, self-interest is expressed as *income* or *wealth maximization*; and for business firms, it is referred to as *profit maximization*.

Self-interest is often confused with selfishness. Critics of market economies argue that encouraging and rewarding self-interested behavior is a basic flaw in such systems. Based on the ideas of social reformers such as Marx and Mao, there have been many experiments in socialism, such as the Fourier settlements in the United States and the Cultural Revolution in China, that have explored alternative ways of organizing economic activity. All of these experimental societies have tried to rebuild societies in such a way that individuals would respond to motivations that

SELF-INTERESTED BEHAVIOR
A basic assumption of economic theory that individual decision makers do what is best for themselves.

MILTON FRIEDMAN (1912)
PAUL A. SAMUELSON (1915)

Milton Friedman and Paul A. Samuelson are two of the best known contemporary economists. They both are recipients of the Nobel Prize in Economics—Samuelson in 1970 and Friedman in 1976. The two men represent polar extremes in their economic policy advice. Samuelson sees an important role for government in the modern industrial society. Friedman advocates a *laissez-faire* economic policy, arguing that the market economy operates very well and that the interventions Samuelson supports cause more harm than good. Samuelson is a leader in the Eastern liberal school in economics, whereas Friedman represents the conservative Chicago School.

Samuelson, a professor at the Massachusetts Institute of Technology (MIT), was awarded an A.B. degree from the University of Chicago and A.M. and Ph.D. degrees in economics from Harvard University. His Ph.D. dissertation, *Foundations of Economic Analysis*, written when he was only 23 years old, still ranks as a monumental work in the application of mathematics to neoclassical economics. Present-day graduate students still study Samuelson's *Foundations*, and many of today's economists were introduced to economics with his *Principles* textbook. Samuelson is largely responsible for making MIT's economics department one of the best in the country.

Friedman is retired from the University of Chicago, where he taught for 30 years, and is presently a Senior Research Fellow at the Hoover Institution at Stanford University. Friedman received an A.B. degree from Rutgers, an A.M. degree from the University of Chicago, and a Ph.D. degree from Columbia University. Friedman has made notable contributions to economic theory, but his policy ideas are readily available in three popular books: *Essays in Positive Economics* (1953), *Capitalism and Freedom* (1962), and *Free to Choose* (1980).

are higher than that of self-interest. In fact, concern for others and for the community as a whole are not incompatible with self-interest because individuals define their own self-interest in terms of what is satisfying to them. Some individuals derive satisfaction from more material possessions, others from leisure or enjoyment of the arts, and still others from helping others and building better communities. Some persons may derive satisfaction from all of these! So self-interested behavior is not inconsistent with volunteer work, charitable contributions, or other activities that may be unselfish but are not, by our definition, unself-interested. This definition of self-interest is broad enough to cover the actions of Albert Schweitzer and Mother Theresa as well as the most unlovable of "greedy capitalists."

When economists use the self-interest assumption to develop theory, they are simply saying that they expect individual behavior to be influenced by costs and benefits. If the cost of a particular course of action declines or the benefits rise relative to alternatives, more people will choose that course of action. For example, if salaries for public school teachers rise relative to those of accountants, we would expect more people to prepare for a teaching career and fewer to study accounting. If the penalty for speeding falls, *ceteris paribus*, we would expect more people to drive faster than the posted speed limit. This is what we mean by self-interested behavior.

Economists do not use the concept of self-interest to predict any one individual's behavior but rather to predict group average behavior. This use of the self-interest assumption is similar to the way insurance companies use attributes of certain groups to predict behavior. Insurance companies study groups and develop norms for these groups—life expectancies, accident rates, or numbers of house fires—that can be used to set prices for insurance policies. These norms say nothing about how likely one particular member of a group is to live past the age of 80, run a car off the road, or have a house burn to the ground.

SOME BASIC FEATURES OF ECONOMIC MODELS

The central goal of economics is to develop a system of theories and models that explains and predicts how the economy works, and to use those theories and models to devise policies to make it work better. All of these theories and models share certain assumptions about how households and firms make decisions about using resources for production and consumption. Although there are many such theories and models, most of them have certain features in common.

Marginal Analysis

MARGINAL ANALYSIS
A technique used to analyze problems in which the results of small changes are examined.

Throughout the remainder of this textbook, we develop and use models that involve **marginal analysis**, a technique used to analyze problems by examining the results of small changes. The concept of the margin is central to economic analysis, although it is probably new to most readers of this textbook.

Marginal refers to the extra, additional, or next unit of output, consumption, or any other measurable quantity that can be increased or decreased by incremental amounts. For example, your grade point average reflects all of the course grades you have received thus far. If you take one additional course, the extra course will raise or lower your grade point average by a small increment. If, for example, your grade point average is 2.9, an *A* or *B* will raise it slightly, whereas a *C*, *D*, or *F* will lower it slightly. The extra, or marginal, unit will raise the average if it is above the average and lower it if it is below. Most economic decisions are made at the margin: Do we consume the extra slice of pizza? Work the extra hour? Produce the extra unit? Take on the extra client in our accounting firm? These are the daily decisions made by households and firms that determine prices, output, and other important economic quantities.

Equilibrium

Equilibrium is a term that you will encounter often in this textbook. You will read about equilibrium prices, equilibrium quantities, equilibrium levels of employment, equilibrium levels of gross national product (GNP), and so forth. Every economic model includes a definition of equilibrium. Each also includes the identification of the forces that can change the equilibrium and that move the system toward a new equilibrium.

The notion of equilibrium in economics is actually borrowed from the physical sciences. A system is in **equilibrium** when it is at rest or when it is moving at a constant rate in a steady direction. That is, all the forces acting on the system are in balance, and there is no tendency to change. Equilibrium carries no sense of being a state that is good or bad, desirable or undesirable. In economics (as in physics or chemistry), if we leave a system alone, equilibrium is where it will come to rest. **Disequilibrium** is a state in which the variables are moving away from old equilibrium values and toward new equilibrium values but have not yet arrived there.

EQUILIBRIUM
When a system or model is at rest or when it is moving at a constant rate in a steady direction.

DISEQUILIBRIUM
A state in which variables are moving toward equilibrium but are not yet at equilibrium—an unstable position.

Comparative Statics

Most of the graphs in this textbook will show the original equilibrium, the new equilibrium, and perhaps some indication of the process by which the market or the economy moves from one equilibrium to another. This kind of analysis is called **comparative statics**. Comparative statics begins by describing the initial equilibrium state of the market (or the economy). This initial state is then compared to some later state in which some element has changed. Thus, comparative statics looks at changes in equilibrium positions between two different time periods.

Another way of looking at comparative statics is to see it as a snapshot of the economy or a part of the economy, for instance a market, and to analyze the relationships that exist. We then change one variable, which causes the economy to move to a new equilibrium. Then we take another snapshot of the economy, and make a similar analysis. We then compare these two snapshots to see what has changed and why. We are comparing static (frozen) pictures of the economy.

COMPARATIVE STATICS
A technique of comparing different equilibrium positions to determine the character of changing relationships between variables.

Endogenous and Exogenous Variables

In developing economic models, we pay particular attention to the individual variables that make up the model. Those variables that a model attempts to explain or determine are called **endogenous variables**. Those variables that have an impact on the endogenous variables but are themselves determined outside the model are called **exogenous variables**. In mathematics (and sometimes in economics), these are referred to as *dependent* and *independent* variables, respectively.

For example, an economic model might attempt to explain how the price of oranges is determined. The price of oranges is endogenous to the model. Some of the other variables in the model, such as the weather in Florida, are exogenous. The weather affects the price of oranges, but the price of oranges does not affect the weather. We would say that price of oranges is endogenous to the model, whereas weather is exogenous (determined by forces outside the model). Unlike simple

ENDOGENOUS VARIABLES
Variables that are explained or determined within a theory or system.

EXOGENOUS VARIABLES
Variables that are determined outside a theory or system.

mathematical models, economic models not only have several exogenous variables but often also have several endogenous variables that affect each other.

Stocks and Flows

In economic analysis, you will often encounter stock variables and flow variables, and it is important to be able to distinguish between the two. A **stock variable** is a variable that is defined at a particular point in time, say, December 31, 1988. A **flow variable** is a variable that is defined over a period of time, say, the year 1988. These are important and often-confused definitions. Let's look at some examples to clarify the distinction.

Savings is a stock, whereas saving is a flow. The amount of money you have in an account is a stock; but the amount you put in per week, per month, or per year is a flow. Income is a flow, whereas wealth is a stock. You may be wealthy if you own a large amount of land, but in order to convert that wealth to an income flow, you must either sell it, plant a cash crop on it, or rent it out. The stock of wealth creates a flow of income.

The national debt is a stock, but the federal deficit is a flow. The size of the national debt, like the size of your savings account, is fixed at any particular time. Whether it increases or decreases depends on the size of the flow variable (the current year's deficit) associated with the stock variable (the accumulated debt from previous deficits). Listen to the debate over the national debt and budget deficits and determine if the participants understand the stock-flow relationship involved.

Primary and Secondary Effects

In economics, we are often analyzing the effect of a change in one variable on other related variables. The **primary effect** is the dominant effect that we are seeking to analyze. For instance, we might want to know how doubling the price of oranges would affect the consumption of oranges. But, in economics everything depends on everything else, so there are **secondary effects**. These effects are the consequence of an economic occurrence, but they are not immediately apparent and may take more time to work through the economy. For example, as a result of doubling the price of oranges, the consumption of cranberry juice might increase, or the consumption of bacon and eggs might decrease. These changes would not be as obvious or as immediately apparent.

Geometry and Algebra

Economics, even at the introductory level, makes extensive use of algebra and analytic geometry, or graphs. The algebra used in this textbook is fairly elementary and should be familiar. The analytic geometry may require some review. If you are unfamiliar with how algebraic relation-

STOCK VARIABLE
A variable that is defined at a point in time.

FLOW VARIABLE
A variable that is defined over a period of time.

PRIMARY EFFECT
The immediate effect of a change in an economic variable.

SECONDARY EFFECT
An effect indirectly related to the immediate effect that is often smaller and only felt with the passage of time.

ships are expressed in graphs, it is important that you take the time to learn it now. An appendix to this chapter reviews the essentials you will need in order to understand the rest of this textbook.

SOME BASIC ELEMENTS
OF THE ECONOMIC APPROACH

The discussion of theories and models suggests that economics is much like other social and physical sciences in its methods. What is unique or different about the economic approach? There are a few particular emphases and ideas that help to set economics apart from other disciplines.

1. Economic theory is **positive**, or nonnormative; that is, it consists of a set of refutable propositions about *what is* rather than individual **normative** value judgments about *what ought to be*. In other words, economic theory strives to be scientific. However, when economists try to apply economic theory to policy questions, it is often difficult to keep their work positive. Economics is a social science, and the outcome of economic analysis can have important social significance. While theory itself is value free, appliers of theory—in this case, economists—are sometimes led into mixing their values with their models and theories to encourage a preferred outcome or policy.

2. Economic theory cannot *predict* the future; it can only explain the consequences of certain occurrences. Economic theory consists of if-*A*-then-*B* types of statements. The prediction that *B* will occur depends on whether or not *A* happens. Theory does not predict the occurrence of *A*; economics is a predictive science, not a crystal ball. Note that, once again, there is a difference between what economics *is* and what many economists actually *do*. Many economists, particularly macroeconomists, spend a great deal of time forecasting future conditions, and to do this they make use of economic theory. To forecast, an economist guesses the likelihood that *A* will occur and then uses economic theory to predict the occurrence of *B*. Sometimes, however, the forecasts are wrong. This doesn't necessarily mean that the economic theory was incorrect but that the forecaster may have been wrong in expecting *A* to occur.

3. Most economists look first to market processes for solutions to social problems. This *market bias* reflects a preference for the freedom and efficiency inherent in decentralized processes. However, most economic theory is applicable to nonmarket economic systems as well, even though the legal and political institutions differ. Economists can apply tools developed to analyze market economies to the workings of socialist economies and a wide variety of nonmarket behavior.

4. Economists pay a great deal of attention to *cost*. This emphasis on cost puts them in conflict with policymakers in other areas. Environmentalists don't like to hear economists talk about the cost of environmental purity in terms of foregone output. College admissions officers seeking students don't like economists reminding students that college not only costs tuition and books but also income not earned while in college.

POSITIVE ECONOMICS
A set of propositions about what is, rather than what ought to be.

NORMATIVE ECONOMICS
A set of propositions about what ought to be; value judgments about the world.

Nobel prize winner Milton Friedman underscored the importance of cost in his famous remark: "There is no such thing as a free lunch. This is the sum of my economic theory. The rest is elaboration."

5. Economists are particularly interested in opportunities to *substitute* among alternatives. Substitution and cost are closely related because the decision to substitute is based on the cost of the various alternatives. Sometimes substitutes are obvious, such as plastic for aluminum or electric heat for gas. Other substitutes are less apparent. Think about a tree, for example, which can substitute for gas or oil as heat or for aluminum siding on houses. Trees can also substitute for air conditioning, front porches, or awnings by providing shade from the heat. An important task of economic analysis is to identify opportunities to substitute and to evaluate the costs of various substitutes.

6. Economists think in terms of incremental, or *marginal analysis*[3], as we discussed earlier in the chapter. The marginal approach means looking at the effects of small increases or decreases in one important variable on other variables.

7. Economists tend to take the *individual*, rather than the group, the industry, or the community as the basic decision-making unit. They regard the behavior of individuals as an important influence on the formulation of public policy and the decisions made in the private sector of the economy. The emphasis on individuals rather than groups reflects the importance of *incentives* in economics. Changes in prices, costs, profits, wages, substitutes, and opportunities are the driving force behind individual economic decisions. It is the individual, not the group or community, that responds to incentives.

THINKING LIKE AN ECONOMIST

As you start to think about problems from an economic perspective, here are some guidelines to help in your thinking about policy proposals.

• Positive, not normative	Try not to confuse what theory tells you will happen with what you *want* to happen.
• Can the market solve it?	Economists tend to prefer market solutions because they are more efficient.
• Costs	I know there is no free lunch, but have I really counted all the costs?
• Substitutes	Where are they? What are they?
• Marginal analysis	What will happen to the next unit, the next buyer, or the next seller?
• Individuals and incentives	What incentives (positive and negative) does this policy create for individual buyers, sellers, and workers?

COMMON FALLACIES

In studying and reading economics, there are some dangerous pitfalls that can lead to false conclusions. There are three such fallacies to

---

3. Remember, *marginal* means extra, or incremental, rather than inferior.

avoid in economics. Consider, for example, the following three statements that could appear in the news and would seem logical to most readers. Each, however, contains an important fallacy.

1. "The stock market closed up today in a day of active trading. Analysts attributed the gain to optimism generated by the recent U.S.-Soviet summit on arms control."
2. "Layoffs in the auto industry were attributed to rising imports of cars, especially from Japan. Union leaders called for renewed emphasis on buying American goods, fearing severe unemployment in all manufacturing industries if the tide of imports continues to rise."
3. "The long-expected decline in college enrollments, caused by fewer high school graduates in the mid-1980s and sharply rising college tuition, has not taken place. College enrollments appear to be stable or rising in contradiction to forecasts."

The Association-Causation Fallacy: *Post Hoc, Ergo Propter Hoc*

The Latin phrase, *post hoc, ergo propter hoc* translates as, "after this, therefore, because of this." We call this the **association-causation fallacy** because association does not imply causation. The fact that *A* changes, then *B* changes does not mean that the change in *A* caused the change in *B*. If there is an increase in the number of students taking driver education programs followed by an increase in accidents involving teenage drivers, we could not conclude that driver education caused more accidents involving teenagers. A statistical or observed association does not imply a causal relationship.

ASSOCIATION-CAUSATION FALLACY
The false notion that association implies causality.

In the first example above, the connection between daily news events and the stock market illustrates this fallacy. Newscasters commenting on the stock market are almost always guilty of this fallacy. They know at the end of the day that the market has either risen or fallen, and they want a causal explanation to report to their news audiences. They can always find such a reason by identifying another important news event of the same day as *the* cause.

The best way to avoid this fallacy is to explore the causal relationship in theoretical terms. Why, in terms of models and theories, should we expect a change in *A* to cause *B* to change in a particular direction? Is there any reason for an arms agreement to affect the stock market? There are sound theoretical reasons why an increase in profits or a decline in interest rates might lead to a stock market boom. However, it is hard to explain the causal connection between arms talks and stock prices. The association-causation fallacy is a good reason for studying and using theory.

The Fallacy of Composition

The second of the three statements illustrates the **fallacy of composition**. This fallacy is the erroneous view that what holds for the parts holds for the whole and vice versa. This does not hold for many economic relationships. In the second example, it is apparent that rising

FALLACY OF COMPOSITION
The false notion that what holds for the parts holds for the whole.

imports hurt auto producers and auto workers as a group. But some auto producers maintained their sales and employment levels, and dealers and mechanics who work with foreign cars probably gained jobs and income. Even if most of the auto industry suffered, the experience cannot be extended to all manufacturing industries. If Americans import more, some American manufacturers will find opportunities to sell more to foreign customers who are earning those dollars; thus, there will be gainers as well as losers. What is true for some auto workers and auto producers is not true for the economy as a whole. The economy has actually been prospering even during some of the worst years for the auto industry.

The *Ceteris Paribus* Fallacy

CETERIS PARIBUS FALLACY
The false notion that arises when an observer fails to recognize that other variables have changed.

As we pointed out earlier, when economists make statements or predictions, they qualify them with the phrase *ceteris paribus*. What happens to the demand for college enrollment when tuition rises, *ceteris paribus*? Economic theory tells us that enrollment should fall. Instead, enrollment has held steady and has even risen slightly. Statement 3 is an example of the **ceteris paribus fallacy**. This fallacy is committed when changes in a variable do not follow the predicted course because we have overlooked the fact that other variables also have changed. Real world economic events do not always happen in a *ceteris paribus* way.

All sorts of variables change simultaneously, and if they aren't correctly sorted out, the analyst will commit the *ceteris paribus* fallacy. In the example given in Statement 3, the rise in tuition and decline in high school graduates should, taken together, have caused a decline in college enrollment. However, at the same time, other influences are at work. Incomes have also been rising. The smaller pool of students have come from smaller families that can afford to educate one or two (but not three or four) children. A growing retired population has provided a new pool of potential students in place of traditional 18-year-old freshmen. These other influences have offset the effects of higher tuition and fewer high school graduates and have allowed college enrollments to increase. The statement is, therefore, wrong because the observer failed to examine the *ceteris paribus* conditions. In this case, as with the other two, a careful application of economic theory will help avoid the fallacy.

A MENU OF POLICY ISSUES

You are about to begin studying what will prove to be one of the most exciting and worthwhile subjects in your formal education. Economic analysis offers insight on topics ranging from crime to inflation, which appear daily on the front pages of newspapers. To set the stage, we offer a few examples of the kinds of policy issues you will be considering. The policy issues we study will be classified as primarily macroeconomic or primarily microeconomic, but keep in mind that almost all topics have both macro and micro elements.

Macroeconomic Issues

Macroeconomic issues are the stuff of headlines. The consumer price index, the federal budget deficit, and the trade balance are all front-page news. Macroeconomic policy is made in Washington, D.C., in a tug-of-war between the President and the executive branch on one side and the leaders of Congress on the other.

Curing Inflation—The Goal of Price Stability

All countries aim to promote price stability. In the 1950s and early 1960s, prices were quite stable in the United States. From the late 1960s until the early 1980s, however, inflation earned regular front-page coverage in the newspapers. Election campaigns were built around inflation as a political problem. Since 1983, the rate of inflation has dropped sharply, and the price index is no longer a media star. However, inflation is likely to recur. A major concern of macroeconomists is the causes of inflation, as well as developing and evaluating policies to promote price stability.

Unemployment—Full Employment

Employment is another important macroeconomic concern. From the viewpoint of the economy, unemployed workers represent lost potential output. From the viewpoint of taxpayers, unemployed workers require food stamps, welfare, or unemployment compensation, creating a burden on others for their support. From the viewpoint of the worker, unemployment means loss of income, of status, and of work experience to enhance future earnings. For many economists, employment is the number one macroeconomic policy priority.

Economic Growth—More is Better

Economic growth is a rise in the quantity of goods and services available. Growth is also a means to create jobs and absorb new entrants into the labor force. Remember, though, that everything has a cost. The costs of rapid economic growth are measured in rapid exhaustion of nonrenewable resources, increased environmental pollution, or other hard-to-measure "quality of life" factors. Often economic growth requires giving up present consumption to provide for the future. Many economists, weighing these costs and benefits, would endorse the cautious title of a book by British economist Wilfred Beckerman, *Two Cheers for Economic Growth.*

Macroeconomic and Microeconomic Issues

Some issues overlap microeconomics and macroeconomics. Here are some examples of issues that involve both macroeconomic and microeconomic policy questions.

Economic Security

The issue of economic security refers to how much income a household or individual has and how dependable that source of income is. Economic security is affected by changes in macroeconomic variables, such as inflation and unemployment. Inflation decreases the value of retirement income and makes people uncertain about their futures. The chance of becoming unemployed is a threat to the economic security of many American workers.

There are also microeconomic dimensions to economic security. One important concern is the effect that programs designed to increase economic security will have on incentives. For instance, if taxes are increased to provide for the old and unemployed, what happens to the incentives of productive workers? Do welfare programs discourage unemployed persons from searching for work?

Regulation: Environment, Safety, and Quality

Government regulations to protect the environment, to make working conditions and products safe, and to guarantee product quality are primarily microeconomic in nature. Such regulations are directed at a particular product or industry. For example, how will the coal industry be affected by requirements to return strip-mined land to its original condition? If housing must meet certain safety standards in wiring and plumbing, will these regulations limit the availability of low-income housing? Will requiring firms to allow maternity leave mean fewer job opportunities or lower wages for young women? Government regulation also has macroeconomic effects. Environmental regulations may slow the rate of economic growth or raise costs and prices and drive up the price index that measures inflation.

International Trade

We usually think of trade between citizens of different countries as a micro issue. Buying a Toyota instead of a Ford, eating bananas from the Caribbean for breakfast, or traveling to old Mexico instead of New Mexico are microeconomic choices made by individuals. But the sum of such individual decisions has macroeconomic effects on output, employment, and prices.

Primarily Microeconomic Issues

The following issues are primarily microeconomic in nature. These are just a few of many microeconomic issues that we will discuss in later chapters.

Special-Interest Groups and Government

Government policies create benefits and costs to different groups of people and change the incentives that individuals face. As a result, all sorts of special-interest groups arise. We are all members of various special-interest groups, no matter how much we may disapprove of their power and influence. Microeconomic theory offers tools to uncover and sort out the impact of special-interest groups working through government on the distribution of income, the mix of products we produce, and the prices we pay.

Labor Unions

Labor unions, like other institutions, have profound effects on markets for workers and for goods and services. Do they raise wages?

Create unemployment? Protect workers? Microeconomics analyzes the influence of unions and explains the public policy debates about encouraging or restricting union activity.

Crime and Punishment

This item may seem misplaced in a list of economic issues. In fact, it is a good illustration of the fruitful application of economic theories based on self-interested behavior, incentives, and marginal analysis to an unlikely policy area. Economists view potential criminals as self-interested persons who respond to incentives to commit crimes or not to commit crimes. Microeconomic models offer insights into what kinds of enforcement and what kinds of penalties are most effective in deterring crime.

In short, the economic approach is a unique way of analyzing the world. Since it is a way of thinking in a logical sequence, and with a set of tools, it provides insight into an endless menu of issues.

THE INTERNATIONAL PERSPECTIVE
THE UNITED STATES AND THE REST
OF THE WORLD

For much of the period from the end of World War II until the mid-1970s, American students learned economics almost as if the United States was on a different planet from the rest of the world. There might have been a chapter or two on international economics at the end of the textbook, which the instructor usually did not have time to cover. Basically, the attitude was that the U.S. economy was so large and the share of foreign trade in U.S. economic activity was so small that the rest of the world could safely be ignored.

In the 1980s, Americans know better. The price of the dollar fell sharply in the late 1970s and contributed to inflation. It rose in the early 1980s, which reduced inflationary pressures, but the higher dollar price made it difficult for American firms to compete with foreign producers. The effects of the international oil cartel on U.S. prices, employment, and economic growth from 1973 until 1985 were very discouraging. Clearly economists could not ignore the macroeconomic effects of the rest of the world.

At the microeconomic level, individual American firms, workers, and consumers have also become increasingly aware of the rest of the world. Americans who eat bananas from Central America on their cereal and drink coffee from Colombia, tea from India, or hot chocolate from Ghana for breakfast start their days in an international world. They are likely to ride to work or school on a Japanese bicycle or in a Japanese car—although the Japanese car may have been built in the United States! When students graduate, it is very probable that they will work for a multinational firm, American or foreign, in the United States or abroad. Their parents may have suffered spells of unemployment in steel, autos, shoes, or textiles related to import competition.

Recognizing the growing importance of the international economy, your authors have chosen not to relegate the rest of the world to the back of the textbook. Each chapter offers an international perspective that extends the material in that chapter to the open, or international, economy.

MAKING POLICY CHOICES

One of the frustrating things about applying economic models to public policy analysis is that it is difficult to decide when the job of the economist ends and the policymaker should take over. When economic methods are used for policy analysis, there is a five-step process.

1. State the problem. Often how a problem is stated determines what tools the economist applies and what solutions are considered. For example, suppose the problem is illegal parking on campus, especially students who park in faculty spaces. Let's follow that problem through the next few steps.
2. Apply the relevant economic model. The economist turns to the toolkit to select the appropriate theoretical model. In this case, there is a fairly simple technique called cost-benefit analysis. It is possible to reduce illegal student parking either by lowering the benefits of illegal parking or by raising the costs.
3. Identify solutions. The most common error at this stage is to leave out some potential solutions. In the case of illegal parking, possible solutions might raise costs with more severe penalties. Do you think a student would park in a faculty space if the fine were $100 instead of $10 or $15? More police officers, increasing the probability of being caught, would also increase costs and discourage illegal parking. The university could also reduce the benefits of illegal parking by providing more bicycle racks, free bus transportation around campus, or shuttle buses from remote student commuter parking lots. Campus officials could even sell reserved parking spaces, and let students and faculty bid for parking rights. You might try some creative brainstorming to suggest others.
4. Evaluate solutions. This is the stage at which the economist shines, pointing to costs, substitutes, incentives, and other economic considerations. The economic model will be helpful in showing how various solutions will affect the amount of illegal parking, who will gain and who will lose, and which solution costs least. More police officers would cost more than higher fines, but higher fines are a burden on students, many of whom have limited incomes. Bicycle racks are cheaper than shuttle buses but are not as helpful to commuting students unless they live very close to campus.
5. Choose and implement solutions. This is *not* the task of the economist, although it is hard to stop after carrying the process this far. The policymaker takes the economist's list of possible solutions with the evaluation and makes a policy choice.

Most of the arguments among economists occur when they overstep the boundaries of scientific analysis and advocate implementing a particular solution to an economic problem. If you look at your daily newspaper or at weekly newsmagazines such as *Newsweek* or *Time*, many of the economic stories are about economists disagreeing over issues. However, you will see in the rest of this textbook that economists agree far more often than they disagree. Disagreements make headlines; agreement isn't news. Throughout this textbook, we will point out those areas in which most economists agree and also where and why they disagree. The toolkit in this textbook represents a broad range of agreement among most economists on how markets work and how individuals respond to incentives.

Economics is an exciting social science. The individual who understands the economic way of thinking will gain insight into an endless array of interesting questions. We wish you well. Let's get on with it!

SUMMARY

1. Economics is the scientific study of how people and institutions make decisions about producing and consuming goods and services and how they face the problem of scarcity.
2. Microeconomics looks at the interactions of producers and consumers in individual markets. Macroeconomics is the study of the economy as a whole and is concerned with aggregates, numbers that are determined by adding across many markets.
3. Economics is both a social science and a decision science.
4. Economic theory is an abstract way of thinking that allows the development of principles, or tools, that can be used to study complex social issues.
5. The self-interest hypothesis is a very basic assumption of economic theory. Although economists recognize that economic behavior is a complex process, it is assumed in economics that human beings pursue their own self-interest.
6. Marginal analysis is a technique used to analyze problems in which the results of small changes are examined.
7. Equilibrium in an economic model is the position toward which the forces within the model naturally tend.
8. Disequilibrium is a state in which the variables are moving away from old equilibrium values and toward new equilibrium values but have not yet arrived there.
9. Comparative statics refers to the analytical technique of examining equilibrium positions at different periods of time in order to study changes that have occurred.
10. An endogenous variable is determined within a theory. An exogenous variable is given outside the theory.
11. A stock variable is defined for a given point in time. A flow variable is defined over a given period of time.
12. A primary effect is the dominant effect of a change in one variable on another related variable. A secondary effect is an effect that occurs in a variable after (or to a lesser extent than) a primary effect has occurred.
13. The economic approach is positive, or nonnormative; it can't tell us what we should or ought to do, but it can make statements of an if-*A*-then-*B* type.
14. Because economics emphasizes how individuals respond to incentives, economists tend to rely on the market to solve many social problems. In analyzing problems, economists spend a great deal of time clarifying options and looking at costs. In examining possibilities for substitution, economists look at costs and benefits at the margin.
15. The association-causation fallacy is the false notion that association implies causality.
16. The fallacy of composition is the erroneous view that what holds for the parts holds for the whole and vice versa.
17. The *ceteris paribus* fallacy is committed when changes in one variable fail to have the predicted effect on another variable because simultaneous changes have taken place in other important variables.
18. A policy decision is analyzed in five steps: state the problem, apply the relevant economic model, identify solutions, evaluate solutions, and choose and implement solutions.
19. Economists agree on many things, but their disagreements are often highlighted. Most of their disagreements are over policy choices rather than economic theory.

NEW TERMS

economics
microeconomics

macroeconomics
social science

decision science
theory

testable hypothesis
model
ceteris paribus
self-interested behavior
marginal analysis
equilibrium
disequilibrium

comparative statics
endogenous variables
exogenous variables
stock variable
flow variable
primary effect

secondary effect
positive economics
normative economics
association-causation fallacy
fallacy of composition
ceteris paribus fallacy

QUESTIONS FOR DISCUSSION

1. Do you think people exhibit behavior patterns that confirm the self-interest hypothesis? Does your own behavior confirm the self-interest hypothesis? Is a charitable contribution or volunteer work a contradiction of the self-interest hypothesis?

2. Why do economists theorize rather than attempt to describe reality exactly?

3. Do assumptions have to be realistic in order for a theory to work?

4. What is the difference between *theory that predicts* and *forecasting*?

5. Develop a theory to explain (predict) student grades in this course. Identify at least one stock variable, one flow variable, one exogenous variable, and one endogenous variable.

6. Identify and explain the fallacy in each of the following statements.
   a. "There was a transit strike in April, and unemployment in the city rose in May. Clearly the transit strike created unemployment."
   b. "The new subway system is finally working, but downtown parking is harder to find than it was before. The subway system hasn't relieved congestion."
   c. "Our state competed heavily to attract industry, and it worked. Our unemployment is down. If all states did the same, national unemployment would fall."

7. Which of the following is a microeconomic quantity or issue, and which is macroeconomic? Which might fall in between the two?

   price of shoes

   level of interest rates

   unemployment in the northeastern states

   number of men aged 18 to 64 in the U.S. labor force

   production of agricultural products

   production of butter

   unemployment in the United States

   number of nurses in the U.S. labor force

   unemployment of carpenters

   unemployment in Tulsa

   average level of prices

   average prices of imported goods

   production of total output

8. Try developing a simple economic model to predict how students will respond to an increase in dormitory rents. What are your assumptions? What will happen to dormitory spaces rented? What will happen to off-campus apartments rented and their prices?

9. Which of the following statements are normative, and which are positive? Rewrite the normative statements to make them positive and the positive ones to make them normative.
   a. "Women earn less than men."
   b. "Defense spending has grown too rapidly in the last decade."
   c. "Because their child-care responsibilities interfere with their work, women with children should earn less than men."
   d. "Twenty-three percent of the federal budget is spent on defense."
   e. "An estimated 14 percent of the U.S. population lives in poverty, according to government standards defining poverty."
   f. "The government is not doing enough to alleviate poverty."

SUGGESTIONS FOR FURTHER READING

Boulding, Kenneth. *Human Betterment*. Beverly Hills: Sage Publications, 1985. This recent book by one of America's best known economic philosophers makes a case for normative analysis where the values behind the analysis are clearly spelled out.

Browne, M. Neil, and John Hoag. *Understanding Economic Analysis*. Newton, M.A.: Allyn and Bacon, 1983, Chapters 1 and 2. These two introductory chapters offer a very readable overview of economic theories and methodology.

Huff, Darrell, and Irving Geis. *How to Lie with Statistics*. New York: W.W. Norton, 1954 (copyright renewed 1982). This classic guide to interpreting and misinterpreting graphs and statistics is must reading for any serious student of the social sciences.

Rhoads, Stephen E. *The Economist's View of the World: Government, Markets, and Public Policy*. New York: Cambridge University Press, 1985. Written by a political scientist, this book looks at both the useful contributions of economics to other social science disciplines and the limitations of economics.

APPENDIX: ECONOMIC RELATIONSHIPS AND GRAPHS

Economic theories and models are often expressed in the form of mathematical relationships among variables. These relationships can be put into the form of algebraic equations, but economists more often express these relationships visually in the form of graphs. Although economics is not *about graphs*, graphs make it possible to illustrate economic theories and models in ways that make them easier to remember and to apply to the real world. Remember that everything that can be said in graphs can also be said in words. Graphs are only an aid to understanding the theory; mastering and applying the theory, not the graph, is what you should be trying to achieve. If you can learn to feel comfortable with these visual representations of economic ideas, reading this textbook and understanding your professor's lectures will be much easier.

Relationship Between Variables

A relationship between two variables, variable X and variable Y, can be expressed in a number of different ways. One is a table of numerical values of X and Y, such as Table 1A–1, showing the various amounts of fertilizer applied per acre and the corresponding yields of corn per acre. What does this table mean? It means that different amounts of fertilizer were applied to different plots of land and that the different plots of land yielded varying amounts of corn.

This relationship could also be expressed in the form of a graph.[a] A graph shows how the quantity of one variable changes when another variable changes. Figure 1A–1 depicts a typical graphing quadrant system.

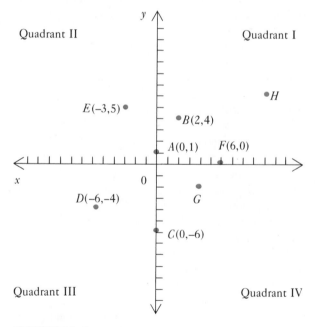

FIGURE 1A–1
QUADRANT SYSTEM
A four-quadrant system makes it possible to represent combinations of positive and negative values in the two dimensions. Point C represents a 0 x-value and –6 y-value. The quadrants are labeled I to IV in counterclockwise direction.

TABLE 1A–1
RELATIONSHIPS BETWEEN VARIABLES

X-Variable Fertilizer (100s of Lbs./Acre)	Y-Variable Corn (Bushels/Acre)
1	1
2	10
3	40
4	80
5	100
6	110
7	115
8	110
9	100
10	70

a. A third way to represent such a relationship is with an equation, $y = f(x)$. We will be using some equations in this textbook but will rely more heavily on graphs to display relationships between variables.

The vertical line is referred to as the **y-axis** (or *vertical axis*), and the horizontal line is referred to as the **x-axis** (or *horizontal axis*). The x-axis and y-axis divide the graph into four quadrants. The place at which the axes intersect is the **origin**. At the origin, the values of both the x-variable and the y-variable are zero. Moving upward from the origin, above the x-axis, the y-variable takes on positive values. Below the x-axis, movement along the y-axis represents negative values for the y-variable. Likewise, as you move away from the origin along the x-axis to the right of the y-axis, the x-variable takes on positive values. To the left of the origin, the x-variable takes on negative values. The graph is divided into four quadrants, with both x and y taking on positive values in Quadrant I and negative values in Quadrant III. In Quadrant IV, x takes on positive values, and y takes on negative values. In Quadrant II, x has negative values whereas y assumes positive values.

You can now locate points on the graph. Each point has a set of **coordinates**, which is a pair of numbers, one representing the x-value and one representing the y-value. For example, Point B on Figure 1A–1 represents the value 2 for the x-variable and 4 for the y-variable. The x-value is always given first. For example, Point E represents x = –3, y = 5. Can you give the coordinates of Points G and H? In this textbook, most of the graphs will appear in Quadrant I because most economic data takes on only positive values.

Now we can plot the relationship between fertilizer and corn output given in Table 1A–1. The first decision to make is to decide which variable goes on which axis. Recall the discussion earlier in this chapter about endogenous and exogenous variables. Fertilizer is the exogenous, or x-variable, on the horizontal axis, whereas corn yield is the endogenous, or y-variable, on the vertical axis.

The next decision is to establish a scale for each axis. We could represent the amount of fertilizer and the output of corn by selecting almost any scale on the axes that we want. The scales do not need to be the same. In this case, the fertilizer units are hundreds of pounds, and the corn units are bushels. Once a scale is established and the axes are clearly labeled, we can plot the coordinates of the points in Table 1A–1 and then connect the plotted points with a smooth curve to produce a graph.

Figure 1A–2 plots the relationship in Table 1A–1 with fertilizer as the x-variable and corn output as the y-variable. The value of the graph is that it gives you a visual picture of the mathematical relationship between the variables. In Figure 1A–2, you can easily see that as fertilizer is increased to 700 pounds per acre, corn output increases. After that, more fertilizer causes a decrease in output. The corn plants grow too rapidly to produce many ears, or the roots suffer fertilizer burn.

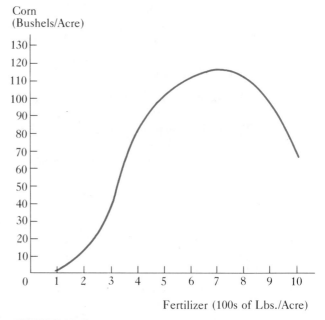

FIGURE 1A-2
FERTILIZER AND CORN OUTPUT
A graph usually is plotted with the dependent variable on the y-axis and the independent variable on the x-axis. On this, as the independent variable—fertilizer—increases, the dependent variable—corn output—first increases and then decreases.

When plotting graphs, economists are not always consistent about plotting the **dependent variable** as the y-variable and the **independent variable** as the x-variable, as we did in this example. Sometimes we cannot clearly identify the dependent and independent variables; we are not sure what causes what or whether or not both variables are caused by something else. A famous diagram in economics called the Phillips curve plots rates of unemployment on the horizontal axis and rates of inflation on the vertical axis for various years. It could just as well have been plotted the opposite way because the graph does not imply that unemployment causes inflation, or inflation causes unemployment, merely that the two are somehow related.

Not all relationships produce as tidy a graph as the fertilizer-corn yield relationship. Sometimes we plot data to see if there is any visual relationship before trying to understand what, if any, is the relationship between the two variables. Figure 1A–3 plots actual data from 1976 to 1986 on the rate of inflation (vertical axis) and the rate of unemployment (horizontal axis) for the United States. Such a plot of actual data is called a **scatter diagram**. Scatter diagrams are useful in searching for possible statistical relationships between two variables. In this diagram, there doesn't seem to be much of a consistent relationship of any kind between the rate of inflation and the rate of unemployment, at least for the years plotted.

Inflation
Rate (%)

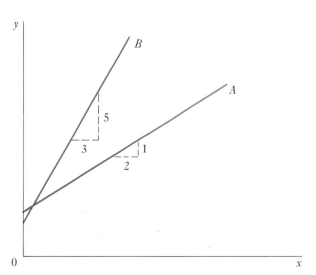

**FIGURE 1A-3
INFLATION AND UNEMPLOYMENT SCATTER DIAGRAM**
A scatter diagram plots the coordinates for the values of two variables that may or may not have a consistent relationship. This diagram plots the values of the unemployment rate and the inflation rate for the United States from 1976 to 1986. It shows no consistent relationship between changes in the two variables.

Source: Council of Economic Advisers, *Economic Report of the President* (Washington, D.C.: U.S. Government Printing Office, 1987).

Positive and Negative Relationships and Slopes

A graph shows how two variables are related. This relationship may be positive or negative. A **positive relationship** means that an increase in the value of the x-variable is associated with an increase in the value

of the y-variable. A **negative relationship** means that an increase in the value of the x-variable is associated with a decrease in the value of the y-variable. Some relationships in economics, such as the fertilizer-corn output relationship in Figure 1A–2, are positive for part of the range and negative for other values of the variables. Most of the economic relationships you will encounter in this textbook, however, are represented by straight lines. A straight line has either a positive slope, as in Figure 1A–4, or a negative slope, as in Figure 1A–5. The **slope** is a measure of the steepness or flatness of the curve. It is the ratio of the change in the dependent (y) variable to the change in the independent (x) variable.

**FIGURE 1A-4
POSITIVELY SLOPED LINES**
The slope of a line is the ratio of the change in the y-value to the change in the x-value. A line sloping upward to the right has a positive slope, indicating a positive relationship between the two variables.

Even though both the lines in Figure 1A–4 are positively sloped, the relationship between the x-variable and the y-variable along line A is very different from the relationship represented by line B. The same amount of change in x leads to a larger change in y along line B than it does along line A. In Figure 1A–4, the slope of line A is equal to $+\frac{1}{2}$ because the y-value changes by one unit for each two-unit change in the x-value. The slope of line B is $+\frac{5}{3}$, or $+1.67$. The steeper slope of line B indicates that a larger change in the value of y will result from a given change in the value of x than along line A. The sign of the slope is also very important because the sign indicates whether the relationship between the two variables is positive or negative. A slope with a positive sign designates a positive relationship. A slope with a negative sign, as in Figure 1A–5, indicates a negative relationship. The slope of the line in Figure 1A–5 is $-1/2$.

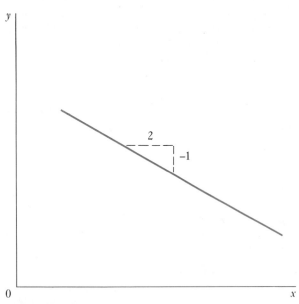

FIGURE 1A-5
NEGATIVELY SLOPED LINE
A negative slope represents a relationship between the variables in which an increase in the value of one variable is associated with a decrease in the value of the other.

Nonlinear Graphs and Maxima and Minima

A straight line graph, like those in Figures 1A–4 and 1A–5, has the same slope along the entire line, but the slope of a curved line varies along the curve. The slope of a curve at a particular point is the slope of the straight line tangent to the curve at the point. A **tangent line** is a straight line that touches a curve at only one point without crossing it. The slope of the curved line in Figure 1A–6 is +1 at Point A and $-1\frac{1}{2}$ at Point C.

The slope of the curve at Point B is equal to 0. This is because a small change in the value of x results in no change in the value of y along the straight line tangent to the curve at Point B. Point B is a **maximum** because the y-variable reaches its highest value at that point. The highest value of y, y_1, is associated with

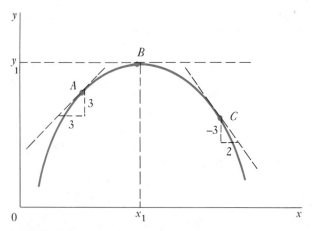

FIGURE 1A-6
NONLINEAR GRAPHS: SLOPE AND MAXIMUM
On a nonlinear graph, the slope changes along the curve. The slope of the curve at any point is the slope of a straight line tangent to the curved line at that point. When the slope is 0, the value of the y-variable is either at a maximum or a minimum. At point B, y is at its maximum value, y_1, when x has the value x_1.

an x value of x_1. Recall that we described self-interested behavior as consumers maximizing satisfaction, resource owners maximizing income, and firms maximizing profit. Being able to find the maximum point is very important in economics.

Sometimes a slope of zero is associated with a **minimum** point rather than a maximum, as in Figure 1A–7. The y-variable assumes its lowest value, Y_1, at Point B in Figure 1A–7, associated with an x-value of X_1.

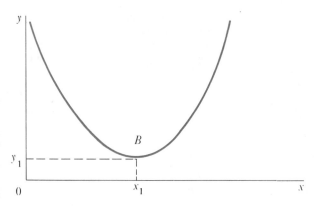

FIGURE 1A-7
NONLINEAR GRAPHS: MINIMUM
This nonlinear graph also has a slope of 0 at Point B. In this case, Point B represents the minimum value of y, y_1, which is associated with an x-value of x_1.

A firm that is trying to minimize costs, or losses, may be interested in finding a minimum point. It is also important to verify whether the point of zero slope is a maximum or a minimum for many kinds of economic questions.

The 45° Line

A geometric construction that proves very useful in economic analysis is a **45° line**, which is a straight line that cuts through the origin of and divides Quadrant I into two equal sections. If both axes are measured in the same units, the values of the x-variable and the y-variable will be equal at any point on the line, and the slope will be $+1$. A 45° line is presented in Figure 1A–8. Suppose, for example, that you want to know whether the value of x was less than, equal to, or greater than the value of y at Point C. A 45° reference line gives you a quick answer to that question; the value of x is less than the value of y at Point C because C lies below the 45° line.

Graphs Without Numbers

The graph in Figures 1A–2 and the scatter diagram in Figure 1A–3 were constructed from a set of numbers. Other graphs in this section only give a few numerical values from which to calculate slopes; Figures 1A–6 and 1A–7 have no numbers on them at all. In economics, graphs of theoretical concepts often use no numbers. For example, we might theorize that there is a negative relationship between price and the quantity demanded of any good that people consume. If price is the y-variable and quantity demanded the x-variable, a negatively sloped line such as the one in Figure 1A–5 could represent this theoretical relationship. It doesn't matter that we don't have specific coordinates to plot; instead we have graphed an abstract idea. Many of the graphs used in economics are of this abstract type.

In working with graphs without numbers, symbols represent line segments and areas. For example, Figure 1A–9 is similar to the graphs that you will study in Chapter 3. The price on the y-axis is designated as the price per loaf of bread, and the quantity on the x-axis is designated as the quantity of loaves consumed per week. Price is then represented by symbols, such as P_1. Quantities are represented by symbols, such as Q_1, Q_2, Q_3, with Q_3 being larger (farther from the origin) than Q_1. If you have studied geometry, you will note that it would be technically correct to refer to quantity Q_1 as quantity

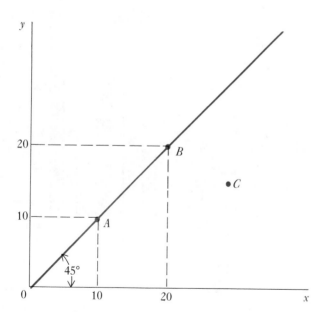

FIGURE 1A-8
THE 45° LINE
A 45° line drawn in the first quadrant has a slope of 1.0. If both axes are measured in the same units, the 45° line shows all points where the x-axis value and the y-axis value are equal.

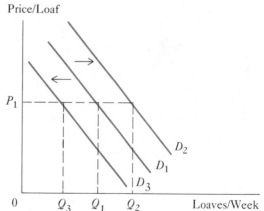

FIGURE 1A-9
EFFECTS OF CHANGES IN TASTES ON THE DEMAND FOR BREAD
Many graphs in economics use symbols rather than numbers on the axes. The notation P_1 represents a hypothetical price, whereas Q_1, Q_2, and Q_3 represent hypothetical quantities.

$0Q_1$. We will, however, use the shorthand Q_1 to minimize the clutter as the graphs become more complicated.

In addition to using symbols to represent quantities, we will also make frequent use of the symbol for delta, Δ, to represent changes in a variable. For example, the symbol ΔQ is a shorthand expression for the change from Q_1 to Q_2 in Figure 1A–9.

Pie Charts and Bar Charts

All of the graphs considered thus far, except for the scatter diagram, represent theoretical relationships of one kind or another. Economists also use graphs to describe the real world. Such graphs might display the allocation of government funds between types of programs; the growth of output or the money supply over time; the different growth rates of imports and exports; and other descriptive statistics.

Two common types of descriptive graphs encountered in economics are pie charts and bar graphs. **Pie charts** are used to show the percentage division of some whole into components. Figure 1A–10 is a pie

chart depicting the sources of household income in 1986. With the arrival of microcomputers, pie charts have become even more popular because they are very easy to create on a computer. This visual representation often conveys a clearer sense of the relative sizes of various components than you could obtain from reading a table of numbers.

Another popular type of descriptive graph is a **bar chart**, such as Figure 1A–11. This diagram describes the behavior of two variables, imports and exports, over a 25-year period with a series of "snapshots." This graph gives a much more vivid impression of how much faster imports have grown than exports than you could derive from a set of numbers.

Theoretical graphs, such as those in Figures 1A–4 to 1A–9, and descriptive graphs, such as Figures 1A–10 and 1A–11, are spread throughout this textbook, as well as textbooks in social sciences and business and popular magazines such as *Newsweek*, *Time*, and *Business Week*. Economics is a very visual subject. Be sure that you feel secure with reading and interpreting graphs before proceeding further.

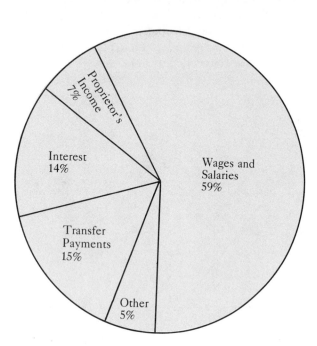

FIGURE 1A–10
PIE CHART OF HOUSEHOLD INCOME, 1986
A pie chart depicts the division of a whole into components (percentage).

Source: *Economic Report of the President*, 1987.

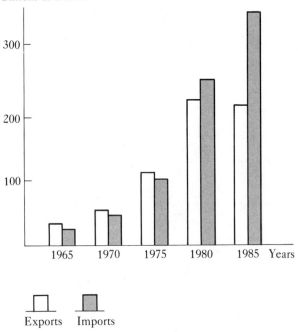

FIGURE 1A–11
BAR CHART OF U.S. EXPORTS AND IMPORTS, 1960 to 1985
A bar chart can be used in a variety of ways to describe economic data in a visual fashion.

Source: *Economic Report of the President*, 1987.

■ Caution: Graphs and Numbers Can Mislead as Well as Inform!

Graphs and statistics can be very informative in putting some concrete, real-world content into abstract models and economic relationships. However, it is very easy to present data in such a way as to mislead readers. The choice of a scale along the axis can make changes look bigger than they really are. The use of averages conceals a great deal of information about variation. For example, three families could have an average income of $25,000 when their respective incomes are $24,000, $25,000, and $26,000. The same average could be the result of three families with incomes of $5,000, $5,000, and $65,000. The same number describes two very different distributions of income.

A classic guide to the use and abuse of numbers and graphs is *How to Lie with Statistics*, by Darrell Huff and Irving Geis. This book has been through numerous paperback editions since it was first published in 1954. This book should be required reading for anyone taking courses in the social sciences. It is a useful guide through the pitfalls of the means, medians, averages, bar charts, surveys, samples, and growth rates that are the daily news of the economic and political worlds. Even if you don't read Huff and Geis' book, however, be very cautious in accepting someone's graphs or numbers. Consider carefully what that person may be trying to persuade you to think or do and how the statistics could be manipulated to put that position in a more favorable light.

CHAPTER 2 ■

■

SCARCITY AND CHOICE

■

■

INTRODUCTION

This chapter is a broad overview of some basic economic questions and how economic systems address those questions. All economic systems have to face the fact of **scarcity**. Human wants and desires for economic goods are vast, relative to the resources available to satisfy them. It is possible to stretch those resources to meet more of those wants through specialization and exchange, but scarcity will still remain. Thus, any economic system needs a method for making choices among different desirable ends.

The process of choosing requires answers to three economic questions. *What* goods and services will be produced and in what quantities? What methods of production and combinations of inputs (*how*) shall be used? *Who* gets what share of the goods produced? Different kinds of economic systems answer these three questions in different ways. Some rely primarily on tradition, others rely on decisions by government officials, and still others rely on the market to answer these questions. Most economies use a combination of these three approaches.

SCARCITY: LIMITED RESOURCES, UNLIMITED WANTS, AND OPPORTUNITY COSTS

We live in a world of limited resources. Some resources, such as oil and coal, are converted to energy and used up in the course of production or consumption. Others are not used up in the same sense but are virtually fixed in quantity, such as land, diamonds, and copper. At any given time, even the quantity of roads, factories, machines, and skilled workers cannot be changed quickly or inexpensively. Limited resources conflict with insatiable human wants.

Wants are said to be **insatiable**—unable to be satisfied— because no matter how much people have, they always want more of *some* goods. Of course, you may know people who seem perfectly content with what they have. However, if you questioned them carefully, you would probably find that they would like cleaner air, more time to play tennis or

SCARCITY
The central economic problem that there are not sufficient resources to produce everything that individuals want.

INSATIABLE WANTS
The fact that there can never be enough of everything to satisfy everyone's wants for all goods and services.

30

golf, or maybe more income that they could give to less fortunate people. Since not all wants can be satisfied, individuals have to pick and choose which wants to satisfy with their limited available resources. In fact, every society is faced with the same problem of scarcity and choice. Without scarcity, there would be no need to make choices about what needs to satisfy, and there would be no need to study economics.

■ Opportunity Costs

Every decision to produce or consume something means sacrificing the production or consumption of something else. For instance, the cost of going to a football game includes the value of what is given up in order to attend. Economists use the term **opportunity cost** to denote the full value of the best foregone alternative. One part of the cost of attending a football game is the price of the ticket, representing the other goods and services you could have purchased with that money instead. Another part of the cost is the most valuable alternative use of those three hours, such as studying for a test. The opportunity cost of attending the game consists of not only the price of the ticket but also the difference in your test score that three more hours of study would have produced. Even if the ticket were "free," it had an opportunity cost.

Opportunity cost has many useful applications in economics. Many people have problems grasping this concept because they are accustomed to thinking of cost as the dollar expenditures on an item or an activity. In economics, however, the concept of cost is much broader, including not only the dollar outlay (the alternative goods you could have purchased) but also the time cost (the earnings or satisfaction you could have produced for yourself in some other activity) and other sacrifices you might have made. Sometimes it is difficult to place a dollar value on these costs, but they are an important influence on economic decisions.

OPPORTUNITY COST
The value of the next best opportunity given up in order to enjoy a particular good or service.

■ Some Applications of Opportunity Cost

There are some applications of opportunity cost close at hand. What is the opportunity cost of attending college to the average student? It's not the dollar figure in your college catalog. The expenditures on books and tuition are certainly part of the opportunity cost. However, the cost of your room, meals, and other incidental expenses is not, because you would have incurred those costs even if you didn't go to college. One important cost is the income you could have been earning during your college years instead of attending classes. For most students, that lost income will eventually be made up in higher future earnings. But what if you were a talented athlete who could play professionally right after high school, as many baseball and tennis players do? Your college education may be costing as much as $100,000 a year in lost earnings. After several years of college, many football and basketball players face the same dilemma. Even if they are straight *A* students, the opportunity cost of completing a degree in terms of foregone income is very high, and it is not surprising that many of them choose to pursue a professional career and postpone or forgo getting a degree.

Another example of opportunity cost is the proposal, frequently put forth by politicians, of two years of universal national service for all young adults. This service would be in the military or some other public-sector job and would pay very low wages. For some, the opportunity cost will be very low because they may have few good alternative employment opportunities. But for someone with athletic skills, an engineering or accounting degree, or other good earnings possibilities, the opportunity cost would be very high. Universal national service is a tax on being young, and the tax is very different for different individuals.

ADAM SMITH (1723-1790)

Adam Smith is generally regarded as the founder of modern economics. He was born in Kirkcaldy, Scotland, educated at the University of Glasgow and at Oxford University in England, and eventually became a professor at Glasgow. *The Wealth of Nations*, published in 1776, marked a break with previous economic thought. Smith stressed the role of individual self-interest in promoting overall welfare. In his view, the "invisible hand" of self-interest leads people to act in socially desirable ways. For example, you know that

when you arrive at a hotel in a new city in the evening, you can count on being able to buy breakfast in the morning because people who hope to make a profit will have restaurants and coffee shops open for your business.

Before Smith, people who wrote on economic issues emphasized what government could and should do to run the economy in the national interest. Smith, however, argued that the role of government should be minimal; it should provide for the national defense, produce and regulate the money supply, and supply a system of laws with swift, efficient justice in the courts. Beyond these activities, private individuals pursuing their own self-interest would provide direction for economic activity; there was no need for government to intervene. For more than a century, Adam Smith's ideas led economists to view the best economic role of government as minimal.

Smith was not naive about the risks of relying on self-interest. He argued that whenever manufacturers of the same product get together, their thoughts rapidly turn to conspiring to raise prices and increase profits. He was opposed to this type of monopoly behavior and thought that government should do nothing to encourage such practices. But as long as the government does not promote monopoly, market forces and competition will limit the ability of firms to take advantage of their customers.

Opportunity cost, which we discussed in this chapter, is another useful concept developed from the work of Adam Smith. He used the example of a village where people could hunt deer or beaver. As he pointed out, the opportunity cost of bagging one deer was the number of beaver that could have been trapped with the same time and trouble. Smith recognized that the only true cost in economics is opportunity cost.

Opportunity Cost and the Choice Curve

We can construct a simple graph to demonstrate opportunity cost and its relationship to choice. Assume that you have $40 to spend, and you are confronted with two choices on which to spend your $40: pizza or Coke®. Pizzas cost $8 each and Cokes cost $2 for a six-pack. Figure 2–1 represents the various combinations of pizza and Coke that you can buy with $40. If you spend the entire $40 on pizza, you could purchase five pizzas (the *y*-intercept in Figure 2–1). Likewise, $40 could purchase 20 six-packs of Coke, as shown by the *x*-intercept in Figure 2–1. Other possibilities lie along the line that connects these two intercepts, showing all possible combinations of pizza and Coke that would exhaust your $40.[1] Of course, all combinations in the shaded area of Figure 2–1 also would be attainable, but these combinations wouldn't exhaust your entire $40. Combinations above and to the right of the line are not attainable because they cost more than $40.

Figure 2–1 illustrates the array of choices and the concept of opportunity cost. The price of one pizza is the same as the price of four six-packs of Coke. The decision to purchase a pizza means the sacrifice of the four six-packs of Coke that could have been purchased instead. Opportunity cost is measured by the slope of the choice line.

For the economy as a whole, the choice is not how to spend income between alternative purchases but how to allocate available resources or factors of production between alternative goods that could be produced. Before we can make this jump from the choice facing individuals to the choice facing the economy, we need to identify the productive resources that an economy has at its disposal.

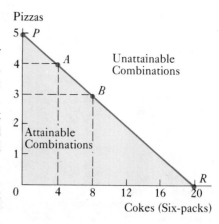

FIGURE 2–1
CHOICE AMONG ALTERNATIVES
If Cokes cost $2 and pizza costs $8, a person with $40 to spend has many attainable combinations of Coke and pizza. The line *PR* represents a boundary between the attainable and unattainable combinations. Along line *PR*, the opportunity cost of one pizza is four Cokes.

LIMITED RESOURCES: THE FACTORS OF PRODUCTION

Economists often use the terms *productive resources* and *factors of production* interchangeably. The **factors of production** are divided into four broad categories: labor, land, capital, and enterprise. All resources that can be used to produce goods and services fit into one of these four categories.

FACTORS OF PRODUCTION
The inputs of land, labor, capital, and enterprise that a firm uses to produce outputs.

Labor

Labor is the factor of production with which you are most familiar. **Labor** is defined as the physical and intellectual exertion of hu-

LABOR
The physical and intellectual exertion of human beings in the production process.

---

1. The line *PR* is a continuous line. It is easy to see why Point *A* or Point *B* in Figure 2–1 represents attainable combinations because Point *A* contains four pizzas at $8 each and four Cokes at $2 each for a total of $40. Likewise, Point *B* represents whole number amounts of Cokes and pizzas. Connecting these points implies that you can purchase fractional units of Coke and pizza; for example, that you could purchase half of a Coke. Since we usually purchase goods in whole units, such as an entire pizza or a full bottle of Coke, it might seem strange to show fractional units as attainable combinations. This is merely a convenient assumption. If the numbers on the axes are large enough—hundreds of pizzas and thousands of Cokes—then there is less of a problem in visualizing the array of combinations as a continuous line.

man beings. The efforts of a professional basketball player, a university professor, and a carpenter are all labor.

Wages are the resource payments that labor receives in exchange for its productive services. Some labor is valued (and paid) more than other labor. Why? One reason is that some labor, like some land, is inherently more productive. Workers are born with different talents and abilities. Some are more intelligent, others are physically stronger or athletically more talented, and still others have artistic or musical ability. It is also possible to make labor more valuable by devoting money and time to improving labor skills. Individuals invest in their labor skills by going to college or practicing basketball. We refer to this development of labor skills as an investment in human capital. **Human capital** is the accumulation of labor-enhancing abilities that increases labor's productivity. A large part of wage differences can be explained by differences in human capital.

Land

The second factor of production is land. **Land,** to an economist, is not merely earth and soil. Rather, it refers to all natural resources that can be used as inputs to production. By this definition, land would include minerals, water, air, forests, oil, and even such intangibles as rainfall, temperature, and soil quality. The income payment to the factor of production land is called **rent.**

A key distinction between land and other productive resources is that land consists of natural resources or conditions unimproved by any human activity. For example, acreage in Arizona that has been irrigated represents more than land. It also represents capital, the third factor of production. Thus, part of the payment that is called rent is a return to land, but part of it may be a return to capital.

Capital

The third factor of production, **capital,** is defined as all aids to production that are human creations rather than found in nature. Capital includes tools, factories, warehouses, and stocks of inventories. Improvements to land—irrigation, landscaping, or adding buildings—are capital, not land. Even part of what we call labor is really human capital if its productivity has been enhanced by investment in human beings.

Capital, like land, receives an income flow; i.e., capital is purchased or rented. The payments to capital are called **interest.** Interest is paid as a reward for giving up present consumption in order to make resources available for the creation of more capital for future production. **Investment** is the act of adding to the capital stock. It includes the purchases of real, tangible assets, such as machines, factories, or stocks of inventories that are used to produce goods and services.

Enterprise

The last factor of production is **enterprise,** which is the service of combining the factors of production to produce goods and services,

---

WAGES
The return to the labor factor of production.

HUMAN CAPITAL
The investment in human beings to improve the quality of labor skills with education, training, health care, and so on.

LAND
Natural resources that can be used as inputs to production.

RENT
The return to the land factor of production.

CAPITAL
The durable, but depreciable, man-made inputs into the production process. Machines, tools, and buildings are examples of capital.

INTEREST
The return to the capital factor of production.

INVESTMENT
Purchases of real, tangible assets, such as machines, factories, or stocks of inventories that are used to produce goods and services.

ENTERPRISE
The input to the production process that involves organizing production, innovation, and risk taking.

taking risk, and introducing new methods and new products (innovation). Entrepreneurs combine the other factors of production by buying or renting these factors to produce a saleable product. The reward for their innovation, risk taking, and organization activities is **profit**.

PROFIT
The return to enterprise as a reward for organizing production, innovation, and risk taking. Profit is the residual after all other factors have been paid.

SOCIETY'S CHOICES: THE PRODUCTION POSSIBILITIES CURVE

A close relative of the "choice" curve of Figure 2–1 is the **production possibilities curve**, which shows the various output combinations of two goods or groups of goods that an economy can produce with its available resources. Underlying this simple economic model are a few assumptions:

PRODUCTION POSSIBILITIES CURVE
A graph that depicts the various combinations of two goods that can be produced with available resources in an economy.

1. All of the economy's productive resources are fully employed. This means that everyone who wants a job has one and that factories, land, and other resources are being used to full capacity.
2. There are only two goods in this economy: missiles and soybeans.
3. The factors of production are homogeneous, or exactly alike. This means that one unit of labor, capital, or land is perfectly substitutable for another unit of the same factor.
4. We are looking at the economy at a particular period of time (the short run). During this time period, both the quantity and quality of resources are fixed, and technology is given.

Table 2–1 shows combinations of missiles and soybeans that the economy can produce, and Figure 2–2 plots the numbers of Table 2–1 on a graph.

TABLE 2-1
PRODUCTION POSSIBILITIES SCHEDULE

Soybeans	Missiles
20	0
16	1
12	2
8	3
4	4
0	5

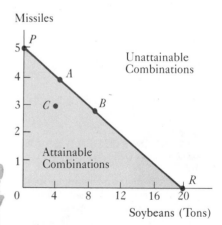

FIGURE 2-2
PRODUCTION POSSIBILITIES CURVE
A production possibilities curve shows combinations of two goods that can be produced in an economy, given resources and technology. Points on the curve represent full employment of resources.

Line *PR* in Figure 2–2 is a **production possibilities curve**. It represents all the attainable combinations of missiles and soybeans that this society can produce with its available resources, all of which are fully employed. Points *A* and *B* represent different combinations of missiles and soybeans, but both are on the production possibilities curve. Points *A* and *B* are both output combinations that the economy can produce with its available resources. Point *C* also is attainable, but since it lies inside of line *PR* it represents unemployed resources. There are points on *PR* that have to be better than *C* because they represent more missiles, more soybeans, or more of both. The economy can do better, i.e., produce more, so *C* is inferior to points on the production possibilities curve.

We can also measure opportunity cost for the economy as a whole along line *PR*. Line *PR* in Figure 2–2 is a straight line. The straight line implies that the opportunity cost of one product in terms of the other, i.e., the number of missiles given up to get another ton of soybeans, doesn't change as the economy moves along *PR*. Each time the production of soybeans is increased by one unit, one-quarter of a missile is sacrificed. The opportunity cost of one more ton of soybeans is one-quarter of a missile, or, conversely, the opportunity cost of one more missile is 4 tons of soybeans.

Constant cost along line *PR* in Figure 2–2 occurs because we assumed that all resources were homogeneous. That is, any unit of labor (or other factor of production) was as productive at producing soybeans as at producing missiles. This assumption produces a straight line production possibilities curve as in Figure 2–2.

Increasing Opportunity Costs

To make the example more realistic, we can drop the assumption of homogeneous factors of production. Table 2–2 shows a different set of combinations of missiles and soybeans that the economy can choose to produce, which are plotted on the graph in Figure 2–3. At Point *A* in Figure 2–3, the economy can produce 10 missiles and 200 tons of soybeans. At Point *B*, the economy can produce more missiles, 100, but can only produce 100 tons of soybeans.

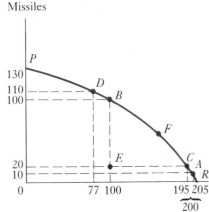

Missiles

Soybeans (Tons)

FIGURE 2–3
PRODUCTION POSSIBILITIES AND INCREASING OPPORTUNITY COSTS
On this production possibilities curve, the opportunity cost of additional units of soybeans increases as the economy becomes more specialized in soybeans; each additional unit of soybeans requires a larger sacrifice of missiles than before (increasing opportunity cost). If the economy is inside the production possibilities curve at some point such as *E*, more of both goods could be produced.

TABLE 2–2
PRODUCTION POSSIBILITIES SCHEDULE

Soybeans	Missiles
205	0
(A) 200 ⎫ −5	10 ⎫ +10
(C) 195 ⎭	20 ⎭
187	30
179	40
169	50
158	60
146	70
133	80
117	90
(B) 100 ⎫ −23	100 ⎫ +10
(D) 77 ⎭	110 ⎭
50	120
0	130

This slight change in assumptions illustrates an important economic fact. If society is at Point *A*, we can get another ten missiles by shifting resources from soybean production to missile production. In the process of moving from Point *A* to Point *C*, we must give up only a small amount of soybeans, 5 units. But if society is at Point *B*, another ten missiles require a larger sacrifice of soybeans, 23 units instead of 5, to get to Point *D*. This curved production possibilities curve illustrates the very important principle of **increasing opportunity costs**—the more missiles you are already producing, the larger the sacrifice of soybeans required to get additional missiles. Table 2–2 shows that at Point *A*, ten more missiles cost 5 units of soybeans, but at Point *B*, producing ten more missiles costs 23 units of soybeans.

INCREASING OPPORTUNITY COST
As production of one good rises, larger and larger sacrifices of another are required.

Increasing opportunity costs are particularly apparent in wartime. As more war goods are demanded, civilian sacrifices become greater. This increasing sacrifice occurs because, initially, the economy uses labor and other resources that are relatively more productive at making missiles and relatively less productive at growing soybeans. As the switch to missiles continues, however, the war economy takes resources that are relatively less productive at making missiles, although they were highly productive at growing soybeans. Soybean production falls by larger and larger amounts, therefore, because more resources are stripped away from soybeans for every extra missile; these resources are increasingly the best the soybean industry has to offer.

Unemployment

Another assumption that we made was that all resources were fully employed. The production possibilities curve can also be used to illustrate unemployment. Suppose the economy is at Point *E* in Figure 2–3, which is inside the production possibilities curve because some workers, factories, land, and machines are unemployed. If the economy could get from Point *E* to Point *C*, it would be possible to have more soybeans (195 instead of 100) with no sacrifice of missiles. Moving from Point *E* to Point *B* means the same amount of soybeans (100) but more missiles (100 instead of 20). Finally, at Point *F*, the economy could produce more of both missiles and soybeans simply by putting idle resources to work. At Point *E*, the opportunity cost of both soybeans and missiles is zero because none of either good has to be sacrificed to increase production of the other.

Both World War II and the Vietnam War made Americans aware of the missiles-versus-soybeans issue. At the beginning of World War II, there were unemployed resources, so it was possible to produce more missiles (war goods) without a sacrifice of soybeans (consumer goods). Eventually, all the idle resources were employed and further expansion of production of war goods required the sacrifice of civilian goods. No automobiles were produced for several years as auto factories switched to military tanks and trucks. Other consumer goods were also in short supply. The Vietnam War in the late 1960s and early 1970s began at a time of relatively little unemployment. Thus, expanding production of military hardware and diverting labor from civilian activities to soldiering led immediately to reduced production of consumer goods. The economy was already on the production possibilities curve when the Vietnam War began.

One of the primary concerns of macroeconomics is to explain how the economy can end up inside the production possibilities curve at a point such as E in Figure 2–3. How can we avoid the idleness and waste of resource unemployment? If the economy finds itself at a point such as Point E, what can be done to get back to the production possibilities curve? The production possibilities curve is a useful way of visualizing these questions.

Economic Growth

Another macroeconomic issue that can be illustrated by the production possibilities curve is economic growth. We drop our assumption of constant technology and a given quantity of resources. As labor becomes more skilled and productive, and as the economy acquires additional machines and plants embodying the latest technology, the production possibilities curve shifts outward from the curve PR to the curve P_1R_1 as in Figure 2–4. If the economy is initially at Point A on PR, it is producing D_1 units of soybeans and C_1 units of missiles. With the growth to P_1R_1, the economy can move to some production point, such as Point B, where it produces both more soybeans (D_2) and more missiles (C_2). Other possible combinations on the new production possibilities curves involve the same amount of one good and more of the other (such as Points E or F) or less of one good and more of the other (such as Points H or J). Regardless of which combination is produced, the important thing about an outward shift in the production possibilities curve from PR to P_1R_1 is that it increases the economy's capacity to respond to human wants.

Additional resources, usually labor or capital, are sources of economic growth. New technology could shift the production possibilities curve outward and account for economic growth. Invention, innovation, resource discovery, and productivity improvements all contribute to economic growth.

SPECIALIZATION AND COMPARATIVE ADVANTAGE

Another way for an economy to go beyond the limited range of production and consumption choices on the production possibilities curve is through specialization and exchange. **Specialization**, or the division of labor, means that individuals will produce one or only a few items, more than they intend to consume, and will trade these items for other things they wish to consume.

Specialization allows individuals to take the fullest advantage of their unique talents and skills. Some people who are stronger and more agile can become professional athletes. Some people who are intelligent and gifted talkers can become lawyers. Others who are intelligent and coordinated can become brain surgeons. The important point is that specialization allows individuals to concentrate on what they do best. They produce more than they could if they tried to engage in a variety of production activities, and enjoy a higher standard of living. By using resources

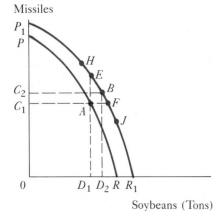

FIGURE 2-4
SHIFTS OF THE PRODUCTION POSSIBILITIES CURVE
An outward shift of the production possibilities curve from PR to P_1R_1 means that the economy can produce more of both goods (economic growth).

SPECIALIZATION
Limiting production activities to one of a small number of goods and services that one produces best in order to exchange for other goods.

more efficiently, more total output can be produced with no increase in resources or breakthroughs in technology. Thus, specialization is another way to improve an individual's standard of living and break the constraints imposed by the production possibilities curve.

Nations, states, and regions also specialize. The phrase *banana republic* used to refer to small Caribbean countries that were heavily specialized in bananas for export. These countries used the earnings from bananas to import and consume a wide variety of products that they did not produce. Other countries are highly specialized in oil, coffee, cocoa, sugar, and other agricultural products and raw materials. Within the United States, pineapples come from Hawaii, oranges from Florida and California, wheat from the midwest and plains states, and peaches from Georgia and South Carolina. Nations, states, and regions also specialize in certain types of manufactures and services; Japan is famous for small cars and electronic products, Switzerland for watches and banking services, and France and Italy for their wines. Small countries in particular can enjoy more goods and a wider range of goods and services through specialization and trade than they could if their consumption were limited to what they produced.

Specialization and Exchange

The benefits of specialization require that people or nations engage in exchange. You could conceivably grow and manufacture all your necessities, but if you specialize, you will need to engage in trade because you give up producing all the other goods and services you need. If you are a successful brain surgeon, you don't have time to spend cutting your own hair, growing your own vegetables, cleaning your own house, or repairing your own car. Much less do you have time to build your house or manufacture your car! One of the characteristics that distinguishes modern industrial societies from earlier times or from less developed countries is the extent of specialization and exchange. Very little of what the average American consumes is produced at home, and very little of what each of us produces is consumed by our own households.

Specialization Based on Comparative Advantage

How do individuals, regions, or nations decide which products to produce for exchange, i.e., how do they answer the question: In what should we specialize? Sometimes the answer is obvious, determined by climate or other resources. In general, the answer lies in the **principle of comparative advantage**, which states that each person, group, or country should specialize in that product or service in which one's opportunity cost of production is lowest. If that principle is followed, the total output of a group of people, an entire economy, or, for that matter, the entire world will be maximized. More total output will result, with no increase in resources or improvement in technology.

Figure 2–5 illustrates comparative advantage using two straight line production possibilities curves for George and Karen. Both can produce various combinations of cookies and hamburgers with their available

PRINCIPLE OF COMPARATIVE ADVANTAGE
The idea that output will be maximized if people specialize in those goods in which their opportunity costs are lowest and engage in exchange to obtain the other goods they want.

resources, as the production possibilities curves illustrate. Before specializing, Karen is producing 30 hamburgers and 10 dozen cookies a month for her own consumption (Point *A* in Figure 2–5), and George is producing 10 hamburgers a month and 40 dozen cookies for himself (Point *R* in the second panel of Figure 2–5). Karen, who has had some valuable experience working in a fast-food restaurant, is better at making hamburgers. Each hamburger she makes only requires sacrificing production of one-half dozen cookies, whereas George's hamburgers cost him 2 dozen cookies per hamburger produced. George has a lower opportunity cost for cookies. Clearly they should specialize.

If they specialize, Karen will produce 50 hamburgers at Point *B*, while George turns out 60 dozen cookies (Point *S*). Total output has increased by 10 hamburgers and 10 dozen cookies. All that remains is to divide up the gains. One combination that would make both better off is to split the increase equally. Karen now consumes at Point *C* in Figure 2–5 and now enjoys 35 hamburgers and 15 dozen cookies. George is consuming at Point *T* in Figure 2–5, with 15 hamburgers and 45 dozen cookies. Both have gained because they can separate consumption at *B* and *S*, respectively, from consumption at *C* for Karen and *T* for George. There is more total output with no new resources and no improvement in technology.

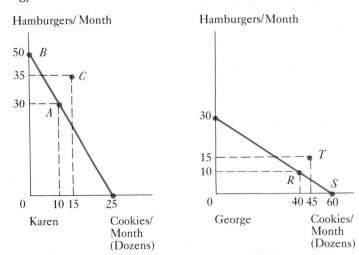

FIGURE 2-5
SPECIALIZATION AND EXCHANGE ON THE PRODUCTION POSSIBILITIES CURVE
When Karen and George specialize, total output increases from 40 hamburgers (Karen 30, George 10) and 50 dozen cookies (Karen 10, George 40) to 50 hamburgers (Karen) and 60 dozen cookies (George). After exchange, both can consume more than before; at Point *C* instead of *A* for Karen and at Point *T* instead of *R* for George.

The principle of comparative advantage is that individuals and nations specialize in these products in which their opportunity cost is lower. It simply states that output will be maximized if everyone produces whatever they produce most efficiently and trades it for what *others* produce more efficiently. We will return to comparative advantage in great detail when we study international economics later in this textbook. However, it is important to keep in mind that comparative advantage is the basis of all trade, not just international trade.

THE PRODUCTION POSSIBILITIES CURVE SHOWS:

- Attainable combinations   along the curve
- Opportunity cost   slope of the curve
- Unemployment   inside the curve
- Economic growth   when the curve shifts to the right

- Gains from specialization and   consumption point outside
  exchange   the curve

THE BASIC ECONOMIC QUESTIONS

The production possibilities curve is useful for visualizing certain macroeconomic concepts, such as unemployed resources and economic growth. It also illustrates such microeconomic principles as opportunity cost and increasing costs of production when nations specialize more heavily in one product relative to the other. The production possibilities curve also illustrates the opportunities for a higher standard of living resulting from specialization and exchange, according to the principle of comparative advantage.

The production possibilities curve shows attainable levels and combinations of output. The production possibilities curve, however, says nothing about how choices are made among these alternative combinations. What determines if a society is at Point B or Point F in Figure 2–4? Closely related to this question is the choice of what input combination to choose, and who receives what share of the chosen output combination. The production possibilities curve poses the basic economic questions of what, how, and for whom.

What, How, and for Whom

The major economic questions are:

1. What combination of goods and services is to be produced? (What)
2. How or with what input combination are the goods and services to be produced? (How)
3. Who will get the goods and services produced, and how much will each person receive? (For whom)

Every society has to answer these basic questions in some way. The three general methods used to answer these questions are tradition, command, and the market.

Tradition, Command, and the Market

Economists divide economic systems into three major types—the traditional economy, the command (planned) economy, and the market economy. Of course, no economy fits neatly into any one of these classification schemes; all economies are mixed economies in that they contain elements of traditional, command, and market-decision processes.

Tradition

TRADITIONAL ECONOMY
An economy in which the fundamental questions are answered by custom or long-standing rules of behavior.

The **traditional economy** answers the fundamental economic questions by appeals to tradition or custom, that is, to how they have been answered in the past. What is produced is whatever parents have taught their children to hunt, to gather, or to plant. The amount of production is, of course, highly dependent on good fortune. The techniques of production (how to produce) are also passed on, with little change, from generation to generation. The answer to the last question, concerning distribution, is also based on tradition. If you have studied cultural anthropology, you know that traditional societies often have rules on how the spoils of the hunt or the harvest are to be divided. Europe in the early Middle Ages was a highly traditional society, with shares of crops assigned to various claimants. There were also obligations for military service or payments to the lord of the manor, established by custom. In a traditional society, the same goods and services are always produced year after year.

You may recognize some elements of tradition that persist even in modern industrial societies such as our own. For example, there are still many small, rural communities almost untouched by modern farming techniques. Some ethnic groups have strong traditions of sons following their fathers' occupations, and women's roles and responsibilities continue to follow tradition in many respects.

Command

COMMAND (PLANNED) ECONOMY
An economy in which the fundamental questions are answered through central command and control.

The **command** (planned) **economy** answers the fundamental microeconomic questions through central command and control. A central planning authority makes all decisions regarding what and how to produce. Individual production units receive detailed plans and orders that carry the weight of law. The question of distribution is answered in the process of determining what and how to produce because planners determine wage rates and the amount of production of consumer goods. This command/plan process is the primary method of organization in the Soviet Union and other countries in Eastern Europe.

In any kind of economy, people plan; that is, they think about the future and make preparations for it. In a command economy, the government plays the primary role in answering the production and consumption questions of the society. This kind of planning is very different from the individual planning that goes on in a market economy, where decision making is less centralized.

Some degree of command and centralized planning exists in all economies, including our own. Federal and state governments play a substantial role in determining what is produced and the manner in which it is produced. Governmental policies also affect the distribution of income, which is the third fundamental question. However, government is not the primary decision maker in the U.S. economy. Most decisions are made by individuals through markets.

The Market

The third type of economic organization is the market economy. The **market economy** relies on incentives and self-interested behavior of individuals to direct production and consumption through market exchanges. Consumers, voting with their dollars, determine what to produce. The result of this voting process determines what goods and services are available.

Suppliers determine how to produce. Since suppliers are self-interested and seek to maximize their profits, they tend to combine inputs so as to produce any good or service at the lowest possible cost. The answer to the *how* question depends on the prices of productive resources. Suppliers will use more of relatively abundant resources because they are relatively cheap.

These goods and services are then distributed to consumers who have the purchasing power to buy them. Households that have more purchasing power (because they own the most valuable productive resources) receive more goods and services. The quantity and quality of the labor skills the individual sells are the most important determinants of individual income because about 75 percent of the income in the United States is labor income. Those with high-quality, scarce skills receive high salaries and can be more of a force in directing production. In a sense, higher earning people have more votes.

One essential condition needed in order to allow undirected markets to answer the basic questions is the institution of **property rights**. Markets will function and exchange will occur only if individual buyers and sellers possess the property rights to the goods and services they exchange. Legal enforcement of property rights and freedom to exchange these rights are essential if a market system is to function well.

In a market system, productive resources are owned by individuals. In order to invest in capital, owners need to be assured that they will be able to claim the ownership of that capital and the products that it produces. They also need to be assured that it will not be taken away by the state or by force or violence, with no recourse for the owner. Even workers will not offer their labor for hire if their contract for payment cannot be enforced or if they know they will be held up and have their earnings stolen. Agreements to use productive resources and to make payments for them have to be protected both from threats of violence or destruction and from the threat that the contract will not be honored by one of the parties. What a market system needs, then, is a legal system or other mechanism that works reasonably well. It would define property rights and enforce them against breach of contract as well as theft and other violations of property rights. Defining and enforcing property rights is an important function of government even in a primarily market economy.

Dealing with Change

One way to compare the workings of these three types of systems is to consider how each system deals with change. As an example,

MARKET ECONOMY
An economy in which the fundamental questions are answered through the market, relying on self-interested behavior and incentives.

PROPERTY RIGHTS
The legal right to a specific property, including the rights to own, buy, sell, or use in specific ways. Markets and exchanges can occur only if individuals have property rights to goods, services, and productive resources.

suppose that an earthquake closes some copper mines so that the supply of copper is suddenly cut in half. A traditional economy would probably have rules governing the distribution of the reduced supply, but little flexibility in adjusting production processes or the output mix. In a command economy, government officials would have to determine the possible effects of this shortage and estimate how long it will last. They then would have to notify all users of copper that they should use less of it. For example, orders would have to be sent to firms producing electric generators to substitute some other metal for copper.

Contrast this process to what occurs in a market system. When the mines close and less copper is available, copper prices rise. Consumers of copper know immediately that the price has gone up. They then search for cheaper substitutes. (All this happens very quickly with no need for government to process and send information.) The market has economized on the amount of costly information needed to make production and consumption decisions.

The Mixed Economy

Clearly the market-decision process has advantages over command and tradition in its flexibility and capacity for dealing with change. However, using the market also has some drawbacks. Many observers criticize the distribution of income that results from the workings of the market, which can create extremes of wealth and poverty. Market systems tend to encourage individualistic, self-interested behavior at the expense of community interests.

Because of the positive advantages of the market-decision process, even primarily traditional or command economies incorporate some elements of markets. Conversely, market economies often make modifications to the pure market system to soften some of the harshness of unbridled capitalism.

MIXED ECONOMY
An economy in which the fundamental questions are answered partly by market forces and partly by government.

The blend of tradition, command, and market-decision methods will vary, but the typical modern industrial economies such as Canada, Japan, the United States, Australia, and some of the nations of Western Europe have mixed economies. In **mixed economies**, the basic decision method is the market, but a significant number of economic choices are made by government bodies. These choices are designed to moderate the outcomes of unregulated market activity while keeping most of the benefits of markets intact. The goal of such policies is to leave economic decisions to the marketplace when it works well but to intervene in the economy when the marketplace leads to unsatisfactory performance. On a macroeconomic level, a high rate of unemployment is an example of an unsatisfactory market result. On a microeconomic level, pollution caused by steel mills is an example of undesirable market outcomes. In both instances, some people argue that a governmental body should step in to correct the unsatisfactory performance of the market and alter its results.

All noncommunist industrial nations are properly categorized as mixed economies. The mix varies significantly between countries. Governments are much more heavily involved in the economy in Sweden and Great Britain than in the United States and West Germany. The differences in governmental involvement reflect differences in political systems and historical experience.

The remainder of this textbook will present economic theory in the context of a mixed, but primarily market, economy. For the most part (until the very end of the textbook), the mixed economy to which we refer is the United States' economy. The economic theory that we develop, however, is universally applicable; what differs is how often and for what purpose different countries choose to intervene in the market.

THE CIRCULAR FLOW OF ECONOMIC ACTIVITY

Chapter 1 discusses the use of models by economists to develop simple descriptions from which wider conclusions and inferences can be made. One model that is often used to describe a market economy is the **circular flow model**. This model provides a good overview of the central concerns of both macroeconomics and microeconomics. The circular flow model is a visual representation of the relationships between factor markets that generate income and product markets in which income is used to purchase goods and services. The first economist to describe such a flow was the French economist Francois Quesnay (1694–1774).

In a pure market economy, there are only two kinds of participants: households and business firms. Firms and households interact in two types of markets, the factor and product markets, as shown in Figure 2–6. Households purchase goods and services produced by firms, creating a flow of dollars to firms in payment for these goods and services. The individual markets in which these exchanges take place, shown in the upper part of Figure 2–6, make up the **product market**. Firms buy factors of production (inputs or resources) from households (who own all the productive resources) in order to produce the goods and services they sell to the households. The total of the individual markets in which these transactions take place, in the lower part of Figure 2–6, is the **factor market**. The flow of productive resources to firms generates a reverse flow of dollar payments (wages, rent, interest, and profits). Quesnay saw such a system as a closed one, in which the flow would be continuous like the circular flow of blood in our bodies.

Sometimes firms and households are one and the same. A family-owned grocery store, a home-based accounting service, or a day-care facility may operate from within the household. For simplicity, we separate them so that households own all factors of production, and firms produce all goods and services.

The circular flow in Figure 2–6 is a very simple model of the way a market economy operates. As we add some of the complications that would make this model more realistic, we will also identify some of the important economic questions that will recur in later chapters.

The first complication is to relax the assumption that the flow of income from firms to households (the lower half of Figure 2–6) and the flow of payments from households to firms (the upper half of Figure 2–6) are equal. If firms pay out all of their revenues to households, and households spend every dollar they receive on purchases of goods and services, then the flows will be equal. But if households save part of their income,

CIRCULAR FLOW MODEL
A visual representation of the relationships between factor markets that generate income and product markets in which income is used to purchase goods and services.

PRODUCT MARKET
Markets in which goods and services produced by firms are sold.

FACTOR MARKET
Markets in which owners of factors of production sell these factors' services to producers.

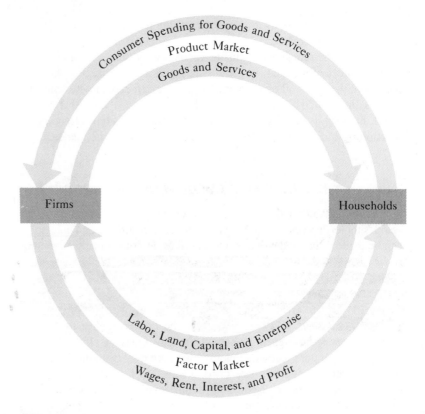

FIGURE 2-6
CIRCULAR FLOW OF INCOME
Households purchase goods and services in the product market and supply land, labor, capital, and enterprise in the factor market. Firms buy the services of these inputs in the factor market, and supply goods and services in the product market.

there is a leakage out of the circular flow. If firms invest (buy new capital equipment) then there is injection into the circular flow. Either an injection or a leakage can change the size of the flow. We will consider injections and leakages in Chapter 5 and throughout the macroeconomics part of this textbook.

A second omission from the simple model is that it doesn't contain a government sector. We know that local, state, and federal governments produce, or cause the production of, goods ranging from schools and libraries to MX missiles. Governments take part of household incomes in taxes and purchase productive inputs from households. Government plays an important microeconomic role because it affects the mix of goods and services to be produced and the distribution of output. In macroeconomics, government actions affect the amount of total production as well as unemployment and economic growth.

The third omission in the simple model in Figure 2–6 is that there are no prices; the broad labels "factor market" and "product market" provide no information about how product prices and factor prices are determined or how producing firms select the mix of products or inputs. These microeconomic questions constitute roughly half of an introductory course in economics.

As you can see, this simple model of a market economy raises more questions than it answers. It is very valuable, however, because it allows us to organize our thoughts about the subject we are going to study. This is the "forest" that you need to keep in mind as we proceed to look at various economic "trees." In later chapters, we will add some refinements to the simple circular flow model and examine how the two sets of markets work. As we saw in Chapter 1, models are an important part of economic analysis because they permit more orderly thinking about the world.

THE INTERNATIONAL PERSPECTIVE
FRANCOIS QUESNAY (1694–1774)

It is easy to get the impression that most economists are American, and the rest are British. Americans tend to be unaware of the great contributions made to economic thinking by economists from non-English-speaking countries. Such European economists as Jean Baptiste Say, Leon Walras, Friedrich Bastiat (French), Karl Menger (Austrian), and Karl Marx (German) had a profound impact on economic thinking in the nineteenth century.

An early and important contribution to economic thinking in the eighteenth century, the concept of the circular flow, was contributed by a French economist. Francois Quesnay was the leader of a group of French economists known as the Physiocrats. The Physiocrats were the first group of economic thinkers to be credited with a school of thought. They were also the first to engage in macroeconomic analysis.

The name *Physiocrats* comes from the French word *physiocrate*, which means "rule of nature." Physiocrats believed that the economy was a part of the natural order and that there were natural laws governing the causes of wealth. They believed that all wealth came from using nature. Farming, fishing, and mining were seen as productive industries. Merchants were seen as parasites because they consumed what farming, fishing, and mining produced, without producing something themselves. Quesnay, a physician (he was Louis XV's doctor), was inspired by William Harvey's discovery that blood circulated in the human body. This led him to develop the circular flow model of the macro economy, which was based on the view that the circulation of resources and products in the macro economy was similar to the circulation of blood in the human body. And, as with the loss of blood, the Physiocrats were concerned about any reduction in this flow.

SUMMARY

1. The economy has finite resources, but human wants are insatiable. This conflict is the fundamental problem of economics—scarcity. We cannot have everything we want; therefore, we must make choices.

2. The factors of production consist of labor, land, capital, and enterprise. Labor receives wages, land receives rent, capital receives interest, and enterprise receives profit.

3. The production possibilities schedule and curve illustrate the problem of scarcity. If society wants more of one good, it must settle for less of another. The cost of extra units of one good is the number of units of the other good sacrificed—opportunity cost.

4. The principle of increasing opportunity costs tells us that the more of one good we have, the greater the amount of other goods that must be sacrificed to get one more unit.

5. The production possibilities curve is useful in describing unemployment (points inside the production possibilities curve), economic growth (shifting the production possibilities curve to the right), and the benefits of specialization and exchange.

6. Individuals and nations can gain a higher standard of living from the same resources if they engage in specialization and exchange. Total output will be larger if individuals, regions, and nations produce those goods for which their opportunity costs are lowest and trade for other things. This is the principle of comparative advantage.

7. Every society must address three basic questions to be answered: what to produce, how to produce it, and for whom to produce. Societies answer these questions through tradition, command, and the market.

8. In different degrees, Western industrial nations have tried to answer the basic economic questions by using a mixed economy, where the government intervenes in the marketplace in an attempt to improve economic performance.

9. The circular flow diagram is a useful overview of the interrelationships found in a market economy.

NEW TERMS

scarcity	capital	traditional economy
insatiable wants	interest	command (planned) economy
opportunity cost	investment	market economy
factors of production	enterprise	property rights
labor	profit	mixed economy
wages	production possibilities curve	circular flow model
human capital	increasing opportunity cost	product market
land	specialization	factor market
rent	principle of comparative advantage	

QUESTIONS FOR DISCUSSION

1. Are wants insatiable? Why or why not?
2. What is opportunity cost? What is increasing opportunity cost?
3. How is opportunity cost involved in the decision to spend spring vacation skiing at Aspen instead of tanning at Fort Lauderdale?
4. Is your college degree an investment in human capital? What is the opportunity cost of your degree?
5. What is the mixed economy approach to handling macroeconomic problems?
6. In what ways are factor markets and product markets similar? In what ways are they different?
7. Why is specialization necessary for exchange and vice versa?
8. Given the following data, plot a production possibilities curve and calculate the opportunity cost of bicycles in terms of boots. Then assume that new technology does the following:
   a. increases the possible output of both boots and bicycles by 50 percent.

   b. increases the amount of bicycles that can be produced by six if all resources are devoted to bicycles but does not change the amount of boots that can be produced.

   Draw the new production possibilities curve in both cases and calculate opportunity costs in both cases.

Bicycles	Boots
10	0
8	10
6	20
4	30
2	40
0	50

9. If you know that the opportunity cost of books in terms of cassettes foregone is 1 book = 2 cassettes, and you know that available resources can produce a

maximum of 100 books, can you draw the production possibilities curve for these two goods? If so, what is the maximum possible output of cassettes? If we choose to produce 40 books, how many cassettes can be produced?

10. Angela and Arthur have been assigned the tasks of filing folders and grading papers. Angela calculates that she can file 50 folders an hour and grade 20 papers. Arthur knows that he can file 25 folders per hour and grade 25 papers. The total assignment for these two work-study students is 100 papers to grade and 200 folders to file. How long will it take if they divide the task equally? How long will it take if

they specialize on the principle of comparative advantage? How much time do they gain?

11. Which of the following represents tradition, which command, and which market decision making?
   a. the military draft
   b. the volunteer army
   c. encouraging daughters to be teachers and nurses
   d. requiring women to be teachers and nurses
   e. offering financial incentives for anyone—male or female—to become teachers or nurses
   f. five generations of farmers on the same land
   g. prohibiting the sale of marijuana
   h. taxing the sale of alcoholic beverages

SUGGESTIONS FOR FURTHER READING

Carson, Robert B. *Economic Issues Today: Alternative Approaches.* 4th ed. New York: St. Martin's Press, Inc., 1986. The introduction gives an overview of alternative values and approaches underlying different economic systems.

Radford, R.A. "The Economic Organization of a P.O.W. Camp." *Economica* (November 1945): 189–201. This classic economics article demonstrates how a market economy quickly established itself in a P.O.W. camp during World War II and highlights the gains from exchange.

CHAPTER 3

SUPPLY AND DEMAND: THE BASICS OF ECONOMIC ANALYSES

INTRODUCTION

Supply and demand is the most basic and most widely used model in economics. Many economists contend that economics is 90 percent supply and demand analysis and that the other 10 percent is the study of what causes supply and demand to be what they are. Economists view **demand** as the desire to consume certain quantities at certain prices, not needs or wants that can be measured in some social or biological way. The concept of "need" is reserved for policymakers and political decision making. For these needs and wants to be demands, they must be viewed as what people actually will do when confronted with different sets of prices. We are not talking about wishes or dreams but about planned expenditures over a period of time backed by purchasing power. Similarly, **supply** refers to what firms actually are willing and able to produce and offer for sale over a period of time at various prices. Supply and demand are flow variables, and it is important to identify the period, e.g., per day, per week, or per year.

DEMAND
The desire and ability to consume certain quantities of goods at certain prices over a period of time.

SUPPLY
The quantity of goods offered for sale over a particular time period at various prices.

DEMAND

Many factors can affect the demand for a good or service. We generally focus on a few, and we separate them into two important categories: price and nonprice determinants. We then choose our words carefully and say that price affects quantity demanded, and the nonprice factors affect demand. We are assuming that price is the most important determinant and that the nonprice determinants are normally held constant. The nonprice determinants are as follows:

1. the tastes of the group demanding the good
2. the size of the group demanding the good

3. the income and wealth of the group demanding the good
4. the prices of other goods and services
5. expectations about future prices or income

Virtually all things that affect demand work through one of these factors. The weather, for example, may affect the demand for bread by changing people's taste for bread. People may eat more cold cut sandwiches instead of hot meals in warmer weather. We study demand by holding all but one factor constant and determining what happens when we change that factor. This method uses the *ceteris paribus* assumption discussed in Chapter 1.

The Law of Demand

First we want to consider what happens when the price of a good or service changes relative to the prices of other goods and services because there is much evidence that price is a very important determinant of demand. In looking at the relationship between price and quantity, we hold constant all of the other factors that affect demand.

ALFRED MARSHALL (1842–1924)

Alfred Marshall was the great synthesizer and expositor of the *neoclassical school of economics*. The neoclassical school consisted of a regeneration of much of classical economics after Karl Marx (and others) had criticized the weaknesses in classical analysis. Most present-day microeconomic theory can be directly traced to this neoclassical school of economic thought.

Born in London, Marshall came to the study of economics by a circuitous route. Marshall was offered a scholarship at Oxford that would have led to the ministry. Instead, he enrolled at Cambridge to study mathematics. Later, Marshall began to study political economy, but he made extensive use of mathematics in developing his economic theory.

Marshall returned to teach at Cambridge. There he belonged to what he called "a small cultural society of great simplicity and distinction." At Cambridge, Marshall generated a tremendous impact on the economics profession. At first, this impact was felt primarily through his influence as a teacher of almost all the major British economists of the early twentieth century. Later, his textbook *Principles of Economics* (1890) influenced still larger numbers of students. Generations of economists learned economics from Marshall's *Principles*. In fact, if you had taken a course in economics before 1950, it is very probable that you would have studied from Marshall's textbook.

LAW OF DEMAND
The quantity demanded of a good or service is negatively related to its price, *ceteris paribus*.

DEMAND SCHEDULE
A tabular listing that shows the quantity demanded at various prices over a particular time period.

The **law of demand** states that the *quantity demanded* of a good or service is negatively related to its price, *ceteris paribus*. In other words, holding all else constant, consumers will purchase more of a good or service at a lower price than at a higher price. As price rises, *ceteris paribus*, consumers will demand a smaller quantity of a good or service. Note that we are saying *quantity demanded*—not demand—is a function of price. This is a critical distinction. Demand refers to a whole set of price-quantity combinations, whereas quantity demanded is the amount we want to buy at a particular price.

A **demand schedule** shows the various *quantities* demanded at various prices over a particular time. How can we generate a demand schedule for an individual? We could develop Mary Jones' demand schedule for potato chips since she already knows all of the *ceteris paribus* conditions for herself (tastes, income, prices of substitutes, and so on). We might suggest various prices and ask her how many bags of potato chips she would buy at each price. Such experiments have been conducted on rats, prisoners, patients in mental hospitals, and students, among other groups. These experiments all support the validity of the law of demand.

The hypothetical demand schedule in Table 3–1 shows Fred Smith's demand for bread. Note again that there is a time dimension; in this case, one week. We cannot answer the question How many loaves will he buy? without specifying per day, per week, per month, per year, or per lifetime. The answers would be very different in each case.

As price falls to very low levels, as in this example, it is possible that Fred Smith would consume large quantities of bread as he substitutes bread for other items he purchases.

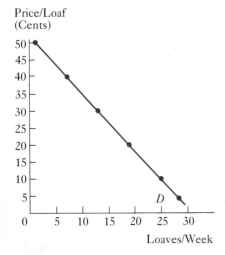

Price/Loaf
(Cents)

Loaves/Week

FIGURE 3-1
FRED SMITH'S DEMAND FOR BREAD
An individual's demand curve shows the quantity that the individual will purchase at different prices.

DEMAND CURVE
A graphical representation of a demand schedule showing the quantity demanded at various prices over a particular time period.

TABLE 3-1
FRED SMITH'S DEMAND FOR BREAD

Price per Loaf (Cents)	Quantity Demanded per Week
50	1
40	7
30	13
20	19
10	25
5	28

Table 3–1 conforms to our law of demand because Fred Smith demands larger quantities of bread at lower prices. We can now convert the demand schedule of Table 3–1 to a graphical representation that we call a **demand curve**. Such a curve is drawn in Figure 3–1. The demand curve is the line graph representing the demand schedule. When we draw a demand curve, we designate the *y*-axis to show the price per unit variable and the *x*-axis to show the quantity per time period variable.[1] It is impor-

1. If graphing the schedule is confusing, review the appendix to Chapter 1. We usually draw linear curves for convenience.

tant to always designate the quantity as quantity per unit of time. In drawing a hypothetical demand curve, this can be done by labeling the *x*-axis as *x/t*, meaning quantity of *x* per time period.

Market Demand

We now have generated a demand schedule and a demand curve representing Fred Smith's demand for bread. We usually are more concerned with the market demand curve for a brand-name bread or even the market demand curve for all bread. A **market demand** curve shows what quantity will be demanded by all consumers in a certain market at various prices. The market demand curve is found by adding all of the individual demand schedules. This involves a horizontal geometric summation of the individual consumer demand curves. For example, to determine the market demand for bread at a price of 40 cents per loaf, we would add Fred Smith's demand for seven loaves to the two loaves demanded by Mary Jones, a loaf demanded by John Stevens, and so on. We calculate that there is a total (market) demand for 10,000 loaves if the price is 40 cents per loaf. This would give us one point on the market demand curve. We could then repeat this procedure (in principle) for every other price. The result is the downward sloping market demand curve shown in Figure 3–2. In practice, market demand curves are not found in this way. Market demand usually is used as a theoretical construct. When an actual demand curve is desired, a statistician would attempt to construct one from observed fluctuations in consumption at different prices.

As price changes in the market, the quantity demanded changes in the opposite direction. In Figure 3–2, 13,000 loaves of bread are purchased at a price of 35 cents per loaf. If price falls to 20 cents per loaf, the quantity demanded increases to 25,000 loaves. If price rises to 45 cents per loaf, the quantity demanded decreases to 5,000 loaves.

Changes in Demand and the *Ceteris Paribus* Conditions

Changes in the *ceteris paribus* conditions change the demand for the good or service. The changes in demand are graphed as a shift in the curve.

Tastes

How do changes in the *ceteris paribus* factors affect the market demand for a commodity? Suppose people's tastes change. Let's assume that people's tastes change in favor of bread because the weather is hot or a fad for vegetarian diets is popular. Such a change in taste is reflected in Figure 3–3 as an increase in demand. An **increase in demand** means that at every price, consumers demand a larger amount than before. The demand curve shifts from D_0 to D_1. The opposite would have occurred if tastes changed away from bread. Such a change in tastes would cause a **decrease in demand**, represented by a shift from D_0 to D_2. A decrease in demand would show up as a shift in the demand curve indicating that at every price, consumers demand a smaller quantity than before.

MARKET DEMAND
The summation of all of the individual consumer demand curves. A market demand curve shows what quantity will be demanded over a particular time period by all consumers in a certain market at various prices.

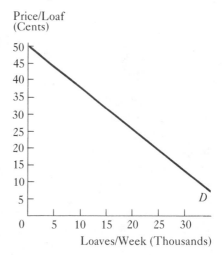

FIGURE 3–2
MARKET DEMAND FOR BREAD
A market demand curve is a graphical depiction of how much will be purchased in the market at various prices. It is the aggregation of all of the individual demand curves.

INCREASE IN DEMAND
A shift in the demand curve indicating that at every price, consumers demand a larger quantity than before.

DECREASE IN DEMAND
A shift in the demand curve indicating that at every price, consumers demand a smaller quantity than before.

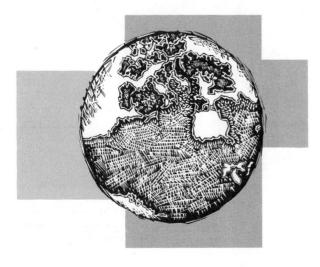

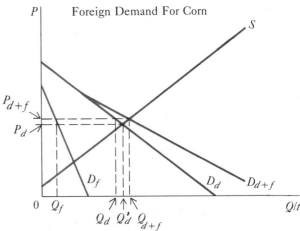

THE INTERNATIONAL PERSPECTIVE ADDING FOREIGN DEMAND AND SUPPLY

Although they will be discussed in detail later in the textbook, it is a simple matter to see how foreign demand and supply can affect domestic markets. Some commodities, in particular those with high transportation costs, will not be traded internationally. Many products, however, have some international demand or supply.

In an open economy, the market demand curve faced by producers is the horizontal summation of the domestic demand for the product and the foreign demand for the product. Consider the market demand for U.S. corn. If there were no foreign demand, the market price would settle at P_d, and corn producers would sell Q'_d tons of corn. (See the Foreign Demand for Corn graph.) When foreign demand, D_f, is added, the price rises to P_{d+f}, and the amount sold rises to Q_{d+f}. The price of corn and the amount of corn sold have both increased. Consumers in the domestic market are paying a higher price because they now pay P_{d+f}. Since the domestic demand curve hasn't shifted and the price has increased, the quantity of corn demanded by domestic consumers will fall. In this example, domestic consumption falls to Q_d.

It appears that domestic corn producers have gained at the expense of domestic corn consumers. After all, consumers now pay a higher price for less corn. This conclusion is correct, but it ignores the other side of the coin. Foreign consumers can only buy the corn if they sell something that earns the currency necessary to pay for the corn. The domestic supply of the product that foreigners sell to pay for the corn will have an effect in other markets.

The second graph, "Foreign Supply of Automobiles," shows the market for automobiles. Without a foreign supply, the domestic price and quantity would be P_d and Q'_d. Adding foreign supply, S_f, changes the equilibrium. There is a decline in price to P_{d+f} and an increase in quantity demanded to Q_{d+f}. In this case, the domestic consumption of automobiles increased by $Q_{d+f} - Q_d$. Domestic consumers have more automobiles at a lower price.

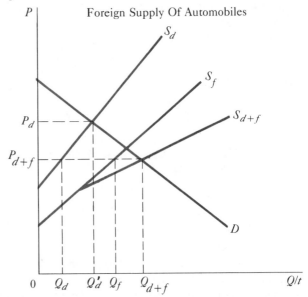

There is an important lesson in this demand and supply exercise. The lesson is that, relative to a no-trading situation, the opening of foreign trade will result in higher prices and less consumption of exported items and lower prices and more consumption of imported items. So there are winners and losers as a result of international trade. But, as you learned in Chapter 2, the principle of comparative advantage shows that the net effect is an expansion of consumption alternatives for consumers in the domestic market.

Size of the Group

The market demand curve, as we saw earlier, is found by aggregating the individual demand curves. Consequently, if the size of the group changes (the number of individuals in the group), market demand will also change. In Figure 3–3, demand curve D_0 might be the demand for automobiles in a state that has a minimum driving age of 17 years. If the law is changed to allow 16-year-olds to drive, the demand curve will shift from D_0 to D_1, as in Figure 3–3. The size of the group has increased; therefore, there has been an increase in the demand for the good. This means that there will be a larger quantity demanded at every price.

Conversely, if the size of the group decreases, there will be a decrease in demand. This would be depicted as a shift from D_0 to D_2. The big reduction in the birth rate in the late 1960s and through the 1970s decreased demand first for baby food and diapers and then for public school teachers. In the late 1980s, it is affecting the demand curves for automobiles and college teachers.

Income and Wealth

Income changes can also shift the demand curve. You might expect that demand for all goods would increase as income increases. However, this is not always true of all goods; it depends on whether the good under consideration is a normal good or an inferior good. A **normal good** is a good for which demand increases as income increases, *ceteris paribus*. If demand falls when income rises, we have an **inferior good**. Most goods are normal goods.

If we define goods quite narrowly, it is possible to identify some inferior goods. Consider, for example, poorer cuts of meat, such as hamburger. If, as an individual's income increases, the individual consumes less hamburger and more steak, hamburger is an inferior good and steak is a normal good. However, although meat or beef in general is still considered a normal good.[2] In terms of demand curves, an increase in income causes demand in Figure 3–3 to increase to D_1 if good x is a normal good. If good x is an inferior good, the shift to D_1 is caused by a decrease in income. The opposite changes in income cause a decrease in demand. Again, consider Figure 3–3. The decrease in demand represented by the shift in demand from D_0 to D_2 would result from a decrease in income if x is a normal good or an increase in income if x is an inferior good.

Changes in wealth have the same effect as a change in income. If the stock market crashes, leaving people less wealthy, the demand for normal goods will decline. When the stock market experienced a significant decline in October of 1987, many analysts predicted a recession. They were expecting a recession because they expected the decline in wealth to cause consumer spending to decrease.

Prices of Other Goods

The fourth determinant that we listed as an influence on demand is the prices of other goods and services. There are two classes of these other goods, complements and substitutes. **Complementary goods** are goods that are jointly consumed. If consuming goods together

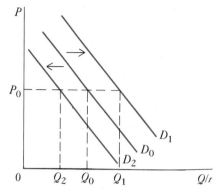

FIGURE 3–3
EFFECTS OF CHANGES IN THE *CERTERIS PARIBUS* CONDITIONS ON THE DEMAND FOR BREAD
If a change causes more to be demanded at every price, the curve will shift to the right, as from D_0 to D_1. A change that causes less to be demanded at every price causes a shift to the left, as from D_0 to D_2.

NORMAL GOOD
A good for which demand increases as income increases.

INFERIOR GOOD
A good for which demand decreases as income increases.

COMPLEMENTARY GOODS
Those goods that are jointly consumed. The consumption of one good enhances the consumption of the other good.

---

2. A good example of an inferior good is an outhouse. As a community's income rises, the demand for outhouses decreases. In the United States, outhouses have almost become obsolete.

SUBSTITUTE GOODS
Goods that replace the consumption of other goods.

enhances the enjoyment of both, such as bacon and eggs, lamps and light bulbs, bicycles and backpacks, or hamburgers and ketchup, we refer to them as complements. Substitute goods have just the opposite relationship. Rather than enhancing the enjoyment of the other good, **substitute goods** replace the consumption of it. Orange juice and grapefruit juice, Coke® and Pepsi®, and Reebok® and Adidas® court shoes would be examples of this type of relationship.

Whether goods are complements or substitutes determines how changes in the price of one affect the other. Figure 3–3 can be applied to the demand for good x (bagels). If the price of complementary good y (lox) goes up, the demand for bagels will decrease, shifting from D_0 to D_2. The reason for this is that consumers will now consume fewer lox because their price is higher and will thus demand fewer bagels at every price. The opposite would occur if the price of lox fell. Consumers would now want to consume more lox and thus will demand more bagels at each price. This would be geometrically depicted as a shift from D_0 to D_1.

Now consider what happens when there is a substitute relationship between the two goods. Good x (Coke) and good y (Pepsi) are substitutes. In Figure 3–3, curve D_0 represents the demand for good x (Coke). The price of good y (Pepsi) now increases relative to the price of Coke. Since this makes Coke more attractive to consumers, they will now demand more Coke at every price. Geometrically, the demand for Coke shifts from D_0 to D_1 in Figure 3–3. If the price of the substitute, Pepsi, decreases relative to the price of Coke, the opposite would happen. Consumers would now find Coke less attractive and would desire less of it at each price as they shift consumption to Pepsi. This is a decrease in demand for Coke, represented by the shift from D_0 to D_2 in Figure 3–3. The shift to substitutes as price rises is an important basis for the law of demand.

You may be tempted to ask if there are goods that are neither substitutes nor complements. In a broad sense, all goods are substitutes for each other because they are all alternatives on which people can spend income. But some are closer substitutes than others. The more easily that good A can be substituted for good B, the more the change in the price of one will affect the demand curve for the other. Consider the effect of a rise in the price of watches on the demand for hot dogs. A rise in the price of watches will have very little effect on demand for hot dogs, but it may affect the demand for clocks, bracelets, or other substitutes.

Often we make the error of assuming a good has no satisfactory substitutes. How often have you heard someone say, "There is no substitute for . . . (victory, success, steak, a car, or any of dozens of other 'irreplaceable' items)." In fact, there are substitutes for everything; if the price of anything rises sharply enough, we will start searching harder for acceptable substitutes.[3] Substitute relationships are studied when discussing elasticity of demand.

Expectations

The last of the changes in *ceteris paribus* factors that affect demand is **expectations**. If individuals expect demand to change in the

EXPECTATIONS
Individual forecasts for the state of the future.

---

3. This point often makes economists seem cynical. Does honesty have a substitute? Yes. If the price becomes "too high," many people (but not all) will become dishonest.

future, they may take action now that they otherwise might postpone. For example, if you expect that the demand for automobiles will be so high next year that their prices will rise, you may decide to buy a car now to avoid the higher price. Other changes in expectations can also affect demand. If you expect your income to be higher in the future, you may demand more goods and borrow to pay for them so that you do not have to delay consumption until your income rises.

Expectations and the effect of expectations on demand can be important in both microeconomics and macroeconomics. If enough people act on an expectation of the future, it will become self-fulfilling. For example, if you expect drought conditions to raise the price of wheat next fall, you will adjust your behavior and buy more wheat now. If enough people agree with your expectations, the price of wheat will rise, affecting the market *before* the growing season is over. Similar effects can occur in the macroeconomy. If groups of consumers think that inflation will continue unabated, they will purchase as many goods as they can now to avoid the higher prices that inflation will bring later. If large numbers of people follow this behavior, they will bring about the very inflation that they expected.

Economists are very careful to distinguish clearly between movements along a demand curve and changes (or shifts) of the curve itself. Movements along the curve are *changes in quantity demanded*, caused solely by a change in the *price* of the good. Changes (or shifts) of the curve are *changes in demand* caused by changes in any of the *ceteris paribus* conditions. There is nothing magical about this language. It is terminology created for convenience. When we diagram a demand curve, we are looking at quantity demanded as a function of price. Price affects the quantity demanded. When we change other factors, these affect demand.

REASONS FOR A CHANGE IN THE QUANTITY DEMANDED

- The quantity of a good or service demanded will *increase* if the price of the good or service *decreases*.
- The quantity of a good or service demanded will *decrease* if the price of the good or service *increases*.

REASONS FOR A CHANGE IN DEMAND

The demand for a normal good or service will *increase* if:

- buyers' tastes change to favor that good or service,
- the number of buyers in the market increases,
- the income or wealth of buyers increases,
- the prices of complementary goods fall,
- the prices of substitute goods increase, or
- buyers' expectations of the future cause them to purchase more now.

The demand for a normal good or service will *decrease* if:

* buyers' tastes change against that good or service,
* the number of buyers in the market decreases,
* the income or wealth of buyers decreases,
* the prices of complementary goods increase,
* the prices of substitute goods decrease, or
* buyers' expectations of the future cause them to delay purchases.

SUPPLY

SUPPLY SCHEDULE
A tabular listing that shows quantity supplied over a particular time period at various prices.

A **supply schedule** shows the various quantities offered for sale at a particular time and at various prices. When examining supply, we again have price as the primary determinant, the one that affects quantity supplied. When we talk about supply, like demand, we have certain *ceteris paribus* factors that can shift the supply curve when they change. We usually concentrate on five other factors that affect supply and shift the curve. These five factors are as follows:

1. the state of technology
2. prices of the factors of production
3. the number of suppliers
4. expectations
5. prices of related goods

Everything that affects supply works through one of these determinants. For example, if there is a natural disaster that destroys large amounts of capital, it will affect supply through its effect on the price of capital. If the price of corn rises relative to wheat, a farmer might decide to grow corn instead of wheat.

The (Not Quite) Law of Supply

Initially we will focus on what happens when the price of the good or service under consideration changes. Assume a *ceteris paribus* situation by holding constant everything but the price of the good or service. We can then state the **(not quite) law of supply** as follows:

(NOT QUITE) LAW OF SUPPLY
The *quantity supplied* of a good or service is *usually* a positive function of price, *ceteris paribus*.

The *quantity supplied* of a good or service is *usually* a positive function of price, *ceteris paribus*.

This means that, holding all else constant, suppliers usually will supply less of a good or service at lower prices; as prices rise, the quantity supplied will increase. It is important to note that *quantity supplied* is a function of price. This distinction is important, as it was in the case of demand. Note also the word *usually*. This is why it is a "not quite" law. There are two exceptions to this relationship. The first is when there is no time to produce more units (for example, theater seats at a sold-out performance) or when a unique supplier no longer exists (for example, paintings by Picasso). In these unusual cases, quantity supplied does not respond to price at all. The second exception occurs in certain areas of production where increased volume allows costs per unit to fall. This can happen when the increased volume of production creates efficiencies in an important input market. For example, as a factory expands, it might cause a trucking firm to relocate. The proximity of the trucking firm could reduce costs to the factory. We will discuss this exception in greater detail in an upcoming chapter.

Table 3–2 shows a hypothetical supply schedule for an individual supplier—Susan Smith's Lemonade Stand. A supply schedule shows the quantity supplied over a period of time at various prices. Like demand, there is a time element attached to the supply schedule. It wouldn't make sense to talk about supply without knowing the period of time. Table 3–2 conforms to the (not quite) law of supply because Susan supplies larger quantities of lemonade at higher prices. The supply schedule of Table 3–2 can be represented graphically by a **supply curve**, as in Figure 3–4. It shows the quantity supplied at a particular time and at various prices. Like graphing demand, price per unit is on the *y*-axis, and quantity per time period is on the *x*-axis. We generally draw supply curves as straight lines for convenience, and they usually are drawn with a positive price (*y*-axis) intercept, indicating that at some low price, suppliers may offer none of the commodity.

TABLE 3–2
SUSAN SMITH'S SUPPLY OF LEMONADE

Price per Glass (Cents)	Quantity Supplied per Day
■	■
5	0
10	5
15	10
20	15
25	20
30	25

■ **Market Supply**

The **market supply** curve can be found by adding all of the individual supply schedules or by a horizontal geometric summation of all of the individual supply curves. Figure 3–5 is a market supply curve for lemonade. It shows the total quantity supplied over a period of time at various prices.

As price changes in the market, the quantity supplied changes as a positive function of this price change. In Figure 3–5, 5,000 glasses of lemonade are supplied at a price of 10 cents per glass. If price falls to 5 cents per glass, the quantity supplied would decrease to zero glasses; if price rises to 20 cents per glass, the quantity supplied would increase to 15,000 glasses. These changes occur because most producers are willing to sell more units if the price rises enough to cover the additional costs of production.

SUPPLY CURVE
A graphical representation of a supply schedule showing the quantity supplied over a particular time period at various prices.

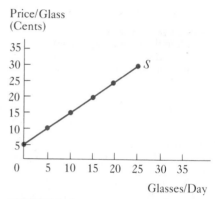

FIGURE 3–4
SUSAN SMITH'S SUPPLY OF LEMONADE
A supply curve for an individual (or an individual firm) graphically depicts how much will be offered for sale at various prices.

MARKET SUPPLY
The summation of all of the individual firm supply curves. A market supply curve shows what quantity will be supplied by all firms over a particular time period at various prices.

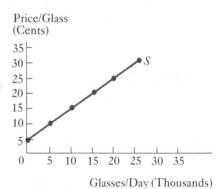

FIGURE 3–5
MARKET SUPPLY OF LEMONADE
A market supply curve is a graphical depiction of how much will be offered for sale at various prices. It is the aggregate of all of the individual supply curves.

Changes in Supply and the *Ceteris Paribus* Conditions

We now can see how other factors affect the supply of a good or service. As was the case for the demand curve, changes in the *ceteris paribus* conditions cause the entire supply curve to shift.

Technology

Suppose technology improves, for instance, and agricultural researchers develop a very inexpensive pill that causes a young steer to double in weight rapidly. This technological advance means that more beef will be supplied at each price. There is an **increase in supply**. That is, a shift in the supply curve indicates that at every price, a larger quantity than before will be provided. An increase in supply is represented in Figure 3–6 as the outward shift from S_0 to S_1. A negative technological change will have the opposite effect. Suppose the government discovers that this drug, now in use for steer fattening, has harmful side effects on humans, and farmers are therefore prohibited from giving it to steers. This will mean that less beef will be supplied at each price. There will be a **decrease in supply**, represented as a shift from S_0 to S_2 in Figure 3–6.

Prices of Factors of Production

Now consider changes in the prices of the factors of production. Recall from Chapter 2 that these factors of production are land, labor, capital, and enterprise. The price paid for the use of land is rent; the price paid for labor services is wages; the price paid for using capital is interest; and the return to enterprise is profit. If the price of a factor—such as labor services used in beef production—goes up, the supply of products using that factor will be affected. It will mean that suppliers will offer less of the good at each price. That is to say, supply will decrease because the costs of production have gone up. Suppose that S_0 in Figure 3–6 represents the market supply of beef. Assume the wage rate of meat cutters increases. This will mean less beef will be supplied at each price; supply will decrease, shifting from S_0 to S_2. Another way of looking at this is to see that before the increase in wages, amount Q_0 was supplied at price P_0. When S_0 decreases to S_2 after wages go up, suppliers will supply the old amount (Q_0) only at a higher price (P_2).

The same principle holds for any factor of production: A rise in the price of a factor of production, *ceteris paribus*, causes a decrease in supply of output. This happens because the producer now will find that the cost of supplying any quantity has increased. After a price rise in a factor of production, less will be supplied at the old price, or the same amount will be supplied only at a higher price. This is graphically represented by a shift in the curve. The opposite is also true. Any decrease in the price of a factor of production will cause an increase in supply. Such an increase in supply is geometrically depicted as a shift from S_0 to S_1 in Figure 3–6.

Number of Suppliers

A change in the number of suppliers (which is another *ceteris paribus* condition) will have a predictable effect on supply. If the number of beef ranchers declines, the supply curve will shift to the left, as from S_0 to

INCREASE IN SUPPLY
A shift in the supply curve indicating that at every price, a larger quantity will be supplied than before.

DECREASE IN SUPPLY
A shift in the supply curve indicating that at every price, suppliers will supply a smaller quantity than before.

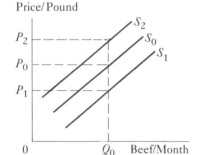

FIGURE 3-6
CHANGES IN THE *CETERIS PARIBUS* FACTORS AND SUPPLY

Changes in a *ceteris paribus* condition can cause the supply curve to shift. A change that would cause more to be supplied at each previous price is an increase in supply and is represented by the shift from S_0 to S_1. A change that causes the supply to decrease is represented by a shift from S_0 to S_2.

S_2 in Figure 3–6. This shift represents a decrease in supply. Conversely, an increase in the number of beef ranchers will cause the supply curve to shift from S_0 to S_1 in Figure 3–6. This represents an increase in supply.

Expectations

As in the case of demand, expectations about any of the *ceteris paribus* conditions or about market price can have an effect on supply. Continuing with the beef example, assume that beef ranchers expect that the price of beef will fall next year because they anticipate a poor grain harvest. This poor grain harvest would make it more expensive to keep beef on feedlots. Beef prices will be lower because ranchers will be slaughtering more cattle. What would this expectation cause ranchers to do? They would bring more cattle to market now before the price falls. If enough ranchers share these same expectations, the supply curve for this year will increase from S_0 to S_1, as shown in Figure 3–6. In this example, the expectation of falling prices created a supply curve shift that caused the price of beef to fall from P_1 to P_2. Next year, with fewer cattle available, the supply curve will shift back to the left.

Prices of Related Goods

As in the case of demand, change in the prices of other goods can have an effect on supply. If the price of a good that is similar in production technique changes, the firm may switch production. We already used the example of a farmer switching from corn to wheat when the relative price of corn increases. In a similar fashion, a sewing factory might switch from men's shirts to babies' nightwear if the price of men's shirts fell and the price of babies' nightwear increased.

REASONS FOR A CHANGE IN THE QUANTITY SUPPLIED

- The quantity of a good or service supplied will *increase* if the price of the good or service *increases*.
- The quantity of a good or service supplied will *decrease* if the price of the good or service *decreases*.

REASONS FOR A CHANGE IN SUPPLY

The supply of a good or service will *increase* if:
- new technology allows the good or service to be produced at lower cost,
- the prices of the factors of production decrease,
- the number of suppliers increases,
- the prices of other goods or services that can be produced with the same resources decrease, or
- suppliers' expectations of the future cause them to produce more now.

The supply of a good or service will *decrease* if:
- the prices of the factors of production increase,
- the number of suppliers decreases,
- the prices of other goods or services that can be produced with the same resources increase, or
- suppliers' expectations of the future cause them to produce less now.

■   ■   ■   ■   ■   ■   ■

MARKET EQUILIBRIUM

We now can combine market supply and market demand schedules or curves for a good or service and determine the market equilibrium. The **market equilibrium** occurs at that price and quantity at which quantity demanded by consumers is equal to quantity supplied by producers. This is also called the *market-clearing* price.

To see how equilibrium comes about, examine Table 3–3. At a price of $2, suppliers *want* to supply 4 million pounds of coffee, and demanders *want* to purchase 8 million pounds. This is a difference of 4 million pounds. The quantity demanded exceeds the quantity supplied by 4 million pounds at a price of $2. This means that at $2, some consumers will not be able to purchase the amount they desire. If markets are allowed to work freely, some consumers will offer more and bid the price up. As the price rises, the quantity supplied will rise, and the quantity demanded will fall. This will continue until the price reaches $3. At $3, the amount consumers wish to purchase is exactly equal to the amount suppliers wish to sell. This is equilibrium. We also say that $3 is the **market-clearing price**.

MARKET EQUILIBRIUM
The price at which quantity demanded by consumers is equal to quantity supplied by producers; also called market-clearing price.

MARKET-CLEARING PRICE
The equilibrium price. It is market clearing because there are no frustrated purchasers or suppliers.

TABLE 3–3
SUPPLY OF AND DEMAND FOR COFFEE

Price per Pound (Dollars)	Pounds Supplied per Month	Pounds Demanded per Month	Difference
1	2 million	10 million	8 million excess quantity demanded
2	4 million	8 million	4 million excess quantity demanded
3	6 million	6 million	equilibrium
4	8 million	4 million	4 million excess quantity supplied
5	10 million	2 million	8 million excess quantity supplied

To see the same process of movement toward equilibrium from the other side of the market, assume a price higher than the market-clearing price. For example, at $4 per pound, suppliers offer 8 million pounds of coffee per month for sale. Consumers only wish to purchase 4 million pounds of coffee per month at that price. We thus have an excess quantity supplied of 4 million pounds per month. Suppliers with unsold coffee will accept a lower price. As the price falls, some suppliers reduce their output (a movement along the supply curve), and some demanders buy more (a movement along the demand curve) as the price falls. This continues until the equilibrium price of $3 is reached. This $3 price again clears the market. It is important to note that the point representing equilibrium price and equilibrium quantity is not simply the point where the amount sold equals the amount bought. Quantities bought and sold are *always* equal. Four million pounds per month were bought and sold at $2 and at $4.

Figure 3–7 shows market demand and market supply curves for coffee, corresponding to the supply and demand schedules in Table 3–3. It demonstrates the same process of moving toward equilibrium, using graphs instead of numbers. The equilibrium price is $3, and 6 million pounds per month are sold at equilibrium. At $4, there is an excess quantity supplied and price will fall, causing the quantity demanded to increase and the quantity supplied to decrease. The opposite happens at a price of $2 per pound.

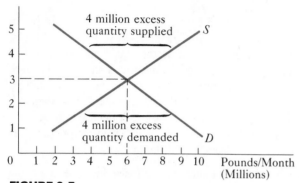

FIGURE 3-7
SUPPLY AND DEMAND OF COFFEE
At equilibrium, the amount demanders wish to purchase is equal to the amount suppliers wish to sell. The price established at equilibrium is called the market-clearing price.

A THEORY OF PRICE FORMATION

The law of demand and the (not quite) law of supply support a very powerful theory of price formation in free markets. That theory is based on the following propositions:

1. Quantity demanded is negatively related to price.
2. Quantity supplied is positively related to price.

When these two propositions are combined, they imply that when the quantity demanded exceeds the quantity supplied, $(Q^d > Q^s)$, price will rise; when the quantity demanded is less than the quantity supplied, $(Q^d < Q^s)$, price will fall; and when the quantity demanded equals the quantity supplied, $(Q^d = Q^s)$, price is at equilibrium. This theory, combined with the possible *ceteris paribus* shifts, produces all of the basic elements of a model of how prices (and quantities) are determined in a market system.

Changes in Demand and Supply

When changes occur in any of the other factors (our *ceteris paribus* conditions) that affect demand, the model can be used to trace the

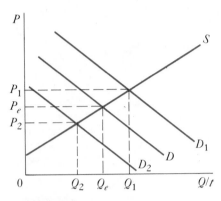

FIGURE 3-8
CHANGES IN DEMAND
An increase in demand from D to D_1 causes equilibrium price to rise from P_e to P_1 and the quantity supplied to increase from Q_e to Q_1. A decrease in demand from D to D_2 causes the equilibrium price to fall from P_e to P_2 and the quantity supplied to fall from Q_e to Q_2.

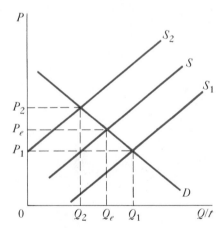

FIGURE 3-9
CHANGES IN SUPPLY
An increase in supply from S to S_1 causes equilibrium price to fall from P_e to P_1 and the quantity demanded to increase from Q_e to Q_1. A decrease in supply from S to S_2 causes price to rise from P_e to P_2 and the quantity demanded to fall from Q_e to Q_2.

effect on market equilibrium. We do this by observing the change in a *ceteris paribus* condition and asking what will be its impact on equilibrium price. Assume first that there is an increase in demand; that is, an upward or rightward shift of the entire curve. This increase in demand could be a result of any of the following:

1. an increase in income if this is a normal good (or a decrease in income if this is an inferior good)
2. a change in tastes in favor of the good
3. an increase in the price of a substitute
4. a decrease in the price of a complement
5. an increase in the size of the group demanding the good
6. a change in expectations

The increase in demand is represented geometrically by an outward shift in the demand curve from D to D_1, as in Figure 3-8. The effect of this increase in demand is to cause the equilibrium price to rise from P_e to P_1. This price increase causes the quantity supplied to increase to Q_1, the new equilibrium quantity. Consumers are now demanding a larger quantity of the good at every price than before the shift in demand.

Now consider a decrease in demand. A decrease in demand means that consumers will demand less of a good at every price. A decrease in demand would result from one of the following:

1. a decrease in income if this is a normal good (or an increase in income if this is an inferior good)
2. a change in tastes away from this good
3. a decrease in the price of a substitute
4. an increase in the price of a complement
5. a decrease in group size
6. a change in expectations

The decrease in demand can be represented geometrically by the leftward shift in the demand curve from D to D_2 in Figure 3-8. The decrease in demand causes equilibrium price to fall from P_e to P_2. As a result of the decrease in price, the quantity supplied falls from Q_e to Q_2.

Changes in any of the factors that affect supply cause shifts in the supply curve. Consider first the factors that cause an increase in supply. This would be caused by a positive change in technology, a decrease in the price of a factor of production, an increase in the number of suppliers, or a change in expectations. The increase in supply would be represented by an outward shift in the supply curve, from S to S_1 in Figure 3-9. This increase in supply would cause the equilibrium price to fall from P_e to P_1. The decrease in price would cause an increase in the quantity demanded from Q_e to Q_1.

A decrease in supply would be geometrically represented by a shift in the supply curve in an inward direction. Such a decrease in supply could result from a negative change in technology; an increase in the price of a factor of production; a decrease in the number of suppliers; or a change in expectations. This decrease in supply is represented by the shift of S to S_2 in Figure 3-9. This decrease in supply causes equilibrium price to rise from P_e to P_2. This increase in price causes the quantity demanded to decrease from Q_e to Q_2.

Shifts and Movements

The supply and demand model is very useful in analyzing a variety of economic issues. Economists in government and business spend much of their time using these basic tools to analyze problems. Later in the textbook, we will examine a range of social and economic issues in terms of basic supply and demand theory. As you apply this model, keep in mind the difference between changes in demand and supply (that is, changes in the position of the curves, or shifts) and changes in the quantity demanded and quantity supplied (that is, movements along the curves). The importance of this difference will become very clear as you attempt to untangle situations in which you proceed through several changes in *ceteris paribus* conditions.[4]

It is also important to remember that we are usually looking for the primary effect, not all of the possible implications of a price change or a change in *ceteris paribus* conditions. For example, if we know that the price of a substitute has gone up, we know that the demand for the good under consideration will increase. We are interested primarily in the most significant response to a change in one of the *ceteris paribus* conditions.

Prices—Fair and Just

The analysis of supply and demand presented in this chapter has been positive rather than normative in that no mention was made about what constitutes a fair or just price or whether certain levels of consumption of certain goods are needed for a just society. Supply and demand theory predicts the impact of an increase in demand for a particular commodity on price and quantity of that commodity. The resulting price increase may mean that some people can no longer afford the item, regardless of how "necessary" or "basic" it may appear to be. The model developed in this chapter does not make any moral judgments about this possibility.

THE MARKET PROCESS: CORNERSTONE OF THE PRIVATE SECTOR

In the previous chapter, we saw that each and every economy must address the *what, how,* and *for whom* questions. The mechanics of the price system—supply and demand—provide important signals to inform, direct, and motivate economic agents in answering these questions.

Functions of Prices

Before proceeding, we should evaluate some of the merits of the price or market system we have analyzed in this chapter. The inform-

---

4. To test yourself, work through these shifts. Determine the effect that changes in supply and demand have on price and quantity. For example, ask yourself: What is the effect on equilibrium of an increase in demand coupled with a decrease in supply?

ing, directing, and motivating functions of prices are critical aspects of a free market system and ones that you shouldn't lose sight of in the mechanics of the model.

Informing

Market prices communicate a great deal of complex information to consumers and producers in a very efficient manner. An increase in demand will cause a market price to rise. The supplier of a product doesn't have to know how consumers value the product being sold, if tastes have changed, or if any one of a myriad of other factors caused demand to change. All that is necessary is that the supplier know that price has risen. When price rises, suppliers increase the quantity supplied without needing to know any other information. Likewise, a consumer need not understand the complexity of production and the costs associated with any particular commodity. All the consumer needs to know is market price. If market price rises, consumers decrease the quantity demanded, economizing on this scarcer commodity. The market price, then, provides all market participants with up-to-the-minute information on the relative scarcity of commodities.

Directing

Market participants act on the information embodied in prices. Prices direct or coordinate this market activity by bringing decisions together. If suppliers are bringing "too much" of a particular product to market, its price will fall and the decisions of consumers and producers will be brought together. Production will increase for those products for which consumers have more intense demands. Firms will produce these goods by bringing resources together in a way directed by the market price of those resources. All of this takes place without any individual or group of individuals telling consumers and entrepreneurs how or why to do it. All of the necessary information is found in the market price.

Motivating

The phrase *for whom* reminds us that price is a powerful motivating factor. Supply and demand establishes a powerful reward structure for all market participants.

Market participants will seek to produce those goods or develop those skills that are highly desired by others. Upon doing so, they will reap the reward of this behavior. All of this happens without the need for any government agency or central planning bureau to tell people what to do. No one has to tell the gas station owner when to be open or where to build a station. No one has to tell a tall and coordinated young person to practice basketball skills. People pursue certain activities because they perceive these activities to be in their own self-interest. This whole process of self-interested response to incentives is what Adam Smith (see Chapter 2 for a biographical inset) referred to as the **invisible hand**.

INVISIBLE HAND
The idea advanced by Adam Smith that individuals pursuing their own self-interest produce socially desirable outcomes.

Allocative Efficiency

According to Adam Smith, the invisible hand informs, directs, and motivates the self-interest of market participants so that they guide resources to produce the goods most wanted by consumers and produce those goods with the most efficient methods and resource combinations possible.

Allocative efficiency is the allocation of resources to produce the goods most desired by society. It is the reason that most economists look to the free market first for solutions to economic problems. Nobel laureate George Stigler has described the free market approach:

The basis of the credo is simply that an economic actor on average knows better the environment in which he is acting and the probable consequences of his actions than an outsider, no matter how clever the outsider may be.[5]

Freedom

The market system has a final attribute that may be its most important. Markets maximize individual freedom by allowing individuals to pursue their own self-interest. One can solve the economic dilemma through the use of a central authority that determines what, how, and for whom. Alternatively, one can opt for voluntary cooperation coordinated by markets. As Nobel laureate Milton Friedman has put it:

So long as effective freedom of exchange is maintained, the central feature of the market organization of economic activity is that it prevents one person from interfering with another in respect to most of his activities. The consumer is protected from coercion by the seller because of the presence of other sellers with whom he can deal. The seller is protected from coercion by the consumer because of other consumers to whom he can sell. The employee is protected from coercion by the employer because of other employers for whom he can work, and so on. And the market does this impersonally and without centralized authority.[6]

Shortcomings of Markets

Although the market is a remarkably efficient tool for the allocation of resources, it does have some drawbacks. Often these drawbacks lead to political action and governmental intervention. This governmental intervention creates a mixed economy rather than a pure market economy.

Transaction Costs

In the supply and demand model, the equilibrium price is a particular price. Consumers are able to buy at this price, and producers are able to sell at this price. In the real world things don't always work this way, because transaction costs exist. **Transaction costs** are costs associated with gathering information about markets (prices and availabilities) for consuming or producing. Organizing, negotiating, and searching take time and involve costs. Firms are organized to solve transaction cost problems on the producing side. For consumers, the existence of transaction costs means that different people pay different prices for the same commodity.

ALLOCATIVE EFFICIENCY
The allocation of resources to produce the goods most desired by society. Free markets produce allocative efficiency.

TRANSACTION COSTS
Costs associated with gathering information about markets (prices and availabilities) for consuming or producing.

5. George J. Stigler, "Economists and Public Policy," *Regulation* (May/June 1982): 16.
6. Milton Friedman, *Capitalism and Freedom* (Chicago: University of Chicago Press, 1981): 14–15.

A familiar example is that gas stations next to expressways and major interstate roads charge higher prices for gasoline than other stations sometimes only a block from the expressway. Why? Transaction costs. Many users of the expressway are unfamiliar with the area and are in a hurry to get on with their trip. The cost of searching for a lower price is higher than the potential saving produced by further searching. As a test of this phenomenon, think about gas prices in a retirement community. We would expect to find lower and more uniform gas prices in a retirement community because the opportunity cost of the customers' time is lower. If you live near Sun City, Arizona (or Florida), or a similar retirement community, check it out!

Other Criticisms

It is argued that the market performs poorly when there is a lack of competition; that is, the quotation from Friedman is not relevant because monopolies interfere with freedom of choice. It is also argued that production and consumption decisions affect outside parties and that these effects can be addressed only through political action to change market outcomes. Pollution is an example.

Still another criticism is aimed at the unequal distribution of income that can be produced by a market system. Some individuals drink champagne and eat caviar while others starve. It is also argued that certain desirable goods, such as education, defense, and highways, are underproduced by the private market.

A final criticism of the market system is that unrestricted free markets lead to instability in output, employment, and prices. If markets are inherently unstable, perhaps government intervention can lead to more stability. Many forthcoming chapters address this question.

Critics range from those who would replace the market system with central direction to a more middle-of-the-road group who sees a division of responsibility between markets and government. It is this latter approach that we will consider in Chapter 4 when we look at the economic role of government.

Alternatives to Market Allocation

It is important to keep in mind that any interference in the equilibrium's ability to adjust will change the allocative outcome of the market. If we don't allow prices to adjust, we must use some other mechanism to allocate scarce resources. Government directives, waiting in line, or appeals to "good behavior" are possible allocative mechanisms. Let's consider three interventions in the market: airport congestion, cab scarcity in New York City, and organ transplant shortages.

Airport Congestion

Airline deregulation is producing lower air fares and as a result American consumers demand a larger quantity of air travel. This has led to a great deal of air traffic congestion, particularly during peak times at major airport hubs. It has also led to a significant increase in the number of delayed flights because there are only so many takeoff and landing "slots" per hour at an airport. The Federal Aviation Administration (FAA) charges a landing fee on a per-landing basis, with the same fee for all time slots. In a market system, the fee would be higher for the most desirable time slots, and passengers who wanted to fly at peak times would have to pay more for their tickets. Instead, the FAA has chosen to substitute its allocative decision making for that of the market. The result? Try leaving Los Angeles or Atlanta at 9:00 Monday morning.

New York City Cabs

The number of cabs and the fares they charge is tightly controlled by the Taxi and Limousine Commission in New York City. In 1987, there were 11,787 cabs in New York City. The owners paid up to $100,000 for the medallion necessary to operate a cab. The city regulates the fares that cab drivers can charge, and these fares are set as a fixed price per mile plus a charge for standing time.

At peak times, it is very difficult to get around in New York, so many cab drivers avoid working during these peak times, making it even more difficult to hail a cab if you need one. The lines of well-dressed theater goers standing forty-deep outside exclusive hotels attest to this allocation problem.

What are the solutions? They could approve more cabs. But if you have paid $100,000 for a permit, would you be in favor of more permits? What about allowing the market to set rates? *Fortune* Magazine suggested that cab drivers be able to change rates at peak times with "some sort of electronic display . . . perched atop the cab that would periodically announce new rates."[7] What would be the effect of such a change in the law? Some riders would be discouraged by higher prices, while some cab drivers would be encouraged by higher fares. Do you think the lines outside the hotels would diminish?

"Free Organs"

Organ transplants have become big business for many hospitals. Certain organs such as hearts, lungs, and eyes are donated at death by organ transplant card holders or concerned relatives. There are other organs, such as kidneys, that can be donated while donors are alive because they have two and can function with just one. As this medical practice has become more popular and more successful, a shortage of organs has developed, and there have been appeals. Some hospitals even have donor seekers who contact relatives of accident victims.

There is a shortage because the price is being held at too low a level. Indeed, the price is zero. One writer, Barry Jacobs, has proposed establishing a market for kidneys.[8] Since individuals can get along quite well with one kidney, Barry Jacobs' proposal is to let individuals who are cash poor and kidney rich sell their kidneys to those who are cash rich and kidney poor.

What kind of response do you think this proposal has received? Well, Representative Andy Jacobs (no relation to Barry), from Indiana, and Senator Albert Gore, from Tennessee, don't like the proposal. They have held hearings to launch legislation that deals with the kidney shortage. They have proposed a new federal program that would

7. "Yellow Power," *Fortune* (September 15, 1986): 144.
8. "Socialized Kidneys," *Fortune* (March 19, 1984): 190.

provide money for a computer organ-marketing system and would finance a 24-hour kidney hotline. It would, however, establish no incentives for donors. This is a particularly interesting example because it shows that markets might be useful in solving some problems that politicians think can only be solved by government. The next chapter examines the role of government in a mixed economy.

SUMMARY

1. Demand depends on the current price of the good or service in question as well as nonprice determinants, including the size of the group demanding the good, the tastes of the consuming group, the incomes of that consuming group, the prices of related goods and services, and the expectations concerning future prices or income.

2. The law of demand states that the quantity demanded of a good or service is negatively related to its price, *ceteris paribus*.

3. Changes in the price of a good affect the quantity demanded of that good; that is, a price change leads to a movement along the demand curve.

4. Changes in the *ceteris paribus* conditions that affect demand cause demand to either increase or decrease; that is, there is a shift in the position of the entire demand curve.

5. When income increases, the demand for a normal good will increase, whereas the demand for an inferior good will decrease.

6. Two goods are complements when a price increase in one will cause a decrease in demand for the other. Similarly, two goods are substitutes if an increase in the price of one good causes an increase in demand for the second good.

7. Supply depends on the price of the good or service being supplied as well as nonprice determinants, including the prices of the factors of production, the

level of technology, the number of suppliers, and expectations.

8. The (not quite) law of supply states that the quantity supplied of a good or service usually is a positive function of its price, *ceteris paribus*.

9. Changes in a good's price affect the quantity supplied of that good. Changes in other factors of production that affect supply cause supply to either increase or decrease. When the prices of factors of production increase, there will be a decrease in supply. A technological advance usually will cause supply to increase.

10. The market-clearing (equilibrium) price is the price at which the amount consumers wish to purchase is equal to the amount suppliers wish to sell.

11. Prices play an important role in informing, directing, and motivating consumers and producers.

12. Markets maximize individual freedom by allowing individuals to pursue their own self-interest.

13. Market shortcomings or failures usually produce a political or governmental solution.

14. Transaction costs result from the fact that organizing, negotiating, and searching take time and involve costs. The existence of transaction costs means that different people pay and are paid different prices.

15. Interference with market outcomes means that scarce goods must be allocated in some other manner than by price signals.

NEW TERMS

demand	normal good	market supply
supply	inferior good	increase in supply
law of demand	complementary goods	decrease in supply
demand schedule	substitute goods	market equilibrium
demand curve	expectations	market-clearing price
market demand	supply schedule	invisible hand
increase in demand	(not quite) law of supply	allocative efficiency
decrease in demand	supply curve	transaction costs

QUESTIONS FOR DISCUSSION

1. How can expectations of economic conditions affect supply?
2. Does the fact that some people appear to buy more of some goods, such as mink coats and diamonds, as their prices go up negate the law of demand?
3. How can the belief in a change in the future availability of gasoline affect the demand for automobiles?
4. Pat, a professional student, failed principles of economics and decided to sell flowers on a street corner to make ends meet. A second flower seller established a business directly across the street from Pat. Pat, unconcerned, came up with the following hypothesis: When supply increases, demand will increase; therefore, I will be just as well off as I was before the second flower seller arrived. Did Pat deserve to fail economics? Why or why not?
5. A market-clearing price is the price at which the amount sold equals the amount purchased. Is this correct?
6. List all of the conditions that can decrease demand or supply.
7. List all of the conditions that can increase demand or supply.
8. Why is it so important to distinguish changes in demand and changes in supply from changes in quantity demanded and changes in quantity supplied?
9. Why do some people shop at convenience stores, knowing that they will pay higher prices, even when a supermarket with lower prices is open in the same block?
10. The following table lists market information that you were able to research for landing slots at the Atlanta airport. If you were going to make a recommendation to the airport manager about pricing the slots to overcome the crowding and delay problem, what would you recommend?

THE MARKET FOR LANDING SLOTS
8:00 A.M. to 9:00 A.M.

Price	Quantity Supplied	Quantity Demanded
$ 0	12	50
$ 250	12	40
$ 500	12	20
$1,000	12	15
$1,500	12	8
$2,000	12	2

SUGGESTIONS FOR FURTHER READING

Friedman, Milton. *Capitalism and Freedom.* Chicago: The University of Chicago Press, 1981. This book presents the case for free markets by perhaps the most respected and passionate advocate of the free market.

Hayek, F.A. "The Use of Knowledge in Society." *American Economic Review* (September 1945): 519–528. This classic, very readable article shows the importance of markets as a source of information and coordination.

North, Douglass C., and Roger LeRoy Miller. *The Economics of Public Issues*, 7th ed. New York: Harper & Row, 1987. An easy to read issues book that uses supply and demand to analyze issues of current interest.

CHAPTER 4 ■
■
THE ECONOMIC ROLE
OF GOVERNMENT
IN A MIXED ECONOMY
■

■
INTRODUCTION

Chapter 3 was an overview of how decisions are made in the market through supply and demand. But not all decisions are made in the market. As we saw in Chapter 3, if the market isn't allowed to function, some other mechanism will have to be substituted. In our economy, many of these other choices concerning the use of resources are made by various levels of government, using political processes instead of market processes. Compared to the United States, there are many countries in the world where far more of the decisions are made by the government and a few where a larger share of the decisions is made by the market. A system in which the majority of economic choices are made in the market, with a significant number also made by governments, is called **mixed capitalism**.

Even in a very market-directed economy, there are some things that the market cannot do or cannot do well. Many economists argue that the market does not do a very good job of protecting us from monopoly, poverty, pollution, inflation, and unemployment. It is also difficult for private markets to give us enough of such goods and services as defense, education, and sewer systems.

Another problem of a market-directed economy is that someone outside the market has to define and enforce property rights. That is, someone has to decide who owns what goods and services and to define their rights to use, buy, and sell those goods and services. U.S. citizens cannot legally own or trade other human beings, drive a car without a license, or build a fast-food restaurant in a residential neighborhood. All of these governmental prohibitions represent restrictions on property rights in the sense that an unrestricted market would allow people to do all of these things. Defining and enforcing property rights is the most basic function of government.

MIXED CAPITALISM
An economy in which most decisions are made individually in the market, with a substantial number made collectively through government.

In this chapter, we will be exploring the size and scope of government activity in our economy. In later chapters, we then will examine in more detail how the market and the government can work, sometimes together and other times at cross-purposes, to improve economic well-being.

■ ■ ■ ■ ■ ■ ■
HOW MUCH GOVERNMENT?

A large part of the nation's income is claimed by government, and a substantial share of output is produced by or for the government. Total government expenditures—federal, state, and local—account for about one-third of our national income. The federal government alone spent $926.2 billion in 1986. State and local governments added another $557.9 billion. Some of this money was spent to produce or to purchase goods and services, such as defense, health care, highways, police, education, and courts.

About two-thirds of total government spending is for goods and services. The rest is for transfer payments. **Transfer payments** are income payments to individuals who provide no goods or services in exchange. Veterans' benefits, welfare payments, unemployment compensation, and Social Security benefits are all examples of transfer payments. Most transfer payments originate at the federal level, although some of them are administered by state and local governments. The debate over which level of government should finance and operate the welfare system, one of the larger components of transfer payments, has been a major issue in the 1980s. Table 4–1 summarizes the major categories of spending at all three levels of government. This Table indicates some division of expenditure responsibilities and also some shared functions, particularly income transfers (such as Social Security and public welfare). Defense and income security are the top priorities for the federal government, whereas education dominates state and local budgets. Interest on the national debt has grown for the federal government as a result of continuing large budget deficits.

TRANSFER PAYMENTS
Income payments to individuals who do not have to provide any goods or services in exchange.

TABLE 4-1
HOW GOVERNMENT SPENT ITS MONEY—1986

Federal ■		State and Local ■	
Social Security	26.9%	Education	33.2%
Defense	27.1	Public welfare	12.6
Interest payments	13.2	Health, hospitals	9.0
Transfers to state and local governments	9.9	Highways	8.1
		Civilian safety	5.4
All other	22.9	All other	31.7
Total	100.0%	Total	100.0%

Source: Advisory Commission on Intergovernmental Relations. *Significant Features of Fiscal Federalism* (Washington, D.C.: U.S. Government Printing Office, 1987).

PAYING FOR GOVERNMENT

Government in the United States has grown faster than the economy as a whole. Between 1949 and 1986, federal government expenditures rose from 15.3 percent of national income to 22.0 percent. During the same period, state and local expenditures rose from 7.8 percent of national income to 13.3 percent.

The major income source for governments at all levels is taxes. The federal government relies mainly on individual income taxes and social insurance taxes (Social Security taxes, workers' compensation taxes, and unemployment insurance taxes). The main revenue sources at the state and local levels are sales taxes and property taxes. Another major revenue source for state and local governments is federal grants-in-aid, which account for a large share of state and local revenues, although far less than in the 1970s. State grants added to federal grants account for 39 percent of local government revenues.

During the 1970s and early 1980s, many states experimented with legalized gambling, lotteries, and other headline-winning revenue sources; but most state and local tax revenues still come from traditional sources. Revenue sources for all three levels of government are listed in Table 4–2.

TABLE 4-2
REVENUE SOURCES FOR GOVERNMENTS, 1986

Federal		State		Local	
Income taxes	41.7%	Sales taxes	19.1%	Property taxes	28.2%
Social insurance taxes	28.7	Income taxes	22.2	Sales taxes	4.1
Other *	7.4	Payroll and other taxes	16.5	Income taxes	2.2
Borrowing	22.2	Other**	19.1	Other**	26.5
		Federal grants	23.1	State and federal grants	39.0
Total	100%	Total	100%	Total	100%

*Includes user fees, revenues from government enterprises, and so on.

**Includes user fees, borrowing, and other miscellaneous sources.

Source: *Significant Features of Fiscal Federalism*, 1987.

Table 4–2 suggests that there is an implicit division of "rights" to revenue sources among federal, state, and local governments. Certain revenue sources may be best suited for national collection because of advantages of size in collection or because a particular tax is easy to evade at the local level but not at the federal level. (Income taxes are a good example of both of these principles.) Since local government services often are provided for property owners (e.g., fire and police protection, streetlights, and sewer service), there is some logic to using the property tax at that level. Also, it is more difficult to avoid property taxes than other kinds of taxes, so it is easier for local governments to rely on that revenue source. State governments are responsible for education and highway expenditures and rely heavily on the sales tax as a revenue resource. This division of revenue sources and responsibilities among the three levels of government is referred to as **fiscal federalism**.

State and local governments sometimes take in more than they spend, as they did in 1986. Some of this revenue included contributions from the federal government in the form of grants-in-aid. The federal government, however, has spent much more than it has received in tax and nontax revenues every year since 1969. We will look at the problem of federal deficits in a later chapter.

FISCAL FEDERALISM
A division of responsibilities and revenue sources between the three levels of government in the United States—federal, state, and local.

THE FUNCTIONS OF GOVERNMENT

The activities of government generally are grouped into three categories: allocation, redistribution, and stabilization. Stabilization and redistribution activities are conducted primarily by government, whereas allocation is a microeconomic activity that is shared between the government and the market. Much of the controversy over what government should do revolves around its allocation activities.

The Allocation Function

Allocation refers to any activity of government that affects the quantity and quality of goods and services produced. Allocation by government includes producing public education; subsidizing higher education; taxing cigarettes; subsidizing farmers; regulating factory and automobile emissions; setting safety standards for cars; placing quotas on steel imports; building highways; and setting prices for electric power produced by private firms. Some, maybe even most, of the allocational activities also have distributional impacts because they increase the incomes of some firms and individuals at the expense of others.

Allocation activities of government generally are justified on the basis of public goods, merit goods, or negative external effects. Some of the allocation function (for example, setting prices for electric power) relates to the regulation of monopoly, a subject we will save for a later chapter.

ALLOCATION
Any activities of government that affect the allocation of resources and the combination of goods and services produced.

Public Goods

Economists define **public goods** as those goods that are nonrival in consumption and not subject to exclusion. What do these technical phrases mean? Think about sunsets and lighthouses. They are nonrival in consumption. *Nonrival* simply means that they are not "used up" in consumption, so the fact that you are watching the sunset leaves no less sunset for me to enjoy. *Exclusion* is the ability to prevent free riders. **Free riders** are people who consume collective goods without contributing to the cost of their production. National defense, streetlights, and mosquito spraying are all services for which it is very difficult, or at least expensive, to prevent or exclude nonpayers from reaping the benefits.

A pure public good enjoys both nonrivalry and nonexclusion. Some economists would extend the definition of a public good to include goods with weak rivalry or high costs of exclusion. Examples include fire

PUBLIC GOODS
Goods that are nonrival in consumption and not subject to exclusion.

FREE RIDERS
People who consume collective goods without contributing to the cost of their production.

services, education, and highways. The problem with all of these is that the benefits spill over to nonpayers as well. As a result, the private market may not produce enough of them because not all of the beneficiaries pay. Note that this extension of the definition of public goods has led to a great deal of expansion in what government does. In fact, all of the examples given are examples of services that have at some times and places been produced in the private sector. Volunteer fire departments in some rural areas still will not put out fires in nonsubcribers' homes. Education through the twelfth grade is produced in both the public and the private sector. Toll roads were the earliest form of highways in New England.

Merit Goods

Merit goods are yet another category of allocation in which the government is involved, although this topic raises much disagreement among economists. **Merit goods are those goods of which consumers will not purchase enough unless forced by government to do so.** Safety features in cars, national health care, and education are examples. We not only offer free public education, but we require that people between certain ages attend school. This is a very normative area. Everyone has his or her own ideas about what other people ought to consume.

Negative External Effects

Finally, along with public goods, there are **public "bads,"** such as noise, litter, and pollution. These are activities in which it is possible for us to pass some of the costs along to other people (negative external effects). People who create noise, litter, hazards, acid rain, and polluted water do not bear the full cost. Too many public bads are produced if decisions are left to private markets and private individuals. A great deal of the regulatory activity that came about in the 1960s and 1970s was designed to reduce these external effects.

The Scope of Allocation by Government

Most economists agree that the government does have some responsibility to produce public goods; to encourage the production of goods with positive external effects; and to discourage the production of negative external effects. But the lines are drawn differently by different people. How big do spillovers have to be before government gets involved? Does the government have to actually produce? Can the production be contracted out to the private sector or be encouraged through subsidies? Do negative external effects have to be addressed by prohibitions or standards? Can the same goals be accomplished better with taxes and fines? An individual's answers to these questions will reflect some underlying values about the relative importance of efficiency, equity, and freedom.

Allocation is carried out mainly by state and local governments. Some public goods must be provided on a national scale—national defense, for example. But many can be provided at the community level, where different groups can choose different combinations of public services. One city may choose more streetlights and snow removal, whereas another may vote for public parks and better roads. Allowing this kind of variety in local choices makes governments more responsive to the values and desires of the people who are paying the bills. This diversity and variety is an attractive feature of fiscal federalism.

MERIT GOODS
Goods that consumers will not buy in sufficient quantities if they are not compelled to do so by government.

PUBLIC "BADS"
Goods for which it is possible to pass some costs along to other people (negative external effect).

The Redistribution Function

The distribution of income in a market economy is based on each person's contributions to production. Exactly how this takes place is the subject of a later chapter, but there is no denying that the distribution of income determined by the market is very unequal. Some people are very wealthy, and others are very poor. One of the most controversial actions of government activity is **redistribution**—taking income from one group and giving it to another through taxes and transfer payments.

When the government taxes individuals with high incomes, these people have less incentive to work, save, and invest to increase output in future years. On the other hand, there are individuals who cannot earn an income through the market. They may be too old, too young, too sick, or too handicapped. There are others who work as hard as they can with the skills and resources at their disposal but who still cannot earn enough money to get by. There is some private redistribution through the Salvation Army and other charitable groups, but private charity is subject to the problem that many people will not participate because they know others will. This problem (which is called the free rider problem) makes income redistribution more or less a public good, which falls within the domain of government. How much income should be redistributed? To whom should it go? How can we redistribute income without destroying work incentives? These are the difficult questions government must answer in deciding whether, how much, and to whom to redistribute income.

The obvious way to redistribute income is to use taxes and transfer payments (mostly under the heading of Social Security and welfare). Most redistribution in the United States is done at the federal level. Redistribution in the form of income security or transfer payments has been the fastest growing area of federal government activity for the last 30 years. Some income redistribution is also done by the state government. However, by redistributing income at the federal level, it is possible to reduce inequality between rich and poor states as well as between rich and poor individuals within states. Furthermore, as we shall see shortly, the federal tax system collects relatively more in taxes from higher income persons. Thus, the taxes to finance transfer payments also are part of a rich-to-poor redistribution because the poor pay little in the way of federal income taxes.

Transfer payments are the most visible form of income redistribution. However, almost everything the government does is redistributive. If increased funds are spent on public education, families with school-age children benefit more than those with no school-age children. Increased health care expenditures benefit those who are sick. Quotas on steel imports benefit steelworkers but not steel users. Expanded student loan programs help college-age people who qualify at the expense of all other taxpayers and would-be borrowers. The fact that it is virtually impossible for the government to spend money on anything without redistributing income makes it very difficult to measure how much redistribution takes place.

Much of the income redistribution that takes place in these indirect ways benefits those who are not poor, i.e., the middle class, and

REDISTRIBUTION
Actions by government that transfer income from one group to another group.

those who are rich. While many conservatives criticize income redistribution because of the effect on incentives, some liberals criticize many government programs as "welfare for the rich." Subsidies for large farms, tax loopholes for real estate and oil and gas producers, and cost overruns in defense that benefit large defense contractors have been especially criticized. Deciding how much redistribution is enough, from whom it should come, and to whom it should go are very difficult political choices.

The Stabilization Function

STABILIZATION
Actions by government to reduce fluctuations in output, employment, and prices.

The last and most recently developed task of government is stabilization. **Stabilization** refers to actions by government to reduce fluctuations in output, employment, and prices. Stabilization is primarily a macroeconomic function. However, the ways in which government goes about stabilizing also have microeconomic effects on the mix of goods produced (allocation) and the distribution of costs and benefits (redistribution).

The Federal government attempts to stabilize the economy by increasing spending or cutting taxes to increase output and employment or by cutting spending and increasing taxes to control inflation. In addition, monetary policy is used to expand or contract economic activity. The two tools of stabilization are monetary and fiscal policy. When spending and taxes are used to stabilize the economy, budget deficits and surpluses are likely to result. Most state and local governments stay within a balanced budget on a yearly basis. The federal government, however, has greater borrowing power and can let considerations of price stability and full employment dictate whether or not the budget is balanced. Between 1958 and 1988, the federal budget has been in deficit for all but two years.

Economists disagree about how stable the private economy would be if it were left alone. Even in earlier periods, when the government taxed and spent a much smaller share of income, there were still cycles in economic activity. Periods of deflation (falling prices) and unemployment alternated with periods of inflation (increasing prices) and rapid growth. Even though cycles have been less severe since World War II, it cannot be stated with certainty that the economy has been more stable with government intervention than it was when the government pretty much left the economy alone.

LAW, ECONOMICS, AND GOVERNMENT

As Adam Smith noted, one of the basic roles of government is to define and enforce property rights. Thus, to an economist, law is the basic framework of any economy. In the United States, government and its effect on the allocation of resources is defined by law and the interpretation of law. In recent years, economists have spent a great deal of time extending economic analysis to explain legal statutes (legislated laws) and judicial decisions (common law).[1] Both types of laws are amenable to economic analysis, although in different ways. *Statute law* is of interest because of the incentives that statutes create and the way that they alter existing property rights. *Common law* changes through judicial decisions; these precedents then alter incentives for decision making. Lawyers are interested in the applications of specific decisions, whereas economists are more concerned with how these judicial decisions affect the economy by altering incentives.

In analyzing law, economists are searching for the economic reasoning implicit in legal decisions. It is most common to divide laws into three major areas. **Property law** relates to the enforcement of property rights. Enforcement of property rights is one of the basic requirements of any economic system. **Tort law** deals with intentional and unintentional wrongs imposed by one party on another. **Contract law** deals with the enforcement of voluntary exchanges.

The relationships between economics and law are important, and in recent years both economists and lawyers have begun to study these relationships. Economics deals with property rights and exchange; the two are perhaps the most basic elements of a market system. Precedents in common law or changes in statutory law will have profound effects on economic activity. Laws (more correctly, the courts' interpretation of laws) determine the private-governmental mixture in our mixed economy.

Property Law

The law in the United States is for the most part compatible with the economic principle that the economy operates more efficiently under a system of exclusive, transferable property rights. The most important exceptions are in two areas in which high transactions costs create market failure or interfere with the efficiency of the market outcome.

The first instance regards incompatible uses of property. Incompatibility exists when the rights of the parties are in conflict. Noise, air, and water pollution are but a few examples. An attractive hazard such as a swimming pool or a construction site is another example.

Often cases involving incompatible uses are treated as matters of nuisance. In many of these cases, the court will simply issue an injunction requiring that the perpetrator of the nuisance cease and desist. This may appear to be the most "fair" or "equitable" solution, but it is not necessarily an efficient solution from an economic viewpoint.

A second exception to the preference for a market solution is the doctrine of **eminent domain**. The principle here is that government has the legal right to purchase property at "fair market value" if it is deemed to be in the public interest. In these cases, the owner's property right is reduced in value because the owner cannot refuse to sell. Condemnation proceedings are court cases in which the government takes the property away from an owner by arguing that the government's rights are

PROPERTY LAW
Law that concerns the enforcement of property rights.

TORT LAW
Law that deals with intentional and unintentional wrongs inflicted by one party on another.

CONTRACT LAW
Law that deals with the enforcement of voluntary exchanges.

EMINENT DOMAIN
A doctrine that gives government the right to buy property at "fair market value" if it is in the public interest.

1. See Richard A. Posner, *Economic Analysis of Law* (Boston: Little, Brown and Company, 1972) and Werner Z. Hirsch, *Introduction to Law and Economics* (New York: McGraw-Hill, 1980).

more important. Most often the condemnation proceeding is used for construction of public goods, such as parks, roads, or dams.

Tort Law

TORT
A wrongful action (or failure to act) that causes damage to the property of another individual.

A **tort** is a wrongful action (or failure to act) by an individual that causes damage to the property of another individual. For example, if reckless behavior on your part damages another person, that person may sue you for damages. Payment of these damages can be justified on the

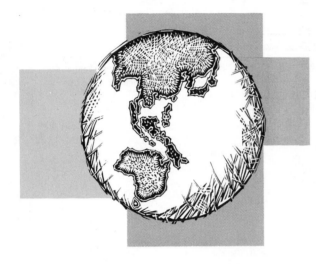

THE INTERNATIONAL PERSPECTIVE THE JAPANESE LEGAL SYSTEM

In this chapter, the way in which the U.S. economy and its legal system interact was discussed. The Japanese legal system is quite different from the U.S. system in that it puts a great deal of emphasis on arbitration and compromise in resolving conflicts. Since most relationships, including economic relationships, are considered social relationships in Japan, there is a great reliance on informal means of settling disputes. The traditional Japanese citizen views being brought to court as a source of personal shame.

The different behavior is most apparent in the area of tort law. The most common way of resolving a damage case is for the injured party to renounce their right to indemnity. The wrongdoer comes to offer apologies and offer a sum of money in compensation. The sum offered is often a token amount and is frequently much less than the value of the damages suffered by the victim. The

victim is moved by the sympathy and sincerity of the responsible party. It is not the amount of the compensation but the sincerity of the responsible party that is socially important. Sometimes the victim is so moved by the sincerity of the responsible party that all compensation is refused. Even in those instances when the victim is not satisfied with the offer of compensation, the courts are avoided. Instead, the victim appeals to someone who has authority to achieve an amicable solution to the disagreement. In this way, both parties are able to save face.

This same attitude about the law extends to contracts. This difference can cause problems in international transactions. The Japanese, with their dislike of the courts' emphasis on conflict, prefer to negotiate a relationship rather than a contract. They can't predict the disputes that may arise, but they prefer to settle the inevitable disputes in an informal manner. They dislike the use of the courts because the courts assign moral fault.

The differences between the United States and Japanese legal systems are striking and underscore differences in the culture of the two countries. The Japanese legal system is very centralized; there are no local or state laws in Japan. This reflects the strong group orientation and concentration of authority in Japan. In the United States, there is much more individualism and disdain for authority. Americans thus view the legal system as a way of asserting their individual rights and are much more likely to resort to the courts to resolve their disputes. These cultural differences bear on economic transactions and must be addressed when doing business with the Japanese. The Japanese have been quick to understand the U.S. system and have adapted to it when doing business in the United States. American business has been slower to adapt to the Japanese system of doing business in Japan.

basis of *equity*; it "restores" the original distribution of income or assets. Payment of these damages can also be justified on the basis of *efficiency*; it makes you bear the costs of your reckless action and thus increases the incentive to be more careful.

The equity issue requires a transfer payment from the wrong-doer to the individual who has been damaged. The efficiency impact is quite different. The law establishes a precedent for the ownership of property rights. Tort law determines who has the property right.[2]

Contract Law

The economics of exchange and contract law are similar in the sense that individuals are presumed to enter contracts only if they stand to gain from those contracts. Parties to certain contracts may end up in court, not because the contracts were bad (for one of the parties) but rather because one party failed to satisfy a provision of the contract. This most often happens when the contractual exchange fails to take place on time or when the cost/benefit calculation of one participant changes.

Contracts usually are not set aside by the courts if the intent of the contract is reasonably clear. On the other hand, the courts have set contracts aside if (honest) mistakes have been committed. If one party has been induced to accept a contract through fraud, duress, or incapacity, the court will refuse to enforce the contract.

Contracts, and court decisions under the common law of contracts, are important in economics because contracts, whether they are expressed or implied, form the basis of exchange. Exchange is influenced by contract law, and contract law creates incentives that affect future exchanges. A simple example can be found at most universities. In recent years, the courts have ruled that a college catalog or a course syllabus represents a contract with a student. This has altered the terms of the production and sale of higher education.

TAXATION

To pay for public goods, merit goods, income redistribution, and the operation of the legal system, government has to raise money. Most government revenues come in the form of tax collections.

What is the best way to tax? There is no good way, but some kinds of taxes do less harm than others. In designing a tax, policymakers look at such factors as equity, incentive effects, visibility, and administrative costs.

The Tax Base

A tax can be levied on almost any base. Most taxes in the United States are levied on the economic bases of income, assets, and

---

2. See Chapter 19 of Allan C. DeSerpa, *Microeconomic Theory: Issues and Applications* (Boston: Allyn and Bacon, Inc., 1985) for a very thorough and readable discussion of the economics of tort law.

spending. Income is the primary tax base of the federal government. Corporate and personal income taxes represented 62.2 percent of all revenues of the federal government in 1986. Income taxes are also an important source of state government revenues. State governments also rely heavily on sales taxes, which are taxes on consumption. Local governments rely mainly on property taxes, which are taxes on wealth.

■ Benefit Versus Ability to Pay

One way to evaluate different kinds of taxes is to consider how groups and individuals should pay. There are two generally accepted principles of how to tax: the benefit principle and the ability-to-pay principle.

BENEFIT PRINCIPLE
The concept that people should pay taxes in relation to the benefits they receive from government programs.

The **benefit principle** is a principle that states that people should pay taxes in relation to the benefits they receive from government programs. The tax is really the fee or the price of the good being supplied by government. In practice, it is often difficult to apply the benefit principle. However, in a few cases, it has worked remarkably well. Highways, for example, traditionally have been financed by a sales tax on gasoline. Since the benefits from roads accrue to motorists, it is appropriate to apply a benefit tax. Further, if you assume that the benefits accrue in proportion to usage, a proportional tax on gasoline would approximate the benefits received. Some state governments have built bridges, tunnels, and highways by charging users a toll on every trip, which is another benefit principle tax.

ABILITY-TO-PAY PRINCIPLE
The concept that people should pay taxes in relation to their capacity to pay as indicated by income, assets, or spending.

The **ability-to-pay principle** is an argument for contribution based on economic capacity to pay, measured by income, assets, or spending. Most people would accept this general principle, but it is difficult to apply in practice. Does twice as much income, for example, imply twice as much in taxes? Three times as much? Do we have to make corrections for family size, illness, or other special circumstances?

■ What Is a Good Tax?

Two of the most important yardsticks used to evaluate tax structures are equity and tax efficiency. By **equity**, we mean the normative concept of fairness. By **tax efficiency**, we mean how a tax affects economic activity.

EQUITY
A normative measure of fairness.

TAX EFFICIENCY
A measure of how a tax affects economic activity.

Equity

The equity of a tax or a tax structure is one of the most discussed topics in any political arena. Because equity is a normative concept, the answer to the question Is it fair? will be different for different people. We must try to answer the question because, as economists, we will be asked to make recommendations. So, to help policymakers, we must develop some ways of describing a tax structure so that decision makers can attempt to measure equity.

REGRESSIVE TAX
A tax that takes a lower percentage of income as income rises.

A tax can be regressive, proportional, or progressive. Table 4–3 shows a regressive, proportional, and progressive tax on three income earners. A **regressive tax** is a tax that takes a smaller share (percentage) of income as income rises. Column 2 gives an example of a regressive tax. Jones pays a higher share of his income (5 percent) than does Brown, who pays only 1 percent of her income.

TABLE 4-3
MEASURES OF TAX SHARE

	Income (1)	Regressive Tax (2)	Proportional Tax (3)	Progressive Tax (4)
Jones	$ 10,000	$ 500 = 5%	$ 500 = 5%	$ 500 = 5%
Smith	$ 80,000	$1,600 = 2%	$ 4,000 = 5%	$ 20,000 = 25%
Brown	$500,000	$5,000 = 1%	$25,000 = 5%	$250,000 = 50%

Sales taxes on food generally are thought to be regressive because the proportion of an individual's budget spent on food declines as income rises. As a result, the tax paid on food declines as income rises. You should note that a regressive tax doesn't require the tax to decline in absolute dollars. Brown paid $5,000, and Jones paid only $500; but Brown's tax, as a percentage of income, was lower. Many people feel that regressive taxes are unfair. In many states and cities, sales taxes on food and medicine have been lowered or abolished because they are seen as particularly burdensome to the poor.

Proportional taxes are taxes that take the same percentage of income from each class of taxpayers. Column 3 of Table 4-3 shows a proportional tax of 5 percent. All individuals pay the same percentage share of income, but the dollar amount increases as income increases.

A **progressive tax** is one that takes a larger share of income from people as their income rises. Column 4 in Table 4-3 represents a progressive tax. The federal personal income tax in the United States is a progressive tax, with rates ranging from 11 percent to 33 percent. Some people argue that progressive taxes are more fair, but the difficulty lies in determining the appropriate degree of progressiveness.

A problem that relates only to progressive taxes is what is known as bracket creep. **Bracket creep** occurs when inflation moves people into higher income tax brackets, even though their real incomes haven't increased.[3] For example, assume that over a given period of time there has been 800 percent inflation. This means that an income of $80,000 now buys what could have previously been purchased for $10,000. According to Column 4 of Table 4-3, the tax rate on this income has risen from 5 percent to 25 percent, even though the individual has the same purchasing power as before the inflation. In other words, in a progressive tax structure, inflation generates more revenue for the government because people creep into higher brackets, even though they are not better off in terms of what their incomes will buy.

Economists look at equity from two different perspectives. **Horizontal equity** in a tax structure is achieved when all taxpayers in a

PROPORTIONAL TAX
A tax that takes a constant percentage of income as income rises.

PROGRESSIVE TAX
A tax that takes a greater percentage of income as income rises.

BRACKET CREEP
A situation in which inflation moves people into higher income tax brackets, even though their real incomes haven't increased.

HORIZONTAL EQUITY
A situation that is achieved when all taxpayers in a certain economic category pay the same tax.

3. A tax bracket is the rate paid on the last or next dollar of income. For example, at 1988 rates, a married couple with a taxable income of $29,750 would pay 15 percent on the $29,750 but would pay 28 percent on each additional dollar up to $71,900.

certain economic category pay the same tax. People with the same income pay the same income tax, and owners of similar houses pay similar property taxes. **Vertical equity** is achieved when individuals of different economic categories pay suitably different taxes. Determination of the correct degree of difference involves a normative judgment of fairness that has to be determined in the political process. Vertical equity is much more difficult to measure than horizontal equity.

VERTICAL EQUITY
A situation in which individuals of different economic categories pay suitably different taxes.

Efficiency

To judge the efficiency of a tax, one has to look at the effect the tax has on the economic activity of the taxpayer. An ideal tax is one that is neutral; a **neutral tax** would cause no distortion in economic activity. However, there is no such thing as a neutral tax because all taxes create some distortion. Income taxes distort choices between work and leisure; sales taxes distort decisions concerned with goods to be consumed; and property taxes affect decisions on home location. A good tax—an efficient tax—is one that least distorts economic activity. In other words, a tax that significantly distorts economic behavior is a bad tax.

NEUTRAL TAX
A tax that causes no distortion in economic activity.

Compliance Costs, Administration Costs, and Visibility

In addition to equity and efficiency, there are some other elements that we might use to judge a tax or a tax structure. Taxes should be visible, and their compliance costs and administrative costs should be low.

For compliance costs to be low means that it should not be difficult or expensive for people to figure out how much tax they owe. Keeping compliance costs low is important because the United States' tax structure requires a great deal of volunteerism, and that system of voluntary cooperation seems to work well. To be sure, if you cheat and defraud the Internal Revenue Service (IRS), you might go to jail, but this is a meaningful threat only because most people cooperate. If there were massive acts of uncooperative behavior, the IRS simply could not cope with the problems that would result.

For administrative costs to be low, we want to raise money for the government at as low a cost as possible. Clearly a tax that uses up all of the funds that are collected to cover the costs of collection is a bad tax.

Visibility refers to the taxpayers' awareness of the taxes they are paying. If taxpayers are less aware of the tax, it is easier for governments to raise money, and government officials may be less careful about how they spend it.

As an example of visibility, consider the following proposition. Do you think federal personal income taxes would be the same if we had to write the government a check every week instead of having the taxes withheld from our paychecks? If people started to think more in terms of their gross pay instead of their net, or take-home, pay, their income taxes would be more visible. Thus, if citizens were reminded more often of the amount of taxes that they pay, some of them probably would demand that taxes be reduced.

Other Considerations

What else might be considered when choosing or designing a tax? Legislators might want to know if the revenues from this tax would hold up during periods of recession (stability). Will they grow as population and demand for government services grow (responsiveness)? Will they discourage some industry or activity that we would like to encourage? A hotel and motel accommodations tax could choke off a budding tourist industry. An income tax can discourage work. High taxes on land and buildings could discourage farming, housing, and land-intensive industrial development. These are efficiency issues.

Table 4–4 looks at the four most important taxes in the United States (those that raise the most revenue) and rates them from 1 (best) to 4 (worst) on each of these criteria. The four taxes are the progressive individual income tax, the sales tax, the property tax, and social insurance payroll taxes. No tax gets a high score on all criteria, which explains why we use a mixture of taxes.

TABLE 4-4
RATING OF MAJOR TAXES

Criteria	Progressive Individual Income Tax	Sales Tax	Property Tax	Social Insurance Payroll Tax
Equity	1	2	4	3
Visibility	3	2	1	4
Cost of administration	2	3	4	1
Responsiveness to economic/population growth	1	3	4	2
Stability	4	2	1	3
Efficiency	1	3	4	2

These ratings are somewhat subjective, particularly for equity and efficiency, which are not very objective criteria to begin with. The federal income tax is given the highest equity rank because it attempts to be progressive, whereas the other three taxes lie in varying degrees between proportional and regressive. The actual degree of progressiveness of the federal income tax is extremely difficult to measure because of all of the adjustments, exclusions, deductions, and credits. The 1986 tax reform, lowering the maximum rate from 50 percent to 33 percent, has made the federal income tax less progressive, but it is still the most progressive of these four taxes. The ratings on the cost of administration criterion are based on the cost to the government; for example, payroll taxes are rated better in terms of cost than are income taxes because the government's administrative cost is lower per dollar collected.

Responsiveness and stability are inversely related criteria, and it is helpful to have some taxes in each category. The federal government, which has the greatest borrowing capacity, is most able to depend on a cyclically unstable income tax in which revenues drop sharply during recessions and rise rapidly during inflation. Local governments, however, need the stable revenues of a tax such as a property tax.

THE INTERNATIONAL PERSPECTIVE
AUSSIES BEAT THE TAX
REFORMER—WILL U.S. BUSINESS
BE AS INGENIOUS?

The 1986 tax reform in the United States dealt a jolt to business lunches, sky boxes in stadiums, and other "extravagant" business expenses because business people can now only deduct 80 percent of their entertainment expenses. The after-tax cost of every $100 business expense rose from around $54 to around $73. Since, as we saw in Chapter 3, demand curves have a negative slope, we would expect that business entertainment expenditures would decline when the after-tax price rose. Don't be too hasty to come to that conclusion. Business is ingenious, and Australian business has demonstrated creative ways of beating similar tax reforms.

In 1985, the labor (liberal) government in Australia introduced tax reform called the Reform of the Australian Taxation Systems. (Many business people referred to the law as RATS.) The law ended most entertainment deductions. The Australian business community was quick to respond. The first "innovation" was table rental. Business rent was still deductible, so businesses rented tables from restaurants that then provided meals and services for the rent. The government passed a new law to stop this. The next innovation was the business seminar. Seminar expenses were deductible, and lunches that "didn't interrupt" were part of the seminar. Again, the government pounced. Advertising expenses were OK. Guess what? Soon waiters' uniforms had corporate logos on them! The lesson seems clear. Business is more ingenious than the government. It shows how difficult "tax reform" is. It also shows how responsive the private sector is to a change in the options available, even though the form the response may take is not easy to predict.

Efficiency is the most difficult criterion to rank because each tax has different efficiency effects. An income tax discourages earning and encourages spending on goods and services that are deductible; it also encourages devoting more resources to tax avoidance than creating income. Sales taxes encourage saving; property taxes encourage accumulating assets in nontaxed forms, usually stocks and bonds rather than houses and cars; payroll taxes discourage working and hiring. The income tax earns the highest rating in this category because it contains many intentional allocation effects that encourage investment, home ownership, charitable contributions, and other "desirable" expenditures.

NONTAX REVENUE SOURCES

Federal grants are an important source of funds for state and local governments, although much less so than in the 1970s when grants were at their peak. The federal government has long provided **categorical grants** to state and local governments for specific purposes, such as the school lunch program, highway construction, and higher education. These grants are highly specific in terms of how state and local governments are

CATEGORICAL GRANTS
Transfer of funds from the federal government to state and local governments for specific purposes.

allowed to use the funds. In recent years, there has been an effort to consolidate some of these numerous and overlapping grant programs into broader block grants. A **block grant** is a transfer of funds from the federal government to state and local governments for use in a general spending category, e.g., education, law enforcement, and health care. Funds in block grants must be spent in a particular category, but there is more flexibility about how the funds are used.

Intergovernmental grants have been the subject of much debate in the last ten years. The current trend is to move away from two extremes. At one extreme is unrestricted revenue sharing, a program in effect from 1972 to 1986 that offered much freedom and flexibility but little accountability, and at the other extreme are categorical grants, which are very restrictive. Block grants, an intermediate alternative, have replaced both revenue sharing and categorical grants. The grant programs of the federal government were particularly controversial in the early 1980s when the federal government was running large deficits. Meanwhile many states were operating on a balanced budget or even experiencing surpluses.

User charges are another source of nontax revenues. A **user charge** is a fee that a governmental unit charges for such services as sewers, parking, or water. User fees are limited to goods that are excludable. It would be hard, for example, to charge a user fee for anything that fits the definition of a public good. For this reason, some economists argue that if a good provided by government can be financed by user charges, then its production should be left to the private market.

Examples of user charges can be found at all levels of government. Postage stamps pay for mail services. Municipal golf courses and tennis courts usually charge for playing time. Many bridges and roads are financed with toll charges, which often continue long after the bridge or road has been paid for!

A third way to finance government spending is by borrowing. All levels of government can borrow, but the biggest borrower is the federal government. The national debt was more than $2 trillion in 1988, representing the total of net federal government borrowing for our entire history. Each time we run a deficit (expenditures greater than revenues), the national debt gets bigger. Needless to say, there are continuing controversies over the size and the effects of the national debt and over running deficits year after year.

ISSUES IN GOVERNMENT SPENDING AND TAXATION

Shortly after being reelected for his second term, President Reagan launched a tax-reform crusade. At the beginning, very few political observers felt it had a chance to pass. To everyone's surprise, the House and Senate both passed the President's tax reform program in 1986. The politically "impossible" was accomplished partly through the strength of Reagan's personal appeal and partly by strong resistance to the lobbying of special-interest groups. What was passed was a new tax law that significantly cuts rates and does away with many deductions and tax shelters.

Although tax reform has attracted much attention, there are many other issues in government spending and taxation that will continue

BLOCK GRANT
Transfer of funds from the federal government to state and local governments for use in a general spending category, such as health care or public education.

USER CHARGE
A fee charged to consumers by governments for the provision of certain goods and services.

to make headlines and provoke argument. The kinds and levels of inter-governmental grants are undergoing review. As part of that process, the federal government is rethinking what expenditure responsibilities belong at each level of government. The deficit, which we will examine more closely in a later chapter, is a continuing source of controversy. The property tax has become a less acceptable form of local government revenue in many areas. Local governments have had to search for replacement revenue sources or cut spending, as they have been pressured into reducing property tax rates.

Most of us enjoy the services that government provides, such as education, highways, defense, and the legal system. None of us likes to pay taxes. Senator Russell Long once stated that the basic philosophy of taxation seems to be: "Don't tax you, don't tax me, tax that man there under the tree." As long as each of us wants to enjoy public services but wants to minimize our own share of the burden by shifting it to others, taxes will be a subject of public controversy.

PRIVATIZATION

PRIVATIZATION
The transfer of governmental activities and/or assets to the private sector.

Privatization is the transfer of governmental activities and/or assets to the private sector. In response to what some observers consider to be excessive growth of government, there has been a movement toward privatization not only in the United States but worldwide. In England, the Thatcher government has perhaps been the most active through a major program of privatizing numerous state-owned industries. In the People's Republic of China, "the reform of the basic tenets of the system" involves elements of privatization. In the United States, privatization has occurred primarily in local governments, but the principle might spread to state governments and the federal government.

The primary motivation for privatization is that it reduces governmental expenditures, yet is politically feasible because it does not eliminate the service. The expenditure reductions come from several sources. Privatization

1. introduces competition and the efficiencies that follow competition.
2. permits smaller localities to join together into more efficiently sized units for purchasing services.
3. removes government from labor negotiations and retirement commitments.
4. transfers revenue-consuming activities to private firms that pay taxes and produce revenues.

There are seven methods that U.S. cities and localities have used to intentionally privatize services. An eighth method is really the result of failure of governments to deliver a quality service. The United Postal Service's (UPS) competition with the post office is perhaps the best example of such a governmental default. Privatization has been a hot topic in the 1980s, and we can expect that it will be an even hotter action item for state and local governments in the 1990s.

METHODS OF PRIVATIZATION

Method	Technique	Advantages	Examples
• CONTRACTING	Competitive letting of bids	Competitive Can be seasonal	Public works Transportation
• FRANCHISES	Grant franchise to operate and charge fee	Completely turn over provision	Garbage pickup Airports
• SUBSIDIES	Help defray costs of private provider	Cheaper than public provision	Cultural arts Youth activities
• VOUCHERS	Coupon to purchase good or service	Can shop in marketplace—competition	Food stamps School lunches
• VOLUNTEERS	Ask people to work for free	No cost services—large pool of people	Tutoring School guards Consulting
• SELF-HELP	Variation on volunteerism	No cost services	Neighborhood watch
• TAX INCENTIVES	Grant tax concessions	Reduces public need to supply	Used at federal level Can have local application
• MARKET COMPETITION	Government failure to provide quality output produces need to supply private response	Reduces public need to supply	UPS Private police

Source: Adopted from John C. Goodman, ed., *Privatization* (Dallas: The National Center for Policy Analysis, 1985), 37.

SUMMARY

1. There are some necessary functions that the market cannot perform or cannot perform well. These include defining and protecting property rights; providing public goods and merit goods; and correcting external effects, bringing about a "fair" distribution of income and stabilization.

2. Allocation by government includes not only the production of public goods but also any activities that affect private decisions about production and consumption, including taxes, subsidies, and regulation.

3. Redistribution changes the unequal distribution of income that results from the market processes. Redistribution occurs mainly through taxes and transfer payments, but any action of government will have distributional effects.

4. Stabilization refers to the activities of government aimed at creating full employment, stable prices, and a satisfactory rate of economic growth. This is the newest function of government.

5. Laws, and changes in laws through court decisions, have important impacts on incentives. These laws and interpretations affect the allocation of resources in a mixed economy.

6. Governments finance their activities primarily with taxes but also with intergovernmental grants, borrowing, and user charges.

7. The most common bases for taxation are income, consumption or spending, and wealth or assets. The principal kinds of taxes in the United States are income taxes, payroll taxes, sales taxes, and property taxes.

8. Taxes can be based on the benefit principle (pay according to benefits received) or the ability-to-pay principle (as measured by income, assets, or spending). Ability to pay is very difficult to measure.

9. Equity usually is measured in terms of progressive, proportional, or regressive taxes, depending on whether the increase in tax as income rises is more than proportional, proportional, or less than proportional.

10. A good tax is efficient, equitable, visible, and inexpensive to administer. Some taxes should be stable in yield, whereas others should be responsive to growth in income and population.

11. Efficiency refers to whether the tax minimizes the distortion of private decision making. Visibility refers to the taxpayers' awareness of the tax payment. Cost is the cost of collection and administration, divided between government and taxpayer.

12. Major tax reform in 1986 lowered tax rates and eliminated many deductions.

13. Privatization of public functions permits public provision of goods and services to be done more efficiently by relying on market (and other) forces. It is the transfer of governmental activities and/or assets to the private sector.

NEW TERMS

mixed capitalism	property law	proportional tax
transfer payment	tort law	progressive tax
fiscal federalism	contract law	bracket creep
allocation	eminent domain	horizontal equity
public good	tort	vertical equity
free rider	benefit principle	neutral tax
merit good	ability-to-pay principle	categorical grant
public "bad"	equity	block grant
redistribution	tax efficiency	user charge
stabilization	regressive tax	

QUESTIONS FOR DISCUSSION

1. Why is the income tax the main revenue source for the federal government, whereas sales taxes are most popular at the state level and property taxes at the local level? Does it have anything to do with how easy it is to move and avoid the tax?

2. What should be the role of the government in providing education? Should it produce, subsidize, or get out of education altogether? Why do you suppose that we provide education through 12th grade "free" (i.e., entirely through taxes) but only subsidize education beyond that level? Does it have anything to do with who gets the benefits?

3. Suppose we were to adopt a flat-rate tax with no deductions, exemptions, or adjustments. What groups would benefit? Who wouldn't benefit?

4. Can you find examples in your own area of services produced in the public sector that are produced elsewhere in the private sector or vice versa? Can you explain why the choice might not be the same in different sections of the country or in communities of different sizes?

5. A hypothetical economy has four individuals who earn the following incomes and pay the following taxes:

	Income	Tax
• Ralph	$ 11,000	$ 605.00
• Maria	100,000	9,100.00
• Roger	78,000	6,464.00
• Carey	29,000	1,869.00

Calculate the tax rates and determine if the rates are proportional, progressive, or regressive.

6. Why do most cities charge for water but not for streetlights or police protection?

7. Classify each of the following government actions as primarily allocation, redistribution, or stabilization:
   a. Cutting taxes to end a recession
   b. Making Social Security payments to the elderly
   c. Paying farmers not to produce corn
   e. Buying paper shredders for government offices

8. City *A* has two kinds of taxes. Tax #1 is only paid by families with children and is used to finance youth recreational activities. Tax #2 is 1 percent of income and is used to finance general city expenditures. Are these taxes based on the benefits principle or the ability-to-pay principle? Explain.

9. Why do states use more than one kind of tax instead of relying on the sales tax, the income tax, or the property tax?

10. Mike pays a sales tax of $100 on his car. Barbara pays a sales tax of $200 on her car. Mike's income is $6,000 and Barbara's is $21,000. Is this a proportional, progressive, or regressive tax? Do you need to know the selling price of the car?

SUGGESTIONS FOR FURTHER READING

Council of Economic Advisors. *Economic Report of the President*. Washington, D.C.: U.S. Government Printing Office, annual. Summarizes spending decisions, program changes, and stabilization activity; contains a great deal of statistics.

McChesney, Fred S. "Government Prohibitions on Volunteer Fire Fighting in Nineteenth-Century America: A Property Rights Perspective." *Journal of Legal Studies* (January 1986): 69–02. Shows some problems of privatization in the pressures to make fire fighting a public service in the late 1800s.

Page, Benjamin I. *Who Gets What From Government*. Berkeley: University of California Press, 1983. An examination of federal programs that shows that the rich pay less in taxes, while the poor get less in benefits than is commonly believed.

Posner, Richard A. *Economic Analysis of Law*. Boston: Little, Brown and Company, 1972. The standard reference for the application of economics to legal issues.

PART TWO

DEMAND AND
CONSUMER CHOICE

CHAPTER 5 ■
■

APPLICATIONS OF SUPPLY AND DEMAND: THE BASIC MICRO TOOLS

INTRODUCTION

This chapter makes use of the basic microeconomic models and theories that we developed in Chapters 1 to 4. These tools of economics can yield profound insights into a variety of social issues. Equipped with these tools of analysis, you can understand diverse issues such as crime, rent control, minimum wages, the energy crisis, and the effects and causes of natural disasters, to name just a few.

THE ECONOMICS OF CRIME: USE OF THE SELF-INTEREST HYPOTHESIS

We can use one of the assumptions from Chapter 1, the self-interest hypothesis, to analyze crime problems and prevention. Assume that criminals are rational people who commit crimes when it is in their self-interest to do so. A criminal calculates the costs and benefits of each crime and commits those crimes for which the benefits exceed the costs. In other words, crime is an economic activity.

The hypothesis is that a criminal calculates costs (C) and benefits (B) of criminal activities and commits those crimes where $B > C$. According to this hypothesis, crime is an economic activity, and the criminal behaves like any other entrepreneur.

The benefits are what the criminal hopes to realize by the activity. We want to place a value on this. In crimes involving the theft of property, this is relatively easy. The anticipated benefit is the anticipated market value of the take. For other crimes such as vandalism, illegal parking, or littering, we have to impute some value to the activity. This value may be nonmonetary in nature; for example, the time saved by parking illegally rather than searching for a legal parking spot.

The cost is the penalty (P) adjusted for the probability (π) that the criminal will be caught, and the penalty will be imposed. So, the prospective criminal compares B to $P \times \pi$. In other words, if the fine for littering is $500, but on the average one will be caught and fined for littering only once every 500 times, the expected cost of littering is $1 ($500 × $^1/_{500}$). The economic model just developed thus suggests that if some people get more than $1 worth of benefit from littering, they will litter.

The Economics of Robbery

This model now can be applied to crimes more serious than littering. If we want to do something about the amount of armed robbery that is taking place in our society, the model offers insight into this crime and its prevention. There are three elements to this model. First, the model says that crime depends on the benefits from the activity so, *ceteris paribus*, as the value of the loot goes up, so will the amount of robbery. Second, it says that as the penalty goes down (with no change in the probability of being caught), criminal activity will go up. Third, it says that if the probability of being caught goes down, *ceteris paribus*, the amount of robbery will go up.

We can now advise policymakers. In order to decrease the amount of armed robbery, policymakers can do any or some combination of all three things. One possibility is to decrease the potential take, or profit. This is difficult to do, but you probably have noticed that most late-night gas stations advertise that they don't keep much cash on hand. That's one way of reducing the "take."

A second possibility is to increase the penalty. Suppose that, if a person is caught robbing a gas station and using a gun during the robbery, the criminal will have the hand that is holding the gun cut off. Increasing the penalty is sometimes difficult because society deems some penalties too severe. In some countries, the hands of robbers are cut off; but in the United States, penalties for robbery usually are limited to prison sentences. Recently in one suburb outside Washington, D.C., the local police chief announced that squad cars would be equipped with rifles with exploding shells (outlawed by the United Nations as being too inhumane for warfare) and that officers had been instructed to shoot first and ask questions later when investigating robberies. Almost immediately, the robbery rate fell in this jurisdiction and increased in adjacent jurisdictions. This result is predicted by the model, which says as the potential penalty rises, criminal activity will fall. Of course, some people might object to this policy even if it does reduce crime. But economic models are positive, telling only what the consequences of such a policy will be. They don't say if it's good or bad in a moral sense.

The third option that could reduce the robbery rate would be to increase the probability of arrest and conviction of would-be robbers. This might be accomplished by more police, speedier justice, television cameras in banks, or other similar measures.

The Economics of the Death Penalty

The preceding analysis has probably led you to the conclusion that economists would argue that the death penalty deters crime. Indeed, a University of Buffalo economist, Isaac Ehrlich, has statistically argued that the death penalty does act to reduce the amount of murder.[1] If you are a doubter, answer this question: Would you ever litter if the probability of getting caught was one in five hundred, and the penalty was death? You would have to place a high value on being able to litter or a low value on your own life if you said yes. However, some people argue that murderers have such a distorted view of reality that they underestimate the probability of being caught, convicted, and sentenced to death. These people argue that the death penalty provides little deterrence. More importantly, just because positive economic theory says the death penalty deters crime, that does not mean that you, or anyone else, has to support the death penalty if you object on moral, or normative, grounds.

The Economics of Illegal Parking

There probably are some of you who are still skeptical about this simple model of crime, so let's analyze a criminal activity that you have probably committed or at least contemplated committing—illegal parking on campus. On almost all college campuses, the quantity of parking spaces supplied is less than the quantity demanded at a zero price; as a result, there are benefits to parking in an illegal parking space. Suppose that the fine for illegal parking is $10, and you find from experience that you get a ticket one out of every four times you park illegally. The expected cost of the crime is thus $2.50 ($10 × 0.25). Now it would be almost impossible to estimate the benefits that accrue to those who illegally park, but since there are many violators, it's clear that benefits are substantial. Assume you are appointed to a committee formed by the university's president to solve the parking problem. Your committee identifies three options: (1) You could lower the benefits by buying shuttle buses to transport students from their parking areas to the classroom buildings; (2) you could increase the likelihood of being caught by hiring more police and increasing the number of times they check the parking areas; or (3) you could raise the cost of the crime. A common way to increase the cost is to tow away illegally parked cars. This raises the cost of the crime significantly because violators now have to pay towing fees in addition to the basic fine. Getting towed involves a great deal of time and trouble as well as expense.

If you still don't believe the model, here is an empirical test you can carry out. Observe the amount of illegal parking on a nice sunny day. Then the next time it rains, observe the criminal activity again. What does the model predict? On rainy days, the benefits of the crime go up,

1. Again, this does not mean that you should necessarily support the death penalty. You can still be opposed to the death penalty on humanitarian grounds even though you accept the implications of the model. For the study, see I. Ehrlich, "The Deterrent Effect of Capital Punishment: A Question of Life and Death," *American Economic Review* (June 1975).

ceteris paribus, because the benefit is the proximity to class plus arriving in class dry. The probability of being caught also goes down, *ceteris paribus*, because campus police don't like to get wet either. The model thus predicts that there will be more illegal parking on rainy days. Check it out—test the model!

Basketball Crime

Recently Professors Robert E. McCormick of Clemson University and Robert D. Tollison of George Mason University applied the model of a market for criminal activity to the basketball arena.[2] They picked basketball as a subject of analysis because there is a great deal of sports data available, and the number of referees (police) increased from two to three in 1978. Their empirical model showed that increasing the number of officials caused fouls to decrease. These results show that the addition of the third referee caused the number of fouls (arrests) to decline by 34 percent. They view this as a lower bound estimate because their data showed that referee competence went up and the number of fouls called declined by 34 percent. They conclude that the crime rate must have decreased by more than 34 percent with a 50 percent increase in the size of the police force.

PRICE CEILINGS AND PRICE FLOORS

Chapter 3 described how free markets reach equilibrium. It is possible for this market process to be interfered with, and this interference is sometimes the result of governmental action. **Price ceilings** are prices imposed by a governmental unit that are set as a limit. The ceiling is a price that cannot be exceeded. **Price floors** are prices established by a governmental unit as minimum prices that cannot be undercut. Price ceilings and price floors cause disruptions in the market-clearing process, and microeconomic tools make it possible to see the effects of these disruptions.

Price Ceilings

A price ceiling that is set below the equilibrium price prohibits the market from clearing. The amount that consumers wish to purchase at the imposed ceiling is greater than the amount suppliers are willing to supply at this price. Figure 5–1 demonstrates this problem. In Figure 5–1, the equilibrium price is P_e and equilibrium quantity is Q_e. The government imposes a price ceiling of P_c. The amount that consumers wish to consume at Price P_c is Q_d, and the amount the suppliers are willing to supply at the ceiling is Q_s. The result is a shortage. A shortage results when the amount that consumers wish to purchase at some price exceeds

PRICE CEILINGS
Prices imposed by a governmental unit that are set as a limit. The ceiling is a price that cannot be exceeded.

PRICE FLOORS
Prices established as minimum prices. A governmental unit sets a price that cannot be undercut.

Price/Unit

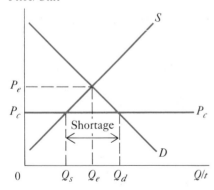

FIGURE 5–1
PRICE CEILING
A price ceiling that is set below the market-clearing price creates a shortage. At the price imposed by the government, potential purchasers demand a larger quantity of the good than suppliers are willing to sell.

2. Robert E. McCormick and Robert D. Tollison, "Crime on the Court," *Journal of Political Economy* (April 1984): 223–235.

the amount suppliers wish to supply. A shortage can occur only on a lasting basis when a price ceiling is in effect. It is important to realize that the shortage is created by the ceiling. Without the ceiling, price would rise, the quantity demanded would decrease, and the quantity supplied would increase until price reaches P_e and the market clears. If the ceiling is to be maintained, government must replace the market with some other way to allocate the goods. Consumers are frustrated as they try to obtain the good or service at the lower price, and some method other than price must be used to determine who will get the good or service—ration coupons, first come-first served, or other nonmarket methods.

In almost all cases where price ceilings are imposed, black markets spring up. **Black markets** are markets in which people illegally buy and sell goods or services subject to price ceilings at prices above the imposed price ceiling.[3] We'll have more to say about black markets a little later.

Rent Control

Price ceilings are used by various levels of government. A later section in this chapter will discuss how price ceilings created a natural gas crisis that is still affecting the economy today. Consider now the effect of price ceilings on apartment rentals.

Many cities, including New York City and Washington, D.C., have imposed price ceilings on apartment rents. This ceiling, imposed by governmental units, is referred to as **rent control**. At first glance, the goals of rent control are admirable; i.e., to keep rents low so that everyone, including the poor, can find a place to live at a reasonable price. For the effect of rent control, refer again to Figure 5–1. At a price less than the market-clearing price, there will be a shortage of rental units. More people will be looking for rental units than the number available. Something other than the market mechanism will now allocate the rental units. The landlord may now impose criteria for choosing among prospective tenants because for any vacancy, the landlord has a number of people waiting in line to rent the apartment. The landlord can now easily discriminate in the choice of a tenant because it is costless to do so. Without rent control, the landlord is more likely to rent to any prospective tenant rather than leave the apartment vacant because the market is clearing. With rent control, the landlord can choose from the backlog of prospective tenants. The landlord can exclude those who are young (or old) or those who have children (or dogs). Since landlords cannot raise rents, they will instead choose tenants who cost the least in terms of damage, noise, complaints, or hassles. The point is that the interference in the market has replaced the nondiscrimination of the market mechanism.

Black Markets

As mentioned earlier, black markets tend to develop when price ceilings are imposed. Assume that the market in Figure 5–2 represents the market for tickets to one of the biggest college football games of the year, the Orange Bowl. The stock of tickets is completely fixed in the short run at the 70,000 seating capacity of the stadium. The athletic

3. You should be able to show why a price ceiling that is imposed *above* the equilibrium price has no noticeable effect on the market.

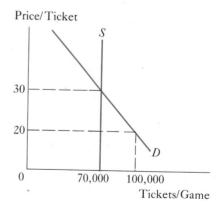

**FIGURE 5-2
THE ORANGE BOWL**
A price ceiling is often imposed by universities in selling tickets to popular events. Such a price ceiling, if it is below the market-clearing price, creates a black market for the underpriced tickets.

department is selling the tickets at a price ceiling of $20 per ticket. For this game, the market-clearing price would be $30, so the $20 imposed price has created a shortage of 30,000 tickets. At that price, there is going to be a larger quantity of tickets demanded than there are tickets. The athletic department has to allocate these tickets by some other means than the market, so it discriminates; selling tickets to those fans who are willing to wait longer in line or those who donate to the booster club. The shortage of tickets will produce a black market. Some of those who are able to get the tickets for $20 will be willing to sell them. These people will engage in black-market activity by selling them to those who are willing to pay more. In the black market for tickets to such events, these black marketers are referred to as *scalpers*. Scalping generally has a bad connotation. But consider that the scalper is performing the service of transferring tickets from people who value other goods more highly than they value the tickets to individuals who value the tickets more highly than other goods. Thus, the scalper is being paid for performing this service.

Why Ceilings?

If price ceilings are so disruptive, why do they exist? One answer is that not all people are hurt by ceilings. Those who are able to purchase the good or service at the artificially low price are better off and they, as a result, approve of the ceiling. In the apartment example, people who already have an apartment and don't want to move would be better off with rent control. These people probably would vote for rent control because it would make them better off. In the ticket example, those who don't mind waiting in line or those who get a ticket because they are a booster like low ticket prices. It is important to realize, though, that price ceilings do not, as is often claimed, generally help the poor. If there is one ticket left at $20 for the big game, who do you think will get it? A poor fan who likes football more than anything else that the $20 would buy or the governor who thinks it would be good politics to be seen at the game? When the market is replaced, another mechanism must be substituted to allocate goods. This mechanism usually depends heavily on power and influence, and thus the poor, who lack power and influence, are not generally helped by the price ceiling.

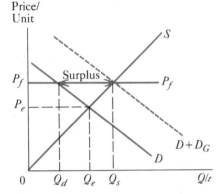

FIGURE 5-3
PRICE FLOOR

If the government imposes a price above the market-clearing price, a surplus will be created. At the higher than equilibrium price, suppliers will desire to sell more units than consumers will be willing to purchase.

SURPLUS

The amount that suppliers wish to supply at some price exceeds the amount that consumers wish to purchase. A surplus can only occur on a lasting basis when a price floor is in effect.

Price Floors

A price floor that is set above the equilibrium price prohibits the market from clearing. The amount that suppliers offer for sale at the imposed floor is greater than the amount consumers wish to purchase at this price. Figure 5–3 demonstrates this case. In Figure 5–3, the equilibrium price is P_e, and the equilibrium quantity is Q_e. The government imposes a price floor of P_f, with the result that the quantity supplied at Price P_f is Q_s, and the quantity consumers demand is Q_d. The higher price has attracted more suppliers into the market, while at the same time has discouraged buyers or caused them to shift to substitutes. The result is a surplus equal to $Q_s - Q_d$. A **surplus** results when the amount that suppliers wish to supply at some price exceeds the amount that consumers wish to purchase. A surplus can only occur on a lasting basis when a price floor is in effect. This surplus is created by the price floor. If the floor didn't exist, price would fall and the quantity demanded would increase. The quantity supplied would decrease until the market cleared.

THE INTERNATIONAL PERSPECTIVE
BLACK MARKETS

During World War II, the U.S. government tried to control the prices of some basic commodities, such as gasoline and sugar. Ration tickets were distributed in order to determine who got the limited supply. These ration tickets were sold on black markets. Since governments at all levels in the United States usually refrain from trying to control prices, there has been little black-market activity in the United States except for that episode. About the only experience you might have with a black market is the occasional resale of tickets to athletic events and concerts. As you saw in this textbook, black-market activity in tickets is usually referred to as *scalping*.

However, if you have traveled or lived outside the United States, you are aware that black markets abound. One important black market is in currencies. Many countries attempt to control the price of their currency in terms of other currencies. Economists refer to this price as the *exchange rate*; we will devote a whole chapter to exchange-rate determination in this textbook. These attempts to control the exchange rate always produce black markets for the foreign exchange. If you have been

to Eastern Europe, the Soviet Union, or Asia, you have probably been approached on the street in a very secretive manner by individuals who want to exchange their currency for dollars at a much better exchange rate than the bank provides.

Currency exchange is not the only kind of black-market exchanges abroad. Even if you haven't traveled there, you have likely heard stories about the black market for jeans in the Soviet Union. If you travel to the Soviet Union, pack a couple pair of extra jeans so you can finance part of your trip out of all the rubles you can earn on the black market for these jeans. But don't get caught!

Governments usually attempt to control a broad range of prices during and after wars. This effort is made more difficult by the fact that consumer goods are usually more scarce during war. Equilibrium prices would therefore be rising rapidly at the same time the government is trying to control them. Perhaps the extreme examples of such controls happened in post-World War II Germany and Japan.

In both Germany and Japan, there were enormous government debts that were financed by monetary expansion. These large increases in the money supply led to severe inflations, but the governments imposed strict controls on food prices, often rationing the caloric intake of individuals. These strict controls led to black markets and the phenomenon of "trekking." Urban residents would leave town to go to the countryside to make black-market deals with farmers. The stricter the controls, the more the trekking grew. It was reported that on one day more than 900,000 residents of Tokyo left town for the countryside. In Germany, the controls came to an end with the Erhard reforms of 1948. With the end of controls, the incentive to trek evaporated. As with most economic forces, there was a secondary effect. Railroad passenger traffic fell immediately to less than 40 percent of the prereform level. This drop in rail traffic was evidence of the volume of the trekking that had been taking place.

Sources: Jerome B. Cohen, *Japan's Economy in War and Reconstruction* (Minneapolis: University of Minnesota Press, 1949); and Lucius C. Clay, *Decision in Germany* (New York: Doubleday & Co., Inc., 1950).

It can be difficult for the governmental unit that imposes a price floor to maintain the floor. Some suppliers will attempt to cut prices in order to sell the desired quantity. The most effective way for the government to prevent this price cutting is to purchase the unwanted quantity supplied. By purchasing the surplus, the government in effect is shifting the demand curve outward to create a new equilibrium at the desired price. In Figure 5–3, the dashed demand curve represents the previous demand curve plus the added governmental demand. Such a shift would allow the price to remain at P_f. The best example of price floors that work in this way are the price supports operated by the Commodity Credit Corporation (CCC) for agricultural products. The Commodity Credit Corporation (CCC) is a government agency that makes loans to farmers as part of the price support programs. The government wants to maintain a price that is above the market-clearing price. To maintain this price floor, it is necessary for the CCC to purchase the grain; the effect of this is to shift the demand curve to the right (as in $D + D_G$ in Figure 5–3) so the higher price can be maintained.

COMMODITY CREDIT CORPORATION (CCC)
A government agency that makes loans to farmers as part of the price support programs.

The Minimum Wage

The minimum wage is a price floor imposed by a governmental unit in the labor market. Again using Figure 5–3, a minimum wage of P_f that is set above the market wage (P_e) causes a surplus of labor ($Q_s - Q_d$). In terms of our analysis, if the minimum wage is set above the market-clearing wage rate, the amount of labor that laborers will supply at that wage will be greater than the amount of labor that firms will wish to employ, resulting in unemployment.

MINIMUM WAGE
A price floor imposed by a governmental unit in the labor market.

Economists generally agree that minimum-wage legislation causes unemployment to be higher than it would be otherwise. This is particularly true for young people, where the market-clearing wage might be significantly lower than the minimum wage. In 1978, Congress raised the wage floor to $2.65 an hour, up from the $2.30 an hour that was set in 1974. In addition, a formula was adopted that ensured automatic increases up to $3.35 an hour in 1981. This action was taken despite the fact that teenage unemployment was almost 18 percent at the time the bill was passed and despite strong statistical evidence from a large number of economists that the increase would raise youth unemployment to even higher levels. Robert Goldfarb of George Washington University and Edward Gramlich, then of the Brookings Institution, independently reviewed eight empirical studies by economists. The studies overwhelmingly agreed that increases in minimum wages would cause increases in unemployment. The studies differed, however, as to how significant the impact would be. They predicted that the 15 percent increase in the minimum wage would increase teenage unemployment anywhere from 3.4 to 5.3 percentage points.[4] In the Reagan years, the minimum wage was not increased, so

4. See Edward M. Gramlich, "Impact of Minimum Wages on Other Wages, Employment and Family Incomes," *Brookings Papers on Economic Activity*, No. 2 (1976): 409–451; and Robert Goldfarb, "The Policy Content of Quantitative Minimum Wage Research," *Industrial Relations Research Association Proceedings* (December 1974): 261–268. These estimates are based on calculating the elasticity of supply and demand for teenage workers.

its impact declined as market wages rose relative to the minimum wage. Recently Senator Kennedy has proposed a $1.60 increase in the minimum wage.

If there is so much agreement among economists about the harmful effects of minimum wages, why are they enacted? The reason is very similar to the one for enacting price ceilings. Not all people are hurt by the wage floor. Some workers, those represented by Q_d in Figure 5–3, receive pay increases when the legislation is enacted. Those who are laid off ($Q_e - Q_d$) or who now seek but are unable to find employment at the new minimum wage ($Q_s - Q_e$) usually don't understand the role of the higher minimum wage in causing their frustration. The result is that it is politically popular among some groups, particularly organized labor, to support minimum-wage legislation. Remember, economics only predicts that minimum-wage legislation causes decreased employment. It does not tell us that minimum-wage legislation is a good or bad thing in other respects. We may decide that it is better to have fewer people employed at a higher wage rate than to have everyone who wants to work employed at a lower, market-clearing wage rate.

A LESSON FROM THE ENERGY "CRISIS"?

To many of you, the energy crisis is a historical curiosity. Indeed, if you are 20 years old, you were not yet in grade school when your parents had to wait in line for gasoline at the height of the energy crisis. Times change, and some gasoline stations have even returned to the practice of giving away road maps to their customers. But, we shouldn't forget or ignore historical mistakes. We should learn from our economic mistakes. There is an old saying: "What goes around, comes around." We should be prepared for future rounds of energy policy and ask what we can learn from past foolishness. Indeed, some policymakers are predicting a second crisis. Secretary of the Interior Donald Hodel warned in 1987 that people would be sitting in gas lines by 1992.

In 1978, President Carter held a fireside chat to talk to the U.S. public about the energy crisis. He declared that the energy crisis was the moral equivalent of war. President Carter ultimately ordered the deregulation of natural gas coupled with a windfall gains tax on large oil companies. President Reagan continued the phased deregulation and eliminated the windfall gains tax in his 1981 tax reform, but problems continue to confront the natural gas market. The tools developed in other chapters can be used to analyze many aspects of the energy "crisis." The natural gas shortage provides a good case study for that purpose.

The Creation of a Crisis: Regulation of Natural Gas

In 1938, Congress passed the Natural Gas Act, and in 1954 the Supreme Court placed all firms selling interstate natural gas under the regulation of the Federal Power Commission (FPC).[5] The law was intended to keep prices "just and reasonable" for consumers by allowing suppliers only a "fair" rate of return. After the 1954 Supreme Court ruling, the FPC attempted to regulate the price received by each individual producer engaged in the interstate sale of natural gas. The system broke down in 1960 when a giant backlog of hearings developed in response to the attempted regulation of more than 4,000 firms. A former Harvard Law School dean has called this "the outstanding example of the federal government in the breakdown of the administrative process."[6] In response to this administrative breakdown, the FPC ruled in 1965 (affirmed by the Supreme Court in 1968) that it would set prices separately for each geographical area and each individual petroleum commodity. This decision took eight years to be implemented, and during this entire period, prices were kept at 1960 levels. This individual commodity approach to pricing is next to impossible to implement because natural gas is jointly produced with crude oil. The FPC method requires that certain costs be allocated to the production of natural gas, even though it is produced in a joint process. Recognizing the administrative history and difficulty of these controls, what were the effects of regulation?

Paul W. MacAvoy, a professor of economics at M.I.T. and a member of President Ford's Council of Economic Advisers, has extensively examined the natural gas industry. In a series of books and articles in professional journals, he has examined the market for natural gas to determine the effects of regulation. MacAvoy concluded that regulation has held prices below free-market levels. Between 1964 and 1967, prices would have been about twice as high without regulation. The result of these artificially depressed prices was that 40 percent fewer new reserves were added to production than would have been added in the free-market context. The result of these lower reserves is painfully obvious. In the absence of the price-rationing function of the market system, there is a shortage. Existing supplies then must be rationed, and consumers (including industry) must substitute more expensive alternative fuels for the cheaper natural gas that is not available. The curious result is that the government, in order to keep the price of natural gas low, produced a shortage that required consumers to buy even more expensive gasified coal, imported liquid natural gas, or some other alternative fuel.

This shortage is shown graphically in Figure 5–4. Assume the price originally set by the FPC was near or at equilibrium. This produced a price represented by P_{1960} and an equilibrium quantity of Q_{1960}. The 1960 decision to set prices on a geographical-area basis resulted in a price ceiling that was not changed for eight years while the case was in litigation. During this period, there were tremendous changes in the *ceteris paribus* demand conditions. For one, income increased substantially during this period. Thus, by 1968 the demand curve had shifted to the curve

5. The brief discussion that follows does not do justice to the complexity of natural gas regulation. The interested reader should see Edward J. Mitchell, *U.S. Energy Policy: A Primer* (Washington D.C.: American Enterprise Institute for Public Policy Research, June, 1974). Mitchell's study cites much of the relevant literature on natural gas regulation. See Mitchell for references to the data and the other studies mentioned.
6. Mitchell, *U.S. Energy Policy: A Primer*, 7.

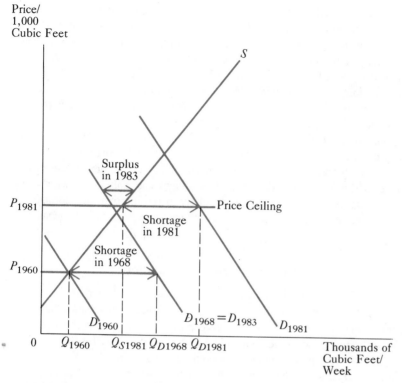

FIGURE 5-4
THE MARKET FOR NATURAL GAS
In 1960, the price P_{1960} was an equilibrium price. The amount consumers *wished* to purchase was exactly the amount suppliers *wished* to sell. A shortage is created if the price is frozen at P_{1960} and demand increases to D_{1968} or D_{1981}. Allowing the price to rise reduces the shortage, but some shortage remains as long as the price is controlled at a level below equilibrium.

represented by D_{1968}, due to rising income, resulting in a shortage. At P_{1960}, the quantity supplied is Q_{1960} and the quantity demanded is Q_{D1968}. We had 40 percent less production than we would have had in a free market. In 1981, the problem was still present. Demand had increased to D_{1981}. To be sure, the FPC allowed the price to rise to P_{1981}, but the price rise lagged behind the demand increase. So in 1981, there was still a government-created shortage because at P_{1981}, the quantity supplied is Q_{S1981} and the quantity demanded is Q_{D1981}.

It is important to realize that the shortage was caused by the price ceiling. Natural gas is scarce, but scarcity and shortage are different concepts. Scarcity simply means that the item is not as plentiful as we would like; with scarcity, rising prices ensure equilibrium. Shortage means that at the prevailing price, the quantity demanded exceeds the quantity supplied. This distinction is important because much of the debate about an energy crisis confuses these two concepts.

The energy industry and the oil industry are topics of hot debate by politicians and analysts. These debates often center on predictions of the dire consequences of the price of oil being too high (as in 1975) or too low (as in 1988)! Predictions of doom for users of energy are not new. As early as the beginning of the nineteenth century, some commentators were predicting the first energy crisis. In the early 1800s, houses were lit by oil-burning lamps. Demand for these lamps was increasing rapidly because of income and population growth. The lamps were fueled by oil from sperm whales. Many people predicted that the whale population would soon be depleted and, therefore, houses would be dark. In other words, they were predicting greater scarcity of this particular product. What happened? Prices rose rapidly, from about 40 cents per gallon to about $2.50 per gallon in 30 years. These higher prices caused the quantity demanded to decrease, as users found substitutes for whale oil. The important point is that a shortage did not occur because prices rose in the face of greater scarcity. Shortages can only occur with artificially imposed low prices. It is particularly disturbing that the shortages of natural gas occurred in a market where there was a potentially large supply.

The Dilemma of Earlier Regulation

Another disturbing consequence of controls is that, even after it is generally recognized that government regulation is creating havoc in important markets, it is politically very difficult to remove the controls. When Congress becomes convinced that the crisis may be the result of regulation, it is politically very unpopular to change the law. Why? Those individuals who are lucky enough, or have enough political power, purchase the natural gas at below-market prices. In 1977, the regulated price of natural gas was $1.34 per thousand cubic feet. At that time, it was estimated that markets would have cleared at $3.00 per thousand cubic feet. People bought gas furnaces, and firms installed gas-driven equipment because of the low operating costs. The dilemma is clear; being an advocate of deregulation makes it appear to consumers as if the deregulator, not the market forces, has produced the sharp rise in fuel bills. Voters might turn against a member of Congress who votes to deregulate. It is important to realize that if Congress had not interfered with the market mechanism in the first place, voters probably would not hold Congress responsible for subsequent higher gas prices after deregulation!

It was a major goal of the Carter administration to lift the price ceiling and the necessary legislation was approved by Congress as The Natural Gas Policy Act of 1978. The Carter deregulation, which was a hard-fought legislative battle, immediately raised prices 25 percent and allowed for a 10 percent increase per year until 1985, when all ceilings on newly found natural gas were removed.

The Shortage Turns to Surplus: And Prices Rise?

The story of the legislated deregulation didn't end nicely in 1985 with the planned removal of all ceilings. Different problems began to surface in late 1982.

The recession of 1981 to 1983 (and warm weather) decreased the demand for natural gas, shifting the curve to D_{1983} in Figure 5–4. (D_{1983} is drawn as the same curve as D_{1968} to keep the diagram as uncluttered as possible.) In fact, in 1983 only about 85 percent of the natural gas produced was consumed. This created a surplus in 1983, as shown in Figure 5–4. In a deregulated market, a surplus should cause prices to decrease. Unfortunately, President Carter's Natural Gas Policy Act of 1978 didn't deregulate all natural gas. Instead, the 1978 Act freed prices on some gas and kept other (old gas) prices at low levels. The immediate effect was that the price of the new gas rose dramatically and a (sort of) equilibrium was reached.

As demand fell, supply and demand analysis predicted that the surplus would push prices downward, but consumers (utilities) were locked into long-term "take or pay" contracts. These contracts stemmed from the old regulated days when utilities would enter into 20-year contracts with gas dealers to share the risk of price fluctuations. The gas suppliers, faced with a surplus, expanded output of the more expensive gas (the new gas) and reduced production of the cheap gas (the old gas). As a result, the price of natural gas rose in a surplus market.

The regulatory nonsense of separating old gas from new gas thus had the effect of raising natural gas prices to consumers, when its intent was to keep prices from rising as much by controlling the price of already-discovered gas.

The natural gas story doesn't end with the complete decontrol of prices in 1985. By 1987, natural gas prices were at very low levels in part because of deregulation but largely due to the collapse of the oil cartel and the significant decline in the worldwide price of oil and related products. Some producers argue that the price would be lower yet if there were competition in the natural gas market. These producers argue that competition is restricted by the pipeline owners who purchase and transport the natural gas of their producing affiliates. The producers who don't own pipelines want a law passed that requires interstate pipeline owners to transport all gas for a posted tariff.

This brief review of natural gas regulation is not meant as a lesson of one industry but as an illustration of the effect that regulation and political interference can have on market forces. Similar regulation can be found throughout the U.S. economy. One need only scan the headlines for this month's crisis, be it the meat shortage, the cement shortage, or the capital shortage. The distortion is very likely caused by well-intentioned interference with market forces.

THE HEALTH CARE INDUSTRY

The rapidly rising price of health care has been receiving considerable attention from journalists and politicians in recent years. In large part, this increased interest is a natural outgrowth of the fact that health care has become one of the fastest growing industries in the United States. Between 1950 and 1980, total expenditures on health care increased from $11 billion annually to more than $200 billion annually, and they are expected to more than triple again between 1985 and 1990. In 1950, these expenditures represented 4.5 percent of total national income, and by 1990 they will represent more than 13 percent of national income. It is possible to analyze the potential problems of the health care industry using the basic economic tools of supply and demand.

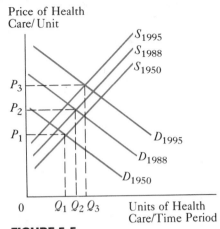

FIGURE 5-5
THE MARKET FOR HEALTH CARE
The health care market is characterized by decreasing supply due to increasing costs and by increasing demand due to rising incomes and the continued aging of our society. As a result, the equilibrium price of health care has been rising rapidly.

Figure 5-5 describes what is happening in the health care industry. The market in 1950 is represented by Supply Curve S_{1950} and Demand Curve D_{1950}. Equilibrium is P_1 and Q_1. Between 1950 and 1988, there were substantial changes in the *ceteris paribus* conditions in the health care market. On the supply side, hospitals and doctors have greatly increased the sophistication of the care they supply. There has been a virtual explosion in technological advances in the industries that make diagnostic, surgical, and therapeutic equipment. This equipment is very expensive and increases the cost of supplying health care (even if it does mean improved health care). The effect of all this improved, expensive care has been to shift the supply curve from S_{1950} to S_{1988} in Figure 5-5.

On the demand side, the changes have been equally significant. First and foremost, the income of U.S. citizens has risen significantly over this period. Assuming health care is a normal good and that the demand for it is income elastic, increased income will increase the demand for health care. The more income elastic this demand, the more significant will be the increase in demand. Second, there has been an increase in Medicare, Medicaid, and employer-provided health insurance. Since, in these cases, payment is made by a third party, the individual demands more health care. Third, the age distribution of the U.S. population has shifted. This will become an even greater problem for health care as Yuppies age. Fourth, the very success of medical health care delivery creates more demand for health care in the future. As the health care of the population improves, the population lives longer. More health care is then demanded because the population is now older, and older people demand more health care. Fifty years ago, many of these people would have died of measles, polio, or tuberculosis before they would have been old enough to develop the maladies now associated with older age. The increased demand for health care is represented by the shift from D_{1950} to D_{1988} in Figure 5-5. The result of these changes in supply and demand has been for price to rise to P_2 and a new level of consumption to be established at Q_2. The magnitude of the shift from P_1 to P_2 can be understood by comparing the price index for medical services to the consumer price index. Between 1950 and 1986, the price index for medical services rose 985 percent. This was 2.2 times more than the increase in the consumer price index.

The Coming Crisis in Health Care

What about the future? Let's speculate as to what might happen. It is likely that the supply curve will continue to shift leftward, representing an increase in the price of the factors of production used to produce health care. It is also likely that demand will continue to increase as incomes rise and the population ages. We would predict, then, that in response to a shift in demand from D_{1988} to D_{1995} and a shift in supply from S_{1988} to S_{1995}, there will be an increase in price to P_3 and an increase in the equilibrium quantity to Q_3. But this prediction supposes that the government does not intervene in this market. A quick review of Congressional interest in the health care industry would be enough to convince you that this is not a realistic assumption. As it stands now, the most likely governmental solution to the rapidly rising prices is twofold. One perennially popular solution is some form of national health insurance. The other is price controls.

Senator Edward Kennedy has made national health insurance a major political issue. Even President Reagan supported catastrophic insurance for older Americans. The economic effects of such a program are easy to predict. Since national health insurance would make health care affordable to more citizens by shifting a large part of the cost to taxpayers in general, it would increase the demand curve even beyond the one represented by D_{1995}. National health insurance would put even greater upward pressure on prices.

While a national health insurance program is seen as an antidote to rising costs, there is also increasing pressure to intervene in the market with price controls. Congress is beginning to talk about the "immorality" of the high price of health care. Price controls have been suggested as a solution. The effect can be predicted by examining Figure 5–5. At a ceiling price of P_2, the effect would be a shortage. The severity of the shortage would depend upon the magnitude of the increase in demand and decrease in supply. We would have the same type of crisis we discussed earlier when examining the natural gas market. An interesting point is that even though Congress demonstrated in the late 1970s that it understood how controls implemented in the 1950s helped create the energy crisis, it is flirting with similar controls for the health care industry.

Does this discussion and an understanding of these basic economic tools mean that economists can't justify supporting a national health program that would ensure health care to all citizens? Not at all! All that economics tells us is that such a program would increase demand and put upward pressure on prices of health care. You may well decide that this upward pressure on prices is worthwhile and that you would support such a program. The contribution of economics is to point out that these pressures are there, that they can't be ignored, and that to resort to controls will probably create a crisis.

M.D.s And The Marketplace[7]

In the mid-1950s, the practice of medicine changed significantly. Before that time, doctors often made house calls, drove Buicks, and were viewed as upper middle class pillars of the community. In 1955, doctors' incomes averaged $16,017. All that has changed: doctors moved to clinics and hospitals, they drove Porsches and Mercedes, and they were viewed by most of us as the privileged rich. Indeed, their mean pretax income jumped to $28,960 in 1965, $58,440 in 1975, and to $108,400 in 1985. That increase represents an increase of 677 percent over a 30-year period, or an average annual increase of 22.5 percent.

Until 1965, the ranks of M.D.s were increasing at about 2 percent per year, and expenditures on medical care were increasing at 10 percent per year. That goes a long way in explaining the 22.5 percent

---

7. Facts and quotes in this section are from "Hippocrates Meets Adam Smith." *Forbes* (February 10, 1986): 63–66.

annual increases in pretax income. But, as we have learned, supply curves slope upward; and these increases created incentives for the number of M.D.s to increase. In 1965, there were 277,600 doctors in the United States, one for every 697 Americans. In 1986, there were 506,000 practicing doctors, one for every 471 Americans.

What has happened? Well, first, the rate of increase in income has slowed dramatically. From 1983 to 1985, pretax mean income rose 2 percent per year. That's drastically below the 30-year average, and a result the model would predict. Medical school applications have declined; in 1975, there were 42,624 applications for 14,579 slots. In 1985, there were 32,893 applications for 16,268 slots. As *Forbes* magazine put it: "Hippocrates meets Adam Smith." These adjustments in price and quantity suggest that the health care "crisis" may have market solutions, and government intervention in national insurance or price setting may not be needed.

A few other adjustments are worth noting. Many doctors have begun to advertise. In 1965, this was considered unprofessional and illegal. Other doctors have added television sets to their waiting rooms to replace year-old magazines. One doctor in Beverly Hills gives her patients beepers that summon them from shopping when their time comes so they don't languish in her waiting room. More of these adjustments can be expected as doctors face the facts of the market.[8]

MICROECONOMICS AND SOCIAL POLICY—THE ECONOMICS OF NATURAL DISASTERS

The use of microeconomics can be demonstrated by looking at an area of social policy that hasn't been scrutinized to a great extent by economists. This example will highlight the **unintended effects** of policy, those effects that are unanticipated by policymakers but which become evident through careful economic analysis. Let's consider a rather comprehensive example of incentive-creating institutions and how policymakers might have avoided some pitfalls by making use of microeconomic analysis.

Economists have, with a few important exceptions, devoted little effort to studying the economics of natural disasters and disaster assistance. There are, however, some important areas in which microeconomics can be brought to bear on the analysis of how people respond to disasters—floods, earthquakes, hurricanes, and other natural catastrophes.

Government Policy

It is clear that government has gotten into the disaster-assistance business very significantly in recent years. Before the mid-1960s, disasters produced little in economic aid from the federal

UNINTENDED EFFECTS
Effects of policy that are unanticipated by policymakers but which become evident through careful economic analysis.

---

8. This section may seem in conflict with the previous section where we argued that the costs of health care were rising. Because doctors' salaries are only a small part of health costs, it is possible for their income to be falling at the same time that health care costs are rising.

dimension. He has also examined racial discrimination, the decision to have children, time allocation, and the pursuit of education as an investment decision.[a] His work on crime prevention, which we have outlined at the very beginning of the previous chapter, came to him as an idea while he was rushing to a student presentation at Columbia University, and he couldn't find a parking place. His thoughts went to the costs, the benefits, and the probability of being caught if he parked illegally. This "intellectual flash" formed the basis for his work on crime prevention.

Gary Becker presently teaches at the University of Chicago. He has also been on the faculty at Columbia University. He received his undergraduate education at Princeton University and his Ph.D. degree from the University of Chicago. In 1967, Becker was awarded the John Bates Clark Award, which is awarded by the American Economic Association to an "outstanding economist under 40 years old." Gary Becker has to be considered to be a good bet to eventually win a Nobel Prize in economics.

GARY BECKER (1930-   )

Gary Becker has, with great innovation, extended the application of microeconomic theory into many areas that had been considered noneconomic. He has examined criminal behavior as a rational economic calculation and the selection of a spouse as an exercise in the demand for characteristics that have an economic

a. See Gary Becker, *The Economic Approach to Human Behavior* (Chicago: University of Chicago Press, 1976); ———, *The Economics of Discrimination* (Chicago: University of Chicago Press, 1957); ———, *Human Capital*, 2d ed. (New York: Columbia University Press, 1975); ——— and W.M. Landes, *Essays in the Economics of Crime and Punishment* (New York: Columbia University Press, 1974); and ———, *A Treatise on The Family* (Cambridge: Harvard University Press, 1981).

government, although private disaster relief for emergency needs was provided by the Red Cross. This is not to say that the federal government did nothing before the 1960s. The federal government did give aid to state and local governments to rebuild schools, hospitals, and roads but little in the way of disaster relief for individuals and businesses. After the mid-1960s, disasters produced massive aid, even though these disasters paled in comparison to the earlier disasters, such as the Galveston hurricane of 1900 that took 6,000 lives. Why the sudden increase in aid? The increased information brought by television coverage and congressional involvement offers a possible explanation. Disasters were brought to the attention of the nation, and local political leaders found they could expect relief since the cost could be spread to all taxpayers. This political cost-sharing game was easy to play, and to mount opposition was to be unsympathetic with disaster victims. As a result, the present policy of massive federal aid to disaster victims has evolved.

Economists, microeconomists in particular, can shed light on several aspects of that policy. One lesson is that if you want to get other people to help you, they have to be reminded of your need. Television news is a good vehicle for such a campaign to "generate a demand for assistance." Recently we saw this every evening during dinner as starving children in Africa were highlighted on the news.

Should Relief Be Given?

This question is moot politically because assistance can and will be given. But what are the consequences of this relief?

The most obvious one is the uneconomic use of our nation's resources. Economic efficiency requires that economic decision makers bear the costs and benefits of their decisions. This implies risk taking. If government policy shifts the risks from the individual to the government, different decisions will be made.

Along with creating sympathy for disaster victims, television also brings this distorted decision making home with increasing frequency. Homes are rebuilt following mud slides in California with little thought given to the possibility of a reoccurrence of the disaster. The same holds for economic activity in flood plains and frequent hurricane paths. The risk of destruction is shifted from the owner to the public, and the taxpayer swallows the consequences.

Some economists have argued that, in the case of floods, the government should not give disaster relief but instead should mandate the purchase of private flood insurance. They argue that such insurance would ensure the efficient use of the floodplain by creating the proper set of incentives. The insurance costs would reflect the risk; in the highest risk areas, insurance would be so expensive that little building would occur. The use of the floodplain would then be determined by markets in such a way that uses for which the benefits exceeded the risk-adjusted cost would not be prohibited. In other words, the floodplain probably would be used for agriculture rather than for housing. What happens instead is that flood assistance distorts incentives, and housing development occurs. In this sense, these floods are artificial (or government-induced) disasters.

One might argue that it would be unnecessary to mandate flood insurance if government simply would cease flood relief because the availability of any form of disaster relief is viewed by many as a form of "free" disaster insurance. On the other hand, private individuals may not purchase disaster insurance, even without the expectation of government relief, because of the huge cost of insurance in disaster-prone areas and the low probability of being a victim.

The conclusion from such analysis and from the generous disaster bills passed by Congress in the late 1960s is clear. Public policy is encouraging uneconomic use of land and, in fact, is contributing to larger disaster losses by subsidizing economic activity in potential disaster areas.

Behavior After Disaster

Yet another interesting economic issue in "disaster economics" is the response of members of the community to disaster victims. The self-interest paradigm of economic analysis would lead us to expect selfish behavior by disaster victims and their neighbors—such phenomena as consumer hoarding, above-market prices by suppliers, and looting of disaster sites. Indeed, in some cases martial law has been enforced to prohibit this behavior, as well as other clearly illegal behavior. Yet many observers have reported helpful, cooperative, and generous behavior in immediate post-disaster periods. This can be explained in terms of self-interested behavior, described in Chapter 1. This explanation lies primarily in informal insurance and alliance activity. In other words, people do unto others as they would have others do unto them in a crisis situation.

An alternative explanation is the cost of not cooperating. Consumers may not loot or hoard, particularly in small communities, because their behavior will be observed and they will be subject to future sanctions if they behave in an "antisocial fashion." Similarly, business firms may not "gouge" consumers because the disaster will be short lived, and they dare not incur the bad feelings that would result. Both the positive informal insurance theory and the negative social sanctions theory explain behavior in terms of a calculation of costs and benefits. You will encounter similar calculations as we study microeconomics. These calculations apply to such diverse aspects of life as committing crime, childbearing, and mothers deciding to work outside the home.

Recovery from Disaster

The long-term economic effects of disaster on communities have been carefully analyzed by economists. The results are consistent and are not surprising. The long-term economic effects of a disaster are not profound, and they leave few lingering economic effects on the local community. Indeed, the speed of recovery often is astonishing.

This rapid recovery is not surprising because economic history has shown rapid recovery from the devastating destruction caused by wars. The economy of the Soviet Union quickly recovered from the great devastation caused by the Bolshevik Revolution starting in 1917 and its protracted civil war. The period of the New Economic Policy restored the economy to its prerevolution level of output in just two years. The post-World War II experience in Western Europe and in Japan was similar. In fact, in many instances new, modern capital was put into place, and economic growth and productivity resumed at faster rates than before. In the United States, the devastation of disaster from Hurricane Fred in Mobile, Alabama, was followed by recovery and increased productivity in astonishingly rapid time.

THE ROAD AHEAD

Microeconomics is concerned about how incentives influence decision making and the way in which institutions and changes in institutions influence incentives and, in turn, the behavior of individuals. This method of looking at markets gives the economist powerful insights into the impact that policymakers have, often an impact very different from what was intended. In order to address more complex microeconomic issues, you will need additional tools beyond supply and demand analysis. The next few chapters develop some of these tools.

■ SUMMARY

1. The basic tools of microeconomics developed in other chapters are useful in analyzing a wide range of social-policy questions.
2. Crime is an economic activity that can be analyzed as a rational decision of the criminal. To decrease criminal activity, one need only decrease the benefits the criminal receives or increase the costs the criminal must pay. This holds for the entire range of crime, from illegal parking to armed robbery or murder.
3. Price ceilings are attempts to keep prices from rising to their equilibrium level. Price ceilings cause shortages, and black markets often develop in response to the shortage. Rent control is an example of a price ceiling.
4. Price floors are attempts to keep market prices from declining below a certain level. Price floors cause surpluses that must be absorbed to prevent the price from falling. Agricultural support prices and minimum wages are examples of price floors.

5. The energy crisis as it pertains to natural gas is a good example of how price ceilings disrupt markets. The lesson is that price ceilings are very difficult to remove even after the damage they cause is well understood. Even after partial deregulation is politically achieved, the effect of past disruptions to the market persists.
6. The health care industry in the United Stated is one of our most rapidly expanding industries. Prices have risen because of increasing demand and increasing costs. There have been political calls for regulation. The lessons of the oil "crisis" may be relevant.
7. Many governmental policies have unintended effects that can be determined by applying microeconomic tools of analysis. For example, analysis of government policy toward disasters shows that the present policy may actually "create" new disasters.

■ NEW TERMS

price ceilings
price floors
shortage

black markets
rent control
surplus

Commodity Credit Corporation (CCC)
minimum wage
unintended effects

■ QUESTIONS FOR DISCUSSION

1. Why does a price ceiling that is set above the equilibrium price have no immediate effect on the market?
2. Can you think of other areas in which models such as the simple economic model of crime might be formulated? What about the economics of the decision to have children? the economics of marriage and/or divorce?
3. How is the minimum wage maintained at higher than market-clearing rates? Why don't the unemployed workers agree to work for lower wages and thereby circumvent the imposed price floor?
4. Many price controls were used in the United States during World War II. Using the models developed in

this chapter, how well do you think they worked?
5. Consider the following "facts" about parking on your campus. You have an 8:00 a.m. class that is distant from the student parking lot. You learn over time that if you park in a faculty spot but move your car by 9:15 a.m., you are ticketed every fourth time you park. The ticket cost is $15. What value are you implicitly placing on that parking space from 8:00 a.m. to 9:15 a.m. if you illegally park? If the university raised the ticket price to $30, would you still illegally park? What effect would a towing policy have on your behavior?

Use the following data to answer Questions 6 through 9. Suppose the total demand and the total supply of winter wheat in March, 1989 on the Chicago grain market are the following:

Price per Bushel (Dollars)	Bushels Demanded (Thousands)	Bushels Supplied (Thousands)
4.65	90	77
4.85	85	78
5.05	80	80
5.25	75	82
5.45	65	86

6. What is the equilibrium price? What is the equilibrium quantity? Why is this the equilibrium? Explain the forces that bring equilibrium about, starting at a price of $5.25.

7. Draw the demand and supply curve from the available data.

8. What would happen if the federal government set a price floor, a support, of $5.45 per bushel? Draw this price floor on the diagram you produced in Question 7.

9. What would happen if the federal government set a price ceiling of $5.45 per bushel? Draw the price floor on your diagram.

10. Usury laws are laws that set maximum interest rates. As such, usury laws are price ceilings in the market for loanable funds. What would happen in states that have usury laws when the equilibrium interest rate exceeds the established interest rate ceiling? Why then are usury laws politically popular?

SUGGESTIONS FOR FURTHER READING

North, Douglass C., and Roger LeRoy Miller. *The Economics of Public Issues.* 7th ed. New York: Harper & Row Publishers, Inc., 1987. Presents innovative, highly readable applications of the basic tools of microeconomics.

Swartz, Thomas, and Frank Bonello. *Taking Sides: Clashing Views on Controversial Economic Issues.* 3d ed. Guilford, CT: Duskin Publishing Group, 1986. Presents opposing viewpoints on controversial issues, including minimum wage and U.S. farm policy.

Vandenbrink, Donna C. "The Minimum Wage: No Minor Matter for Teens," *Economic perspectives,* Federal Reserve Bank of Chicago (March/April 1987). A current survey of the data on teenage unemployment and the minimum wage.

CHAPTER 6 ■
■
ELASTICITY: MEASURE OF RESPONSIVENESS

■

■
INTRODUCTION

Chapter 3 developed the tools of supply and demand and in the previous chapter, we applied those tools to a range of important issues. This chapter expands on these concepts and develops another tool of the microeconomist, the elasticity measurement. **Elasticity** is a measure of the *sensitivity* or *responsiveness* of quantity demanded or quantity supplied to changes in price (or other factors). We will develop several elasticity measures and then demonstrate their usefulness in discussions of public policy.

ELASTICITY
A measure of the sensitivity or responsiveness of quantity demanded or quantity supplied to changes in price (or other factors).

■ ■   ■   ■   ■   ■   ■
SUPPLY AND DEMAND, AGAIN

Supply and demand are basic to economic analysis. It is worth reviewing them before beginning to expand your kit of economic tools.

When developing the concept of demand, we stressed the distinction between shifts in demand curves and movement along demand curves. Any movement along a demand curve is in response to a change in price and is referred to as a *change in quantity demanded*. Any shift of the demand curve is called a *change in demand.* These changes in demand are in response to changes in one or more of the other *ceteris paribus* conditions that underlie the demand curve—the tastes of the group demanding the good, the size of the group, the income and wealth of the group, the prices of other goods and services, or expectations concerning any of these *ceteris paribus* conditions.

In a similar fashion, there is an important difference between changes in supply and changes in quantity supplied. The term *change in quantity supplied* indicates to the economist that the change that occurred was in response to a change in price. The phrase *change in supply* means that the change occurred not because of a change in price, but because of a change in one or more of the other *ceteris paribus* conditions affecting supply—the prices of the factors of production, the number of sellers, the technology used to produce the good, or expectations about any of these conditions.

These economic principles and new terminology are useful in explaining economic happenings. Figure 6–1 is a diagram of the market supply and demand for automobiles. Given *ceteris paribus* conditions and ignoring differences in quality, size, and mileage, the market determines an equilibrium price of P_1 and quantity sold of Q_1. Now suppose the price of gasoline increases—a movement along the demand curve for gasoline. Since gasoline and automobiles are complements, you know that the increase in the price of gasoline is going to cause the demand for automobiles to shift from D_1 to D_2 in Figure 6–1. That is, with gasoline now more expensive, people will reduce the amount of driving they do. This reduces the demand for automobiles. This decrease in demand causes the price to fall to P_2 and the quantity supplied to decrease to Q_2 because of the shift in the demand curve for autos. Remember that quality and other factors are held constant, so the decrease in demand for automobiles could represent a change to smaller autos, or an average consumer trading autos every four years instead of every three years.

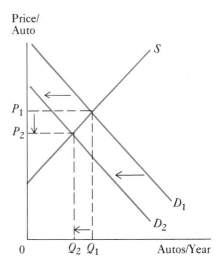

FIGURE 6-1
THE MARKET FOR AUTOMOBILES
If the price of gasoline, a complementary product to automobiles, rises, there will be a decrease in the demand for automobiles. The price will fall from P_1 to P_2, and the equilibrium quantity will decrease from Q_1 to Q_2. We say there has been a decrease in the quantity supplied.

ELASTICITY AS A GENERAL CONCEPT

Elasticity measures the way one variable responds to changes in other variables. The *dependent variable* is the variable that changes in response to some other variable, called the *independent variable*. In formula form, the dependent variable (y) is written as a function of one or more independent variables (x), as in equation (6–1).

$$(6-1) \qquad y = f(x_1, x_2, x_3, \ldots, x_n)$$

Elasticity measures how the y variable responds to changes in any one of the different x variables. The formula to determine this responsiveness can be expressed in equation (6–2):

$$(6-2) \qquad E_1 = \frac{\%\Delta y}{\%\Delta x_1}, \; E_2 = \frac{\%\Delta y}{\%\Delta x_2}, \ldots, E_n = \frac{\%\Delta y}{\%\Delta x_n}.$$

E denotes elasticity, and the formula says that elasticity is the percentage change in the dependent variable (y) divided by the percentage change in the particular independent variable we are examining (x) in the denominator.

In examining demand, economists are interested in how the quantity demanded responds to changes in price (the Δ symbol represents change) and how the quantity demanded responds to changes in the other *ceteris paribus* factors that affect demand. The quantity demanded of Good a (Q_a^d) is thus the dependent variable, and the independent variables are the price of a (P_a), income (I), tastes (T), the price of complements (P_c), and the price of substitutes (P_s). We can thus rewrite equation (6–1) as

$$Q_a^d = f(P_a, I, T, P_c, P_s).$$

It is now possible to determine how Q_a^d responds to any of the factors by holding all but one of them constant and calculating the elasticity coefficient using equation (6–2). For example, to see how quantity demanded responds to price, we would calculate

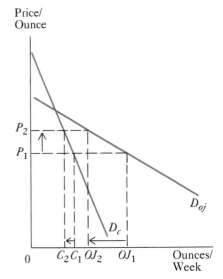

FIGURE 6-2
DEMAND CURVES WITH DIFFERENT ELASTICITIES
Demand curves may have different elasticities. The same price change has a much greater impact on the quantity of orange juice demanded, so the demand for orange juice is more elastic than the demand for coffee.

$$E_d = \frac{\%\Delta Q_a^d}{\%\Delta P_a},$$

where E_d is the coefficient of price elasticity of demand. This formula gives us the price elasticity of demand. **Price elasticity of demand** is the measure of the responsiveness of the quantity demanded to changes in price.

PRICE ELASTICITY OF DEMAND
A measure of the responsiveness of the quantity demanded to changes in price.

PRICE ELASTICITY OF DEMAND

In the late 1800s, the famous English economist, Alfred Marshall, developed the concept of elasticity to compare the demands for various products. When comparisons are made, it is necessary to concentrate on the *relative* responsiveness of the quantity demanded to price changes rather than concentrating on the absolute responsiveness. Relative comparisons make it possible to measure and then describe the sensitivity of the demand relationship. To understand this concept, examine Figure 6-2. Two demand curves are drawn—one is the demand curve for coffee, the other is the demand curve for orange juice. Although the price increases by the same amount for each curve, there are different changes in the quantity demanded. The two goods have different sensitivities to the price change; that is, they have different elasticities.

The **coefficient of price elasticity of demand (E_d)** is the numerical measure of price elasticity of demand. It is the percentage change in quantity demanded divided by the percentage change in price. The equation for the price elasticity of demand is, as you have seen,

COEFFICIENT OF PRICE ELASTICITY OF DEMAND (E_d)
The numerical measure of price elasticity of demand. The percentage change in quantity demanded divided by the percentage change in price.

$$E_d = \frac{\%\Delta Q_a^d}{\%\Delta P_a}.$$

Since percentage change is the change in the variable divided by the base amount of the variable, this can be rewritten as

(6-3) $$E_d = \frac{\dfrac{\Delta Q_a^d}{Q_a^d}}{\dfrac{\Delta P_a}{P_a}}.$$

With most demand curves, the elasticity coefficient varies along the curve; however, some demand curves have a *constant* price elasticity of demand. We shall first examine three special cases before looking at more typical demand curves.

Figure 6-3 depicts a vertical demand curve, showing that quantity demanded is totally unresponsive to changes in price. As price changes from P_1 to P_2, there is no change in the quantity demanded. The elasticity coefficient is:

Price/Unit

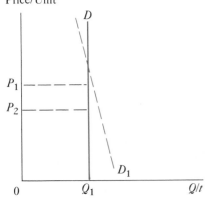

FIGURE 6-3
PERFECTLY INELASTIC DEMAND CURVE
On a perfectly inelastic demand curve, such as D, the quantity demanded has no responsiveness to changes in price. A relatively inelastic demand curve, such as D_1, is a demand curve that is not very responsive to changes in price.

$$E_d = \frac{\dfrac{\Delta Q^d}{Q_1}}{\dfrac{\Delta P}{P_1}} = 0.$$

This is a limiting case that violates the law of demand and is not known to exist in the real world. This curve is called a perfectly inelastic demand curve. **Perfectly inelastic** describes a price elasticity of demand coefficient of zero. There is no response in quantity demanded to changes in price. The demand curve is vertical. Although it doesn't exist in the real world, there may be demand curves that are very close to it, such as curve D_1, represented by the dashed line in Figure 6-3. This curve is a *relatively* inelastic demand curve. A highly inelastic demand exists for goods such as heart medicine for someone with a heart condition. Individuals who purchase these goods probably do not respond very much to changes in price, particularly if they are wealthy.

Figure 6-4, depicts a horizontal demand curve, another limiting case. At P_1, or at any price below P_1, an infinite quantity of the good would be demanded; if price rises above P_1, the quantity of the good that would be demanded is zero. Calculating the coefficient for a price change from P_1 to P_2, yields:

$$E_d = \frac{\dfrac{\Delta Q}{Q_1}}{\dfrac{\Delta P}{P_1}} = \infty.$$

Such a curve is called a perfectly elastic demand curve because the response to changes in price is infinite or perfect. **Perfectly elastic** describes price elasticity of demand coefficient of infinity. The quantity demanded responds in an infinite way to a change in price. The demand curve is a horizontal line. A curve such as D_1, the dashed demand curve in Figure 6-4, is a *relatively* elastic demand curve. A highly elastic demand curve exists for the wheat production of an individual farmer in the United States. The price of a bushel of wheat is determined by the market. At that price (or any lower price), all of the farmer's wheat that is available will be demanded. But if a farmer raises the price even slightly, demand for that farmer's wheat will go to zero.

A third kind of demand curve is drawn in Figure 6-5. The mathematical term for this curve is a rectangular hyperbola. Any percentage decrease or increase in price is met by an exactly equal percentage increase or decrease in the quantity demanded. This means that the elasticity coefficient at any point along the demand curve is equal to one. For example, if you calculated the elasticity coefficient for a price change from P_1 to P_2, you would find that:

$$E_d = \frac{\dfrac{\Delta Q}{Q_1}}{\dfrac{\Delta P}{P_1}} = 1$$

Such a curve is referred to as unit elastic. **Unit elastic** describes price elasticity of demand coefficient of one.

Most demand curves are not shaped like the curves in Figures 6-3, 6-4, or 6-5. Most straight line demand curves have a shape similar to the one drawn in Figure 6-6. Demand curve D in Figure 6-6

PERFECTLY INELASTIC
A price elasticity of demand coefficient of zero. There is no response in quantity demanded to changes in price. The demand curve is vertical.

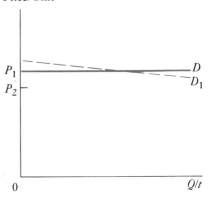

FIGURE 6-4
PERFECTLY ELASTIC
DEMAND CURVE
On a perfectly elastic demand curve, the quantity demanded has an infinite response to changes in price. If price rises above P_1, no amount of the good will be purchased. If price falls to P_2, all that is available will be purchased. A relatively elastic demand curve is a demand curve that is very responsive to changes in price.

PERFECTLY ELASTIC
A price elasticity of demand coefficient of infinity. The quantity demanded responds in an infinite way to a change in price. The demand curve is a horizontal line.

UNIT ELASTIC
A price elasticity of demand coefficient of one. The change in quantity demanded responds at the same rate as any change in price. The demand curve is a rectangular hyperbola.

Price/Unit

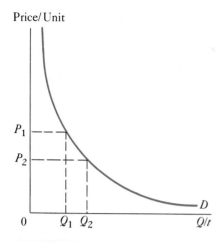

FIGURE 6-5
UNITARY ELASTIC
DEMAND CURVE

A unitary elastic demand curve is a rectangular hyperbola. A change in price brings about an equal relative change in quantity demanded.

ARC ELASTICITY
Average elasticity over the space between two points.

POINT ELASTICITY
The responsiveness of quantity demanded to price at a particular point on a curve.

has a *range* of elasticity coefficients from infinitely elastic (at the *y*-axis intercept) to infinitely inelastic (at the *x*-axis intercept). When the coefficient is *less* than one, demand is *inelastic* because the percentage change in quantity demanded is less than the percentage change in price. When the coefficient is *greater* than one, demand is *elastic* because the quantity demanded changes relatively more than price. Of course, there are degrees of responsiveness. The larger the coefficient, the greater the responsiveness.

The best way to understand elasticity is to calculate some elasticity coefficients. Using Figure 6-6 and the associated demand schedule in Table 6-1, it is possible to calculate elasticity coefficients for the demand curve. First, however, there are two important technicalities.

The first problem is to decide whether elasticity is to be calculated at a single point or between two points. The elasticity between points is actually the *average* elasticity over the space between the points. This is called **arc elasticity**. Many economists use a different, but related, concept called **point elasticity**. This refers to the responsiveness of quantity demanded to price at a particular point on a curve, a concept

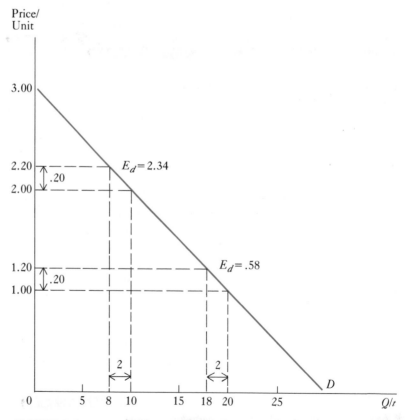

FIGURE 6-6
STRAIGHT LINE DEMAND CURVE WITH CHANGING ELASTICITY
A straight line demand curve has changing elasticity coefficients from the *y*-axis intercept to the *x*-axis intercept.

A GUIDE TO ELASTICITY COEFFICIENTS

Numerical Coefficients	Responsiveness of Quantity Demanded to a Change in Price	Terminology
• $E_d = 0$	None	perfectly inelastic
• $0 < E_d < 1$	Quantity demanded changes by a smaller percentage than the percentage change in price	inelastic
• $E_d = 1$	Quantity demanded changes by a percentage equal to the percentage change in price	unit elastic
• $1 < E_d < \infty$	Quantity demanded changes by a larger percentage than the percentage change in price	elastic
• $E_d = \infty$	Quantity demanded goes to zero or to all that is available.	perfectly elastic

derived from differential calculus.[1] Mathematically, elasticity is measured at a point by assuming infinitesimally small changes in price and quantity demanded. However, when you use arithmetic to calculate particular coefficients, you are working with a sizable, discrete change and use arc elasticity.

TABLE 6-1
DEMAND SCHEDULE FOR FIGURE 6-6

Price	Quantity Demanded
$0.50	25
1.00	20
1.20	18
1.40	16
1.60	14
1.80	12
2.00	10
2.20	8
2.40	6
2.60	4
2.80	2
3.00	0

1. Elasticity at a particular point can be measured using the formula:

$$E_d = \frac{dQ}{dP} \times \frac{P}{Q}$$

A second technicality is that the formula will always produce a negative number because demand curves are negatively sloped. This means there is an inverse relationship between the variables. In practice, economists ignore the minus sign and consider an E_d of –5 larger than an E_d of –4. That is, price elasticities are quoted as absolute values. It will be important later, when considering other elasticity measures, to keep track of the sign but not for price elasticity of demand.

The demand schedule of Table 6–1 can be used to calculate some price elasticity of demand coefficients. The formula again is

$$E_d = \frac{\text{percentage change in quantity demanded}}{\text{percentage change in price}}$$

For analytical purposes, this reduces to

$$E_d = \frac{\dfrac{\Delta Q}{\dfrac{(Q_1 + Q_2)}{2}}}{\dfrac{\Delta P}{\dfrac{(P_1 + P_2)}{2}}}$$

Since we are calculating arc elasticity, we need averages. It is necessary to divide the sum of the beginning price and ending price by two and to divide the sum of the beginning and ending quantity by two. If an average quantity and average price were not used as the bases, and instead the beginning or ending price and quantity data were used, the formula would produce different elasticity measures between the same two points.

We will now compute the elasticity coefficients for two different changes on the demand curve in Figure 6–6. First, the elasticity coefficient for the increase in price from \$1.00 to \$1.20:

$$E_d = \frac{\dfrac{20 - 18}{\dfrac{(20 + 18)}{2}}}{\dfrac{1.00 - 1.20}{\dfrac{(1.00 + 1.20)}{2}}}$$

$$E_d = \frac{\dfrac{2}{19}}{\dfrac{-0.20}{1.10}}$$

$$E_d = \frac{0.105}{-0.182}$$

$$E_d = 0.58$$

Now for the elasticity coefficient for the increase in price from \$2.00 to \$2.20:

$$E_d = \cfrac{\cfrac{10 - 8}{(10 + 8)}}{\cfrac{2.00 - 2.20}{(2.00 + 2.20)}}$$

$$E_d = \cfrac{\cfrac{2}{9}}{\cfrac{-0.20}{2.10}}$$

$$E_d = \frac{0.222}{-0.095}$$

$$E_d = 2.34$$

Recall that economists ignore the minus sign and just look at the absolute value of price elasticities of demand.

Notice that the elasticity is different at different points along this constant slope demand curve. In fact, all constant slope or linear demand curves except those that are perfectly vertical or horizontal have points that range from elastic to unit elastic to inelastic. On a demand curve, such as the one shown in Figure 6–7, all points above Price P_1 (which corresponds to the midpoint on a straight line demand curve) have an elasticity coefficient greater than one and are elastic; at Price P_1, the elasticity is equal to one (unit elasticity); and all points below P_1 have an elasticity coefficient less than one and are inelastic.

To demonstrate how important it is to average the quantity base and the price base, calculate the effect of an increase in price from $1.00 to $1.20 and then of a decrease in price from $1.20 to $1.00 using equation (6–3), which does not use an averaging technique. If you do this, you will get different elasticity coefficients. Often when examining a demand curve or schedule, we don't know if the price is decreasing or increasing. The average, or arc, elasticity between two points is found by employing the averaging technique.

This example also clearly demonstrates that elasticity is an entirely different concept from the geometric concept of slope. The demand curve in Figure 6–6 has a constant slope, but the elasticity coefficients you calculated varied along the curve.

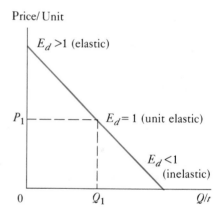

FIGURE 6-7
VARYING ELASTICITY
DEMAND CURVE

A straight line demand curve has varying elasticity coefficients from the y-axis intercept to the x-axis intercept. At all prices above the unit elastic price (P_1), demand is elastic. At all prices below the unit elastic price, demand is inelastic.

Elasticity and Substitutability

Price elasticity of demand depends, in large part, on the number of substitutes a product has. If a product, such as table salt, has relatively few substitutes, it will tend to have a relatively inelastic demand. This is just another way of saying that the quantity demanded of a good like table salt isn't very responsive to changes in price over a wide range of prices. The elasticity coefficients for a general category of commodities will be lower than for a specific commodity. For example, the coefficient of the elasticity of demand for salt in general will be lower than the coefficient of the elasticity of demand for Morton salt.

Another determinant of elasticity is time. The longer the period of time consumers have to adjust, the more elastic the demand becomes. The reason for this is that there are more opportunities to modify behavior and substitute different products over a longer time period. A good example would be the price elasticity of demand for natural gas. In the short run, it is likely to be very inelastic; but over time, as industry and homes convert to other sources of energy, the price elasticity will increase. Table 6–2 lists estimated elasticity coefficients for some commonly purchased items.

TABLE 6-2
SELECTED ESTIMATED ELASTICITIES

Item	E_d
Fresh tomatoes	4.60
Medical care	3.60
Canned tomatoes	2.50
Airline travel	2.40
Radios and televisions	1.25
Automobiles	0.80

Source: Adapted from Dean A. Worcester, Jr., "On Monopoly Losses: Comment," *American Economic Review* (December 1975): 1016.

Price Elasticity of Demand and Total Revenue

TOTAL REVENUE
The quantity of a good or service that a firm sells, multiplied by its price.

Demand curves illustrate price and quantity relationships. Quantity, or the number of items sold, multiplied by price equals the **total revenue** generated. The relationship between total revenue and price elasticity of demand can be used to understand how firms set and change prices. In order to grasp the relationship, consider a famous illustration in economics. The French mathematician and economist Antoine Augustin Cournot wondered what the owner of a mineral spring should charge for the spring's water, which was desired for its healing powers. Cournot assumed that the spring cost nothing to operate, it produced an unlimited quantity of output, and the owner wanted to be as wealthy as possible under the principle of self-interest.

To determine the correct price, Cournot first recognized that a price change has two (opposite) effects on total revenue. The first effect is that a price decrease, by itself, will decrease total revenue. The other is that with a price decrease, quantity demanded increases, thus increasing total revenue. The net effect of these two changes on total revenue depends on whether the relative price decrease exceeds the relative increase in quantity demanded or vice versa. This is exactly the information that the price elasticity of demand coefficient provides.

To see this principle in numerical form, consider Figure 6–6 and Table 6–1 once more. At a price of $2.00, the total revenue (*TR*) is $20.00. An increase in price from $2.00 to $2.20 causes *TR* to fall from $20.00 to $17.60. *TR* drops because the 10 percent increase in price caused an even greater percentage decrease in quantity demanded. The elasticity was greater than one. Conversely, if price rises from $1.00 to $1.20, *TR* increases from $20.00 to $21.60 because the percentage increase in price is greater than the percentage decrease in quantity demanded. The elasticity is less than one.

To see this principle in a more general way, consider Figure 6–8. On both demand curves, the price falls from P_1 to P_2, and output increases from Q_1 to Q_2. This change causes the total revenue to change. Some revenue is lost, and some revenue is gained due to the price change. In Figure 6–8, the crosshatched area represents revenue that has been lost and the shaded area represents revenue that has been added. In the case of the relatively elastic curve, Panel (*b*) of Figure 6–8, the decrease in price has brought about an increase in total revenue; in Panel (*a*), the decrease in price has brought about a decrease in total revenue.

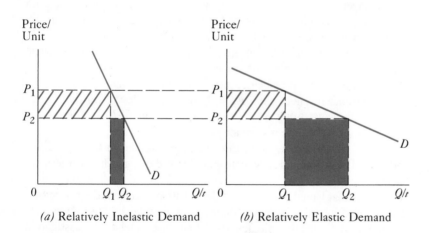

(*a*) Relatively Inelastic Demand   (*b*) Relatively Elastic Demand

FIGURE 6-8
CHANGES IN TOTAL REVENUE
Equal price changes bring about different changes in total revenue, depending on the relative elasticities of the demand curve. If the curve is relatively inelastic, a decrease in price will bring about a decrease in total revenue; and if the curve is relatively elastic, the same decrease in price will bring about an increase in total revenue.

In other words, you can determine what will happen to total revenue when price changes if you know the elasticity coefficient. A reduction in price will always cause an increase in quantity demanded, but total revenue will decrease with inelastic demand and increase with elastic demand. Likewise, a rise in price will cause total revenue to fall with elastic demand and to rise with inelastic demand.

ELASTICITY AND TOTAL REVENUE

Price Change	Quantity Demanded Change	Elasticity	Total Revenue
▪	▪	▪	▪
• Rise	Decrease	$E_d > 1$	Decrease
• Rise	Decrease	$E_d = 1$	Unchanged
• Rise	Decrease	$E_d < 1$	Increase
• Fall	Increase	$E_d > 1$	Increase
• Fall	Increase	$E_d = 1$	Unchanged
• Fall	Increase	$E_d < 1$	Decrease

The answer to Cournot's question is that the owner of the mineral spring should not try to charge the highest possible price or sell the largest possible amount. The owner should set price where the elasticity coefficient is *unitary*. To see why, imagine that the price is where the elasticity is, say, 0.5, or inelastic. If the owner raises the price, quantity demanded will decrease, but by only one-half the rate of the price increase, so revenue will rise. On the other hand, if the $E_d = 2$, or is elastic, the owner should decrease the price. If the price is lowered, the quantity demanded increases at twice the rate of the price decline. The owner will maximize total revenue when $E_d = 1$, or is unit elastic. So the mineral spring water owner would set a price of P_1 in Figure 6–7. At Price P_1, the area $P_1 \times Q_1$ represents maximum possible total revenue.

A good example of this principle occurred in the U.S. airline industry. The airline industry, believing that the demand for air travel was inelastic, had historically been against deregulation of the industry and the lower fares that would result. When deregulation occurred, the revenues of the airline companies increased dramatically despite the lower fares. The experience indicates that the demand for air travel is relatively elastic, or at least much more elastic than the airlines had thought. This is not to say that the airline industry does not have problems. Many new carriers entered after deregulation. Competition has driven prices below costs for some carriers, and many mergers and some bankruptcies have resulted.

Perhaps the best example of all time is that of Henry Ford and his introduction of the automobile. When Ford entered the manufacturing scene, automobiles were a curiosity for the rich. Ford's strategy was to make autos for the average person through mass production—but he had to sell them. He found that by reducing prices, he sold more autos and increased profits. In the process, Ford Motor Company revolutionized production. In the early years of the Model T, Henry Ford said: "Every time I reduce the charge for our car by one dollar, I get a thousand new buyers."[2]

2. *Forbes* (January 12, 1987): 26.

Price Elasticity of Demand and Public Policy

For many years the U.S. government, primarily through the office of the Surgeon General, has pursued a policy of trying to discourage cigarette smoking.[3] We could argue over whether it is appropriate for government to try to intervene in personal decisions, such as smoking, but it is nevertheless true that various levels of government are doing so.

In the early 1980s, the city of San Francisco made national news by forcing firms to provide smoke-free environments for workers. Such policies are now so common that they are no longer newsworthy. Many states and some local governments have required public places, such as restaurants, to set up no smoking sections and have prohibited smoking altogether in other public places, such as hospitals and doctors' offices.

Let's consider a hypothetical situation using the concept of price elasticity of demand to make policy recommendations to policymakers. Let's begin by assuming that the president decides to declare an all-out "war on cigarette smoking." In addition, assume that the president calls in the secretary of Health and Human Services and tells the secretary that cigarette smoking should be cut by 25 percent in the next year. You have recently been hired as an economist at the Department of Health and Human Services. Upon returning to the office, the secretary asks you to write a memo outlining a plan to accomplish this goal.

You consider this "war" and advise the secretary that you do not think that prohibitions and warnings work. You have studied enough economics to be convinced that the only way to solve this "problem" is to unleash market forces that create the incentives that will accomplish the desired policy goal. (Remember, you are facing this question as a positive economist, without any normative considerations of whether or not this policy should be carried out.)

You return to your office to begin work on your memo. You decide that the best way to bring about the desired reduction in smoking is to let the market do it. The best way to accomplish this is to raise price by putting an additional federal excise tax on cigarettes. Your job is now relatively simple: determine the appropriate tax.

You need data on cigarette consumption and how it responds to changes in cigarette prices. The data are not that difficult to find. In January, 1983, the federal excise tax on cigarettes was doubled. This was a temporary increase that was made permanent in 1986. As a result, the average price of a pack of cigarettes increased from $.73 to $.93. During this same period, domestic consumption declined by 4.6 percent. To make the problem manageable, you make a *ceteris paribus* assumption that this decline in consumption was due solely to the price change. Using this information, you calculate the price elasticity of demand to be $E_d = 0.19$, or relatively inelastic.

It is now a simple matter to compute the tax necessary to have the desired impact on consumption. You know that the president wants to

3. Evidently the Surgeon General feels that smoking is only a problem for U.S. citizens because the warning about smoking being hazardous to your health is printed only on cigarettes manufactured for domestic consumption. Cigarettes manufactured for export do not contain the warning unless it is required by the government of the importing country.

cut consumption by 25 percent and that the present average price of a pack of cigarettes is $1.42. You need only to substitute into the formula to determine the tax:

$$E_d = \frac{\%\Delta Q}{\%\Delta P}$$

$$0.19 = \frac{0.25}{\%\Delta P}$$

$$\%\Delta P = \frac{0.25}{0.19} = 1.32 = 132\%$$

You can now write your memo. In order to have the 25 percent decrease in quantity demanded, it is necessary to have a 132 percent increase in price. The required additional excise tax would, therefore, be $1.87 per pack of cigarettes ($1.42 × 132 percent), making the price of a pack of cigarettes $3.29.

In this hypothetical case, you have used a simple economic tool in the same way that economists giving policy advice would use it. Although it was hypothetical, the data were real and the estimates were based on sound theory. In fact, the National Bureau of Economic Research, Inc. (NBER) suggested such a solution to the "smoking problem." An NBER study showed that the coefficient of the elasticity of demand was quite high for young males so that the price mechanism could significantly alter the use of cigarettes by young males. The NBER study showed that the coefficient was much lower—more inelastic—for young females. In a similar study, NBER researchers looked at the demand for beer. They found that 1,000 lives could be saved annually (car accidents) by a tax on beer of approximately $2.00 per case. Their simulation showed that such a tax would be much more effective in reducing beer consumption and saving lives than raising the drinking age to 21, which simulations showed would be expected to save 555 lives annually.[4]

OTHER DEMAND ELASTICITIES

As we saw at the beginning of this chapter, it is possible to calculate the elasticity of almost anything because what an elasticity coefficient measures is the responsiveness of one measurable quantity to another. There are two other demand elasticity coefficients that are quite common in economics.

INCOME ELASTICITY OF DEMAND
A measure of the way in which quantity demanded responds to changes in income.

The first is the **income elasticity of demand**. This measures the way in which quantity demanded responds to changes in income, assuming all other things, including price, are held constant. The formula is expressed as

$$E_I = \frac{\text{percentage change in quantity demanded}}{\text{percentage change in income}}.$$

The sign of the coefficient is important for income elasticity. If the sign is negative, indicating an inverse relationship between income and

4. *Fortune* (October 27, 1986): 127.

demand, the good is said to be an inferior good. If the sign is positive, the good is a normal good.

For normal goods, the same designations are used for the elasticity coefficient as before. If the coefficient is greater than one, $E_I > 1$, the good is income elastic. If $E_I < 1$, the good is income inelastic. Goods that have high and positive income elasticities are usually thought to be luxury goods. Indeed, the concept of income elasticity of demand is used as a definition of what a luxury good is. Necessities, such as food, have a low, but positive, income elasticity coefficient. Luxuries, such as meals in restaurants, have a high income elasticity coefficient.

Income elasticity is useful to producers in forecasting sales. If producers can forecast changes in consumer income and know what the income elasticity of demand for their product happens to be, they can estimate how much more to produce. This is one of the reasons firms are interested in economic forecasts.

The other elasticity concept is **cross elasticity of demand**. Cross elasticity measures the responsiveness of changes in the quantity demanded of one product to changes in the price of another product. If cross elasticities are equal to anything but zero, the goods are related; they are either complements or substitutes. Two goods that are completely unrelated (independent of one another) would have a zero cross elasticity of demand. The formula can be stated as

$$E_{ab} = \frac{\text{percentage change in quantity demanded of Good } a}{\text{percentage change in price of Good } b}.$$

If the sign of E_{ab} is negative, the relationship is an inverse one; an increase in the price of Good b will bring about a decrease in the quantity demanded of Good a. A negative cross elasticity coefficient would thus indicate that Good a and Good b are complements. A positive coefficient would indicate a substitute relationship between Good a and Good b because an increase in the price of Good b will lead to an increase in the quantity demanded of Good a. The size of the coefficient tells how strong the complementary or substitute relationship is between the two goods. In later chapters, cross elasticity will be useful in defining markets and industries because it is a measure of how closely goods are related.

CROSS ELASTICITY OF DEMAND
A measure of the responsiveness of changes in quantity demanded for one product to changes in the price of another product.

PRICE ELASTICITY OF SUPPLY

The principles that we developed in examining the elasticity of demand are applicable to supply schedules and supply curves. **Price elasticity of supply** is a measure of the responsiveness of the quantity supplied to changes in the price. The **coefficient of price elasticity of supply** (E_s) is the numerical measure of price elasticity of supply. The equation for the coefficient of price elasticity of supply is

$$E_s = \frac{\text{percentage change in quantity supplied}}{\text{percentage change in price}},$$

which again reduces into the more workable formula of

PRICE ELASTICITY OF SUPPLY
A measure of the responsiveness of the quantity supplied to changes in the price.

COEFFICIENT OF PRICE ELASTICITY OF SUPPLY (E_s)
The numerical measure of price elasticity of supply. The percentage change in quantity supplied divided by the percentage change in price.

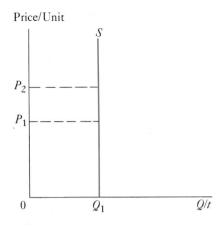

FIGURE 6-9
PERFECTLY INELASTIC
SUPPLY CURVE

A perfectly inelastic supply curve is a
vertical line. It would exist if suppliers
supplied a fixed amount of a commodity
on a market, regardless of any changes in
its price.

$$E_s = \frac{\dfrac{\Delta Q_s}{Q_s}}{\dfrac{\Delta P}{P}}.$$

As with demand elasticity, when $E_s = 1$, supply is unit elastic.
If $E_s > 1$, it is elastic; and if $E_s < 1$, it is inelastic. The analogy to price
elasticity of demand stops there. A major difference is that the coefficient
of price elasticity of supply usually is positive because supply curves normally have positive slopes. Since the curves are positively sloped, the
relationship between elasticity and total revenue established for price elasticity of demand doesn't hold; higher prices result in higher total revenue,
regardless of whether supply is elastic or inelastic.

Special cases of supply curves are classified as perfectly inelastic, unit elastic, or perfectly elastic. Consider Figure 6–9. The quantity
supplied is totally unresponsive to changes in price. It is perfectly inelastic.
Examples of perfectly inelastic supply curves are infrequently found, but in
the very short run it is often impossible to produce more of a good regardless of what happens to price. This inability to produce more will affect
the supply curve, which depicts the amount people are willing to supply at
various prices. Consider the price of Rembrandt paintings, for example, or
the supply of Rose Bowl tickets. A rise in the price of Rembrandt paintings
(even in the long run) or Rose Bowl tickets (in the short run) does not
cause the quantity supplied to increase. These supply curves are perfectly
inelastic.

Figure 6–10 shows a perfectly elastic and a unit elastic supply
curve, respectively. S_1, a horizontal line, is a perfectly elastic supply curve.
Any straight line supply curve that is drawn through the origin, as is S_2 in
Figure 6–10, is unit elastic over its entire range. The reason for this is
that the percentage changes of the two variables are always equal to each
other. Throughout their range, other linear, or straight line, supply curves
are elastic if they intersect the price axis above the origin and inelastic if
they intersect the quantity axis to the right of the origin. This is true even
though elasticity changes along both curves. Two such curves are drawn in
Figure 6–11.

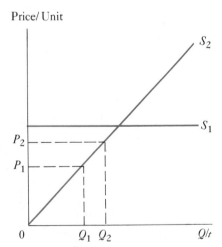

FIGURE 6-10
UNIT ELASTIC SUPPLY CURVE
AND PERFECTLY ELASTIC
SUPPLY CURVE

A perfectly elastic curve is a horizontal
line. A change in price produces an
infinite response in the quantity supplied.
A straight line supply curve drawn through
the origin has a unitary coefficient of
elasticity along the entire curve.

Price Elasticity of Supply and Cost

Price elasticity of supply is very dependent on the costs of
production and how these costs change as the output of a good or service
is increased. If costs rise rapidly as output is expanded, the quantity supplied will not be very responsive to changes in price; the supply curve will
be inelastic. Alternatively, if costs don't increase very much as output is
increased, the rise in price will increase the profits of supplying firms and
the output response could be significant. This would be the case for an
elastic supply curve. The relationship between price elasticity of supply
and the costs of production is so intertwined that we will return to this
discussion when we study production and cost.

Price Elasticity of Supply and Time

Elasticity of supply is the measure of responsiveness of quantity supplied to changes in price. The major factor affecting this responsiveness is the availability of inputs that can be attracted away from other uses. Another factor is the time period under consideration. As the time period increases, the possibility of obtaining new and different inputs to increase the supply increases. In our two examples of fixed supply, Rembrandt paintings and Rose Bowl tickets, you will recognize that in the long run the stadium could be expanded and the quantity of tickets increased; Rembrandts, however, have a perfectly inelastic supply because additional inputs don't exist.[5]

These two factors—availability of inputs and time—affect elasticity of supply. Normally the elasticity of supply coefficient becomes larger as the time frame increases and is larger for products that use relatively unspecialized or abundant inputs.

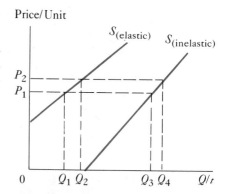

FIGURE 6-11
INELASTIC AND ELASTIC SUPPLY CURVES
A straight line supply curve that intersects the *y*-price axis will be elastic over its entire length, and a straight line supply curve that intersects the *x*-quantity axis will be inelastic over its entire length.

POLICY APPLICATIONS

It is possible to use elasticity to examine all sorts of real-world situations. Two useful examples are the volunteer army and college recruiting. These situations may seem miles apart but, as economics often demonstrates, there are more similarities than differences.

Military Recruiting

Suppose that you are hired as an adviser to the Secretary of Defense and are instructed to determine how to make the volunteer army work better. This is an important task because there is increasing pressure to reinstate the draft. You are told that the army is presently enlisting 57,500 volunteers per month, but 30 percent more are needed to keep the ranks at full strength. If you could calculate the elasticity of supply, it would be a simple matter to determine the pay increase necessary to reach full strength. Note that you don't even need to know what the present level of pay happens to be if you can calculate the elasticity.

During the early 1970s, when the United States had a military draft and President Nixon proposed doing away with it, the military commissioned many elasticity studies, and there is no reason to believe that the elasticity coefficients have changed. These studies agree on an $E_s = 1.25$. Working from $1.25 = {}^{0.30}/\%\Delta P$, you can report to the secretary that the army can meet its personnel requirements by raising pay levels by 24 percent ($24\% = {}^{0.30}/_{1.25} \times 100$).

But before you report this figure, you have some second thoughts. You realize that elasticity of supply will be different for different people. Not all potential volunteers are equally available; the more intelli-

5. This isn't quite correct because some individuals who own Rembrandt paintings will become suppliers as price gets higher.

difference between the value of exports and the value of imports. This decline in the trade deficit would have come about because imports had become more expensive to Americans, causing the quantity of imports demanded to decrease. It would have taken more dollars to buy a given amount of foreign currency. At the same time, U.S. exports to foreigners became cheaper, causing the quantity of exports demanded to increase. The experience, however, at least in the short run, was that the deficit remained high. The explanation is to be found in the differences between short-run and long-run elasticities.

In the short run, the demand for imports is very price inelastic. So when the value of the dollar falls, making imports more expensive, the quantity demanded falls, but not very much. Similarly, foreign demand for exports is inelastic, so when price falls, the quantity demanded increases, but not very much. As time passes and importers in the United States have more time to adjust to the increased prices of foreign goods and foreigners have more time to adjust to the lower prices of U.S. exports, the trade balance will come back into equilibrium.

The short-run phenomenon is that a cheaper dollar may make the trade deficit worse before it gets better. This curious result comes from the fact that short-run elasticities are much lower that long-run elasticities. Economists have come to call this worsening of the balance of trade in the face of a cheaper currency, the *J-curve effect*. It is called a J-curve because the trade deficit initially gets worse before it turns around and improves. Although this is a technical economic concept, it is terminology that has been quickly adopted into the jargon of newswriters. As a result, you are quite likely to see the term J-curve if you read the *Wall Street Journal* or other business publications.

THE INTERNATIONAL PERSPECTIVE
THE PRICE ELASTICITY OF
IMPORTS AND EXPORTS

When a country runs a surplus or deficit in its balance of trade, adjustment in the value of its currency is one way in which balance in its trade can be restored. In the early part of the 1980s, the value of the dollar had risen considerably in terms of other currencies, particularly the currencies of our European trading partners. As Americans began importing more foreign goods, however, the supply of dollars rose. Since the value of the dollar is determined on markets, the large supply of dollars caused the value of the dollar to decline relative to these European currencies. Between 1985 and 1988, the value of the dollar fell by about 50 percent.

The decline in the value of the dollar should have had the effect of decreasing the trade deficit, which is the

---

gent have more options in civilian jobs and colleges and would probably be less responsive to the pay increase because their opportunity costs are higher. This leads you to forecast that a simple pay increase for all potential enlistees might change the mix of enlistees and attract fewer intelligent ones.

You gather more data and find that at present, the army breaks its personnel into three groups—Mental Categories I and II, Mental Category III, and Mental Category IV, based on how high they score on the Armed Forces Qualifying Test. The test is similar to an intelligence test, with Categories I and II being the highest. Assuming the present army has one-third of its strength from each group, and estimating from past experience that the elasticity coefficients for the three groups are 0.5, 1.25, and

2.0, you now have some important policy information to report. If the pay raise of 24 percent that you calculated was to go into effect, the number of Mental Category IV enlistments—which have the highest elasticity because the volunteers have fewer options—would increase by 48 percent. Meanwhile, the number of Categories I and II enlistments would increase by only 12 percent. This would mean the ability (as measured by mental category) of the army would decrease substantially.

To counteract this problem, you could suggest a differential pay increase. Assuming you want to keep enlistments by mental category at the present share, you could now calculate the needed increases. Pay for Mental Categories I and II would have to go up by 60 percent ($0.5 = {}^{0.30}/\%\Delta P$), Mental Category III pay would have to go up by 24 percent ($1.25 = {}^{0.30}/\%\Delta P$), and Mental Category IV pay would only need to go up by 15 percent ($2.0 = {}^{0.30}/\%\Delta P$). As you can see, imaginative application of this simple tool can have important implications for policy. This example, though hypothetical, is very similar to exercises that were actually performed in the early years of the volunteer army.

ANTOINE AUGUSTIN COURNOT
(1801-1877)

Antoine Augustin Cournot was one of the first economists to view economic theory as a set of tools that could be used to analyze economic and social problems. Cournot showed that both supply and demand determine price, and that, in time, price influences both supply and demand. Cournot used two-dimensional diagrams to demonstrate these relationships.

Cournot is now recognized as a great economist, but this was not always the case. He had one of the great original minds in economic theory, but his life was a tragic one. Cournot studied mathematics at the Ecole Normale in Paris. He had an insatiable appetite for reading, which he pursued despite very poor eyesight that eventually resulted in blindness. While a student, Cournot worked as a secretary to one of Napoleon's generals. In 1834, with the help of the famous statistician Poisson, Cournot became a professor of mathematics at Lyons. In 1838, Cournot published his great work in mathematical microeconomics, *Researches into the Mathematical Principles of the Theory of Wealth*. This book did not have much impact and was hardly noticed. Some sources indicate that not a single copy was sold! In later years, as his sight was failing, Cournot published less mathematical versions of his previous work, which were more widely read. When Cournot died in 1877, his highly original and innovative work in economic theory was largely unnoticed.

The irony of Cournot's life is that, although he was not well known during his own lifetime, his version of economics as a set of highly mathematical tools that could be used to examine a large number of social problems is very close to the thinking of most present-day economists. If Cournot were to return today, he surely would be surprised to see how his radical vision has come to be the traditional role of the contemporary economist.

Recruiting Students

Just as it is important for the military to recruit volunteers to make the volunteer army work, it is important for firms to recruit new employees and for colleges and universities to recruit new students. For many years, colleges didn't pay too much attention to this problem because the post-World War II baby boom produced a seemingly endless supply of new students. Many campuses significantly expanded their facilities during this boom period. This was particularly true at state-supported institutions. This "bubble" in the population is now past college age, and demographic data show that the college-age population has been declining throughout the 1980s and into the 1990s. This presents serious problems to both private and state-supported institutions of higher learning. Private institutions must attract students because tuition is the primary source of revenue. Public institutions also demand students because their state funding is tied to the number of students they have enrolled. Like the military, both public and private colleges also are concerned about attracting bright individuals.

Colleges face essentially the same problem as the military. It is a little easier to view it from the standpoint of the college student as a demander of college services. (Since the number of students who "buy" becomes the supply of students to colleges, it is also possible to view the problem as a problem of supply.) The demand curve is like any other demand curve; it has a negative slope. If colleges raise the price, students will decrease the quantity of educational services they demand, and the number of students will be lower than before the price increase.

The situation is a supply and demand problem with elasticity considerations. To attract the best and brightest students in a competitive world, colleges have to lower their prices. But if they lower their prices to everyone, they "give back" revenue to other students who aren't the best and the brightest while significantly lowering their operating revenues. Can you think of a solution? The solution is exactly the same as in the volunteer army example. Colleges lower the price to some selected students—those whose demand is more price elastic because they have more good alternatives—by giving scholarships and other types of financial aid.

WHO PAYS WHAT TAX: AN EXERCISE IN ELASTICITY

If you listen to the rhetoric of the debates over taxation, you know it is quite confusing. Consumers often are convinced that they ultimately pay all taxes, yet business often fights hard to prevent tax increases on their products. If consumers pay all taxes, why should business care if it is taxed or not? The answer is not simple. The correct answer to the question of who ultimately pays what tax is, "It depends." It depends on the supply and demand conditions in the relevant markets. This is another exercise in elasticity.

An **excise tax** is a tax that is placed on the purchase or consumption of a particular item, such as liquor, cigarettes, or electricity. Excise taxes can be specific, being placed on one particular item, such as

EXCISE TAX
A tax that is placed on the sale of a particular item, such as liquor, cigarettes, or electricity.

cigarettes, or they can be general, being placed on a broad class of goods, such as food.

Let's examine a case in which there are normally sloped supply and demand curves, as in Figure 6–12, which illustrates the market for beer. Beer is a good example because excise taxes are often placed on items such as alcohol and cigarettes that there are "moral" strictures against consuming. Assume the market settles on a price of $3.00 per six-pack, with X_e six-packs per week representing the equilibrium quantity. Now suppose the government places a tax of $1.00 per six-pack on beer and collects this tax from producers. This means that the supply curve will shift up by the amount of the tax. The costs of production for the beer producer have been increased $1.00 per six-pack. One way to view the tax is that the producer must pay $1.00 per six-pack for the permission to produce beer. In terms of Figure 6–12, the supply curve shifts up at all points by $1.00. The post-tax supply curve is S_t. Equilibrium price will rise to $3.50 per six-pack, and the new equilibrium quantity is X_t. But note that this new price is less than the old price plus the tax. If the entire tax had been shifted forward to consumers, the consumer would now pay the old price of $3.00 plus the tax of $1.00, or $4.00 per six-pack. It is also clear that the amount of money the producer actually keeps has fallen.

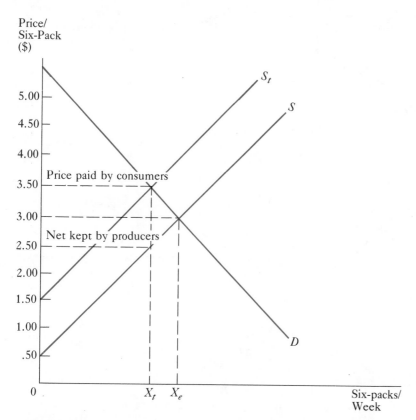

FIGURE 6-12
AN EXCISE TAX ON BEER
A per-unit tax on a commodity causes the supply curve to shift up by the amount of the tax. Less of the commodity is purchased at a higher price. Part of the tax is borne by consumers, and part of the tax is borne by producers.

Before the tax, the producer kept $3.00 per six-pack, but now the producer keeps $2.50 per six-pack ($3.50 price minus the $1.00 tax). The tax caused prices to rise, which meant the quantity demanded fell. The beer producers must sell the lower quantity at a lower received price than before. In this example, then, part of the tax was paid by consumers and part was paid by producers. Each paid half of the excise tax.

The amount of the tax that each pays depends on the supply and demand elasticities for the goods being taxed. To see this more clearly, examine the four panels in Figure 6–13. Using Figure 6–13, we can easily see how the elasticity of supply and the elasticity of demand affect the tax incidence. Tax incidence is the economist's phrase for who really pays the tax. **Tax incidence** is the place where the tax burden of any tax actually rests. It includes those who pay the tax after all shifting has occurred.

Panel (*a*) of Figure 6–13 shows a normally sloped supply curve and a perfectly inelastic demand curve. When the excise tax is

TAX INCIDENCE
The place where the tax burden of any tax actually rests; those who pay the tax after all shifting has occurred.

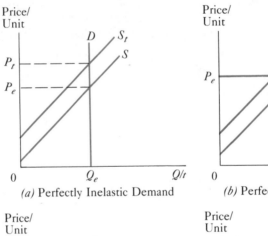
(a) Perfectly Inelastic Demand

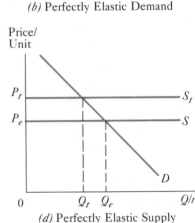
(b) Perfectly Elastic Demand

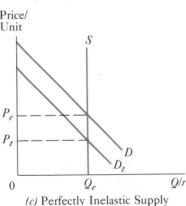
(c) Perfectly Inelastic Supply

(d) Perfectly Elastic Supply

FIGURE 6-13
ELASTICITY AND TAX INCIDENCE
Tax incidence, or who pays the tax, can be easily determined in the case of perfectly elastic or perfectly inelastic demand and supply curves. With perfectly inelastic demand [Panel (*a*)], the consumer pays the entire tax. With perfectly elastic demand [Panel (*b*)], the producer pays the entire tax. With perfectly inelastic supply [Panel (*c*)], the supplier pays the entire tax. With perfectly elastic supply [Panel (*d*)], the consumer pays the entire tax.

placed on the good, the supply curve shifts to S_r. The result is that price rises from P_e to P_r. Price has risen by the full amount of the tax, and the equilibrium quantity is unchanged. In this case, the incidence of the excise tax falls fully on the consumers of this good. The tax has been shifted forward to consumers by the full amount of the tax.

Panel (b) of Figure 6–13 shows a normally sloped supply curve and a perfectly elastic demand curve. The post-tax supply curve is S_r. After the tax is imposed, price is unchanged at P_e, and equilibrium quantity falls to Q_r. Since the price to consumers is unchanged, the producer is paying the entire tax. The incidence of the tax falls fully on the suppliers of this good.

The principle demonstrated in the first two panels of Figure 6–13 is clear: The more inelastic the demand for a good, the more any excise tax placed on the good will fall on consumers of that good. Conversely, the more elastic the demand curve, the more any excise tax placed on the good will fall on the producers of that good.

In order to see the effects of supply elasticity, it is necessary to alter the geometric presentation slightly. The usual way to represent a tax increase on a graph is by a parallel increase in the supply schedule. However, we can also represent a tax increase by a parallel decrease in the demand schedule. D is still what consumers are willing to pay for various quantities, including the tax, but D_t is the demand curve as the producer sees it, after the tax has been subtracted. In the case of perfectly inelastic supply, it is necessary to use the alternative of shifting the demand schedule because it is impossible to shift the supply schedule.

In Panel (c) of Figure 6–13, the tax does not affect the quantity, which is determined by the perfectly inelastic supply curve. The industry views the demand curve as the curve with the amount of the tax subtracted from the price. The equilibrium quantity is unchanged after the shift, and the price the firm receives falls from P_e to P_r. In other words, the entire amount of the tax has been paid by the suppliers of the good.

Panel (d) shows a perfectly elastic supply curve. An excise tax shifts the supply curve to account for the higher price at each output. After the shift, the price of the item has increased from P_e to P_r, the exact amount of the tax. In this case, consumers are paying the entire tax. Less is being sold, so some producers may be worse off in that sense, but consumers are paying more for Q_r, and this increased amount is exactly equal to the amount of the tax.

This exercise in shifting supply and demand curves demonstrates some general characteristics of excise tax incidence:

1. The more inelastic the demand, the more price rises, meaning that the tax falls more heavily on consumers.
2. The more elastic the demand, the less price rises, indicating that the tax falls more heavily on producers.
3. The more inelastic the supply, the more the tax is paid by producers.
4. The more elastic the supply, the more price rises, and the more the tax is paid by consumers.

The answer to the question of who pays the excise tax should now be clear. The answer again is, It depends. It depends on the relative elasticities of supply and demand for the good on which the tax is placed.

These elasticities depend on substitutability and are related to how consumers make choices among competing goods when prices change. In the next chapter, you will develop a theory of consumer choice that explains this process of adjustment.

SUMMARY

1. Elasticity is the measure of the sensitivity or responsiveness of quantity demanded or quantity supplied to changes in price (and to changes in other *ceteris paribus* factors).
2. Linear demand curves, except for those that are perfectly vertical or horizontal, have points on them that range from elastic to inelastic and one point that is unit elastic.
3. Price elasticity of demand is a measure of substitutability. The more substitutes an item has, the more elastic demand will be. This simply means that consumers have more options and, as a result, respond more readily to changes in price.
4. As time increases, elasticity of demand increases because individuals have more opportunity to substitute other goods.
5. Total revenue is dependent on elasticity because a demand curve is a price-quantity relationship, and total revenue is price times quantity. When price changes, the quantity demanded changes, and this changes total revenue. The amount of the change in total revenue will depend on the responsiveness of consumers to changes in price, and this is precisely what elasticity measures.
6. Income elasticity measures the responsiveness of changes in quantity demanded to changes in income.
7. Cross elasticity of demand measures the responsiveness of changes in the quantity demanded of one good to changes in the price of other goods.
8. Price elasticity of supply is a measure of the responsiveness of changes in quantity supplied to changes in price.
9. As time increases, the elasticity of supply increases because the longer the time period, the more chance there is for adjustments to take place.
10. The concepts of supply, demand, and elasticity can be used to determine tax incidence. The more inelastic the demand for a product and the more elastic the supply, the greater the amount of the tax paid by the consumer. Conversely, the greater the elasticity of demand for a product and the more inelastic the supply, the more the tax is paid by producers. Relative elasticities determine tax incidence.

NEW TERMS

elasticity
price elasticity of demand
coefficient of price elasticity of demand (E_d)
perfectly inelastic
perfectly elastic

unit elastic
arc elasticity
point elasticity
total revenue
income elasticity of demand
cross elasticity of demand

price elasticity of supply
coefficient of price elasticity of supply (E_s)
excise tax
tax incidence

QUESTIONS FOR DISCUSSION

1. A recent issue of *The Wall Street Journal* ran an article entitled "Chicago's Troubled Transit System Takes Unorthodox Steps to Attract Commuters." This "unorthodox" step was to reduce fares. What does this indicate about what the head of the Illinois State Department of Transportation thinks about the price elasticity of demand for the transit system?

2. To demonstrate the importance of calculating average price changes and quantity changes when determining elasticity, use the correct formula for calculating a change in price from $2.20 to $2.40 in Table 6-1. Then calculate it again as a price increase from $2.20 and as a price decrease from

$2.40, without using the averaging formula. Explain the difference in your answers.

3. Would the elasticity of demand for Pepsi be higher or lower than the elasticity of demand for soft drinks in general? Why?

4. Why is public policy that is aimed at decreasing the importation of oil frustrated by the fact that demand for gasoline is income elastic and price inelastic?

5. During the energy crisis, *The Wall Street Journal* ran a headline, "Europe's Drivers Don't Reduce Gasoline Use Despite Soaring Prices." What was wrong with the headline, given data from the article that showed that gas prices were up 120 percent, and the general level of inflation was up 140 percent?

6. If the government wants to place a tax on a certain commodity for the purpose of generating revenue, should it look for goods that have relatively inelastic or relatively elastic demand curves?

7. The demand schedule below can be used to create a total revenue schedule by multiplying price times quantity demanded. Do so by completing a total revenue column. Then create a fourth column in which you estimate the price elasticity of demand based on the movements of price and total revenue.

Price	Quantity Demanded	Total Revenue	Coefficient of Price Elasticity of Demand
■	■	■	■
$0.50	25		
1.00	20		
1.20	18		
1.40	16		
1.60	14		
1.80	12		
2.00	10		
2.20	8		
2.40	6		
2.60	4		
2.80	2		
3.00	0		

8. If a firm were the only seller of the product represented by the demand schedule in Question 7, what would you do if the price were $20 when you took over the marketing department?

9. The price of Good x increases from $1.10 to $1.15, and the quantity of Good y consumed increases from 1,100 units to 1,750 units. What is the cross elasticity of demand? What does this imply about Goods x and y?

10. If the coefficient of the cross elasticity of demand for Good a and Good b is infinite, what kind of goods are Good a and Good b?

SUGGESTIONS FOR FURTHER READING

Browning, Edgar K., and Jacquelene M. Browning. *Microeconomic Theory and Applications*. 2d ed. Boston: Little, Brown and Co., 1986. This book contains a good treatment of elasticity, with problems to be solved.

Lindsay, Cotton Mather. *Applied Price Theory*. New York: The Dryden Press, 1984. A well-written, intermediate price theory textbook with many elasticity applications.

CHAPTER 7

DEMAND AND CONSUMER CHOICE

INTRODUCTION

We have spent a considerable amount of time using demand and supply curves to develop predictions about the outcome of market processes. Most of our analysis made use of market demand curves, which we derived by aggregating individual demand curves. Since these individual demand curves form the bedrock of microeconomic analysis, we need to consider the factors that underlie the individual consumer's demand curve.

The first approach economists took in examining consumer demand—the classical approach—involved the concept of measurable utility. We will use this approach to examine some problems and suggest some applications for demand analysis. The second approach to consumer demand—indifference curve analysis—is discussed in an appendix to this chapter.

CHOICE, VALUE, AND UTILITY THEORY

The idea that households and firms must make choices because of scarcity is the fundamental notion of economic analysis. We now want to expand on that analysis to determine why consumers react in the way that they do. Why does a person demand a certain good or service? An obvious answer is that the good or service is expected to satisfy some need or desire of the consumer. Economists are content with this superficial answer.

There may be moral or ethical dimensions to the desires people have. Why do people want to buy guns? pornography? narcotics? sports cars? liquor? cigarettes? These are questions to which psychologists, moralists, and many others devote a great deal of attention. But economists generally are not interested in why desires exist or why people should buy some goods and not others. It is not because they think such questions are unimportant. Indeed, such questions may be more important than the questions economists try to answer, such as, What would happen to the sales of Porsches if their price increased by $1,000? or, What would happen to the sales of potatoes if the price of wheat went up $1 per bushel? Economists accept the fact that people have a certain psychological or ethical makeup and, without approving or disapproving of it, start their analysis from there.

Economists' view of consumer choice is based on five propositions about the psychology of consumer behavior. These five propositions are:

1. Individuals (or households) must make choices because they have limited income and are forced to choose which of their many wants to satisfy.
2. Individuals make *rational choices* when they make these consumption decisions, i.e., they weigh costs and benefits and make the decision that gives them the most satisfaction.
3. Individuals make these choices with imperfect information. In other words, they don't know (with certainty) all the attributes of the goods they are choosing to consume.
4. As increasing amounts of particular goods are consumed, the additional satisfaction gained from an additional unit becomes smaller.
5. Many goods have characteristics that make them satisfactory substitutes for other goods.

All of these statements may seem simple and obvious, but they will enable us to make some powerful conclusions about the nature of demand.

INCOME AND SUBSTITUTION EFFECTS

The law of demand, which you studied in Chapter 3, states that as the price of a good or service declines, the quantity demanded increases, *ceteris paribus*. This law is true because of two effects that take place as a result of the price decline.

The first is called the **substitution effect**. When the price of a good or service falls, the good or service becomes less expensive relative to all other goods. As a result, more of it is purchased because it has become a better substitute for these other goods as it has become cheaper. Steaks and ground beef are a good example. As the price of steaks falls, more people will switch from ground beef to steaks.

The second reason that more of the good or service is purchased is called the **income effect**. When the price of a good or service falls, *ceteris paribus*, the household's real income, or purchasing power, rises. That is, after buying the same amount as before (of the good for which price has fallen), the household has more income left over. With this higher real income, more of all normal goods will be consumed; thus, the consumption of the good that experienced the price decline also will increase (if it is a normal good). These income and substitution effects are important forces, which will become clearer in this chapter.

SUBSTITUTION EFFECT
When the price of a good falls, it becomes less expensive relative to all other goods and more of it is consumed, substituting for other goods.

INCOME EFFECT
When the price of a good or service falls, *ceteris paribus*, the household's real income rises, and the consumer buys more of all normal goods.

■ The History of Utility Theory: The Diamond-Water Paradox

In the development of economic theory, early economists often posed questions that they then debated. One of the popular topics of the day was what determined value. Adam Smith wrote that value could mean either *value in use* or *value in exchange*. He posed (in 1776) what became known as the diamond-water paradox by writing:

The things that have the greatest value in use have frequently little or no value in exchange; and on the contrary, those which have the greatest value in exchange have frequently little value in use. Nothing is more valuable than water: but it will purchase scarce anything; scarce anything can be had in exchange for it. A diamond, on the contrary, has scarce any value in use; but a very great quantity of other goods may frequently be had in exchange for it. [1]

DIAMOND-WATER PARADOX
The problem that classical economists faced when they argued that value in use could not determine price (demand) because diamonds, while less useful than water, are more expensive than water.

The **diamond-water paradox** was the problem that classical economists faced when they argued that value in use could not determine price (value in exchange) because diamonds, while less useful than water, are more expensive than water. The discussion concerning the diamond-water paradox went on for a long time. Many famous mathematicians, economists, and philosophers took part in the debate. In large part, the confusion over the diamond-water paradox concerned the distinction between total units and marginal units and arguments over what the term *useful* meant.

In the 1870s, William Stanley Jevons, Carl Menger, and Leon Walras, all writing separately, solved the paradox by developing a theory in which demand and utility came to the forefront. Their solution serves a major role in developing the theory of consumer demand.

Part of the debate underlying the diamond-water paradox was an argument over whether value (or price) was determined by supply or demand. In a famous analogy, Alfred Marshall, the great British economist, said that you could no more say whether supply or demand determined value than you could say which blade of a pair of scissors did the cutting. Thus, value (or price) is determined by the interaction of supply and demand.

Let's consider the influence of demand on value first, and leave supply for later chapters. Demand theorists used the notion of utility. In economics, if an individual wants a commodity, then that commodity has utility. **Utility** is the satisfaction an individual receives from consuming a good or service. Thus, the same commodity may have a great deal of utility for one person and none or very little for some other person. Like beauty, utility is in the eye (or mind) of the beholder.

UTILITY
The satisfaction that an individual receives from consuming a good or service.

Utility is strictly an ex ante concept; that is, utility measures the way an individual feels about a commodity *before* the individual buys or consumes it. You may see a cake in a bakery window and have great desire for it—that's utility. If you buy and eat the cake, you may get sick and receive no satisfaction from its consumption—that's irrelevant economi-

---

1. Mark Blaug, *Economic Theory in Retrospect* (Homewood, IL: Richard D. Irwin, Inc., 1968); writes that Smith, in what may be the greatest understatement in the history of economic thought, conceded that his explanation of value was obscure.

cally. Utility is the satisfaction you *expect* to get, not what you actually get. The reason for this distinction is that we use utility in the development of the demand curve, and the demand curve shows the amounts that people will buy based on anticipated satisfaction, not the amounts of satisfaction actually received after having made the purchase.

A good unit for the measurement of utility, like pounds or gallons or miles, does not exist; but since utility is unique to the individual, an arbitrary (and imaginary) unit called the **util** can be employed. The economists who conceived this theory did not seem too concerned over the measurability and ability to add these measures of utility.

UTIL
An arbitrary unit used to measure utility.

■ Total Utility and Marginal Utility

As long as no attempt is made to compare the number of utils of different people, this is a satisfactory measuring device. A preference function ordering a consumer's desire to consume differing amounts of goods is called a **utility function**. For example, suppose you try to construct your utility function for some commodity, say a particular brand of soft drink. First, choose a convenient time period, a day for this example. Then, for one unit (one can) of Coke per day, assign a number of utils, say 20. (You can choose any number at all: 1; 1,000; $1/10$; $47^1/2$.) Ask yourself, if I get 20 utils from one can, how many would I get if I consumed two cans of Coke per day rather than just one? Suppose, after much reflection, you say 38. Ask yourself the same question about three cans of Coke per day, four, five, six, and so on.

UTILITY FUNCTION
A preference function ordering a consumer's desire to consume differing amounts of goods.

TABLE 7-1
UTILITY SCHEDULE FOR COKE

Cans of Coke per Day ■	Total Utility ■	Marginal Utility ■
0	0	0
1	20	20
2	38	18
3	54	16
4	67	13
5	77	10
6	84	7
7	88	4
8	89	1
9	87	-2
10	82	-5

Marginal utility is the amount of utility that an additional unit of consumption adds to total utility. The formula for marginal utility (MU) is

$$MU = \frac{\text{change in total utility}}{\text{change in quantity consumed}}.$$

MARGINAL UTILITY
The amount of satisfaction provided by one more or one less unit of consumption.

Marginal utility is the change in satisfaction provided by one more or one less unit of consumption. In Table 7-1, the marginal utility is determined by calculating how much each additional can of Coke adds to total utility. For example, the first can of Coke adds 20 utils to total utility. The fourth can of Coke adds 13 utils to total utility. This is found by subtracting the total utility of consuming three Cokes from the total utility of consuming four Cokes (67 − 54 = 13).

Principle of Diminishing Marginal Utility

The important characteristic of the schedule shown in Table 7-1 is that, while the total utility becomes larger the more you consume per day (up to a point), the additions to total utility from each additional unit consumed become smaller. This feature—the fact that additional, or marginal, utility declines as consumption increases—is called diminishing marginal utility.

DIMINISHING MARGINAL UTILITY
The fact that additional satisfaction or utility declines as consumption increases. Less satisfaction is obtained per additional unit as more units are consumed.

The principle of **diminishing marginal utility** states that for a given time period, the greater the level of consumption of a particular commodity, the lower the marginal utility. In other words, as you consume more units of a commodity, the additional units yield less of an addition to total utility than the preceding units did. For instance, the seventh Coke is expected to provide less additional pleasure than the sixth Coke. This principle is reflected in Table 7-1 and Figure 7-1. In Table 7-1, marginal utility falls from 20 utils for the first Coke to 18 utils for the second Coke. The seventh Coke only adds four utils to total utility.

Figure 7-1, Panel (*b*), shows the marginal utility curve that corresponds to the total utility curve in Panel (*a*). Note that when the total utility curve reaches its maximum, marginal utility is zero. This makes sense because if total utility is to decline, marginal utility must become negative. In Table 7-1, total utility reaches a maximum at eight because the ninth Coke has a negative marginal utility. The only way a total of anything can decline is for changes in that total to be negative.

Utility and Consumer Behavior

The concepts of utility and price now can be combined to show how consumers make choices in the marketplace. When choosing, consumers are confronted with a range of items and also a range of prices. You may not choose the item that has the greatest utility because the price and your income are also important factors. In other words, consumers don't always buy their first choice. You may prefer a Porsche to a Chevrolet, but you may purchase the Chevrolet. The explanation for this behavior lies in price and utility.

Suppose, for example, you are considering purchasing a six-pack of soft drinks. You are presented with the three possibilities shown in Table 7-2. Coke is your first choice because it yields the most utility. But the relevant question is not which soft drink has the most utility, but which has the most utility *per dollar*. Therefore, you choose to buy a six-pack of Pepsi. This choice implies that the extra satisfaction of Coke over Pepsi is

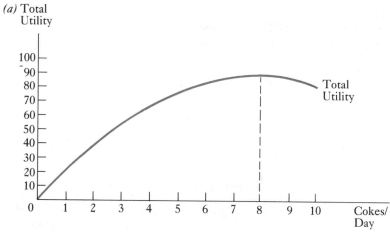

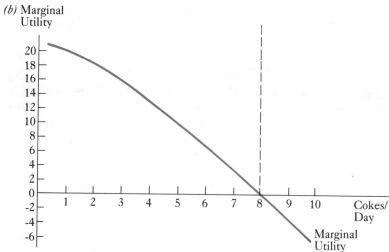

FIGURE 7-1
TOTAL AND MARGINAL UTILITY
Total utility increases as consumption increases to a certain level, in this case
eight Cokes per day, and then it declines. When total utility is increasing,
marginal utility is declining, illustrating the principle of diminishing marginal
utility. At the point where total utility begins to decline, marginal utility is
negative.

not worth $.75, but the extra satisfaction of Pepsi over 7-Up is worth the
extra $.25 it costs. Thus, in deciding how to spend your money, you look
at marginal utility per dollar rather than marginal utility alone. You do this
because money is the common denominator. Dollars can be used to buy
any available good. So for the last dollar you spend, you want to choose
the item with the highest utility per dollar; and in so doing, you economize
by getting the most satisfaction per dollar. There are other things you can
do with the extra $.75. You are saying in this example that $.75 spent on
something other than Coke will yield more additional utils than the difference between the utility of Coke and the utility of Pepsi, but that $.25
spent on other goods will not yield more utils than spending it on Pepsi
instead of 7-Up.

TABLE 7-2
HYPOTHETICAL UTILITY-PER-DOLLAR COMPARISONS

Choice	Marginal Utility (Utils)	Price	*MU* per Dollar
Coke	30.0	$3.00	10
Pepsi	27.0	2.25	12
7-Up	20.0	2.00	10

Maximizing Total Utility

The self-interest hypothesis implies that individuals will act to maximize their total utility. To see how marginal utility and price influence how a consumer maximizes total utility, consider an example with only two goods, Coke and pizza, where a unit of Coke costs $.50 and a unit of pizza costs $1. The consumer's utility schedules for the two goods are presented in Table 7-3. The consumer has a given amount of income, called a budget constraint. A **budget constraint** is a given level of income that determines the maximum amount of goods that may be purchased by an individual. Let's endow this consumer with $13 worth of purchasing power, and see how that income will be allocated between the two goods so as to achieve maximum utility.

BUDGET CONSTRAINT
A given level of income that determines the maximum amount of goods that may be purchased by an individual.

TABLE 7-3
UTILITY SCHEDULE

Coke				Pizza			
Quantity per Week (Cans)	*MU* (Utils)	*MU/P* (P = $.50)	*TU* (Utils)	Quantity per Week (Pizza Pieces)	*MU* (Utils)	*MU/P* (P = $1.00)	*TU* (Utils)
1	15	30	15	1	32	32	32
2	14	28	29	2	31	31	63
3	13	26	42	3	28	28	91
4	12	24	54	4	$24^{3}/_{4}$	$24^{3}/_{4}$	$115^{3}/_{4}$
5	11	22	65	5	$20^{1}/_{4}$	$20^{1}/_{4}$	136
6	$10^{3}/_{4}$	$21^{1}/_{2}$	$75^{3}/_{4}$	6	18	18	154
7	$10^{1}/_{4}$	$20^{1}/_{2}$	86	7	17	17	171
8	10	20	96	8	16	16	187
9	9	18	105	9	14	14	201
10	8	16	113	10	12	12	213
11	7	14	120	11	11	11	224
12	$6^{1}/_{2}$	13	$126^{1}/_{2}$	12	9	9	233

The first dollar will be allocated to pizza because pizza yields 32 utils of satisfaction compared with 29 utils for a dollar's worth of Coke. The next dollar spent also will be for pizza because it yields 31 utils, which is still greater than Coke, the alternative purchase. In other words, the consumer buys two pieces of pizza before buying any Coke. The third dollar is spent on Coke because the 29 utils of satisfaction gained from purchasing two Cokes are greater than the 28 utils that are yielded by a third pizza piece. The process continues until the income of $13 is spent. In maximizing total utility, the consumer will spend $5 on ten cans of Coke and $8 on eight pieces of pizza. This allocation produces 300 utils of satisfaction—the maximum total utility that can be purchased with $13 of income. You cannot find an expenditure pattern that will produce more satisfaction (try reducing Coke consumption by two cans and increasing pizza consumption by one piece or vice versa).

The consumer's choices are based on a maximization rule that says that total utility is maximized when the last dollar spent on Good A yields the same utility as the last dollar spent on Good B. In algebraic form, total utility is maximized where,

$$\frac{MU_A}{P_A} = \frac{MU_B}{P_B}.$$

Thus, the marginal utility of a can of Coke, when ten cans per week are consumed, is 8 utils, and the price of Coke is $.50, so

$$\frac{MU_{Coke}}{P_{Coke}} = \frac{8}{\$.50},$$

or 16 utils per dollar. For pizza, at the optimum consumption rate, the MU is 16 and the price is $1, so

$$\frac{MU_{pizza}}{P_{pizza}} = \frac{16}{\$1},$$

or 16 utils per dollar.

This can be generalized to include all goods by saying an individual maximizes utility where

$$\frac{MU_x}{P_x} = \frac{MU_y}{P_y} = \ldots = \frac{MU_n}{P_n}.$$

Of course, individuals don't spend all their income on goods. Sometimes individuals hold money (let's use $\$$ as the symbol) as they do any other commodity. With money, the equation for maximization is

$$\frac{MU_A}{P_A} = \frac{MU_B}{P_B} = \frac{MU_\$}{P_\$}.$$

Since the price of one dollar is one dollar, $MU_\$/P_\$$, can be simply written as $MU_\$$.

Thus, total utility is maximized where

(7–1) $$\frac{MU_x}{P_x} = \frac{MU_y}{P_y} = \ldots = \frac{MU_n}{P_n} = MU_\$.$$

Utility maximization is the way a consumer adjusts consumption, given a budget constraint and a set of prices, in order to attain the highest total amount of satisfaction. Equation (7–1) is a very complete expression for utility maximization. It has been extended to include all commodities, including money, and says that in order to maximize total utility, the marginal utilities per dollar of expenditures have to be equal and

UTILITY MAXIMIZATION
The way a consumer adjusts consumption, given a budget constraint and a set of prices, in order to attain the highest total amount of satisfaction.

also have to equal the marginal utility of money. If this is not the case, a change in consumption patterns, for a given budget constraint, can produce more satisfaction. This is just a formal way of saying that people allocate their income so as to yield the most satisfaction possible. When utility is being maximized, the additional satisfaction from any use of $1 will equal the additional satisfaction from any other use of $1. When this is not the case, the individual can reallocate personal income from one good to another and gain more satisfaction.

To see how a given consumption pattern can be adjusted to achieve maximum utility, return to Table 7–3. Let's give the individual a $9 income and say that $3 worth of Coke and $6 worth of pizza are consumed. The expression

$$\frac{MU_{Coke}}{P_{Coke}} = \frac{MU_{pizza}}{P_{pizza}}$$

doesn't hold because

$$\frac{10^{3}/_{4}}{.50} > \frac{18}{1}.$$

The individual isn't maximizing utility because the last dollar spent on Coke yields more utils than the last dollar spent on pizza. The individual should reallocate consumption outlays. By giving up one dollar's worth of pizza, the consumer would lose 18 utils but would gain 20 utils by spending one more dollar on Coke. Total utility would thus rise by 2, and

$$\frac{10}{.50} = \frac{20}{1} \; (20^{1}/_{4} \text{ rounded off})$$

the consumer is maximizing.

■
Marginal Utility and the Law of Demand

Utility theory makes it possible to derive an individual's demand curve for a good. Suppose that there are only two goods, x and y. Remember, demand curves are drawn with the *ceteris paribus* assumption, so income, tastes, and the prices of all other goods (Good y) are held constant. The consumer is initially in equilibrium, maximizing utility when

$$\frac{MU_x}{P_x} = \frac{MU_y}{P_y}.$$

At this equilibrium, MU_{x1} corresponds to the consumption of x_1 units of x in Figure 7–2. The price of x_1 is represented by P_1 in Figure 7–2. So the equation now should be written

$$\frac{MU_{x1}}{P_1} = \frac{MU_y}{P_y}.$$

Now lower the price of x to P_2. This throws the expression out of equilibrium because the denominator on the left side is now smaller, making the left side of the expression larger:

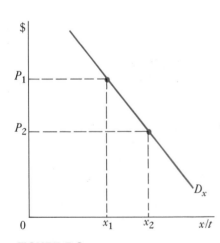

FIGURE 7-2
DEMAND CURVE FOR GOOD X
When price falls from P_1 to P_2, the consumer's utility maximization is thrown out of equilibrium. Equilibrium will be restored if the consumer increases consumption to x_2.

$$\frac{MU_{x1}}{P_2} > \frac{MU_y}{P_y}.$$

To get the expression back into equality, the individual has to lower the value of the left side of the expression and/or raise the right side. How can this be done? If the individual consumes more of x, MU_x will decline because of the principle of diminishing marginal utility. As consumption moves to x_2 on Figure 7-2, the marginal utility of x_2 falls. Furthermore, more of x will mean some reduction in the consumption of y. As consumption of y falls, MU_y rises. When this happens, the expression will move toward

$$\frac{MU_x}{P_x} = \frac{MU_y}{P_y}.$$

Utility-maximizing behavior requires that when the price of commodity x falls (as from P_1 to P_2 in Figure 7-2), the consumer will increase the consumption of x. Since this is necessary for utility maximization, it demonstrates that the demand curves of individuals must have a negative slope; that is, the lower the price, the greater the quantity demanded.

PROBLEMS WITH UTILITY THEORY

There are two major difficulties with a demand theory based on utility. They center on the indivisibility and immeasurability of utility. The theory works well enough to describe the consumption of certain kinds of goods, such as Cokes or pizzas. When considering the purchase of an automobile or a home, however, it is difficult to talk about additional units because the purchase is what economists call *lumpy*. It is difficult to consume a part of a house or a part of a car, while it is possible to consume part of a six-pack of Coke. The theory is somewhat weakened, then, by the fact that the consumer can't make continuous decisions about successive amounts of consumption.[2]

A greater problem is the inability to measure utility. We have proceeded as if there were a way we could strap a meter to a consumer and with exactness measure the utility expected from consuming one more Coke. This is, of course, not possible. Psychology has not yet developed to such a technological level. But before you reject utility theory as useless, remember that it is a theoretical tool. It really isn't that important for the theory to be able to measure utility. The purpose is to develop a better understanding of why and how quantity demanded will change when prices change, not about how utility changes.

2. This problem with utility theory is really not such a debilitating flaw. Consumers still can make adjustments even with most lumpy purchases. Consider a house as an example. Suppose the individual decides after the purchase that the house is too large and that other purchases would yield more marginal utility. Over time, expenditures on the house can be lowered by a lessening of routine maintenance so that more can be spent on the other goods that yield a higher marginal utility. Buying a smaller house, buying one at a less desirable location, or renting are also available alternatives.

SOME APPLICATIONS OF UTILITY THEORY

You have practiced and observed utility maximization even though you may not have thought of it in the formal terminology of economics. Suppose, for a moment, you are organizing the beer concession for a club fund-raising event. There are two ways to finance the concession. You can charge an admission fee to the event and then allow unlimited consumption, or you can charge a set price for each beer, say $.50 per glass. Utility theory predicts different levels of consumption and hence different requirements for planning the supply. In the first case, beer drinkers will consume beer until the marginal utility per glass is zero because the price per additional glass is zero. In the second case, beer drinkers will consume beer until the marginal utility per glass equals the marginal utility of $.50. You can predict, then, that there will be more drunken, rowdy behavior if the party is financed by an admission charge. If you don't agree with this analysis, reflect back on group parties you have observed. Were the most rowdy ones the pay-as-you-go type or the admission type?

This may seem like an insignificant example because the consumption of beer isn't a very earth-shaking issue. So let's change the good from beer to medical services. If the government decides to provide *free* national health care, what do you predict will happen to the consumption of these services?[3] Of course, people will consume them until the marginal utility of the last unit is zero. This is exactly what tends to happen in a prepaid or tax-financed health care program. If you have ever participated in such a program in the military, at a university, or under a health maintenance plan, you probably have consumed more of these services than before. Since the services do not have a charge per visit, more are consumed. You also may have noticed that with the "free" system, the waiting time is usually longer, the waiting rooms are less comfortable, and the workers are less congenial than with a fee-for-service system.

The Diamond-Water Paradox Solved

Adam Smith (and others) argued that utility (and thus demand) could not be a determinant of price because diamonds, while less useful than water, are more expensive than water. The paradox disappears if you distinguish between total utility and marginal utility. The total utility of water is high, but since there is a great deal in existence and large quantities are consumed, its marginal utility is low. The total utility of diamonds, on the other hand, is relatively low, but since diamonds are rare, their marginal utility is high. Price, then, is determined by marginal utility, not total utility. Economists say that marginal utility determines value in exchange (price) and that total utility determines value in use. Scarcity, then, is related to value through utility. If something has a low marginal utility at all quantities consumed, it will have a low price, regardless of how scarce it is; but if something is relatively scarce and has a high marginal utility, it will be valuable and hence will be expensive.

3. By *free*, we mean there is no monetary cost to the patient, i.e., price is zero.

Utility Theory and the Uneasy Case for the Progressive Income Tax

Many noneconomists believe that money and income are subject to diminishing marginal utility. This idea is one of the main arguments (but not the only one) for a progressive income tax based on the principle of diminishing marginal utility. This argument assumes that it is possible to measure utility and further that we can make **interpersonal utility comparisons**. Such comparisons are attempts to compare utility between consumers. One way around comparing different people's utility is to assume that individuals all have the same utility schedule for equal increments of income. With these two assumptions, proponents of the progressive income tax argue that society can maximize total utility by taking income away from the high-income individuals who have lower marginal utilities of income and transferring it to the low-income individuals who have higher marginal utilities of income.

Proponents of a progressive income tax who apply principles of individual utility maximization to the society as a whole are on very shaky ground, however. First of all, economists are in agreement that interpersonal utility comparisons are meaningless. People are different. There really is no accounting for taste. There is no way you can prove that an additional $100 of income gives less satisfaction to actress Linda Evans than to an unemployed auto worker. In fact, Linda may get more satisfaction because she is such an expert consumer. It is impossible to prove that one individual gets more or less satisfaction from an increment to income than does any other individual.

A second and more fundamental problem with this analysis is that it assumes a diminishing marginal utility for income. This proposition cannot be verified. The principle of diminishing marginal utility, you will remember, states that the marginal utility of a *particular commodity* declines as consumption is increased. Increased income, however, represents an increase in the consumption of all goods. If wants are insatiable, there is no reason to believe that the principle of diminishing marginal utility holds for money. Even so, it is probably the case that most people think that money has diminishing marginal utility. What about you? Do you think a $100 bill would give your "rich" economics instructor more or less satisfaction than it would give you?[4]

INTERPERSONAL UTILITY COMPARISONS
Attempts to compare amounts of utility between consumers.

Shopping for Bargains

Economists have used the concept of utility-maximizing behavior to analyze search or shopping behavior. The idea is that a buyer will search for bargains until the expected value or utility savings equals the cost of continued searching.

Several predictions can be made from this theory. The first is that the larger the amount individuals expect to save, the longer they will continue to search. In other words, the bigger the item in terms of your

4. For a comprehensive treatment of this subject, see Walter J. Blum and Harry Kalven, Jr., *The Uneasy Case for Progressive Taxation* (Chicago: University of Chicago Press, 1970).

budget, the more you will shop around. You will search longer for a good price on an automobile than you will for a good price on a loaf of bread. As a result, we would expect that price differences on bigger budget items would be smaller than price differences on smaller budget items. The reason for this is that the search process will drive high-price sellers out of business or cause them to reduce their prices.

We also might expect that where search costs are higher, prices could be higher without driving sellers out of business. Have you ever noticed that prices of gasoline are higher near freeways than in towns? We can explain this phenomenon with our theory. Users of freeways are going somewhere, often in a hurry. Their search costs are high; they therefore do less shopping around and as a result pay higher prices.

WILLIAM STANLEY JEVONS (1835–1882)

William Stanley Jevons had one of the greatest minds in the history of economic thought. Jevons combined utility theory with marginal analysis and applied it to consumer choice. He thus constructed the theory that underlies the theory of demand, much as we have done in this chapter.

Jevons was both an esoteric intellectual and a practical economist. He was born in Liverpool and studied chemistry and mathematics at University College, London.

Financial problems forced him to move to Australia to accept a job with the Sydney Mint. He spent five years in Australia, during which time he became very interested in political economy. In 1859, he returned to the University of London and studied political economy until 1865. In 1865, he published a book, *The Coal Question*, which thrust him into prominence in economic circles. His most famous book, *Theory of Political Economy*, was published in 1871.

Jevons accepted a professorship at Owens College, Manchester, in 1866, where he worked on a wide range of intellectual pursuits, from statistical analysis of commodity prices to very abstract economic theory. He even developed a sunspot theory to explain business cycles. His work generated a great deal of interest in political circles, but Jevons himself had little impact on economic policy or economic thought. This was largely because of his personal habits. He was, perhaps, the original "strange professor." He once wrote to his sister that he had never attended a party "without impressing upon all friends the fact that it is no use inviting me." He didn't regret this solitude; in fact, he argued that reserve and loneliness are necessary to develop ideas. He felt that social intercourse insured that thoughts would "never rise above the ordinary level of the others." A colleague of Jevons wrote: "There never was a worse lecturer, the men would not go to his classes, he worked in flashes and could not finish anything thoroughly, the only point about Jevons was that he was a genius."

Unfortunately for economics, Jevons died at the early age of 47. At the time of his death, Jevons was working on a massive book entitled *Principles of Economics*. The book, of course, was never completed.

CONSUMER SURPLUS

Consumers often benefit because in a market economy, they are able to purchase a good or service by sacrificing something that is worth less to them than the value of what they receive. **Consumer surplus** is the utility derived from a purchase in excess of the market-determined price. Utility theory provides a measure of consumer surplus.

Consider the demand curve for a single consumer or group of homogeneous consumers in Figure 7–3. At price P_1, the individual will consume Q_1 units of the good. From the discussion of utility-maximizing behavior, the marginal utility of the last unit purchased is equal to the price of the unit. This means that the marginal utility of each previous unit purchased was greater than price P_1. The consumer would have been willing to pay higher prices for those previous units, so at the market price of P_1, the consumer receives a bonus in terms of utility on all units but the last one. The total purchase is worth more to the consumer than the total amount (price times quantity) that is paid. This extra utility gained is called consumer surplus and is represented by the shaded area in Figure 7–3. This will be an important concept when we study monopoly. For an application of consumer surplus in international trade, be sure to read the International Perspective in this chapter.

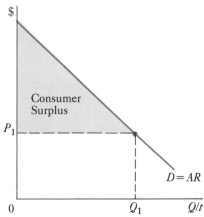

FIGURE 7–3
CONSUMER SURPLUS
Consumer surplus is the difference between the total utility received from the purchase of a product and the total revenue generated by the product.

CONSUMER SURPLUS
The benefit derived from a purchase in excess of the market-determined price.

THE INTERNATIONAL PERSPECTIVE
TARIFFS AND CONSUMER SURPLUS

Tariffs have many effects. They reduce the efficiency of resource allocation, they redistribute income between countries and between producers and consumers within countries, and they raise revenue for the countries that impose them. All of the economic effects of tariffs are important and will be discussed in the chapter on international trade. It is possible, however, to use the concept of consumer surplus developed in this chapter to see how tariffs affect consumer well-being.

The graph in this box is similar to Figure 7–3. S_d represents the domestic supply curve and S_w the world supply curve. World supply is perfectly elastic at the World Price P_f. Consumers are demanding quantity $0D$, of which quantity $0A$ is sold by domestic producers and quantity AD is imported. The triangle P_fHS_w represents consumer surplus. What happens if the government imposes a tariff (excise tax) equal to t? The price rises by the amount of the tariff to P_t, creating a new supply curve, S'_w. Consumers now purchase $0B$ from domestic producers and BC from foreign producers.

Consumer surplus is now represented by the triangle $P_tHS'_w$. There has been a reduction in consumer surplus equal to the difference in the two triangles, represented by the cross-hatched area. What this exercise demonstrates is that the imposition of a tariff permits producers to sell more of a product at a higher price and that governmental revenues rise by the amount of the tariff times the imported quantity (BC), but consumers experience a decline in consumer surplus.

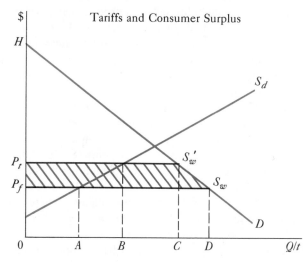

ADVERTISING AND MARKETING

The theory developed in this chapter explains a great deal about demand and consumer equilibrium. It does not say anything about the role of advertising and marketing. Advertising and marketing are difficult topics for economists to deal with because the analysis assumes a consumer is an informed, rational, utility maximizer. Advertising and marketing are not, however, inconsistent with those basic assumptions.

Advertisers spend a great deal of time trying to alter tastes and perceptions. If enough tastes and perceptions can be changed, the demand for the firm's product can be increased. Changes in tastes do not mean that the consumer is not rational. Even without advertising, tastes would change over time with changes in age, education, and other factors. Some tastes even change regularly with the change of season. Economists, however, usually begin their analysis by accepting tastes as a given.

Advertisers also spend a great deal of time generating information for consumers about prices. This behavior of advertisers fits into the description of search behavior that we previously developed. If the cost of information falls, the cost of the search falls and consumers will do more searching. As a consequence, they may alter their purchasing patterns and buy from lower cost sellers.

Much advertising is directed toward making consumer demand more inelastic by convincing buyers that similar products are not satisfactory substitutes for the one being advertised. In the jargon of this chapter, advertisers attempt to widen the spread between the utility of their product and the utility of potential substitutes. From what you have learned in this chapter, you can see that if this strategy succeeds, advertisers can charge a higher price for their product without losing many sales.

EXPERIMENTAL ECONOMICS: ECONOMICS ACCORDING TO RATS

Economics is beginning to borrow from experimental psychology. Economists at the University of Arizona and Texas A&M University, among others, are carrying out work in a lab setting to test some fundamental propositions in economics.

At the University of Arizona, Vernon Smith has conducted research on market behavior using human subjects, usually students. At Texas A&M, economists Ray Battalio and John Kagel have experimented with human and animal subjects. In mental hospitals, these economists did experiments with token economies. Patients were paid tokens for tasks and were free to spend these tokens on personal items. Some of the results of these investigations were fascinating. They found that the distribution of income earned was closely parallel to that in the U.S. economy. Perhaps even more startling was the fact that earning differences between male and female patients were similar to those in the "real" economy.

This led the two economists to experiment with rats. They found that rats trained to do "work for pay" (i.e., hit a bar for food) reduced their work effort after some point, choosing more leisure over additional income. They also found that among low-income rats (those that had to work hard for a little food), such work reduction patterns were more common. These experimental results are consistent with behavior patterns of individuals in nonlaboratory situations.

SUMMARY

1. When price falls, the quantity demanded increases because of income effects and substitution effects.
2. Total utility is the total amount of satisfaction expected from consuming an item.
3. Marginal utility is the addition to total utility from consuming one more or one less unit of a good.
4. Consumers, in deciding among items, choose those items with the highest marginal utility per dollar.
5. An individual maximizes total utility by consuming all items so that the marginal utilities per dollar spent are equal.
6. Utility theory is useful in explaining how much effort people will make to search for bargains.

7. Utility theory has been criticized on the grounds that utility is not measurable and that items consumed are not perfectly divisible, as the theory of utility maximization requires. Despite these criticisms, utility theory is a useful tool for analyzing consumer behavior.
8. Consumer surplus is a measure of the benefits derived from a purchase in excess of the price that is paid.
9. Marketing and advertising can be viewed as attempts to reduce search costs and change tastes. Attempts to alter tastes are not in conflict with the theory learned in this chapter.

NEW TERMS

substitution effect	util	budget constraint
income effect	utility function	utility maximization
diamond-water paradox	marginal utility	interpersonal utility comparisons
utility	diminishing marginal utility	consumer surplus

QUESTIONS FOR DISCUSSION

1. Does something have to be useful to have utility? What does it mean for a good or service to be useful?
2. What is happening if the price of a good, such as a petroleum product, is increasing without a decrease in consumption?
3. Does the fact that water is inexpensive and diamonds are expensive conflict with the theory developed in this chapter? Explain.
4. If the marginal utility of one good is four and the price is $2, and the marginal utility of another good is five and its price is $1, is the individual consumer maximizing total utility? If not, how could more utility be obtained?

5. Does advertising increase or decrease the utility you get from consuming certain goods? Is this good or bad?
6. What would you expect to happen to a normal consumer's total utility curve for bacon if the surgeon general established a link between bacon and cancer? How would this announcement affect the demand curve for bacon?
7. The following table shows the marginal utility that Roger gets from buying various amounts of cola, pretzels, nuts, pizza, and holding dollars. Assume that Roger has an income of $106 and that the prices of the respective products are $18, $4, $6, and $24.

Units of Cola	MU	Units of Pretzels	MU	Units of Nuts	MU	Units of Pizza	MU	$	MU
1	72	1	15	1	24	1	36	1	5
2	54	2	12	2	15	2	30	2	4
3	45	3	8	3	12	3	24	3	3
4	36	4	7	4	9	4	18	4	2
5	27	5	5	5	7	5	13	5	1
6	18	6	4	6	5	6	7	6	$1/2$
7	15	7	$3^{1}/_{2}$	7	2	7	4	7	$1/4$
8	12	8	3	8	1	8	2	8	$1/8$

What quantities of cola, nuts, pretzels, and pizza will Roger purchase? How many dollars will he hold?

8. The material in this chapter shows rational consumer behavior. Is it ever rational to be irrational?

9. Observers of the wealthy often comment on the fact that they waste a lot of things, e.g., food, but are very careful in their use of time. Is this irrational behavior?

10. Explain graphically how a demand curve can be derived from indifference analysis.

■ SUGGESTIONS FOR FURTHER READING

Browning, Edgar K., and Jacquelene M. Browning. *Microeconomic Theory and Applications*. 2d ed. Boston: Little Brown and Company, 1986. A very well-written intermediate microeconomic theory textbook.

Easterlin, Richard A. "Does Money Buy Happiness?" *Public Interest* (Winter 1973): 3–10. A short essay that challenges the notion that more goods mean more utility (happiness).

APPENDIX: AN ALTERNATIVE APPROACH TO CONSUMER CHOICE: INDIFFERENCE ANALYSIS

The marginal utility theory discussed in this chapter was unsatisfactory because it required precise numerical values to be assigned to alternatives (cardinal utility). The next innovation in the economic theory of choice was based on ordinal utility. **Ordinal utility** requires only that the utility of the choices can be ranked. Instead of saying, "The next slice of pizza has 30 units of utility" or "The next Coke has 25 units of utility," the consumer needs only to be able to say, "I prefer another slice of pizza to another Coke."

In the late 1800s, Italian economist Vilfredo Pareto and British economist F.Y. Edgeworth, working separately, developed another approach to consumer behavior theory based on ordinal utility—**indifference analysis**—that is the subject of this appendix. It wasn't until 1939, when Nobel prizewinning British economist Sir John Hicks published his classic book *Value and Capital*, that this analysis became popular with economic theorists and teachers. The theory swept the economics profession, and for a while, marginal utility analysis fell into disrepute.

Pareto, Edgeworth, Hicks, and others were not trying to discredit utility analysis but rather were proposing an alternative way of viewing consumer behavior. The major improvement of this theory is that it does not require the ability to measure utility. All that is necessary is that consumers are able to rank bundles of goods in the order, from low to high, in which they prefer them.

■ Indifference or Preference

Indifference and preference seem to fit more closely the way consumers actually make decisions than does marginal utility. Individuals make choices between bundles of goods. For example, you might choose be-tween four tickets to a football game and two tickets to a concert. In indifference analysis, the consumer is viewed as making choices between collections of goods and ser-vices. The only assumption is that the individual is able to state preferences for different bundles of commodities or to profess indifference between some of them. In other words, confronted with a choice of going to a movie or a football game, the individual might rank the football game as a preferred choice. Or the individual might say, "I don't have a preference. I'm indifferent be-tween the two choices."

Suppose Mary is considering different com-binations of cans of Coke and slices of pizza, as indi-cated in Table 7A–1. Combination *A* contains 16 Cokes and 3 slices of pizza. When Combination *B* is offered to Mary, which contains 12 Cokes and 4 slices of pizza, she states that neither Combination *A* nor Combi-nation *B* is preferred over the other; they are equal in the amount of satisfaction she expects to derive and, there-fore, is indifferent between the two cartons. Offering Mary the choice among Combinations C, D, and E yields the same response, or indifference. Mary has indi-cated that all five combinations of pizza and Coke yield the same amount of satisfaction. We have created an **indifference set** for her.

This indifference set can be geometrically represented by drawing an indifference curve. An indif-ference curve corresponding to the indifference set in Table 7A–1 is drawn in Figure 7A–1. An **indiffer-ence curve** shows all combinations of the two commod-ities among which a consumer is indifferent.

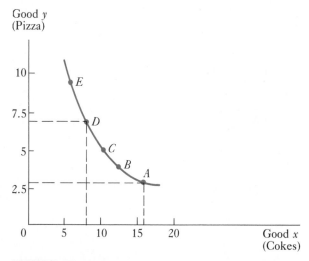

FIGURE 7A-1
INDIFFERENCE CURVE
Indifference curves represent combinations of two goods among which the consumer is indifferent. All combinations on the same indifference curve represent the same level of satisfaction.

TABLE 7A-1
MARY'S INDIFFERENCE SET

Combinations	Good x (Cans of Coke)	Good y (Slices of Pizza)
■	■	■
A	16	3
B	12	4
C	10	5
D	8	7
E	6	9

Indifference curves are negatively sloped be-cause if a consumer is to be indifferent, all points on the curve must represent equal amounts of utility. This means that if more of one good is added to the com-

bination, some of the other must be removed. Each combination represents a trade-off. In Mary's case, if Combination *B* has more pizza than Combination *A*, it must have less Coke, since the bundles are to yield the same level of satisfaction. If one combination has more pizza and more Coke than any other, or if it has more of one good without having less of the other, it would be preferred and the consumer would no longer be indiffer-ent. This is yet another way of saying that more is pre-ferred to less.

The indifference set represented by a higher indifference curve is preferred to that represented by a lower indifference curve. As Mary moves from I_1 to I_2 to I_3 to I_4 in Figure 7A–2, she receives more satisfaction. Such a series of indifference curves is called an **indiffer-ence map.** Every individual consumer has such a map, and movement to higher curves on the map represents a gain in utility.

The typical indifference curve for two goods will have some curvature and some degree of convexity. The convexity feature means that as a consumer attains more units of one good and fewer units of the other good, it takes more and more units of the more abun-dant good to compensate for the loss of one unit of the good that is becoming more scarce. (See Figure 7A–3.)

At Point *A*, the individual is consuming rela-tively large amounts of *y* and small amounts of *x*. In order to compensate for a reduction in consumption of

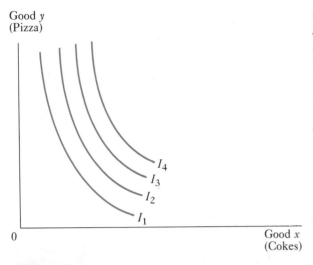

Good y
(Pizza)

I_4
I_3
I_2
I_1

0   Good x
                                                (Cokes)

FIGURE 7A-2
INDIFFERENCE MAP
An indifference map is a set of indifference curves, each
corresponding to a different level of satisfaction. Higher
curves on the map represent higher levels of satisfaction.

one unit of y, the person would only require two units of
x in order to be satisfied with such a trade; but at Point
B, since less of y and more of x are being consumed
compared to Point A, it will take a larger quantity of x
(five units) to compensate for the loss of one unit of y.
At Point C, the individual now consumes a large amount
of x and very little y, so to give up 1 unit of y, 20 units of
x would be needed to retain the same utility as before.

Why do economists expect such preference
relations to hold? First, upon reflection most of us would
say that this is the way we would behave in this trade-off
situation. Second, the opposite proposition seems highly
unlikely. It would say that the less you have of a good,
the less you would want of it relative to other goods; and
the more you had of a good, the more valuable additional
units of it would become. Indifference curves reflect the
concept of diminishing marginal utility in both goods
without assigning numerical values to utility.

Diminishing Marginal Rates of Substitution

The trade-off ratio along the indifference
curve is called the marginal rate of substitution. The
marginal rate of substitution (MRS) of x for y,
MRS_{xy}, shows the willingness of the consumer to substitute between the goods; that is,

$$MRS_{xy} = \frac{\text{number of units of } y \text{ given up}}{\text{number of units of } x \text{ gained}}.$$

In Figure 7A–3, the MRS_{xy} at Point A is $1/2$;
that is, one unit of y must be sacrificed to gain two units
of x. At Point B, the MRS_{xy} is $1/5$ and at Point C, it is
$1/20$. The declining value of MRS_{xy} is a reflection of the
**principle of diminishing marginal rates of substi-
tution**, showing that as more of one good (x) is substituted for the other good (y), the value of Good x in
terms of Good y declines.

Budget Constraints

An indifference map makes it possible to
compare points representing combinations of Goods x
and y to determine whether the individual prefers one
such combination or feels indifferent among several. All
points on any single indifference curve are equivalent
to each other in utility, even if utility cannot be measured. Points on indifference curves located to the right
and above other indifference curves are preferred
combinations.

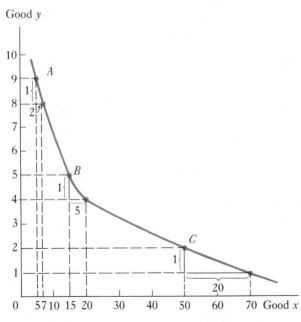

Good y

FIGURE 7A-3
CONVEXITY FEATURE OF INDIFFERENCE CURVES
A typical indifference curve is convex to the origin. This
convexity means that it takes increasingly larger amounts of
the abundant good to compensate for losses of the good that
is becoming more scarce.

Which combinations of commodities are actually attainable for Mary? The answer depends on the income available to her and on the prices of the commodities. Keep in mind that Mary faces prices that are determined in markets and she cannot influence them. Income constrains her from buying all that might be desired. Her income is her budget constraint and, when drawn on the indifference map, is called the *budget line*.

We limit the analysis to two goods (you could think of one of the goods as "all other goods"). To remain consistent with our earlier example, assume that Mary can consume either slices of pizza or cans of Coke. Suppose she has a disposable income (*DI*) of $10.00 and now pizza and Coke sell for $1.00 and $.50, respectively, per unit. The construction of the budget line is illustrated in Figure 7A–4. If she spends the entire income (*DI*) on pizza, she can buy ten slices of pizza. This number is determined by dividing income by the price of the good

$$\frac{DI}{P_y}$$

In this case,

$$\frac{\$10.00}{\$1.00} = 10 \text{ slices of pizza.}$$

Thus, 10 is the *y*-intercept. The *x*-intercept is calculated in the same manner:

$$\frac{DI}{P_x} = \frac{\$10.00}{\$.50} = 20 \text{ cans of Coke.}$$

A straight line connecting the two points that represent buying all of Good *y* (pizza) or all of Good *x* (Coke) will show all possible combinations that Mary can purchase with a given income level. For example, $10 will buy five slices of pizza and ten Cokes or six slices of pizza and eight Cokes. Any combination outside (to the northeast of) the line is unattainable at that income level; it is outside her budget constraint. In other words, the budget line is the dividing line between those combinations that are attainable and those that are unattainable at a given level of prices and a given level of income.

Changes in Income and Changes in Prices

The budget line was developed holding prices and income constant. How do changes in income and prices affect the budget line? An increase in income means that more of both goods can be purchased, if prices stay the same. A doubling of income means that twice as much of both goods can be purchased, if prices remain constant. Increases in income are represented by a parallel outward shift of the budget line. Decreases in income are represented by a parallel inward shift of the budget line. Two such shifts are shown in Figure 7A–5.

A change in the price of one good only affects the maximum amount of that good that can be

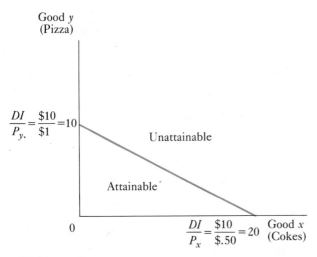

FIGURE 7A–4
BUDGET LINE
A budget line graphically depicts the consumption combinations that are attainable with a given level of income. Any combination above the line is unattainable.

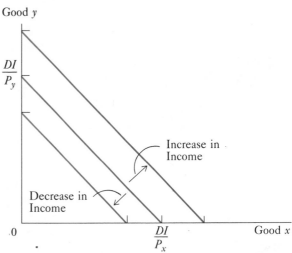

FIGURE 7A–5
THE EFFECT OF INCOME CHANGES ON BUDGET LINES
An increase in income is represented by an outward parallel shift of the budget line. A decrease in income is represented by an inward parallel shift of the budget line.

purchased, not the maximum amount of the other good that can be purchased. If the price of Coke rises and Mary spends all her income on pizza, the price rise has had no effect on the amount of pizza purchased. A price rise, then, will only affect the budget line intercept of the good that has experienced the price rise. Such a change is shown in Figure 7A–6. A price rise for Good x from P_{x1} to P_{x2} causes the budget line intercept to move closer to the origin, reflecting the fact that less x can now be purchased with the constant income. A decrease in the price of Good x to P_{x3} would mean more x could be purchased and the intercept would move away from the origin, reflecting increases in the potential consumption of Good x.

Price changes cause the slope of the budget line to change. The slope of the budget line is $\Delta y/\Delta x$. Notice that the slope is the negative of the ratio of the vertical intercept to the horizontal intercept, or

$$-\frac{\dfrac{DI}{P_y}}{\dfrac{DI}{P_x}}$$

which is equal to

$$-\frac{P_x}{P_y}.$$

So, we can say that the slope of the budget line changes when the ratio of prices changes. A change in income, on the other hand, represents no change in relative prices, so the slope of the budget line remains the same, as reflected by the parallel shifting of the budget line described above.

■ Maximization of Consumer Satisfaction

Adding a budget line to an indifference map makes it possible to demonstrate maximization of consumer satisfaction, as in Figure 7A–7. At Point A on Indifference Curve I_2, the budget line and Indifference Curve I_2 are tangent. Any Point on I_3, such as Point B, is preferred to Point A because higher indifference curves represent higher levels of utility. However, Point B is not attainable because it is outside the budget line. Point C on I_1 is attainable, but a point on Indifference Curve I_2 also is attainable, and any point on I_2 represents more satisfaction than any point on I_1. Mary wants to reach the highest attainable indifference curve. The highest attainable curve would be one that is tangent to the budget line because no higher indifference curve can be reached with the given income and prices. So in this example, Mary is maximizing utility, or is in equilibrium, at Point A on Indifference Curve I_2.

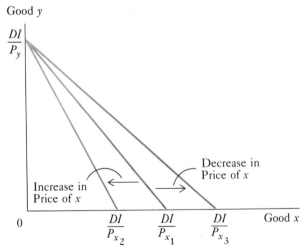

FIGURE 7A-6
THE EFFECT OF PRICE CHANGES ON BUDGET LINES
An increase in the price of one good changes the slope of the budget line because if all disposable income is spent on the item, less of it can be purchased. As a result, the intercept of the budget line will shift closer to the origin. The opposite holds for a decrease in price.

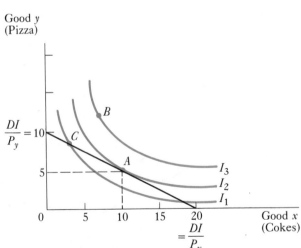

FIGURE 7A-7
CONSUMER MAXIMIZATION
An individual maximizes consumer satisfaction where the budget line is tangent to the highest attainable indifference curve.

You should remember from geometry that two curves that are tangent have equal slopes at the point of tangency. At the point of tangency between the indifference curve and the budget line, the marginal rate of substitution is equal to the ratio of the price of x to the price of y; that is,[a]

$$MRS_{xy} = \frac{P_x}{P_y}.$$

This may seem like a great deal of theoretical mumbo jumbo, but the common sense of it is that the marginal rate of substitution expresses the willingness of the consumer to trade a certain amount of x for a certain amount of y, and the slope of the budget line reflects the market's willingness to trade a certain amount of x for a certain amount of y. The impersonal forces of the market impose the relative price on the consumer, so the consumer adjusts consumption amounts in such a way that his or her trade-off is the same as that of the market.

Look at Figure 7A–8. Suppose you are consuming 15 units of y and 5 units of x (you are at Point A). According to your indifference curve (I_1), you would be willing to give up five units of y if you received two additional units of x; but the market is willing to give you five units of x in exchange for five units of y (note Point B). We would expect to see you consuming less y and more x. In fact, you will be able to increase your utility by moving in the direction of the tangency of some higher indifference curve and the budget line.

Consumer Reaction to Income Changes

The real value of indifference curve analysis is that it allows us to study the reaction of consumers to price and income changes. Using the indifference map and the budget line, we can trace through the adjustment process that takes place when a household experiences a change in income. In Figure 7A–9, if the consumer's income is DI_1, and x and y sell for P_x and P_y respectively, the optimum utility is at Point A. A decrease in income is represented by DI_0, and two increases in income are represented by DI_2 and DI_3. The respective optimum positions representing tangencies of a budget line and an indifference curve are Points B, C, and D. Connecting these points generates an **income-consumption curve** that shows how consumption of the two goods changes as income changes. Recall the discussion of the income elasticity of demand. The income elasticities of both Good x and Good y in Figure

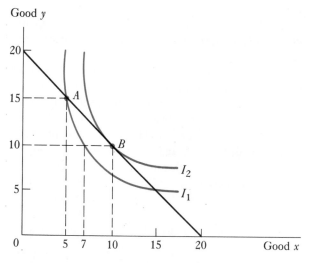

Good y

FIGURE 7A-8
TANGENCY SOLUTION ONCE AGAIN
Lower indifference curves that are within the budget constraint represent lower levels of utility than the highest, but still attainable, indifference curve.

a. Technically, MRS_{xy} is equal to the negative of the slope of the indifference curve. The price ratio, as we have seen, is the negative of the slope of the budget line. Therefore, at the (equilibrium) point of tangency between the indifference curve and the budget line, $MRS_{xy} = P_x/P_y$.

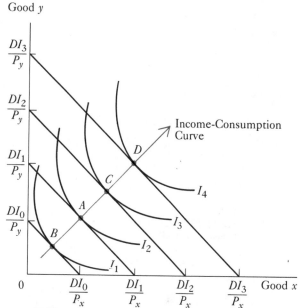

Good y

FIGURE 7A-9
INCOME CHANGES AND THE INCOME-CONSUMPTION CURVE
An income-consumption curve traces the response of consumption combinations to changes in income.

7A–9 are positive because consumption of both goods increases as income increases. (Remember that a positive income elasticity indicates that a good is a normal good. An inferior good would have a negative income elasticity since, in that case, as income increases, consumption of the good decreases.)

Figure 7A–10 shows a case where one commodity, Good x, is a normal good for this person until the individual's income reaches DI_3. But, when income increases above DI_3, less x is bought as income increases. So x is a normal good up to Point A and then becomes an inferior good as the income-consumption curve bends backward. There is nothing derogatory about the term inferior. A daily newspaper might be considered an inferior good; as income falls, a person buys the paper more often because it is a less expensive form of entertainment and also because it offers job listings. Remember, also, that a normal good to some people may be an inferior good to others.

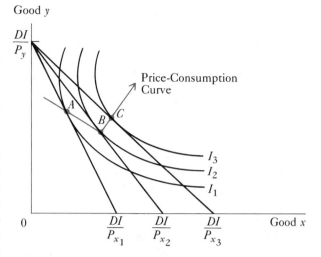

FIGURE 7A-11
PRICE-CONSUMPTION CURVE
A price-consumption curve depicts how consumption changes when relative prices change.

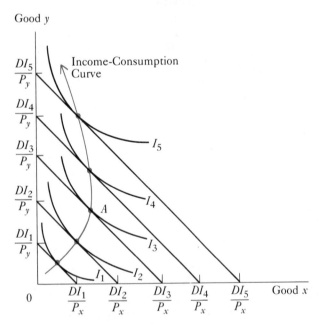

FIGURE 7A-10
INCOME-CONSUMPTION CURVE
FOR AN INFERIOR GOOD
The income-consumption curve for an inferior good bends backward, indicating that less of the good is consumed as income increases beyond a certain level.

Consumer Reaction to Price Changes

Let us now see how the optimum consumption combination will be affected by price changes. Initially the consumer is at the point of maximum utility (Point A in Figure 7A–11). As the price of x falls from P_{x1} to P_{x2}, the budget line rotates out to intersect the x-axis at DI/P_{x2}, and the consumer now has a new optimum at Point B on Indifference Curve I_2. Another decrease in price to P_{x3} allows the consumer to reach a still higher indifference curve, I_3, and a new optimum at Point C. Connecting the points produces a **price-consumption curve**, which shows how consumption changes when relative prices change.

The theory behind this change in consumption patterns is the income and substitution effects once again. When the price of a commodity falls, there are two forces at work to cause the consumer to increase purchases of that commodity. First, when the price of a good falls, the market trade-off between this good and other goods (or the substitution rate) changes. This is the *substitution effect*. Second, the individual has a larger real income, meaning that with the same nominal income, more of both (or all) commodities can be purchased (and will be purchased as long as the good is not an inferior good). This is the *income effect*.

Indifference Analysis and the Law of Demand

Indifference analysis can be used to derive an individual's demand curve and demonstrate the law of demand. This demonstration is a *ceteris paribus* experiment in which the price of one commodity is changed. Figure 7A–12, Panel (*a*), shows an indifference map and a budget line for Goods x and y. The consumer is at

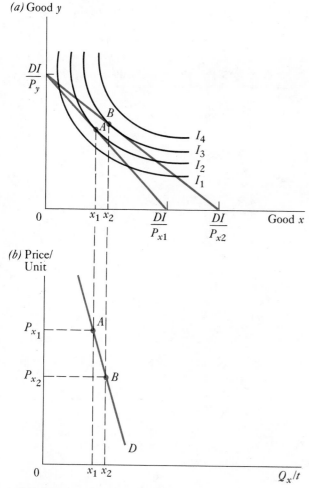

FIGURE 7A-12
DERIVING A DEMAND CURVE
When the price of Good x decreases, the consumer can
reach a higher indifference curve. This increased
consumption of Good x at a lower price means that the
demand curve must have a negative slope.

an optimum at Point A. At Point A, the individual consumes x_1 units of x at a price of P_{x1}. Price and quantity of Good x are plotted on Panel (b). Now let the price of x fall to P_{x2}. As before, this decline in price causes the budget line to rotate outward. A new optimum is reached at Point B, where the new budget line is tangent

to indifference curve I_3. The change in price has caused the quantity demanded to increase from x_1 to x_2. This increase in quantity demanded also is plotted on Panel (b). The line connecting two price-quantity points in Panel (b) is a demand curve, and this demand curve has the usual negative slope.

PART THREE

MARKETS

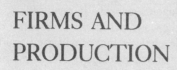

CHAPTER 8

FIRMS AND PRODUCTION

INTRODUCTION

The next two chapters set the stage for examining the behavior of firms. Before we can analyze firms as sellers of products in different types of markets, it is necessary to understand firms as purchasers of factors of production. The firm buys factors of production (the terms *factors of production* and *inputs* are used as synonyms) and attempts to transform them into marketable outputs. This chapter examines the transformation process, which economists call **production**.

PRODUCTION
The transformation of inputs into marketable outputs.

THE FIRM IN THEORY

It is easy to take the existence of firms and firm organization for granted because we have all had dealings with all types of firms. We need to stop, however, to ask why firms exist. Economic theory recognizes that firms exist to accomplish economic objectives and are organized in different ways to meet specific objectives.

Households As Firms

In many ways, households compete with firms. If firms exist to organize production and if households also organize some production, there are aspects of household activity that are similar to the activities of firms. Firms put "things" together to make other "things" that have economic value. Households clearly do likewise. Households cook meals, as do restaurants; households make clothes, as do tailors; households organize entertainment, as do movie theaters.

An interesting economic question is why households don't do everything for themselves. Why don't they make their own automobiles, for example? That's an easy one. They don't make their own automobiles because it is more efficient for them to buy automobiles from other firms.

163

It gets more difficult when we ask why households don't make their own granola or build their own homes. The answer is that some do. And as the price of granola and homes (produced by firms) increases, more households will compete with organized firms to produce their own products for consumption.

In fact, as relative market prices change, the amount of production carried out by households changes. In recent years, many households have started to grow their own vegetables in response to both rising food prices and the lifestyle changes that emphasized gourmet cooking with high-quality, organically grown vegetables. This home production, in turn, affected the demand for products of organized firms that produced canning equipment and related products.

What Business Firms Do

Firms are organizations that plan production. They assign tasks, monitor those tasks, and generate incentives that reward individuals for completing those assigned tasks. We have just seen that households fit into this definition. An important question is why there are so many different-sized firms. At one extreme, households behave like very small firms, and at the other, governments can serve as extremely large, multipurpose firms. In the Soviet Union, the government acts as a single firm in that it plans, organizes, and provides the incentives. Within the category of business firms, there is great diversity. Many firms in the U.S. economy are **vertically integrated**, which means they combine many steps in the production process. For example, they may grow cotton, weave cloth, print the cloth, and finally sew it into garments. Other firms not vertically integrated may simply make garments. Still other firms are **horizontally integrated**, which means that they combine many production operations in the same industry. Still other firms are **conglomerates**, which means that they consist of many, often quite unrelated, activities.

Economic theory should help explain why these different organizations can all exist in a market economy. Part of the answer to this question can be found in the incentives that bring about firm organization. Professor Ronald Coase, in a now-famous article, showed that transaction costs create firms.[1] He argued that buying and selling imposes costs. **Transaction costs** are costs associated with the conduct of a business; organizing and negotiating involve costs. These transaction costs are minimized by the formation of firms. What Coase was talking about was the fact that a buyer and seller in a market economy must continually explore options. Buyers must search for quality and price. Sellers must monitor the demands of buyers.

The transaction costs of these activities often can be reduced by carrying out more research and exploration within a firm. Workers agree to join a firm that provides a workplace, incentives, and guidelines. The firm exists because it economizes the transaction costs. But the organization also faces constraints. Costs may rise as the size and complexity of the firm increase. Thus, smaller firms (maybe even households) will be-

VERTICAL INTEGRATION
The combination of many steps in the production process.

HORIZONTAL INTEGRATION
The combination of many production operations in the same industry.

CONGLOMERATE
The combination of many unrelated operations in a single firm.

TRANSACTION COSTS
Costs associated with the conduct of a business; organizing and negotiating involve costs.

1. Ronald Coase, "The Nature of the Firm," *Economica* (November 1937): 286–405.

come potential competitors. In other words, firms exist in many organizational forms and sizes because different forms and sizes make efficient use of information in reducing transaction costs for different kinds of production activities.

Recent developments in this theory of firm organization have added other elements to the reasons why firms exist. Armen Alchian and Harold Demsetz, both of UCLA, have added some new insights.[2] There are two important elements to their analysis. First, firms exist because the production of many types of products is more efficiently carried out by teams than by individuals. **Teams** are groups of employees that work together to produce something. Firms exist to organize teams to exploit these economies. Secondly, in team production that is not organized in a firm (e.g., volunteer activities), it is difficult to measure the contribution of the individual team members, and there are incentives to **shirk**; i.e., to not put forth the agreed-to effort.

The firm exists to reward individuals for team effort and to monitor shirking behavior. Management is primarily responsible for developing organizational forms that use both negative and positive incentives in order to limit shirking.

THE BUSINESS FIRM IN PRACTICE

The **business firm** is organized by an entrepreneur or group of entrepreneurs to combine inputs of raw materials, capital, labor services, and organization technology to produce marketable outputs of goods and services. Firms are parts of industries. There are many ways to define an **industry**, but, in general, what economists mean by an industry is a group of firms producing similar or related products. For example, the automobile industry might include just the big three—General Motors, Ford, and Chrysler. Or we might extend the coverage to include all foreign makers and all small domestic producers. The industry also might include firms that supply parts, materials, and services to automobile producers or to automobile consumers. There are no absolute rules on how to define a particular industry. The definition usually depends on the purpose or the particular problem or issue being studied.

In the United States, firms are organized primarily in one of three ways. These categories are legal, not economic, and they differ mainly as to the legal liability of the owners. There are some interesting economic questions that arise because of the differences in treatment under the law, but these are not important at this point.

Sole Proprietorships

In the **sole proprietorship** form of enterprise, no legal distinction is made between the owner and the firm. The financial resources of the firm are limited to those of the individual owner and what can be

TEAMS
Groups of employees that work together to produce something.

SHIRK
Not putting forth agreed-to effort.

BUSINESS FIRM
An organization formed by an entrepreneur to transform inputs into marketable outputs.

INDUSTRY
A group of firms producing similar or related products.

SOLE PROPRIETORSHIP
The form of business enterprise in which no legal distinction is made between the firm and its owner.

2. Armen A. Alchian and Harold Demsetz, "Production, Information Costs and Economic Organization," *American Economic Review* (December 1972): 777–795.

borrowed from friends or financial institutions. Thus, the profits and losses accrue solely to that individual. Success of the firm is success of the owner; bankruptcy of the firm is bankruptcy of the owner. This intimate relationship usually means a constant involvement of the owner with the affairs of the firm; and obviously, there are great incentives for hard work and diligence.

Compared to other forms of business enterprise, a proprietorship can go into or out of business very easily. In certain lines of business, government approval is required, as licenses or permits may be needed; but typically, the single proprietor starts and ends a business by simply doing so. More than 75 percent of the business firms in the United States are sole proprietorships. Most farmers and many small firms, especially in retailing and services, are sole proprietorships. Although dominant in numbers, sole proprietorships account for only 10 percent of annual business sales.

Partnerships

PARTNERSHIP
The form of business enterprise in which there is more than one owner, and the firm does not have a legal existence separate from the owners.

Partnerships are similar to sole proprietorships except they have more than one owner, and the firm does not have a legal existence separate from the owners. There are more personal and financial resources available to a partnership than if only one person formed the firm. Each partner brings to the relationship special skills, knowledge, energy, and decision-making powers. Offsetting these advantages are the inevitable frictions that arise in operating the firm. Partners have to agree on the proportions of ownership owned by each partner, which may be dictated by the amounts of funds contributed, the amounts of work, or the amounts of other kinds of value contributed (such as ideas or patents). Joint rights and responsibilities have to be agreed upon. The partners share in any profits but also share legal liability for any debts incurred by the enterprise.

The disadvantages of the partnership arrangement apparently outweigh the advantages, since less than 10 percent of the business organizations and only 5 percent of annual sales in the United States are accounted for by this form of business. Like sole proprietorships, firms organized as partnerships tend to be quite small; they are typically found in professional services—medicine, law, consulting, and some financial services.

Corporations

CORPORATION
The form of business enterprise in which stockholders are the legal owners of the firm. The legal liability of the stockholders is limited.

The dominant form of business organization in the United States, measured in any way except by absolute number, is the *corporate* form. A **corporation** is the form of business enterprise in which stockholders are the legal owners of the firm. The legal liability of the stockholders is limited. Corporations account for slightly less than 15 percent of business firms but about 85 percent of annual business sales.

A corporation is a more formal and complex organization than the others. Owners of a corporation are called **stockholders**. Their numbers may run into the hundreds of thousands, although some corporations have only a few stockholders. The stockholders vote, according to the number of shares held, for a board of directors, which in turn appoints officers of the corporation to manage the corporation along the guidelines set by the charter of incorporation and the directors. A **board of directors** consists of the individuals elected by the stockholders of a corporation to select the managers and oversee the management of the corporation.

One of the strengths of the corporate form of business organization is the relative ease of acquiring capital, either by issuing additional shares of **stock**, which are certificates demonstrating ownership in the corporation; by borrowing through the issuance of **bonds**, which are interest-bearing certificates issued by governments or corporations; or by borrowing directly by loans from banks or other financial agencies. (Only the third option can create outside funding for partnerships and proprietorships.)

The attractiveness of the corporation as a form of organization stems from the fact that the stockholders of the corporation are the legal owners and have rights to the profits, but their legal liability is very limited. **Limited liability** refers to the fact that the stockholders of a corporation cannot be sued for failure of the corporation to pay its debts; only the corporation itself can be sued. This limited liability aspect is the critical advantage of the corporate form of business. In fact, in many countries corporations are referred to as limited liability companies and often have the letters *Ltd.* after the name of the firm to stress this feature to anyone who might deal with the enterprise. The letters *Inc.* (Incorporated) after the name of a firm in the United States mean the same thing. A stockholder cannot be sued for failure of the corporation to pay its debts; only the corporation can be sued. Thus, the corporation, defined in law as a legal person in its own right, can go bankrupt without the owners going bankrupt. Of course, if individuals have most of their wealth in the stock of one corporation, they might go bankrupt because the stock would no longer have any value.

A second and very important attraction of corporate organization is the ease of transferring ownership. Ownership rights can be transferred through the sale of stocks, and markets (stock exchanges) have evolved to facilitate the transfer. The costs of transfer of ownership are for this reason significantly lower for corporations than for partnerships or sole proprietorships.

Different types of ownership cause managers of firms to behave in different ways. For instance, an owner-manager of a single proprietorship may make decisions that are different from those of the hired manager of a large corporation. For now, we will ignore these differences and assume that firms, however they are organized, exist for only one purpose: to increase the wealth of owners. To do this, firms try to maximize their profits. This assumption of profit maximization makes it possible to develop a powerful predictive theory about the economic effects of different market structures.

STOCKHOLDERS
The owners of a corporation.

BOARD OF DIRECTORS
The individuals elected by the stockholders of a corporation to select th managers and oversee the management o the corporation.

STOCKS
Certificates of ownership in a corporation

BONDS
Interest-earning certificates issued by governments or corporations as a method of borrowing money.

LIMITED LIABILITY
The fact that the stockholders of a corporation cannot be sued for failure of the corporation to pay its debts; only the corporation itself can be sued.

THE INTERNATIONAL PERSPECTIVE LABOR-MANAGED FIRMS AND WORKERS SELF-MANAGEMENT IN YUGOSLAVIA

In the United States, there have been a few experiments with labor-managed firms. In contrast, almost all firms in Yugoslavia are owned and managed by the workers.

In the United States, this phenomenon exists in a few craft industries and has been attempted in a few. in-stances when manufacturing plants were about to close, mostly in the steel industry. The closest parallel to a labor-managed firm in the United States is profit-sharing by labor in some industries. In Yugoslavia, the workers own the plant and decide how it will be managed through councils. This is an interesting concept for a socialist country because worker democracy is closer to Marxist philosophy than the state-owned and -managed firms that exist in most communist countries. The interesting question is how such organization and control by workers affects incentives and ultimately the economic development of the country.

Entrepreneurs maximize profits. If the firm is owned by workers, is something other than profit going to be maximized? Worker self-management means that workers would seek to maximize wages and other benefits that they can capture while they are with the firm. Since workers have no ownership rights in the firm that they can sell, they will opt for a management policy that increases the short-term income of the firm at the expense of policies that would increase the firm's value over time. This bias will tend to reduce the firm's investments which in turn (in the aggregate) reduces the long-term economic growth of the country.

For more on this topic see: John H. Moore, *Growth With Self-Management* (Stanford: Hoover Institution Press, 1980).

Enterprise, Entrepreneurs, and the Firm

The factor of production enterprise is provided by the entrepreneur. The entrepreneur is the founder and often the guiding spirit of the business firm. Many business schools are even offering courses in entrepreneurship. But what is it that entrepreneurs do? The textbook answer is that they identify consumer demands, they organize production, they allocate resources, and they acquire real capital assets. In the process, they take risks and are rewarded with profits if they have good hunches or go bankrupt if they are wrong. Many more go bankrupt than get fabulously wealthy, yet we read in the newspapers about the most successful. A *Fortune* survey about getting rich in America concluded that "most successful entrepreneurs didn't start out as fortune seekers; they were pursuing visions, not the almighty buck."[3]

3. Monci Jo Williams, "How the Wealthy Get That Way," *Fortune* (April 13, 1987): 38.

ENTREPRENEUR EXTRAORDINAIRE: LIZ CLAIBORNE

Elisabeth Claiborne Ortenberg started with a dream of designing clothes for professional women. She hoped to get her name on the label and build a success-ful small business. By paying great attention to detail and marketing what she did, she instead created a Fortune 500 firm.

Liz Claiborne and her husband Arthur Ortenberg started what is now Liz Claiborne, Inc., in 1976. It is by any account a marketing success. She was one of the first to have the idea of designing fashionable clothes for professional women. The clothes are designed with the intent to look good on the body style of American professional women, rather than runway models. There is a constant flow (six changes a year) of fresh designs that are not faddish.

Claiborne and her husband work ten-hour days in Manhattan. She oversees the designers and he, as *Fortune* magazine reports, is the man behind the door, "intellectual and godlike." *Fortune* reports that they both are "intense, a bit arrogant, and obsessed about the high quality of Liz Claiborne clothes."

The Ortenbergs, like most entrepreneurs, work long hours with single-minded dedication to their idea. They then market what they produce with superb results. They concentrate on their firm, leading relatively simple lives. When asked the value of her 4.3 percent share in Liz Claiborne, Inc., she responded "a couple of million." The correct answer—over $80 million!

Source: "The Years 50 Most Fascinating Business People," *Fortune* (January 5, 1987).

THE NONPROFIT FIRM

Economic models assume that firms exist to maximize profits or wealth, but there are increasingly large numbers of firms that are organized as nonprofit organizations. These firms are conspicuously different from for-profit firms in that they do not have a residual claimant. A **residual claimant** is economics jargon for individuals, or groups of individuals, who share profits (if any). Another way of saying this same thing is that it is difficult to determine who owns these nonprofits. We can separate these nonprofits into two categories: private sector and government sector.

RESIDUAL CLAIMANT
Individuals, or groups of individuals, who share profits.

Nonprofit—Private Sector

The first category is nonprofit, private sector firms; these firms are not part of, or sponsored directly by, a governmental unit. They exist for many reasons; most of them are engaged in private transfers (e.g., health clinics and soup kitchens) or providing collective goods that cannot conveniently be provided through government.

The manager (organizer) of these private nonprofits usually receives a salary for managing the firm. Economists would expect more shirking behavior in these firms because the manager cannot convert increased efficiencies into profits that affect his or her salary. This shirking behavior has been documented by economists. Ken Clarkson of the University of Miami found that nonprofit hospitals devoted more budget expense to supervisory positions than for-profit hospitals did.[4] The chief manager of a nonprofit hospital also was much less concerned with the price and productivity of equipment. Automatic, across-the-board pay increases were more frequently used in nonprofit hospitals. This method of determining raises is a type of shirking behavior because it is hard work to separate good employees from bad employees.

Most economists would argue that these nonprofit firms have significant organizational disadvantages that introduce the inefficiencies we have been discussing. Yet they have grown rapidly in recent years. Why, given this managerial inefficiency, have they become such a popular form of organization?

Earl Thompson of UCLA has suggested an answer.[5] Thompson points out that most nonprofit firms are associated with charitable organizations. He concludes that contributors to these charitable organizations usually are remote from the production of the product or service they are supporting. While they pay for the products or services, they normally are not the beneficiaries of those services. These contributors would have a difficult time monitoring the manager of the charitable firm; they wouldn't know if the manager was using their gift to produce the charitable product or if the manager was simply "taking their gift home" in the form of higher wages. Thompson argues that the way around this problem is to specify a certain salary to the manager.

Thompson concludes that one reason for the growth of nonprofit private firms in some sectors is that the inefficiencies caused by the lack of managers who are profit seekers are less costly to contributors than is monitoring manager behavior. As a result, charitable donors tolerate some inefficiency in nonprofit firms in preference to supporting the provision of these services through the for-profit sector.

It is also true that tax laws play a role in encouraging the formation of nonprofit organizations. In some cases, individuals can create nonprofit firms that produce output they desire to consume for themselves. They can then support this production through tax deductible, charitable contributions. You might, for example, create a nonprofit organization to support the training of Olympic athletes and make gifts to this nonprofit organization tax deductible.

---

4. Kenneth W. Clarkson, "Some Implications of Property Rights in Hospital Management," *Journal of Law and Economics* (October 1972): 363–384.

5. Earl Thompson, "Charity and Nonprofit Organizations," *The Economics of Nonproprietary Organizations*, ed. K.W. Clarkson and D.C. Martin (Greenwich, NJ: JAI Press, 1980): 125–128.

Nonprofit—Government Sector

Everyone does business with some governmental firms. Often these governmental firms compete directly with private, for-profit firms. The U.S. Postal Service competes with the United Parcel Service and Federal Express. City and county hospitals compete with private hospitals. Municipal golf and tennis clubs compete with private country clubs. City bus lines compete with private cab companies. Let's not forget the competition between public and private colleges and universities. The list goes on and on.

How do these governmental firms compare with the private firm we are studying? To begin, like the private nonprofit firm, there is no profit and no residual claimant to that profit. Secondly, the manager of the governmental nonprofit usually has little control over price. If a price is charged, the price setting usually is done by a board or some political entity. The price is often substantially below the operating costs of the firm.

In addition, the "customer" often has many ways to influence the behavior of the organization. Unless the government forbids competition, the customer can buy from private firms or can exert influence through the political process.

The tendency to shirk is certainly prevalent in governmental firms for the same reasons given for the private nonprofit firm. In addition, a bureaucratic manager can advance by being "better" than other bureaucratic managers. In many instances, causing your agency to grow is taken as a sign of success and for advancement. We will discuss this bureaucratic incentive in a later chapter.

It generally is held by economists that the quality of products produced by governmental nonprofit firms is often below that of similar private sector, for-profit firms. This results from the fact that prices of the government firm are usually lower, and customers often will choose the low-priced product, even though it is of lower quality. Research on Veterans Administration hospitals relative to private, for-profit hospitals confirms this observation.[6]

Nonprofits: What About Their Profits?

In recent years, many private and governmental nonprofit organizations have entered into profit-making activities. These profit-making activities are often euphemistically labeled "excess of revenues over expenses." Hospitals are selling health-related equipment, universities are selling in-company training programs, university presses are looking for "best sellers," alumni groups are selling tours, and churches are selling condos at religious theme parks.

Profits from such activities aren't taxed because they are intertwined with the nonprofit organizations' noncommercial activities. In addi-

6. See C.M. Lindsay, "A Theory of Government Enterprise," *Journal of Political Economy* (October 1976): 1061–1077.

tion, these nonprofit organizations often have access to referrals and free space for doing business. They can also use bulk mail compared to first-class in the private sector. This presents a cost advantage to these firms over private sector firms in the same business.

Delegates to the 1986 White House Conference on Small Business voted that nonprofit organizations using their tax exempt status to compete with the private sector was the number three problem facing small business. It ranked third after liability insurance problems and governmentally mandated employee benefits.

This subsidized competition from nonprofit organizations has become such a significant problem for private sector firms that they have put pressure on the U.S. Congress to change the law as it relates to profit-making activity on tax exempt nonprofit organizations. In 1987, the House Ways and Means Committee held comprehensive hearings on the tax status of nonprofit organizations. As one witness, a travel agent from New Jersey put it, "I'm not opposed to the Girl Scouts having an annual cookie sale, but if the Girl Scouts want to open a cookie store next door to a Mrs. Fields cookie store, they should have to pay the same taxes."[7]

ECONOMIC EFFICIENCY

The firms that produce most of the U.S. output are private, profit-maximizing firms. The entrepreneur must combine the factors of production efficiently if the firm is to maximize profits. To do this, entrepreneurs must decide among competing ways of producing a given output. Suppose, for example, the printer, in deciding how to produce this textbook, was faced with the alternatives listed in Table 8–1. The production engineer has told the production chief that 100,000 copies of this textbook could be produced in any of four ways. The engineer has determined the alternative ways to produce the textbook; it is now up to the entrepreneur to decide how to actually produce the textbooks. The entrepreneur must have a decision rule in order to select a production alternative. This is where profit maximization comes into play. Without profit maximization as a goal, the entrepreneur would have to choose on some other basis—perhaps on a physical-units basis. The method that would minimize the inputs in a physical sense would be Method *A*, which uses the fewest inputs. This method of choosing is based on technical efficiency. **Technical efficiency** refers to a method of production that minimizes physical usage of inputs according to some specific rule. A drawback of this method is that it compares physical units of machines, acres of land, and worker-years of labor.

Such a method might be used in a command economy, such as the Soviet Union. A market system, however, puts the inputs into dollar terms and lets the entrepreneur choose the least-cost method of producing. The least-cost method is based on **economic efficiency**. The least-cost method, or the economically efficient method, would always be chosen by the entrepreneur because of the assumption of attempted profit maximization. In Table 8–1, the entrepreneur would choose Method *C* to

TECHNICAL EFFICIENCY
A method of production that minimizes physical usage of inputs according to some specific rule.

ECONOMIC EFFICIENCY
The least-cost method of production.

7. "Profits? Who, me?" *Forbes* (March 23, 1987): 108.

TABLE 8-1
ALTERNATIVE WAYS TO PRODUCE 100,000 COPIES
OF THIS TEXTBOOK

	Capital (Machines) ■	Labor (Worker-Years) ■	Land (Acres) ■	Output ■
METHOD: A	5	5	1	100,000
B	4	10	1	100,000
C	3	15	1	100,000
D	2	25	1	100,000

- Price of:

  Capital Services $30,000 per Machine
  Labor Services $ 4,000 per Worker-Year
  Land Services $10,000 per Acre

- Cost of:

  $A = \$150,000 + 20,000 + 10,000 = \$180,000$
  $B = \$120,000 + 40,000 + 10,000 = \$170,000$
  $C = \$ 90,000 + 60,000 + 10,000 = \$160,000$
  $D = \$ 60,000 + 100,000 + 10,000 = \$170,000$

produce the textbooks. Regardless of the price of the textbooks, Method *C* maximizes profits (or minimizes losses) because costs are minimized.

PRODUCTION FUNCTIONS IN THE SHORT AND LONG RUN

A **production function** is a description of the amounts of output expected from various combinations of input usage. It usually is expressed in tabular or graphic form, but it also can be shown by a mathematical formula. The production function describes a technical or technological relationship. The input combinations and their corresponding output quantities, which make up the production function, are determined by engineers, agronomists, chemists, and other technical experts. Only the best input combinations are included. For example, it might be that an output of 100 units of a commodity could be produced by 5 units of capital, 20 units of labor, and 2 units of land, or by 6 units of capital, 30 units of labor, and 3 units of land. The second combination is inferior to the first because it takes more of all inputs to produce the same output. That method of production would be ignored. The production function is a reflection of the best technology available for a given level of output in the production process.

Usually entrepreneurs are interested in only a portion of the production function. For instance, it is often convenient to ask what would happen to total production if all but one of the inputs were at a given, fixed level and only the remaining input was allowed to change in amount. Then it is possible to distinguish between fixed factors and variable factors. **Fixed factors** are the factors of production that cannot be varied in the short run, such as the size of the plant. **Variable factors** are the factors of production that can be increased or decreased in the short run. Which

PRODUCTION FUNCTION
A description of the amounts of output expected from various combinations of input usage.

FIXED FACTORS
The factors of production that cannot be varied in the short run, such as the size of the plant.

VARIABLE FACTORS
The factors of production that can be increased or decreased in the short run.

factors are fixed and which are variable usually depends on the problem under consideration, although in many cases it is natural to think of the land and the buildings of a firm (the physical plant) as the fixed factors and labor as the variable factor.

When economists distinguish between fixed and variable factors, they consider what is called the short run. The **short run** is the period of time too short to vary all the factors of production. The **long run** is the period of time in which all inputs, including plant and equipment, can be varied. *Short-run* decisions are those concerning the profit-maximizing use of the existing plant and equipment. The plant is used more intensively by increasing the amount of variable factors, such as labor or additional machines. *Long-run* decisions are those concerning the selection of a plant size that will maximize profits.

These different time horizons may not correspond to time in the calendar sense. Some industries may be able to increase in size very rapidly. In some cases, contractions can occur more quickly, depending on whether the plant and equipment are adaptable for use in other industries. It is primarily for convenience of analysis that decisions are classed as being either short-run or long-run decisions. Keep in mind that these decisions are inherently interrelated. Once a long-run decision to build a plant of a certain size is made, a whole series of short-run decisions are influenced because they must deal with this certain-size plant.

Increasing and Decreasing Returns

As more and more units of a variable factor are added to a set of fixed factors, the resulting additions to output eventually will become increasingly smaller. This economic phenomenon is referred to as the **principle of diminishing returns**. It is plausible that returns are eventually diminishing because, otherwise, all the wheat needed to feed the world could be produced on one acre of land by just adding more seed, more fertilizer, more water, and more labor to that acre of land.

The principle of diminishing returns is a fascinating and pervasive phenomenon. The principle is almost never contradicted in real-world observations. Why is it that a tree grows more slowly as it grows larger? Why do little pigs put on more weight from a given amount of corn than do big ones? Why is it more costly to add a floor to a 20-story building than to a 10-story building? Why is it that adding water to parched soil yields remarkable results whereas adding the same amount of water to already moist soil may add very little to the crop? Why is it that if a firm adds a worker when the labor force is already large, the increase in output is less than if one is added at a time when the labor force is small? These are only a few examples of the principle of diminishing returns.

Note that diminishing returns is a short-run phenomenon and says nothing about the long-run production function. It only says that if more and more variable input is added to a fixed factor, after awhile the return will decline. Think of your own experience in studying for exams. The output is your score on a test, and the variable factor is the time you spend studying. Assume you could get a score of 55 percent without studying. One hour of studying boosts your score to 66 percent; two

---

SHORT RUN
The period of time too short to vary all the factors of production. Short-run decisions are those concerned with using the existing plant more or less extensively.

LONG RUN
The period of time in which all inputs, including plant and equipment, can be varied.

PRINCIPLE OF DIMINISHING RETURNS
As more and more units of a variable factor are added to a set of fixed factors, the resulting additions to output eventually will become increasingly smaller.

hours, to 75 percent; three hours, to 80 percent; four hours, to 84 percent; five hours, to 86 percent, and so on. You see that each additional variable input (each hour spent studying) produces a smaller increment in output (improvement in test score) than the previous input. In this example, the first hour produced an improvement of 11 percentage points; the second hour, 9 points; the third, 5 points, and so on. You see a diminishing return to studying. It is up to you to decide when the return for an additional hour of studying is not worth the opportunity cost of that hour in terms of the other things you could be doing. So you see, even deciding how much to study is an exercise in rational economic choice that reflects the law of diminishing returns.

Average and Marginal Relationships

A very important relationship between average values and marginal values always holds. Think of your grade point average. If your grade in this course (the marginal grade) is below your grade point average for all courses taken, your average will fall. If your grade in this course is above your grade point average, your average will rise. The same holds for every marginal-average relationship. If a basketball player's lifetime shooting percentage (average) is higher this week than last week, you know that in the intervening (marginal) games, the player has shot a higher-than-average percentage. If the average is rising, the marginal must be above average; or putting it the other way around, if the marginal is above average, it will pull the average up. If the average is falling, the marginal must be below the average.

The important marginal/average relationship in production is between marginal physical product and average physical product. In order to describe more precisely the relationship between inputs and outputs, economists use the concept of the marginal physical product. **Marginal physical product (MPP)** is the change in physical output that is produced by a unit change in a factor of production. The marginal physical product of labor, for example, is the change in total output per unit change in the use of labor service. Formally,

$$MPP_L = \frac{\Delta TPP}{\Delta_L},$$

where MPP_L is the marginal physical product of labor, ΔTPP is the change in the total physical product, and Δ_L is the change in the number of units of labor employed. The **average physical product (APP)** of a factor of production is simply the total physical product divided by the number of units of the factor employed. The **total physical product (TPP)** is the amount that a firm produces in physical units. For example, the average physical product of capital is

$$APP_K = \frac{TPP}{K},$$

where APP_K is the average physical product of capital and where K is the number of units of capital used.

MARGINAL PHYSICAL PRODUCT (MPP)
The change in physical output that is produced by a unit change in a factor of production.

AVERAGE PHYSICAL PRODUCT (APP)
The total physical product (output) divided by the number of units of a factor used.

TOTAL PHYSICAL PRODUCT (TPP)
The amount that a firm produces in physical units.

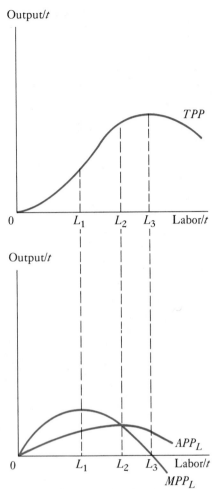

Table 8–2 shows these relationships arithmetically in the form of a short-run production function. All the factors of production are fixed except labor. Labor, the variable input, can vary between one and ten units. You can see, by examining Table 8–2, that as more variable input is added to the fixed inputs, output goes through three distinct stages. When the first three units of labor are added, output increases at an increasing rate, which is another way of saying that the marginal physical product is increasing. Adding the fourth unit of labor causes output to increase but by a smaller amount than the third unit of labor produced. The marginal physical product is now declining. The eighth unit of labor produces no increase in output, and the ninth unit of labor causes total output to actually fall.

TABLE 8–2
PRODUCTION RELATIONSHIPS

Variable Input (Units of Labor)	Total Output (Units of Product)	Marginal Product	Average Product
1	6	6	6.0
2	14	8	7.0
3	24	10	8.0
4	32	8	8.0
5	38	6	7.6
6	42	4	7.0
7	44	2	6.3
8	44	0	5.5
9	42	–2	4.7
10	36	–6	3.6

FIGURE 8–1
PRODUCT CURVES
When *TPP* is increasing at an increasing rate, *MPP* is increasing. When *TPP* is increasing at a decreasing rate, *MPP* is diminishing. When *TPP* is at a maximum, *MPP* is equal to zero.

Figure 8–1 shows these same relationships in graphical form. From 0 to L_1 units of labor, total product of labor is increasing at an increasing rate. This means that marginal physical product and average physical product are also increasing. At L_1, the marginal physical product of labor reaches its maximum. From L_1 to L_3 units of labor, total physical product is increasing at a decreasing rate. This is the region of diminishing returns. The marginal physical product of labor is declining throughout this range. At L_2, the average physical product of labor is at its maximum. At L_3 units of labor, the total physical product reaches its maximum; adding further units of labor produces no more output. The marginal physical product of labor is equal to 0 at L_3.

THE CHOICE OF INPUTS

We now can use the concept of production functions and diminishing marginal productivity to consider the choice of a production method. Earlier in this chapter, we demonstrated the concept of economic efficiency by showing how a printer might choose to produce this text-book. We can now add complexity and realism to this example.

Assume that we are again looking at the production of text-books by a firm that is of a given size. This means that the firm is in the short run and, as a result, the firm size cannot be altered. Let's further assume, to start, that there are only two variable inputs, labor and printing presses. Table 8–3 shows the quantities of labor and printing presses and their corresponding marginal physical products. You can see from the numbers of marginal physical products that this firm is in the range of diminishing marginal product. This corresponds to the range between L_1 and L_3 in Figure 8–1.

TABLE 8-3
FACTOR INPUTS AND THEIR MARGINAL PHYSICAL PRODUCTS

Variable Input— Labor (Units)	Marginal Physical Product— Labor (MPP_L)	Variable Input— Presses (Units)	Marginal Physical Product— (MPP_P)
■	■	■	■
7	6	5	10
8	5	6	9
9	4	7	8
10	3	8	6
11	1	9	3
12	0	10	0

The production question facing the firm is to determine which combination of labor and presses will produce the largest amount of text-books for a given cost outlay. Let's say that presses cost $2 per unit per day, and labor units cost $1 per unit per day and that the firm has a budget of $26 per day.

The firm will maximize output by purchasing labor and presses until the marginal physical products per dollar spent are equal. This is written as:

$$\frac{MPP_L}{P_L} = \frac{MPP_P}{P_P}.$$

In our numerical example, the firm would use ten units of labor and eight presses per day because:

$$3/\$1 = 6/\$2.$$

You can easily see why this maximizes output, given a spending constraint of $26. Substitute two units of labor for one press, for example. If one less press is used, two units of output are lost, and if two more units of labor are added, only one unit of output is added; so the firm has lost a unit of output with this alternative mix of inputs.

We now can see that a firm maximizes output by choosing its mix of inputs so that the marginal physical product of a dollar's worth of each input is equal to the marginal physical product of a dollar's worth of every other input. If MPP_a/P_a > MPP_b/P_b, the firm reallocates its inputs to use more a and less b. As the firm uses more of Input a, it will drive down the marginal physical product of a and bring equality between MPP_a/P_a and MPP_b/P_b. This can be generalized to include all inputs by saying that the firm maximizes its production for a given cost outlay by producing where,

$$\frac{MPP_a}{P_a} = \frac{MPP_b}{P_b} \cdots \frac{MPP_n}{P_n}.$$

You will note that the principles developed here are very similar to those developed for utility analysis. In the utility analysis example, the consumer maximized utility with given income or a budget constraint. Here, the firm maximizes output given a cost constraint. The principles of maximization are the same.

PRODUCTION RELATIONSHIPS AND INPUTS
- At least one factor input is fixed in the short run.
- All factor inputs are variable in the long run.
- Marginal physical product of an input is the change in output produced by a one-unit change in that input.
- Diminishing returns is a short-run phenomenon.
- If marginal physical product is negative, total physical product is declining.

ON TO COSTS

The principles of production are a foundation for analyzing costs. In the next chapter, we will see how production functions, and in particular the principle of diminishing returns, relate to the cost functions firms face.

SUMMARY

1. Firms are organized by entrepreneurs to produce outputs by combining inputs. The entrepreneur does this in such a way as to maximize profits.
2. Nonprofit private sector firms and nonprofit governmental firms face different incentives than for-profit firms because nonprofit firms have no residual claimants.
3. While single proprietorships are the dominant form of business organization by number, corporations account for about 85 percent of annual business sales in the United States.
4. Economic efficiency means selecting that combination of resources that minimizes the cost of produc-

ing a certain output.
5. A production function is the technical relationship between factors of production and outputs.
6. In the short run, some factors are fixed; but in the long run, all factors are variable.
7. In the short run, as variable factors are added to the fixed factor, the firm may experience increasing returns at low levels of output but eventually will incur diminishing returns at some higher levels of output.
8. Firms choose their input mix from the production function to maximize output subject to cost constraints.

◼ NEW TERMS

production	partnership	production function
vertical integration	corporation	fixed factors
horizontal integration	stockholders	variable factors
conglomerate	board of directors	short run
transaction costs	stocks	long run
teams	bonds	principle of diminishing returns
shirk	limited liability	marginal physical product (*MPP*)
business firm	residual claimant	average physical product (*APP*)
industry	technical efficiency	total physical product (*TPP*)
sole proprietorship	economic efficiency	

◼ QUESTIONS FOR DISCUSSION

1. How does the short run differ from the long run? What would be the short run in farming? in the lemonade-stand business? in electricity generation?

2. Is there a parallel between diminishing utility in consumption and diminishing returns in production? Describe any similarities you see.

3. List some of the differences you have observed between firms in the private profit-seeking sector and nonprofit firms that produce the same good.

4. In professional sports, there are very few player-coaches; yet many players become coaches immediately after their playing days end. Can you think of any reasons why this may be the case, based on our theories of why firms are formed and what managers do in these firms?

5. Suppose the following production function describes three ways to produce 1,000 shirts.

	Capital (Sewing Machines) ◼	Labor (Sewer— Weeks) ◼	Land (Acres) ◼	Output (Shirts) ◼
A	4	60	1/5	1,000
B	10	10	1/5	1,000
C	30	5	1/5	1,000

If you were the plant manager of this sewing factory, which method of production would you choose?

6. If the cost basis of the capital services of sewing machines is $3,000 per 1,000 shirts and the wage rate is $6.25 per hour (40-hour week), which method of production would you choose?

7. What would happen if your sewing factory were successfully unionized and the union contract specifies a wage rate of $10.65 per hour?

8. The price of land was irrelevant to your decision in Questions 6 and 7 because the plant was going to consume 1/5 of an acre of land in all three methods of production. What would be your reaction if the governor in a neighboring state offered you free land in an industrial park and forgave all property taxes on that land for ten years?

9. Classify each of these mergers as either a vertical, horizontal, or conglomerate merger.

   a. An oil company buys a chain of gas stations.

   b. A cosmetics company buys a financial institution.

   c. An airline buys a travel agency.

   d. An airline buys an interstate bus line.

   e. A movie company buys a television studio.

   f. A supermarket chain buys a rental car company.

10. Quality circles and similar management techniques that increase worker involvement in the manufacturing process have become popular and are sometimes referred to as the Japanese style of management. Do such "styles" of management fit the team-shirking analysis of production that was presented in this chapter?

◼ SUGGESTIONS FOR FURTHER READING

Leftwich, Richard H., and Ross D. Eckert. *The Price System and Resource Allocation*. 9th ed. Hinsdale, IL: The Dryden Press, 1985; and Cotton M. Lindsay. *Applied Price Theory*. Hinsdale, IL: The Dryden Press, 1984.

These two intermediate price theory texts develop the material found in this chapter in much greater detail.

White, Michelle J., ed., *Nonprofit Firms in a Three Sector*

Economy. Washington, D.C.: Urban Institute Press, 1981. A collection of articles looking at the behavior of private nonprofit firms.

APPENDIX: PRODUCER CHOICE: ISOQUANTS AND ISOCOSTS

If you have not already done so, you should study the appendix to the chapter entitled "Demand and Consumer Choice." That appendix describes indifference analysis and budget constraints applied to consumer choice. A very close analogy using isoquants and isocosts can be used to analyze producer choice. An **isoquant** (called a producer indifference curve by some economists) is a curve that shows all combinations of the quantities of two inputs that can be used to produce a given quantity of output. Along a particular isoquant, the amount of output produced remains the same, but the combinations of inputs vary. There is a separate isoquant for each level of output.

Isoquant Curves

Suppose Eric, an entrepreneur, is considering the use of different combinations of capital and labor, as indicated in Table 8A–1. Combination *A* contains 16 units of labor (measured in person years) and 3 units of capital (measured in number of machines used per year). Combination *B* uses 12 units of labor and 4 units of capital. He states that neither Combination *A* nor Combination *B* is preferred over the other; they are equal in the amount of output he expects to produce and, therefore, in the absence of prices, he is indifferent between the input combinations. When Eric expands the choice to input combinations *C*, *D*, and *E*, he has the same response because they all produce the same output,

1,000 dozen shirts. These production choices can be geometrically represented by drawing an isoquant curve. An isoquant curve corresponding to the production choices in Table 8A–1 is drawn in Figure 8A–1. The isoquant curve shows all combinations of the two inputs that produce a given output.

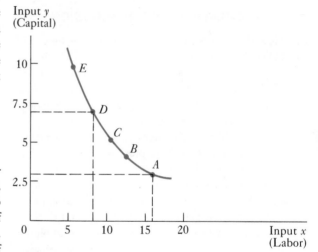

FIGURE 8A-1
ISOQUANT CURVE
Isoquant curves represent combinations of two inputs that produce the same output. All combinations on the same isoquant curve represent the same level of output.

A production function represented by a higher isoquant curve is associated with larger quantities of output. As Eric moves from I_1 to I_2 to I_3 to I_4 in Figure 8A–2, more output is being produced.

The typical isoquant curve for two inputs will have some curvature, reflecting imperfect substitutability between inputs. It will have a negative slope, which means that for the output to be equal along the curve some extra amount of one input is necessary to compensate for the loss of some amount of the other. Saying the same thing in another way, every combination of two inputs represented on the same isoquant curve will have more of one of the inputs but less of the other than any other combination on that isoquant curve.

TABLE 8A-1
ERIC'S PRODUCTION CHOICES TO PRODUCE 1,000 DOZEN SHIRTS

Combinations	Input *x* (Labor)	Input *y* (Capital)
A	16	3
B	12	4
C	10	5
D	8	7
E	6	9

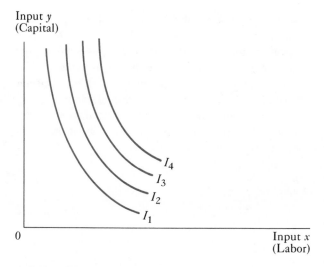

FIGURE 8A-2
ISOQUANT MAP
An isoquant map is a set of isoquant curves, each corresponding to a different level of output. Higher curves on the map represent higher levels of output.

The curvature (convex to the origin) means that as a producer uses more units of one input and fewer units of the other input, it takes more and more units of the more abundant input to compensate for the loss of one unit of the input that is becoming more scarce.

Diminishing Marginal Rates of Substitution

The trade-off ratio along the isoquant curve is called (as before with indifference curves) the *marginal rate of substitution*. The marginal rate of substitution of x for y, MRS_{xy}, shows the willingness of the producer to substitute between the inputs; that is,

$$MRS_{xy} = \frac{\text{number of units of } y \text{ released}}{\text{number of units of } x \text{ substituted}}.$$

Just as with indifference curves, the convexity feature of the isoquant is a reflection of the the principle of diminishing marginal rates of substitution, showing that as more of one input (x) is substituted for the other input (y), the value of Input x in terms of Input y declines.

Cost Constraints

An isoquant map makes it possible to compare points representing combinations of Inputs x and y

so as to determine whether the producer prefers one such combination. All points on any single isoquant curve represent the same level of output. Points on isoquant curves located to the right and above other isoquant curves are combinations that produce greater levels of output.

Which combination of inputs should this producer choose? The answer depends on the budget available to that producer and on the prices of the inputs. Keep in mind that the producer faces input prices that are determined in markets. The producer cannot influence these prices. Total costs constrain the producer from buying all that might be desired. For every possible cost constraint, there is an *isocost line*. "Isocost" means equal cost. An **isocost line** identifies all combinations of inputs the firm can purchase for a given total cost. This concept is analogous to the budget line in indifference analysis.

A straight line connecting the two points that represent buying only Input y or only Input x will show all possible combinations that can be employed with a given cost outlay. Any output outside (to the northeast of) the line is unattainable at that cost outlay; it is outside the budget constraint. In other words, the isocost line is the dividing line between those output levels that are attainable and those that are unattainable at a given level of prices and a given cost outlay. An isocost line is shown in Figure 8A–3. The intercept on the axis of each representing each input is determined

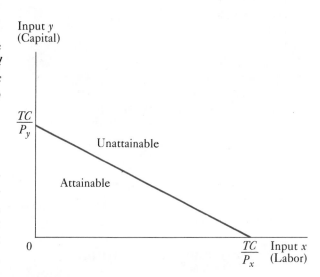

FIGURE 8A-3
ISOCOST LINE
An isocost line depicts the input combinations that are possible with a given level of cost outlay. Any combination outside (to the northeast of) the line is unattainable.

by dividing the total cost outlay by the price of that input. The slope of the isocost curve is therefore the ratio of the per-unit costs of the alternative inputs.

■ Changes in Cost Outlay and Changes in Prices

The isocost line was developed holding prices and total cost outlay constant. How do changes in total cost outlay and prices affect the isocost line?

An increase in cost outlay means that more of both inputs can be purchased, if prices stay the same. A doubling of cost outlay—or the firm's budget—means that twice as much of both inputs can be purchased, if prices remain constant. Increases in cost outlay are represented by a parallel outward shift of the isocost line. Decreases in cost outlay are represented by a parallel inward shift of the isocost line. Two such shifts are shown in Figure 8A–4.

A change in the price of one good only affects the total amount of that input that can be employed, not the total amount of the other input that can be purchased. A price rise, then, will affect only the isocost line intercept of the input that has experienced the price rise. Such a change is shown in Figure 8A–5. A price rise for Input x from P_{x1} to P_{x2} causes the isocost line intercept to move closer to the origin, reflecting the fact that less x can now be employed with the constant cost outlay. A decrease in the price of Input x to P_{x3} would mean more x could be employed and the intercept would move away from the origin, reflecting increases in the potential employment of Input x.

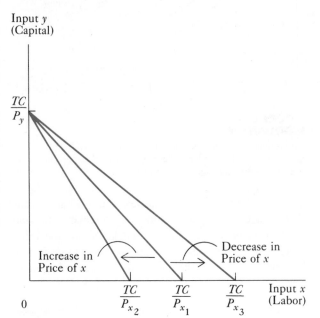

FIGURE 8A-5
THE EFFECT OF INPUT PRICE CHANGES ON ISOCOST LINES
An increase in the price of one input changes the slope of the isocost line. An increase in price means that if all of the firm's cost outlay is spent on the input, less of it can be purchased. As a result, the intercept of the isocost line will shift closer to the origin. The opposite holds for a decrease in price.

FIGURE 8A-4
THE EFFECT OF COST OUTLAY CHANGES ON ISOCOST LINES
An increase in cost outlay is represented by a parallel outward shift of the isocost line. A decrease in cost outlay is represented by an inward parallel shift of the isocost line.

Price changes cause the slope of the isocost line to change. Notice again that the slope is the negative of the ratio of the prices of the two inputs, or $-(P_x/P_y)$.

The slope of the isocost line changes when the ratio of the input prices changes. A change in total cost outlay, on the other hand, represents no change in relative prices, so the slope of the isocost line remains the same, as reflected by the parallel shifting of the isocost line described above.

■ Choosing the Optimum Combination of Inputs

Drawing the isocost line on the isoquant map makes it possible to demonstrate the choice of input combination, as in Figure 8A–6. At Point A on Isoquant Curve I_2, the isocost line and Isoquant Curve I_2 are tangent. Any point on I_3, such as Point B, is preferred to Point A because higher isoquant curves represent higher levels of output. However, Point B is not attainable because it is outside the isocost line. Point C on I_1 is attainable, but a point on isoquant curve I_2 also is attainable, and any point on I_2 represents more output than any point on I_1. The producer wants to reach the highest attainable isoquant curve. The highest attainable curve would be one that is tangent to the isocost line because no higher isoquant curve can be reached with the given cost outlay and prices.

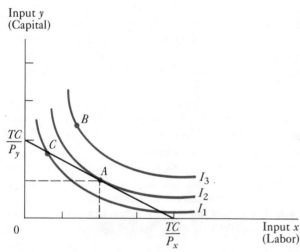

Input y
(Capital)

FIGURE 8A–6
THE CHOICE OF INPUT COMBINATIONS
A producer maximizes output for a given cost outlay where the isocost line is tangent to the highest attainable isoquant curve.

You should remember from geometry that two curves that are tangent have equal slopes at the point of tangency. At the point of tangency between the isoquant curve and the isocost line, the marginal rate of substitution is equal to the ratio of the price of x to the price of y; that is,[a]

$$MRS_{xy} = \frac{P_x}{P_y} .$$

The common sense of this equation is that the marginal rate of substitution expresses the willingness of the producer to substitute a certain amount of x for a certain amount of y, and the slope of the isocost line reflects the market's willingness to trade a certain amount of x for a certain amount of y through their prices. The impersonal forces of the market impose the relative price on the producer, so the producer adjusts the choice of inputs in such a way that his or her trade-off is the same as that of the market.

The Firm's Reaction to Price Changes

Figure 8A–5 showed how price changes affect the isocost line. We now can see how the optimum combination of inputs will be affected by price changes. Initially the producer is at the point of maximum output (Point A in Figure 8A–7). As the price of x falls from P_{x1} to P_{x2}, the isocost line rotates out to intersect the x-axis at TC/P_{x2}, and the producer now has a new optimum at Point B on Isoquant Curve I_2. Another decrease in price to P_{x3} allows the producer to reach a still higher isoquant curve, I_3, and a new optimum at Point C. Connecting the points produces an expansion path, which shows how the input combination changes when relative input prices change.

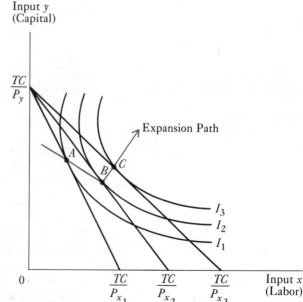

Input y
(Capital)

FIGURE 8A–7
THE FIRM'S EXPANSION PATH
An expansion path depicts how the firm's choice of inputs changes when relative prices change.

a. Technically, MRS_{xy} is equal to the negative of the slope of the isoquant curve. The price ratio, as we have seen, is the negative of the slope of the isocost line. Therefore, at the (equilibrium) point of tangency between the isoquant curve and the isocost line, $MRS_{xy} = P_x/P_y$.

CHAPTER 9

THE COSTS
OF PRODUCTION

INTRODUCTION

In the previous chapter, we examined firm organization and production. We developed the concept of a production function and the idea that the firm chooses its mix of inputs from a production function. These choices translate into costs and cost functions. This chapter is devoted to studying the cost relationships that result from production decisions.

We also saw in the last chapter how the entrepreneur attempts to minimize costs to achieve economic efficiency. But we need to be careful how we define cost. Costs of inputs are expressed in terms of their *opportunity cost*. You were introduced to opportunity cost earlier in our study, and now you need to apply it with a vengeance. Measuring costs this way can be a problem if you are not used to thinking in terms of opportunity cost and are more used to thinking in terms of explicit cost. **Explicit costs** are accounting costs or money outlays. **Implicit costs** are those additional costs implied by the alternatives given up. In sum, when we talk of costs, we include all the opportunity costs, not just the part that is explicit.

Some examples can make this clearer. Suppose you have the option of working two hours of overtime at $10 an hour or going to a concert that costs $5. The cost of attending the concert is the $5 ticket *plus* the $20 you could have earned working overtime. Attending the concert will cost you $25. The explicit cost is $5; the implicit cost is $20. Suppose your rich aunt in Great Britain gives you her "old" Rolls Royce that is worth $100,000. She doesn't care what you do with it. You are excited because now you can drive an exciting car at very low cost. You need only pay for gas, oil, and repairs. Right? No! You have forgotten to include a calculation for the implicit cost. If you sold the car, you could invest the $100,000. You could put the money in a high-yield account that earns 10 percent per year. In other words, you are giving up $10,000 in implicit costs per year if you choose to drive the Rolls. The cost is $10,000 plus the explicit cost of gas, oil, insurance, and repairs. Do you still want to drive the Rolls?

EXPLICIT COST
Accounting cost or money outlay.

IMPLICIT COST
Cost measured by the value of alternatives given up.

184

ACCOUNTING PROFIT AND ECONOMIC PROFIT

In Chapter 3, Susan Smith's lemonade stand provided an example of a firm as a supplier. Now imagine that we can obtain Susan's account books in order to calculate her profits. Let's say she had total sales of $15,000 for the summer. Her books say that she has accounting (explicit) costs of $11,500. Her **accounting profit** is $3,500, determined by subtracting her explicit costs from her total sales. These are the profits reported for tax purposes. But economists think that these profits give a misleading view of the firm's health because they ignore implicit costs. If Susan's skills and talents are worth $2,000, then her opportunity cost, which is her implicit costs plus her explicit costs, would be $14,000. She would be earning an economic profit of $1,500. **Economic profit** is the difference between total sales and the total of explicit and implicit costs of production. If entrepreneurs do not earn a profit that is at least equal to their opportunity cost, they will leave that endeavor because they can do better elsewhere.

Opportunity Cost and Normal Profit

The opportunity cost of capital and enterprise is referred to as **normal profit**. A normal profit represents the rate of return that is necessary to keep capital and enterprise in an industry. Say, for example, a normal rate of return is 12 percent. Then a firm earning a 12 percent rate of return is earning zero economic profits because its capital and entrepreneurial resources could earn 12 percent elsewhere. The concept of normal profit is important in setting prices for public utilities (private regulated monopolies). If an electric utility is not granted a price increase and the rate of return on capital falls below the normal rate of return, capital will leave that industry because it can earn its opportunity cost elsewhere.

In other words, normal profit is part of the implicit cost structure of firms. Just like the "free" Rolls Royce, a firm's capital, even if it is paid for, represents wealth that could be sold and invested elsewhere. The calculation is, in principle, exactly the same as in the Rolls Royce example.

Figure 9–1 shows the relationship between these concepts. Total revenue is the same in both bars, but the difference between economic profits and accounting profits is the implicit costs.

A correct definition of costs is important because economists use costs and profits to predict behavior. When economic profits are positive, economists predict that firms will enter an industry; when negative, firms will leave; and when zero, firms will remain. Economic profit serves as a signal to call forth entry into or exit out of an industry. If a firm isn't earning normal profits in its present industry, the resources of this firm will flow to an industry where normal returns can be earned. If more than normal returns are earned in an industry, resources will be attracted to it.

The Use of Accounting Profits in Economic Analysis

Economic theory is based on the concept of economic costs and economic profit, but these data aren't usually available in doing real-

ACCOUNTING PROFIT
The difference between explicit costs and total sales.

ECONOMIC PROFIT
The difference between total sales and the total of explicit and implicit costs of production.

NORMAL PROFIT
The opportunity cost of capital and enterprise. This is the level of profit that is necessary for a firm to remain in a competitive industry.

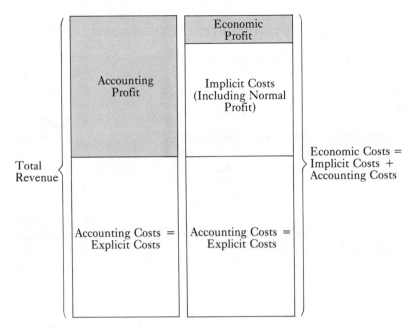

FIGURE 9-1
ECONOMIC PROFIT AND ACCOUNTING PROFIT
Economic profit is different from accounting profit by the amount of implicit costs.

world analyses. Economists are very suspicious of accounting costs and accounting profits for at least two reasons. The first has to do with the way in which accounting costs are gathered, and the second has to do with the discrepancy between accounting costs and economic costs.

There is a host of things that can be done to manipulate accounting profits. Since income tax is paid on profits, firms have incentives to make profits look as small as possible for the Internal Revenue Service and as large as possible for potential investors. Some flexibility in measuring profits comes from the significantly different ways that firms can account for items whose value is estimated subjectively. In 1984, *Fortune* magazine asked experts at several "Big Eight" accounting firms how they could "pump up" the profits of a mythical $10 billion-a-year company. These experts reported that different accounting techniques could boost reported profits as much as 15 percent.[1] These techniques fall into three categories: changing approved accounting methods, manipulating managers' estimates of costs, and changing the time periods in which costs are paid and revenues are received.

Even though economists argue that accounting data do not reflect economic reality and can be manipulated, economists still must make use of accounting data when they study the economy. The use of the data is subject to much debate by economic researchers. Some argue that studies that use accounting data are meaningless. Others hold that accounting data are all that is available, and as long as economists make

1. Ford S. Worthy, "Manipulating Profits: How It's Done," *Fortune* (June 25, 1984): 49–54.

careful use of the data, it is worthwhile.[2] This debate will go on as long as economists do such studies.

COST IN THE SHORT RUN

The production function relates inputs to outputs. The inputs have prices and represent costs to the firm. These prices are determined in factor markets and may or may not be affected by the actions of the firm itself. Given the prices of inputs and the production function, we can derive cost data for the firm. Although the derivation can be done formally, we will show the relationship between the two geometrically and then derive the costs in a simpler fashion. We will leave the formal derivation to more advanced texts and courses.

Cost Defined

Total cost (*TC*) is simply the sum of all the costs of production for a given level of output. A total cost profile for a hypothetical firm is given in Column 4 of Table 9–1. Total cost is made up of two components: total fixed cost (*TFC*) and total variable cost (*TVC*). **Total fixed costs (*TFC*)** are the costs of the fixed factors of production and, therefore, do not vary in the short run. These total fixed costs will be the same regardless of how many units of output the firm produces. **Total variable costs (*TVC*)** vary directly with output, increasing as more output is produced. This happens because more variable factors have to be purchased if more output is to be produced. Total fixed costs and total variable costs are represented by Columns 2 and 3 in Table 9–1. Note that *TFC* + *TVC* = *TC*. We assume that for every level of output, the firm has already identified that combination of inputs that minimizes the *TVC* associated with producing that level of output. Why should the firm pay a higher *TVC* than it has to? (The firm cannot change *TFC* in the short run.)

Given the information in Columns 1 through 3, the rest of the columns are computed as follows:

Average total cost, (*AC*), is the total cost of producing an output, divided by that level of output. Thus,

$$AC = \frac{TC}{Q}.$$

Likewise, **average fixed cost (*AFC*)** is total fixed costs of production divided by the number of units of output, and **average variable cost (*AVC*)** is the total variable cost divided by the number of units of

TOTAL COST (*TC*)
The sum of all the costs of production for a given level of output.

TOTAL FIXED COST (*TFC*)
The cost of the fixed factors of production. Total fixed cost does not vary in the short run.

TOTAL VARIABLE COST (*TVC*)
The total of costs that vary directly with output, increasing as more output is produced.

AVERAGE TOTAL COST (*AC*)
Total costs of production divided by the number of units of output.

AVERAGE FIXED COST (*AFC*)
Total fixed costs of production divided by output. Average fixed costs decline as production is increased.

AVERAGE VARIABLE COST (*AVC*)
Total variable cost divided by the number of units of output.

---

2. The most recent exchange in this debate was kicked off by George J. Benston, "The Validity of Profits-Structure Studies With Particular Reference to the FTC's Line of Business Data," *American Economic Review* (March 1985): 36–67. Thirteen economists responded to Benston's article in the March 1987 issue of the *American Economic Review*. Also see Franklin M. Fisher and John J. McGowan, "On the Misuse of Accounting Rates of Return to Infer Monopoly Profits," *American Economic Review* (March 1983): 82–97. A series of comments in opposition to their position can be found in the June 1984 issue of the *American Economic Review*.

TABLE 9-1
COST FOR A HYPOTHETICAL FIRM

(1) Output per Week (Q)	(2) Total Fixed Cost (TFC)	(3) Total Variable Cost (TVC)	(4) Total Cost (TC)	(5) Average Fixed Cost (AFC)	(6) Average Variable Cost (AVC)	(7) Average Total Cost (AC)	(8) Marginal Cost (MC)
0	60	0	60		0		0
1	60	40	100	60	40	100	40
2	60	76	136	30	38	68	36
3	60	108	168	20	36	56	32
4	60	140	200	15	35	50	32
5	60	175	235	12	35	47	35
6	60	216	276	10	36	46	41
7	60	262	322	$8^4/_7$	$37^3/_7$	46	46
8	60	312	372	$7^1/_2$	39	$46^1/_2$	50
9	60	369	429	$6^2/_3$	41	$47^2/_3$	57
10	60	430	490	6	43	49	61

output. *AFC*, *AVC*, and *AC* appear in Columns 5, 6, and 7 of Table 9–1, respectively.

MARGINAL COST
The change in total cost from producing one more (or one less) unit of output.

Marginal cost (MC) is the change in total cost as a result of producing one more (or one less) unit of output. Therefore,

$$MC = \frac{\Delta TC}{\Delta Q} = \frac{\Delta TVC}{\Delta Q}.$$

Marginal costs are really marginal *variable* costs because there are no marginal fixed costs; the change in fixed costs when output changes is zero.

Cost Curves

We can draw a series of cost curves for the production function described by the numerical data given in Table 9–1. The curves are drawn smoothly to better emphasize the relationship between the curves.[3]

The total fixed cost, total variable cost, and total cost curves are drawn in Figure 9–2. The shapes of the total cost curve and the total variable cost curve are determined by the shape of the production function. As the amount of the variable factor is increased, output increases and total costs increase. If output increases more rapidly than factor cost, total cost (as well as total variable cost) increases at a decreasing rate, and returns are increasing. In Figure 9–2, this is what is happening in the production function as output increases from zero to Q_1. From Q_1 to higher levels of output, output increases less rapidly than the factor cost increases, so total cost (along with total variable cost) increases at an increasing rate. The principle of diminishing returns is operating.

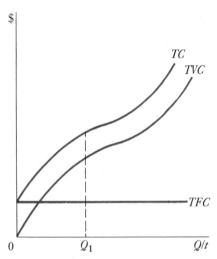

FIGURE 9-2
TOTAL COST CURVES
The shapes of the total cost curve and total variable cost curve are a reflection of the production function. From zero output until an output of Q_1, total cost and total variable cost increase at a decreasing rate. Beyond output Q_1, diminishing returns set in and these costs increase at an increasing rate.

3. Drawing the curves smoothly assumes that the gaps between the discrete points in Table 9–1 can be filled in with a continuous curve.

Consider this simple example. Suppose that a firm hires one more worker and output increases by ten units. The variable cost increases by the wage of that worker (for a given time period). Now, if it takes two workers to increase output by ten more units, total variable costs would increase by the wage rate times two. Clearly the cost has increased at an increasing rate.

Now, let's look at average costs. Figure 9–3 shows the *AFC*, *AVC*, *AC*, and *MC* curves of a hypothetical firm. The *AFC* curve declines continuously, getting closer and closer to the *x*-axis of the graph. This decline occurs because fixed costs are constant, and average fixed costs are calculated by dividing a constant cost amount by an ever-increasing quantity. The *AFC* thus becomes smaller and smaller as output increases.

AVC first declines and then increases, as does *AC*. This U-shape represents at first increasing returns and then diminishing returns to the variable inputs. The variable inputs are being added to the fixed-size plant. This is represented by the output up to Q_1 in Figure 9–3.

Beyond Q_1, returns to the variable factors decline. We have reached diminishing returns. Increasing returns imply decreasing average costs and diminishing returns mean increasing average costs. The *AVC* and *AC* curves are U-shaped because of decreasing costs (increasing returns) for small levels of output and eventual increasing costs (diminishing returns) for higher levels of output. *AC* declines sharply at first because *AFC* drops rapidly and then more slowly.

It is very important to note that the *MC* curve intersects the *AC* and *AVC* curves at their lowest points: Points *A* and *B* in Figure 9–3. This relates to our earlier discussion of the average-marginal relationship. For the average curves to be declining, the marginal cost must be below the average cost; and in order for the average to be rising, the marginal cost must be above the average cost. This requires that the marginal cost and average cost be equal when the average curve is at its minimum point. Think back to the example of how your grade point average goes up or down depending on the grade in an added (marginal) course. Also, notice that when the marginal cost curve starts to rise as output is increased, it is still below the average variable cost curve; thus, average variable cost is still falling. An average value falls as long as the marginal value is below it, regardless of whether the marginal value is falling or rising.

The Relationship Between Product Curves and Cost Curves

At the start, we said that cost curves could be derived from production functions. This is an advanced topic in economics, but you can see the relationship between a production function, represented by product curves, and cost curves in Figure 9–4.

Panel (*a*) of Figure 9–4 reproduces the marginal physical product and average physical product curves from the previous chapter. Panel (*b*) represents the cost curves that are derived from the production function that produced the product curves. The marginal cost curve is a mirror image of the marginal physical product curve. At those output levels where marginal physical product is increasing, reflecting increasing returns, marginal cost is decreasing. When the marginal physical product curve is at

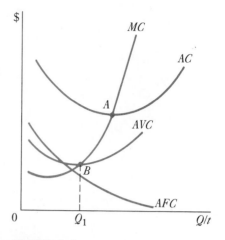

FIGURE 9–3
MARGINAL AND AVERAGE COST CURVES
Average fixed cost declines continuously. Average variable cost declines, reaches a minimum, and then increases (as does average cost), resulting in a U-shaped cost curve. The marginal cost curve intersects the average variable cost and average cost curves at their minimum points.

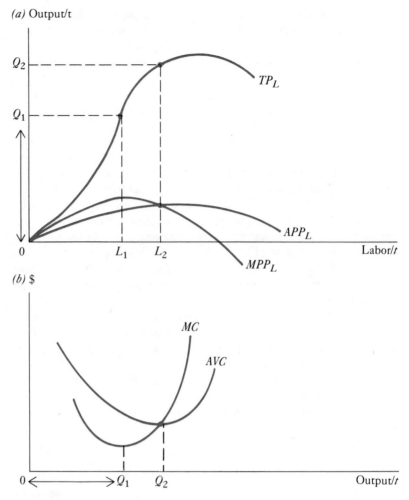

(a) Output/t

(b) $

FIGURE 9-4
THE RELATIONSHIP BETWEEN PRODUCT CURVES AND COST
CURVES

The cost curves are mirror images of the respective product curves. When the product curve is increasing, the cost curve is decreasing, and vice versa. Q_1 units on the vertical axis of Panel *(a)* is the same Q_1 as that on the horizontal axis of Panel *(b)*. The L_1 in Panel *(a)* represents units of labor required to produce Q_1, which represents units of output.

its maximum, marginal cost is at its minimum point. When marginal physical product is declining, reflecting diminishing returns, marginal cost is rising.

Similar relationships hold for the average physical product and average variable cost curves. When average physical product is increasing, average variable cost is decreasing, and when average physical product is decreasing, average variable cost is increasing. The maximum and minimum points also coincide with each other.

This relationship is simple logic because the cost curves are simply a monetary measure of inputs needed to produce a given output, while the production function measures outputs out of a given amount of inputs. Given prices of resources, increasing returns have to mean decreasing costs and diminishing returns have to mean increasing costs.

COST IN THE LONG RUN

In the long run, all factors are variable; therefore, there are no fixed factors of production. As a result, there are no fixed costs; all costs are variable. In fact, the long run is defined as that period long enough to vary all inputs.

The most important long-run decision is what size plant to build. Each plant size is represented by a short-run AC curve, so the long-run decision is the selection of the desired short-run average cost curve. The decision will be based on the output the firm expects to produce. Figure 9–5 illustrates this decision. Suppose that the technological factors (given by the production function) are such that only three plant sizes are feasible. These plants are represented by AC_1, AC_2, and AC_3 in Figure 9–5. The long-run decision of which short-run curve to operate on would depend on the planned output of the firm. If output is to be less than Q_1, then the plant represented by AC_1 should be built because it represents the plant size that will produce any output level between zero and Q_1 at a per-unit cost that is lower than it would be for any other plant size. Likewise, if outputs between Q_1 and Q_2 are planned, the plant represented by AC_2 should be built. If outputs greater than Q_2 are planned, plant AC_3 should be built.

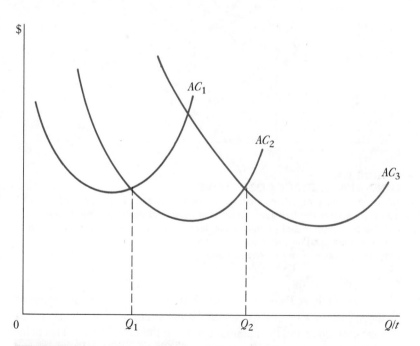

FIGURE 9-5
ALTERNATIVE PLANT SIZES
The determination of which size plant to build is a long-run decision of the firm. This decision is the selection of the desired short-run cost curve.

It is likely that more than three alternative plant sizes are available, and in the planning stage they would all be examined. Assume the firm faces all the alternative short-run curves depicted in Figure 9–6. All the possible short-run curves are tangent to a curve that is sometimes referred to as a planning curve. A **planning curve** is the long-run average cost curve. In the planning stage, a short-run curve tangent to the long-run curve can be selected. It is called a planning curve because in the planning stage, any point on the curve could be chosen by building a certain-size plant. Such a planning curve, more commonly called the long-run average cost curve, is shown in Figure 9–6. The **long-run average cost curve** (*LRAC*) represents the lowest attainable average cost of producing any given output. It is a curve tangent to all the possible short-run cost curves. For example, if you knew you were going to produce exactly Q_0 units of output, plant size AC_4 would have the lowest average cost of doing so.

PLANNING CURVE
The long-run average cost curve. In the planning stage, a short-run curve tangent to the long-run curve can be selected.

LONG-RUN AVERAGE COST CURVE (LRAC)
The lowest attainable average cost of producing any given output. A curve tangent to all the possible short-run cost curves.

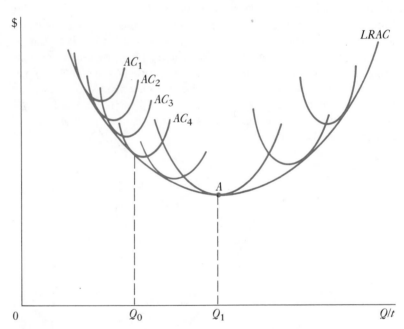

FIGURE 9-6
LONG-RUN AVERAGE COST CURVE
All the possible short-run cost curves are tangent to the planning curve. This planning curve is the long-run average cost curve and represents the lowest attainable average cost of producing any level of output. The optimal plant size would be found at Point *A*, where the minimum point on the short-run average cost curve is tangent to the long-run average cost curve at its minimum point.

OPTIMAL-SIZE PLANT
The plant represented by the short-run average cost curve with the lowest attainable per-unit costs.

Only at Point *A* in Figure 9–6, which represents an output of Q_1 units, is there a tangency between the minimum point on the short-run average cost curve and the minimum point on the *LRAC* curve. This point is referred to as the optimal-size plant. This is the **optimal-size plant** because it represents the short-run *AC* curve with the lowest attainable per-unit costs.

Economies and Diseconomies of Scale

The *LRAC* curve drawn in Figure 9–6 is U-shaped. This U-shape means that, at first, as plant size and firm output increase, long-run average costs fall. After a certain point (Point *A* on Figure 9–6), however, bigness starts becoming costly. As the plant continues to increase in size, average cost begins to rise. Economists refer to these changes in long-run average cost due to increased plant size as economies and diseconomies of scale. **Economies of scale** are declines in long-run average cost that are due to increased plant size. **Diseconomies of scale** are increases in long-run average cost that are due to increased plant size. As scale (plant size) increases, economies (cost savings) result. After a while, further growth results in diseconomies (higher costs).

ECONOMIES OF SCALE
Declines in long-run average cost that are due to increased plant size.

DISECONOMIES OF SCALE
Increases in long-run average cost that are due to increased plant size.

THE INTERNATIONAL PERSPECTIVE
ECONOMIC DEVELOPMENT AND
ECONOMIES OF SCALE

Manufacturing is quite often subject to economies of large scale over a relatively large output range as depicted in Figure 9–7 in this chapter. As a result of these large scale economies, policymakers have argued that manufacturing in less developed countries needs to be protected from foreign competition if it is to get a toehold in the domestic market and someday be able to compete with industry in already developed countries.

This argument, called the *infant industry argument* by economists, was vehemently advocated by Alexander Hamilton, the first Secretary of the U.S. Treasury in George Washington's cabinet. Hamilton (1755–1804) was a promoter of economic growth and of a strong federal government.

Hamilton argued that it would be exceedingly difficult for the U.S. economy to develop in a system of free trade because Great Britain already possessed entrenched manufacturers with established trade networks. He argued that the only way U.S. firms could compete with developed foreign firms was with the "interference and aid" of the federal government. These infant industries could stand on their own after a "nursing period." An important element of this argument is that the new firm needs to grow to a size at which it enjoys economies of scale before it faces foreign competition.

The infant industry argument is used by many countries today. Indeed, it is the sort of policy advocated by Hamilton that many observers point to when they examine the Japanese experience with industrialization in the postwar period. The argument is that Japanese government and business leaders defined a few key industrial sectors. They nurtured these key areas with subsidies and high-tariff barriers until they attained economies of scale and low enough long-run average costs to be competitive on world markets.

The difficulty with the infant industry argument should be obvious. How can politicians recognize promising industries in advance? Many less developed countries may aspire to produce their own automobiles, have their own steel plants, or even manufacture main frame computers. But, unless these industries have a domestic market that is large enough to attain economies of scale that make them cost competitive on world markets, the government will have to protect the industry into old age. The fear is that subsidized infant industries will only grow into senile subsidized industries.

Economies and diseconomies of scale are distinct from increasing and decreasing returns. Increasing and decreasing returns are the result of using a given size plant more or less intensively in the short run. Economies and diseconomies of scale result from changes in the size of the plant in the long run.

It is easy to see how economies of scale result from an increase in plant size. As a firm increases its scale of operations, it usually can employ more specialized machinery, and jobs can be more specialized. Equipment can be used more efficiently. By-products of the operation that might be uneconomical to recover, or exploit, in a small-scale plant may become significant for a large operation. A large firm is often able to obtain quantity discounts and to purchase more precise amounts of intermediate products from other firms. Even political influence of economic value is more likely to accrue to a large, rather than a small, firm. These are just a few of the factors that account for the negative slope of the *LRAC* curve as the scale of plant increases.

Diseconomies of scale are perhaps harder to grasp, although anyone who has dealt with giant bureaucracies, public or private, will have seen evidence of them. Diseconomies result primarily from the fact that as an organization becomes very large, communication and coordination become more difficult and time consuming, and control from the top diminishes. So when a firm has taken advantage of most of the gains to be achieved by growing larger, managerial inefficiencies set in and the *LRAC* curve turns upward with further growth.

Optimal-Size Plants in the Real World

Figure 9–6 depicted a smooth *LRAC* curve that had a single optimal-size plant corresponding to an output of Q_1. If we look around in the real world, however, we see many different firms operating side by side in the same industry. Steel, for example, is produced by both very large and very small firms.

Economists have spent much time investigating economies of scale. The range of actual *LRAC* curves is represented in Figures 9–7, 9–8, and 9–9. Figure 9–7 shows economies of scale over a large range of output. This situation occurs in the auto industry where there are a few very large firms. The optimal-size plant in Figure 9–7 would be Q_1, which conceivably might represent all the normal sales of the industry. In some industries, a natural monopoly occurs. A **natural monopoly** is a monopoly that emerges because of economies of scale. The size of the market is such that there is room for only one optimal-size firm. Many public utilities (gas and electric), for instance, need to have all the sales in a market in order to become large enough to be of optimal size.

In Figure 9–8, a large number of different-size plants can be optimally sized. Distinctly different-size firms can all produce efficiently in the same industry at the same per-unit (or average) cost. In Figure 9–8, any firm producing an output between Q_1 and Q_2 would be efficient, and if the demand for the product were large enough to support many firms of this size, a very competitive situation would exist. This situation prevails in many industries, such as textiles, publishing, and packaged food products.

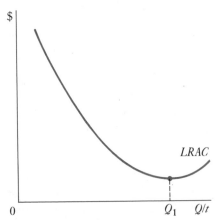

FIGURE 9-7
ECONOMIES OF SCALE AND A FEW VERY LARGE PLANTS
When economies of scale exist over large ranges of output, one large plant or a few large plants are most efficient.

NATURAL MONOPOLY
A monopoly that emerges because of economies of scale. The size of the market is such that there is room for only one optimal-size firm.

Figure 9–9 shows rapidly achievable economies of scale and then rapid diseconomies of scale. This kind of *LRAC* would be the case when all the firms in an industry are of a very similar size. The optimal-size plant in Figure 9–9 is the one whose short-run *AC* curve hits a minimum point at Q_1.

The concept of economies of scale is important. If the bigness of a firm is due to economies of scale, it is efficient to have production carried out by large firms. However, these large-scale firms may exert monopoly pricing power so that consumers do not benefit from scale economies. We will return to this problem in some detail when we examine some actual studies of economies of scale and monopoly power in selected industries.

PROFIT MAXIMIZATION

The choice of scale of plant is one of several decisions that determine a firm's profits. The firms examined here and in the next three chapters are all profit-maximizing firms. What does profit maximization mean in terms of production decisions? It means that in the short run, the firm will attempt to choose the output that maximizes the difference between total revenue and total cost. **Total revenue (TR)** is the price an item sells for multiplied by the number of units sold. **Marginal revenue (MR)** is the change in total revenue from selling one more (or one less) unit.

Profit will be maximized where *MR* = *MC*. Anytime *MR* is greater than *MC*, total revenue is increasing faster than total cost when output and sales are increased. This means that profit is increasing (or losses are decreasing). If output is decreased when *MR* > *MC*, total revenue would decline by more than total cost declines, so profit would fall. In other words, anytime *MR* > *MC*, if output were increased, total revenue would increase more than total cost would increase, and profit would increase.

On the other hand, if *MC* > *MR*, an increase in output and sales would cause total cost to increase more than the increase in total revenue, so profit would fall. A decrease in output and sales would reduce costs more than revenues, so profit would increase. So far, the rule is that if *MR* > *MC*, expand production and sales; and if *MC* > *MR*, decrease production and sales. If *MR* = *MC*, it would be unprofitable to either increase or decrease production.

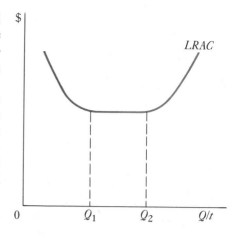

FIGURE 9–8
MANY OPTIMAL-SIZE PLANTS OF DIFFERENT SIZES
A range in the output of the optimal-size plant can exist. When this situation exists, plants of distinctly different sizes can all produce efficiently in the same industry.

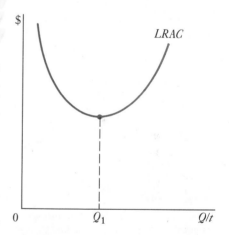

FIGURE 9–9
MANY OPTIMAL-SIZE PLANTS OF SIMILAR SIZES
If there is a unique minimum point on the long-run average cost curve, all the plants will be similar in size.

TOTAL REVENUE (TR)
The price an item sells for multiplied by the number of units sold.

MARGINAL REVENUE (MR)
The change in total revenue from selling one more (or one less) unit.

RULES FOR PROFIT MAXIMIZATION
- *MR* > *MC*   Expand Output
- *MR* = *MC*   Profits Maximized, Output Unchanged
- *MR* < *MC*   Reduce Output

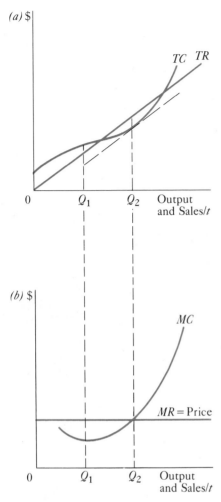

FIGURE 9-10
PROFIT MAXIMIZATION UNDER CONDITIONS OF PURE COMPETITION
Profit is maximized where marginal cost is equal to marginal revenue. The vertical distance between total revenue and total cost is greatest, Panel (*a*), at the same level of output where marginal cost equals marginal revenue, Panel (*b*).

PRESENT VALUE
The capitalized value of an item to be paid for or sold in the future. A future value discounted to the present.

DISCOUNTING
The technique of calculating present values by adjusting for interest that would be earned between now and some specific future time.

The operational rule for profit maximization, then, is to produce that output at which marginal revenue equals marginal cost (*MR = MC*). The directive to produce where *MR = MC* is just another way of saying, "Produce where total profit is at its maximum," or alternatively, "Produce where total revenue exceeds total cost by the largest amount." These are simply different ways of saying the same thing. Generally the *MR = MC* rule is the most convenient one with which to work.

It's easy to see this same relationship on a graph. In Figure 9–10, the firm is a *price taker*, which means that the price is given as far as this firm is concerned. Thus, the total revenue curve in Figure 9–10, Panel (*a*), is a straight line from the origin, and the *MR* curve in Panel (*b*) is a horizontal line, equal to the price of the product. The total cost curve is consistent with the law of diminishing returns beyond Output Q_2. (From zero output to Q_2, the cost curve represents increasing returns and decreasing average costs.)

The vertical distance between *TR* and *TC* is greatest at output Q_2; at that point the slopes of *TR* and *TC* are equal. The slope of *TR* is *MR* and the slope of *TC* is *MC*, so it is clear that *MR = MC* at output Q_2. This can be seen clearly in Figure 9–10, Panel (*b*). Note that if output were decreased from Q_2, *MC* would fall below *MR*, and *TR* would fall by more than *TC*, so profit would fall. If output increased from Q_2, *TC* would increase more than *TR*, and *MC* would be greater than *MR*, so again profit would fall. Profit is at a maximum at Q_2.

This decision rule, to produce that output where marginal revenue equals marginal cost, will come up again and again, so it is important to make sure you understand it. It will always be true that maximum profit will be obtained by operating at that point where *MR = MC*.

PRESENT VALUE

So far, the discussion of costs and the movement from the short run to the long run has ignored uncertainty and differences between present and future income. It is important to keep in mind that when the entrepreneur makes the decision of which plant to build, based on forecasted production, there is much uncertainty surrounding that decision. To make these forecasts, a great deal of information must be gathered and many factors must be considered.

Production decisions (or, for that matter, most economic decisions) affect costs and revenues over a number of periods of time. The decision maker needs a way of comparing revenues and costs in different time periods because a dollar cost or a dollar revenue today is not the same as a dollar cost or a dollar revenue next year or ten years from now.

To compare future dollars (costs or revenues) for different periods with present dollars, firms calculate the present value of these future dollars. **Present value (*PV*)** is the capitalized value of an item to be paid for or sold in the future. It is a future value discounted to the present. **Discounting** is the technique of calculating present values by adjusting for interest that would be earned between now and some specific future time. It works simply and has many important uses in daily life.

Buccaneers reported to be worth $8.2 million. According to sources, the contract was the highest ever given to a rookie and the third largest in NFL history.

Let's calculate the present value of Testaverde's contract using a 10 percent interest rate and assuming (for simplicity) that his salary is paid in one lump sum on December 31 of each year. The Associated Press reported the salary to be received each year and the part of the salary that was to be deferred. The calculations below show that the reported $8.2 million is really worth $5.02 million. This is still a very lucrative contract; it may be the third best in football. But it is worth $3.18 million less than the headlines declared.

PRESENT VALUE AND SPORTS HEADLINES

Sports salaries are high, and the sports headlines often are filled with the reported value of contracts. This is not a new phenomenon. Babe Ruth was once asked by a reporter how he could justify the fact that he earned more than President Herbert Hoover. His reply was, "I had a better year than he did." As lucrative as these contracts seem to be, they are not what they appear. Sports contracts are for multiple years, and often payments are stretched far into the future.

Many people feel that Vinny Testaverde has the potential to be the greatest quarterback of all time. In 1987, he signed a six-year contract with the Tampa Bay

TESTAVERDE'S SALARY

Year	Salary in Millions of Dollars	Present Value in Millions of Dollars (10% Discount Rate)
Signing Bonus	1.00	1.00
1. 1987	1.35	1.23
2. 1988	.35	.29
3. 1989	.35	.26
4. 1990	.35	.24
5. 1991	.35	.22
6. 1992	.35	.20
Deferred Payments:		
7. 1993	.25	.13
8. 1994	.45	.21
9. 1995	.65	.28
10. 1996	.85	.33
11. 1997	.85	.30
12. 1998	1.05	.33
TOTAL:	8.20	5.02

Source: Associated Press wire story, 11 April 1987.

We live in a society where you can save (refrain from consumption) and receive interest as a reward for your saving. As a result, you are always better off delaying a payment of a fixed sum that you must make and speeding up a payment of a fixed sum you are to receive. For example, suppose you owe your friend $100, and your friend doesn't care when you pay off the debt within the next year. If the interest rate is 10 percent, you could take $90.90, put it in the bank, and in one year pay off the $100 debt because you would receive back from the bank the $90.90 you deposited *plus* interest of $9.10. In other words, the present value of the $100 debt to be paid in one year at 10 percent interest is only $90.90.

Another way of saying this is that the $90.90 you put in the bank today will be equivalent to the $100 you pay to your friend a year from now. Conversely, if you were owed $100, you would want the money now so you could put $100 in the bank and have $110 at the end of a year. Two principles emerge from this example of discounting. The first is: the higher the interest rate, the lower the present value. The second is: the longer the time period, the lower the present value.

The formula for calculating present value is

$$\frac{V_t}{(1 + r)^t},$$

where V_t is the value in year t, r is the interest rate, and t is the number of years. The formula is rarely used in calculations, however, since present value tables, like Table 9–2, are readily available. This table shows the present value of one dollar received in various future years (up to 50 years) at different interest rates. You can easily read the table to see, as in the previous example, that the present value of $100 for one year at a 10 percent interest rate is $90.90 (0.909 × $100).

TABLE 9–2
PRESENT VALUE OF $1.00

Year	3%	4%	5%	6%	7%	8%	10%	12%	15%	20%	Year
1	.971	.962	.952	.943	.935	.926	.909	.893	.870	.833	1
2	.943	.925	.907	.890	.873	.857	.826	.797	.756	.694	2
3	.915	.890	.864	.839	.816	.794	.751	.711	.658	.578	3
4	.889	.855	.823	.792	.763	.735	.683	.636	.572	.472	4
5	.863	.823	.784	.747	.713	.681	.620	.567	.497	.402	5
6	.838	.790	.746	.705	.666	.630	.564	.507	.432	.335	6
7	.813	.760	.711	.665	.623	.583	.513	.452	.376	.279	7
8	.789	.731	.677	.627	.582	.540	.466	.404	.326	.233	8
9	.766	.703	.645	.591	.544	.500	.424	.360	.284	.194	9
10	.744	.676	.614	.558	.508	.463	.385	.322	.247	.162	10
11	.722	.650	.585	.526	.475	.429	.350	.287	.215	.134	11
12	.701	.625	.557	.497	.444	.397	.318	.257	.187	.112	12
13	.681	.601	.530	.468	.415	.368	.289	.229	.162	.093	13
14	.661	.577	.505	.442	.388	.340	.263	.204	.141	.078	14
15	.642	.555	.481	.417	.362	.315	.239	.183	.122	.065	15
16	.623	.534	.458	.393	.339	.292	.217	.163	.107	.054	16
17	.605	.513	.436	.371	.317	.270	.197	.146	.093	.045	17
18	.587	.494	.416	.350	.296	.250	.179	.130	.081	.037	18
19	.570	.475	.396	.330	.277	.232	.163	.116	.070	.031	19
20	.554	.456	.377	.311	.258	.215	.148	.104	.061	.026	20
25	.478	.375	.295	.232	.184	.146	.092	.059	.030	.0105	25
30	.412	.308	.231	.174	.131	.0994	.057	.033	.015	.0042	30
40	.307	.208	.142	.0972	.067	.0460	.022	.011	.0037	.0006	40
50	.228	.141	.087	.0543	.034	.0213	.008	.003	.0009	.0001	50

Applications of present value calculation surround you in your day-to-day life. Let's look at an example. Suppose that on your first job as project manager, you are given the task of planning a new phase of operations. The engineer tells you the operation can be built in any of three ways and over a period of three years, but the firm's cash outlay will be spread out differently over the years. The alternatives are listed in Table 9–3. All alternatives are equal in the sense that they do not affect the operation of the project and have the same date of completion, and all payments are made at the end of the year. Each plan costs $600. Which should you choose? The only way to determine which alternative will maximize profit is to use present value analysis and discount the future dollar amounts. Using Table 9–2, we can calculate the present value of each amount in Table 9–3. The present values, using a 10 percent interest rate, are in parentheses in Table 9–3. We can then total the present value amounts to find the least-cost method of production, which turns out to be Alternative *C*. The present value of Alternative *C* is 5 percent less than Alternative *A* and 9 percent less than Alternative *B*, meaning a substantial savings for the firm.

TABLE 9-3
PRESENT VALUE EXAMPLE (10 PERCENT INTEREST RATE)

Alternative	Cost in Year 1	Cost in Year 2	Cost in Year 3	Total Cost
■	■	■	■	■
A	$200.00	$200.00	$200.00	$600.00
	(181.80)	(165.20)	(150.20)	(*PV* = 497.20)
B	$400.00	$100.00	$100.00	$600.00
	(363.60)	(82.60)	(75.10)	(*PV* = 521.30)
C	$100.00	$100.00	$400.00	$600.00
	(90.90)	(82.60)	(300.40)	(*PV* = 473.90)

A profit-making firm that expects to be in business for awhile will try to maximize profits, but it will maximize the present value of profits over a period of several years, not just the current period. The concept of present value is very important in business decisions *and* is not understood by many decision makers. It is often joked that the first year of an MBA degree program should be devoted solely to getting students to understand and make use of present value.

■
SUMMARY

1. Economists calculate both implicit and explicit costs of production. Implicit costs are those costs implied by alternatives given up, and explicit costs are expenditure, or accounting, costs.

2. When total costs (both implicit and explicit) are equal to total revenues, economists say there is zero economic profit. This means the firm is covering all opportunity costs, including a normal return to enterprise. When costs exceed revenues, firms and resources will leave an industry in order to earn the opportunity cost associated with those resources.

3. In the short run as variable factors are added to the fixed factor, the firm may experience increasing returns at low levels of output but eventually will incur diminishing returns at some higher levels of output.

4. Increasing and diminishing returns account for the U-shape of the short-run average cost curve.

5. The U-shape of the long-run average cost curve is

due to economies and diseconomies of large-scale production.

6. Profit maximization means that an entrepreneur will produce that level of output that equates marginal cost and marginal revenue, thus insuring that total revenue exceeds total cost by the largest possible amount.

7. Present value calculations are techniques for making dollar amounts to be received or paid in the future comparable with dollar amounts in the present.

NEW TERMS

explicit cost
implicit cost
accounting profit
economic profit
normal profit
total cost (*TC*)
total fixed cost (*TFC*)
total variable cost (*TVC*)

average total cost (*AC*)
average fixed cost (*AFC*)
average variable cost (*AVC*)
marginal cost (*MC*)
planning curve
long-run average cost curve (*LRAC*)
optimal-size plant

economies of scale
diseconomies of scale
natural monopoly
total revenue (*TR*)
marginal revenue (*MR*)
present value
discounting

QUESTIONS FOR DISCUSSION

1. Why are cost curves normally U-shaped both in the long run and in the short run?

2. What is a normal profit? Why is it necessary for a firm to earn a normal profit?

3. The famous epigram of the Chicago School of Economics is: There is no such thing as a free lunch. What does this mean?

4. At what size do universities start experiencing diseconomies of scale? What does the existence of many different sizes of universities indicate about the optimally sized university?

5. Does a university have to reach a certain size to have an efficient (winning) sports program? How would you gather empirical evidence on this?

6. What is the difference between diminishing returns and diseconomies of scale?

7. Would you rather win $6 million in a lump sum or $1 million a year for ten years? Use a present value table to find an answer.

8. Give an example of an explicit and an implicit cost associated with your college education. Why does college attendance and, even more so, graduate school attendance increase when economic times are bad, and unemployment rates are high?

9. Complete the table at the top of page 483. You will be referring back to it when you answer questions at the end of the next two chapters.

10. Graph *AFC*, *AVC*, *AC*, and *MC*. Why does *MC* cut the *AVC* and *AC* at their low points?

SUGGESTIONS FOR FURTHER READING

Leftwich, Richard H., and Ross D. Eckert. *The Price System and Resource Allocation*. 9th ed. Hinsdale, IL: The Dryden Press, 1985; and Cotton M. Lindsay. *Applied Price Theory*. Hinsdale, IL: The Dryden Press, 1984. These two intermediate price theory texts develop the material found in this chapter in much greater detail.

(1) Total Output Q/Day	(2) Total Fixed Cost TFC	(3) Total Variable Cost TVC	(4) Total Cost TC	(5) Average Fixed Cost AFC	(6) Average Variable Cost AVC	(7) Average Total Cost AC	(8) Marginal Cost MC
■	■	■	■	■	■	■	■
0	$10.00	$ 0	$ 0	—	—	—	—
1			15.00				
2						9.00	
3					3.33		
4			21.00				
5							2.00
6		16.00					
7							4.00
8					3.13		
9			41.00				
10							7.00
11			56.00				

CHAPTER 10 ■
■
PURE COMPETITION

■
INTRODUCTION

The last two chapters have developed the principles of production and the general cost relationships derived from the production process. Any firm making production decisions will relate potential, or forecasted, revenues to these costs in order to determine output levels. However, the forecasted revenues will depend on the market conditions faced by the firm.

The next three chapters will look at four different models, referred to as *market structures*. The first model discussed is the model of pure (or perfect) competition. **Pure competition** is the market structure in which there are many sellers and buyers. The firms produce a homogenous product, and there is free entry and exit of these firms to and from the industry. It is important to keep in mind that this is a theoretical model. It does not precisely describe reality but rather allows the development of tools that indicate what determines price and quantity when conditions are close to those of pure competition. The purely competitive model is the abstract ideal to which we will compare other market structures. This purely competitive model underlies the basic supply and demand model developed earlier.

■ ■ ■ ■ ■ ■ ■
CHARACTERISTICS OF PURE COMPETITION

There are six basic assumptions for the model of pure competition. In developing the theory, we assume these six characteristics exist in the market in which the firm is selling its product.

The first assumption is that there is a large number of sellers in the industry. No particular number is specified as being large: a large number means there are so many sellers of the product that no single seller's decisions can affect price. A wheat farmer would be an example of this. No single wheat farmer can influence the price of wheat. The farmer could sell the entire crop or none of the crop, and as far as the farmer could tell, it wouldn't affect the price one bit because the market is so large relative to any single producer.

PURE COMPETITION
The market structure in which there are many sellers and buyers. The firms produce an homogeneous product, and there is free entry and exit of these firms to and from the industry.

The second assumption is that there is a large number of buyers. Again, a large number means that no one buyer can affect the price in any perceptible way. In other words, no single purchaser has any **market power**.

The third assumption is that purely competitive firms produce a homogeneous product. The product of one firm is no different from the products of other firms in the industry. Since this is the case, purchasers have no preference for one producer over another. If you are a miller and want to purchase wheat, you don't care if Farmer Jones or Farmer Smith produced the wheat—a bushel of Number 1 winter wheat is a bushel of Number 1 winter wheat!

The fourth, and very important, assumption is that there is free entry into, and free exit out of, the industry. This means that if one firm wishes to go into business or if another firm wishes to cease production, they do so without governmental or any other kind of constraint. Keep this assumption in mind because it is crucial in distinguishing pure competition from monopoly, which we will examine in the next chapter.

The last two assumptions are that there is perfect knowledge and perfect mobility of resources. These assumptions are even more unrealistic than the others because resources are ordinarily costly to move, and information is costly to acquire. The effect of these two assumptions is that when economic profits exist, firms will find out about these profits and enter the industry. Even if these assumptions are far from reality, the resulting model is valuable because it shows what adjustments would take place in an ideal setting.

These six assumptions, for the most part, were those of Adam Smith, who developed the general outline of the perfectly competitive model in his book, *The Wealth of Nations*, more than two centuries ago. The graphic models in this chapter were first developed by Alfred Marshall. In the nineteenth century, the model of perfect competition was the dominant way of looking at problems of determining prices and output levels. The study of other market structures, which we will examine in the next two chapters, arose later.

■ ■ ■ ■ ■ ■ ■
COMPETITIVE ADJUSTMENT IN THE SHORT RUN

Recall that a profit-maximizing firm always produces that quantity for which marginal cost is equal to marginal revenue. Now that we know what cost curves look like, we need to determine what the competitive firm's marginal revenue curve looks like. Since the firm is small relative to the market, and its product is indistinguishable from the product of other firms, the purely competitive firm views itself as having no influence on market price. If the purely competitive firm wants to sell any of its output, it must sell at the market price. For this reason, the firm is referred to as a price taker. A firm in pure competition is a **price taker** because it has no influence on price. It can sell any amount at the market-clearing price. The firm takes the market price as its selling price. If it sets a higher price, none of its output will be sold because buyers can purchase an identical product for the lower market price elsewhere. By the same token, it makes no sense to sell below market price because the firm can sell all it wants to sell at the established market price.

MARKET POWER
The ability of firms or buyers to affect price. Large numbers of buyers and sellers ensure that no one buyer or seller affects price.

PRICE TAKER
A firm in pure competition is a price taker because the firm views itself as having no influence on price. It can sell any amount at the market-clearing price.

The market demand and supply curves and the firm's resultant demand curve are drawn in Figure 10–1. Market demand (*D*) and supply (*S*) curves are such that the market equilibrium price is P_1. If the market is in equilibrium, the purely competitive firm can sell as much of the product as it wishes at Price P_1. From the firm's viewpoint, the demand curve is perfectly elastic at Price P_1.

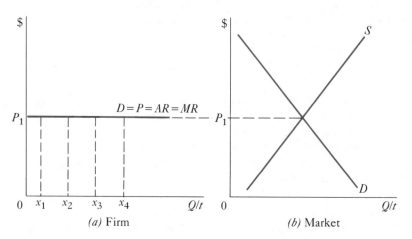

FIGURE 10-1
ELASTIC DEMAND AT MARKET EQUILIBRIUM
A firm's demand curve in pure competition is perfectly elastic at the market equilibrium price.

AVERAGE REVENUE
Total revenue divided by the quantity sold. A demand curve is an average revenue curve.

The demand schedule a firm faces is, at the same time, its average revenue schedule. If, for example, the price consumers pay in a market is $15, the average revenue a seller receives is also $15. Thus, as price changes along a market demand curve, the average revenue that sellers receive is also changing. Total revenue of a firm is the price times the quantity sold ($TR = P \times Q$). **Average revenue** is total revenue divided by the quantity sold. It is the revenue per unit sold, which is the price of the product. A demand curve is an average revenue curve. In the case of pure competition, price does not vary with output, so $AR = {(P \times Q)}/{Q} = P$ is a constant. The firm's perfectly elastic demand curve in Figure 10–1 is also a perfectly elastic AR curve.

Marginal revenue is the change in total revenue from selling one more (or one fewer) unit ($MR_n = TR_n - TR_{n-1}$). In Figure 10–1, the change in total revenue, if sales increase from x_1 to x_2 to x_3, etc., is $P_1(x_2 - x_1)$, $P_1(x_3 - x_2)$, etc., where each change in *x* is one unit of *x*. In other words, in the case of a perfectly elastic demand curve, such as the firm's demand curve in Figure 10–1, $D = P = AR = MR$. The marginal revenue curve of a perfectly elastic demand curve is the same as the demand curve. The demand curve is always the average revenue curve for any market structure, but it is equal to the marginal revenue curve only in perfect competition.

REPRESENTATIVE FIRM
A typical or "average" firm in pure competition.

Using marginal cost and marginal revenue, we now can determine how the firm will adjust its output in the short run. The market and a representative firm are depicted in Figure 10–2. A **representative firm** is a typical or "average" firm in pure competition—one of the many similar firms in this market. In Figure 10–2, the representative firm's marginal cost curve also is drawn. This firm maximizes profits by producing x_1 when the price per unit is P_1 because at x_1, $MR = MC$. Now assume the market demand increases to D_1. This causes the market price to rise to P_2 and the firm's demand curve, average revenue curve, and marginal revenue curve to change to $D_1 = AR_1 = MR_1$. The firm responds by increasing its output level to x_2, where $MR_1 = MC$. We see in Figure 10–2 that the firm's short-run marginal cost curve is the same as its short-run supply curve. **A short-run supply curve** is a supply curve in the short run—the period in which the size of the plant cannot be varied. In pure competition, the short-run marginal cost curve is the short-run supply curve.

SHORT-RUN SUPPLY CURVE

The supply curve in the short run—the period in which the size of the plant cannot be varied. In pure competition, the short-run marginal cost curve is the short-run supply curve.

(a) Firm   *(b)* Market

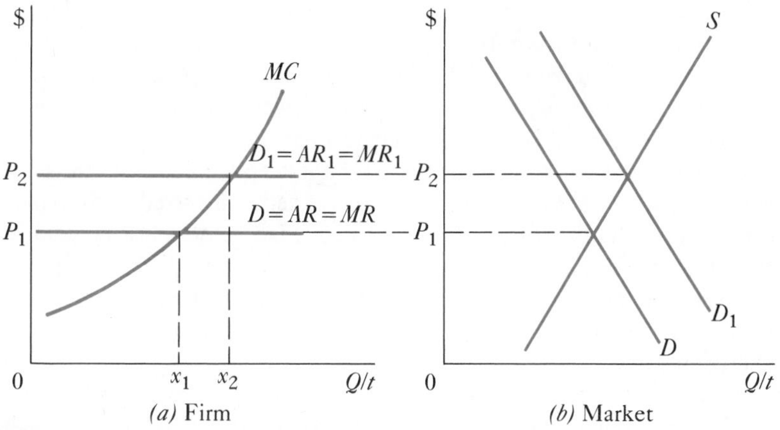

FIGURE 10-2
PROFIT MAXIMIZATION
An increase in demand in the market causes equilibrium price to rise. The demand curve the firm faces adjusts by the amount of the increase in price, and the firm increases its output to equate *MC* and *MR*. The adjustment process is such that the firm's *MC* curve is its short-run supply curve.

We have, in fact, been looking at the supply curve of the firm all along. As market price rose, the firm increased its output along its marginal cost curve. Further increases or decreases in price would cause further movements along the marginal cost curve or the short-run supply curve. Shortly, we will see how these short-run supply curves relate to the industry (or market) supply curve.

Profits, Losses, and Shutting Down

We have just seen how a firm adjusts in the short run to changes in market demand, but we don't yet know whether this firm is making a profit or a loss and how large this profit or loss is. To find out, we need to add to the graph the average cost curve, which we encountered in the last chapter. Also, in order to decide if the firm should continue to produce if losses are encountered, we need to add the average variable cost curve.

In Figure 10-3, the firm is maximizing profit by producing x_1 at Price P_1 where $P = MR = MC$. The average cost of producing x_1 can be seen to be x_1C in Figure 10-3. The total cost of producing x_1 is represented by the area of the rectangle $0P_1Cx_1$.

Total revenue is also $0P_1Cx_1$, so $TR = TC$. This firm is thus making zero economic profits, although it is meeting its opportunity costs. Remember that total cost includes *normal profit*, which is the return on capital and enterprise necessary to keep firms in the industry.

If the firm's average cost curve is as drawn in Figure 10-4, the average cost of producing x_1 would be x_1A. Total revenue is still P_1 times x_1, or the area $0P_1Bx_1$. Total cost is now $0CAx_1$. $TR > TC$, so there is an economic profit equal to CP_1BA in Figure 10-4. Alternatively, if the average cost curve is represented by the one drawn in Figure 10-5, the average cost of producing x_1 would be x_1A. Total revenue is $0P_1Bx_1$, and total cost is $0CAx_1$. In this case, $TC > TR$, so losses are being incurred. The loss is equal to P_1CAB in Figure 10-5.

Should the firm in Figure 10-5 continue to produce, and if so, for how long? After all, it is suffering a loss, which means the factors of production employed by this firm could earn more in some other use. Revenues are less than opportunity costs. But keep in mind that this is the short run, which means that some factor is fixed. This fixed factor represents fixed costs that cannot be eliminated. Fixed costs must be paid in the short run even if production ceases. We need to include the AVC curve to determine the conditions under which the firm should cease production because variable costs are the only ones under the firm's control in the short run.

The short-run cost curves of a firm are depicted with several equilibrium points represented in Figure 10-6. At a price of P_1, which represents a marginal revenue of MR_1, the firm maximizes profits by producing x_1. At P_1, the firm is making an economic profit because total revenue ($0P_1Ax_1$) is greater than total cost ($0C_1Dx_1$). At Price $P_2 = MR_2$, the firm would produce x_2 and make zero economic profit because TR ($0P_2Bx_2$) is equal to TC ($0C_2Bx_2$). Examine carefully what happens when price falls to P_3 and marginal revenue to MR_3. The profit-maximizing or loss-minimizing output is now x_3. At Output x_3, losses are incurred because total revenue is now $0P_3Sx_3$, and total cost is $0C_3Ex_3$. Losses are thus represented by the rectangle P_3CES. The question the firm needs to answer is: Should it produce and incur this loss or should it cease production? Remember, if production is halted, fixed costs must still be paid. In Figure 10-6, if price is P_3, the firm is earning a total revenue of $0P_3Sx_3$, and its total variable costs are $0P_3Sx_3$ ($TVC = AVC \times Q$). In other words, the firm is covering (exactly) its total variable costs and losing an amount equal to its total fixed costs. It must pay the fixed costs even if it shuts down, so at P_3 the firm is indifferent about shutting down or continuing to produce. But if price falls below P_3, the firm will shut down because shutting down will minimize losses. By shutting down, only total fixed cost is lost, instead of total fixed cost plus some portion of variable costs if it continued to produce. The minimum or low point on the AVC curve (S in Figure 10-6) is called the **shutdown point** because if Price (MR) falls below the minimum point on AVC, the firm loses less by ceasing production.

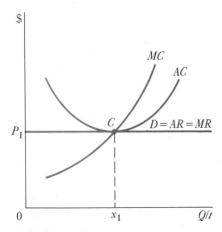

FIGURE 10-3
A FIRM EARNING ZERO ECONOMIC PROFIT
The average cost curve is used to determine if the firm is making an economic profit. If AR (price) is equal to AC, the firm is making zero economic profit.

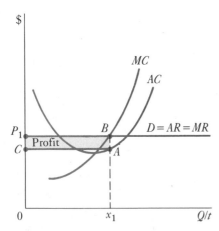

FIGURE 10-4
A FIRM EARNING AN ECONOMIC PROFIT
If the firm's AR is greater than its AC at the level of output being produced, the firm is making an economic profit.

SHUTDOWN POINT
The level of output at which the firm minimizes its losses by ceasing operation.

Consider Price $P_4 = MR_4$ in Figure 10–6. The $MC = MR$ rule tells the firm that at P_4 it should produce Output x_4. However, at x_4 the firm is losing P_4C_4GF ($0P_4Fx_4 - 0C_4Gx_4$). Total revenue of $0P_4Fx_0$ does not cover the total variable cost of producing x_4, which is x_4H times x_4. In other words, the firm is losing more than total fixed cost. It is making variable cost outlays that it wouldn't have to make if it stopped production entirely. The firm would be better off to shut down and only incur its fixed costs.

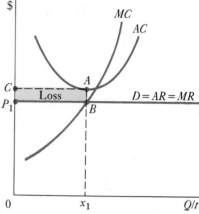

FIGURE 10-5
A FIRM SUFFERING A LOSS
If the firm's AC is greater than its AR at the level of output being produced, the firm is incurring a loss.

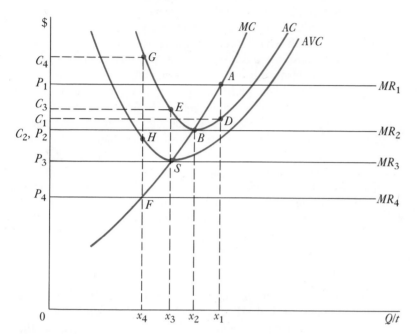

FIGURE 10-6
THE SHUTDOWN POINT
If average revenue is greater than average variable cost, the firm will be able to cover total variable costs and make a payment toward total fixed costs. If price falls below average variable costs, the firm will lose less money if it shuts down than if it continues to produce.

Consider now the earlier statement that the firm's marginal cost curve represents its short-run supply curve. This statement is not exactly correct. A firm's short-run supply curve is represented by its marginal cost curve only *above* Point S, the shutdown point. Below Point S, the firm would produce no output, so only the part of the marginal cost curve above the minimum point on the AVC curve is the firm's supply curve.

The theory has just told us that in the short run, the firm will shut down when price falls below AVC; it says nothing about the real-world timing of such a shutdown. The answer is more difficult in reality than in theory. It depends on many factors, including time and anticipated changes. Consider just two.

First, imagine yourself the owner of a sporting goods store in a ski area or a beach area. Shutdown may be a seasonal decision. If revenues fall below average variable costs (sales clerks, electricity, etc.) in the off-season, you may close up, bearing only your fixed costs (such as rent on the store) until crowds return and your revenues increase. In this case, shutdown does not mean you are moving your investments in plant and equipment into other businesses, only that you lose money in certain seasons and you lose less money if you shut down. In this case, you fully intend to reopen for business when the snow flies or the temperature sends people to the beaches. Past experience helps you to determine about what week to shut down and when to reopen.

Second, imagine yourself as the owner-manager of a steel mill. The price of steel has fallen below your average variable costs of production. In the short run, you shut down (if laws and union contracts allow you to do so) because the short run is too short a time period for you to vary your plant size (which is one way of saying that you can't move your fixed resources in this time period). However, if you are convinced that this low price is a permanent situation, you will begin to liquidate. You will sell equipment and attempt to sell your buildings and other fixed assets. As you succeed in doing this, you are moving to the long run.

To review, note that the minimum point on the AC curve is the least-cost combination, and the minimum point on the AVC curve is the shutdown point. The MC curve above the AVC curve is the purely competitive firm's supply curve. Also keep in mind that these are all short-run phenomena. We will trace the long-run adjustment later.

A Numerical Example

The same short-run adjustments can be seen with the aid of a numerical example. Table 10–1 reproduces some of the production cost data used in the last chapter. Assuming that different market prices are the result of different market equilibrium situations, it is possible to calculate the response the firm would make to these changes. In Table 10–2, six different market prices corresponding to different market conditions are assumed. When the market price is $61, the new demand and marginal revenue curves the firm faces are perfectly elastic at $61. The firm would then produce ten units ($MR = MC = \$61$) and earn an economic profit of

TABLE 10-1
PRODUCTION DATA

Output	AVC	AC	MC	TC
1	$40	$100	$40	$100
2	38	68	36	136
3	36	56	32	168
4	35	50	32	200
5	35	47	35	235
6	36	46	41	276
7	$37^3/_7$	46	46	322
8	39	$46^1/_2$	50	372
9	41	$47^2/_3$	57	429
10	43	49	61	490

$120. This numerical example corresponds to the geometric example in Figure 10–4. At a market price of $46, the firm maximizes profit where $MR = MC = \$46$, which is at an output of seven units. Since $TR = TC$ at seven units, there is zero economic profit. This situation corresponds to Figure 10–3. When market price falls to $41, the firm reacts by decreasing its output to six units ($MR = MC = \$41$), and at six units it incurs a loss of $30. This economic loss corresponds to Figure 10–5.

The firm will continue to produce in the short run unless price falls below $35 because the minimum point on the AVC curve is at $35. To see why, examine the adjustment when market price falls to $32. At $32, the firm would produce four units, but if it does, it loses $72 ($TR = 4 \times \$32 = \$128$; $TC = 4 \times \$50 = \$200$; and $\$128 - \$200 = -\$72$). If it shuts down, the firm loses only $60 in total fixed cost, as the total variable cost (TVC) would have been $140 if production had taken place ($TVC = 4 \times \$35 = \$140$; $TFC = \$200 - \$140 = \$60$). So it loses less if it ceases production. At any price less than $35, the firm will shut down.

TABLE 10-2
PRODUCTION DECISIONS

Market Price (MR)	Firm's Output	TR	TC	Firm's Profits
$61	10	$610	$490	$120
50	8	400	372	28
46	7	322	322	0
41	6	246	276	–30
35	5	175	235	–60
32	4	128	200	–72

A Market Supply Curve

We now can look at the interaction between supply and demand in the market in terms of the relationship between the firm's marginal cost curve and the market supply curve. The firm's marginal cost curve represents its output response to increased market prices. If we were to add (horizontally) all the individual supply curves, we would construct the market, or industry, short-run supply curve. The market supply curve is simply the aggregate of all the firms' supply curves. The short-run market supply curve, then, is the aggregate of all the firms' marginal cost curves that lie above their average variable cost curves. In the long run, more firms can enter an industry as a response to economic profits. The market supply curve will shift to the right because it is now made up of more individual firm supply curves. Conversely, as firms leave an industry due to losses, the market, or industry, supply curve will shift to the left, representing a decrease in supply. This time the decrease is due to the fact that there are fewer individual firm supply curves to be summed.

THE LONG RUN: CONSTANT, INCREASING, AND DECREASING COSTS

To trace the adjustment process when firms have time to alter their fixed inputs, and when new firms can enter the industry, consider the example in Figure 10–7. The black D_1 and S_1 lines in Figure 10–7, Panel (*b*), show the industry in equilibrium. The industry is in long-run equilibrium when there are no economic forces working that would cause it to expand or contract (or that would cause the price to change). In Figure 10–7, Panel (*a*), the firm is making zero economic profit at Price P_1 and Output x_1. Let's assume this representative firm is one of 1,000 identical firms, so the market supply curve (S_1) in Figure 10–7, Panel (*b*), is the summation of 1,000 *MC* curves (above the *AVC* curves). Since these firms are making zero economic profits at P_1, the industry is in equilibrium with an industry output of Q_1 and each firm producing x_1, where $1,000 \times x_1 = Q_1$. Now suppose there is an increase in market demand to D_2. Let's say this increase is brought about by an increase in consumers' real income and the good under consideration is a normal good. When market demand shifts to D_2, market price rises to P_2, and the demand curve facing the firm rises to be perfectly elastic at Price P_2. The firm's new demand curve is represented by D_2, AR_2, and MR_2. These changes are represented by colored lines.

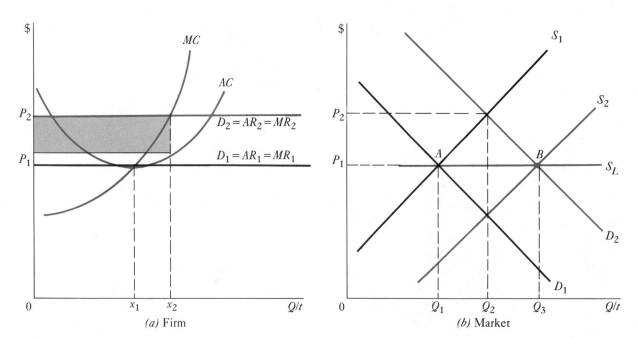

(*a*) Firm   (*b*) Market

FIGURE 10-7
AN ADJUSTMENT TO AN INCREASE IN DEMAND
An increase in market demand will cause price to rise and the demand curve the representative firm faces to shift upward. Economic profits will result, and new firms will enter in response to this profit. As new firms enter the industry, the market supply curve shifts to the right, causing price to fall to the point at which the representative firm is again earning zero economic profit.

The firm's initial (short-run) response is to increase its output to x_2 because $MR_2 = MC$ at Output x_2. Thus, the initial increase in market demand (from Q_1 to Q_2) is met by each of the 1,000 firms increasing their output from x_1 to x_2. Note, however, that each firm is now making an economic profit equal to the shaded area in Figure 10–7, Panel (a). Economic profit, you recall, means that factors of production are earning more than their opportunity cost. This profit means the industry is out of equilibrium. Other firms are going to attempt to grab some of this profit. The existence of profit is the signal for new firms to enter this industry.

Since free entry and perfect knowledge are assumed to be characteristics of pure competition, entrepreneurs will be aware of this profit and will enter the industry. As firms enter the industry, the market supply curve will shift because it now is the summation of the 1,000 original MC curves plus the MC curves of the new entrant firms. In fact, firms will keep entering the industry until equilibrium (zero economic profit) is restored. This is illustrated in Figure 10–7. If all firms have the same costs (that is, all firms are exactly like this representative firm) and if nothing happens to change these costs (in Figure 10–7, we assume that this is the case), equilibrium will be restored when the price has been reduced to P_1, the original equilibrium price. If the new equilibrium price is P_1, and industry output is Q_3, each firm is producing x_1, and the summation of the firms' output (1,000 + the new number of firms times x_1) is equal to the industry output, which is Q_3. Connecting the market equilibrium points, Points A and B in Figure 10–7, gives the industry's long-run supply curve (S_L). This curve represents what firms will supply after all adjustments have taken place.

You can check your understanding of this adjustment process by going through the adjustments to a decrease in demand. Figure 10–8 illustrates this process. The industry is initially in equilibrium at Price P_1 and Output Q_1. Firms are making zero profits and producing x_1 units of output. Something or someone, perhaps the government, says the product is dangerous to people's health. This news causes demand to decrease to D_2, represented by the dashed line in Figure 10–8, Panel (b). Market price falls to P_2, and industry output falls to Q_2. In the short run, firms adjust their output to x_2, where $MC = MR_2$. At x_2, however, firms are incurring losses represented by the shaded area. (P_2 is above AVC, so the firm continues production.) The industry is now out of equilibrium. Just as profits were the signal for firms to enter, losses are the signal for firms to exit the industry. Entrepreneurs move their factors to the production of other commodities, seeking to earn their opportunity cost elsewhere. We assumed perfect knowledge, so the entrepreneurs will know where they can earn at least normal profit. As firms leave the industry, the short-run market supply curve will shift because it is now derived by adding up fewer firms' MC curves. Firms will leave the industry until those remaining firms have zero economic profits. Equilibrium is restored when the market supply curve shifts to S_2 so as to restore a price of P_1. Industry output is now Q_3, with each of the remaining firms producing x_1 units of output. As before, the long-run supply curve (S_L) can be found by connecting the industry's equilibrium points, which are represented by Points A and B in Figure 10–8, Panel (b).

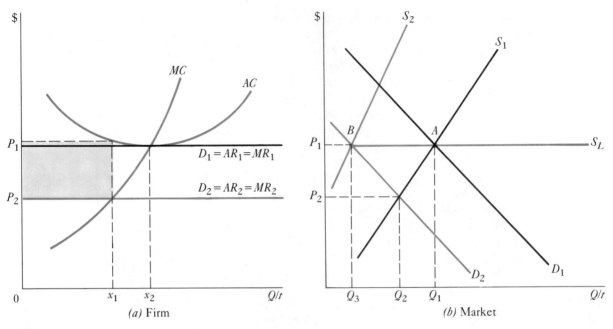

FIGURE 10-8
AN ADJUSTMENT TO A DECREASE IN DEMAND
A decrease in market demand will cause price to fall and the demand curve the representative firm faces to shift downward. Losses will be incurred and some firms will leave the industry. As some firms leave the industry, the market supply curve shifts to the left, causing price to rise until a remaining representative firm is earning zero economic profit.

CONSTANT COST INDUSTRY
An industry in which expansion of output does not cause average costs to rise. The long-run supply curve is perfectly elastic.

The adjustment traced in Figures 10–7 and 10–8 assumed that factor prices, and thus costs, were unaffected by the quantity of output the industry produced. This meant that as firms entered the industry (Figure 10–7) or exited the industry (Figure 10–8), the price of the factors of production did not change and, as a result, the cost curves didn't change. When this is so, the industry is referred to as a constant cost industry. **A constant cost industry** is an industry in which expansion of output does not cause average costs to rise. In a constant cost industry, as more steel, labor, electricity, or whatever is purchased, the cost of those inputs does not increase. Constant costs would probably be the case where the industry's purchase of inputs is small relative to the market supply of these inputs. If the industry's use of inputs is small relative to the market supply, the increased demand for inputs would not increase the price of these same inputs. For example, take the home computer industry. If profits exist and firms enter, these firms will demand more inputs. They will demand more plastic, more labor, and more microchips. If all the computer-producing firms use an insignificant fraction of the total consumption of these inputs, the increase in demand will not cause the price of plastic, labor, and microchips to rise.

Figures 10–7 and 10–8, then, represent contractions and expansions in constant cost industries. The short-run response to a contraction in demand was a decrease in price. An expansion in demand produced a short-run increase in price. The market adjustment, however, returned price to its original level, with fewer firms in the case of the contraction or additional firms in the case of the expansion. The long-run supply curve in a constant cost industry is thus perfectly elastic, even though the short-run supply curve has a positive slope.

Increasing Cost Industries

Sometimes an expansion in industry output will cause costs to increase in the long run. In this case, as an industry expands output and demands more inputs, the increased demand will cause prices to rise in the input markets. For example, an increase in demand for chicken causes new firms to enter the chicken industry and to demand more chicken coops, chicken pluckers, land, and plastic wrapping paper. If the increased demand causes the price of chicken coops, chicken pluckers, land, or plastic wrapping paper to rise, the average production costs of the firm will increase as a result of the increased demand for chicken. Also, less efficient factors and firms may be drawn into the industry. These conditions describe an increasing cost industry. An **increasing cost industry** is an industry in which expansion of output causes average costs to rise in the long run.

INCREASING COST INDUSTRY
An industry in which expansion of output causes average costs to rise in the long run. The long-run supply curve has a positive slope.

Figure 10–9 illustrates the long-run adjustment process in an increasing cost industry. The industry is originally in equilibrium at Price P_1 and Output Q_1. Each firm is producing x_1. Market demand increases to D_2 and, as a result, market price rises to P_2. The firm's demand is now represented by $D_2 = AR_2 = MR_2$. The firm's short-run response is to

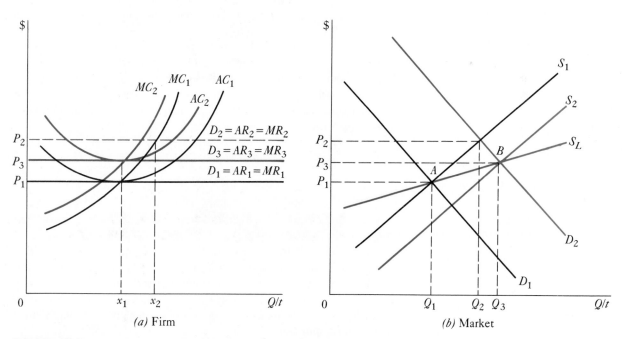

(a) Firm

(b) Market

FIGURE 10-9
AN ADJUSTMENT IN AN INCREASING COST INDUSTRY
When demand increases in an increasing cost industry, the firms that enter the industry bid up the prices of the factors of production for all firms in the industry. As a result, price does not return to the previous equilibrium. Instead, a new equilibrium with the representative firm earning zero economic profit is established at a price above the old equilibrium but below the initial increase in price.

increase output to x_2, where $MC_1 = MR_2$. Industry's output is now Q_2. At this increased output, two things will happen. First, new firms will enter the industry because of the economic profits that now exist. Second, costs will rise as a result of the increased demand for inputs. This rise in cost is represented by the upward shift in the marginal and average cost curves to MC_2 and AC_2 in Figure 10–9, Panel (*a*).

This upward shift of *MC* and *AC* is drawn on the assumption that all costs increase proportionally. In most cases, this would not be exactly true, since some inputs (the scarcer ones) would rise faster in price. However, the illustration is clearer if we assume all factor prices rise proportionally, and this assumption does not seriously affect the analysis. Firms, as purchasers of inputs, are likely to have a significant influence in some input markets and an insignificant one in others. In the previous example, as the demand for chicken increased and firms entered the industry, there may have been no effect on the price of land but a significant effect on the wages of chicken pluckers. It is also possible that firms that are less efficient at producing the good in question will be attracted to the industry. In this case, the representative firm would now have higher costs, indicating less efficient production.

The net result of the increased number of firms and increased costs is a rightward shift in the short-run market supply curve. The supply curve shifts to the right because there are more firms' *MC* curves to add up, but it will not shift as far to the right as it did in the constant cost case because costs have risen for every firm. A new short-run market supply curve will be created when equilibrium is reached at Price P_3, where firms are no longer making profits. Industry output is now Q_3, and each firm is producing x_1 where $MR_3 = MC_2$.

As before, the long-run supply curve connects the industry's equilibrium points on a series of short-run supply curves. Connecting Points *A* and *B* in Figure 10–9, Panel (*b*), produces a long-run supply curve (S_L) with a positive slope, indicating an increasing cost industry. We will leave it to you to diagram the adjustment process reflecting a decrease in demand for an increasing cost industry.

Decreasing Cost Industries

DECREASING COST INDUSTRY
An industry in which an expansion of output causes average costs to fall in the long run. The long-run supply curve has a negative slope.

To complete the analysis, we must examine a decreasing cost industry. A **decreasing cost industry** is an industry in which an expansion of output causes average costs to fall in the long run. A real-world example is difficult to find. In a decreasing cost industry, as more firms enter the industry, causing the demand for inputs to increase, input prices fall. This implies that there are economies of scale in an industry that is supplying an input to the industry under examination. For example, as more electricity is demanded, more efficient generators are built and the price of this input falls.

Figure 10–10 demonstrates this adjustment process. The market equilibrium price, P_1, is determined at the intersection of the market demand and supply curves, D_1 and S_1. The firm is in equilibrium producing x_1 at Price P_1. Now suppose there is an increase in the price of a

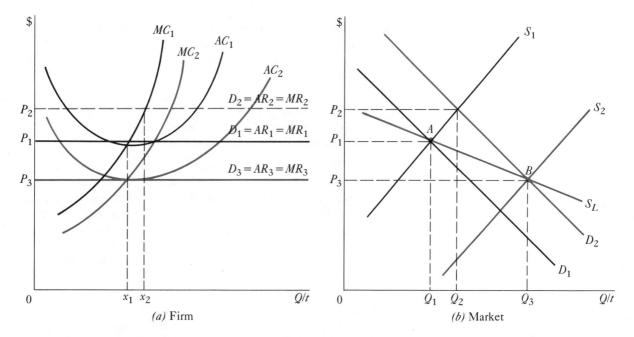

FIGURE 10-10
AN ADJUSTMENT IN A DECREASING COST INDUSTRY
When demand increases in a decreasing cost industry, the firms that enter the industry cause the prices of the factors of production for all firms in this industry to fall. As a result, a new equilibrium price is established that is below the initial equilibrium price.

substitute good. This means that demand for the good in question increases to D_2. The short-run response is for price to rise to P_2. This changes the firm's demand curve to D_2, AR_2, and MR_2. The representative firm responds by increasing its output to x_2, where $MR_2 = MC_1$. Profits now exist and new firms will enter this industry. As new firms enter, two things happen. First, the market supply curve will shift to the right because it is now composed of more MC curves. Second, as industry output increases, costs fall. In Figure 10–10, Panel (*a*), the decrease in costs is assumed to be a proportional decrease in the cost of all inputs. Again, this assumption is not essential, but it is convenient because it simplifies the graph. If costs decrease with industry expansion, it is more likely that this decrease would be a result of a decline in the price of a major input rather than a proportional decline in the price of all inputs. The decrease in costs for the representative firm is shown in Figure 10–10, Panel (*a*), as a shift from AC_1 to AC_2 and from MC_1 to MC_2.

   The decrease in cost and increase in supply cause price to fall. A new equilibrium at a price such as P_3 will be reached. At P_3, the representative firm faces Demand Curve D_3. Equilibrium is reached at Output x_1 where $MC_2 = MR_3$. No economic profits exist.

   As before, the long-run supply curve connects the equilibrium points in the market. These points are represented by Points *A* and *B*. The long-run industry supply curve is represented by the S_L curve in Figure 10–10, Panel (*b*). The curve has a negative slope. This would mean that an increase in market demand would eventually lead to a new equilibrium at lower product prices. Decreasing cost industries thus have negatively sloped long-run supply curves. (The short-run supply curves are still positively sloped, since they are the aggregate of firms' *MC* curves.) Industries with decreasing costs are theoretically conceivable but very unlikely. We leave diagramming the effects of a decrease in demand to you.

COMPETITIVE EQUILIBRIUM: WHAT'S SO GREAT ABOUT PURE COMPETITION?

The nature of pure competition is such that the firm and industry are driven to equilibrium at zero economic profit. Herein lies the appeal of pure competition as a standard against which to judge other market structures. Economists view this equilibrium as an ideal, or a social optimum. In equilibrium, resources are optimally allocated among competing uses. Figure 10–11 shows a firm in equilibrium. At equilibrium, price (P) is equal to average cost (AC) and also is equal to marginal cost (MC).

First, consider $P = MC$. This means that allocative efficiency is being achieved and that the resources of the firm are being allocated exactly as consumers wish. It means that firms are expanding production exactly to the level desired by consumers. If $P > MC$, it would mean that the firm was not putting enough resources into the production of the good in question. Consumers would be willing to pay more (P) than it costs to produce another unit of the good (MC). If $P < MC$, too many resources are being devoted to the production of the good. Consumers would not be willing to pay as much as it costs to produce another unit of the good. In other words, where $P = MC$, the correct amount of resources is being devoted to producing the good.

Second, consider $P = AC$. This means that firms are only earning normal profits. There is no incentive for firms to enter or leave the industry. It is important to note the role of profits in the purely competitive model. Economic profits serve as the signal for firms to move in and out of an industry. When profits exist, entrepreneurs rush in to attempt to capture them; the industry is forced to equilibrium. Likewise, when losses are present, firms leave to earn higher returns elsewhere. Equilibrium is attained due to the profit-seeking nature of firms. In equilibrium, there is efficiency. It is not because of some altruistic behavior on the part of the entrepreneur that the firm is efficient; rather, the entrepreneur is assumed to be a profit maximizer interested solely in individual self-interest, and this brings about efficiency. In the competitive model, self-interest and the quest for profits produce the efficiency that benefits consumers. The firm is not striving for efficiency but for profits. When economic profits have served their signaling function, they disappear.

Third, consider $MC = AC$. This means that AC is at a minimum and, therefore, the firm is using the least-cost combination of inputs. The variable resources are being combined as efficiently as possible.

In the long run, the short-run average cost curve (AC) also will be tangent to the long-run average cost curve at its minimum point, $AC = LRAC$, as in Figure 10–12. This means that all firms are at the most efficient size and are also combining variable resources efficiently. The firms are using the least-cost combination of inputs and at the optimal

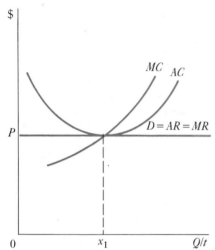

FIGURE 10-11
THE EQUILIBRIUM CONDITION
In short-run equilibrium, allocative efficiency is met. This means that the resources of the firm are being allocated as consumers wish.

WHAT EQUILIBRIUM IN PURE COMPETITION MEANS

- $P = MC$ Production is at the level consumers say (through the market) they want.
- $P = AC$ Firms are earning normal profits. There is no movement into or out of the industry.
- $AC = MC$ Firms are using the least-cost method of production.

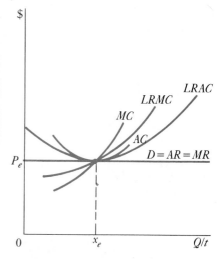

FIGURE 10-12
LONG-RUN EQUILIBRIUM
In long-run equilibrium, average cost is equal to long-run average cost. This means that all firms are at the technically efficient size and are also combining variable resources efficiently. This is the ideal of efficiency to which we compare all other market structures.

plant size. All firms must be efficient, or they will be driven from the market by losses. If any one firm is more efficient than normal, or more efficient than the representative firm, it will be able to make an economic profit even though the other firms don't.

At long-run equilibrium, then, we have $P = AC = MC = LRAC = LRMC$. The purely competitive model is the ideal of efficiency to which we will compare other market structures.

EXAMPLES OF PURE COMPETITION

Perhaps the closest any market can come to the model of pure competition in the U.S. economy are the markets for various agricultural products. In these markets, there are large numbers of buyers and sellers and there is a homogeneous product. This homogeneity is reflected in the fact that there are no brand names associated with most farm products. In addition, there is relatively free entry into and exit out of the industry. Anyone with capital or the ability to borrow capital can enter the agriculture industry. There are very few, if any, educational requirements in the sense of having a degree or passing a test and little in the way of licenses or inspection codes. So, if you don't like thinking in abstract terms all the time, you can use agriculture as an industry and a wheat farm as a firm to illustrate the theory of pure competition. Of course, the example is not perfect, because resources tend to be immobile in agriculture, and the model assumes relatively mobile resources. Agriculture is, however, a reasonably good example of pure competition.

In recent years, the financial services industry has become very close to the model of a purely competitive industry. The services that the financial industry markets offer are very homogeneous. A checking account at a financial institution in a given city is pretty much the same as a checking account anywhere else. In addition, the Depository Institutions Deregulation and Monetary Control Act of 1980 opened up entry into this industry. As a result, insurance companies, stockbrokers, and savings and loan institutions all began to compete with commercial banks for checking account business. One of the results is that customers now get interest on their checking accounts. This market entry was beneficial to consumers and drove bank profits down to normal levels.

The model of pure competition is not meant to be a perfect description of reality. Nor is it, in every case, the ideal state that society should be striving to reach. In certain industries, it may be too costly to bring about the necessary conditions to make that industry purely competitive, in which case we would accept less than the ideal. The model of pure competition is a tool for the economist. The economist can compare the real-world situation to the hypothetical world of pure competition to determine what would be the case if pure competition existed. In this sense, pure competition is a benchmark, or yardstick, by which economists can measure the costs of other market structures.

LARGE NUMBERS OF BUYERS: COMPETITION ON THE BUYER'S SIDE

This chapter has concentrated on developing a theory of firms in perfect competition, or competition on the sellers' side of the market. The assumption of many sellers produced a situation where all sellers perceive the demand curve they face to be perfectly elastic at the market price. Keep in mind that at the beginning of this chapter, we also assumed large numbers of buyers, so many that none possessed market power.

Concentrating on the firm should not obscure the importance of competition on the buyers' side of the market. In order for markets to be competitive, there must be enough buyers so that none can affect the price by withholding purchases or increasing purchases. A competitive market cannot be "cornered" by buyers with market power or wealth. A competitive market is too big and too impersonal to be influenced by single buyers.

THE REPRESENTATIVE FIRM AND ECONOMIC PROFIT IN PURE COMPETITION

We have just studied the model of pure competition in detail. It showed that in situations in which free entry exists, profits will be driven to normal rates of return. Yet we all know of individuals who have become rich in industries that are very competitive and that have relatively free entry. How can this happen without totally invalidating this model of competition? To see how returns in excess of normal can exist in the long run, even under pure competition, we must introduce some new concepts.

Economic Rent

Rent is a familiar term. You pay rent on your apartment. But economists have a special (and very different) meaning for the term rent. **Economic rent** is a payment to a factor of production in excess of the opportunity cost of that factor of production. Let's say, for example, you are trained as a teacher and can earn $20,000 per year as a teacher; but you also have beautiful teeth and can do toothpaste commercials, and in this endeavor you earn $50,000 per year. Economists would say that $30,000 of your income is economic rent because it is the amount by which your earnings exceed your opportunity cost. Presumably, you would

ECONOMIC RENT
A payment to a factor of production in excess of the opportunity cost of that factor of production.

THE INTERNATIONAL PERSPECTIVE
CULTURE AND ENTERPRISE

In many countries throughout the world, markets are not as well developed as they are in the United States. Many institutions have strong holds on culture and affect production, distribution, and consumption.

The laws of supply and demand still hold in these countries, but customs, systems of land tenure, village and family organization, religious practices, and corruption all impact on the functioning of markets.

The evolution of entrepreneurs and profit maximization are affected by these cultural differences. In poor countries, entrepreneurs may lack the help of markets for standardized components, materials, labor, and capital. If individuals are not inherently risk takers, the reaction may be to say "no" to new business opportunities. Indeed, in some cultures risk taking is viewed as unacceptable behavior and minorities have become the entrepreneurs. Jews played this role in medieval Europe, as did the Chinese in some countries in South America and Indians in Africa. This cultural bias is a serious problem in many less developed countries that lack a strong entrepreneurial class. Also, if the ruling structure of society diverts from the encouragement of entrepreneurial development toward the stability of a traditional society, the effect is to slow economic growth. Often in such traditional societies, a trauma that replaces the traditional society produces a spurt of economic growth. The trauma of World War II and its shakeup of the power structure in Japan is a case in point.

do the commercials for $20,001 per year since then you would be earning more than your opportunity cost. Economic rent, then, is more general than economic profit. Since we defined economic profit as revenue in excess of all the implicit costs (including normal profit) and explicit costs of production, economic profit is rent to entrepreneurs. Entrepreneurs will earn only normal profits in pure competition because new entry will drive out all but the normal rate of profit. But it is possible that economic rents to other factors of production will exist. We now need to relate the concept of economic rent to the model of pure competition.

Representative Firms and Economic Rents

The theory of pure competition uses a representative firm that was one of many firms with cost structures that were similar. This is clearly not always realistic. Consider agriculture as an example. Some farmland is far superior to other farmland. It is more fertile, it gets more rainfall, or it is located where the weather is warmer. This will affect the farmer's costs of production. There will always be economic rent earned on the more fertile land. In other competitive industries, location, family connections, or more talent will make firm's cost structures different, creating economic rents.

Differential Rent Theory

The important thing is that economic rent does not weaken the theory of pure competition. In 1817, classical economist David Ricardo reconciled the existence of economic rents with competition by developing the idea of differential rent theory. He was concerned with the fact that fertile farmland was paid a higher rent than poor farmland.

Consider, for example, the cost and revenue functions of the two farms graphed in Figure 10–13. The market is represented in Panel (*c*). Supply and demand are such that market price is *P*. Farm *A*, in Panel (*a*), is earning zero economic profit ($P = AC_a$). Farm *B*, represented in Panel (*b*), is earning an economic profit equal to the shaded area. This economic profit comes from the fact that the land used to produce Product *x* is much more fertile for Farm *B*. As a result, the costs of production are lower.

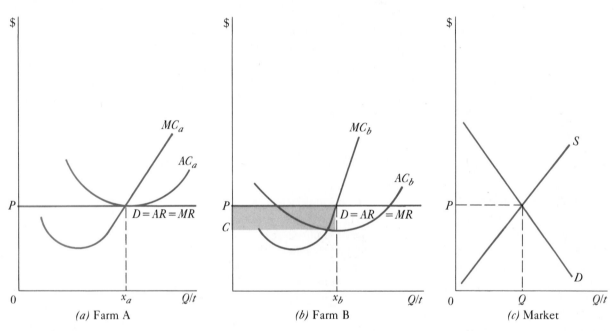

FIGURE 10-13
DIFFERENTIAL RENTS IN PURE COMPETITION
Farms *A* and *B* both face perfectly elastic demand curves at Price *P* determined in Panel (*c*). Because its land is more fertile, Farm *B* has lower average costs and earns a profit shown by the shaded area in Panel (*b*). That profit will be converted to economic rent as competition for the fertile land bids up its price.

Farmers would be willing to pay the owner of the land owned by Farm *B* a higher price for being able to farm this land. This higher price becomes a cost of production to Farm *B* because economic rent for the more fertile land will rise as farmers seek to either purchase or lease this land. Even if the owner of the land is also the farmer, economic rent is still a cost of production because the owner could lease the land to other farmers.

DAVID RICARDO (1772–1823)

David Ricardo may have been the most in-fluential of all the classical economists. Despite his lack

of formal education, he quickly became a leading intellectual of his time. His experience is in contrast to that of almost all the other classical economists who had pursued rigorous programs of formal education. In 1814, Ricardo retired to devote his time to political economy. In 1819, he became a member of Parliament and, with the help of James Mill (father of the great economist John Stuart Mill), founded the Political Economy Club of London. This club became the forum in which the classical economists discussed their ideas.

Ricardo was a prolific writer of letters and pamphlets intended to influence policy discussions on economic matters. His chief formal work, *On the Principles of Political Economy and Taxation*, was published in 1817. He is best remembered for his statements on the principles of comparative advantage and his support of free trade, which are only a part of his comprehensive work. In fact, much of his early interest in economics was generated by his interest in international trade and his interest in showing the benefits of such trade. Ricardo also developed a labor theory of value that greatly impressed Karl Marx, who extended and radicalized Ricardo's theory. Ricardo developed the differential rent theory presented in this chapter.

The result of differential rent to factors of production is that rents rise on more productive factors, which equalizes the average costs of production among firms. In other words, the economic profit for Farm B is a result of a superior factor of production, in this case land. The user of the factor (it could be the owner of the farm or someone else) will receive this rent. When the rent is paid, AC_b will, in fact, rise until the shaded area of Farm B disappears.

The point that emerges is that competitive firms may appear to earn economic profits, i.e., more than a normal rate of return, but these returns are economic rents to factors of production, not economic profits. In many cases, the firm's entrepreneur is the owner of these factors and, as a result, the rent looks like an economic profit. In fact, many times the entrepreneur has specialized skills that form the basis for the firm. The return to these special skills is an economic rent to the special factor input, not an economic profit. The concept of economic rent is an important one that will be discussed in more detail in several of the upcoming chapters.

SUMMARY

1. Pure competition is characterized by large numbers of buyers and sellers, homogeneous products, ease of entry into and exit from the industry, perfect knowledge, and mobility of resources.

2. The firm in a purely competitive market faces a perfectly elastic demand curve at the price determined by equilibrium in the market.

3. The firm's short-run supply curve is its short-run marginal cost curve above the minimum point on the average variable cost curve, otherwise known as the shutdown point.

4. Long-run adjustments to changes in market demand are dependent on the cost characteristics of the industry under consideration. Since entry is easy, additional firms will enter as long as economic profits are present. As a result, economic profits, brought about by an increase in demand, will lead to new entry.

5. An industry can be characterized by constant, increasing or decreasing costs. The slope of the long-run supply curve will depend on which of these different cost situations prevails.

6. In equilibrium, $P = AC = MC = LRAC = LRMC$. This condition describes the efficiency ideal to which other market structures are compared.

7. Profits are the force that drives the model to efficiency. The firm is not seeking efficiency but profits. This search for profits produces the efficiency that characterizes the model of pure competition.

8. Large numbers of buyers ensure that no single buyer can influence price in a competitive market.

9. Economic rent is a payment (return) to a factor of production over the opportunity cost of that factor.

10. Competitive firms may appear to be earning long-run economic profits, but these returns are economic rents to specific factors of production in that firm rather than economic profits.

NEW TERMS

pure competition
market power
price taker
average revenue (AR)

representative firm
short-run supply curve
shutdown point
constant cost industry

increasing cost industry
decreasing cost industry
economic rent

QUESTIONS FOR DISCUSSION

1. Show how the long-run market supply curve will be determined by short-run supply adjustments in an increasing cost industry.

2. Diagram a situation showing a market in equilibrium and a representative firm. Then show a decrease in market demand. Trace through the short-run and long-run adjustment, assuming this is a decreasing cost industry.

3. "If the price of wheat doesn't rise, farmers will lose money and the long-run price will be even higher." Discuss this often-heard argument.

4. Why does profit maximization bring about efficiency?

5. What situations cause long-run supply curves to be positively sloped?

6. Explain in your own words why your firm might keep producing in the short run even if you were incurring a loss.

7. What does it mean to say that in pure competition, long-run equilibrium means that $P = AC = MC = LRAC = LRMC$?

8. Explain how the return to a good location for a firm (for instance, a gas station) in pure competition does not violate the conclusion that economic profits are driven to zero by new entry.

   Return to the Table you completed in question 9 of the preceding Chapter. Use the data in that Table to answer questions 9 and 10. (The data will also be used in the next Chapter.)

9. Assume that the data from question 9 in the last chapter represents the unit-cost data for a purely competitive firm in a constant cost industry. What would the firm produce in the short run if the market price is $7.00. Why? What is the economic profit or loss? If this is a representative firm, where is the market price going to settle?

10. What would happen if market price fell to $2.50? Why?

■ SUGGESTIONS FOR FURTHER READING

Leftwich, Richard H., and Ross D. Eckert. *The Price System and Resource Allocation*. 9th ed. Hinsdale, IL: The Dryden Press, 1985. Develops the graphical analysis of the material in this chapter in great detail.

Stigler, George J. "Perfect Competition, Historically Contemplated." *Journal of Political Economy* (1957). Reprinted in Edwin Mansfield. *Microeconomics: Selected Readings*. New York: W.W. Norton and Sons, Inc., (1975): 167–187. A classic article that reviews the historical development of the theory of perfect competition.

Stigler, George J. *The Theory of Price*. 4th ed. New York: Macmillan Publishing Co., 1987: Chapter 10. A classic introductory price theory text.

CHAPTER 11 ■

■

MONOPOLY

■

■
INTRODUCTION

Pure monopoly is at the other end of the market continuum from pure competition in the sense that pure competition has many firms and pure monopoly has but one. The word *monopoly* is derived from the Greek words *mono* for "one" and *polein* for "seller." **Monopoly** is the market structure in which the firm is a single seller of a product that has no close substitutes. It is necessary that there be no close substitutes to ensure that there is only one firm in the industry. If a close substitute product exists, the firm is not a single seller.

Pure monopoly is a theoretical model and as with pure competition, real-world examples are almost nonexistent. The theory is still useful, however, as a tool to examine real-world situations. The definition of a pure monopoly as a single seller of a product with no close substitutes makes finding examples quite difficult, but there are many firms that we can say have monopoly power. **Monopoly power** is the ability to exercise some of the economic effects predicted in the model of pure monopoly. In the last chapter, we described firms in pure competition as price takers. In this chapter you will see that, because it has some control over price, a monopoly is a price searcher. **A price searcher** is a firm that sets price in order to maximize profits. A price-searching firm has monopoly power. It searches for the price-quantity combination that will maximize profit.

Perhaps the best example of monopoly in U.S. history is the Aluminum Company of America, which, prior to World War II, was the only aluminum producer in the United States. But even this falls short of pure monopoly because aluminum does have some close substitutes. For example, soft drinks can be put into glass bottles, steel cans, or plastic containers; golf clubs can be made with steel shafts; and not long ago tennis players got along with wooden racquets. Before worrying too much about finding a *real* monopoly, let's analyze adjustment under monopoly and then compare the allocation of resources under pure monopoly to those under pure competition.

MONOPOLY
The market structure in which there is a single seller of a product that has no close substitutes.

MONOPOLY POWER
The ability to exercise some of the economic effects predicted in the model of pure monopoly.

PRICE SEARCHER
A firm that sets price in order to maximize profits. A price-searching firm has monopoly power.

DEMAND AND MARGINAL REVENUE

In the last chapter, the purely competitive firm faced a perfectly elastic demand curve and, as a result, price (or average revenue) and marginal revenue were equal. However, a monopolistic firm faces the *market* demand curve because the firm is the single seller and is, therefore, the industry. This distinction is very important because market demand curves have negative slopes. Since the demand curve has a negative slope, the marginal revenue curve will lie below the demand curve, which is also the average revenue curve. The common sense reason that the marginal revenue curve lies below the average revenue curve is that the monopolist must lower price in order to sell more units of output. Price reductions apply to *all* units of output that the monopolist sells, not just the last or marginal unit. Each additional unit sold thus adds to total revenue by the amount it sells for—its price—but takes away from total revenue by the reduction in price on each of the previous units sold; so, this change in revenue (the marginal revenue) must be less than price.

An arithmetic example of the relationship among average, total, and marginal revenue for a monopoly firm is presented in Table 11-1. When three units are sold, the total revenue is $186 (3 × $62). In order to sell four units, the monopolist must reduce the price from $62 to $60. Total revenue will then increase by $60 because an additional unit is being sold for $60, but it will also decrease by $6 because the first three units now sell for $2 less each (for $60 each rather than for $62). The net result is that the monopolist has added $54 ($60 – $6) to total revenue by reducing the price from $62 to $60. Notice that marginal revenue is $54 and price (average revenue) is $60 for four units. Marginal revenue has to be smaller than average revenue whenever there are previous units that suffer a price reduction.

TABLE 11-1
DEMAND AND MARGINAL REVENUE RELATIONSHIPS

Units Sold	Price (Average Revenue)	Total Revenue	Marginal Revenue
1	$64	$ 64	$64
2	63	126	62
3	62	186	60
4	60	240	54
5	58	290	50
6	56½	339	49
7	55	385	46
8	52	416	31
9	47	423	7
10	40	400	–23

This relationship can be seen graphically in Figure 11-1. When demand is inelastic, decreases in price will cause total revenue to

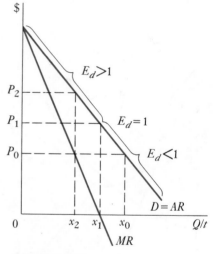

FIGURE 11-1
DEMAND AND MARGINAL REVENUE

The marginal revenue curve lies below the average revenue curve in the case of a negatively sloped demand curve. In drawing the relationship between average and marginal revenue, the marginal revenue curve will intersect the x-axis exactly halfway between the origin and the point where the average revenue curve intersects the x-axis. Demand is elastic above P_1 and inelastic below P_1.

decline. If total revenue is declining, additions to total revenue must be negative, i.e., *MR* is negative. In Figure 11–1, a reduction in price below P_1 will decrease total revenue because marginal revenue is negative. This corresponds to the inelastic portion of the demand curve. Conversely, a reduction in price from P_2 to P_1 would increase total revenue because the demand curve is elastic in this range.

Think back to the discussion of elasticity and Cournot's problem of the mineral spring. In that problem, the monopoly owner of a mineral spring with no production costs set price at the point where the price elasticity of demand was unitary. We can now see this same principle using the profit maximization rule of *MR* = *MC*. If costs are zero, the *MC* curve would lie along on the horizontal axis. In Figure 11–1, the monopolist would maximize profits by producing x_1 at Price P_1, where *MC* = *MR* = 0. Since monopolists are profit maximizers, they produce that quantity where *MR* = *MC* and sell the product for whatever the market will pay. The demand curve shows what price buyers will pay for an output of x_1. The mineral spring monopolist will increase sales of the product as long as marginal revenue is positive, since it costs nothing more to produce another unit. You should note that this does *not* mean the mineral spring monopolist sells as much as possible but rather sells the quantity that maximizes profit. In this case, it happens that the quantity where profit is maximized is at a marginal revenue of zero, since costs are zero.

PRICE AND OUTPUT DECISIONS UNDER MONOPOLY

In the more general case, where costs are positive, the monopolist searches out the profit-maximizing output by equating marginal costs and marginal revenue. The purely competitive firm is a price taker; the monopoly firm is a price searcher. A monopolist searches for the profit-maximizing price, not the highest price. We can see this process graphically by looking at cost relationships under monopoly.

Figure 11–2 shows a monopolist producing a certain good for which the market demand is *D*. *MR* is derived from *D*. The monopolist's *AC* curve and *MC* curve are also given. The monopolist will maximize profit by producing x_1 units because at that level of output, *MR* = *MC*. If *MR* > *MC* (that is, if output is less than x_1), the monopolist can increase profits by expanding output because additions to output cause total revenue then to increase by more than total cost rises. On the other hand, if *MR* < *MC* (that is, if output is greater than x_1), the monopolist would contract output because additions to output add more to total cost than to total revenue.

After choosing Output x_1, the monopolist will search for the highest price it can charge and still sell that amount of output. In Figure 11–2, this price is P_1. The monopolist can sell Output x_1 at Price P_1 because the demand curve in Figure 11–2 shows that P_1 is the maximum that consumers will pay for Output x_1.

At P_1 and x_1, the monopolist is making an economic profit. The average revenue (price) is P_1. C_1 is the average cost, so $P_1 > C_1$ and thus the monopolist is making a profit of $P_1 - C_1$ on each unit for a total

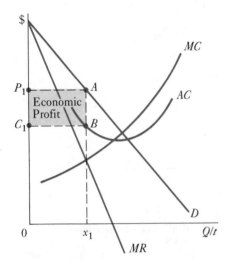

**FIGURE 11-2
THE PROFIT-MAXIMIZING
POSITION OF A PURE
MONOPOLIST**

The profit-maximizing monopolist will produce Output x_1, where *MR* = *MC*. Since average cost is less than average revenue (price) for Output x_1, this monopolist is making an economic profit.

profit of $(P_1 - C_1)(x_1)$. In Figure 11–2, total cost is represented by rectangle $0C_1Bx_1$, and total revenue is represented by rectangle $0P_1Ax_1$. *TR* minus *TC* equals economic profit, or rectangle C_1P_1AB. Since the cost curves include both explicit and implicit costs, this profit means that the monopoly firm is making more than its opportunity cost. That is, the firm is earning more than is necessary to keep its resources employed in this industry—it is making an economic profit.

Price and output can also be determined numerically. Table 11–2 combines the revenue data of Table 11–1 and the cost data of the chapter on production. The monopolist would maximize profits at seven units, where $MC = MR = \$46$. Price would be \$52 because the demand curve (*AR*) indicates that seven units will sell for \$52 each. At a price of \$52, total revenue is \$364 (7 × \$52) and total cost is \$322 (7 × \$46), which means that the monopolist is making a profit of \$42 (\$364 − \$322). If you don't believe this is maximum profit, construct an eighth column for Table 11–2 and call it profit. Calculate the profit at each level of output from one to ten units, and you will see it is maximized at seven units because at seven units, $MR = MC$.[1]

TABLE 11–2
A MONOPOLIST'S COST AND REVENUE DATA

Output and Sales	Total Cost	Average Cost	Marginal Cost	Average Revenue	Total Revenue	Marginal Revenue
0	60	—	—	—	0	—
1	100	100	40	58	58	58
2	136	68	36	57	114	56
3	168	56	32	56	168	54
4	200	50	32	55	220	52
5	235	47	35	54	270	50
6	276	46	41	53	318	48
7	322	46	46	52	364	46
8	372	$46\frac{1}{2}$	50	51	408	44
9	429	$47\frac{2}{3}$	57	50	450	42
10	490	49	61	49	490	40

The Monopolist's Supply Curve

A supply curve shows how much output will be supplied at any price. In order to determine a supply curve, it is necessary to show that at a given and unique price, a firm will supply a given and unique output, which is independent of the demand curve. A monopoly firm does not

---

1. If you undertake such a calculation, you will find that profit is \$42 at an output of six units and at an output of seven units. This result is obtained from the fact that in numerical examples, we use discrete data. The principle is that profit maximization implies producing where $MC = MR$, but a unique point only exists when dealing with continuous functions and using calculus. In this example, the actual profit-maximizing output would be somewhere between six and seven units of output.

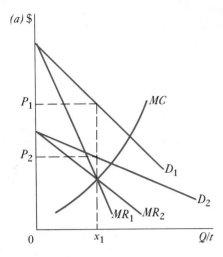

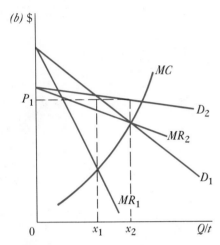

FIGURE 11-3
ONE OUTPUT—TWO PRICES OR ONE PRICE—TWO OUTPUTS

It is possible to trace out a supply curve only if we can show a unique price, associated with a certain output. In Panel (*a*) there are at least two prices, P_1 and P_2, consistent with Output x_1. Likewise, in Panel (*b*) there are at least two outputs, x_1 and x_2, consistent with Price P_1. We cannot draw the monopolist's supply curve.

BARRIERS TO ENTRY

Natural or artificial obstacles that keep new firms from entering an industry.

have a supply curve in the same sense that a purely competitive firm's marginal cost curve can be viewed as its supply curve. A monopolist sets the price at the profit-maximizing output, so it doesn't make sense to ask how much will be supplied at various prices. For a monopoly, the profit-maximizing output, where $MC = MR$, will depend on the location and shape of the demand curve.

Examine Figure 11–3. In Panel (*a*), two different prices, P_1 and P_2, could be consistent with Output x_1, depending on where the market demand curve is located. The marginal revenue curves that are derived from the demand curves D_1 and D_2 both intersect the monopolist's marginal cost at the same level of output. In Panel (*b*), two different output levels, x_1 and x_2, could be produced at Price P_1, depending on whether market demand is represented by D_1 or D_2.

The analysis of Figure 11–3 shows that it is impossible to identify a supply curve for a monopolist. There is no way to predict what the monopolist will do without knowing the exact nature of the demand curve. In this sense, then, the monopolist has no supply curve. The predictive powers of the economist are, therefore, considerably limited in an analysis of monopoly. Economists can no longer say, *ceteris paribus*, that an increase in demand will cause price to rise.

Profits and Barriers to Entry

If the monopolist is earning profits, other entrepreneurs will want some of the profits the monopolist is receiving. As a result, there will be pressure from new firms entering the industry. But wait! A monopoly is a single seller producing a product for which there are no close substitutes; if there is new entry, there is no longer a monopoly. If a monopoly is to persist, there must be some forces at work to keep new firms from entering. **Barriers to entry** are natural or artificial obstacles that keep new firms from entering an industry.

Economies of scale provide a *natural barrier* to entry. If the long-run cost curves are such that an optimal-size plant occurs only when the firm is very large relative to the size of the market, there may be room for only one cost-efficient firm in the industry. If there are significant economies of scale, one firm that gets bigger than any of the others will be able to undersell them. In such a case, the bigger firm will cut its price below that of its rivals and capture their customers. Eventually the large firm will become the only firm in the industry. When just one firm emerges in this way—and this happens in very few industries—the firm is called a *natural monopoly.* Public utilities such as telephone, electric, and cable television fit this category. The government recognizes that these are natural monopolies and therefore regulates them. Problems associated with such regulation will be discussed in a later chapter. Natural monopoly is very uncommon, some economists argue that even public utilities are not really natural monopolies. If the occurrence of a natural monopoly is rare, then most of the monopoly power that exists in our economy must be due to artificial barriers.

An *artificial barrier* to entry is one that is contrived by the firm (or someone else) to keep others out. It doesn't take much imagination to come up with a list of such barriers. The least sophisticated, but perhaps the most effective, would be the use of violence. Say you have a monopoly on the illegal numbers racket in South Chicago. If a new entrepreneur ("family") moves in to reap some of these profits, you simply blow them away—very effective! This sort of tactic may sound preposterous, but business history contains many examples of such activity. The early history of oil exploration and drilling is one example in which violence was used, and private armies were often a must.

On a more civilized level, it may be possible to erect artificial barriers that are legal, or at least quasi-legal. If exclusive ownership of all the raw materials in an industry could be captured, entry could be controlled by not selling to potential new entrants. The reason that the Aluminum Company of America enjoyed a monopoly before World War II was because it controlled almost all the known sources of bauxite, the essential ore for the production of aluminum.

A present-day example of the existence of artificial barriers occurs in the sale of diamonds. The de Beers Company of South Africa controls most of the world's diamond supply. They effectively control the mining of new diamonds and have a significant influence on price. Even in this case there is competition because all diamonds produced in the past are potential competitors. If de Beers manipulated production to drive price "too high," individuals might enter the market as suppliers by selling any diamonds they presently own.

Another technique for creating artificial barriers is a patent on a process or machine that is vital in production. Patent rights give sole authority to use the process or machine to the holder of the patent. The problem with a patent is twofold. First, it expires after 17 years in the United States, and then everyone is entitled to use the idea. Second, to get a patent, detailed plans on how the item is produced must be provided, and these plans are available to potential competitors at the Library of Congress. So it appears a patent is not a very effective entry barrier to anyone who is willing to risk a lawsuit brought by the offended patent holder (and patent holders don't always win their cases). A good alternative to patents is secrecy. If a firm can keep its vital process secret, it can keep new firms out of its industry. So now you know why there is barbed wire around research and development offices, why you aren't told the formula for Pepsi Cola, and why corporate spying is big business.

Government and Barriers to Entry

In the final analysis, it is very difficult to be a monopolist because it is very hard to keep new entrants out of your industry—unless you can get the government to help you. Let's look briefly at two industries where firms have significant market power: the steel industry and the taxicab industry.

Suppose that firms in the U.S. steel industry are earning economic profits. Firms that are producing steel in other countries see profits being earned and gear up to export steel to the United States to earn some of these profits. In effect, these foreign steel firms are entering the U.S. industry. The domestic firms then appeal to Congress or the president to keep these foreign firms out (to block their entry), and tariffs or quotas are then put into effect. These tariffs or quotas serve as artificial barriers to entry by raising the price of foreign goods or prohibiting their sale in the United States.

Next, consider the taxicab industry. You probably consider this to be a competitive industry since you can see Yellow Cabs, Checker Cabs, and some generic-brand cabs on the street every day. But, if you decide to start a cab business, you might be in for some trouble. Suppose you already own a car, so the entry costs are relatively small. All you need to do is to mark your vehicle so that it can be recognized as a cab, and perhaps install a meter. However, you will need a permit, which in some cities will be very difficult and expensive to obtain. If you operate as a "jitney," an underground cab that avoids city regulations, you will make the existing monopoly cab owners very unhappy. The end of this story is that in many cities, cabs are a monopoly enterprise and it is government that protects the monopoly.

In these examples, government supplied the artificial barrier to entry. Federal, state, and local governments all restrict entry and thereby ensure protected market positions. It should not be too surprising that many instances of corruption in government have centered on the granting of monopoly privileges. A government official or agency protects a monopoly by keeping competitors out, and the monopolist often is willing to pay for this with campaign contributions, favors, or outright bribes, such as direct cash payments, free vacations, or jobs for relatives.

If monopoly power persists for a long period of time, there is very likely to be some explicit or implicit government support of that monopoly. Monopoly profits are a very powerful and attractive force, and new entry is very difficult for the firm alone to block. As a result, monopolies usually try to enlist governmental support of one kind or another.

IS MONOPOLY BAD?

No entrepreneur wants to sell in a purely competitive industry. A firm that can create a successful monopoly can be rewarded with persistent profits. (This ability to use power in markets is stressed in marketing and management courses—hence, there are no marketing courses for wheat farmers!) Obviously monopoly is good for the monopolist, but monopoly can be bad for society.

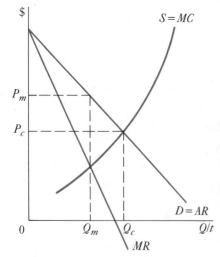

FIGURE 11-4
PRICE OUTPUT DETERMINATION UNDER PURE MONOPOLY AND PURE COMPETITION

The monopolist, equating marginal cost and marginal revenue, produces Output Q_m at Price P_m. If this same industry were competitive, the price would be P_c and output would be Q_c.

How Monopoly Compares to Pure Competition

To see what's so bad about monopoly, let's examine Figure 11-4. First, suppose that Figure 11-4 represents a purely competitive industry. The market demand curve is that faced by the numerous sellers, and the MC curve is the summation of all the individual firms' marginal cost curves. The competitive price and output would be P_c and Q_c. Now, suppose that the industry is monopolized by one firm that has bought up all the individual competitive firms but still has the same cost curves. The monopoly firm, then, would face the same cost conditions that the aggregate of competitive firms faced. The *market* supply curve would become the monopolist's marginal cost curve because it would be the summation of the purchased firms' marginal cost curves. Likewise, the monopoly firm faces the *market* demand curve and its corresponding marginal revenue curve. The monopoly firm will produce Q_m at Price P_m. In this case, it is a very simple matter to contrast pure monopoly with pure competition. The monopolist produces a smaller output ($Q_m < Q_c$) and charges a higher price ($P_m > P_c$) than do the purely competitive firms. This is possible because entry into the industry is blocked. Since new firms cannot enter, consumers are not getting the optimal amounts of those goods that are produced by monopolized industries. Monopoly restricts output. This is the principal economic argument against monopoly.

The monopolistic output and price, then, represent misallocation of resources if the monopoly has the same cost conditions as the aggregate of the competitive firms. Note that the misallocation under monopoly might even be worse if, in buying up the individual firms, the monopoly introduced some inefficiencies of large-scale management. Such inefficiencies would cause an upward shift of the cost curves in Figure 11–4.

This misallocation of resources is illustrated in Figure 11–5. The monopoly is in equilibrium producing x_1 at a price of P_1. Monopoly profits, which are total revenue minus total cost, are represented by rectangle CP_1AB. Let's examine closely what is going on at this equilibrium. First, Price P_1 is greater than average cost (which is x_1B per unit); that is, $P_1 > AC$. This means that economic profits are being earned. Second, price is greater than marginal cost ($P_1 > MC$), which means the value consumers place on the last unit (P_1) exceeds the opportunity cost of producing it (MC). From a welfare point of view, more should be produced, but the monopolist prohibits that from happening by restricting entry. Third, average cost at Output x_1 is greater than marginal cost at x_1; $AC > MC$. This means that x_1 is not being produced using the least-cost combination of factors. The monopolist is not forced to be fully efficient, although the firm does produce its actual output for the lowest cost possible. You can easily see, then, what we mean when we say that monopoly misallocates resources.

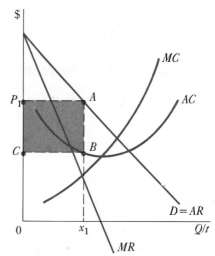

FIGURE 11–5
MONOPOLY MISALLOCATION OF RESOURCES
A monopoly misallocates resources because price is greater than marginal cost. This means the value consumers place on the item exceeds the opportunity cost of producing it.

MONOPOLY AND COMPETITION

Monopoly	Pure Competition
■	■
• One firm	• Many firms
• Barriers to entry	• Free entry
• $P \neq AC$, Profits exist	• $P = AC$, Only normal profit
• $MC \neq AC$, Not at least cost combination	• $MC = AC$, At least cost combination

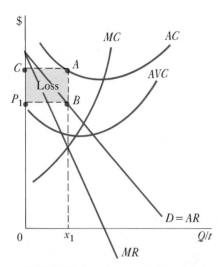

FIGURE 11-6
A MONOPOLY SUFFERING LOSSES
The monopolist might suffer losses in the short run. If $AC > AR$, the monopolist is suffering a loss.

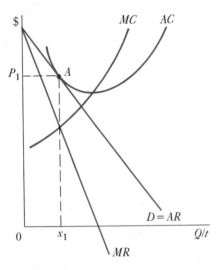

FIGURE 11-7
A MONOPOLY EARNING NORMAL PROFITS
It is possible that a monopoly might only earn normal profits. In this instance, there is no incentive for other firms to enter the industry, and there is no need for barriers to entry.

Monopoly, Profits, and Price

A monopoly is not a license to make profits. If the U.S. government granted you an absolute monopoly in the sale and manufacture of Conestoga wagons, if the Israeli government granted you the sole right to sell bacon in Tel Aviv, or if you had a monopoly in the sale and manufacture of Fieros, you might lose money. High costs or insufficient demand may cause the monopolist to lose money. Still, there is a common misconception that a monopoly situation guarantees profits.

Figure 11–6 shows a monopoly suffering a loss. The monopoly is producing x_1 and charging the profit-maximizing price, P_1. Average costs of producing x_1 are x_1A per unit. As a result, the monopolist is incurring losses equal to rectangle P_1CAB. Since the demand curve is below the average cost curve, there is no way to avoid losses. The next question is, will the monopolist continue to produce? If price is above AVC, as is the case in Figure 11–6, the monopolist will be better off in the short run to continue producing. In the long run, if demand does not increase, the monopoly will go out of business. The presence of losses indicates that the factors are not earning their opportunity cost. The factors will move to more productive uses.

Just as monopolists can suffer losses, it also is possible that a monopoly might earn only normal profits. Figure 11–7 illustrates this case. The monopoly is producing x_1 and charges P_1. TR is equal to rectangle $0P_1Ax_1$. In this instance, the monopoly is earning its opportunity cost, and there will be no incentive for other firms to try to enter this industry or for this firm to leave the industry. $P = AC$, which means that producers are not earning economic profits. It still is the case, however, that $P > MC$, indicating that more units should be produced.

You can see, then, that monopolies don't always make profits. In fact, they often can incur losses and go out of business. Also, monopolists do not charge the highest price possible. Remember the mineral spring example? Monopolists charge the *profit-maximizing* price, and this price will depend on the demand conditions, and costs, in that industry.

Monopoly in the Long Run

The monopolist, unlike the purely competitive firm, can continue to earn economic profits in the long run. As long as the entry barriers remain, economic profits can be maintained. Long-run maintenance of entry barriers is very difficult, however, because the economic profits will attract new firms, substitute products, and new processes to compete for those economic profits. In principle, then, even with government help, the power of any single monopoly is likely to decline in the very long run.

Real-World Monopolies

We have pointed out that there are no examples of pure monopoly in the real world. The theoretical definition prohibits this. There are, however, firms with monopoly power, and the monopoly model is useful in explaining the behavior of these firms. Public utilities, for example, are considered natural monopolies and are regulated as a result. State trading monopolies that are set up by some nations to engage in international trade also are monopolistic. Local monopolies are another form of real-world monopoly. A **local monopoly** is a firm that has monopoly power in a geographic region. Even though close substitutes exist, the distance between sources of supply creates monopolies. If you grew up in a small, remote town, there may have been only one movie theater or perhaps only one grocery store. A firm in such a situation is a local monopoly because the substitutes are costly in the sense that you must travel to reach them. In all these real-world examples, we can use the model of pure monopoly to examine the effects of monopoly power.

MONOPOLY POWER AND PRICE DISCRIMINATION

In analyzing monopoly behavior, we have assumed that the monopolist charges the same price to all consumers and the same price for all units sold to a particular consumer. If, on the other hand, the monopolist is able to charge different consumers different prices, or charge a particular consumer different prices depending on the quantity purchased, the monopolist is practicing **price discrimination**. Price discrimination, when it succeeds, is a way to expand monopoly profits. First, we will examine a monopolist practicing price discrimination with one consumer, and then we will examine a case where price discrimination means different prices for different consumers.

When we examined the demand curve earlier in the textbook, we discussed the concept of utility. Figure 11–8 reproduces the figure used there to explain the concept of consumer surplus. Consumer surplus is the extra utility gained because some consumers end up paying less for an item than they would be willing to pay for it. Consumers purchase an item until the marginal utility of the last dollar spent on an item is equal to the marginal utility of a dollar spent on any other good, or the utility of holding the dollar. The marginal utility of previously purchased units was greater than the price paid for those units because they were all purchased at the price of the last unit. The consumer would have been willing to pay higher prices for these units, so at Price P_1 in Figure 11–8, the consumer was receiving a "bonus" in terms of utility. This extra utility is called *consumer surplus*. The shaded area in Figure 11–9 represents this consumer surplus.

A monopoly producer might be able to deal separately with the consumer for each unit purchased. In terms of Figure 11–9, the monopolist could say, "You may buy Q_1 units for P_1, $Q_2 - Q_1$ units for P_2, $Q_3 - Q_2$ units for P_3, and $Q_4 - Q_3$ units for P_4." By doing this, the monopolist has extracted most of the consumer surplus and converted it into revenue for the firm. Compare the shaded areas in Figure 11–9 to the shaded area in Figure 11–8. Both represent consumer surplus. In Figure 11–9, by charging different prices for different amounts of consumption, the monopolist has expropriated much of the consumer surplus. It is theoretically possible for the monopolist to get all of this consumer surplus by charging different prices for each unit.

LOCAL MONOPOLY
A firm that has monopoly power in a geographic region. Even though close substitutes exist, the distance between sources of supply creates monopolies.

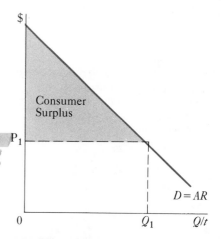

FIGURE 11–8
CONSUMER SURPLUS
Consumer surplus is the difference between the total utility received from the purchase of a product and the total revenue generated by the product. It exists because the marginal utility of each previous unit purchased was greater than Price P_1.

PRICE DISCRIMINATION
The practice of charging different consumers different prices, or a particular consumer different prices, for different quantities purchased.

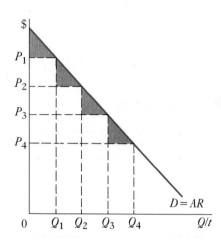

**FIGURE 11-9
A DISCRIMINATING MONOPOLIST**
A discriminating monopolist can
expropriate most of the consumer surplus
by charging different prices for different
amounts of consumption.

A second type of price discrimination occurs when a monopolist can separate markets and charge different prices to different groups of consumers. If the monopolist can separate the markets and prevent resale, it can price discriminate by adjusting output for the different demand elasticities in the two markets. The monopolist does this by equating marginal revenue in each submarket. If marginal revenue is not equal in each submarket, a switching of output between markets would increase total revenue. Given any level of sales, profit is increased by selling in the submarket where a given extra unit of sales adds most to total revenue; i.e., where marginal revenue is highest. So the monopolist would sell first where marginal revenue is highest and maximize profits when marginal revenue (rather than price) is the same in all markets.

Price Discrimination in Practice

In practice, we see the first type of price discrimination only crudely practiced. It requires the seller to have the power to separate sales on a unit-by-unit basis. This form of price discrimination is what is being practiced when multiples of a product can be purchased for a total that is less than the per-unit price times the number purchased. "Artichokes 40¢, two for 65¢" and "Coffee 50¢, refills a quarter" are examples of this type of price discrimination.

The second type of price discrimination only requires that the seller be able to separate markets according to the elasticity of demand in these different markets. Examples of such price discrimination abound. Bookstores offer lower prices to professors than to students; airlines charge lower fares for students and vacationers than for businesspeople; university athletic departments offer lower priced tickets to students and faculty; medical doctors charge different patients different fees for the same service; and senior citizens get discounts on all kinds of items from drugs to theater tickets. Consider plane fares. If you fly to Europe and stay for 14–21 days, the fare is cheaper than if you stay for less than 14 days. If you stay a month or longer, flights are even cheaper. Why? Which class of consumers of air transportation have the most inelastic demand? Business travelers, of course, who tend to travel on tight schedules and have bosses who don't want them sight-seeing in France for 14 days! With airline deregulation, major carriers have developed sophisticated techniques to set and change fares. *Business Week* reported that in 1985, American Airlines had over 100 traffic analysts working three shifts seven days a week. They do this to juggle fares to "match the bargain offerings of low-cost rivals while protecting their full-fare business."[2]

It should be clear that two conditions are necessary in order to practice price discrimination. First, it must be possible to separate consumers into groups that have different demand elasticities. These groups need to be economically identifiable (if it costs too much to identify the groups, discrimination might not pay). So when economists talk about price discrimination, they're not talking about creed, color, or sex, unless certain creeds, colors, or sexes have different demand elasticities for certain products. Many times, age is used to identify groups with different

2. *Business Week* (2 December 1985): 34.

THE INTERNATIONAL PERSPECTIVE MULTINATIONAL CORPORATIONS AS MONOPOLIES IN FOREIGN COUNTRIES

Many multinational companies are very large relative to the countries in which they operate. It is conceivable that a company may have worldwide net sales that are larger than the GNP of the country in which it is operating. These multinationals have significant monopoly power in small host countries.

Small less developed countries face a political dilemma in bargaining with large multinational companies. At the onset of operations, a country may have very little bargaining power with the multinational because the company can "shop around" for hospitable governments. If the country's policymakers want to pursue economic growth, they may have to agree to the multinational's terms. But as time passes and the company invests more fixed capital assets in the country, the host government

can increase taxes and appropriate more of the monopoly profits. However, a delicate balance must be maintained because taxes and government controls diminish the profitability of investment and future investment, from the multinational and other multinationals may be hindered by changes in the host countries' business climate.

Controls on multinationals can take several forms. Some countries impose foreign exchange regulations that require the foreign firm to convert earnings at exchange rates that are different from market exchange rates or to repatriate their earnings in locally produced goods rather than in currency. This requires the foreign firms to buy local products and export them to countries with freely exchangeable currencies. Other countries (notably India) require foreign companies to divest their assets over time by selling them to native investors. This is a form of expropriation with compensation. Still other countries specify local content laws that force the foreign firm to purchase a certain percent of the components in a manufacturing process from domestic sources. Finally, although it may be illegal (or if not illegal, at least hushed), in some countries, or more correctly, politicians in some countries may require bribes as a condition for doing business. This is not uncommon in countries with dictatorial governments.

In a small country, multinational companies not only exert monopoly power but also must confront monopoly power exerted by the host government. In this situation, it is not always clear who wins.

The political and economic dilemmas faced by multinational corporations and host governments have even come to the United States. For decades, U.S. policymakers were only confronted with one side of the problem, that of U.S. corporations in foreign countries. Recently, however, the United States has become a host country for foreign, primarily Japanese, investment.

demand elasticities. In the case of airfares, the classes of consumers are separated by length of stay. Businesspeople seldom travel to a destination for more than a few days; rarely do they travel for more than 14 days.

The second major requirement for price discrimination is that the monopolist *must* prevent the resale of goods or the movement of customers between markets. Consider the case of charging different prices to different classes of consumers for tickets for a college football game. It only works if the lower priced customers are prohibited from reselling their tickets. If not, the college is no longer a monopolist in the sale to the higher priced market. Is it any wonder that the athletic department requires you to show your picture I.D. card *and* your ticket at the gate? The higher priced ticket holders are only required to present their tickets. Price discrimination works well where resale is very difficult. Medical doctors are very successful in practicing price discrimination because they have easily recognizable submarkets with different elasticities (by income and insurance category) *and* because resale is almost always ruled out. Services are good candidates for price discrimination because it is very difficult to resell a service.

There are many examples of this kind of price discrimination. It often is the case that the seller justifies price discrimination as helping a group. For example, doctors might claim they practice price discrimination (charging less to some groups) in order to "help" the poor. Students or senior citizens might be charged less because "We want to help them out." In reality, this price discrimination is practiced because it increases profit.

Consider but a few examples. Time-of-day price discrimination includes matinee performances of cultural events and movies, bowling alley use, and lunch and dinner menus. In all these cases, demand is more inelastic at night because some consumers are limited to night consumption. Magazine publishers charge higher prices for magazines purchased at newsstands than for subscriptions. Sometimes subscription prices are $^1/_3$ the price of newsstand prices. Newsstand demand is more inelastic because it is a spur-of-the-moment, unplanned purchase. Book publishers charge much higher prices for hardcover novels than for softcover versions of the same novel. They separate the markets by publishing the softcover version after the hardcover market has been satiated. Some colleges charge in-state and out-of-state tuition because it is very easy to separate these two markets. Has your car ever broken down when you were out of town? Your demand is very inelastic; you have little information about services available, and you are easy to identify as a one-time customer (you even may have an out-of-state license plate). What do you think happens? You're right! You will pay much more than a local person with car trouble would pay.

Price Discrimination: Gainers and Losers

Price discrimination does have a positive side effect because it usually will cause output under monopoly to increase. We saw earlier in this chapter that monopoly is undesirable because it restricts output. If a monopoly can, however, sell output one unit at a time, output will be pushed to the point where $P = MC$. This is just common sense because the monopolist restricts output in order to keep price from falling. If price will only fall on the additions to output (not other units), production will be pushed to the point where $P = MC$. This is the same solution as is obtained in pure competition. The difference, of course, is that more of the benefit accrues to the monopolist. Price discrimination converts consumer surplus into monopoly profits, making monopolists wealthier and consumers worse off.

On another level, many people believe price discrimination is unfair or immoral because it involves different prices for the very same product. Why should an airplane ticket be cheaper because someone is a tourist rather than a business traveler? Why should professors get their books and pens for lower prices than students? Why should students pay less for a football ticket than nonstudents?

Interestingly, it is sometimes the group that benefits from price discrimination that complains. Price discrimination is common in international trade because the separation of national markets often is easy to maintain. Tariffs and transportation costs can help prevent resale. When firms in a country sell in a foreign market at a lower price than they do at home, they are engaging in price discrimination. Demand in the foreign country may be more elastic than domestic demand because there is more competition, and, therefore, more good substitutes are available. The foreign monopolist sells to foreigners at a lower price than at home. The U.S. Treasury calls this practice **dumping**. Dumping occurs, for example, when the Japanese sell televisions in the United States at a lower price than they sell the same sets at home. The odd thing is that dumping has an unfavorable connotation. When the Japanese dump televisions in the United States, the U.S. government takes action against Japan. This is curious because Japanese firms are giving U.S. consumers a better deal than Japanese consumers.[3] Complaining about the lower price is a little like writing to the school paper to say that you, as a student, don't like the fact that you can get tickets to the big game for one third the regular price. Seen from another angle, however, dumping is an objectionable practice. You can understand why domestic manufacturers don't particularly approve of foreign competitors selling in this country more cheaply than in their own home market.[4]

DUMPING
The practice of selling in foreign markets at lower prices than in domestic markets. This is a form of price discrimination.

Price Discrimination and Monopoly

The concept of price discrimination was developed in connection with the study of monopoly, but price discrimination is not limited to monopoly. Price discrimination will never occur in pure competition but could occur in monopolistic competition and oligopoly, which we will study in the next chapter. However, since the opportunity to use price discrimination will be limited if consumers have good substitutes, it is easiest to discriminate under monopolistic conditions.

THE COSTS OF MONOPOLY

We have carefully developed the point that a monopoly misallocates resources by contriving shortages—producing less than the competitive output to create monopoly profits. There are, however, other costs associated with monopoly. Figure 11–10 depicts a monopoly firm with constant marginal costs and, thus, constant average costs. Constant marginal costs and average costs are assumed for simplicity.

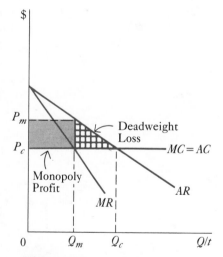

FIGURE 11–10
THE DEADWEIGHT LOSS OF MONOPOLY
A monopoly converts some consumer surplus to monopoly profit. The crosshatched area, however, represents consumer surplus that is lost to the economy. It is the deadweight loss associated with monopoly.

3. In fact, the dumping case concerning Japanese television sets was a rarity in that the initial complaint came from Japanese consumers.
4. There may be some other objections to dumping. The government may fear that the Japanese are selling below cost to drive U.S. firms out of business in an attempt to corner the market on televisions. Or the Treasury may fear Japan is transmitting macroeconomic disturbances to the United States by weakening the U.S. television industry. But the bottom line is that we are objecting to someone selling us goods too cheaply.

The monopolist will produce Output Q_m and set price at P_m. A purely competitive structure would have produced an output of Q_c at Price P_c. As a result of restricting output, the monopolist earns a monopoly profit equal to the shaded area. This shaded area represents a transfer from consumers (in terms of lost consumer surplus) to the monopolist (in terms of monopoly profit). This, however, is not the only cost the monopoly creates.

Deadweight Loss

The crosshatched triangle in Figure 11–10 represents lost consumer surplus that was not converted into monopoly profits. This lost consumer surplus is received by no one. Consumers have lost it because the monopoly has restricted output, but it has not been received by anyone in the economy. The lost consumer surplus is referred to as the deadweight loss of monopoly. A deadweight loss is comprised of the lost gains from trade due to monopoly restriction of output. It is a deadweight loss because nothing is received in exchange for the loss; it is equivalent to throwing a valuable resource away.

Many years ago, Arnold C. Harberger of the University of Chicago attempted to measure this deadweight loss of monopoly.[5] He estimated that deadweight loss (he referred to it as the welfare loss from monopoly) was quite small, and that in 1954, only about one tenth of 1 percent of GNP was lost due to the deadweight loss effect. This small fraction of GNP amounted to about $1.50 for each U.S. citizen in 1954. Since Harberger's study, other economists have attempted to measure this loss, and most of their estimates are also small. The other estimates tend to congregate in the range of 1 percent of GNP being lost. This is still a surprisingly low figure, although it is ten times larger than Harberger's original estimate.[6] Harberger's work implies that, if we ignore the transfer from consumers to monopolists (the captured consumer surplus), monopoly has little effect on welfare.

DEADWEIGHT LOSS
The lost gains from trade due to monopoly restriction of output.

Monopoly Rent Seeking

Gordon Tullock of George Mason University argues that these deadweight loss estimates are likely to underestimate the costs of monopoly. Tullock argues that since the monopoly profits captured (the consumer surplus expropriated) are potentially huge, monopolists spend a great deal of time, effort, and resources in establishing a monopoly.[7] He developed his argument by drawing an analogy to theft. If thieves steal $100

5. See A.C. Harberger, "The Welfare Loss From Monopoly," *American Economic Review* (May 1954): 77–87. For a recent study confirming Harberger's result and summarizing many other studies, see Micha Gisser, "Price Leadership and Welfare Losses in U.S. Manufacturing," *American Economic Review* (September 1986): 756–767.

6. For a review of these other studies, see F.M. Scherer, *Industrial Market Structure and Economic Performance*, 2d ed. (Chicago: Rand McNally, 1980), Chapter 17.

7. G. Tullock, "The Welfare Costs of Tariffs, Monopolies and Theft," *Western Economic Journal* (now *Economic Inquiry*) (June 1967): 224–232.

million, they transfer that $100 million from victims to themselves. This transfer is just like the transfer of consumer surplus. But thieves invest time, effort, and resources on guns and getaway cars. In addition, victims invest money on protecting themselves from theft. Both of these costs are wasted from the viewpoint of society as a whole. Tullock argues that the same holds true for monopoly. Monopolists "waste" resources (from a societal viewpoint) in seeking to establish a monopoly, while society expends resources trying to break up and prevent monopolies. The efforts and resources expended by those attempting to establish monopolies to earn monopoly profits have become known as **monopoly rent seeking** and is a cost of monopoly because these resources are no longer available to produce goods and services. We will spend more time discussing rent seeking in greater detail in a future chapter.

MONOPOLY RENT SEEKING
The efforts and resources expended by those attempting to establish monopolies to earn monopoly profits.

■ X-Inefficiency

Still another cost of monopoly has been identified by Harvey Leibenstein of Harvard University.[8] Leibenstein argues that while competitive firms are forced to be efficient by the market, this does not hold true for monopolies. Since the monopoly is not punished by the market for slack management, the monopoly will tend to have more managerial "looseness" than a competitive firm. This looseness will manifest itself in corporate jets, limousines, expense accounts, and golden parachutes. Leibenstein coined the term **x-inefficiency** to describe the inefficiency associated with the "slack" management of monopoly. The monopoly escapes the market discipline and is therefore less conscious of management efficiencies. Leibenstein estimated this cost to be as high as 2 percent of GNP.

X-INEFFICIENCY
The inefficiency associated with the "slack" management of monopoly. The monopoly escapes the market discipline and is therefore less conscious of management efficiencies.

■ ■ ■ ■ ■ ■ ■ WHO RUNS THE FIRM? ALTERNATIVES TO PROFIT MAXIMIZATION

We have consistently assumed that firms are profit maximizers. This assumption makes it possible to predict how the firm would adjust to changes in demand in the two distinct market structures of pure competition and pure monopoly.

The profit-maximizing assumption might have seemed reasonable for competitive firms, but what happens in the realm of monopoly power and giant firms run by professional managers? We saw earlier that corporations account for about 85 percent of the annual business sales in the United States. Yet corporations are run by hired managers, not owners. Managers might operate by some principle other than profit maximization. This proposition is sometimes referred to as the **separation of ownership and control** and simply means that managers who control corporations may behave differently than would owner-managers. This different behavior will result only if the managers have different goals *and* if owners can't control managers.

SEPARATION OF OWNERSHIP AND CONTROL
Corporations are run by hired managers, not owners. These managers might operate by some principle other than profit maximization. This behavior results if managers have goals different than the owners' and if the owners cannot control the managers.

8. H. Leibenstein, "Allocative Efficiency vs. X-Inefficiency," *American Economic Review* (June 1966): 392–415.

HERBERT SIMON (1916-   )

Herbert Simon was born in Milwaukee, Wisconsin, and educated at the University of Chicago. Simon has held teaching positions at the University of California, the Illinois Institute of Technology, and the University of Pittsburgh. He is presently at Carnegie-Mellon University. Simon has never held a teaching post as an economist. Instead, he has held professorships in

political science, administration, psychology, and information sciences. He is an economist in the broadest sense of the word, like the early classical economists.

In awarding the 1978 Nobel Prize in Economics to Simon, the Royal Swedish Academy paid particular attention to his work, which was concerned with the development of alternatives to profit maximization. The committee made the following statement in its official announcement:

"In his epoch-making book, *Administrative Behavior* (1947), and in a number of subsequent works, he (Simon) described the company as an adaptive system of physical, personal, and social components that are held together by a network of intercommunications and by the willingness of its members to cooperate and to strive towards a common goal. What is new in Simon's ideas is, most of all, that he rejects the assumption made in classic theory of the firm as an omnisciently rational, profit-maximizing entrepreneur."[a]

Simon has had an important impact on more academic disciplines than any of the other Nobel Prize winners in economics. His work in management science and public administration is credited with bringing scientific approaches to the study of management. Herbert Simon is perhaps the best example of an economic theorist who has made a major impact on business and public administration.

a. "The Nobel Memorial Prize in Economics," *The Scandinavian Journal of Economics*, 81, no. 1 (1979): 72–73.

The hypothesis that behavior deviates from profit maximization is based on organizational theory, which you probably have studied if you have taken a course in social psychology or management. The hypothesis assumes that management will follow standard procedures even if these procedures result in lower profits. Managers of big business are seen as bureaucrats who react conservatively to avoid mistakes and to cover their liability, much as managers in the military, the federal bureaucracy, or any large organization do. Those who argue that a firm does not maximize profits offer several competing alternatives to the standard profit-maximization hypothesis. Let's look briefly at some of these.

SATISFICING

Management does not seek to maximize profits but rather seeks target levels of output and profits that are satisfactory to the ownership interests.

The **satisficing** hypothesis argues that the management of a firm does not seek maximum profits but rather looks for certain target levels of output and profits that are satisfactory to the ownership interests. Ownership interests might include size or market share, altruism or philanthropy, or other goals. Unfortunately, in order to perform empirical tests of this hypothesis to determine its validity, it would be necessary to specify what a firm's target happens to be; otherwise any result that is found would be consistent with satisficing behavior. The proponents of the satisficing hypothesis have not as yet found a way to do this. As a result, the predictive value of the hypothesis is very low.

One goal that might be substituted in place of profit maximization is religious or racial discrimination. Firms may sacrifice some profits in order to sell to, or hire, the type of people with whom they identify. A very interesting test of this hypothesis was conducted several years ago by Armen Alchian of UCLA and the late Reuben Kessel of the University of Chicago. They classified Jewish and non-Jewish graduates of the Harvard Business School according to the market structures in which they were employed. In the years examined, 36 percent of the graduates were Jewish. Comparing the employment of these Harvard MBAs in monopolized and relatively competitive industries, they discovered that the monopolized category was 18 percent Jewish, and the competitive category was 41 percent Jewish. This evidence is consistent with the hypothesis that monopoly power makes discrimination against minorities easier (less costly) and points to yet another cost of monopoly power.[9]

Thomas DiLorenzo of George Mason University has argued that rational profit maximizing behavior of managers of private monopolies will not be more lax than that of their counterparts in competitive firms. Monopoly managers will try just as hard because they get to share in monopoly profits in the form of salary increases and increased expenditures on managerial perquisites.[10]

Another alternative hypothesis has been suggested by William Baumol of Princeton University. Baumol argues that given some numerical level of profits, the managers' primary goal is to increase the *sales* of the firm. In essence, Baumol is saying that managers are rewarded by stockholders, according to the relative size of their firm in the market, for increasing the firms's relative share of the market, say, from 15 to 20 percent. This is called the **constrained sales maximization** hypothesis. The implication of this hypothesis is that monopoly might not be as bad as we concluded earlier. If sales, rather than profits, are the primary goal of a monopoly, the firm will lower prices and increase output. The lower prices and increased output will result in less misallocation of resources than we had predicted with profit maximization.

A rejoinder to these competing hypotheses is the long-run profit maximization hypothesis. **Long-run profit maximization** is the argument that even if managers follow satisficing behavior or constrained sales maximization, they do so only because it leads to higher profits in the long run. Following this hypothesis, if the firm maximizes sales, it is doing so because this will lead to higher profits in the long run. Likewise, if the firm is concerned with social responsibility and philanthropic or altruistic projects, it may find its long-run profits maximized. The problem with this hypothesis is that unless we specify a distinct time period, almost any behavior could be consistent with long-run profit maximization. The the-

CONSTRAINED SALES MAXIMIZATION
Occurs when a manager's primary goal is to increase the sales of the firm because managers are rewarded by stockholders for increasing the firm's relative share of the market.

LONG-RUN PROFIT MAXIMIZATION
The argument that even if managers follow satisficing behavior or constrained sales maximization, they do so only because it leads to higher profits in the long run.

9. A. Alchian and R.A. Kessel, "Competition, Monopoly, and the Pursuit of Money," in H.G. Lewis et al., *Aspects of Labor Economics* Princeton, NJ: Princeton University Press, 1962.
10. Thomas J. DiLorenzo, "Corporate Management, Property Rights, and the X-istence of X-inefficiency," *Southern Economic Journal* (July 1981): 116–124.

ory then becomes a cataloging exercise; there is no way to refute such a theory because it is consistent with everything and, therefore, can predict or explain nothing.

Before we go too far afield in developing a list of behavioral hypotheses about firm behavior, we need to think back to our discussion of what theory is and what it does. Theory abstracts from the real world by concentrating on the important aspects or effects of a phenomenon. If profit maximization is a valid assumption, it will yield reasonably accurate predictions about firm behavior. The profit-maximization assumption is a cornerstone of many hypotheses that have been empirically tested and found to be valid. Alternative assumptions have yet to be rigorously tested.

FALLACIES AND FACTS ABOUT MONOPOLY

In this chapter, we have developed a model of monopoly. Although there is no such thing as a pure monopoly in the real world, there are firms that have monopoly power, and the monopoly model is useful in describing monopolizing behavior. Since there are so many misconceptions about monopoly, it is worthwhile to review a few of the fallacies and facts we have studied in this chapter.

Fallacy—Monopolies Charge the Highest Possible Price

The public often believes that monopolies charge the highest possible price and "rip off" the public. This view is often promulgated by the press and by consumer lobby groups. We have, however, seen in this chapter that monopolies produce the profit-maximizing output and then sell that output on the market at a price constrained by the market demand curve.

Fallacy—Monopolies Always Earn (High) Profits

A similar, but slightly different, view is that monopolies always earn profits. We have seen in this chapter that some monopolies earn profits, some earn normal profits, and others suffer losses. To be sure, monopolists try to earn profits, but if demand changes, they might lose money. The key difference between monopoly and competition is that monopoly profits can persist because they don't lead to new entry. In instances where monopolies suffer losses, however, the resources will flow to other industries. In some cases, the government has tried to keep unprofitable monopolies from going out of business.

Fallacy—Monopolists Don't Have to Worry About Demand

It is a commonly held belief that monopolists don't have to worry about demand. Some social critics have even suggested that monopolists can manipulate demand. We have seen, however, that monopolists are constrained by the market demand for the good or service they produce. Their search for the price that maximizes their revenue is strictly tied to that demand curve.

Fact—Monopolies Charge a Price Higher Than Marginal Cost

We have seen in this chapter that a monopoly restricts output in order to earn economic profits. This output restriction means that price is greater than marginal cost. Compared to pure competition, monopolies are less efficient in allocating resources in accordance with consumer preferences.

Fact—Monopolists Produce Where Demand Is Elastic

It is often mistakenly felt that a monopoly will produce where a demand is inelastic, but we have seen that monopolies will always raise price if demand is inelastic. Every monopoly will always be producing in an elastic portion of its demand curve.

Fact—Monopolies Do Not Have Supply Curves

As we have seen in this chapter, a monopoly is a price searcher. The monopoly establishes the profit-maximizing output and then sets price equal to average revenue. As a result, the concept of a supply curve is meaningless. This lack of a supply curve makes our theory of monopoly less useful than the theory of pure competition because we cannot easily depict supply responses to demand shifts.

Fact—Monopoly Ultimately Faces Competition

When we develop the theory of pure monopoly, we assume that the firm faces little or no competition because we begin with a single firm producing a good with no close substitutes. In reality, however, the monopolist that earns a profit will be pursued by potential competitors, and the natural or artificial barriers to entry will be difficult to maintain. As a closing note, it is appropriate to quote Alfred Marshall, the great expositor of neoclassical economics, on this subject:

It will in fact presently be seen that, though monopoly and free competition are really wide apart, yet in practice they shade into one another by imperceptible degrees: that there is an element of monopoly in nearly all competitive business: and that nearly all the monopolies, that are of any practical importance in the present age, hold much of their power by an uncertain tenure; so that they would lose it ere long, if they ignored the possibilities of competition, direct and indirect.[11]

11. Alfred Marshall, *Industry and Trade*, 4th ed. (London: Macmillan & Co., 1923): 397.

CONTESTABLE MARKETS

CONTESTABLE MARKETS
Markets that may be comprised of large firms, but these firms are efficient because easily reversible entry is possible.

A number of economists, primarily affiliated with Princeton University, New York University, and Bell Laboratories, have developed a new theory of industry structure that they call contestable markets. **Contestable markets** are markets that may be comprised of large firms, but these firms are efficient because easily reversible entry is possible.[12] This theory attempts to bring more reality to microeconomics by analyzing large multi-product firms. The theory is very complex because of the authors' heavy reliance on mathematical models, but the insights produced are essentially quite simple.

The basic idea is that potential entry constrains the behavior of large firms and makes them efficient. Using this contestability theory, these economists argue that it is no longer necessary to assume that there are large numbers of firms, each a price taker, acting as if their production had no impact on the market in order to obtain efficiency. If "easily reversible" entry is possible, efficiency can be shown to exist with large-scale production. In the past, this large-scale production might have been labeled monopoly.

Elizabeth Bailey, a proponent of contestability theory, was a commissioner at the Civil Aeronautics Board during the Carter administration. She suggested that contestability in the airline industry was enough to ensure efficiency because capital consists mostly of aircraft, and capital costs can be recovered from a particular market with little loss. In other words, entry into a particular air travel market is easy. She argued that even if an airline route were flown by only one airline, it is unlikely that monopoly prices would be charged because monopoly prices would elicit entry by contesting airlines. In this theory, it is the recovery of capital costs (or the amount of sunk cost) rather than economies of scale that is important.

Critics of this theory argue that there really is not that much new here. They argue that the model is not much different from models that show that the possibility of entry limits the pricing behavior of monopolists. Regardless of who wins the intellectual battle, it is important to note that entry conditions are important in both theories. Monopoly cannot persist in open markets, and whether one refers to this as competition or contestability makes little difference for public policy.

SUMMARY

1. Pure monopoly is a market situation in which there is a single seller of a product with no close substitutes.
2. The monopoly firm faces a negatively sloped demand curve and a marginal revenue curve that lies below that demand curve.
3. The monopolist maximizes profits by producing the output at which $MC = MR$ and sets the price at which exactly that amount of output can be sold. Since price often is greater than average cost in the monopoly case, economic profits often exist.
4. The monopolist is sometimes able to erect barriers to entry that allow profits to exist in the long run. These barriers are very difficult to maintain and, as a result, monopolists often appeal to the government for help in maintaining entry barriers.

12. William J. Baumol, John C. Panzar, and Robert D. Willig, *Contestable Markets and the Theory of Industry Structure* (New York: Harcourt, Brace, Jovanovich, Inc., 1982).

5. Monopolies produce a lower output at a higher price than do competitive firms. At equilibrium, the monopoly firm is producing at a level of output where $P \neq AC \neq MC$.

6. Monopoly power is not a guarantee of profits. Some monopolies go out of business because of persistent losses; others make only normal profits.

7. A monopoly can increase its revenues if it practices price discrimination. For price discrimination to be successful, the monopolist must have customers with different demand elasticities, and they must be separated and prohibited from reselling the product.

8. The costs of monopoly include the misallocation of resources, the deadweight loss, monopoly rent seeking, and x-inefficiency.

9. The satisficing hypothesis and the sales maximization hypothesis are both derived from the idea of the separation of ownership and control. They argue that hired managers, as opposed to owner-managers, attempt to maximize sales or meet *satisfactory* profit targets rather than maximize profits.

10. Although no examples of *pure* monopoly exist, the model of pure monopoly is useful in analyzing monopoly power.

11. The theory of contestable markets argues that large firms are forced to efficient outcomes if capital is freely movable in these markets.

NEW TERMS

monopoly	dumping	satisficing
monopoly power	deadweight loss	constrained sales maximization
price searcher	monopoly rent seeking	long-run profit maximization
barriers to entry	x-inefficiency	contestable markets
local monopoly	separation of ownership and	
price discrimination	control	

QUESTIONS FOR DISCUSSION

1. Explain in your own words why marginal revenue is less than average revenue under conditions of monopoly.

2. Should business firms be socially responsible? Respond to the argument that they should maximize profits and leave social responsibility to elected and appointed officials.

3. List as many barriers to entry as you can. Which are the most effective?

4. Why will a monopolist never attempt to produce in the inelastic portion of the demand curve?

5. Should government subsidize monopolies that are losing money to keep them in business?

6. Is the phenomenon of trading stamps in grocery stores a form of price discrimination? If so, how does it work?

7. The following table describes the demand curve faced by a monopoly firm. Complete the *MR* column of the table.

Price	Quantity Demanded	MR
10	0	
9	1	
8	3	
7	4	
6	5	
5	6	
4	7	
3	8	

8. Assume that the unit cost data that you calculated in question 9 in Chapter 9 represents the cost data of this monopoly firm. How much would the monopolist produce in the short run? Why? What price would the monopolist charge.

9. What is the monopoly profit?

10. What will happen in the long run?

■ SUGGESTIONS FOR FURTHER READING

Asch, Peter. *Industrial Organization and Antitrust Policy*, revised ed. New York: John Wiley and Sons, Inc., 1983. The first chapter of this industrial organization book contrasts monopoly and competition.

Browning, Edgar K., and Jacquelene M. Browning. *Microeconomic Theory and Applications*. 2d ed. Boston: Little, Brown and Co., 1986. Chapters 11 and 12 present a more in-depth treatment of monopoly theory.

CHAPTER 12 ■

■

MONOPOLISTIC COMPETITION AND OLIGOPOLY

■

■
INTRODUCTION

The last two chapters have examined the two poles of the theoretical spectrum of market structures. At one extreme is pure monopoly, and at the other is pure competition. There are no perfect, theoretically correct real-world examples of either polar case, but for many years all real-world industry structures were analyzed by appealing to these two models. In the 1930s, theories were developed that filled out the spectrum. As we saw earlier, the space between these two poles is called *imperfect competition*. Economists further divide imperfect competition into monopolistic competition and oligopoly. We will study these two market structures in this chapter.

The theory of monopolistic competition usually is associated with Edward Chamberlin and Joan Robinson. Chamberlin was a Harvard professor who published a book in 1933 entitled *The Theory of Monopolistic Competition*. Joan Robinson, at Cambridge University in England, published *The Economics of Imperfect Competition*, also in 1933. (Robinson, who died in 1983, was only 30 years old when this classic was published!)

At approximately the same time that Chamberlin and Robinson were developing their concepts of monopolistic competition, German economist Heinrich von Stackelberg published a book entitled *Market Structure and Equilibrium* (1934). It discussed the idea of interdependence between firms and formed the basis of the model of oligopoly. Oligopoly, the other form of imperfect competition, is the market structure in which there are few firms. The scarcity of sellers is the key to firm behavior in oligopoly. In oligopoly, firms realize that their small number produces mutual interdependence. As a result, each firm will forecast or expect a certain response from its rivals to any price or output decision that it might initiate. We will examine the oligopoly model after we study monopolistic competition.

MONOPOLISTIC COMPETITION

The model of monopolistic competition describes an industry composed of a large number of sellers. Each of these sellers produces a product that is **differentiated**, which means that the products have either real or imagined identifiable characteristics that are different from each other. This differentiation can take many forms. It might be that the salespeople are nicer, that the packaging is prettier, that the credit terms are better, or that the service is faster. It could even be that a famous person is associated with the product, such as Whitney Houston endorsing Diet Coke, or Bill Cosby promoting Jell-O instant puddings. It is important to note that a product is differentiated if consumers view it as different. Chemists tell us that aspirin is aspirin, that there is no difference among the brands. Yet if consumers view the brands as different, there is product differentiation.

In monopolistic competition, the industry is characterized by a large number of firms, each producing a differentiated product. Another very important assumption is that entry into this industry is relatively easy. New firms can enter the industry and start producing products that are similar to those already being produced. In his original description of monopolistic competition, Chamberlin called the market for a good that was differentiated, but that had a large number of close substitutes, a **product group**. Chamberlin characterized monopolistic competition as the large-group case where there was rivalry between many firms in a product group.

You probably will recognize monopolistic competition as the market structure of many firms that you are familiar with, since retail firms often fit this description. Monopolistic competition is generally what most people think of when they think of competition. Pure competition, with its homogeneous products, simply does not fit the popular idea of competition in which firms are scrambling to make their products different.

Short-Run Adjustment

Analysis of the short-run position of the monopolistically competitive firm is remarkably similar to the analysis of the monopolistic firm. Figure 12–1 shows a representative firm's demand curve. When we depicted pure competition, we started with the market and derived the representative firm's demand curve. In monopolistic competition, we begin with a representative firm, rather than with the market. With product differentiation, each firm faces its own unique demand curve. The firm's demand curve in Figure 12–1 is negatively sloped, unlike the perfectly elastic demand curve of the purely competitive firm. This slope is caused by the differentiated nature of the product the firm is producing. If the product's price is raised, the firm will not lose all its customers because some will continue to prefer this product to substitutes that are close but not perfect. Likewise, if price is lowered, the firm will gain customers, but some customers will remain loyal to the products produced by other firms.

The elasticity of the demand curve is a measure of the degree of differentiation within the industry. If the goods are only slightly differentiated, then they are close substitutes and each firm's demand curve will be

DIFFERENTIATED PRODUCT
A good that has real or imagined identifiable characteristics that are different from other goods.

PRODUCT GROUP
A classification for a set of goods that is differentiated but has a large number of close substitutes.

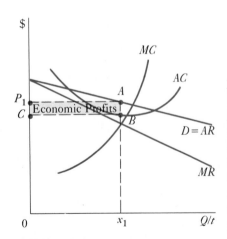

**FIGURE 12-1
SHORT-RUN PROFITS IN
MONOPOLISTIC COMPETITION**
In the short run, economic profits as depicted by the shaded area can exist in monopolistic competition. These profits will cause new firms to enter the industry.

very elastic. If the products are highly differentiated, the demand curve will be relatively inelastic, indicating that the firm could more easily raise price without losing many customers. Its customers are more loyal. Think of the aspirin example. If some people are willing to pay more for Bayer than for Brand X aspirin because they think it is different, the makers of Bayer will be able to raise price without losing a large number of customers. Bayer will be limited in price flexibility by the amount of differentiation it is able to create. As price goes higher and higher, fewer people will be willing to pay for the differentiation. Some people may be willing to pay 10¢ more for Bayer than for a different brand, but as price is raised higher, more and more people will shift to the other brands.

The demand curve in Figure 12–1 has a negative slope, indicating product differentiation; but the curve is very elastic, indicating that there are many good substitutes. Since the curve is negatively sloped, the marginal revenue curve will lie below the demand (average revenue) curve for the same reasons that it did in the case of pure monopoly. The firm will, of course, maximize profits at Price P_1 and Output x_1, where marginal revenue is equal to marginal cost. The firm in Figure 12–1 is earning economic profits because average revenue, P_1, exceeds average cost, C. Total revenue is represented by rectangle $0P_1Ax_1$, and total cost is represented by rectangle $0CBx_1$. Economic profits are thus shown by the shaded rectangle CP_1AB.

This analysis is very similar to the one developed in the previous chapter for monopoly in the short run. The most significant difference is that the demand curve is very elastic. The monopolistically competitive firm is, in one sense, a mini-monopolist over a product with close substitutes. The key to whether it is more like a competitive firm or more like a monopoly depends on what happens in response to the economic profit.

Long-Run Adjustment

What about long-run equilibrium in monopolistically competitive industries? In Figure 12–1, we saw a short-run equilibrium with economic profits. Joan Robinson thought the analysis ended here, with the firm able to earn economic profits in the long run. We will diverge from her analysis by allowing new firms to respond to these economic profits.

Since we assumed that entry into monopolistically competitive industries is relatively easy, new firms will enter the industry. As firms enter the industry, the demand curve that is faced by any single representative firm will shift to the left because the new firms will be attracting customers away from firms already in the industry. This is what happens in an area, for example, when a new retail grocery store opens. It draws customers away from the existing firm. Its demand curve will continue to shift down and to the left as new firms enter, and new firms will enter as long as economic profits are to be made. Long-run equilibrium will occur when all firms are earning zero economic profit (or normal profit). Such an equilibrium is depicted in Figure 12–2. Price is P_1 and output is x_1. Total revenue and total cost are represented by rectangle $0P_1Ax_1$. There are no economic profits being earned, and no additional firms will attempt to enter this industry.

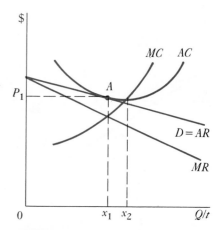

FIGURE 12-2
LONG-RUN EQUILIBRIUM IN MONOPOLISTIC COMPETITION
Since entry into monopolistically competitive industries is relatively easy, there can be no long-run economic profits. Firms will enter until the existing firms are earning only normal profits.

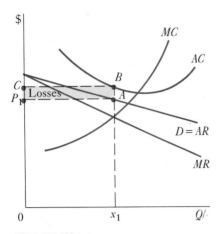

FIGURE 12-3
SHORT-RUN LOSSES IN
MONOPOLISTIC COMPETITION

Short-run losses as shown in the shaded area will cause some firms to exit the industry. Firms will exit until the existing firms are earning normal profits, as in Figure 12-2.

EXCESS CAPACITY

Underutilization of existing plant size. In monopolistic competition, the firm produces less than the efficient capacity of the plant.

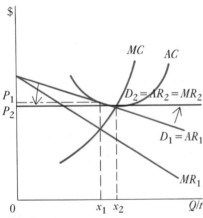

FIGURE 12-4
EXCESS CAPACITY

Excess capacity results from the negative slope of the demand curve. As the demand curve becomes more elastic, the excess capacity diminishes and disappears when the curve becomes perfectly elastic. The excess capacity is a result of product differentiation.

Of course, too many firms might enter the industry in the mistaken anticipation of economic profits. If this happens, losses will be realized, and some firms will leave the industry as the long-run adjustment proceeds. Figure 12-3 shows a monopolistically competitive firm making losses of P_1CBA. Firms would respond by leaving the industry, which would cause the demand curves faced by the remaining firms to increase (shift up and to the right) until the equilibrium shown in Figure 12-2 is restored. The long-run adjustment process under monopolistic competition produces a situation in which zero economic profits exist.

Monopoly and Competition

As we have just seen, the theory of monopolistic competition borrows from the theory of pure monopoly and the theory of pure competition. In the short run, the monopolistically competitive firm is a mini-monopolist producing the profit-maximizing output and searching for the price that can be charged for this output. The long run sees the economic profits disappear as new firms enter the market, causing the demand curve of each firm to shift to the left because market demand is shared by more firms. This result is similar to the long-run outcome in pure competition. The market structure is thus at once both monopolistic and competitive. That explains the name monopolistic competition.

Excess Capacity

In long-run equilibrium, the monopolistically competitive firm chooses an output that does not fully utilize existing plant size. This underutilization, called **excess capacity**, is depicted in Figure 12-2. The profit-maximizing output was seen to be x_1, where $MR = MC$. This is not, however, the output that would have resulted under pure competition, because under pure competition the firm uses the least-cost combination of inputs. The least-cost combination is where average cost is at a minimum and is the socially optimal output because it represents maximum attainable efficiency. This efficient output is represented by x_2 in Figure 12-2. In other words, in long-run equilibrium, the monopolistically competitive firm produces less than the quantity that efficiently uses the full productive capacity of the firm.

Is excess capacity a bad thing? To answer this, it is necessary to understand what causes it. The firm is producing less than the socially ideal output because it maximizes profits by producing a lower output. This lower output is a result of the fact that the demand curve for the monopolistically competitive firm is downward sloping. We can see this by examining Figure 12-4. Begin with Demand Curve D_1. The monopolistically competitive firm would produce Quantity x_1 at Price P_1. Now make the demand curve more elastic by rotating it, as in Figure 12-4. As the demand curve becomes more and more elastic and finally perfectly elastic, as in D_2, the output would increase to the socially efficient Output x_2 to be a result of the negative slope in the demand curve. This negative slope, you recall, is a result of the product differentiation. The excess capacity, therefore, results from product differentiation.

JOAN ROBINSON (1903–1983)
EDWARD CHAMBERLIN (1899–1967)

Joan Robinson and Edward Chamberlin are given joint credit for developing the theory of monopolistic competition. Chamberlin published his *Theory of Monopolistic Competition* (1933) six months before Robinson published *The Economics of Imperfect Competition* (1933). Chamberlin, in later years, was preoccupied with trying to differentiate his ideas from Robinson's. Robinson is reported to have commented on Chamberlin's anguish over her receiving joint credit by saying at one point, "I'm sorry I ruined his life."

Chamberlin was born in the state of Washington but attended high school in Iowa, where he was an all-around student and a successful athlete. He later attended the University of Iowa, then went to the University of Michigan to study, and ultimately received his Ph.D. at Harvard. He taught at Harvard until his death.

Joan Robinson developed her ideas quite independently of Chamberlin (they did not know each other) while a junior faculty member at Cambridge University. After the appearance of her path-breaking book, Robinson expanded her interests and research over a wide range of economic policy issues. Robinson was an outspoken critic of the market system. Her more recent antimarket publications include *An Essay on Marxian Economics* (1956), *Economic Philosophy* (1962), and *Freedom and Necessity* (1970).

Both Robinson and Chamberlin have had a significant impact on economics, but their careers were strikingly different. Chamberlin's career was characterized by a single pursuit: the development of the theory of monopolistic competition. Few economists have applied themselves to so singular a purpose and yet achieved fame. Perhaps this singleness of purpose in part explains Chamberlin's pain at having to share his fame with Robinson. Unlike Chamberlin's, Robinson's interests were wide ranging. After contributing to micro theory, she worked with Keynes and helped to develop macroeconomics. Subsequently, she became a fiery social critic with varied interests.

Robinson thought that economic analysis should begin with monopoly and that pure competition should be studied only as a special case. Robinson was one of the first economists to draw marginal cost curves the way we do now. Her account of monopolistic competition was different than that of Chamberlin's and what we examined in this chapter. Robinson thought it natural for profits to exist in the long run.

It might be argued that this excess capacity is not necessarily a bad thing because consumers willingly accept the extra cost in return for the benefits of product differentiation that result. It would indeed be a very boring world without product differentiation. We might all be wearing khaki-colored shirts, for example.

How should we evaluate this argument? The major problem lies in separating desired from undesired product differentiation. A consumer who is faced with considerable product differentiation, but little price competition, is not able to choose whether or not to pay extra to get the differentiated product. This isn't likely to be too important a problem when there are many firms, however, as in monopolistic competition. Consider aspirin. If the only products in the industry were Anacin, Bufferin, and Excedrin, the consumer really would not have a low-price choice, since these brands compete almost exclusively by advertising rather than by lowering prices. But the consumer does have a choice of lower priced aspirin brands. So in choosing Anacin over Brand X, we can say that the consumer voluntarily chooses the product differentiation. In this case, product differentiation seems to be a good thing because the consumer is maximizing individual utility by making that choice. If, on the other hand, there are no options for lower priced products and the consumer must choose among those products that compete only through advertising, then the consumer may not have a choice about bearing the cost of the differentiation except, of course, by doing without the good altogether.

Product Differentiation and Advertising

The firm in monopolistic competition will try to differentiate its product in order to shift its demand curve to the right and to make it more inelastic by developing consumer loyalty. The firm will advertise as well as make changes in color, style, quality, and so on. This advertising can inform consumers about higher quality, or it can develop brand loyalty, either of which creates differentiation. Competing with rivals through advertising, style changes, color changes, and techniques other than lowering price is referred to as **nonprice competition**.

NONPRICE COMPETITION
Competing through advertising, style changes, color changes, and techniques other than lowering price.

Advertising does not necessarily cause an increase in price. Even though costs rise with advertising, it is possible that the increased output that advertising generates could result in lower prices because of economies of scale. You can see this by examining Figure 12-5. In Figure 12-5, AC_1 represents a firm's long-run average costs before advertising. With sales of x_1, the price consumers pay is P_1. Advertising raises costs, as represented by AC_2, but if output increases because the firm gains sales by advertising, price can fall to P_2 because of economies of scale. On the other hand, if sales stay at x_1, price will rise to P_3.

If a firm, by effective use of nonprice competition, can successfully differentiate its product so that other firms' products do not seem to be satisfactory substitutes, the firm can earn economic profits in the long run. Such a firm has in essence turned its share of the monopolistically competitive market into a long-run mini-monopoly in the sense that these profits could exist in the long run and not be driven to zero by new entrants.

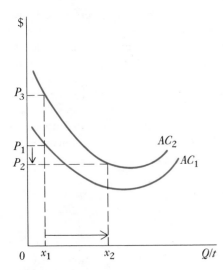

FIGURE 12-5
ADVERTISING AND A POSSIBLE DECLINE IN PRICE
AC_1 represents long-run average costs without advertising. AC_2 represents costs made higher by advertising. If the firm increases output from x_1 to x_2 because of advertising, it is possible for price to the consumer to fall from P_1 to P_2. If sales do not increase, price will rise to P_3.

Consider McDonald's as an example. Fast-food preparation is a monopolistically competitive industry. There are large numbers of firms, and entry is relatively easy. If a firm is able to successfully differentiate its product so that consumers don't consider the products of other firms as close substitutes, the firm is then able to earn long-run profits because it can keep would-be competitors out of its segment of the industry. For example, McDonald's can't keep firms out of the hamburger market, but it can keep firms out of the McDonald's hamburger market. If enough people believe there's nothing like a Big Mac, this persistent brand loyalty might allow McDonald's to maintain economic profits in the long run. Remember—Joan Robinson thought this would be the equilibrium state.

It is easy to determine how successful a firm is at this type of differentiation by examining its prices relative to its competitors' prices. You may go to McDonald's if a Big Mac costs $.15 more than the competition, but would you if it were $.55 more or $1.15 more? There is some price at which the other products will become good substitutes. That price is a measure of the effectiveness of product differentiation. It may be that a Big Mac is worth more to you because it has a higher quality, or it may be that it is worth more only because McDonald's has a very successful advertising and public relations program. The point is that it doesn't matter what causes the differentiation; the economic impact is that McDonald's can earn an economic profit in the long run.

RESOURCE ALLOCATION IN MONOPOLISTIC COMPETITION

The theory of monopolistic competition has several implications for the allocation of resources that are different from the societal ideal developed in pure competition. First, even at the long-run equilibrium with zero economic profit, there will be excess capacity. This means that price will be greater than marginal cost. Consumers are paying only the average costs of production, but these costs are higher than the most efficient level of production would produce.

Second, if costs are the same under pure competition and monopolistic competition, prices will be higher in monopolistic competition. Third, firms in monopolistic competition will provide a wider variety of styles, colors, qualities, and brands. These choices are, unfortunately, related to the product differentiation and excess capacity that caused average costs to be higher.

Fourth, there will be advertising and other forms of nonprice competition. This outcome is not necessarily bad; to the extent that advertising adds to satisfaction and as long as the product is voluntarily purchased, it can be a good thing. Some social critics consider any advertising that does more than convey information to be a bad thing. As economists, we would argue that advertising is undesirable only if people don't have the option to consume alternative goods.[1]

OLIGOPOLY

The last of the four market structures is oligopoly. Oligopoly is important because we observe so many examples of it. **Oligopoly is the situation in which there are few firms. Since there are few firms, the actions of the firms are interdependent.**

In some people's minds, oligopoly and monopoly are essentially the same. Among economists, this view is expressed by John Ken-

OLIGOPOLY
The market structure in which there are few firms. This causes firms to recognize their interdependence.

1. The theory of monopolistic competition has been criticized by Professor George Stigler as not offering any additional insights or predictions to firm behavior. Stigler admits that monopolistic competition is more descriptive of the real world, but he argues that the theory of pure competition offers the same insights and predictions. See G. Chris Archibald, "Chamberlin Versus Chicago," *Review of Economic Studies* (October 1961): 1–28.

SHARED MONOPOLY
The idea that oligopolists coordinate and share markets to act as a monopoly.

neth Galbraith. Galbraith argues that, "So long as there are only a few massive firms in an industry, each must act with a view of the welfare of all."[2] This view, which is not widely shared among economists, regards oligopoly as shared monopoly. **Shared monopoly** is the idea that oligopolists coordinate and share markets to act as a monopoly.

Most economists view oligopoly behavior as more complex and difficult to analyze than monopoly. The difficulty stems from the mutual interdependence that characterizes oligopoly. As a result, economic analysis of oligopoly often includes heavy doses of descriptive economics, and stresses institutional factors. We will describe some types of oligopoly behavior and give examples of each.

PURE OLIGOPOLY
An oligopoly that produces a homogeneous product.

Oligopolistic industries sometimes are categorized by the type of product they produce. Oligopolies may produce either homogeneous or differentiated products. An oligopolistic industry that produces a homogeneous product is referred to as a **pure oligopoly**. The distinction is important because pure oligopolies have a single price for the output of all the firms. An example of a pure oligopoly would be the cement industry. As a consumer, you would be indifferent to which firm produced the sack of cement you purchase.

DIFFERENTIATED OLIGOPOLY
An oligopoly that produces a heterogeneous or differentiated product.

PRICE CLUSTERS
Groupings of prices for similar, but not homogeneous, products.

As opposed to a pure oligopoly, a **differentiated oligopoly** produces goods that are different. The auto industry is a good example. In differentiated oligopolies, there are **price clusters**, which are groupings of prices for similar, but not homogeneous, products. The range of prices within these clusters will depend on the amount of product differentiation. The more differentiated the products, the greater the price divergence. Tight price clusters indicate very little differentiation.

OLIGOPOLY COLLUSIVENESS

Perhaps the most useful classification tool for analyzing oligopolies is the system of definitions proposed by Fritz Machlup of New York University.[3] Machlup divided oligopoly behavior into three classes, which are based on the degree of communication, coordination, and collusion among the new firms. **Communication** refers to the firms' ability to signal their intentions to each other; **coordination** refers to the firms' ability to relate their production decisions to the other firms in the industry; and **collusion** refers to agreements between the firms in an industry to set a certain price or to share a market in certain ways. It should be obvious that the abilities to communicate, coordinate, and collude will depend on the number of firms. As the number of firms increases, the cost of keeping communication open will increase.

COMMUNICATION
Firms' ability to signal their intentions to each other.

COORDINATION
Firms' ability to relate their production decisions to those made by other firms in an industry.

COLLUSION
Agreements between firms in an industry to set certain prices or to share markets in certain ways.

Machlup's list suggests dividing oligopolies into three categories. The first category is one that is characterized by formalized market coordination. The second is characterized by informal market coordination. The third category displays no market coordination.

2. John K. Galbraith, *American Capitalism*, 2d ed. (Cambridge: The Riverside Press, 1956), 83.
3. Fritz Machlup, *The Economics of Sellers' Competition* (Baltimore: Johns Hopkins Press, 1952).

■ Formalized Market Coordination: Cartels

Organized, collusive oligopolies are cartels. **Cartels** are groups of independent firms that agree not to compete but rather to determine prices and quantity jointly. Perfect cartels are able to behave as a monopoly behaves. They correspond to Galbraith's concept of a shared monopoly.

In striving for joint profit maximization, the cartel must set prices, outputs, and marketing areas. However, the cartel can't always set these variables so that each individual firm in the cartel is maximizing its own profits. Examine Figure 12–6 to see this more clearly. In Figure 12–6,

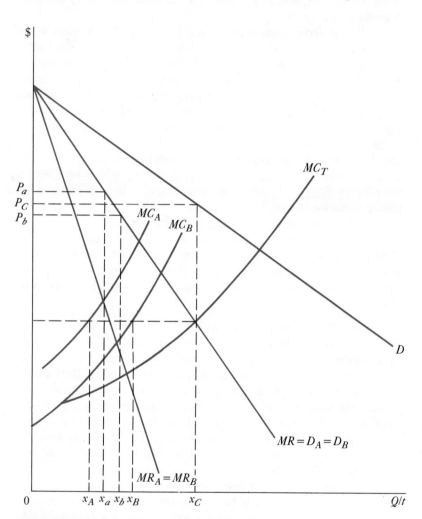

FIGURE 12-6
CARTEL PROFIT MAXIMIZATION
Joint profit maximization by the two firms would occur where $MC_T = MR$. This would establish a price of P_C and output of x_C. The cartel must now force Output x_A and x_B from firms A and B, respectively. The cartel must force this behavior because individual profit maximization, assuming each firm could view one half of the market represented by demand curve (D) as its own, would establish a price of P_a and Output x_a for firm A and a price of P_B and Output x_b for firm B. The cartel must compel firm A to reduce its production and firm B to expand its production relative to its individual maximizing output.

there are two firms, *A* and *B*, in a cartel that produces a homogeneous product. The marginal cost curves of each firm are MC_A and MC_B, respectively. MC_T is the horizontal summation of MC_A and MC_B. The cartel would maximize profits, behaving exactly as a monopoly, by producing x_C where $MR = MC_T$. This output level results in a price of P_C.

Now the centralized cartel must enforce this solution by requiring Firms *A* and *B* to produce x_A and x_B, respectively. The difficulty is that neither firm is at its individual profit-maximizing output. If each firm views one half of the market as its own, its demand curve would be represented by *MR* in Figure 12–6[4]; their profit-maximizing outputs would be where $MC_A = MR_A$ and $MC_B = MR_B$. Firm *A* would produce x_a, and Firm *B* would produce x_b.

In short, profit maximization for the cartel as a whole is not necessarily consistent with profit maximization for each individual cartel member. In the example in Figure 12–6, Firm *A* would prefer to produce *more* and sell it at a *higher* price and Firm *B* would prefer to produce *less* at a *lower* price. The example here points out the most important problem faced by cartels. The problem is that joint cartel profit maximization and individual firm profit maximization are often in conflict. As a result, a cartel is very unstable.

Perhaps the greatest danger a cartel faces is that members find it in their own self-interest to cheat on the cartel. **Chiseling** refers to cheating on a cartel arrangement by lowering prices in an attempt to capture more of the market. If, for example, a cartel agrees on a set price, such as P_C in the previous example, individual members may attempt to give secret price cuts and capture more of the market. If either Firm *A* or Firm *B* believes the other is untrustworthy, it will have more of an incentive to chisel. As the number of firms increases, it becomes increasingly likely that individual firms will become suspicious of the other cartel members.

Cartels in the Real World

The history of cartels is not impressive. They usually have held together for only short periods of time, primarily because of chiseling. In the few cases where cartels have had long-term success, there usually has been direct government participation. Once governments are involved, it becomes more difficult to chisel because government can police and penalize this behavior. The amount of chiseling, it should be clear, is closely related to the number of firms comprising a cartel. The fewer the firms, the more closely the cartel will be able to monitor behavior to determine if a firm is chiseling.

Other factors can help cartels control the problem of chiseling. For example, if the number of buyers is small and if the prices are widely publicized, the cartel members will not worry so much about one of their own members chiseling. Also, if the cartel is successful in acting as a monopoly and earning higher than normal profits, it must create barriers to entry; otherwise, new firms might enter the market and compete with the cartel. Let's briefly examine a few cartel-type organizations to see what elements affected their success or failure.

CHISELING
Cheating on a cartel arrangement by lowering prices in an attempt to capture more of the market.

---

4. Remember that $MR = 1/2D$. So if each firm views half the market as its own, the demand curve that each firm faced would be identical to the market *MR* curve.

Organized, collusive activity in private industry in the United States usually has been invalidated by the courts. However, General Electric and Westinghouse engaged in secret conspiracies in the late 1950s to act as a cartel. They decided on a scheme that allowed them to rotate low bid submissions on government contracts where the job was awarded to the low bidder. The most famous scheme depended on the phases of the moon. At every phase of the moon (every two weeks), the firm designated to be the low bidder would gain the right to that contract because the other firm would submit an uncompetitive, high bid. This plan worked well because there were only two firms dealing with one buyer, the federal government. Each firm would know if the other was cheating because the bids would be made public. In this case, the government was inadvertently helping the cartel overcome the chiseling problem.

At the other end of the spectrum, as far as firm numbers are concerned, was an attempt to form a cartel known as the National Farm Organization (NFO). The farm industry for milk and beef production is composed of large numbers of firms, and the NFO cartel only included about 10 percent of these firms. In 1967 and 1968, the NFO attempted to act as a producer cartel. In two separate actions—one to raise milk prices and the other to raise beef prices—the NFO tried withholding actions. In order to raise prices, cartel members would destroy milk and keep cattle away from the market. If the NFO members had been successful in raising prices, the nonmembers who continued to produce and sell would have been the beneficiaries and would have reacted to these higher prices by expanding output in response. Additionally, as prices began to rise, there would have been tremendous pressure to chisel on the withholding action. In fact, the chiselers would have benefited much more than the members who refused to chisel. The realization of this possibility resulted in violence. Cattle scales were blown up. Withholding farmers sat in the roads to keep chiselers from taking their products to market. Some chiselers even resorted to taking cattle to market in house trailers to avoid detection. The lesson is clear. A cartel with many members will find it very difficult to be successful.

Cartels are much more common in Europe than they are in the United States. In Europe, cartels are permitted and often encouraged by governments. In Nazi Germany, all the major industries operated as cartels, and in present-day Western Europe, the Common Market Commission is actively promoting cartels in steel, textiles, and shipbuilding.

Cartels are—with one exception—illegal in the United States. The one exception, based on the Webb-Pomerene Act of 1921, allows the formation of cartels when they are necessary to participate in foreign trade. These Webb-Pomerene cartels have not been successful in raising prices, primarily because of the large number of firms participating.

OPEC—A Decade of Success

Without question, the most successful cartel in recent years is the Organization of Petroleum Exporting Countries, known as OPEC. In the 1950s, international oil companies controlled a major portion of the world's oil supply. These companies frequently engaged in active price competition. In an attempt to stop such price competition, the Arab governments, along with a few non-Arab governments, formed OPEC in 1960. At first, OPEC enjoyed little success. But this changed in 1973, as the Arab-Israeli war heated up, and the Arab countries banded together. On January 1, 1973, the price of oil was $2.12 per barrel. Of this $2.12, $1.52 went to the governments involved. By January 1, 1974, the price was $7.61 with $7.01 going to the governments. By January, 1975, the price was about $10.50. By 1982, the price had risen to $35.00.

How did this cartel, which had been in existence with a few members since 1960, come to flex its muscles in 1973? At that time, importing governments helped by posting prices and dealing with the OPEC governments in open forums where the individual members could be less fearful of chiseling. More important, however, Saudi Arabia was willing to cut back its production of oil to allow other members to sell all they wanted to produce at the high prices set by the cartel.[5] In 1984, after production had to be cut back by 5 million barrels a day to prevent the cartel from collapsing, Saudi Arabia's willingness to bear this cost began to weaken.

The price began to fall. The January, 1984, spot price of oil was $29 per barrel, down from the 1982 high of $35. The slide continued. In January 1987, the spot price of oil was $13 per barrel. As prices fell, chiseling became more common. The predictions made by economists in the 1970s that the cartel eventually would weaken started to come true. In 1986, Nobel Prize winner Milton Friedman wrote an editorial entitled "Right at Last, an Expert's Dream" reminding readers that he had predicted in 1974 that OPEC would not last very long.[6]

As we discussed earlier, all cartels face two problems. The first is chiseling, or secret price cutting. OPEC is facing this problem in the presence of oil surpluses. Some of the Persian Gulf countries, notably Kuwait, the United Arab Emirates, and Qatar, are now experiencing cash flow problems. These countries started grandiose development schemes when their oil revenues were in excess of $264 billion per year. Their revenues are now significantly down due to the decreased price and decreased sales. There is extreme pressure to sell more oil to maintain these development projects.

The second problem a successful cartel faces is new entry. Large amounts of new oil are coming on stream from non-OPEC sources. In addition, other sources of energy, such as solar and nuclear energy, which were uneconomical when oil was $2 per barrel, are now economical at the current high price of oil. The entry of nonoil competition has been slow to develop, but the future should prove even more difficult for OPEC as new firms producing oil and other competing products enter and challenge the cartel's cohesiveness.

In addition to the new oil supplies, the high oil prices also have had an effect on quantity demanded. The decade of OPEC's dominance resulted in adjustments in consumer demand. This is perhaps most evident in the increased fuel efficiency of automobiles.

The impact of new oil supplies and reordered consumption patterns is evident in the statistics. In 1973, OPEC's share of world oil production was 56 percent. In 1975, its share was 51 percent; in 1980, 45 percent; and in 1984, 35 percent. In 1987, OPEC's share had fallen to 30

---

5. An interesting side issue is that much public criticism was leveled on the oil companies rather than the OPEC members. This is odd because the cartel profits are not going to the oil companies but to the governments of the OPEC member countries.

6. Milton Friedman, "Right at Last, an Expert's Dream," *Newsweek* (March 10, 1986): 8.

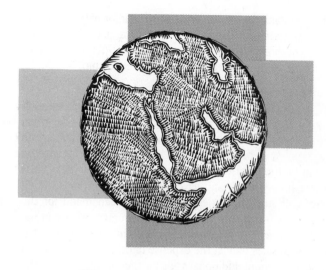

THE INTERNATIONAL PERSPECTIVE
COMMODITY CARTELS

Commodity cartels have a long history of failure. In the 1950s, commodity agreements, which are essentially cartels of commodity producing countries, existed for tin, coffee, sugar, and wheat. The success of OPEC in 1973, which was documented in this chapter, reenergized some of these cartels as many commodity exporting countries tried to emulate OPEC. The result was a flurry of activity that produced the following official organizations in addition to The Organization of Petroleum Exporting Countries (OPEC):

International Bauxite Association (IBA)
Intergovernmental Council of Copper-Exporting Countries (CIPEC)
International Sugar Association (ISA)

International Tin Council (ITC)
Organization of Banana Exporting Countries (OBEC)

In addition, there were attempts in the late 1970s and early 1980s to organize cartels in iron ore, nickel, rubber, tungsten, molybdenum, cobalt, columbium, and tantalum.

Several lessons can be learned from the experience of these commodity cartels and in particular the success of OPEC. These lessons are that to be successful, a commodity cartel must:

1. have few members,
2. produce a product with few substitutes (have inelastic demand),
3. have buoyant world demand (have high income elasticity),
4. pursue a moderate pricing policy,
5. have at least tacit approval of consuming nations, and
6. have effective sanctions against chiselers.

Most cartels have great difficulty with 4, 5, and 6 and, as a result, break down rather quickly.

The effects of cartels are often mixed up with economic development and world politics. Cartel member countries tend to be less developed countries, and the consuming nations tend to be developed countries. The reasons for the formation of the cartels are often put in terms of a "fair" price that will redistribute from rich to poor countries. The rhetoric concerning producer cartels is therefore about redistribution. Cartels are anticonsumer. Some of those consumers live in high-income countries, while many may be poor people in poor countries. The OPEC oil price hike caused more hardship in poor countries than it did in rich countries.

percent. This declining share of production signaled the weakening of the cartel better than any other piece of data. If a cartel is going to set prices, it must control production.

Informal Market Coordination

Informally coordinated oligopolies practice unorganized and unstated attempts to practice joint actions. Such **tacit collusion** is a much weaker form of collusion than that of formally organized oligopolies or cartels. It is weaker because all the incentives to chisel are still present, but organized techniques to guard against the chiseling are not. Tacit collusion is found in U.S. industry because cartels are clearly illegal under U.S. antitrust laws. Informal cooperation among oligopolistic firms can, in part, be viewed as an attempt to form cartels while avoiding antitrust laws.

TACIT COLLUSION
Unorganized and unstated attempts to practice joint action.

Collusion in such oligopolies usually takes the form of informal agreements to behave in certain ways. Often these agreements arise naturally, without any need for clear-cut organization. The most common form of tacit, informal agreement is based on some form of price leadership.

Price Leadership

Price leadership is the practice of industry pricing in which other firms typically follow the initiative of a particular firm, the price leader. The firm that is the most influential in an industry is called the **dominant firm**, which may be the largest firm. It also can be the *low-cost* firm, which may not be the largest firm in the industry. Price leadership is most effective where firms are few and have clearly similar products (e.g., the auto, cigarette, and steel industries). It helps if the demand for the product is price inelastic since this will further discourage price cutting. When the demand curve for the industry is perfectly inelastic, a firm that chisels on price will gain sales only at the expense of other firms because a lower price will not bring about additional sales for the industry. Thus, the conflict between firms will be sharper when demand is not very responsive to price cuts.

The Dominant Firm

In price leadership by the dominant firm, that firm sets a profit-maximizing price, and the other firms divide up the market at that same price. The other firms, known as the **competitive fringe**, act much like firms in pure competition. This result can be seen by examining Figure 12–7. The market demand curve for the product is represented by D. The marginal cost curve of the dominant firm is MC_d, and the summation of all the other fringe firms' marginal cost curves is MC_f. The fringe firms will make production decisions as price takers and will always produce where price is equal to their marginal cost. MC_f can thus be viewed as their supply curve. The demand curve that the dominant firm faces can then be derived by horizontally subtracting the amount supplied by the fringe firms (MC_f) from the market demand curve. This subtraction gives the dominant firm's demand curve, D_d, and its marginal revenue curve, MR_d. The dominant firm now will set a profit-maximizing price and output of P_1 and x_d. Once Price P_1 is determined, the fringe firms view this price much as competitive firms view the market price. The fringe firms will produce x_f units at the Market Price P_1 because for them $P_1 = MR$, and they will produce where $MR = MC_f$. The sum of production of the dominant firm (x_d) and of the fringe firms (x_f) satisfies the market demand of x_m at Price P_1.

This model of price leadership is applicable to the oil industry, where there is a small group of dominant firms and a large number of small fringe firms. Dominant firm price leadership also appears to have prevailed at one time or another in the aluminum, automobile, and cigarette industries.

Historical Price Leadership

In a few cases, particularly in mature industries, it is possible for a firm to emerge as the price leader because it is convenient for the other firms in the industry to follow the leader and thus coordinate their pricing. This type of price leadership is very similar to cartel behavior. Its intent is collusion—to achieve industry-wide profit maximization. Histori-

PRICE LEADERSHIP
The practice of industry pricing in which other firms follow the pricing initiatives of a particular firm, the price leader.

DOMINANT FIRM
The most influential firm in an industry, usually the price leader.

COMPETITIVE FRINGE
The sometimes substantial number of small competitors in markets with one large, dominant firm.

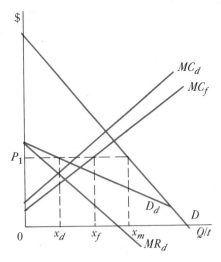

FIGURE 12-7
DOMINANT FIRM WITH COMPETITIVE FRINGE FIRMS
The dominant firm views a part of the market, D_d, as its own. D_d is determined by subtracting the competitive fringe supply curve, MC_f, from the market demand, D. The dominant firm then produces where $MC_d = MR_d$, setting Price P_1 and producing x_d units. The fringe firms then face a perfectly elastic demand at P_1, and produce x_f units where $P_1 = MR = MC_f$.

cal price leadership, however, is unorganized and thus not illegal in the United States. This type of price leadership was rampant within U.S. oligopolies. General Motors was the recognized price leader in autos, U.S. Steel in steel, and DuPont in chemicals. In the last ten years, the price leadership of these domestic oligopolies has been severely limited by foreign competition.

Successful Price Leadership

In order to be successful—that is, in order to raise industry profit levels—price leadership must produce a kind of cartel but still avoid legal sanctions. This means walking a tightrope because, as the tacit collusion embodied in price leadership becomes successful, the incentive to chisel increases. As a result, most successful price leadership situations that are not the dominant firm type occur in industries in which there are only a few firms. The record of such tacit collusion shows that such industries are characterized by rigid prices; and price changes, when they occur, are generally small. Such industries are usually those that blame price increases on rising costs and that can punish firms who do not follow the price increase. The steel and auto industries are two examples. In these industries, potential chiselers know they cannot easily get away with not following the price leader.

CHARACTERISTICS OF IMPERFECT COMPETITION

Monopolistic Competition

■

- Many sellers of similar, but differentiated products
- Economic profits can exist in the short run
- $P = AC$ in the long run
- Excess capacity exists in the long run, $P > MC$
- Nonprice competition increases product differentiation

Oligopoly

■

- Few sellers of homogeneous or differentiated products
- Interdependence leads to attempts at communication, coordination, and collusion
- Cartels may be formed to determine industry pricing and output
- Price leadership may be used to coordinate industry pricing
- The price leader may be a dominant firm
- Nonprice competition increases product differentiation

The Gary Dinners

The way in which cartels can be held together informally is clearly demonstrated by what have come to be known as the Gary Dinners. In 1901, U.S. Steel put together mergers that made U.S. Steel the dominant firm, supplying 65 percent of the domestic steel market. From

1907 to 1911, Judge Elbert H. Gary, chairman of the board of U.S. Steel, held a series of dinners for executives of competing companies.

Judge Gary explained that the close communication *and contact* developed at these dinners ". . . generated such mutual *respect and affectionate regard* among steel industry leaders that all considered the obligation to cooperate and avoid destructive competition *more binding . . . than any written or verbal contract*."[7] Efforts to prosecute U.S. Steel's behavior for antitrust violations were unsuccessful.

In recent years, there haven't been any reported "informal" gatherings as effective as the Gary Dinners, but trade associations, country clubs, and other such business and social gatherings can serve as a forum for developing cooperative behavior among potential competitors.

No Market Coordination

Unorganized, uncollusive oligopolies are characterized by independent action. These oligopolies practice profit maximization independently but are affected by the action and response of their rivals. Each firm tries to anticipate the response of its rivals and then takes the predicted response into account when making decisions. Economists tried to develop a model for this behavior in the early 1800s; and in 1838, A. Augustin Cournot (1801–1877) published a theory of duopoly (a market with only two firms). His theory and the theories that followed up to the post-World War II period, while interesting, were unsatisfactory because they assumed that the rival firm would not react to the action of the firm being analyzed. The post-World War II developments in oligopoly theory rest heavily on mathematical game theory. Game theory is a relatively new field of mathematics that can provide insights into oligopolistic behavior.

Game Theory

GAME THEORY
A mathematical technique that can provide insight into oligopolistic behavior. "Players" try to reach an optimal position through strategic behavior that takes into account the anticipated moves of other players.

Game theory, a theory of rational decision making under conditions of uncertainty, was first developed by John von Neumann (1903–1957) and Oskar Morgenstern (1902–1977) in a book entitled *The Theory of Games and Economic Behavior*.[8] In game theory, "players" try to reach an optimal position through strategic behavior that takes into account the anticipated moves of other players. Game theory describes very accurately how oligopolists behave.

Standard microeconomic decision-making theory is based on the assumption that the outcomes of various decisions are known with certainty. Game theory suggests rational solutions when the outcomes are uncertain. Games usually are described as being either zero-sum or nonzero-sum. Zero-sum games are those in which one player's gain is another player's loss. Nonzero-sum games open the door to collusion or

---

7. F.M. Scherer, *Industrial Market Structure and Economic Performance* (Chicago: Rand McNally, 1980): 170. Italicized passages are Judge Gary's actual words taken from a government antitrust brief.

8. For a detailed and highly mathematical treatment of game theory, see John von Neumann and Oskar Morgenstern, *The Theory of Games and Economic Behavior* (Princeton, N.J.: Princeton University Press, 1949). For a short survey on game theory, see Scherer, *Industrial Market Structure and Economic Performance*, 160–166.

cooperative action because all players may gain (or all may lose) from a certain course of action. This aspect of game theory has proved very useful in the study of oligopoly markets in which each participant must take into account the reactions of its competitors.

One of the most famous nonzero-sum games is called the Prisoner's Dilemma. The name comes from a situation in which two criminals are interrogated separately. Each criminal knows that if neither confesses, both will go free. However, if one confesses and implicates the other, he or she can go free and the other will be convicted. The interrogator then offers each criminal the opportunity to confess and go free. The rational course of action for the self-interested criminal is to confess and implicate the other. Since both will be motivated in this way, both will confess and the outcome of both rational decisions will make both worse off. They would both be better off if they could engage in collusion. The same lesson holds for oligopolistic firms.

The Kinked Demand Curve

One explanation of why prices in oligopolistic industries tend to be less flexible than prices in other market structures was presented by Paul Sweezy when he was a professor at Stanford University. Sweezy hypothesized that price rigidity exists because the firms in an oligopoly face a **kinked demand curve.** The demand curve has two sections because the firms come to believe that if they cut prices, their rivals will follow the price cut and, as a result, the price cut will not produce much of an increase in sales. A price increase, on the other hand, will not be followed and will, therefore, result in a significant loss of sales to the firm raising its price. As a result, once a price is reached, it tends to remain in effect for long periods.

You can see the effect of a kink in the demand curve by examining Figure 12–8. A kink in the demand curve, D, comes about at Point A (or at Price P) because the other oligopoly firms will match any price decrease, making the demand curve below Point A relatively inelastic; the firm won't increase sales very much by decreasing price. Any increase in price above P will have the opposite effect. Competing firms will not match the increase and, as a result, the demand curve above Point A will be relatively elastic. At the kink in the demand curve, the corresponding marginal revenue curve, MR, will be discontinuous, meaning it has a break in it from B to C in Figure 12–8. This break allows a large variation in marginal cost, from B to C, with no effect on the profit-maximizing price, P, or output, x. For example, marginal cost could change from MC to MC_1 with no effect on price and output. Sweezy used this result to explain why prices were so rigid in oligopoly.

Nonprice Competition

All oligopolists, whether organized or unorganized, compete in dimensions other than just the price dimension. In formulating models, economists tend to treat goods as homogeneous and view competition as occurring primarily through price adjustments. In the real world, however, competition can take other forms. Firms can change the quality, color, texture, design, size, advertising, and a host of other attributes of a product. Even an apparently homogeneous product can be differentiated by the quality of customer service.

KINKED DEMAND CURVE
A model used to explain price rigidity under oligopoly. The kink comes from pricing behavior in which other firms' price cuts, but not price increases, are matched.

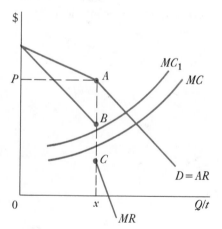

FIGURE 12–8
THE KINKED DEMAND CURVE
In this model, the firm faces a kinked demand curve, D, because prices above P will not be matched, while prices below P will be matched. The kink creates a discontinuity in the marginal revenue curve, which causes the price to be very rigid at the kink (P).

extensively in the field of industrial organization, but the similarities end there.

George Stigler is the personification of the "Chicago School" of free-enterprise capitalism. He received a B.B.A. degree from the University of Washington, an M.B.A. degree from Northwestern University, and a Ph.D. from the University of Chicago. In 1982, Stigler was awarded the Nobel Prize in economics. Paul Sweezy is an American Marxist. He was awarded a B.A. degree and, in 1937, a Ph.D. in economics from Harvard University.

Both economists are coeditors of prestigious journals that are at opposite ends of the ideological spectrum. Stigler is coeditor of the *Journal of Political Economy*, and Sweezy is coeditor of the *Monthly Review*. Stigler's views are best delineated in *The Theory of Price* (1966) and *Organization of Industry* (1968). Sweezy's views can be found in *The Dynamics of U.S. Capitalism* (1972), *Introduction to Socialism* (1968), and *Modern Capitalism and Other Essays* (1972).

Stigler and Sweezy have clashed over Sweezy's use of the kinked demand curve to explain why prices in oligopolistic industries are more stable than prices in other market structures. This model has been devastatingly attacked by Stigler, who argues that Sweezy's theory is wrong and that his observation that prices in an oligopoly are more stable than in other market structures does not stand up to empirical investigation.

GEORGE STIGLER (1911–   )
PAUL SWEEZY (1910–   )

George Stigler and Paul Sweezy represent polar extremes in economic analysis. Both have written

An oligopolistic firm may resort to nonprice competition in an attempt to increase its market share.[9] We can apply the model of oligopoly behavior to these other types of competition. For example, a firm contemplating a new advertising program will need to consider whether the program will increase its market share or prompt a rival to undertake a similar program. In the first instance, the program may be worthwhile. In the second, it probably would only increase costs without creating a larger market share. Thus, even with nonprice competition, oligopoly firms are interdependent and need to consider the reactions of rivals.

Factors Facilitating and Limiting Oligopoly Coordination

We have seen that there are benefits to be gained by oligopolists who can coordinate output and pricing decisions, whether such coor-

9. Sometimes quality changes act as inverse price changes. For example, if the price of a candy bar remains at 25 cents but the amount of chocolate or almonds has been decreased, this is equivalent to an increase in price. Oligopolists often engage in this kind of disguised price changing because it seems to provoke less response from rivals.

dination is formal or informal. As we have seen, there are strong forces pulling in opposite directions. It is worthwhile to review those factors that facilitate, and those that limit, oligopoly coordination.

The Number of Firms
The number of firms has the most obvious impact on the probability of formal or informal coordination and collusion. As the number of firms increases, the perceived impact of any individual firm's actions decreases, and the incentive to coordinate diminishes. In addition, as the number of firms increases, the cost of coordinating and policing the agreement increases. It is obvious that as the size of the group increases, the probability that it will include a maverick also increases. All tendencies have the same effect; as the number of firms increases, the likelihood of effective coordination diminishes rapidly. Some economists have suggested that after the number of firms reaches ten, it is likely that they will ignore each other's actions, making coordination less feasible.[10]

Entry Barriers
Entry barriers play a key role because they are related to the number of firms. An oligopoly will not be able to practice effective coordination if it can't limit entry. New firms will destroy oligopoly coordination and erode any economic profit created by the coordination. The lesson is a simple one: If strong entry barriers (including barriers created by government) exist, the possibility of coordination exists; if strong entry barriers are weak, coordination is highly unlikely.

The Size of Firms
If the oligopolistic industry is dominated by one firm, or if several of the firms are large relative to the remaining firms, the possibility of coordination is enhanced. Coordination would only necessitate agreement by the dominant firm or firms.

Secrecy
Coordination requires the elimination of secret deals so that uncooperative behavior can be punished. Monitoring chiseling behavior is easier in an environment in which secret deals don't stay secret long. As we have seen, it is often the case that government has aided cooperative agreements by requiring the full disclosure of contract details.

Unstable or Fluctuating Demand
If demand fluctuates or is otherwise unstable, oligopolists will have difficulty determining if changes in their own demand are the result of market forces, or alternatively, the competitive behavior of a rival. As a result, unstable or fluctuating demand will make cartel coordination more difficult.

Product Heterogeneity
The more homogeneous products are, the easier it will be to coordinate the sale of those products. As product differences increase, firms will be unable to determine if the price concessions of rivals are attempts to chisel or whether they are due to actual differences in product characteristics.

---

10. See Scherer, *Industrial Market Structure and Economic Performance.*

Industry Social Structure

We already have seen that the maturity of an industry can affect coordination. The social structure of an industry is also important for coordination. Do the leaders know and trust each other? Do they get together at meetings? Do they play golf and engage in other recreational pursuits? If they do, coordination might be easier. We must be very careful here. Socializing does not mean that entrepreneurs are not competitive. What appears to be cooperation may be a subterfuge for future chiseling on a coordination effort. Remember, if an oligopolist can get all the others to agree and then can chisel on the agreement, it can be very profitable.

Antitrust Activity

The U.S. antitrust laws make coordination illegal. If these laws are vigorously enforced, it will make coordination more costly; this will serve to limit attempts at coordination.

■ ■ ■ ■ ■ ■ ■
MARKET STRUCTURES IN REVIEW

This chapter concludes the discussion of the four market structures in the theory of the firm. Table 12–1 summarizes some of the important variables that differentiate the market structures we have examined. The key to understanding the theory of the firm is a solid understanding of monopoly and pure competition. Oligopoly and monopolistic competition expand the theories of monopoly and pure competition and, in effect, demonstrate that we can generalize from the pure models to real-world situations.

TABLE 12-1
SUMMARY OF MARKET STRUCTURES

Type of Market	Number of Firms	Product Differentiation	Control Over Price	Amount of Nonprice Competition	Examples
Pure Competition	Large numbers	Homogeneous product	None	None	Agriculture is reasonably close
Monopolistic Competition	Many	Slightly differentiated	Some	Advertising and product differentiation	Retail trade and service industry
Oligopoly	Few	Homogeneous *or* differentiated product	Some to considerable	Advertising and product differentiation	Autos, steel
Monopoly	One	Unique product (no close substitutes)	Considerable	Public relations	Some utilities and aluminum before 1945

■ SUMMARY

1. Monopolistic competition is a market situation characterized by many producers of a heterogeneous product.
2. Key assumptions in the model of monopolistic competition are: large numbers of producers, product differentiation, and relative ease of entry. This means that economic profits can exist in the short run, but entry of new firms will insure a long-run equilibrium with zero economic profit.
3. Because of product differentiation, a firm at equilibrium produces less than the socially optimal output. This underproduction is referred to as excess capacity.
4. Monopolistically competitive firms produce a smaller output at a higher price than firms (with the same costs) engaged in pure competition.
5. Marginal cost is not equal to average, long-run equilibrium cost in monopolistic competition.
6. Oligopoly is the market structure in which there are only a few firms producing goods that are either homogeneous or differentiated.
7. Because there are so few firms in an oligopoly, they are interdependent, and they take this interdependence into account in their economic decision making.
8. Oligopolies can be divided into three classes: oligopolies characterized by formalized market coordination (cartels), oligopolies characterized by informal market coordination, and oligopolies characterized by no market coordination.
9. Cartels are threatened by chiseling behavior on the part of individual members of the cartel. The larger the number of firms in the cartel, the more difficult it is for the cartel to hold together.
10. Successful cartels historically have often used governments to police the cartel.
11. Price leadership is common in oligopolies where formalized market coordination is not possible. Price leadership can be by a dominant firm or, in mature industries, by a historical leader.
12. Oligopolies are characterized by extensive use of nonprice competition.
13. Barriers to entry are important in oligopoly, just as they are in monopoly.
14. There are economic forces working to limit coordination and to facilitate coordination. These forces pull in opposite directions.

■ NEW TERMS

differentiated product	differentiated oligopoly	tacit collusion
product group	price clusters	price leadership
excess capacity	communication	dominant firm
nonprice competition	coordination	competitive fringe
oligopoly	collusion	game theory
shared monopoly	cartel	kinked demand curve
pure oligopoly	chiseling	

■ QUESTIONS FOR DISCUSSION

1. Firms in monopolistic competition only earn normal profits in the long run, unless they can successfully convince consumers that their product is really different. List as many examples of product differentiation as you can. Do you think the differences are real, imagined, or created? Does product differentiation make any economic difference?
2. Are there any significant differences between the model of pure competition and monopolistic competition? What assumption is different?
3. What is excess capacity? Is it a good or a bad thing?
4. Is the NCAA (National Collegiate Athletic Association) a cartel? How do some universities (firms) chisel on the cartel? Why do they do this?
5. Explain how the expectation of new entry would limit cartel formation.
6. How would you expect the number of firms in a cartel to affect the probability of its success? Why?

What differences in the model are created by this changed assumption?

7. In what sense is monopolistic competition like monopoly and in what sense is it like competition?

8. What does the kinked demand curve imply about the oligopolists' response to the price behavior of rivals? What does the kinked demand curve model say about prices in oligopolistic industries? On what grounds has the model been criticized?

9. How would you characterize the market in which the major television networks compete with each other? Are NBC, CBS, and ABC monopolists, oligopolists, or monopolistically competitive? How do they compete with one another?

10. Suppose that advertising in an oligopolistic market does not increase the total volume of sales but only the distribution of each of the oligopoly firm's sales. How does this fit the prisoner's dilemma model?

SUGGESTIONS FOR FURTHER READING

Breit, William, and Roger L. Ransom. *The Academic Scribblers: Economists in Collusion.* 2d ed. New York: The Dryden Press, 1983. Covers the ideas of several of the economists discussed in this chapter.

Friedman, James W. *Oligopoly Theory.* New York: Cambridge University Press, 1984. A thorough study of oligopoly theory using numerical examples.

Scherer, F.M. *Industrial Market Structure and Economic Performance.* Chicago: Rand McNally, 1980. This is a reference book for industrial organization, market structure, and antitrust. This book contains a good review of monopolistic competition and oligopoly theory.

CHAPTER 13 ■
■

THEORY IN THE REAL WORLD: AMERICAN INDUSTRY AND U.S. ANTITRUST POLICY

■

INTRODUCTION

The preceding chapters examined four theoretically distinct types of market structures. In this chapter, we will apply these theoretical models to the real world and examine the extent of monopoly power in U.S. industry. To do this, we need first to determine what constitutes an industry. We then can attempt to determine whether a particular industry is monopolistic and what elements contribute to this monopoly power. Only then can we examine public policy options to address any monopoly power that might exist. This chapter, then, will take you into empirical industry studies to develop a real-world appreciation of the monopoly problem. **Industry studies** are investigations of particular industries to determine the degree of competitive behavior in the industry. As a separate subfield of economics, this area of investigation is sometimes referred to as *industrial organization*.

Once it is determined that an industry possesses some degree of monopoly power, it may be desirable to control or mitigate the worst aspects of that monopoly power. Monopoly power could be destroyed through antitrust action, monopoly profits could be taxed away, or the monopoly could be regulated and thus forced to behave in some prescribed fashion. Or it might even be better to do nothing about the monopoly power. This chapter will examine the theory and practice of regulation and then the development and record of U.S. antitrust laws. It will conclude with an assessment of the record of regulation and antitrust policy and an examination of recent trends in merger activity in U.S. industry.

INDUSTRY STUDIES
Investigations of particular industries to determine the degree of competitive behavior in the industry.

269

■   ■   ■   ■   ■   ■   ■

WHAT IS AN INDUSTRY?

We have, up to this point, been using the term industry without carefully defining what an industry is. In general, an *industry* is a group of firms producing the same, or at least similar, products. The difficulty with this definition centers on the degree of dissimilarity allowed before the two products are thought of as being produced in different industries. Consider the container industry. Are firms producing glass bottles and aluminum cans similar enough to be included in the same industry? How about including firms making paper cups or even pewter mugs in this industry? Most consumers regard pewter mugs and paper cups as quite different. If you are willing to pay substantially more for a pewter mug than for a paper cup, you regard them as being distinct products. What about a plastic Ronald McDonald® glass? Is it closer to a paper cup or a pewter mug? We raise these questions to demonstrate that whatever answers we reach will be arbitrary to some degree. Therefore some people, even some economists, may disagree with a particular classification of two products as belonging to the same industry, or to different industries.

One of the principles developed earlier, cross elasticity of demand, could be useful in determining whether products belong to the same industry or different industries. We saw earlier that if the coefficient of the cross elasticity of demand between two products is positive, the goods are substitutes.[1] Goods that are close substitutes have a positive and very high cross-elasticity of demand coefficient. If economists could agree on a cross elasticity coefficient that would represent goods from the same industry—again, an arbitrary decision—they could then use this figure in a very mechanical fashion to define an industry.

The problem of assigning firms to industries becomes even more difficult if you consider that some multiproduct firms produce a variety of goods that might be included in different industries. In which industry is a firm that produces coffee in addition to soap and cake mixes? Informed judgments and somewhat arbitrary definitions are necessary in order to move from the world of theory into the real world of industry studies.

There is a standard set of data available from the U.S. Census Bureau in which these judgments have already been made. The Census Bureau collects and classifies data according to the **Standard Industrial Classification (SIC) system**.[2] The SIC system divides the economy into about 400 four-digit industries. These four-digit groups can then be aggregated into three-digit or two-digit groups, or disaggregated into five-digit (or even seven-digit) product classes. Table 13–1 presents an example of how a product becomes more specific as the industry group is disaggregated. The purpose of such a system is to organize groups of processes, products, and materials into a workable, consistent classification. This SIC system is the basis for studies referred to in the remainder of this chapter.

STANDARD INDUSTRIAL CLASSIFICATION (SIC) SYSTEM
A system devised by the U.S. Census Bureau for classifying industries. The SIC system divides the economy into about 400 four-digit industries.

1. $E_{x,y} =$ (percentage change in quantity demanded of good x)/(percentage change in price of good y).
2. See U.S. Bureau of the Budget, *Standard Industrial Classification Manual* (Washington, D.C.: U.S. Government Printing Office, 1976).

TABLE 13-1
SAMPLE STANDARD INDUSTRIAL
CLASSIFICATION SYSTEM CODES

Code Number		Designation	Name
Two-digit	20	Major Industry Group	Food & Kindred Products
Three-digit	201	Industry Group	Meat Products
Four-digit	2011	Industry	Meat Packing Plants
Five-digit	20111	Product Class	Fresh Beef

Source: U.S. Bureau of the Budget, *Standard Industrial Classification Manual* (Washington, D.C.: U.S. Government Printing Office, 1976).

INDUSTRY STRUCTURE

Once the hurdle of defining an industry has been overcome, it is then possible to determine its market structure, i.e., where it lies on the continuum from perfect competition to monopoly. As we saw earlier, this structure will depend critically on a number of elements in that particular industry. Of these elements, degrees of concentration and conditions of entry are especially important. Concentration and entry interact in such a way that entry barriers make for a more concentrated industry, but for the moment, let's consider them separately.

Concentration Ratios

Concentration refers to the extent to which a certain number of firms dominate sales in a given market. Measures of concentration have, for many years, been a primary tool of industry studies. A **concentration ratio** is used by economists to provide an index of the relative degree of concentration in an oligopolistic market. To calculate a concentration ratio, the economist takes all the firms in a particular four-digit SIC code and calculates the percentage of that industry's total sales accounted for by a certain number of firms.[3] For example, a four-firm concentration ratio would measure the percentage of sales in an industry accounted for by the largest four firms. Other commonly used concentration ratios are for the largest firm, the three largest firms, the eight largest firms, and so on. Most industry studies employ four-firm ratios. Table 13–2 gives four-firm concentration ratios for a few industries.

It could be argued that the percentage of sales is not the best measure of concentration in an industry. You might instead want to calculate concentration ratios using percentage of assets, percentage of employees, or value of shipments. The various measures of concentration are all highly correlated, however, so it really isn't that crucial which type of ratio you select.

CONCENTRATION RATIO
An index of the relative degree of concentration in an oligopolistic market.

---

3. Prelaw students might anticipate a strategy for defense in antitrust cases. The defense, of course, would prefer to have concentration ratios calculated on the basis of the most general category possible to ensure that any one firm has a small share of the sales in the industry.

TABLE 13-2
FOUR-FIRM CONCENTRATION RATIOS—SELECTED INDUSTRIES

Product	Concentration Ratio
■	■
Automobile	94%
Chewing Gum	93
Window Glass	89
Sewing Machines	82
Detergent (household)	80
Tires	71
Canned Beer	66

Source: Federal Trade Commission, *Selected Statistical Series* (Washington, D.C.: U.S. Government Printing Office, 1986).

As we discussed earlier, the more concentrated an industry, the more likely it is that there will be a recognized interdependence and joint action of either a collusive or noncollusive nature. When a four-firm concentration ratio exceeds 40 to 50 percent, the degree of interdependence is likely to be very high.

Entry Barriers

Entry conditions are the second element affecting market structure. If entry barriers are high and the industry is highly concentrated, it is more likely that joint action can be undertaken to create monopoly profits. We saw earlier that cartels are very unstable and that profits will strongly attract new firms into the industry. But if concentration is high and entry is blocked, the existing firms will be in a better position to restrict output, raise price, and maintain persistent profits.

The Herfindahl Index

HERFINDAHL INDEX
An index of concentration that takes into account all the firms in an industry.

The U.S. Justice Department recently has taken a great deal of interest in the **Herfindahl Index,** a summary index of concentration to replace the more traditional concentration ratios.[4] The Herfindahl Index takes into account the market shares of all of the firms in an industry, not just the market share of the largest few firms.

The Herfindahl Index is the sum of the squares of market shares in an industry. The formula to calculate the Herfindahl Index is:

$$H = (S_1)^2 + (S_2)^2 + \ldots (S_n)^2,$$

where H is the Herfindahl Index and S_1 through S_n are the market shares of individual firms 1 through n. These market shares total 100 percent.

Table 13-3 shows how the Herfindahl Index is calculated and compares the index to a four-firm concentration ratio for two hypothetical

4. The Herfindahl Index was developed by Orris Clemens Herfindahl in his 1950 Ph.D. dissertation at Columbia University.

industries. Note that both industries have four-firm concentration ratios of 96 percent, but Industry A has a much higher Herfindahl Index (8116) than Industry B (2304). The table demonstrates that the Herfindahl Index gives a much higher "score" to industries that have a firm or group of firms that are relatively large. This higher weight for large firms is the result of squaring the individual market shares to construct the index. In Table 13–3, the four-firm concentration ratios are equal, but the Herfindahl Index shows Industry A is 3.52 times more concentrated than is Industry B.

TABLE 13–3
CALCULATING THE HERFINDAHL INDEX

Industry A			Industry B		
Firm	Market Share (percent)	Square of Firm's Market Share	Firm	Market Share (percent)	Square of Firm's Market Share
1	90	8100	1	24	576
2	2	4	2	24	576
3	2	4	3	24	576
4	2	4	4	24	576
5	1	1	5	1	1
6	1	1	6	1	1
7	1	1	7	1	1
8	1	1	8	1	1

Four-Firm Concentration Ratio = .96 or 96%. Herfindahl Index = 8116.

Four-Firm Concentration Ratio = .96 or 96%. Herfindahl Index = 2304.

An industry that has ten equal-sized firms each having 10 percent of the market would have a Herfindahl Index of 1000. As we saw in the previous chapter, most economists would classify such an industry as being workably competitive. We shall see later in this chapter how the Herfindahl Index was used by the Justice Department in the 1980s.

The Number Equivalent

Professor M.A. Adelman of MIT has developed another property of the Herfindahl Index. The **Number Equivalent** is the reciprocal of the Herfindahl Index (1 divided by the Herfindahl Index). It shows the theoretical number of equal-sized firms that should be found in an industry. In Table 13–3, Industry A theoretically would have 1.2 equal-sized firms, while Industry B would have 4.3 such firms. Adelman would conclude that, *ceteris paribus*, Industry B would be more competitive than Industry A because Industry A has a higher likelihood of collusion.

NUMBER EQUIVALENT
The reciprocal of the Herfindahl Index used as a measure of the theoretical number of equal-sized firms that should be found in an industry.

CONCENTRATION AND PERFORMANCE

At first glance, it seems that the number of concentrated, oligopolistic industries in the U.S. economy is high. But just how concentrated is U.S. industry? And does concentration make any difference? In other words, would you as a consumer be better off if U.S. industry were generally less concentrated and, hence, perhaps more competitive?

Studies of Concentration Trends

Given the difficulty of defining industries and the fact that any classification scheme requires arbitrary judgments, it is not surprising that studies have reached widely differing conclusions on the degree and trend of concentration in U.S. industry. The studies can be divided roughly into three groups.

One group of studies, which investigated trends in concentration in the first half of the twentieth century, concluded that there had been a pronounced increase in industrial concentration in the United States. This group of studies is associated with and represented by the work of Gardiner Means, who looked at the assets of the 200 largest nonfinancial corporations. Means found that between 1909 and 1933, the percentage of total assets controlled by the 200 largest nonfinancial corporations increased from 33.3 percent to 54.8 percent. In contrast, a second group of studies done more recently by the Federal Trade Commission, using the same methodology as Means, show that the percentage of assets controlled by the 200 largest nonfinancial corporations has not changed since 1950.[5]

The studies that found increased concentration were also challenged in a third group of studies begun by G. Warren Nutter. Nutter argued that between 1901 and 1937, industrial concentration declined in the United States. His studies were attacked on the grounds that they depended crucially on data from 1899, which he took as a starting point. Critics argued that these early figures were suspect because of the poor quality of data for that period. Later, Nutter's figures were updated and extended by Henry A. Einhorn. Einhorn used Nutter's figures for 1939 as a benchmark and sought to determine if concentration had changed between 1939 and 1958. He divided firms in the economy, as Nutter had earlier, into three categories: (1) monopolistic; (2) workably competitive; and (3) governmental. The two researchers had to use judgment as to what "monopoly," "workably competitive," and "governmental" mean and how to determine into which of these three categories a particular firm fits. Einhorn then, like Nutter, sought to determine if the share of production originating in each of the three structures had changed. Einhorn concluded that between 1939 and 1958, roughly 60 percent of national income was generated by firms producing in a workably competitive structure. The monopolistic sector declined slightly, and the governmental sector in-

5. Gardiner Means, National Resources Committee, *The Structure of the American Economy* (Washington, D.C.: U.S. Government Printing Office, 1939). Norman R. Collins and Lee E. Preston, "The Size Structure of the Largest Industrial Firms," *American Economic Review* (December 1961). Adolf A. Berle and Gardiner C. Means, *The Modern Corporation and Private Property* (New York: Macmillan Co., 1933). Richard Duke, "Trends in Aggregate Concentration," FTC Working Paper No. 61 (June 1982).

creased slightly. The conclusion of the Nutter-Einhorn research is that market concentration in the twentieth century has been surprisingly stable.[6]

Can we draw any conclusions from these seemingly conflicting studies? At one extreme in the debate is the position that the level of monopoly power has been stable. At the other end of the debate is the position that concentration in U.S. industry increased dramatically in the early part of this century, and that it has also increased since World War II but at a much slower pace than in the early 1900s.

Keep in mind that these measures of concentration are all aggregate measures, i.e., they measure concentration at the national level. These measures may understate the degree of monopoly power in U.S. industry because they ignore or understate the power of local and regional monopolies. The food distribution industry is a good example. At the national level there is a good deal of competition between supermarket chains. However, in some regions the concentration ratios are much higher: in some markets there is a virtual monopoly. Thus, the national figures might lead some to conclude that the industry is workably competitive, whereas the regional or local figures might suggest that the industry consists of a series of local monopolies.

The Merger Wave of the 1980s

The mid-1980s have witnessed what many observers think is the greatest reshuffling of corporate assets in U.S. history. Between January 1983 and January 1987, 12,200 companies worth at least $490 billion changed hands. If the merger and acquisition rate continues at that pace, every publicly held company would be turned over to new owners by the year 2001.[7]

This supercharged business environment created a host of strategies that generated a whole list of imaginative names to describe merger activity and defensive strategies:

1. Scorched earth: The target tries to make itself less attractive, perhaps by selling off some of its best assets.
2. Pac-man: The target changes roles and attempts to take over the original pursuer.
3. Poison pill: The target makes itself more expensive than it is worth through the issuance of additional preferred stock with special voting rights.
4. Shark repellent: Amendments to a corporate charter such as supermajority requirements or staggered terms for board members that make it harder to gain control of a board of directors.
5. Golden parachute: Large payments guaranteed to top executives in case of a takeover; intended to encourage top executives to operate in the best interests of the stockholders.

---

6. G. Warren Nutter and Henry A. Einhorn, *Enterprise Monopoly in the United States: 1899–1958* (New York: Columbia University Press, 1969).
7. *Business Week* (12 January 1987): 38. For a detailed report of the 200 largest mergers and acquisitions in 1986 see *Business Week* (17 April 1987).

6. White knight: A friendly alternative to a hostile pursuer; usually agrees to retain current management.

7. Greenmail: Repurchase of stock acquired by a hostile investor at prices significantly above the market. There have been lawsuits by stockholders to prevent management from paying greenmail because it depresses the value of other stock.

This terminology and the accompanying publicity is common during the current merger wave. For the most part public and political opinion thought the merger wave was, as the terminology indicates, bad for the economy. In 1987, a Louis Harris poll indicated . . . "the American people are fed up with takeover raiders. Such types are viewed as little better than predators."[8] Most of the corporate raiders and many economists see the situation differently. They see takeovers as a catalyst that is necessary to spur complacent managers. Often a company is completely restructured in the wake of a takeover or attempted takeover. Companies have eliminated whole layers of management after they are the victim of a takeover or to prevent a takeover. This debate is very likely to continue. It seems likely that Congress will develop new legislation to address what many view as excesses in this latest merger movement. State governments are already passing state antitakeover laws. In April 1987, the Supreme Court upheld Indiana's antitakeover law.

The Market Concentration Doctrine

In the light of the recent merger movement, which has probably increased concentration to some degree, we should examine the implicit presumption that concentration, *per se*, is undesirable. This dislike of concentration has become commonplace among industrial organization economists. The reason is that economists typically see a sequence of events running from (1) the structure of the industry to (2) the behavior of firms in that industry and then to (3) the performance of the industry itself. According to this line of thought, a highly concentrated structure will produce the antisocial behavior and unsatisfactory performance expected of a monopoly. The industrial organization economist, therefore, examines the structure of an industry to predict behavior of prices and output restriction. This structure-conduct-performance chain has been termed the Market Concentration Doctrine.

MARKET CONCENTRATION DOCTRINE
A hypothesis that holds that the degree of concentration in an industry is a reliable index of monopoly behavior and performance in that industry.

The **Market Concentration Doctrine** holds that the degree of concentration in an industry is a reliable index of monopoly power and, consequently, is likely to be associated with undesirable monopoly behavior and performance. Strict application of this doctrine might lead policymakers to suggest antitrust action or some other form of control when concentration ratios reach a certain level. Before examining policy action against monopoly, let us first examine the assumptions behind this doctrine.

Administered Prices

Those who support the Market Concentration Doctrine base their arguments primarily on two empirical observations. The first is that

8. *Fortune* (27 April 1987): 10.

prices are more rigid (less flexible) in concentrated industries, and the second is that profit rates and concentration are positively correlated. Supporters of this doctrine believe that both rigid prices and higher profit rates reflect the effects of monopoly power associated with high degrees of concentration.

The lack of price flexibility in concentrated industries was first found by Gardiner Means, whose findings are described in a now-famous monograph.[9] Looking at data from 1926 to 1933, he argued that price movements in different industries varied in frequency. In some industries, prices changed very often, and in others, prices tended to be constant for relatively long periods of time. He labeled the prices that were relatively rigid, or changed only infrequently, as **administered prices**. Later he demonstrated that these administered prices were related to the degree of concentration in the industry.[10]

This early work by Means has had a significant influence on discussions of public policy toward industry. As might be expected, it was subjected to close scrutiny. As is usually the case with empirical work, the data and methodology used by both sides in the debate have been criticized. Competing researchers criticized Means's study because his data were gathered from reports submitted by firms to the Bureau of Labor Statistics. Since firms reported at different intervals, his reported price flexibility (or inflexibility) might simply reflect a different frequency of reporting.[11] Other researchers claimed that the Bureau of Labor Statistics' data were composed of prices *asked* by firms and that the relevant data are prices *paid* by consumers.[12] Since oligopolists often want to hide their price cuts from their competitors, they often grant buyers secret cuts on posted prices. For this reason, there could be significant discrepancies between prices asked and prices paid.

Even though this question of administered prices has been scrutinized by economists for some time, we do not yet have a scientific conclusion. The standard textbook conclusion is that there is a loose association between concentration and price inflexibility. This conventional wisdom has become part of public policy debates, but the economist, in the capacity of scientist, would be hard put to prove this relationship.

ADMINISTERED PRICES
A term coined by Gardiner Means to describe price inflexibility in concentrated industries. Means labeled prices that were relatively rigid, or changed only infrequently, as administered prices.

Concentration and Profit Levels

The second element of the Market Concentration Doctrine is that profits and concentration ratios are positively correlated. The theoretical basis for this relationship between concentration and profits is that a small number of firms finds it easier to behave collusively. The empirical

9. Gardiner Means, *Industrial Prices and Their Relative Inflexibility*, Senate Document 13, 74th Congress, 1st Session (17 January 1935).

10. National Resources Committee, *The Structure of the American Economy* (Washington, D.C.: U.S. Government Printing Office, 1939).

11. U.S. Congress, Joint Economic Committee, *Government Price Statistics*. Hearings before the Subcommittee on Economic Statistics of the Joint Economic Committee, 87th Congress, 1st Session (1961).

12. George J. Stigler and James K. Kindahl, *The Behavior of Industrial Prices* (New York: National Bureau of Economic Research, 1970).

link between concentration and profits began with the work of Joe Bain.[13] Bain found, although he had some reservations, that profit rates and concentration ratios were positively correlated for a sample of 42 manufacturing industries. Bain also found that when the concentration ratio exceeded 70 percent, there was a significant increase in average profit rates. George Stigler, on the other hand, conducting similar research, found there was no clear-cut relationship between concentration ratios and profit rates.[14] In his study, Stigler defined an industry as concentrated if the four-firm concentration ratio for the value of output exceeded 60 percent. Other studies examining the same hypothesis concluded that there is a weak, but positive, relationship between concentration and profit rates.[15]

There has been debate about the tendency for profits to be higher in concentrated industries over the years. President Johnson's Task Force on Antitrust Policy concluded that such a correlation exists:

The adverse effects of concentration on output and price find some confirmation in various studies that have been made of return on capital in major industries. These studies have found a close association between high levels of concentration and persistently high rates of return on capital. It is the persistence of high profits over extended time periods and over whole industries rather than in individual firms that suggest artificial restraints on output and the absence of fully effective competition. The correlation of evidence of this kind with very high levels of concentration appears to be significant.[16]

This conclusion has been challenged by the University of Chicago's Yale Brozen and others.[17] Brozen recalculated many of the old studies using data from later time periods. He found that with the passage of time, there was a tendency for rates of profit in concentrated industries to converge with those of less concentrated industries. Rates of profit increased in the industries that previously had below-average profit levels and decreased in the industries with above-average profit levels. Thus, the concentration-profit hypothesis, like the concentration-price rigidity hypothesis, is challenged on two of its most important tenets. There appears to be some evidence to dispute the conventional wisdom that concentration ratios are a good predictor of monopoly behavior, especially over time.

Why is this issue important? It is important because present policy proposals to reformulate antitrust law use market concentration as a guide. If concentration is illegal, *per se*, in part because concentration is taken as an indicator of monopoly behavior and performance, many industries may be restructured by the courts simply because they are concentrated. If, instead, these industries are concentrated because there are economies of scale, or because they have better, more aggressive managers

13. Joe S. Bain, "Relation of Profit-Rate to Industry Concentration: American Manufacturing, 1936–1940," *Quarterly Journal of Economics* (August 1951).

14. George J. Stigler, *Capital and Rates of Return in Manufacturing* (Princeton, NJ: Princeton University Press, 1963).

15. For a review of these studies, see Harold Demsetz, *The Market Concentration Doctrine* (Washington, D.C.: American Enterprise Institute for Public Policy Research, 1975).

16. White House Task Force on Antitrust Policy, *Role of the Giant Corporation* (Washington, D.C.: U.S. Government Printing Office, 1967), 883.

17. Yale Brozen, "The Antitrust Task Force Deconcentration Recommendation," *Journal of Law and Economics* (October 1970): 279–292.

or more innovation, why break them up? In such cases, antitrust activity would only serve to introduce inefficiencies into the economy.

In short, the challenges to the Market Concentration Doctrine are significant enough that it should be examined more closely. It is particularly important that economists reach a scientific consensus on this important issue before policymakers take public action to restructure U.S. industry on the basis of a Market Concentration Doctrine that has not been empirically validated.

POLICIES AIMED AT MONOPOLY POWER

In the remainder of this chapter, we will discuss policy aimed at correcting the problems associated with monopoly power. We have just seen that there is disagreement over the connection between concentration and monopoly behavior; nevertheless, in most policy questions a high level of concentration is taken as implying monopoly behavior.

The Case Against Monopoly

In the chapter on monopoly, we examined in detail the costs associated with monopoly. The arguments in favor of policy against monopoly are directed at mitigating these costs. You should review the chapter on monopoly if you are unclear as to what these costs are.

The Case for Monopoly

There are at least two arguments that have been made in support of monopoly power. These arguments concern countervailing power and the promotion of technical progress.

Countervailing Power

John Kenneth Galbraith has developed the notion of **countervailing power**. He argues that monopoly power produces power on both sides of the market, and these two powers countervail, or offset, each other. According to Galbraith, the U.S. economy is made up of big unions, big government, and big firms. In bargaining with each other, these big units are equally powerful. While Galbraith did not develop the concept of countervailing power as a defense of monopoly, other economists have used it for that purpose.

In superficial ways, this argument has some appeal. We see concentrated tire manufacturers dealing with concentrated automobile producers. Large retail chains purchase from concentrated industries that manufacture the products they sell, and labor unions are most successful in concentrated industries, e.g., steel, autos, and mining. Consumers are, however, left out of this bargaining process, as Galbraith points out. The costs associated with monopoly still hold for the consumer. In essence, countervailing power only redistributes the monopoly profit among monopoly sellers, monopoly buyers, and monopoly unions.

COUNTERVAILING POWER
The notion put forward by Galbraith that monopoly sellers and monopoly purchasers offset each other's power in bargaining with one another.

**JOHN KENNETH GALBRAITH
(1908-   )**

John Kenneth Galbraith is perhaps the best known contemporary social critic who happens to be an economist. His fame results, in part, from his ability to write economics in clear English and from his generally entertaining and witty writing style. However, many economists are not sympathetic to his economic analysis because he often criticizes in sweeping generalities. His arguments are rarely stated as precise, testable hypotheses. As a result, it is almost impossible for Galbraith to present scientific evidence for his arguments or for his critics to refute them. In a stinging review of Galbraith, Robert Solow of MIT argues that economists are "little thinkers" while Galbraith is a "big thinker." Solow went on to illustrate his criticism of Galbraith by referring to

. . . the old story of the couple that had achieved an agreeable division of labor. She made the unimportant decisions: what job he should take, where they should live, how to bring up the children. He made the important decisions: what to do about Jerusalem, who should be admitted to the United Nations, how to deal with crime on the streets.[a]

John Kenneth Galbraith was born in Canada and received a B.S. degree from the University of Toronto. He received a Ph.D. in agricultural economics at the University of California, Berkeley, in 1934. Galbraith went immediately to Harvard as an instructor, where he remained until his recent retirement. Galbraith, unlike many economists, is very politically active. He has been chairperson of the Americans for Democratic Action and was an early and outspoken critic of the Vietnam War. President John Kennedy, who knew Galbraith from his days at Harvard, appointed him ambassador to India.

Galbraith has written a large number of books on both economic and noneconomic matters. The most important economic books are *American Capitalism: The Concept of the Countervailing Power* (1956), *The Affluent Society* (1958), *The New Industrial State* (1967), and *Economics and the Public Purpose* (1973). These books and Galbraith's other works on economics all have a common theme, which has come to be referred to as *Galbraithian economics.* This theme is that monopoly power is the dominant force in the U.S. economy, and these powerful firms control and manipulate input prices, demand, and governmental policy. The control of the economy is now in the hands of a technostructure (scientists, engineers, and trained managers) rather than the entrepreneur of conventional economic theory. Galbraith's economics calls for an enlarged government to control this unrestricted power.

a. Robert Solow, "Son of Affluence," *Public Interest* (Fall 1967): 100.

Innovation

Some economists, most notably the famous Austrian-born economist Joseph Schumpeter, and later John Kenneth Galbraith, have argued that monopoly, or at least oligopoly, is more conducive to technological innovation than is competition. They argue that the costs of monopoly power are offset by the dynamic innovation that monopolistic firms introduce into the economy. Schumpeter called his conclusion that monopoly power leads to innovation "shocking," since traditional economic analysis showed that monopoly would not be innovative because it did not face the pressure of competition.[18]

Years later Galbraith sounded the same theme, that monopoly power and bigness promote innovation:

In the modern industry shared by a few large firms, size and the rewards accruing to market power combine to insure that resources for research and technical development will be available. The power that enables the firm to have some influence on prices insures that the resulting gains will not be passed on to the public by imitators (who have stood none of the costs of development) before the outlay for development can be recouped. In this way, market power protects the incentive to technical development.[19]

The proposition that bigness allows a financial commitment to research and development is an attractive one. For years, General Electric advertised that progress was its most important product. But what are the facts? The facts, or more correctly the case histories, of invention and innovation are not so convincing. Researchers have found that the majority (as high as 2/3) of important inventions are the products of individuals working independently and had nothing to do with support from large research labs funded by giant corporations.[20]

REGULATION OF MONOPOLY—THEORY

We have seen that monopoly power is present in the U.S. economy, and we have seen that from the point of view of an optimal allocation of resources, monopoly is a bad thing. Society may decide that it is best to regulate a monopoly rather than restructure a monopolistic industry. Two common ways to do this are through price regulation and taxation.

Consider the monopoly represented in Figure 13–1. The monopoly is maximizing its profits by producing Q_1 at Price P_1. Assume that the government wants to force the firm to produce the same amount that would be produced if this were a purely competitive market, that is, to produce where the marginal cost curve intersects the demand curve. If the government set a price ceiling of P_2, the monopoly would react by producing Q_2 units of output because the demand curve that the monopoly faces would now be represented by line P_2AD. The firm, as always, produces where $MC = MR$, and MR is equal to line P_2A because demand is perfectly elastic for segment P_2A. The setting of such a price ceiling is sometimes called marginal cost pricing. **Marginal cost pricing** is a theoretical technique for forcing a monopoly to behave more like a competitive firm by regulating the monopoly price so that it is equal to marginal cost. Note that by regulating monopoly this way, per-unit profits decrease from C_1P_1

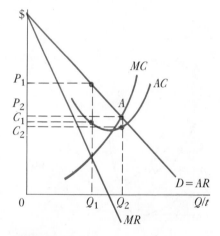

FIGURE 13-1
MARGINAL COST PRICING
If the regulator imposes a price of P_2, the monopoly would produce Q_2 units of output. Per-unit profits would decrease from C_1P_1 to C_2P_2.

18. Joseph Schumpeter, *Capitalism, Socialism, and Democracy*, 2d ed. (New York: Harper and Row, 1942), 81–82.
19. John Kenneth Galbraith, *American Capitalism*, 2d. ed. (Boston: Houghton Mifflin Company, 1956), 86–87.
20. See John Jewkes, David Sawers, and Richard Stillerman, *The Sources of Invention* (New York: St. Martins Press, 1959).

MARGINAL COST PRICING
A theoretical technique for forcing a monopoly to behave more like a competitive firm by regulating the monopoly price so that it is equal to marginal cost.

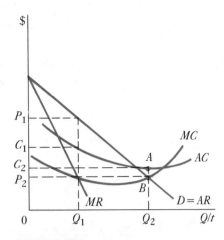

FIGURE 13-2
MARGINAL COST PRICING
AND LOSSES

If the regulator sets a price of P_2, the monopolist would lose C_2P_2 per unit of output sold. The monopolist would thus only produce if the regulator subsidizes it.

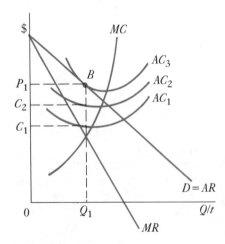

FIGURE 13-3
TAXING THE MONOPOLY

A license fee on the monopolist will be viewed as a fixed cost and will increase average cost but not marginal cost. In this way, the monopoly profit can be taxed away with no effect on output.

to C_2P_2. Why not lower the price below P_2, because every decrease in price between P_1 and P_2 will increase output even more? The problem is that for output levels greater than Q_2, every unit produced costs society more than it is willing to pay ($MC > P$). This larger output is just as inefficient as monopoly behavior when $MC < P$, and the cost of an extra unit is less than society is willing to pay.

Now let us introduce a more realistic example, a natural monopoly. Remember, a natural monopoly is one that results from a constantly declining average cost curve. Consider Figure 13–2. The profit-maximizing monopolist produces Q_1 at Price P_1 and receives C_1P_1 profit per unit. Now impose a regulated price of P_2 on the monopolist. At P_2, it appears the monopolist would increase output to Q_2. But note, at Price P_2 and Output Q_2, the monopolist would lose C_2P_2 per unit sold. Price is below average cost so the monopolist would leave the industry. In other words, the optimal output from society's viewpoint is now where $MC = MR$, but this output forces losses on the monopolist.

This output could, however, be feasibly produced if the government would make up the loss, P_2C_2AB, in Figure 13–2. The monopolist then would produce the desired output, Q_2 at Price P_2. The problem with this solution is that if the government subsidizes the industry out of general tax revenues, it is transferring income from taxpayers to the consumers of the good. Most people (except consumers of the particular good) would view such a transfer as an inequitable redistribution of income. The trick, then, for the would-be price regulator is to set price equal to MC at the point where the MC curve intersects the demand curve, but only if price is equal to or greater than average cost for that level of output. This might not be possible in the case of a natural monopoly.

Now let's see how taxation could be used to regulate monopoly power. Suppose government officials impose a license fee (tax) on the monopolist as in Figure 13–3. Before the tax, the monopoly is producing Q_1 at Price P_1. The relevant average cost curve is AC_1. The monopolist is earning profits of C_1P_1 per unit. If the monopolist is charged a fee for the right to do business, the fee represents an increase in the firm's fixed cost. The AC curve shifts up by the amount of the fee to AC_2. The monopolist still maximizes profits by producing Q_1 at Price P_1, but profits have been reduced to C_2P_1 per unit. Note that it is possible to set the tax or fee so as to capture all the monopoly profit and shift average cost to AC_3 in Figure 13–3. However, no increase in output occurs.

Although there are practical difficulties with both methods of regulating monopoly, they have quite different effects on the industry. Price regulation can cause the monopolist to produce the purely competitive output at a lower price. Taxation, on the other hand, leaves price and output unchanged. A tax simply captures the monopoly profit for the public coffers. It should be clear, then, that from the viewpoint of the allocation of resources, price regulation is preferred because it increases output and lowers price. The tax only corrects for the effect of monopoly on the distribution of income. The monopoly profit does not accrue to the monopolist and is spent on governmental projects. In this sense, there is still an impact on the distribution of income because consumers still pay "too much" for the product.

The Lerner Index of Monopoly Power

The theory of regulation just discussed suggested a policy of marginal cost pricing as one way to correct for monopoly misallocations. That proposal is based on the theoretical notion presented in the last two chapters that the degree of monopoly power is measured by the gap between marginal cost and price. Using this concept, Abba P. Lerner developed an index to measure monopoly power. The **Lerner Index of monopoly power (LMP)** measures the gap between price and marginal cost as a proxy for monopoly power. The index is calculated as

$$LMP = \frac{price - marginal\ cost}{price}.$$

In a purely competitive industry, LMP would be zero because price would equal marginal cost. If monopoly power is present, LMP would take on positive values because price would exceed marginal cost, and as the gap between price and marginal cost increases the value of the index rises. Using LMP would permit the researcher to compare the monopoly power of firms.

The LMP is a valuable theoretical construct, but the difficulty of determining marginal cost limits its value in applied work. If average cost data are used as a proxy for marginal cost data, the results are misleading. Purely competitive firms might even appear to have monopoly power in the short run because price could be greater than average cost, even while it is equal to marginal cost.

REGULATION OF MONOPOLY—PRACTICE

We saw in the previous chapter that attempts at regulation often increase the power of oligopolies as the regulatory bodies are "captured" by the industry. There is, however, an additional problem that is relevant to setting prices to regulate monopoly output. Regulators may not be able to determine marginal costs and must, therefore, turn to the alternative of regulating price on the basis of average cost information. In addition, such average cost pricing solves "the problem" of natural monopoly that we saw in Figure 13–2.

The usual practice is to allow the firm a markup as a percentage of average cost of production. This most common form of price regulation is referred to as **cost-plus pricing**. This type of regulation creates some distortions. If the monopolist is allowed to charge a price, say, 10 percent above average cost, the firm has less incentive to minimize cost, although consumer demand gives the firm some incentive not to let price get too far out of hand.

Perhaps the best example of this form of behavior is in the present regulatory environment for the utility industries—electricity, gas, water, and so forth. Since utilities are considered natural monopolies, they are regulated for the public interest. Such regulation is on an average-cost-plus markup basis. This markup policy is often called a fair rate of return. A **fair rate of return** is the idea that a regulated industry must earn a

LERNER INDEX OF MONOPOLY OF POWER (LMP)
An index that measures the gap between price and marginal cost as a proxy for monopoly power.

COST-PLUS PRICING
The practice in price regulation of allowing firms a markup on average costs of production. This is the most common form of price regulation.

FAIR RATE OF RETURN
The idea that a regulated industry must earn a normal profit, or it will go out of business.

normal profit, or it will go out of business. Under such a regulatory policy, utilities have less real incentive to cut costs than do profit-oriented firms, whose profits increase whenever costs decrease.

Some communities have debated whether or not utilities should be allowed to advertise their product. The argument against such advertising is that it simply raises average costs and results in higher prices to consumers. The argument in favor of such advertising is that it increases demand, which leads to more output at lower average cost and resulting lower prices. Our analysis tends to support the first argument. Interestingly, our self-interest model of individual behavior would predict that a certain group in the community would support utility advertising. Any guesses? Of course, it would be the news media. The news media have strongly supported utility advertising, often on the grounds of ensuring free speech.

Regulation not only makes a firm less cost conscious, but it also can raise the actual cost of doing business. The costs of compliance (and noncompliance) with regulation could mean that less is produced at higher prices because costs are higher. In this case, regulation is counterproductive to the goal of making monopolies produce a larger output. Regulation is also rarely limited to price regulation. Most often, regulatory bodies interfere in a wide range of firm decision making. Regulation often changes the firm into a quasi-governmental firm, rather than a firm that responds to market forces.

ANTITRUST LAWS IN THE UNITED STATES

Around the turn of the century in the United States, there was a substantial increase in the growth of large business organizations. This period saw the establishment of legal arrangements such as **trusts**, which were organizations set up to control the stock of other companies through boards of trustees, and **holding companies**, which were single firms set up for the sole purpose of owning and thus controlling other firms. Trust and holding companies enabled the robber barons, as they have been called by economic historians, to control and coordinate the activities of many previously independent firms. At first, this new form of business was viewed as a natural outgrowth of the industrial revolution in the United States. Social Darwinism—a popular social theory at the time—justified such behavior. Social Darwinism applied Charles Darwin's theory of the evolution of the species, often summed up as a belief in the survival of the fittest, to business enterprise. Under that view, stronger firms were justified in getting bigger by "gobbling up" or driving out the smaller ones.

Eventually the public began to view some of these arrangements with suspicion. One of the earliest organized groups to vigorously oppose the trust movement was the *National Grange*. The Grange, organized in 1867, was opposed to trusts, in particular the railroad trust, because of the high monopoly prices it set and also because it was able to practice price discrimination in the hauling of agricultural produce.

In response to the Grange and other similar populist political movements against trusts, several states enacted antitrust statutes that

TRUSTS
Legal organizations set up to control the stock of other companies through boards of trustees.

HOLDING COMPANIES
Firms set up for the sole purpose of owning and controlling other firms.

regulated businesses chartered in the state. These state statutes failed because corporations were able to seek out less restrictive states in which to gain charters. Two of the more hospitable states were New Jersey and Delaware. Eventually the antitrust sentiment became so widespread and intense that by 1888, both national political parties had an antitrust plank in their presidential platform.

In 1890, Congress passed the **Sherman Antitrust Act**. The Sherman Act had two major provisions. Section 1 of the act declared every contract, combination, or conspiracy in restraint of trade to be illegal. Section 2 made it illegal to monopolize or attempt to monopolize.[21] This was the first antitrust law. The language of the law is strong, but it is also vague, and the courts took years to determine its scope. We shall trace some of the important decisions, but first we will examine other antitrust laws.

The **Clayton Act**, passed in 1914, made illegal certain business practices that could lead to monopoly. It prohibited a company from acquiring the stock of a competing company if such an acquisition would "substantially lessen competition."[22] The act also prohibited tying contracts and price discrimination. **Tying contracts** are agreements between producers and retailers whereby a retailer must agree to stock certain items as a prerequisite to being allowed to handle other items. In 1936, the **Robinson-Patman Act** amended the Clayton Act to make predatory pricing illegal. **Predatory pricing** is the act of selling below cost to destroy competitors. Although the Clayton Act prohibited the acquisition of competing firms through stock purchase, it could be circumvented because it did not prohibit acquisition of physical assets. The **Celler-Kefauver Antimerger Act**, passed in 1950, made it illegal in certain circumstances for a firm to merge with another by purchasing its assets, and thereby strengthened the Clayton Act.

In 1914, Congress passed the **Federal Trade Commission Act**. This act set up the Federal Trade Commission (FTC) to police unfair and deceptive business practices. Initially, the FTC had many powers, but the Supreme Court, in 1919, denied it the power to issue cease and desist orders without judicial review. In 1938, the FTC Act was amended by the **Wheeler-Lea Act** that added the term "unfair or deceptive acts or practices in commerce" to the list of FTC transgressions. The **Hart-Scott-Rodino Antitrust Improvement Act** amended the FTC Act in 1970. It required that firms contemplating a merger notify the FTC and the Department of Justice *prior* to consummating the merger or acquisition. In recent years, the FTC has worked closely with the Justice Department in antitrust matters.

SHERMAN ANTITRUST ACT
Passed in 1890, the first antitrust law. Section 1 of the act declared every contract, combination, or conspiracy in restraint of trade to be illegal. Section 2 made it illegal to monopolize or attempt to monopolize.

CLAYTON ACT
Passed in 1914, it prohibited the acquisition of the stock of a competing company if such an acquisition would "substantially lessen competition."

TYING CONTRACTS
Agreements between producers and retailers whereby a retailer must agree to handle certain items as a prerequisite to being allowed to handle other items.

ROBINSON-PATMAN ACT
A 1936 act that amended the Clayton Act to make predatory pricing illegal.

PREDATORY PRICING
The act of selling below cost to destroy competitors.

CELLER-KEFAUVER ANTIMERGER ACT
A 1950 act that made it illegal in certain circumstances for a firm to merge with another by purchasing its assets. This act strengthened the Clayton Act.

FEDERAL TRADE COMMISSION ACT
A 1914 act establishing the Federal Trade Commission to police unfair and deceptive business practices.

WHEELER-LEA ACT
A 1938 act amending the FTC Act to make unfair or deceptive acts or practices in commerce illegal.

HART-SCOTT-RODINO ANTITRUST IMPROVEMENT ACT
A 1970 act amending the FTC Act to require firms to report mergers or acquisitions to the FTC and Department of Justice prior to their consummation.

21. Section 1: Every contract, combination in the form of trust or otherwise, or conspiracy, in restraint of trade or commerce among the several States, or with foreign nations, is declared to be illegal. . . . Section 2: Every person who shall monopolize, or attempt to monopolize, or combine or conspire with any other person or persons, to monopolize any part of the trade or commerce among the several States, or with foreign nations, shall be deemed guilty of a misdemeanor. . . . (Sherman Antitrust Act, Sec. 1, 26 stat. 209, 1890).

22. For a publication covering the technical details of all these laws, see J. G. Van Cise, *Understanding the Antitrust Laws* (New York: Practicing Law Institute, 1973).

UNITED STATES ANTITRUST LAWS

Act (year passed)	Major Provision(s)
SHERMAN ANTITRUST ACT (1890)	Makes it illegal to monopolize or attempt to monopolize. Makes contracts, combinations, or conspiracies in restraint of trade illegal.
CLAYTON ACT (1914)	Prohibits the acquisition of the stock of another company if it will substantially lessen competition. Prohibits tying contracts and price discrimination.
ROBINSON-PATMAN ACT (1936)	Amendment to the Clayton Act that makes predatory pricing illegal.
CELLER-KEFAUVER ANTIMERGER ACT (1950)	Amendment to the Clayton Act that makes it illegal to purchase the assets of another company if it will substantially lessen competition.
FEDERAL TRADE COMMISSION ACT (1914)	Established the FTC to police unfair and deceptive business practices.
WHEELER-LEA ACT (1938)	Amendment to the FTC Act that makes unfair or deceptive trade practices illegal.
HART-SCOTT-RODINO ANTITRUST IMPROVEMENT ACT (1970)	Requires that the FTC and Justice Department be notified prior to mergers or acquisitions.

The History of Antitrust Enforcement

It took some time for the courts to determine the scope of the Sherman Act. In particular, the phrase "in restraint of trade" needed a legal definition. Under a strict economic definition, any firm with monopoly power (that is, power to restrict output or to increase price) would be guilty of restraint of trade. In two famous 1911 cases against Standard Oil and American Tobacco, the courts interpreted the law using the rule of reason. The **rule of reason** said that monopolies that behaved well were not illegal. In effect, the Supreme Court defined—some might say rewrote—the Sherman Antitrust Act to make only "unreasonable" restraints of trade illegal. The test of reasonableness was itself difficult to define. The court held that the existence of competitors was sufficient to demonstrate reasonable behavior. In 1920, U.S. Steel, despite its dominance in the steel industry, was found not to be an unreasonable monopoly. The court stated that the law did not make mere size an offense.

RULE OF REASON
Indicated that monopolies that behaved well did not violate the Sherman Antitrust Act. The court held that the existence of competitors was sufficient to demonstrate "reasonable behavior."

In 1945, after 13 years of litigation, this rule of reason was dropped. Judge Learned Hand ruled in a case against Alcoa Aluminum that size itself *was* enough to prove the exercise of monopoly power. The change was so fundamental that commentators later referred to the ruling as the "new Sherman Act." The Alcoa case was based on estimates of market power and structural aspects of the industry. In such cases, the way in which an industry is defined is extremely significant and in fact to a large degree determines defense and prosecution strategies. As you might guess, the defense would prefer the industry to be broadly defined, both geographically and by the number of products included, since such a definition tends to reduce the importance of any one firm in any particular industry.[23]

23. For some examples of the ridiculous lengths that definitions of the relevant market can go to suit legal purposes, see Franklin M. Fisher, "Diagnosing Monopoly," *Quarterly Review of Economics and Business*, (Summer 1979): 7–33.

THE INTERNATIONAL PERSPECTIVE
ANTITRUST ABROAD

Antitrust activity as discussed in this chapter is not found in most other countries. Interestingly, after World War II, the U.S. government imposed U.S. type antitrust policies against the defeated powers, Japan and Germany. United States occupation forces set up new governments in Germany and Japan. They imposed stringent antitrust measures aimed at deconcentrating industry. There were two stated goals. The first was to punish leading industrial groups for their wartime complicity, and the second was to weaken the German and Japanese industrial base so they would be less able to pursue future wars.

This second objective is ironic because of its contradiction with domestic United States policy and antitrust thinking at the time. United States domestic policy was to pursue antitrust to limit monopoly power and make the United States economy *more* efficient, but at the same time our foreign policy was to break up German and Japanese trusts to make them *less* efficient. The curiosity is compounded by the fact that after the United States decided that Japan and Germany should be allowed to grow economically, to counter Soviet expansion in the cold war period, the first policy changed was the antitrust policy. One might legitimately ask what caused policymakers to view concentration as good for Germany and Japan and bad for the United States.

Except for these two cases of divestiture imposed temporarily on Germany and Japan, there are no other antitrust laws in other countries that are concentration-based and lead to the possibility of divestiture. In the mid-1970s there was vigorous debate about proposed legislation for divestiture in Japan, but it was not enacted. Japan's trading conglomerates, called **sogo shosha**, are informal associations of industrial, financial, and commercial companies. They could not exist under U.S. antitrust laws.

Much of the relevant law in Europe is based on the Treaty of Rome that established the European Economic Community. Individual countries tend to monitor the activities of "market-dominating" firms and regulate their price setting ability. The emphasis is not on "breaking up" monopolies or potential monopolies but rather preventing the abuse of any market power. A typical remedy would be a price rollback and government approval of future price increases. European governments often monitor the prices, costs, and profit rates of large firms.

After the Alcoa decision, the way in which a market was defined became critical. The DuPont Cellophane case in 1956 gave further indication of what the courts thought about markets. The Justice Department filed suit against DuPont for monopolization of the cellophane market because DuPont controlled 75 percent of the U.S. market. The Supreme Court ruled in favor of DuPont, accepting the argument of DuPont's lawyers that the relevant market was not cellophane, but rather flexible wrapping materials that included waxed paper, aluminum foil, and vegetable parchment. The court said that products that are "reasonably interchangeable" must be included in the definition of market. DuPont controlled only 20 percent of this "reasonably interchangeable" set of products.

In 1975, the U.S. Justice Department won a case against Xerox that also centered on market definition. At that time, Xerox controlled

90 percent of the plain-paper copier market. The courts ruled that Xerox must share its patents with competitors in order to increase competition in this market.

In 1982, the Justice Department's case against IBM, initiated in 1969, was dismissed. The case began when the Justice Department accused IBM of monopolizing the "general purpose computer and peripheral-equipment industry." In 1969, IBM controlled 70 percent of the large mainframe computer market and 40 percent of the office equipment market. When the case was dismissed, IBM still controlled 70 percent of the mainframe computer market but was experiencing substantial competition in office equipment and minicomputers. This case, like the others, centered on market share; but the trend seems to be toward defining markets in a much broader way.

Another significant change has taken place much more recently. The Sherman Antitrust Act provides that private parties who are victims of monopoly under Sections 1 and 2 are entitled to sue for **treble damages**. In other words, if a firm is convicted under the Sherman Antitrust Act, individuals can recover three times the damages they have sustained. This provision was intended to stimulate private lawsuits by firms or individuals who had been victims of price discrimination, but historically it was of very little practical importance. Recently, however, consumer groups have become very active on this front and have brought many "class action" lawsuits under the provisions of the antitrust laws. Consumer groups bring action on behalf of the entire class of consumers, and treble damages in these cases can be very large.

The courts, as we have seen, have made some significant changes in enforcement, but the courts only rule on cases brought before them. In general, there have been very few antitrust cases brought by damaged firms or individuals. This raises an important question: Who brings most antitrust cases? The decision on whether to bring a case or not rests largely with the Antitrust Division of the Department of Justice. This decision is made by a presidential appointee, the assistant attorney general for antitrust. Antitrust policy therefore reflects the desires of the president. Theodore Roosevelt campaigned as the great "trust-buster." He set up the Antitrust Division and his administration brought the first cases.

Franklin Roosevelt's first term saw virtually no activity on the antitrust scene. On the contrary, in the early Depression years of the first Roosevelt administration, the government actually fostered anticompetitive practices through the National Recovery Administration (NRA). The **National Recovery Administration (NRA)** was a major New Deal program aimed at business recovery. The NRA was anticompetitive since it allowed and encouraged agreements between firms. The NRA tried to set up cartels in virtually every industry, but they eventually were declared unconstitutional. In 1937, the Roosevelt administration changed its position. Thurman Arnold, the assistant attorney general for antitrust, vigorously pursued antitrust cases, including the Alcoa case, which ultimately reversed the rule of reason.

Both the Eisenhower and Kennedy administrations pursued active antitrust programs. President Johnson's administration represented a retreat from vigorous antitrust policy, although the IBM case that dragged on for well over a decade was filed at the end of his administration. Presi-

TREBLE DAMAGES
A provision under the Sherman Antitrust Act that victims of monopoly can recover three times the damages they have sustained.

NATIONAL RECOVERY ADMINISTRATION (NRA)
A major New Deal program aimed at business recovery. The NRA was anticompetitive since it allowed and encouraged agreements between firms and was eventually declared unconstitutional.

dent Nixon's first assistant attorney general, Richard McLaren, vigorously worked to restrict conglomerate mergers. McLaren ultimately resigned because of political interference by Nixon forces in the International Telephone and Telegraph case. The interference clearly demonstrated that antitrust prosecution is very much a political decision.

Thomas E. Kauper, who served as President Ford's assistant attorney general, pursued an active antitrust policy. He launched a major case against AT&T and tripled the number of price-fixing cases filed. He also was instrumental in changing the law to make price fixing a felony instead of a misdemeanor, as it had been under the Sherman Act.

President Carter appointed John Shenefield as his assistant attorney general for antitrust. Shenefield promised at his confirmation hearings to use the antitrust law to change the concentration of power. Shenefield also promised to attack the notion of *shared monopoly*, in which very few firms control an industry, and to speed up the litigation process so cases would not drag on for dozens of years. Very little was accomplished along these lines, because the Reagan appointees were of a much different philosophy and abruptly changed the policy.

The Reagan administration stepped into an environment that had been growing increasingly intense in pursuing antitrust enforcement. Reagan's appointees made it clear that the Reagan administration did not equate big business with bad business practices. William Baxter, Reagan's first assistant attorney general for antitrust, believed that the purpose of antitrust activity should be to promote efficiency. To this end, Baxter argued that government should not interfere with most vertical mergers (mergers in which a company integrates its production backward toward its source of supply or forward in its marketing chain). He also felt that conglomerate mergers, in which a company buys a firm unrelated to its existing business, should be allowed. Baxter argued that vertical mergers and conglomerate mergers seldom foster price fixing and do not reduce competition. On the other hand, Baxter approved of tough action against horizontal mergers, in which a firm acquires a competitor.

Baxter purged the Antitrust Division of many previous practices including Richard Nixon's attack on conglomerates and Jimmy Carter's attack on shared monopoly. Reagan's first chairperson of the Federal Trade Commission (FTC), James C. Miller III, engineered a similar policy change at the FTC. These changed attitudes had a considerable influence on the merger movement of the 1980s. Most observers feel that many of these mergers would never have been permitted by previous administrations.

Halfway through the Reagan administration, the cast of policymakers changed with the usual shift of emphasis. President Reagan appointed Paul McGrath to succeed Baxter as assistant attorney general for antitrust in 1984. McGrath's first act was to veto the proposed LTV-Republic Steel merger, a horizontal merger between two competing firms. This action came as a surprise to the executives and antitrust lawyers for both firms, who were confident that Baxter and Miller (who had been replaced by Daniel Oliver, a lawyer) would not have opposed it.

In 1986, the promerger policies of the Reagan administration were supported by the Supreme Court, which ruled that antitrust laws were not meant to prevent mergers just because they create larger, more formidable competitors. The Supreme Court decision overturned two lower court decisions in allowing Cargill to buy Spencer Beef, combining the second and third largest beef packing companies.

■ The Role of Economic Variables in Case Bringing

Economists and lawyers have begun to statistically analyze the case-bringing activity of the Antitrust Division of the Justice Department. The first such study was conducted by Richard Posner and was published in 1970.[24] Posner found that in the first eight decades of the Sherman Act, 1,551 cases were brought by the Justice Department. Antitrust activity can also be initiated by the Federal Trade Commission and even by private citizens. Posner found that, contrary to popular belief, the statistics do not bear out the contention that antimonopoly activity of the FTC has increased over time. However, the number of cases brought by private citizens has increased continuously and significantly since 1949.

Antitrust enforcement by the individual states also has been stepped up. This change, in part, has resulted from a bill signed into law by President Ford in September 1976. This law allows state attorneys general to sue suspected price fixers for treble damages on behalf of citizens. Politics enter here also. State attorneys general are often campaigning for re-election or for higher office. They will bring lawsuits for publicity value but will be careful to avoid lawsuits against powerful groups whom they need to count on in future elections. Cases are often brought against out-of-state firms. This approach creates good publicity but doesn't damage in-state business support for the attorney general who aspires to higher office.

Although antitrust cases usually are very protracted, with many lasting as long as five and six years, the success rate of the Justice Department is very high. The success rate is much lower in FTC and in private cases. However, the remedies the court imposes have been far from successful in terms of restoring competition. In civil cases, the remedy has often taken the form of regulation. If we view the goal of antitrust as restoring competition, then regulation is in fact an admission that competition cannot be restored. The problems that regulation introduces make it a very unsatisfactory remedy.

On the criminal side, the decisions are notoriously weak as far as penalties are concerned. Not until the late 1950s was an individual sentenced to jail for price fixing. In 1960, seven more executives were sentenced to jail. In the few cases in which sentences have been imposed, the terms have been very short. In addition, the fines levied have been too small to have much of a deterrent effect. Although there has been more rhetoric about bigger fines and tougher prison terms for white-collar crimes, this sentiment has not permeated antitrust decisions.

Posner's study spawned some attempts to examine the determinants of antitrust activity. Posner himself pointed out that antitrust activity did not seem to be related to economic conditions in the country. He

---

24. Richard A. Posner, "A Statistical Study of Antitrust Enforcement," *Journal of Law and Economics* (October 1970).

also examined the influence of politics by looking at the party affiliation of the president. He found that the political party in the White House does not seem to affect the number of cases initiated. This, of course, does not mean that politics does not affect the Justice Department's antitrust decisions, only that the amount of political interference has not, on the average, been too much affected by which party holds the presidency.

William Long, Richard Schramm, and Robert Tollison analyzed case-bringing patterns of the Justice Department and found that cases were more likely to be brought in larger industries as measured by sales.[25] Other variables that may more meaningfully indicate monopoly power, such as profit rates on sales and concentration, were found to play a less important role in explaining Justice Department cases. John Siegfried has found that economic variables have little influence on the cases filed by the Justice Department.[26] The work of Siegfried and Peter Asch suggests that the Justice Department case-bringing criteria are complex and difficult to forecast using economic variables.[27] This complexity and the insignificance of economic considerations is probably not surprising, given the political nature of the Justice Department.

The Economic Consequences of Antitrust Activity

In addition to looking for an economic explanation of Justice Department case bringing, economists have begun to examine the economic consequences of antitrust activity. Several of these empirical studies are informative. Asch and J. Seneca found that firms that were known to be engaged in collusion were (to their surprise) less profitable than firms that were not known to be in collusion.[28] Robert Feinberg argued that these statistical results were actually the deterrent effect of antitrust case bringing.[29] Desoung Choi and George Philippatos found that antitrust case bringing caused pricing restraint but that this pricing restraint decreased with the number of times the firm had been indicted.[30] This finding implies a diminishing return to case bringing against a single firm, an implication that any student studying beginning economics should be able to predict. Finally, and again not too surprisingly, Kenneth Garbade, William Silber, and Lawrence White have found that the announcement of an antitrust suit against a firm has a negative impact on the stock price of that firm.[31]

25. William F. Long, Richard Schramm, and Robert Tollison, "Economic Determinants of Antitrust Activity," *Journal of Law and Economics* (October 1973).

26. John J. Siegfried, "The Determinants of Antitrust Activity," *Journal of Law and Economics* (October 1975).

27. Peter Asch, "The Determinants and Effects of Antitrust Activity", *Journal of Law and Economics* (October 1975).

28. Peter Asch and J.J. Seneca, "Is Collusion Profitable?" *The Review of Economics and Statistics* (February 1976).

29. Robert Feinberg, "Antitrust Enforcement and Subsequent Price Behavior," *The Review of Economics and Statistics* (November 1980).

30. Dosoung Choi and George Philippatos, "The Financial Consequences of Antitrust Enforcement," *The Review of Economics and Statistics* (August 1983).

31. Kenneth Garbade, William Silber, and Lawrence White, "Market Reaction to the Filing of Antitrust Suits: An Aggregate and Cross Sectional Analysis," *The Review of Economics and Statistics* (November 1982).

The actual record of antitrust activity does not present an encouraging picture. We have seen that even though there is a reasonable success rate for cases brought, the litigation is a long process, and the civil remedies available seldom restore competition. Moreover, the criminal sanctions have been applied with so little vigor that they probably have very little deterrent effect.

Two Systems of Belief About Monopoly

In recent years, the policy discussion of monopoly has been undergoing revision. Harold Demsetz of UCLA has argued that there are two systems of belief about monopoly.[32] One system views private sector monopoly as a major threat to the economy. This view is that of proponents of the Market Concentration Doctrine. Proponents of this view think such monopolies should be aggressively regulated and pursued by strictly defined antitrust policy. The other system, which Demsetz calls the *new learning*, views the more serious economic threat as coming from monopolies that are nurtured, sponsored, and protected by government. Protection from this type of monopoly calls for deregulation and less governmental control. The new learning system is helpful in understanding antitrust activity in the 1980s because it represents the Reagan administration's view of monopoly.

REGULATION—THE ALPHABET DEPARTMENTS

Regulation at the federal level has resulted in a host of regulatory agencies aimed at protecting consumer welfare. The acronyms for these agencies read like somebody spilled their alphabet soup. The list includes the CAB, EEOC, EPA, FCC, FDA, FTC, ICC, NHTSA, OSHA, and the SEC. These agencies grew very rapidly in the 1960s and 1970s. The Reagan administration ran on a platform of getting these agencies "off the backs" of corporate America. The Reagan administration produced a significant decrease in the budgets and the employment of these agencies. Presumably, lower budgets and fewer people mean less regulation.

In many cases, the regulatory agencies that were formed for consumer protection actually inhibit competition and innovation. Before airline deregulation, the Civil Aeronautics Board (CAB) set fares and prohibited new entry. The Food and Drug Administration (FDA) tightly controls innovation and new entry in drug markets, often creating a situation where U.S. citizens must travel to foreign countries if they want access to innovative medical procedures and drugs. On a local level, most cities regulate taxi cabs by setting minimum prices, controlling entry, or both. The list could go on and on. Ironically, in many instances regulatory agencies set up for consumer protection are responsible for the monopoly power that exists in the regulated market. Many companies defend the

---

32. Harold Demsetz, "Two Systems of Belief About Monopoly," in H. Goldschmid, H. M. Mann, and J.F. Weston, (eds.), *Industrial Concentration: The New Learning* (Boston: Little, Brown, and Co., 1974).

regulatory status quo because they already have met the regulations, and these regulations serve as an effective barrier to new entry and new competition. These firms are the government-protected monopolies that Demsetz identified.

COMPETITIVENESS

In the months preceding the 1984 presidential election, the concept of a national industrial policy became popular. In 1987, many of these same proposals reappeared and became popular under the new political buzzword competitiveness. In the 1988 presidential election, every candidate was forced to have a policy on competitiveness, and many state governors created councils on competitiveness.

Those who propose a national economic policy seem to draw their ideas from the success of the Japanese economy. There is a belief that the success of the Japanese stems from the government working closely with private industry and taking steps to insure that private industry is successful. The idea in part is that government should take steps to back industrial "winners" to make them even more successful. Such proposals rest on the premise that the U.S. economy is in serious decline, that other countries (notably Japan) have had a positive experience with industrial-governmental "partnerships," and that the political structure can forge a consensus on what such a policy for the United States should look like. Regardless of the form that policies on competitiveness take at the federal level, they represent increased governmental intervention in the market. Proponents of such a policy are quick to point out that the United States already has a kind of industrial policy because every action of government in taxing and spending rewards some participants in the economy and penalizes others. These individuals argue that a coordinated and intentional policy would be preferable to what we have at present. A competitiveness policy, however, envisions a more active role for government in our mixed economy than most market-oriented economists would find acceptable.[33]

The competitiveness rhetoric at the state level has a different meaning. Policymakers at the state level have become very involved in economic development activities. Almost every state has a state development board that aids the governor in recruiting new firms to the state. These firms are recruited from other states and foreign countries. Government officials use all types of tax breaks and other incentives to lure new firms to their states. In this context, competitiveness can mean making state tax law, other state regulatory activity, and state services competitive with other states. Such competition puts a check on state government because if state officials create an environment that is hostile to business, firms will migrate to more friendly states.

---

33. For a thorough review of the industrial policy debate see R. D. Norton, "Industrial Policy and American Renewal," *Journal of Economic Literature* (March 1986).

ALTERNATIVES FOR CONTROLLING INDUSTRY

There is a substantial amount of monopoly power, or at least concentration, in U.S. industry, and monopoly power is detrimental from society's point of view. Unfortunately, attempts to control monopoly or to restore competition through antitrust enforcement have not produced the desired results. There does, however, seem to be at least one policy action that, if vigorously followed, could increase competitive pressures without endangering the efficiency produced by economies of scale. This policy action is based on the earlier discussion of industrial concentration and the threat of new entry. If public policy could actually support new entry by actively dismantling *artificial* barriers to entry, competitive pressure would increase. In many cases, the threat of new entry alone would be sufficient to alter the behavior of existing oligopolistic industries. These artificial barriers are both privately and publicly imposed. Vigorous enforcement of present antitrust law should be sufficient to remove private-entry barriers. Deregulation in the airline industry meant the removal of barriers sanctioned and enforced by government. The removal of these barriers caused market forces to introduce competitive pressure, a less drastic and more productive outcome than what results from courtroom interference and restructuring.

SUMMARY

1. Industries are defined by SIC codes, prepared by the Department of Commerce. These SIC codes can be used to calculate concentration ratios, which are measures of the degree to which markets are concentrated.

2. Herfindahl Indexes have been proposed as better measures of monopoly power than simple concentration ratios because they account for all of the firms in the industry.

3. There is no conclusive evidence on the concentration trend in U.S. industry. Some researchers have found the concentration level in U.S. industry to be quite stable.

4. The merger movement of the mid-1980s led to a whole set of new terminology to describe corporate raiders and takeovers.

5. The Market Concentration Doctrine, stating that the structure of an industry determines its ultimate performance, is accepted by many policymakers. If this is true, it would simply indicate that concentrated industries should be restructured. However, there is a good deal of debate concerning the degree to which concentration leads to higher profit rates and more rigid prices. Although most economists still accept the Market Concentration Doctrine, competing evidence warrants more study before basing policy decisions on this doctrine.

6. Countervailing power and innovation are sometimes argued to be positive aspects of monopoly power.

7. Regulation of monopoly leads to cost-plus pricing, which destroys cost-minimizing incentives.

8. Taxation of monopoly is an alternative to regulation. It simply captures monopoly profit without affecting price or output.

9. A Lerner Index measures the percentage difference between price and marginal cost, which is perhaps the "best" measure of monopoly power. The unavailability of marginal cost data limits its use.

10. U.S. antitrust law began with the Sherman Antitrust Act in 1890. The Sherman Act and succeeding laws have been applied with varying vigor and success.

11. The record of antitrust enforcement is not too impressive. Litigation takes a long time and rarely restores competition. Politics plays an important role in antitrust activity.

12. Competitiveness became the political buzzword in the late 1980s. At the federal level, it is industrial policy in new clothes, but at the state level it relates to economic development.

■ NEW TERMS

industry studies
Standard Industrial Classification (SIC) system
concentration ratio
Herfindahl Index
Number Equivalent
Market Concentration Doctrine
administered prices
countervailing power
marginal cost pricing

Lerner Index of Monopoly Power (LMP)
cost-plus pricing
fair rate of return
trusts
holding companies
Sherman Antitrust Act
Clayton Act
tying contracts
Robinson-Patman Act

predatory pricing
Celler-Kefauver Antimerger Act
Federal Trade Commission Act
Wheeler-Lea Act
Hart-Scott-Rodino Antitrust Improvement Act
rule of reason
treble damages
National Recovery Administration (NRA)

■ QUESTIONS FOR DISCUSSION

1. Should profits be used as a measure of monopoly power? Should concentration be used as a measure of monopoly power? Discuss the wisdom of using either or both.

2. What would happen in a regulated industry if price were set so that the firm would not earn a normal rate of return?

3. If all prices in an industry are identical, is this evidence of an antitrust violation?

4. Do concentration ratios tell you anything about changes in conglomerate merger activity?

5. Assume that the table below represents data from the soft drink industry.

	Annual Sales (in dollars)
Firm 1	$400,000,000
Firm 2	300,000,000
Firm 3	200,000,000
Firm 4	150,000,000
Firms 5–35	300,000,000

What is the four-firm concentration ratio for this industry?

6. Now assume that the entire soft drink industry is made up of the first four firms listed in question 5. What is the four-firm concentration ratio? What is the Herfindahl index? What is the Number Equivalent? What does the Number Equivalent tell you?

7. What would happen to the concentration ratios in question 5 if we defined the industry as the beverage industry? As the name brand, nationally advertised soft drink industry?

8. Why is it so difficult to regulate a natural monopoly?

9. Why do some economists favor deregulation as a way of dealing with monopoly rather than "better" or "tougher" regulation?

10. Make a case for active antitrust policy and then argue that monopoly is not so bad and we shouldn't worry too much about it.

■ SUGGESTIONS FOR FURTHER READING

Adams, Walter, and James Brock. *The Bigness Complex: Industry, Labor, and the American Economy.* New York: Pantheon, 1986. A critique of bigness by two economists unabashedly opposed to bigness. They argue that the bigger the company, the more likely it will be protected and helped by government.

Asch, Peter. *Industrial Organization and Antitrust Policy.* New York: John Wiley and Sons, Inc., 1986. A textbook that gives detailed accounts of important antitrust cases.

Newcomb, Peter. "No One Is Safe." *Forbes* (13 July 1987): 121–160. An account of how the largest firms ebb and flow so that concentration is in flux.

Reich, Robert B. *Tales of A New America.* New York: Times Books, 1986. A topical new book on competitiveness by one of the advocates of industrial policy.

Scherer, F.M. *Industrial Market Structure and Economic Performance.* Chicago: Rand McNally & Company, 1980. A source book with detailed references to the literature on regulation and antitrust matters.

"Symposia: Horizontal Mergers and Antitrust," and "Symposium: Takeover," *The Journal of Economic Perspectives* (Fall 1987 and Winter 1988, respectively). These two issues of the new Journal of the American Economic Association contain eight very readable essays on horizontal mergers and takeovers.

PART FOUR

FACTOR

MARKETS

■

CHAPTER 14

MARGINAL PRODUCTIVITY THEORY AND LABOR MARKETS

■

INTRODUCTION

Income is earned through ownership of any (or perhaps all) of the factors of production. Most individuals receive income from their labor; many others own land or capital, or are entrepreneurs. Flows of personal income accrue to all these factors. In most discussions, much more attention is given to the equity aspects of the distribution of personal income than to the reasons for this distribution. This chapter discusses labor markets and explains why the distribution of labor income is what it is. In a later chapter we will discuss actions that can be taken if society doesn't like the distribution of income that is produced by the market process. The following discussion is a theoretical explanation of how labor income is determined in a market system.

The demand for labor is, of course, analogous to other types of demand that we have studied. In previous chapters we discussed product markets, in which firms or individuals sell the goods and services they produce to consumers. Now we want to examine labor markets, which are the markets in which firms buy—or rent—the services of labor from individuals who are supplying these labor inputs. We can go far in understanding this market by using the same tools we developed to study product markets. There are, however, some differences between labor markets and product markets, and we will concentrate on these differences.

THE FIRM IN TWO MARKETS

In previous chapters, we examined the circular flow as a starting point. It is worthwhile to pause briefly to return to that earlier discussion. Figure 14–1 reproduces Figure 2–6 from Chapter 2. It shows the firm involved in two markets: the product market and the factor market.

We have just spent a great deal of time studying the theory of the firm in the product market, the upper half of the circular flow. We now will turn our attention to a detailed discussion of the lower half, the theory of the firm in one part of the factor market, the labor market.

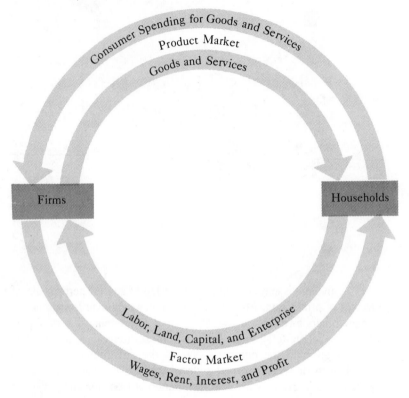

FIGURE 14-1
THE CIRCULAR FLOW OF INCOME
Households purchase goods and services and supply land, labor, capital, and enterprise. Firms buy these factors of production and supply goods and services. In the product market, goods and services are exchanged; and in the factor market, factors of production (resources) are exchanged.

■   ■   ■   ■   ■   ■   ■   ■
DIFFERENCES IN LABOR MARKETS

DERIVED DEMAND
A demand that is the result of the demand for another product. For example, the demand for labor is derived from the demand for the good that the labor produces.

The demand for labor has three features that make it somewhat different from the demand for a product. The first is that it is **derived demand**. A firm demands labor because the labor can be used to produce goods which consumers are demanding. The demand for labor is thus derived from the demand for the product it produces. If there were no consumer demand for milk, there would be no demand for milkers. This holds true for all factors of production. They are only valuable to a firm if they help produce products that consumers value.

INTERDEPENDENT DEMAND
The demand for a factor of production depends on the amount of other factors that the firm plans to use.

The second unusual feature of the demand for labor is that it is **interdependent** with the demand for other factors. In other words, the amount of labor that is demanded will depend on the amounts of other factors a firm plans to use. The amount of labor a firm demands depends on the amount of land and capital that will be used with the labor.

The third special feature is that the demand for labor is in part **technologically determined**; that is, the demand will depend on techniques of production and on technological progress, or the production function. The production function tells how much labor is needed to produce a certain level of output, given a certain technique of production and the other factors of production used.

You will see these basic elements unfold as we examine marginal productivity theory. **Marginal productivity theory** is a theory originally developed by John Bates Clark that explains how the distribution of income comes about. Each factor is paid according to its contribution, or its marginal productivity. We shall follow Clark's precedent by developing the theory in terms of labor supply and demand. The theory holds for all factors of production, but most interest centers on labor and the returns to labor.

TECHNOLOGICALLY DETERMINED DEMAND
The demand for a factor of production is determined by the techniques of production and the level of technology used.

MARGINAL PRODUCTIVITY THEORY
A theory originally developed by John Bates Clark that explains how the distribution of income comes about. Each factor is paid according to its contribution, or its marginal productivity.

LABOR MARKETS— DIFFERENCES FROM PRODUCT MARKETS

- Demand is derived.
- Demand is interdependent.
- Demand is technologically determined.

THE MARKET FOR LABOR WHEN BOTH PRODUCT AND FACTOR MARKETS ARE PURELY COMPETITIVE

Remember that a demand curve graphically depicts the relationship between price and quantity demanded. A demand curve for labor shows how much labor will be demanded at various wages. In order to develop a theory about the market demand for labor, we start by asking how much labor an individual firm will employ at various wage rates. Then we aggregate the results across firms in the same way that we added individual demand curves to find the market demand for a product.

The Demand for Labor

We shall begin with a firm that is selling its product in a perfectly competitive product market and buying its labor in a perfectly competitive labor market. This means that the firm will take the price of its product *and* the price of labor as given. The firm has no effect on product prices or on wage rates.

We need to determine the firm's demand for labor. Suppose the production function is such that, as the firm increases the amount of labor employed, *ceteris paribus*, the increases in the amount of total product become smaller. This product function reflects the principle of diminishing marginal productivity, which we discussed earlier when we looked at costs. Holding constant the quantities of the other factors, land and capital, it is possible to determine how the firm's output is related to the quantity of labor it uses. As the firm employs more labor in combination with fixed amounts of the other factors, the additional amounts of output per additional unit of labor eventually decline. If this were not the case, it would be theoretically possible to grow the entire world's supply of wheat on one acre of land just by employing more workers.

The amount of total physical product associated with various amounts of labor inputs for a hypothetical firm is given in Column 2 of Table 14–1. This output depends on the technical relationship found in the production function. Once we know the total product, we can determine how much extra product is produced when labor inputs are added, i.e., the marginal physical product (MPP_L) of that unit of labor. It is the marginal physical product because the output is in physical units, e.g., number of autos or pounds of coal.

TABLE 14–1
THE DEMAND FOR LABOR IN PURELY COMPETITIVE PRODUCT MARKETS

(1) Units of Labor	(2) Total Physical Product	(3) Marginal Physical Product of Labor (MPP_L)	(4) Product Price	(5) Total Revenue	(6) Value of Marginal Product of Labor (VMP_L)	(7) Marginal Revenue Product of Labor (MRP_L)
■	■	■	■	■	■	■
1	10	10	$2	$20	$20	$20
2	18	8	2	36	16	16
3	24	6	2	48	12	12
4	28	4	2	56	8	8
5	30	2	2	60	4	4

VALUE OF THE MARGINAL PRODUCT (VMP)
The value of the marginal product is found by multiplying the marginal physical product by the price at which the firm can sell the product.

MARGINAL REVENUE PRODUCT (MRP)
The amount that an additional unit of the variable factor of production adds to a firm's total revenue.

To put a market value on the output, we simply multiply the amount of the product by the price at which the firm can sell it. This value is called the **value of the marginal product** of labor (VMP_L); it appears in Column 6 of Table 14–1. The VMP_L, which is $P \times MPP_L$, is a measure of the value that each unit of labor adds to the firm's product. The **marginal revenue product** of labor (MRP_L) is the amount that an additional unit of the variable factor of production, in this case labor, adds to the firm's total revenue. It is found in Column 7 of Table 14–1. Marginal revenue product is found by multiplying MR by MPP_L. You will note that in pure competition in the product market, the $VMP_L = MRP_L$. They are equal because the product price remains constant, $P = MR$, so $VMP_L = MRP_L$. The firm can produce and sell as much as it wants at the market-determined price, which is $2 in this example. When the firm faces a given price, marginal revenue is exactly equal to price, as it was in the model of pure competition. Later in this chapter we will see how VMP and MRP behave when there is monopoly power in the product market.

The VMP_L and the MRP_L are plotted on a graph, as in Figure 14–2. The MRP_L is the firm's demand curve for labor. The MRP_L shows the value of each additional unit of labor to the firm. Thus, the MRP_L graph is the demand curve for labor. It shows how much labor the firm will purchase at various prices (wage rates). If you know the price of labor, you will be able to determine how much labor the firm will purchase.

The Supply of Labor

The market supply curve of labor (S_L) is the aggregate of all the individual supply curves, showing how much labor is available at different wage rates as in Figure 14–3. This supply curve of labor, like most supply curves, is upward sloping. As wage rates in an occupation rise, more people will want to enter that line of work. In general, as wages rise, more people will choose to give up leisure in favor of more income, and more workers will be attracted to the market.

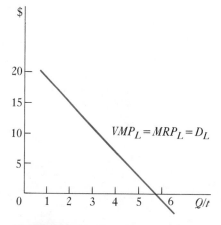

FIGURE 14-2
THE DEMAND FOR LABOR IN PURELY COMPETITIVE PRODUCT MARKETS
The marginal revenue product of labor curve is the firm's demand curve for labor. When the firm's product market is purely competitive, the MRP and the VMP are identical.

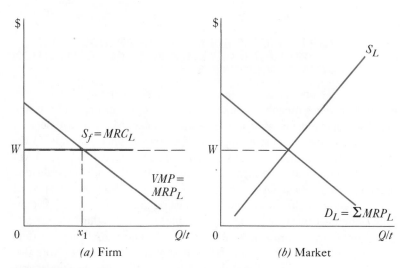

(a) Firm   *(b)* Market

FIGURE 14-3
PERFECTLY COMPETITIVE LABOR MARKET
The firm faces a perfectly elastic supply curve in a perfectly competitive labor market. If the supply curve is perfectly elastic, the marginal resource cost curve is also perfectly elastic. The firm can purchase as much labor as it wants at the market-determined wage rate.

We began by assuming that this firm was in a purely competitive factor market. Pure competition in the resource market means the firm can purchase labor at the market wage without affecting the wage. The equilibrium price W is the wage rate. The firm can now purchase as much labor as it wishes at W. The supply curve the firm faces, represented by S_f in Figure 14–3, is thus perfectly elastic at W. If the supply curve the firm faces is perfectly elastic, the cost of each additional unit of labor is the same, or constant. The cost of each additional unit of a productive resource (in this case, labor) is the **marginal resource cost** (MRC). For a firm in a perfectly competitive labor market, the marginal resource cost curve of labor, MRC_L, is the same as the labor supply curve.

MARGINAL RESOURCE COST (MRC)
The cost of each additional unit of a productive resource.

■ Equilibrium

The MRC_L curve is the supply curve the firm faces because it shows the relationship between price and additional units of labor being offered. A profit-maximizing firm will employ or purchase a resource until $MRP = MRC$. If a factor adds more to revenue than to cost (if $MRP > MRC$), it will be profitable for the firm to purchase more units of the factor. However, if the factor adds more to cost than to revenue (if $MRP < MRC$), the firm should purchase fewer units. The firm will hire laborers until the amount they add to total cost (MRC_L) is exactly equal to the amount they add to revenue (MRP_L). In Figure 14–3 the firm would employ x_1 units of labor at wage rate W. In terms of the numerical example in Table 14–1 the firm would employ four units of labor if the market wage was $8 per unit. If the market wage was $4 per unit, five units of labor would be employed.

■ ■ ■ ■ ■ ■ ■ THE MARKET FOR LABOR UNDER MONOPOLY IN PRODUCT MARKETS AND PURE COMPETITION IN FACTOR MARKETS

We now want to assume that the firm under consideration sells its product under monopoly conditions. A numerical example of the monopolist's demand for labor is presented in Table 14–2. The difference between this and the first example is that product price (Column 4) declines as the firm produces and sells more of its product. VMP_L and MRP_L are calculated in the same manner as before. VMP_L is simply the valuation of the labor's marginal physical product, so $VMP_L = MPP_L \times P$ (Column 3 times Column 4). MRP_L is found by calculating the change in total revenue from additional units of labor. For example, when the third worker was added, total revenue rose from $162 to $192. Thus, MRP_L for the third worker is $192 – $162 = $30. MRP_L is shown in Column 7. Note that now $VMP_L > MRP_L$ for all but the first unit of labor, because under monopoly, product price is greater than marginal revenue.

TABLE 14-2
THE DEMAND FOR LABOR IN MONOPOLISTIC PRODUCT MARKETS

(1) Units of Labor	(2) Total Physical Product	(3) Marginal Physical Product of Labor (MPP_L)	(4) Product Price	(5) Total Revenue	(6) Value of the Marginal Product of Labor (VMP_L)	(7) Marginal Revenue Product of Labor (MRP_L)
■	■	■	■	■	■	■
1	10	10	$10	$100	$100	$100
2	18	8	9	162	72	62
3	24	6	8	192	48	30
4	28	4	7	196	28	4
5	30	2	6	180	12	–6

We have graphed both a VMP_L curve and an MRP_L curve in Figure 14–4. The MRP_L curve is the firm's demand curve for labor. This firm, like the previous firm, will employ labor until $MRP_L = MRC_L$. Although the firm is selling its product in a monopolistic product market, it is purchasing labor in a competitive labor market.

The firm and the market are diagrammed in Figure 14–5. The market demand curve is, as before, found by summing the MRP_L curves for all firms purchasing this type of labor. The market supply (S_L) is the sum of individual supply curves of workers. The market-determined wage is W. This firm can purchase as much labor as it desires at W since the supply curve facing it, S_f, is perfectly elastic at W. Since S_f is perfectly elastic, MRC_L is constant. The firm maximizes profits where $MRC_L = MRP_L$, so the firm hires x_1 units of labor. You will note from Figure 14–5 that the monopolist pays W, the market wage. The fact that $MRP_L <$ VMP_L does not mean the monopolist exploits labor by paying too little— the monopolist has to pay the market wage just like any other employer in this market. Instead, it means that the monopolist employs fewer laborers than similar competitive firms would employ. Recall from the chapter on pure monopoly that the monopolist restricts output to keep price high. The result of this output restriction in the factor market is that the monopolist restricts input usage in order to restrict output. If this were a competitive firm rather than a monopolist, it would want to be on the VMP_L curve (which would then also be the MRP_L curve) and hire x_2 workers.

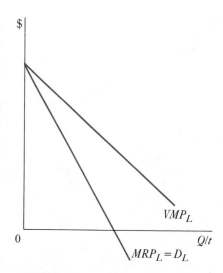

FIGURE 14-4
THE DEMAND FOR LABOR WITH MONOPOLY IN PRODUCT MARKETS
When the firm has monopoly power in the product market, the MRP_L curve will lie below the VMP_L curve. This is because under monopoly, product price is greater than marginal revenue and so $P \times MP_L$ is greater than $MR \times MP_L$.

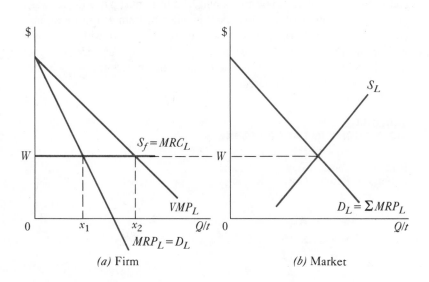

(a) Firm   (b) Market

FIGURE 14-5
A MONOPOLISTIC FIRM FACING A PERFECTLY COMPETITIVE LABOR MARKET
A firm with monopoly power in product markets and in a perfectly competitive labor market will face a perfectly elastic supply curve. The firm will hire units of labor until the marginal revenue product of labor is equal to the marginal resource cost of labor.

■   ■   ■   ■   ■   ■   ■

MONOPSONY

We have looked at competitive and monopolistic firms demanding labor in competitive labor markets. Now we want to consider the case in which the firm has market power in the labor market. We have assumed to this point that the purchasing firm has no effect on wage rates. But what if the firm does affect wage rates, so that as the firm hires more labor, the wage rate rises? We refer to such a firm as having monopsony power. The word **monopsony** comes from a Greek word meaning "one purchaser." Just as a pure monopoly is a single seller of a product, a pure monopsony is the single purchaser of a particular factor.

We will begin by assuming that we know what the firm's MRP_L curve is, as in Figure 14–6. It doesn't matter if this firm is selling its product in a competitive market or a monopolistic market, although it's hard to imagine a monopsonist without some degree of monopoly power in the product market. We also know the market supply curve of labor to this firm, S_L. Table 14–3 provides a numerical example of the monopsony supply curve to further your understanding of Figure 14–6. The market supply curve, S_L, is the labor supply curve the firm faces because the firm is the market for this labor by the definition of monopsony. If this were a competitive market, a wage rate of W_c and employment of Q_c would have resulted. However, since the firm faces the upward-sloping supply curve, S_L, the marginal resource cost curve for labor (MRC_L) lies above the S_L curve, as in Figure 14–6. To see why this is the case, refer to Table 14–3. The supply curve is, of course, the graphical representation of Columns 1 and 2. Since the curve is upward sloping, the firm must pay a higher wage rate as it hires more labor. This result is different from a firm hiring in a competitive labor market. The total wage costs go up with additional workers in this case for two reasons. First, the wage must rise to attract more labor. Second, wage costs rise because all laborers receive a higher wage as more workers are hired.

MONOPSONY
A single purchaser of a factor of production.

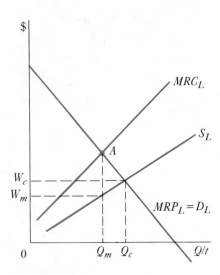

FIGURE 14-6
MONOPSONY

The monopsony firm faces the market supply curve for labor. Since this curve has a positive slope, the marginal resource cost curve lies above it. The monopsonist thus hires Q_m units of labor at a wage rate of W_m.

TABLE 14-3
MONOPSONY IN LABOR MARKETS

(1) Units of Labor	(2) Wage Rate	(3) Wage Cost	(4) Marginal Resource Cost (MRC_L)
■	■	■	■
1	$ 5	$ 5	$ 5
2	6	12	7
3	7	21	9
4	8	32	11
5	9	45	13
6	10	60	15
7	11	77	17
8	12	96	19
9	13	117	21
10	14	140	23

The amount that each additional unit hired adds to wage expenses is the marginal resource cost. You can see by comparing Columns 2 and 4 that the curve representing Column 4 will lie above the supply curve, as shown in Figure 14–6. The firm, as before, maximizes profits where $MRP_L = MRC_L$. This would be at point A on Figure 14–6, where the firm employs Q_m units of labor. But MRC is not the wage rate. Remember, the supply curve tells you what has to be paid to hire Q_m units of labor. The firm will pay W_m. Note that $W_m < W_c$, so the monopsonist is paying a lower wage than would have been paid in a competitive labor market. We refer to this situation as monopsonistic exploitation. **Monopsonistic exploitation** is the underpayment of wages due to monopsony power. Labor receives less than it would receive in competitive markets. This does not mean that workers are forced to work at wage rates below what they are willing to accept. Rather, the monopsonist simply restricts input just as the monopolist restricts output.

MONOPSONISTIC EXPLOITATION
The reduction in wages due to monopsony power. Labor receives less than it would receive in competitive markets.

Monopsony in the Real World

Are there any real-world examples of pure labor monopsony? No, because all labor has some alternative employment. Pure monopsony, like pure monopoly, is a theoretical extreme. There are, however, real-world examples of monopsony power. You are probably familiar with the song about the miner who owes his soul to the company store. This song was written about mining companies and how they dominate the labor market as the major employer in certain areas. "Company towns"—small towns with only one major employer such as Pullman, Illinois, where railroad sleeping cars were manufactured—were common in the early twentieth century. A large university in a small town would be another good example of monopsony power. If you compared university secretarial salaries for similar-sized schools in cities with labor pools of varying size, you would find that where the university dominates, the salaries are lower. Why? Monopsony power.

Perhaps the best example of monopsony in our present economy exists in professional sports. Congress has granted sports leagues exemptions from the antitrust laws that we discussed in an earlier chapter. This exemption allows the leagues to hire as monopsonists by drafting players and maintaining control through reserve clauses.[1] As a result, wage rates for these athletes are lower than they would be if the teams competed for players on an open or at least freer market. A study of the economics of baseball by Gerald Scully found empirical evidence of monopsonistic exploitation in that sport. In Scully's research, he found that the typical MRP of star pitchers in 1969 was \$405,300, while the typical salary was only \$66,800.[2] Think about the case of Michael Jordan, a basketball player. He receives a very high salary, but consider what he adds to the league in

---

1. Reserve clauses have been and are being challenged. Players can now play out their options, thus reducing the monopsony power of the owners.
2. G.W. Scully, "Pay and Performance in Major League Baseball," *American Economic Review* (December 1974): 915–930.

terms of marginal revenue. He fills up the arena for practically every game he plays.[3] His salary is surely less than his *MRP*.

In the early 1980s the formation of the United States Football League (USFL) had a profound effect on salaries in professional football. The new league introduced competition for players and the effect was startling. In 1983, rookie salaries jumped an average of 52 percent over 1982 salaries. Many of football's general managers called this trend an "economic disaster" and blamed it on players, agents, and other teams. If they had studied economics, they would have realized it was due to the breaking of their monopsony. When the USFL folded, the upward pressure on football salaries declined.

Except for these special cases, where there are buyers of very specialized labor skills, there are few instances of significant monopsony power. In general, improved transportation and communication in U.S. labor markets have increased labor mobility, and with increased labor mobility there is decreased monopsony power. If miners are aware of job possibilities in other areas and in other occupations, the mine will be forced to pay a competitive wage. Indeed, if even a small percentage of miners are willing to pull up stakes, the mine will be forced to pay competitive wages. Complete labor mobility isn't needed to reduce monopsony power; it's enough to have mobility only at the margin.

Monopsony Power and Minimum Wages

We saw earlier that the minimum wage is a price floor set above the market-clearing price and, as such, causes a surplus, or unemployment, in the labor market. This conclusion is not always correct, because a minimum wage can cause employment to increase in a monopsonistic market. Consider the monopsony market shown in Figure 14–7. The monopsonist would employ Q_m units of labor at wage rate W_m. Now suppose a minimum wage of W_1 is imposed. A segment of the market supply curve is replaced by a horizontal line at W_1, the imposed minimum wage. In effect, the monopsonist is forced to accept the minimum wage. The market supply curve is now represented by the line W_1AS_L. The marginal resource cost for labor is now W_1A, because the supply curve is perfectly elastic in the range W_1A. At a wage rate of W_1, Q_1 would be employed.

If the minimum wage selected is W_2 instead of W_1, the supply curve the firm faces is W_2BS_L. The firm would face perfectly elastic supply and *MRC* curves in the relevant range. In this case, the firm would employ Q_m units of labor at wage rate W_2. You can see that if the minimum wage that is imposed lies between W_m and W_2, more employment at a higher wage rate will result.

What we have just analyzed is an exception to the case where minimum wages have undesirable effects. Be careful, though; this result only holds when there is monopsony power in the labor market, and a

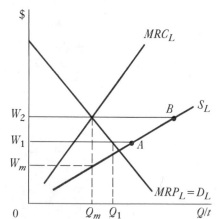

FIGURE 14–7
MONOPSONY POWER AND MINIMUM WAGES

A minimum wage of W_2 in a monopsonistic labor market changes the market supply curve from S_L to W_2BS_L. The marginal resource cost curve is the same as the supply curve along W_2B, the perfectly elastic portion.

3. *Sports Illustrated* reported that the Milwaukee Bucks realized an additional $700,000 profit during Kareem Abdul-Jabbar's first season. His salary was $250,000. So you can see, Abdul-Jabbar's $MRP_L > MRC_L$. Although salary figures are not available for Michael Jordan's 1986–1987 year with the Chicago Bulls, *Sports Illustrated* reported in December, 1987, that Jordan brought in 276,996 additional fans over the previous season. At the average ticket price of $13.14, that represented $3.71 million in marginal revenue.

monopsony is relatively rare except in certain labor markets for specialized skills, such as basketball players. Most empirical studies of the effects of minimum wages show that the monopsony model is not an important exception to the negative effects of a minimum wage on employment.[4]

THE DETERMINANTS OF THE ELASTICITY OF LABOR DEMAND

At the beginning of this chapter, you saw that the demand for labor had features making it somewhat different from the demand for a product. These same features influence the elasticity of the demand for labor. It is worth considering these differences because they determine how the quantity of labor demanded will respond to changes in the wage rate. In other words, the demand for labor has an elasticity coefficient just like the demand for products, but this coefficient is influenced by the same features that influenced the demand for labor.

Elasticity of Product Demand

If the wage rate falls, the cost of producing the product will also fall. There will, as a result, be a decline in the selling price of the product. As this price declines, consumers will increase their consumption of the product. The price elasticity of demand for the product determines how much more of the product consumers will purchase in response to the decline in price. Thus product price elasticity affects the price elasticity of the demand for labor. If the product demand is elastic, the firm will hire more labor in order to increase production to respond to the increased quantity demanded by consumers. In other words, the larger the increase in quantity demanded of the product, the larger will be the increase in quantity demanded of the labor input. This means, quite simply, that the more elastic the demand is for the final product, the more elastic will be the demand for the labor used to produce that product.

Share of Labor in Factor Cost

The second element that affects the elasticity of demand for labor is a bit more complicated. To begin, assume that only labor is used to produce the product. Labor costs are 100 percent of product cost. If the price of labor falls 10 percent, the cost of production falls 10 percent, and price (in pure competition) falls 10 percent. Being more realistic, let labor constitute only 50 percent of cost. Then if the price of labor falls 10 percent, the costs of production would fall only 5 percent. In other words, the more significant labor cost is in the production of a product, the more a change in the wage rate will affect the cost of production and the price of that product. As a result, the larger the share of wages in the total cost of production, the greater will be the elasticity of demand for labor.

4. See Jack Hirshleifer, *Price Theory and Applications*, 4th Ed. (Englewood Cliffs, N.J.: Prentice-Hall, Inc., 1988), 336–340, for a review of these empirical studies.

JOHN BATES CLARK (1847-1938)

John Bates Clark was the first U.S.-born economist to achieve an international reputation as an economic theorist. He was a reformer and an activist who helped form the American Economic Association, later becoming its third president.

Clark was born and raised in Providence, Rhode Island. He graduated from Amherst College in 1872. He studied economics at the University of Heidelberg and the University of Zurich. Upon his return to the United States, Clark taught political economy at Carleton College and then moved to Smith College, Amherst, Johns Hopkins, and finally to Columbia, where he taught political science from 1895 to 1923. After 1911, he became very active in pacifist causes and was the first director of the Carnegie Endowment for International Peace.

The nature of Clark's interests in economic theory reflect the times in which he lived. The American Industrial Revolution caused Clark to examine problems of production and distribution. Clark concentrated his attention on developing a positive theory based on the competition of rational, self-interested people, as illustrated in his book *The Distribution of Wealth* (1899). This approach was a radical change from Clark's earlier work, *The Philosophy of Wealth* (1887), in which he attacked the "hedonistic" assumptions of the classical economists. His influence on later economists is in large part due to the analytical tools he developed.

John Bates Clark's status in the U.S. economics profession is recognized in the awarding of a John Bates Clark Prize by the American Economics Association. Every two years, this prize is awarded to an economist under the age of 40 who has made a significant contribution to economic theory. The list of winners reads like a *Who's Who* of the U.S. economics profession.

Opportunities for Factor Substitution

In actual production, a great deal of substitutability exists among the factors of production. We discussed this possibility in detail when we talked about production. The choice of which combination of factors of production to use depends, as we saw earlier, on the prices of these factors. As the price of labor increases, entrepreneurs will substitute capital and land to the extent that substitution is permitted by the production function.

Consider what happens when the wage rate falls. To the extent that labor can be substituted for other factors of production, more labor will be hired. The greater the degree of substitutability in production, the greater will be the price elasticity of factor demand.

CHANGES IN FACTOR DEMAND

The demand curve for labor, like the demand curve for products, can shift in response to changes in underlying conditions. Two of the most important causes of such shifts are changes in demand for the product and changes in the employment of the other factors of production.

Changes in Product Demand

The demand for labor is derived demand from the demand for the product it is used to produce. To see this more clearly, return to Table 14–1 and Table 14–2, which show the situation for a competitive and monopolistic firm, respectively. Suppose there were an increase in demand in the product market, with the market demand curve shifting to the right. This would cause the product price to increase for the competitive firm, and the value of the marginal product of labor would be larger for all quantities. The MRP_L for the competitive firm, Column 7 in Table 14–1, would increase in proportion to the increase in product price. In most cases, an increase in demand would also increase the monopolist's MRP_L compared to the figures shown in Table 14–2.[5] The MRP_L curve would shift outward for either kind of firm, representing an increase in the demand for labor.

In a competitive labor market, each firm would want to hire more labor at the existing wage rate. The market demand for labor could increase, raising both the level of employment and the wage rate. The amount by which the market wage increases would depend on how large this industry is relative to the labor market. If the industry is small, there may be only an imperceptible increase in wages; but if it is large, the wage rate could rise significantly. In a monopsonistic market, the result would also be an increase in wages and an increase in employment.[6]

Other Inputs

A second important cause of shifts in factor demand results from the fact that the demands for different factors are mutually interdependent. Refer again to Table 14–1 and Table 14–2. Suppose the capital stock of the firm is doubled. If labor and capital used together are complementary in the sense that an increase in capital makes labor more productive, each unit of labor will now have a larger physical product. In Table 14–1 and Table 14–2, the figures in Column 2 will increase, which will cause the MPP_L to increase, which will cause the MRP_L to increase. The MRP_L curve has shifted outward, signifying that the demand for labor has increased. This is what is meant by complementarity; an increase in usage of one factor raises the MRP of the other.

Increased productivity resulting from an increased capital stock can have several effects. Consider first what happens if the capital stock expands in one firm but has no industry-wide effects. The firm's demand curve (MRP_L) would increase (shift to the right) in Figures 14–3 and 14–5 without any (noticeable) effect on the market demand curve,

5. We can create cases in which the demand facing the monopolist increases at every price, but marginal revenue, and hence marginal product, actually fall so that the demand for labor falls.

6. You should work through the geometry of such increases.

because the firm is trivial in size relative to the industry. The result would be that the firm would employ more units of labor at the market-determined price.

Alternatively, consider the effect of an industry-wide increase in the capital stock. All firms in the industry have an increase in capital, causing their individual MRP_L curves to increase. The industry MRP_L curve also increases, and more labor is employed at a higher wage rate. Such a situation is graphically depicted in Figure 14–8. The initial equilibrium occurs where the firm employs x_1 units of labor at the market wage of W_1. The industry is employing Q_1 units of labor. Now there is an industry-wide increase in capital. The firm's MRP_L curve shifts to MRP'_L. Since all the firms in the industry have experienced this increase in MRP_L, the industry labor demand curve also will increase, as from D_L to D'_L in Figure 14–8. The market wage rises to W_2. As a result, the horizontal supply curve that the individual firm faces shifts from S_f to S'_f. The firm now will employ x_2 units of labor at wage rate W_2. Industry employment has risen from Q_1 to Q_2. The important point is that the response of the firm to an increase in its capital stock was to hire more workers at higher wages because the increase in the stock of capital increased the marginal productivity of the workers. The demand for the factors, labor and capital, can thus be seen to be interdependent.

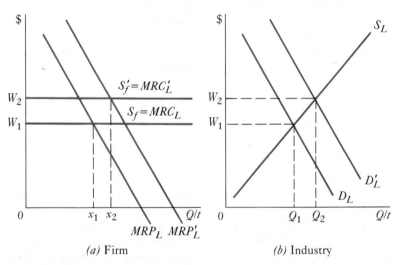

FIGURE 14-8
AN INDUSTRY-WIDE INCREASE IN CAPITAL
An increase in the capital stock will increase the productivity of labor if capital and labor are complementary factors. This increase in productivity will shift the marginal revenue product curve from MRP_L to MRP'_L and the market demand for labor from D_L to D'_L.

INVESTMENT IN HUMAN CAPITAL

In this chapter you examined marginal productivity theory as it applied to labor markets. It was demonstrated that labor became more productive and wages rose when the labor was used with more capital.

The notion of capital is, however, broader than that of a physical tool. Capital is anything used to increase the flow of output. Economists have therefore come to define human capital as anything such as health, vigor, education, or training that can be enhanced by "investment" and that increases the productivity of the individual in which it is embodied.

Just as a firm can increase its investment in physical capital, an individual can invest in human capital. An individual's decision to seek additional education is analogous to an entrepreneur's decision to purchase a new piece of equipment. In both cases, the investment is productive if the return (properly discounted) exceeds the cost (properly discounted).

Higher Education As an Investment

Your decision to seek higher education is a form of investment. The costs are the direct costs—tuition, fees, and books, etc.—plus the foregone opportunity costs, primarily lost income (which an individual could earn instead of going to college). The return is the present value of the increased earnings flow caused by the investment in education.

The anticipated future wage rate will have a profound impact on the type and amount of education that is pursued. For example, if wages of accountants rise relative to those of engineers, economists would expect more students to study accounting. Wages in professions that require long periods of study will have to be higher to attract students, for two reasons. First, students studying for long periods of time (like medical doctors do) forego a great deal of present income. Second, their future income is a longer way off. As you saw when we studied present value, income a long way into the future is worth a great deal less than income now. Viewed in this light, the incomes of doctors are not as high as they first appear. C. M. Lindsay of Clemson University has studied the rate of return to medical education. He found that when doctors' incomes are properly discounted and the hours worked are calculated correctly (doctors work longer hours than many other professionals), the return to investment in medical education earns a normal return.[7]

Important insights can be gained by viewing education as an investment in human capital. This analysis does not deny that people attend universities and colleges for other reasons. Some engage in education for its consumption value. For example, retired people returning to school are not investing in human capital because their productive years have ended. Instead, they are acquiring education for its consumption value. There are many consumption-related elements to education, ranging from enjoyment of literature and fine arts to the thrill of solving a tricky problem in logic. There are also many consumption activities related to being a student. If you are a member of a fraternity or a sorority, or have attended the "big game" weekend, you are familiar with some of these consumption benefits.

Not everyone makes career decisions on a strictly economic basis, and we don't want to imply that you should. You are going to spend

7. C. M. Lindsay, "Real Returns to Medical Education," *The Journal of Human Resources* 8, no. 3 (1973): 321–348.

the rest of your life working. Why not pick out an occupation or profession that you find enjoyable? This discussion of human capital and education is similar to many policy areas in economics. An economic model of human capital formation may seem dehumanizing, but you shouldn't take it that way. It is really a different way of viewing a complex process and it will give you important insights. Let's build on some of those insights.

Human Capital and Race

The concept of human capital and differences in wage rates relate to the question of race (or sex) discrimination. The important economic question is how much of the white/black income difference is the result of discrimination and how much it is a market phenomenon, the result of differences in human capital.

Many economists have examined changes in black/white income differences from a human capital perspective. In 1955, Morton Zeman's doctoral dissertation at the University of Chicago began the debate over the cause of black/white income differences.[8] Zeman examined the effects of schooling and on-the-job training, two elements of human capital formation, on income differences. He reported that while increases in schooling and training increased the incomes of both whites and blacks, they increased the earnings of whites more. In other words, the rate of return to investment in human capital appeared to be higher for whites. Zeman's work implied that income differences were the result of different pay for the same skill (i.e., discrimination) and that increasing the schooling of blacks would do little to change relative income differences between whites and blacks.

As time passed and more data became available in the 1960s, Zeman's result appeared to be confirmed. Blacks gained access to more schooling, yet income differences seemed to become more pronounced. In 1974, Finis Welch of UCLA brought attention to a human capital explanation of income differences.[9] Welch showed, using newly available and more extensive data, that rates of return to education were in fact as high for blacks as for whites.

James P. Smith of the Rand Corporation studied the effects of race and human capital formation using historical records.[10] Smith found that the story of black education after the Civil War had important implications for income differentials in a human capital approach.

Before the Civil War, every southern state had laws prohibiting the schooling of slaves. As a result, 95 percent of all black southerners were illiterate in 1860. At the end of the Civil War, the differences in average schooling of blacks and whites were enormous. Smith reports that whites of either sex (on the average) finished four to five more years of schooling than did blacks. In the first two decades after the war, blacks

8. Morton Zeman, "A Comparative Analysis of White and Non-White Income Differentials" (unpublished dissertation, University of Chicago, September, 1955).

9. Finis Welch, "Education and Racial Discrimination," in Orley Ashenfelter and Albert Rees (eds.), *Discrimination in Labor Markets* (Princeton: Princeton University Press, 1974).

10. Smith, J.P. "Race and Human Capital," *American Economic Review* (September 1984): 865-898.

began to close this gap and the stage was set for the eradication of black illiteracy. In the next two decades (1886 to 1906), however, black schooling made little progress, and human capital formation of whites outstripped that of blacks. This was the result of two factors: the disenfranchisement of blacks in the South and the spread of high school education as the normal level of education for whites in the North. Finally, Smith found that from 1906 to 1950, the differences in education between blacks and whites continually narrowed.

Smith concludes that education, or human capital formation, profoundly affects racial income differences but that a great lag exists. Smith shows that interruptions in the progress of black schooling in the early 1900s are still influencing income differentials. The lesson of this research is that the key to further narrowing wage and income differentials between the races (or sexes) will depend in large part on the availability of education and on-the-job training. It further shows that such changes are slow and evolutionary.

COMPARABLE WORTH

Comparable worth is the idea that there should be equal pay for jobs that require similar levels of training, responsibility, and other characteristics of "worth." It has been a very popular political issue in the 1980s. Comparable worth is a response to the fact that women earn an average of about 64.8 percent of what men earn, and are heavily concentrated in nursing, teaching, retail sales, secretarial, and clerical work. The comparable worth or pay equity argument is criticized heavily by many economists. Nevertheless, it is a politically controversial issue and thus worth examining in detail.

The Comparable Worth Argument

Advocates of comparable worth argue that the Equal Pay Act of 1963 and the Civil Rights Act of 1964, which required equal pay for equal work, did not go far enough. They claim that these laws are inadequate because female average pay is less than 65 percent of male average pay. Comparable worth advocates argue that there should be equal pay for jobs requiring similar levels of training, responsibility, and other characteristics of "worth."

Comparable worth advocates propose replacing market-determined wages with a planned or administered pay structure. The comparable worth argument is based on two propositions: the existence of sex discrimination and monopsony power in labor markets. If there is discrimination on the basis of race or sex, and federal laws prohibit discrimination in pay in the same job category, then an indirect way to perpetuate discrimination is to separate jobs into categories. These categories would be predominately black or white, or male or female, and pay different wages to jobs with similar skills and responsibilities. Since competition would undermine such subtle discrimination, it could only persist if there is monopsony power in the labor market.

COMPARABLE WORTH
The idea that there should be equal pay for jobs that require similar levels of training, responsibility, and other characteristics of "worth."

THE INTERNATIONAL PERSPECTIVE
U.S. IMMIGRATION POLICY AND
WAGE RATES

Give me your tired, your poor,
Your huddled masses yearning to breath free,
The wretched refuse of your teeming shore,
Send these, the homeless, tempest-tossed to me:
I lift my lamp beside the golden door.

-Inscription on the Statue of Liberty-

The United States is a country of immigrants and descendants of immigrants. All of us learned about our "melting pot" nation in grade school. In the early 1800s Europeans, mostly from Western Europe, flooded into the United States. In the late 1800s, a wave of Chinese immigrated to California. In the early 1900s, a huge flood of immigrants arrived from Southern and Eastern Europe. The most recent large inflows of immigrants have been from Cuba after Castro's rise to power, from Southeast Asia after the U.S. disengagement from Vietnam, and from Central America. Large numbers of those coming from Central America are illegal immigrants, making them distinct from most of the other waves of immigrants.

Each influx of immigrants caused a great debate among Americans who were already citizens. The debate was always the same: whether or not to shut the door to new immigrants. Often the answer was yes, and new restrictions were passed. There was the Chinese exclusion law in 1882, the "Gentlemen's Agreement" with Japan in 1907 (halting the immigration of Japanese), and, in 1921 and 1924, the national-origin quotas. The quotas were designed to freeze the ethnic composition of the United States by limiting the entrance of any one nationality to a small percentage of the number of people of that nationality who were already here. The Quota Law of 1921 limited immigration from any Eastern Hemisphere country to 3 percent of the foreign-born persons from that country living in the United States in 1910. In 1924, the Immigration Act Origins law set an annual quota of 2 percent of each country's United States' residents in 1920. In 1965 Congress did away with the national-origin quotas and placed an overall limit on immigrants of 290,000.

Many of the reasons for the political activity to restrict immigration are racist in origin. Many groups support immigration of those who are like themselves but are opposed to altering the racial or national origin mix of the country. This motivation was clear in the 1924 Immigration Act.

There is at least one economic motivation for restricting immigration. For each skill level it makes the supply of labor much more elastic, putting downward pressure on wage rates. It isn't surprising that organized labor groups are often opposed to liberalizing immigration policy. In fact some states even prohibit the transfer of certain occupational skills within the United States. For example, a Certified Public Accountant in Wisconsin who plans to move to Arizona will not be licensed until he or she passes the Arizona CPA exam. This clearly reduces the supply of accounting services in Arizona, and as a result, accountants in Arizona have higher incomes than they would otherwise.

In October 1986, the U.S. Congress passed an immigration reform bill that offered citizenship to illegal aliens who could prove they entered the United States before January 1, 1982, but imposed strict penalties on employers who hire illegal aliens. This law will likely put upward pressure on wage rates in unskilled labor markets of the South and Southwestern states, where illegal aliens compose a significant, albeit undocumented, share of the work force.

Human Capital Again

The chief difficulty with comparable worth as a way of determining wages is that it substitutes bureaucratic judgments about differences in jobs for the judgment of the marketplace. Shifts in supply and demand for particular products and services, subtle differences in skills, occupational attractiveness, and other market determinants of wages in specific occupations are difficult to identify and can change more rapidly than bureaucratic wage setting can accommodate.

The comparable worth argument not only disputes the validity of the marginal productivity theory of wage determination, but also ignores the fact that less human capital is an important part of the explanation for lower salaries for women. Some observers claim that women bring less human capital to the market. Less human capital could be the result of less education and on-the-job training, or it could be the strength, vigor, dependability, and health of women in general. Historically, females have invested less in education and training than have men. As a result, the average market value of their skills is lower. However, as in the previous section in which we discussed the education of blacks, the gap between male and female education rates is closing. Over the last 30 years, women have been enrolling in colleges and completing degrees at rates approaching those of males. These figures are familiar to you if you are a student in a business college. The number of students studying business has increased dramatically, an increasing percentage are women. The economics of this trend is simple. As human capital equalizes, wage differentials between men and women should decline. We will explore this issue further in the chapter on income distribution.

MARGINAL PRODUCTIVITY AND INCOME

The analysis in this chapter has served to point up an important conclusion of marginal productivity theory. That is, in a competitive labor market, the productivity of labor determines the wage rate. In turn, the productivity depends on the inherent productive qualities of labor, the quantity of the labor employed, and the amounts of cooperating factors being used. This is another way of saying that the distribution of income is determined by the relative marginal revenue products of the different factors of production. Since wages determine incomes of laborers, more productive laborers will have higher incomes. Laborers that are less productive will have lower incomes.

John Bates Clark, the original expositor of this theory, claimed that it presented a "morally correct" outcome of economic activity. Whether or not it is morally correct is not the province of economic theory. Theory is positive, and says nothing concerning whether the income distribution which results is a good one. Rather, the theory indicates that if labor markets are competitive, labor will receive returns based on each laborer's productivity. If we don't like the outcome, we can then work to change it through political action (a topic that will be discussed in a later chapter), but theory does indicate that output will be maximized in societies in which labor is paid according to its marginal productivity.

SUMMARY

1. The firm is a supplier in the product market and a demander in the factor market.

2. The demand for labor is a derived demand. It is determined by the amount of other factors used, as well as by technology.

3. A firm demands labor because labor is productive. The marginal revenue product curve is the firm's demand curve for labor.

4. In a competitive labor market, the firm faces a perfectly elastic labor supply curve. When the labor supply curve is perfectly elastic, the marginal resource cost curve is the same as the labor supply curve.

5. A monopoly firm in product markets uses less labor than a competitive industry would use, because the firm restricts inputs in the process of restricting output.

6. A monopsony is a single purchaser of an input. Monopsony results in fewer units of labor being purchased at less than the perfectly competitive wage, because the marginal resource cost curve lies above the supply curve. Because the monopsonistic wage is below a competitive wage, we refer to the difference as monopsonistic exploitation. Improved mar-

ket information and mobility of workers greatly reduce monopsony power.

7. The elasticity of demand for labor is greater: (a) the greater the price elasticity of demand of the product it is used to produce; (b) the more important labor is in the cost structure of the product; and (c) the greater the opportunity for factor substitution.

8. The decision to pursue more education can be viewed as an investment decision that adds to the stock of human capital.

9. Blacks historically have invested less in human capital that have whites. Indeed, before the Civil War, blacks were prohibited by law from receiving an education. As education rates of blacks and whites converge, the human capital argument predicts that income levels also will converge.

10. The comparable worth movement calls for equal pay for jobs of equal worth, or equal skills and responsibilities.

11. Marginal productivity theory explains how the distribution of labor income is determined in a market economy. It says nothing about the normative appropriateness of this distribution.

NEW TERMS

derived demand
interdependent demand
technologically determined demand
marginal productivity theory

value of the marginal product
    (VMP)
marginal revenue product (MRP)
marginal resource cost (MRC)

monopsony
monopsonistic exploitation
comparable worth

QUESTIONS FOR DISCUSSION

1. Can you describe a situation that might constitute monopsonistic exploitation? What would you recommend as a correction?

2. The demand for accountants has skyrocketed in recent years and the salaries of accountants have increased significantly. Is the demand for accountants a derived demand? If so, from what?

3. Why are professional athletes opposed to reserve clauses?

4. Can you characterize your decision to attend college in human capital terms? Include your opportunity costs and projected income. Will continued invest-

ment be required to keep your human capital from depreciating?

5. How could the potential of career interruptions have an impact on starting salaries and create a difference between female and male earnings?

6. Firms operate in both the factor market and the product market. Does the market situation in the product market affect the market situation in the factor market? In other words, is a monopolist always a monopsonist or vice versa?

7. In words, how does an entrepreneur decide how much labor to employ?

8. How is a change in the quantity of labor demanded different than a change in the demand for labor?

9. Does the fact that undergraduate students with high grade-point averages are highly sought by big-eight accounting firms have any impact on the supply of accounting professors?

10. How can the elasticity of demand for the product that labor is producing affect the elasticity of demand for that labor?

■ SUGGESTIONS FOR FURTHER READING

Bergmann, Barbara R. *The Economic Emergence of Women*. New York: Basic Books, 1986. An argument for comparable worth made by the economist who chaired the Committee on the Status of Women in the Economics Profession of the American Economics Association for a number of years.

Leftwich, Richard H., and Ross Eckert. *The Price System and Resource Allocation*. 9th ed. Homewood, IL: The Dryden Press, 1985. Chapters 15 and 16 provide a standard treatment of factor markets at the intermediate level.

CHAPTER 15 ■

■

THE LABOR MOVEMENT IN THE UNITED STATES

■

INTRODUCTION

After looking at factor markets in theory, we now can examine the effect that unions have on the factor market for labor. Unions generally have goals that are social and political as well as economic. For the most part, U.S. unions have concentrated on economic goals and have pursued objectives such as high salaries, job security, good pensions, and, of course, good jobs for union leaders. The most important goal has been to raise wages, and we will concentrate on the effects unions have had on the wage rate. We will begin with a theoretical look at unions to determine how they attempt to raise wages. We then will look at the empirical evidence of the success of unions in raising wages and discuss at whose expense these increased wages have come. Finally, we will take a look at the history of the labor movement in the United States and examine recent trends in the labor movement.

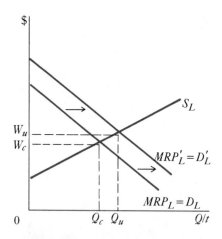

FIGURE 15-1
UNION GOAL—INCREASE DEMAND FOR UNION LABOR
One way in which a union can raise its members' wages above competitive levels is to increase the demand for union labor. An increase in demand from D_L to D'_L would increase wages from W_c to W_u. This increase in demand causes employment to increase.

THE ECONOMICS OF UNION GOALS

Unions have been formed for all sorts of reasons, many of which are social and political as well as economic. As we shall see later in this chapter, the only lasting U.S. labor unions are those that have concentrated on economic goals. When we speak of economic goals, the bottom line is the real income of union members. It is largely correct, though oversimplified, to think of unions as existing to increase the wages of their members. Unions do pursue goals other than wage maximization, such as shorter hours and better working conditions. These goals also have the effect, *ceteris paribus*, of increasing the well-being of union workers. If wages are unchanged and working conditions have improved, the worker has received an increase in real income. In order to increase wage rates in a competitive labor market, such as those shown in Figures 15–1 and 15–2, the union must do one of two things. It must either increase the demand for labor (such as to D'_L in Figure 15–1) or decrease the supply of labor (such as to S_u in Figure 15–2).

318

Increasing the demand for labor is very difficult for the union. Remember that D'_L in Figure 15–1 depends both on the demand for the product the labor produces and on the productivity of the labor. One way for the union to increase the demand for labor is by increasing the demand for the product the firm produces. Unions have run programs to influence people to "buy union-made" and to decrease imports, thus attempting to increase the demand for domestically-produced (union) products. Unions have encouraged educational training programs aimed at increasing productivity and thus increasing the demand for labor. The unions also have tried to persuade the government to help by buying union-made goods and also by using macroeconomic policy to increase the demand for union-produced goods. All things considered, however, it is very difficult for unions to increase the demand for labor. In some instances, unions have been successful in keeping demand from falling by forestalling the elimination of jobs in declining or dying industries. One approach is the practice of **featherbedding**, or insisting on required jobs that management claims are unnecessary or redundant. A good example of featherbedding is the case of railroad firemen. The advent of diesel and electric power made the fireman obsolete, but unions were successful in maintaining the job. However, even this kind of success may be only temporary because it speeds the decline of an already dying industry, and the decline of the industry ultimately weakens the union.

Because of the difficulties of changing demand, unions often work more on the supply side of the market, attempting to shift the supply curve, as from S_L to S_u in Figure 15–2. Historically, many of the "social goals" of unions also have had the effect of restricting the supply of labor. Unions have sought to reduce immigration, limit child labor, encourage compulsory and early retirement, enforce a shorter workweek, and enact minimum wage legislation. Whatever else you may think of these goals, they all make economic sense for unions if the goal is to increase the union wage rate.

Regardless of whether a union works on demand (Figure 15–1) or supply (Figure 15–2), it has the same effect on wages. In both cases, successful union activity will cause the wage rate to rise. The effect on employment, however, is quite different. An attempt to increase demand, as shown in Figure 15–1, will cause employment in the industry to rise. If, however, the union tries to decrease supply, as in Figure 15–2, employment in the industry will decline. Since unions are much more effective at reducing supply than at increasing demand, the first economic implication of unions is that they probably reduce employment in those markets that they successfully organize.

TYPES OF UNIONS

In examining unions from a theoretical point of view, we can reduce the different kinds of unions to two basic types, *exclusive* and *inclusive*. An **exclusive union** is a union that restricts supply and maintains a higher-than-competitive wage by excluding workers from the profession. Because of this exclusion, the wage rate is higher in that part of the work force than it would be in the absence of the union organization. Figure

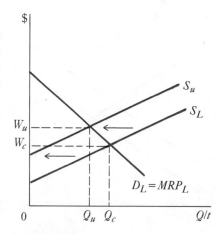

FIGURE 15-2
UNION GOAL—DECREASE SUPPLY OF LABOR
One way in which a union can raise its members' wages above competitive levels is to decrease the supply of labor. A decrease in the labor supply from S_L to S_u will cause wages to rise from W_c to W_u. This decrease in supply causes employment to decrease.

FEATHERBEDDING
The maintenance of jobs that management claims are unnecessary or redundant. Unions often insist on featherbedding in industries that are declining.

EXCLUSIVE UNION
A union that restricts supply and maintains a higher-than-competitive wage by excluding workers from the profession. Craft unions are exclusive unions.

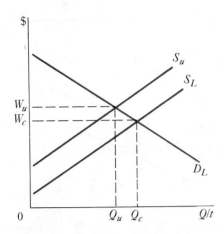

FIGURE 15-3
AN EXCLUSIVE UNION
In an exclusive union, union membership is a precondition for employment. As a result, the union can exclude membership and decrease the supply of labor.

CRAFT UNIONS
Unions composed of skilled workers, such as plumbers and carpenters.

INCLUSIVE UNION
A union that attempts to organize all the workers in an industry and maintain a strong bargaining position vis-à-vis management.

INDUSTRIAL UNIONS
Inclusive unions such as the Steelworkers, Autoworkers, and Teamsters that gain power by organizing all (or a large share) of the workers in an industry.

15–3 represents such a union. Supply Curve S_L represents the competitive supply of labor, and D_L represents the demand for labor. In the absence of any union organization, the wage rate would be W_c, and Q_c units of labor would be employed. The exclusive union attempts to exclude workers from the industry and thus shift the supply curve to S_u. If the union were to succeed in doing this, the wage rate for union workers would be W_u, and the number of workers hired would be Q_u.

The key, then, to an exclusive union is that it restricts entry into the profession. Examples of exclusive unions are **craft unions**, which are unions composed of skilled laborers, such as plumbers and carpenters. These unions very often require workers to serve apprenticeships and internships in order to become members.

It should be obvious that a successful exclusive union is very powerful because increases in the wage rate results directly from the exclusionary tactics. The union doesn't need to bargain, coerce, or threaten to strike. Its power to exclude competing workers is sufficient to cause the market wage to increase. The power of the union is difficult to challenge once the exclusion has been established.

It is difficult to exclude workers from the union. When wages rise, there will be pressure from other workers to seek employment in these trades. This natural economic force makes it necessary for the union to be able to control licensing. In particular, many successful exclusive unions find it easier if they can get the government to help them by requiring a worker to earn a license or permit to be a member of the trade. If the union can then gain control of this licensing function, it has an automatic way of excluding labor. This is one way in which plumbers and electricians have maintained their union power. Professional associations, such as the American Medical Association or the American Bar Association, have many of the same effects on the labor market for their members as do craft unions. Entry is restricted through licensing and control over professional schools.

The **inclusive union** is quite different in that it attempts to organize all the workers in a particular industry and maintain a strong bargaining position vis-à-vis management. These inclusive unions, sometimes referred to as **industrial unions**, include the United Steelworkers, the United Auto Workers, and the Teamsters. The goal of an inclusive union is to bring all workers in an industry into union membership and, as a result, present a strong bargaining position to management. Additionally, it is important that an industrial union organize most of the firms in an industry. Otherwise, nonunionized firms will enjoy a cost advantage and be able to undersell union-organized firms. This competitive disadvantage will create an incentive for nonunionized firms to try to break the union. Such union organization has been most successful in oligopolistic markets where there are fewer firms in which the labor needs to be organized.

The inclusive union is represented by Figure 15–4. The competitive wage and employment are W_c and Q_c, respectively. The union organizes the industry and bargains a wage, W_u. W_u has the same effect as a minimum wage in this industry, and employment will be Q_u. It should be clear that the ability of the inclusive union to raise wages depends on the strength of its bargaining stance, which will, of course, depend on its membership as a share of employment in the particular industry. It is important that an inclusive union have a significant membership in the particular industry in which it operates because its success depends on its ability to threaten the firms in that industry.

Bilateral Monopoly

The inclusive union has been most successful in industries that are very concentrated. The firms in these industries may possess monopsony power in labor markets. **Bilateral monopolies** are monopolies dealing with each other as buyers and sellers, such as a monopoly labor union selling labor to a monopsonistic firm. Such bilateral monopolies exist in the steel, auto, and farm machinery industries, where there are both big unions and big oligopolies. This situation is depicted in Figure 15–5. In the absence of the union, the monopsony firm would employ Q_f units of labor at a wage rate of W_f. The competitive wage and employment would have been W_c and Q_c. In the absence of monopsony power on the part of the purchaser, the union will press for a wage of W_u because the monopoly union faces a demand curve for its product (labor supply) of D_L. The marginal revenue of the union is thus represented by MR. The union maximizes its gains where MR is equal to MC or at a wage rate of W_u and employment level of Q_u. The result of this process is logically indeterminate; that is, the model will not theoretically explain what the resulting wage will be. All we can say is that the wage will be between W_f and W_u. Whether it is closer to W_f or to W_u depends on the relative bargaining strengths of the union and the monopsony firm. Note that if the wage is anywhere between W_m and W_f, employment with unionization in a monopsonistic industry will increase the employment over the nonunion level Q_f. The monopsonist hired fewer workers than would have been the case with competition. If the union is successful in bargaining a wage rate of W_c (the competitive rate), employment will rise to Q_c. You will note that this result is very similar to the effect of a minimum wage in a monopsonistic market, which was discussed in the last chapter.

Do Unions Raise Wages?

Regardless of the power of a union, there will be constraints on the degree to which it can influence wages. Competitive pressure from nonunion labor inputs and the possibility of substituting other factor inputs will always put limits on union demands. A good example would be a union organizing migrant workers. In response to higher wages resulting from the union, the farmer substitutes machinery for labor. A second powerful restraint exists in the product market. If unions raise wages, costs and prices rise. Consumers will react to the increased price and will shift consumption to nonunion products; the demand for union-made products, and thus for union labor will then fall. These constraints are always present, and the union can do very little to offset them.

Given these limitations, how successful have unions been in increasing the wages of their members? The difficulty in answering this question lies in separating wage differences based on productivity differences from those based solely on union power. The path-breaking empiri-

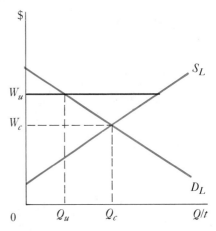

FIGURE 15–4
AN INCLUSIVE UNION

In an inclusive union, the union attempts to organize all labor in the industry and then to bargain a wage. This bargained wage works like a price floor (or minimum wage) in this labor market.

BILATERAL MONOPOLY

Monopolies dealing with each other as buyers and sellers, such as when a monopoly labor union sells labor to a monopsonistic firm.

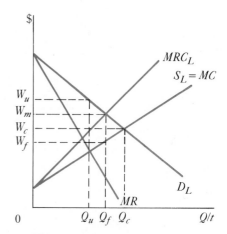

FIGURE 15–5
BILATERAL MONOPOLY

In a bilateral monopoly, a monopolistic seller, the union, sells labor to a monopsony firm. The wage rate will be logically indeterminate, depending on the relative bargaining strengths of the two participants.

cal study in this area was done by H. Gregg Lewis, then at the University of Chicago. Lewis based his study on data from the 1940s and 1950s. He found that union workers with similar productivity characteristics received on average from 10 to 15 percent higher wages than nonunion workers.[1] Later studies using Lewis's techniques and more recent data indicate that union salaries are 15 to 25 percent higher for workers with similar productivity characteristics.[2] These same studies also indicate that craft unions are more successful in raising wages than are inclusive unions.

In 1980, C.J. Parsley of the University of Guelph published an extensive review of empirical studies on the effects of unions on wages.[3] His survey for U.S. studies is summarized in Table 15-1. Parsley's review shows that wages are consistently higher in unionized sectors. Parsley, however, sounds an important warning note. He argues that the previous studies only showed that high wages and unionization were correlated. He argues that a correct statistical approach would show that wages affect unionization rather than unions affecting wages. In other words, workers may unionize after the wages are already higher. He points out, however, that his argument is paradoxical if laborers join unions because they believe that unionization affects wages!

TABLE 15-1
EFFECTS OF UNIONS ON WAGES

Author	Time Period of Data	Industry or Occupation	Effect on Union Wages
Lewis (5 studies)	1923–1958	Industrial Workers	0–25%
Throop (2 studies)	1950–1960	Selected Industries	25%–29.7%
Personick	1972	Construction	35%–70%
Personick & Schwenk	1971	Shirt Manufacturing	7%–16%
Ashenfelter	1961–1966	Firemen	6%–16%
Schmenner	1962–1970	Public Employees	12%–15%
Weiss	1959	Craftsmen—Operators	6%–8%
Stafford	1966	Various Occupations	–8%–52%
Boskin	1967	Various Occupations	–5.3%–24.7%

Source: C.J. Parsley, "Labor Union Effects on Wage Gains: A Survey of Recent Literature," *Journal of Economic Literature* (October 1980); and H. Gregg Lewis, *Union Relative Wage Effects: A Survey, 1986* (Chicago: University of Chicago Press, 1986).

Where do these higher wages come from? Your first reaction may be that they come out of business profits, but can this be so? Let's reflect back on the theory developed in earlier chapters. Wages are a cost of production. If markets are characterized by competition (pure or mo-

1. H. Gregg Lewis, *Union Relative Wage Effects: A Survey*, (Chicago: University of Chicago Press, 1986).
2. See M.J. Boskin, "Unions and Relative Real Wages," *American Economic Review* (June 1972); and P.M. Ryscavage, "Measuring Union-Nonunion Earnings Differences," *Monthly Labor Review* (December 1974).
3. C.J. Parsley, "Labor Union Effects on Wage Gains: A Survey of Recent Literature," *Journal of Economic Literature* (October 1980).

nopolistic), the increased cost will result in higher prices because in the long run, with or without unions, the average firm will only be earning normal profits. If the firm possesses some monopoly power, the higher labor costs might reduce monopoly profits, but part of the increased costs will be passed forward in higher prices. Additionally, regardless of the firm's market structure, the increased costs of union-made products will cause the quantity demanded of their output to decrease (below what it would have been without a union). The reduction in output in unionized industries means a loss of jobs in those industries so there are now more nonunion workers. Wage rates will fall in the nonunion sector. The supply of nonunion workers increases as the supply of union workers decreases. This analysis indicates that the increased wages of union workers are paid partly by consumers in the form of higher prices for union-made goods *and* partly by nonunion workers in the form of lower wages. Again, Lewis has done empirical research in this area and concludes that nonunion wages are 3 to 4 percent lower because of union-increased wages in the organized labor sector.[4]

Unions and Productivity

As we saw earlier in this chapter, if unions could raise the *MRP* of labor, the firm's demand for labor would increase and wage rates would rise. Increasing the demand for labor is difficult to do. The traditional view is that unions are not successful at raising worker productivity but in fact introduce inefficiencies that decrease the *MRP* of labor.

Examples of these inefficiencies are well known. We are familiar with work rules that require certain jobs be performed by certain workers. A light bulb can't be changed by a custodian because the work rules require that the job be performed by an electrician; or the display for a convention *must* be unloaded by a teamster. Earlier we discussed featherbedding, which would be another form of inefficiency. Still another way unions can introduce inefficiency into the economy is through disruptive strikes. Strikes cause production to fall, and strikes in major industries can even cause production to be disrupted in related industries. The third way unions introduce inefficiency depends on the wage-increasing effects we just discussed. If unions raise wages above competitive levels, they must restrict entry into those occupations, and output is lost in those industries.

These three arguments about union effects on productivity are widely held among economists. However, in a recently published book, Richard Freeman and James Medoff, both economists at Harvard University, argue that unions increase productivity because of the effect unions have on worker turnover.[5] They argue that unions give workers a "voice/response" mechanism that enables management and workers to iron out problems. This mechanism, they argue, "changes the employment relationship from a casual dating game, in which people look elsewhere at the first serious problem, to a more permanent 'marriage' in which they seek

4. Lewis, *Union Relative Wage Effects.*
5. Richard B. Freeman and James L. Medoff, *What Do Unions Do?* (New York: Basic Books, 1984).

to resolve disputes through discussion and negotiation." Freeman and Medoff go on to argue that this "marriage" produces more skilled, loyal employees who have higher levels of productivity. In fact, they argue, this increased productivity is between 20 percent and 25 percent higher in the unionized manufacturing sector of the U.S. economy.

Do Unions Cause Inflation?

We have just seen that unions cause wages to be higher in unionized industries and lower in the nonunion sector. We also saw that unions cause prices to be higher in unionized industries. But do unions cause inflation? The answer is *no*! Unions are only affecting the relative prices across industries—not the absolute level of prices. Of course, unions bargain for higher wages and businesses raise prices in inflationary times, but these are responses to the inflation, not causes of the inflation. In fact, the empirical evidence indicates that union wages rise less rapidly during the early part of an inflation than do nonunion wages.[6] This is partly because the unions are unaware in the early part of the inflation of how high the inflation will be. Even if unions correctly anticipate inflation, they may already have committed themselves to long-term contracts with wage increases less than the inflation rate. When these contracts expire, the unions try to make up for the inflation in their wage demands, and it sometimes appears as if they are responsible for the inflation, rather than the victims of it who are trying to catch up.

There are some indirect ways in which union activity can be inflationary. If unions are successful in raising wages above competitive levels in one sector of the economy, employment in that sector will fall. If the unemployed labor from that sector of the economy is unable to find employment in other sectors, unemployment rates will rise. Then, if policymakers pursue an expansionary monetary and fiscal policy to reduce the unemployment rate in response to union pressures, inflation might result. In this sense, then, unions may encourage an inflationary bias in macro policy.

A second way that unions might have an inflationary influence is through a successful effort to raise wages faster than productivity increases. Again, unemployment would tend to result, putting pressure on policymakers to pursue expansionary policies. Keep in mind, though, that unions and businesses do not cause inflation—government policymakers cause inflation through expansionary monetary and fiscal policy.

A SHORT HISTORY OF THE LABOR MOVEMENT

In the early 1900s, the U.S. economy shifted rapidly from a largely agrarian society to an industrial society. By 1910, employment in industry exceeded employment in agriculture. The industrial labor force grew rapidly, and labor organizers attempted to capitalize on this growth. In 1914, about 7 percent of the work force was unionized. Growth in the

6. See Albert Rees, "Do Unions Cause Inflation?" *The Journal of Law and Economics* (October 1959).

labor force and growth in unionization were accompanied by a rapidly rising real wage rate. The real wage rate advancement was largely attributable to rapid growth in technology and in the human capital of the wage earner. Both union and nonunion labor made substantial wage advances during this period.

The Early Unsuccessful Years

To better understand the labor movement in the United States, we must view it in its historical perspective. In the early 1800s, the labor movement was unsuccessful in organizing significant numbers of workers, although its operations were largely limited to eastern cities in the United States. During this period, the workday changed from a sunup to sundown situation to a 10-hour day. Workers still spent 12 hours on the job but received two 1-hour (mid-morning and mid-afternoon) breaks.

It became apparent by the mid-1800s that a coordinated national effort to organize labor was necessary if unions were to be successful. Even if labor could successfully raise wages above free market equilibrium wage rates in a certain area, the gains would be short-lived. Labor from other regions of the country would produce cheaper goods that could be shipped via the rapidly growing, low-cost transportation network. The U.S. Constitution forbids any interference with interstate commerce, so regions or states could not place tariffs on the goods imported from other regions or states. Thus, all or most of the labor in the firms of a particular industry had to be organized if unionization was to be successful.

The first successful attempt at organizing a national union was made by William H. Sylvis. Sylvis had been treasurer of the short-lived Iron Molders International Union and in 1867 founded the National Labor Union. The **National Labor Union** was involved in political action and espoused the eight-hour day, arbitration, and cooperatives, where union members owned the firms in which they worked. The union published a journal, *The Workingman's Advocate*, as a political voice. The union grew rapidly to a membership of 600,000 but quickly fell apart after Sylvis's death in 1869. Organizers learned an important lesson from the experience of the National Labor Union—the political environment of the time prevented reform legislation that would lead to labor advancement.

In 1869, the **Knights of Labor** was organized by Uriah Stevens as a secret society. The secrecy was to protect members from reprisals by management. As might be expected, the secrecy led to much suspicion and bad public relations and, as a result, secrecy was dropped in 1879. The Knights' greatest accomplishment was to win the first major strike in U.S. history. The Knights won a strike against the Wabash, Missouri-Kansas-Texas, and Missouri Pacific railroads, which were owned by Jay Gould, the personification of a capitalist robber baron. But by the turn of the century, the Knights had become unimportant as a labor force. The reasons for its demise were important for future labor organizations. The Knights' philosophical goal for political reform was to abolish the wage system and replace it with worker cooperatives. It thus had a reformist political agenda rather than "bread and butter" economic goals. These

NATIONAL LABOR UNION
The first successful union in the United States that had a national scope. Founded in 1867 by William Sylvis, the union quickly grew to 600,000 members but fell apart rapidly after Sylvis's death in 1869.

KNIGHTS OF LABOR
Organized by Uriah Stevens in 1869, the Knights of Labor was a secret organization. It won the first major strike in the United States against the railroad industry. The organization had political reformist goals, which led to its demise.

AMERICAN FEDERATION OF LABOR (AFL)
Founded by Samuel Gompers in 1886, the AFL was the first business union. The AFL was an exclusive union organized for skilled workers.

BUSINESS UNION
Samuel Gompers's description of a union that worked for economic goals without wanting to change or destroy the business organization or the political environment in which it worked.

UNITED MINE WORKERS (UMW)
The industrial union for mine workers.

WILDCAT STRIKES
Local strikes that are unauthorized by the national union.

political reformist goals, coupled with some unsuccessful large strikes and some violent cases of sabotage, contributed to the union's failure.[7]

The **American Federation of Labor (AFL)** was founded in 1886 by Samuel Gompers.[8] The Federation was primarily organized for the skilled worker and was an exclusive union movement. It also was the first business union, an approach that overcame many of the problems the earlier national unions had faced. A **business union** was Samuel Gompers' description of a union that worked for economic goals without wanting to change or destroy the business organization or the political environment in which it worked. Gompers was, above all, pragmatic; he set a single goal of economic gains for his union members, with no social-reformist goals. Gompers thought it necessary that national labor leaders be supreme and have sole authority to call strikes and control membership dues. This principle has remained important in the U.S. labor movement to the present day.

Business and labor are not always at odds. In some cases, union organization brings stability to an industry, and in other cases an oligopolistic industry may even use labor power to help monopolize the industry. Before the days of the United Mine Workers, mine operators had a very difficult time with labor because miners were (and are) a very independent lot. The **United Mine Workers (UMW)** is the industrial union for mine workers; under the leadership of John L. Lewis, it brought organization *and* discipline to labor. When Lewis ordered the miners back to work, they went back to work! In recent years, however, the United Mine Workers' leadership has not been able to exercise such strong control and **wildcat strikes**, which are local strikes unauthorized by the national union, have been frequent. The point is that management is not necessarily hostile to union organization. Unions and management often have worked together to lobby for reduced pollution control legislation, to curb imports, and even to urge tax cuts for business.

Having briefly examined these early unions, we can now sketch the labor movement in a more general historical framework. Early progress, as we have seen, was not rapid. This can be attributed in large part to the massive immigration of the period. The early hostility of management toward organized labor was understandable, since it was easy to break strikes and even labor organizations with the steady supply of young, healthy, and eager workers who poured in from Europe.

World War I and the accompanying prosperity marked the beginning of success for American unions. Membership increased steadily during this period, and the image of unions started to improve. Much credit for this is due to Gompers, who served on President Wilson's Advisory Commission of the National Council of Defense. Unions were, however, flexing their muscles during the war period, and there were many strikes in 1917. These strikes were largely a reflection of the war-

7. The Knights of Labor were linked to the infamous Haymarket bomb-throwing incident in Chicago in which seven policemen were killed. Eight anarchists were arrested. One was a Knight and the local union refused to expel him because of his involvement. This caused many people to link the Knights with the most radical elements of the labor movement, which was politically costly to the labor movement, as well as to the Knights of Labor.
8. Technically, Gompers founded the Federation of Organized Trades and Labor Unions in 1881, which is regarded as the precursor of the American Federation of Labor.

SAMUEL GOMPERS (1850–1924)

Samuel Gompers is often called the father of the American labor movement. Gompers was born in a very poor section of East London, England. He quit school after four years and was apprenticed to become a cigar maker like his father. When he was 13, his family moved to the United States and lived in a two-room tenement next to a cattle slaughterhouse in New York's lower east side. He continued his career as a cigar maker, leaving home at the age of 17 to get married. His wife and 14 children experienced much misery and violence because of his devotion to the labor movement.

Gompers joined the Cigar Makers' International Union and aided in the development of the local chapter. In 1874, he was elected president of the local. He was ousted seven years later by socialist opponents.

In December 1886, Gompers helped found the American Federation of Labor (AFL) and became its first president. By 1904, membership had grown to nearly two million. Much of the union's success was due to Gompers's abilities. Although in his younger days Gompers had been a radical, he realized that to succeed in America, the labor movement had to shed its radical-socialist image. Gompers worked hard to overcome the bad publicity for organized labor generated by the management of large corporations and fed by the activities and radical-activist tactics of other unions, such as the International Workers of the World (IWW). Gompers joined the National Civic Federation, an association of wealthy eastern capitalists, editors, professional people, and corporation officers. The National Civic Federation particularly emphasized that labor union strength did not undermine U.S. business and that strong business was good for labor.

Perhaps the best evidence of Gompers's success was his acceptance by the political establishment. He proved that labor leaders were respectable members of the establishment, not communist radicals seeking to overthrow U.S. capitalism. During World War I, President Wilson appointed Gompers to the advisory commission to the Council of National Defense, and in 1919, at the Versailles Peace Conference, Gompers served as chairperson of the Commission of International Labor Legislation.

generated inflation and booming labor demand and the effect this inflation had on long-term union contracts. In 1918 labor was successful in negotiating an eight-hour day and collective bargaining rights in exchange for a no-strike agreement. As a result, labor emerged from World War I stronger than it had ever been.

The postwar period brought increased inflation and more activity to increase wages via strikes. The **Industrial Workers of the World (IWW)** was an international union that organized steelworkers after World War I. These workers were unskilled laborers and thus not members of Gompers' Federation. The IWW had been associated with several prominent socialists and was regarded as a radical movement. At this time, the Russian Revolution and the fear of a worldwide Bolshevik revolution gripped the United States. The IWW subsequently went on

**INDUSTRIAL WORKERS
OF THE WORLD (IWW)**
An international union that organized U.S. steelworkers after World War I. The IWW was viewed as a socialistic organization in the United States, and this contributed to its demise.

strike against U.S. Steel and lost. The breaking of the strike was a major victory for steel companies, who successfully branded the union leaders as socialists who were attempting to overthrow capitalism. The breaking of the U.S. Steel strike had more significance than one would normally attribute to a single strike. The union's failure, coupled with the recession of 1920 to 1922, halted what had been a steady rise in union prestige and membership.

The 1920s proved to be a bad time for the labor movement. The Republican presidents, Harding, Coolidge, and Hoover, were probusiness, and business at that time was aggressively opposed to organized labor. The government sanctioned **yellow-dog contracts** in which the employee had to agree to refrain from union activity as a precondition of employment and which allowed the firm to discharge the worker for violation of the agreement. In addition, the courts were hostile to union activity. This hostility was apparent in the ease with which management was able to receive court injunctions. An **injunction** is a court order in labor-management disputes that is often used to order labor back to work. A section of the Clayton Act (1914), which had been hailed by Samuel Gompers as the Magna Carta of labor because it limited the use of injunctions against labor, was declared unconstitutional.

YELLOW-DOG CONTRACTS
Contracts in which an employee must agree to refrain from union activity as a precondition for employment.

INJUNCTIONS
Court orders in labor union-management disputes to order labor to stop some activity or return to work.

Success and Power

These bad times for unions were swept away with the election of Franklin D. Roosevelt in 1932. Roosevelt campaigned as the friend of the worker, and the legislation that was proposed and passed during Roosevelt's terms established the bond between organized labor and the Democratic party, that still exists today. The two key pieces of legislation were the Norris-La Guardia Act (1932) and the Wagner Act (1935). The **Norris-La Guardia Act** and the **Wagner Act** were laws passed that vastly strengthened the power of labor unions and set the stage for their rapid development. Jointly, the two acts gave workers the right to organize and made illegal any interference with this right.

Under the Norris-La Guardia Act, yellow-dog contracts were outlawed. Injunctions against unions and their activities were limited to unlawful acts, and businesses were required to engage in collective bargaining and to bargain in good faith. Thus, the most common union-bashing tactic of employers was thwarted by the Norris-La Guardia Act. Court-issued injunctions had been used to stop union strikes, boycotts, and other activities. The intent of the statute was to make the federal government neutral with respect to labor policy. Compared to past practices, this was a substantial stimulus to union activity.

The Wagner Act made it federal policy that every worker should "have full freedom of association, self-organization, and designation of representatives of his own choosing, to negotiate terms and conditions of his employment." The act also established the **National Labor Relations Board (NLRB)**. The NLRB was empowered to investigate employer unfair labor practices and to determine legitimate bargaining agents for labor when there were competing unions. This act was challenged in the courts and declared to be constitutional by the Supreme Court. Under

NORRIS-LA GUARDIA ACT
A law passed in 1932 that vastly strengthened the power of labor unions by limiting the court's use of injunctions in labor-management disputes.

WAGNER ACT
A law passed in 1935 that gave employees the right to organize and bargain collectively and outlawed certain employer unfair labor practices.

NATIONAL LABOR RELATIONS BOARD (NLRB)
Established by the Wagner Act (1935), the NLRB was empowered to investigate employer unfair labor practices and to determine legitimate bargaining agents for labor when there were competing unions.

these laws, private-sector workers were given the right to organize without interference from management. In practice, if organizers can get 30 percent of the work force in a particular place of employment to sign authorization cards, the NLRB steps in and conducts a vote. If the majority of workers support the union, the management of that company must recognize the union and bargain with it.

About this time, a debate was going on within the AFL concerning whether or not it should organize unions in mass-production industries such as steelworking, automobile manufacturing, and mining. The AFL was primarily an organization of craft unions and decided not to promote unions in these industries. As a result, a number of affiliated unions broke away in 1935 and formed the Committee for Industrial Organization. Shortly thereafter the name was changed to the **Congress of Industrial Organizations (CIO)**. John L. Lewis, the colorful, forceful head of the United Mine Workers, became the first president.

World War II and the 1950s

The wartime boom economy brought a number of serious strikes. The Wagner Act had given unions more legal power, and the coffers of union treasuries were full. Unions flexed their muscles and a wave of strikes causing substantial work stoppages followed. The unions were successful in achieving sizable settlements. But public sympathy began to shift away from organized labor and, as a result, Congress passed the **Taft-Hartley Act** in 1947, which was designed to reverse some of the labor excesses created by the Wagner Act. President Truman vetoed the act, but Congress overrode the veto, reflecting the antiunion political atmosphere.

The Taft-Hartley Act shifted some legal rights back to employers. **Closed shops,** in which workers were forced to become union members before employment, were made illegal. **Union shops,** in which union membership was necessary for a worker to remain employed, remained legal under the Taft-Hartley Act, but individual states were given the right to pass **right-to-work laws.** Right-to-work laws allowed people to hold jobs without belonging to unions. These laws obviously undermined union power. We saw earlier in this chapter that inclusive unions must organize and present a unified front if they are to be successful in bargaining with management. Right-to-work laws greatly undermined the ability of an inclusive union to present this united front.

Taft-Hartley also required unions to bargain in good faith, and featherbedding and secondary boycotts were outlawed. **Secondary boycotts** are union actions to stop one employer from doing business with another employer. A secondary boycott is more powerful than a picket line because it involves actions against and pressures on third parties. In other words, a union not only boycotts a certain product or firm, which would be a *primary* boycott, but it also boycotts firms (and their products) who do business with the firm the union has an action against. In certain instances, the president was empowered to call 80-day cooling-off periods before strikes. During this 80-day period, mediation is attempted by a government-appointed fact-finding board.

CONGRESS OF INDUSTRIAL ORGANIZATIONS (CIO)
An affiliation of industrial unions that was organized when the AFL decided not to promote unions in the mass-production industries.

TAFT-HARTLEY ACT
Passed in 1947 over President Truman's veto, the act was designed to reverse some of the labor excesses created by the Wagner Act. The Taft-Hartley Act shifted some legal rights back to the employers.

CLOSED SHOPS
Firms where workers must be union members before employment.

UNION SHOPS
Firms where union membership is necessary for a worker to remain employed.

RIGHT-TO-WORK LAWS
State laws that allow people to hold jobs without belonging to unions.

SECONDARY BOYCOTTS
Union actions to stop one employer from doing business with another employer. This involves action to create pressures on third parties.

MEDIATION
Third-party intervention in a strike. The mediator attempts to keep the parties together and talking by offering suggestions and clarifying issues.

ARBITRATION
A third party hears the arguments of both management and labor in a labor dispute, studies their positions, and renders a decision. In binding arbitration, the sides must abide by the decision.

AFL-CIO
The merged American Federation of Labor and Congress of Industrial Organizations. The merger took place in 1955 and gave labor a more unified political stance.

LANDRUM-GRIFFIN ACT
The act, passed in 1959, aimed at curbing union power; it made unions more democratic, restricted Communist party members and convicted felons from union leadership, and made picketing illegal under certain circumstances.

AMERICAN FEDERATION OF STATE, COUNTY, AND MUNICIPAL EMPLOYEES (AFSCME)
One of the few unions that grew in the 1970s. A union of public employees.

Mediation is third-party intervention into the strike. The mediator attempts to keep the parties together and talking by offering suggestions and clarifying issues. This procedure is distinct from arbitration. In **arbitration**, a third party hears the arguments of both management and labor in a labor dispute, studies their positions, and renders a decision. If the dispute has been submitted to *binding* arbitration, both parties must abide by that decision.

Union leaders fought the Taft-Hartley Act as a "slave labor law" every step of the way, and union leaders continue to campaign to reverse some of its provisions. Despite the Taft-Hartley Act, however, unions have continued to show great strength, which is enhanced by careful and well-organized political activity.

In 1955, the American Federation of Labor and the Congress of Industrial Organizations merged to form the **AFL-CIO**. This gave the labor movement a more unified stance under the leadership of Walter Reuther and George Meany. The **Landrum-Griffin Act**, passed in 1959, was a response to further public concern over union power and certain questionable practices. The act made unions more democratic, prohibited Communist party members and convicted felons from union leadership, and strengthened the Taft-Hartley Act by making picketing illegal under certain circumstances.

Since 1960

The 1960s and 1970s saw a decline in the unionized share of the labor force, partly as a result of the fact that the economy was becoming more service-oriented and less manufacturing-oriented. Thirty-five years ago, almost 40 percent of the U.S. labor force was unionized. Today, less than 20 percent is unionized. Some observers forecast that by 1990, relative union membership will be at the level it was before the wave of unionization in the mid-1930s.

One notable exception has been a dramatic increase in the membership of public employee unions. The **American Federation of State, County, and Municipal Employees (AFSCME)** was one of the few unions that grew in the 1970s. In the early 1970s, under the leadership of Jerry Wurf, AFSCME was politically active. However, in 1977 the union lost its first major battle in a confrontation with Mayor Maynard Jackson of Atlanta. The union's garbage workers affiliate struck the city of Atlanta. Much as in 1920, when U.S. Steel broke the IWW, Mayor Jackson refused to bargain with the local AFSCME chapter and hired strikebreakers. Unemployment problems in the city aided the strikebreaking, and the jobs were quickly filled. In August, 1981, President Reagan dealt the public sector union movement another blow when, in response to an unauthorized strike, he disbanded the Professional Air Traffic Controllers Organization (PATCO).[9]

9. For an up-to-date review of the public sector union movement see Richard B. Freeman, "Unionism Comes to the Public Sector," *Journal of Economic Literature* (March 1986).
10. Audrey Freedman, "What Has Happened to Unions?" *Bell Atlantic Quarterly* (Autumn 1985): 11.

The real-world operation of labor-management relations does not always run the way a review of the law would indicate. The NLRB is often slow to act and sometimes slow to rule in cases of unfair labor practices. The battleground of labor-management relations has shifted to the South where much of the new industrial growth in this country is taking place. It is also mainly in the South that right-to-work laws are found. Some observers attribute at least part of the faster growth of industry in the South to right-to-work laws.

There has been little in the way of new labor legislation since the Landrum-Griffin Act, except, for increases in the minimum wage. The Reagan Administration successfully fought increases in the minimum wage. Senator Kennedy proposed a boost to $3.85 an hour in 1988 and going in steps to $4.65 an hour in 1990. This would be the first increase since 1981. Labor has campaigned vigorously against some aspects of the Taft-Hartley Act, and these campaigns are worth watching. The two most important pieces of legislation that organized labor currently favors are (1) the repeal of right-to-work laws and (2) the common situs picketing bill, which grants any union the right to picket an entire construction job even when the union represents only a small part of the labor used on the project.

In late 1978, President Carter signed the Humphrey-Hawkins Act into law. The **Humphrey-Hawkins Act** was an amendment to the Employment Act of 1946 that set specific targets for output, employment, and prices. The original bill, which included public sector jobs to guarantee employment, was highly praised by organized labor, but the bill that finally passed Congress was viewed by many labor leaders as meaningless. The bill set national goals to reduce unemployment to 4 percent in 1983 and to cut inflation to 3 percent in 1983 and to zero by 1988. The bill

HUMPHREY-HAWKINS ACT
A 1978 amendment to the Employment Act of 1946 that set specific targets for output, employment, and prices.

SUMMARY OF LABOR LAWS

Statute (Year)	Major Provisions
NORRIS-LA GUARDIA ACT (1932)	Outlawed yellow dog contracts and made picket lines and secondary boycotts legal. Limited injunction against labor to illegal acts and required management to bargain in good faith with unions.
WAGNER ACT (1935)	Established right to form unions and set up NLRB.
TAFT-HARTLEY ACT (1947)	Made closed shops illegal. Permitted union shops but also allowed states to pass right-to-work laws.
LANDRUM-GRIFFIN ACT (1959)	Strengthened Taft-Hartley and made unions more democratic.
HUMPHREY-HAWKINS ACT (1978)	Set employment targets, but they were nonbinding.

defined full employment as the right of full opportunity for useful employment at fair rates of compensation for all individuals able and willing to work. The bill was regarded by labor as merely symbolic because it did not include any means to reach the goals specified, particularly more public sector jobs, but rather left them all to future legislation.

The 1980s

The situation of organized labor in the 1980s has been affected by President Reagan's policy toward the union movement. His first term was represented by antagonism toward unions, perhaps best exemplified by his dismantling of PATCO. President Reagan's appointments to the NLRB have reversed earlier NLRB decisions that were more favorable to organized labor. These new decisions began in December, 1983, when Reagan appointees gained a majority on the five-man board. The theme of these reversals has been to make it more difficult for labor to receive favorable rulings. For example, the NLRB ruled that all grievance procedures must be exhausted before an appeal to the NLRB is allowed and that the NLRB cannot force a company to bargain with a union unless the union proves it represents a majority of the workers.

The decade of the 1980s has been a period of decreased influence of union power. NLRB data show that in 1965, unions won 60 percent of the certification elections they held. In 1986, that number was less than 20 percent. This decline is the result of active policy on the part of industry to fight unionization, coupled with increased sophistication of labor consultants who advise industry on how to prevent union-forming activity. In 1987, the Bureau of Labor Statistics reported that union membership had declined by 2.8 million members between 1980 and 1986. This figure represented a drop in the unionized work force from 23 percent to 18.1 percent of the total labor force.

Nowhere is the weakness of the labor movement more obvious than in the recent wage settlements. In part because of increased pressure from imports, and in some sectors because of deregulation, companies sought lower wage contracts with unions in attempts to be more competitive. What evolved was a system of two-tier labor contracts. In these contracts, which were very popular in the mid-1980s, the union agreed to accept lower wages for future employees as a way of maintaining the higher salaries of existing members. These contracts created significant differentials in pay. A new pilot for TWA was paid $22,000, while a pilot with seniority on foreign routes was paid $110,000. The Giant Foods contract called for $6.96 per hour for "old hires" and $5.00 per hour for "new hires." The same type contract at Briggs & Stratton produced a differential wage of $5.50 per hour for new workers to $8.00 per hour for "old" workers. The strategy started to backfire on union leaders in 1987. They learned that new union members eventually become old union members, and they form powerful voting blocs. They pay the same union dues, and they resent being treated differently.

THE INTERNATIONAL PERSPECTIVE
THE FOREIGN POLICY
OF THE AFL-CIO

During the Reagan Administration, one would have thought from the rhetoric that the AFL-CIO and the president were the bitterest of enemies. After all, Reagan cut the budget of the U.S. Department of Labor and destroyed the union of the air traffic controllers when he fired more than 11,000 controllers when they went out on strike. But in foreign policy, the AFL-CIO and the President were strange bedfellows. In fact, in the year 1985 alone the AFL-CIO spent $43 million in 83 foreign countries, often on anticommunist projects. Many of these projects sound as if they came from a spy novel. A union in El Salvador complained that it was undermined by the AFL-CIO because it criticized Jose Napoleon Duarte, who was supported by Reagan. In another instance, a private group, *Prodemca*, supported by AFL-CIO officials, sponsored tours of the United States by *Contra* leaders.

AFL-CIO spending in foreign countries is done through four operating groups, The American Institute for Free Labor Department, The African-American Labor Center, The Asian-American Free Labor Institute, and The Free Trade Union, all of which are part of the AFL-CIO's International Affairs Department. In 1985 the four groups spent $43 million. This sum was almost equivalent to the AFL-CIO's domestic U.S. budget of $45 million that same year. The $43 million in expenditures were financed partly from union dues ($5 million) but mainly from U.S. government funds ($38 million). Most of the government funds were transfers from the U.S. Agency for International Development.

In 1984, $20,000 of government funds channeled through the AFL-CIO went to fund a union in Panama. The Panamanian union used the money to fund an election rally that featured the candidates supported by the military. The U.S. Ambassador to Panama, Everett Briggs, sent a cable to the U.S. State Department accusing the AFL-CIO of meddling in Panama's election. He wired that "the embassy requests that this harebrained project be abandoned before it hits the fan." One might wonder why the AFL-CIO has a foreign policy and moreover why that foreign policy is supported with U.S. tax revenue.

Source: *Business Week* (4 November 1985): 92–96.

The union movement in the United States faces severe challenges in the 1980s. Business is increasingly antiunion and is developing sophisticated antiunion tactics. The Reagan administration reversed labor's earlier favorable political treatment. Finally, the structure of the U.S. economy is changing in such a way that there are fewer jobs in the industries that have traditionally been unionized. Union leaders have been slow to grasp the implication of the changing structure and the internationalization of the U.S. economy. In 1988, only 26 percent of manufacturing workers were unionized, while 38.7 percent of transportation, communication, and public utility workers and 35.7 percent of government workers were unionized. In the private sector, only 15.3 percent of the work force was unionized.

Despite this change, many union leaders still think of themselves as representing "old style" unions. This attitude is reflected in an article by labor economist Audrey Freedman where she reports on an

AFL-CIO gathering she attended. The chairperson broke the attendees into two groups by saying: "The real unions—steelworkers, boilermakers, etc.—go into the room next door. Pantywaist unions—communications workers, teachers—stay here."[10] What we have seen in this chapter is that the "pantywaist" unions have grown, and the "real" unions have shrunk. Many labor leaders are unaware of or unwilling to accept this fact and have not come to grips with the fact that any growth in the union movement will have to come in the white collar and service trades.

The Broad Sweep

As the union movement developed in the United States, several motives for unionization were evident. These different motives are reflected in union goals. Some unions were **welfare unions** (the Knights of Labor) that had lofty ideals of social welfare and sought these goals by advocating an end to the wage system and the establishment of worker cooperatives. Other unions were **revolutionary unions** (the International Workers of the World) that sought changes in the social order. Still others were business unions (the American Federation of Labor) that eschewed social and political goals and sought only to better the economic status of their members. History indicates that it is this third type that has been successful and able to survive in the U.S. economic system.

The movement and the struggles of these different types of unions fit into three clearly identifiable periods. The early period from the 1700s until 1930 might be called the *repression phase* because of the hostility of the government and the courts. This was a difficult time for union organization and one in which the successes of unions were few and far between. The period from 1930 to 1947 might be termed the *encouragement phase*. Government support and key labor legislation greatly increased the power and prestige of unions. Unions reached their peak period of influence during this period. The period since 1947 and the Taft-Hartley Act would properly be labeled the *intervention phase*. Government has intervened in labor disputes, has taken away some of labor's earlier gains, and has attempted to put big business and big labor on a more equal footing. It is possible that we are now in a fourth stage where the basic underpinnings of the labor movement are in a state of flux, the membership mix is changing, and unions are being challenged by government at all levels.

FORCES THAT STRENGTHEN UNIONS

We can draw on what we have learned in earlier chapters to identify the economic forces that would work to make unions stronger.

Market power in the product market means that the firm has some degree of control over the price of its product. As a result, it has less incentive to fight attempts at unionization. One would therefore expect that unions would be more successful in monopolistic or oligopolistic industries.

The previous chapter discussed the determinants of the elasticity of factor demand. The elasticity of demand for union labor affects

WELFARE UNIONS
Unions that had lofty ideals of social welfare and sought to establish worker cooperatives.

REVOLUTIONARY UNIONS
Unions that sought changes in the social order.

the strength of the union directly. The more inelastic the product demand, the more inelastic will be the demand for labor and the stronger the union can be.

The share of labor cost in total cost is the second determinant of the elasticity of the demand for labor. The smaller the share of labor cost in total cost, the more inelastic the demand for labor will be and, as a result, the stronger the union will be.

Factor substitutability also affects factor demand elasticity. The fewer opportunities the firm has to substitute other factors for labor in production, the more inelastic the demand for labor will be and, again as a result, the union will be stronger.

FORCES THAT WEAKEN UNIONS

In a similar fashion, any factor that increases the competitiveness of the economy (decreases monopoly power) or increases the elasticity of demand for labor will work to weaken union power. These factors need little discussion because they are the reverse of the factors just discussed that strengthen unions. However, there are a few additional factors that have played an important role in recent years and deserve special mention.

Right-to-Work Laws

Twenty states, mostly southern and southwestern, have right-to-work laws. These laws, coupled with favorable tax laws, abundant labor supplies, and nice weather, have attracted a movement of industry from what has been called the "rust belt" to the "sun belt." This movement presents severe competition for unions and undermines their strength. The products that these largely nonunionized workers produce compete with union-made products and weaken northern, unionized firms. The unions have responded by attempting to unionize these workers, but firms in right-to-work states have successfully resisted these attempts. A recent examination of organizing activity in right-to-work states concludes that union organizing is reduced by 50 percent in the first five years after passage of right-to-work legislation and that union membership is reduced by 5 to 10 percent.[11] Table 15–2 on page 336 lists the states that have passed right-to-work legislation.

Deregulation

The increased deregulation of certain industries undermines labor union strength in those industries. This trend is most obvious in the transportation industry, which underwent significant deregulation in the early 1980s. Deregulation makes a previously regulated monopoly subject

11. David Ellwood and Glenn Fine, "The Impact of Right-to-Work Laws on Union Organizing," *Journal of Political Economy* (April 1987): 250–273.

TABLE 15-2
RIGHT-TO-WORK STATES

State	Year of Legislation
Alabama	1953
Arizona	1946
Arkansas	1944
Florida	1944
Georgia	1947
Iowa	1947
Kansas	1958
Louisiana	1976
Mississippi	1954
Nebraska	1946
Nevada	1951
North Carolina	1947
North Dakota	1947
South Carolina	1954
South Dakota	1946
Tennessee	1947
Texas	1947
Utah	1955
Virginia	1947
Wyoming	1963

to competition, and the deregulated firms may find it hard to compete if labor has previously bargained for higher-than-competitive wage rates. This change has been most startlingly evident in the airline industry. Prior to deregulation, $100,000-plus salaries were common for airline captains. Postderegulation airlines were offering much lower salaries. Continental Airlines, for example, declared bankruptcy, reorganized, tore up pilots' contracts, and offered starting salaries of $43,000. In addition, airlines moved pilots to 40-hour, 5-day weeks, requiring them to do administrative work when not flying. American West Airlines, one of the new carriers that entered the industry in the competitive environment, offered pilots $32,500 and received 4,000 applicants for 29 positions.

The lesson is an important one. Regulation protects monopoly and unions. Don't be surprised to see unions fighting deregulation.

Imports

Imports, like deregulation, undermine monopoly power and union power in some industries. The steel and auto industries are cases in point. The United Auto Workers has been successful over the years in negotiating wage contracts that are significantly above competitive wage rates. These high wages make the U.S. auto industry less competitive on world markets. Foreign autos are thus a threat to the union strength as they represent competition. As auto imports increased and auto profits fell in the early 1980s, the United Auto Workers found wage negotiations increasingly difficult. The unions and the automakers joined ranks and went to Washington to plead, successfully, for import restraint.

SUMMARY

1. Exclusive unions are more likely to be successful than inclusive unions at raising wages.

2. Evidence indicates that unions have been successful in raising wages and that this success has come primarily at the expense of consumers and nonunion labor, not at the expense of business profits.

3. It has been argued that unions add to productivity because they reduce employee turnover.

4. Whether unions contribute to inflation is an important question. Politicians blame labor unions for inflation, but the evidence doesn't support this.

5. Early unions had reformist political goals and were largely unsuccessful. When Samuel Gompers turned the American Federation of Labor toward strictly economic goals, he was successful. It wasn't until 1932, with the election of Franklin Roosevelt, that unions received active encouragement from government. The Norris-La Guardia Act (1932) and the Wagner Act (1935) greatly enhanced the power of unions. The Taft-Hartley Act (1947) and the Landrum-Griffin Act (1959) diminished the power and put unions and management on a more equal footing.

6. In recent years, union membership has declined as a percent of the labor force except in public employee unions, where it has grown.

7. The Reagan administration and its appointees to the NLRB have reversed several rulings favorable to unions.

8. Factors that enhance monopoly power and make the demand for labor more inelastic increase the strength of unions.

9. Factors that make the economy more competitive weaken union strength. Right-to-work laws, imports, and deregulation all fit in this category.

NEW TERMS

featherbedding
exclusive union
craft unions
inclusive union
industrial unions
bilateral monopoly
National Labor Union
Knights of Labor
American Federation of Labor (AFL)
business union
United Mine Workers (UMW)
wildcat strikes
Industrial Workers of the World (IWW)

yellow-dog contracts
injunctions
Norris-La Guardia Act
Wagner Act
secondary boycotts
National Labor Relations Board (NLRB)
Congress of Industrial Organizations (CIO)
Taft-Hartley Act
closed shop
union shop
right-to-work laws

mediation
arbitration
American Federation of Labor and the Congress of Industrial Organizations (AFL-CIO)
Landrum-Griffin Act American Federation of State, County, and Municipal Employees (AFSCME)
Humphrey-Hawkins Act
welfare unions
revolutionary unions

QUESTIONS FOR DISCUSSION

1. Do unions raise wages? If so, at whose expense?

2. Is there a difference in the way inclusive unions and exclusive unions organize an industry? Which is more difficult?

3. Explain the differences between closed shops, union shops, and right-to-work laws.

4. Suppose that César Chavez is successful in organizing the grape pickers in California. What will be the likely effect on the price of California wine? What will be the likely effect in the number of grape pickers employed? Does the fact that the United States-Mexico border is relatively easy to cross and that the supply of undocumented workers is relatively elastic have any impact on Chavez's organizing costs?

5. Has union strength in the North had any impact on business activity in the South?

6. Public unions have increased in strength, yet many states and the federal government forbid public unions from going on strike. Can you think of any reasons why this should be so? Is a police officer in Los Angeles any different than a bank guard in Los Angeles?

7. Is the American Medical Association (AMA) a union?

8. Unions are often simplistically viewed as simply bargaining for higher wages for their members. What other things do unions do?

9. In the fall of 1987, the Players Association of the National Football League went on strike. The strike lasted 4 weeks and was unsuccessful from the players point of view. Why?

10. How do unions affect the distribution of labor income?

■ SUGGESTIONS FOR FURTHER READING

Dulles, Foster Rhea. *Labor in America: A History*. New York: Thomas Y. Crowell Co., 1966. A well-written history of the early years of the U.S. labor movement.

Freeman, Richard B., and James Medoff. *What Do Unions Do?* New York: Basic Books, 1984. A study that claims unions are good for America because they increase productivity.

Hirsch, Barry T., and John T Addison. *The Economic Analysis of Unions: New Approaches and Evidence*. Boston: Allen & Unwin, Inc., 1986. An evaluation of the literature on the economics of labor unions. A good source of information with over 30 pages of bibliography.

Wendland, Michael F. "The Calumet Tragedy." *American Heritage* (April/May 1986): 38–48. A vivid historical account about union busting in Northern Michigan in 1913. The activity resulted in deaths and ultimately the making of a ghost town.

CHAPTER 16 ■
■

RENT, INTEREST, AND PROFIT

■

■
INTRODUCTION

In an earlier chapter, labor markets were used to illustrate the marginal productivity theory of factor pricing. There are, of course, other factors of production that generate income for their owners. Most of the points we have made will hold for these other factors. Firms demand the services of land and capital because land and capital are productive, the demand being derived from the demand for the product that they help produce. It would be a waste of your time to repeat the analogy between labor and the other factors, so instead we will discuss differences between these other factor markets and labor markets. In turn, we shall examine rent and interest, the payments to the ownership of the services of land and capital. We will conclude with a discussion of profits.

■ ■ ■ ■ ■ ■ ■
LAND AND RENT

The property income that has generated the most political interest in the United States is rent. To begin, we must define the concepts of land and rent. To the British economists of the 1700s and 1800s, *land* was the input in the productive process that was fixed by nature. Such assets as arable acreage, water, oil, and coal all would qualify as land. Recall if something is in fixed supply, its supply curve is perfectly inelastic, as in Figure 16–1. If the supply is perfectly inelastic, the price is determined by changes in demand only, which is known as a **demand-determined price**. In Figure 16–1, if the demand is D_0, the price is zero. As the demand increases to D_1, D_2, and D_3, the price rises to P_1, P_2, and P_3, respectively. These prices are called *rent*. We must, however, be careful with this term, which is defined as the payment for the productive services of land, not the price of the land itself. The price of the land would be the present value of the expected future flow of these payments for each year's productive services.

DEMAND-DETERMINED PRICE
If supply is perfectly inelastic, the price is determined by changes in demand only.

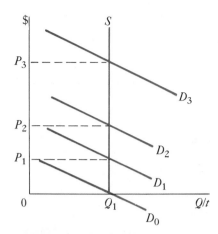

FIGURE 16-1
THE SUPPLY OF LAND
If the supply of land were perfectly inelastic, the price of land would be demand determined.

SINGLE TAX
A tax on land proposed by Henry George to capture the economic rent on land.

Economic Rent

The idea of rent can be generalized to apply to any factor. Economic rent is technically a payment greater than the amount necessary to bring the factor into productive use. In other words, in Figure 16-1, all the payments to land are rent because the amount Q_1 is fixed, and the payments don't bring any more land into existence. This market is different from the labor market supply curves earlier, in which higher wage rates increase the quantity of labor supplied, and the marginal workers entering the market do so only at the higher wage rate. The essential difference between labor and land in this regard is that humans have alternatives to work, such as leisure, which have utility.

The concept of economic rent is controversial because it is a surplus being paid to the owner of the factor of production. This surplus could be taken away with no change in economic activity. For example, suppose actor Harrison Ford's skills are such that he has only two work alternatives: being a carpenter and earning $35,000 per year or being an actor and earning $5,000,000 per film or $2,500,000 per year. Under such circumstances, he is earning economic rent. If the two occupations are equally attractive to him, he could be paid $35,001, and he would remain an actor.[1] We could then tax away $2,464,999 of his salary, and he would not change his behavior. An idea similar to this was suggested by Henry George as a method of raising money to conduct governmental activity.

The Single Tax

In 1879, Henry George (1839–1897) wrote a book entitled *Progress and Poverty*, which suggested a single tax on land. A **single tax** is a tax on land proposed by George to capture the economic rent on land. George's book was widely read; he may even be the best known U.S. economist of all time (if we measured this by the percentage of the population familiar with his book). George ran for mayor of New York City on the idea of his single tax and came very close to winning. He argued that the return to land was a *surplus* of unearned income and should be taxed away by the government. The proposal rested on two basic presumptions. First, the rent was unearned, and landowners were receiving the return simply because they held good land. If you think about this, it has political appeal. Why should someone get rich just because his or her grandfather happened to stake a claim on a piece of land that was located in a future population center? Second, the confiscation of this rent would not affect economic activity because the supply was perfectly inelastic. In other words, the tax wouldn't cause less land to be supplied, as an income tax causes less labor to be supplied. George became a social reformer and argued that this land tax should be the only tax that government collects. His followers became known as the single taxers, some of whom are still active today.

---

1. Competition for actors has kept Ford's salary above $35,001.

HENRY GEORGE (1839-1897)

Henry George may have been the most widely read economist of all time. George's book, *Progress and Poverty* (1879), was a best seller—it sold millions of copies. If measured by sales as a percentage of the population, George's book would be the most popular economics book of all time.

Henry George was born in Philadelphia in a lower middle-class environment. He had almost no formal education and went to sea at age 14. He ended up in San Francisco and became a journalist. His interests in political economy were fueled by his experience as a journalist. In California, George ran for the legislature but was defeated, in large part because of his strong opposition to state subsidies for railroads.

During this period, George was a devoted reader, and he turned his hand to writing books that combined economics and social commentary. Between 1870 and 1886, he published numerous books and articles, but *Progress and Poverty* brought him international fame. In it, George argued for a single tax on land because landowners contributed nothing to the productivity of the land. Rising land values were explained by general economic growth and westward expansion. George's single tax rested on the proposition that such a tax would not change the allocation of the land and, furthermore, that it was inequitable for landowners to get rich while people who did not own land remained poor. George argued that there was no reason that landowners should get rich by the simple economics of increased demand brought about by the westward expansion of the U.S. population. The increasing value of the land, George argued, was in no way determined or affected by the owners of the land. In this sense, George was arguing that the rising value of land was a "windfall" profit, much in the same way that President Carter argued that deregulation of oil creates "windfall" profits for holders of oil reserves.

George's book and his idea of a single tax made him immensely popular. In 1886, he re-entered politics. This time he ran as the Labor and Socialist parties' candidate for mayor of New York City. George was so popular that it took a major coalition of other parties to defeat him. He ran again in 1897 but died during the campaign. The Henry George School of Social Science, which still promotes the ideas of Henry George can be found at 5 East 44th Street in New York City.

Economic Functions of Rents

The single tax movement died for political reasons (landowners are a strong political force) but also because of some severe theoretical problems. First, one could argue with the proposition that the quantity of land is fixed. Remember, when we draw a demand or supply curve, we hold quality constant. It is possible for land to be improved in the quality dimension, thus increasing the quantity of land of a particular quality. Anyone who has seen agriculture in the Arizona or California deserts can attest to this fact. Increasing payments for land causes more land to be irrigated and increases the quantity of arable land supplied. If the return to land were taxed away, this incentive to improve land would be gone. Similarly, swamps can be drained and land can be reclaimed from the sea with dikes, as in the Netherlands. For example, several years ago there was a proposal to build a new airport near downtown Chicago. The idea was to build a dike in Lake Michigan, pump out the water, and build an airport at the bottom of the lake. Such projects would not even be contemplated if George's tax were operative.

Second, rents serve a very important function, even if they don't influence the quantity of land in existence. George argued that the rent the landowner receives plays no part in creating incentives for landowners to supply land. But the other side of the transaction is different. The payment made by the user of the land (the firm) rations the land between competing uses and ensures that the land is put to its highest valued economic use. For example, suppose there is a choice acre of vacant land near your school. What should this land be used for—a McDonald's, a massage parlor, a church, or a dump? In a market system, the decision will be determined by who is willing to pay the most. In other words, the market rations between competing uses for the land. If payments are not made, a universal planning system would have to be implemented to determine allocation among competing uses of the land.[2]

The Capitalization of Rent

Rent is an income flow to the owner of land in payment for its current use. Often, however, economists speak of the price of land as a lump-sum price at which title to the resource is exchanged. This is easy to do as there is a simple relationship between the value of a piece of land, or any resource, expressed as a lump sum or a flow. The market price of a piece of land is the capitalized value of the rent. **Capitalized value** is the present value of the stream of future rent payments.

CAPITALIZED VALUE
The present value of the stream of future rent payments.

The capitalized value is the amount of money that would earn the annual rent if invested at the market rate of interest. It can be calculated using the technique presented in the chapter on firms and production. Changes in the stream of rent payment will thus have an impact on the capitalized value. This has had a very visible impact on farmland in recent years. For a farmer, the rent from farmland is the income that is produced from farming that land. When farm income falls, the capitalized value of the farmland falls. In some midwestern states, the selling price of farmland fell by over 50 percent in the mid-1980s. To compound the misery for farmers, many of them had their land, which was falling in value, as collateral for bank loans.

Locational Rents

In the chapter on pure competition we discussed differential rent theory. The topic arose because firms in pure competition may appear

---

2. The perceptive reader will note that zoning commissions in part play this role in a mixed economy. To the extent that they don't allow the most economic use of a piece of land, they are taxing the owner's potential income from that land.

to be earning economic profits, but these returns are economic rents to resources owned by the entrepreneur. Perhaps the most basic kind of such a rent is a locational rent. If the seller of a good or service can locate so that the cost of transportation for customers is lower at the sellers location than at the competing location, the advantageously located seller can charge a higher price. If you could find out the location of the interchanges on a new interstate highway, you could buy the land and make a huge profit after the highway is announced. Ocean-front property has a higher market price than does land next to a sewage plant. An acre of land is more expensive in New York City than in Fair Play, South Carolina. These are all examples of locational rents.

CAPITAL AND INTEREST

The capital market is the market in which the capital factor of production is exchanged. The term is, however, used in a number of ways. Capital in its economic definition is the tangible equipment, the machinery and buildings, that is used to produce other things. In its popular usage, the capital market consists of those markets in which funds (money) for the purchase of the physical capital are borrowed and loaned.

Roundabout Production

People produce goods so that they can consume. In this sense, the object of all production is consumption. Nonetheless, it is apparent that even the most primitive societies produce tools for production so that they can ultimately increase their output and consume more. These tools are capital, and the production of the tools that enhance production is sometimes referred to as **roundabout production**. The capital goods that are produced are purchased, or rented by firms, as factors of production. The firm borrows the money to rent or purchase capital in the market for loanable funds.

The Demand for Capital

Firms demand capital because it is productive. We could derive a marginal revenue product curve for capital just as we did for labor. Such a curve is drawn in Figure 16–2. The difference you will note is that the demand for capital is expressed as a demand for funds to purchase this capital. It is important to realize that the demand for capital is not a demand for money itself but rather a demand for physical capital.

The price of borrowing money is the interest rate. In Figure 16–2, there will be higher rates of capital formation by firms at lower rates of interest. You can see this more clearly by examining Figure 16–3, which shows the firm and the market in the market for loanable funds. The supply of loanable funds comes out of business and personal savings. Firms accumulate funds out of profits in order to invest them, and individuals save in order to consume more in future periods. At higher interest

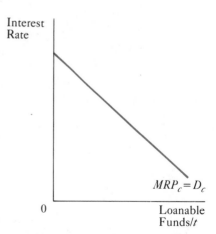

ROUNDABOUT PRODUCTION
The production of capital goods (tools) that enhance productive capacity and ultimately allow increased output.

FIGURE 16–2
THE DEMAND FOR CAPITAL
The marginal revenue product curve for capital is the firm's demand curve for capital.

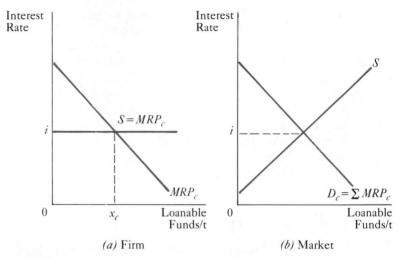

FIGURE 16-3
THE MARKET FOR LOANABLE FUNDS
The supply of capital to the firm is perfectly elastic at the interest rate set in the market for loanable funds. The firm then invests in capital until the marginal revenue product of capital is equal to the market rate of interest.

rates, people will save more because the present foregone consumption will allow greater consumption in the future. As a result, there is a normal upward-sloping supply curve.

In Figure 16–3, the market demand for capital is the summation of all the individual firm demand curves which are, of course, the marginal revenue product curves for capital. The market rate of interest, i, determines the supply of capital available to a firm in a competitive capital market. The supply to the firm is perfectly elastic at the market rate of interest, which makes the marginal resource cost curve perfectly elastic. We can then determine the amount of capital formation for the firm, which in this case is x_c.

Interest Rates, Inflation, and Risk

The analysis has proceeded as if there were only one rate of interest, which you know is not the case. The important question is: What interest rate are we looking at? This is one of the areas in economics where there is an important intersection between macro and micro economics, and in order to answer this question, we have to distinguish between the real rate of interest and the nominal rate of interest. Let's look at the nominal rate first. The rate that we observe, or the market rate, is the nominal rate. Of course, we don't observe just one interest rate. We observe a whole family of interest rates, depending on who the borrower is and how much risk the lender perceives there is of not getting interest and principal payments, as well as on how long the repayment period is. Short-term loans ordinarily carry lower rates than long-term loans. Risky borrowers pay more than safe, dependable borrowers. For this reason, when we are looking for a single interest rate to give us an indicator of how the market is doing, we generally use the U.S. Treasury bill (T-bill) rate. This is the rate the government, the least risky borrower possible, pays on its short-term borrowing.

Interest rates generally rise and fall together, so it's reasonable to pick out one important interest rate and use it as a proxy for the overall level of interest rates. The difference among rates, however, will vary over the course of the business cycle. As private borrowers begin to look riskier relative to the government as borrower, lenders will be more reluctant to lend to them and more inclined to buy T-bills. The rate to private borrowers rises relative to the T-bill rate. The difference between the T-bill rate and the rate to private borrowers for the same length of time is called the *risk premium*. Risk premiums vary from borrower to borrower, but they generally rise during recessions and fall during expansions.

The real rate of interest isn't observed. The real rate of interest is the nominal rate of interest minus the expected rate of inflation. When lenders set an interest rate, they consider inflation as well as risk. If prices are rising, the dollars they are being repaid will be worth less and less with each successive payment. They want to get back, not the number of dollars that they lent plus some interest, but the purchasing power that they lent plus some interest. Similarly, borrowers are making calculations on their side of the market of what a loan really costs them, considering that they can repay with depreciating dollars. Thus, an inflation premium will be included in the nominal interest rate.

INTEREST RATES RISE (FALL)

- When inflation increases (decreases)
- With riskier (safer) loans
- For longer (shorter) time periods
- When the demand for loanable funds increases (falls)
- When the supply of loanable funds decreases (increases)

Competition for Capital

The interest rate allocates loanable funds among competing firms and among competing uses exactly as the wage rate allocates labor services. If we expand on this idea a little, you can see why some economists are so concerned with the federal deficit. Consider the fact that there are more than just business firms demanding loanable funds. There are two other important groups in this market for loanable funds. Consumers demand loanable funds to finance the portion of their consumption based on credit. They borrow to buy homes, furniture, automobiles, and college educations. The other demander of loanable funds is the government. At all levels, federal, state, or local, governments borrow loanable funds. The market for loanable funds is, therefore, composed of three important segments which are added to give D_L in Figure 16–4. The market for loanable funds is represented by a supply of S_L and a demand of D_L, which is the summation of the household demand for loanable funds, the business demand for loanable funds, and the governmental demand for loanable funds. The resulting interest rate is i, and a representative firm adds x units of capital to its capital stock.

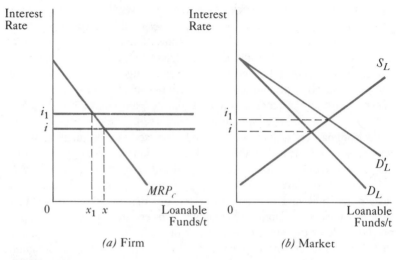

(a) Firm   (b) Market

FIGURE 16–4
CROWDING OUT
The market demand for loanable funds is composed of household, business, and governmental demand for funds. An increase in governmental borrowing will cause the market rate of interest to rise. The firms' response to this increased price of capital is to decrease the quantity demanded. We then say firms have been crowded out of capital markets.

What happens, *ceteris paribus*, when the government increases its borrowing? Government demand increases, causing total demand to increase to D'_L. The interest rate rises to i_1. This higher interest rate means that the supply curve to the firm has shifted up by the amount of the increase from i to i_1. The net result is that the firm will decrease its investment from x to x_1. The government has crowded some businesses (and households) out of capital markets. Interest rates allocate funds among the three uses, and when the government bids them up, households and businesses will get fewer of these funds.

Many political and business leaders are very worried about **crowding out**. They believe this crowding out is a very real burden of the federal deficit. They argue that the large amounts of borrowing by the government bids up the interest rate and attracts investment funds away from business. When this happens, business does not grow as much as it would have and the productivity of the economy suffers. Remember the preceding discussion of how increases in the capital stock raise the overall demand for labor. Crowding out would have the effect of keeping the demand for labor from growing as fast as it would have and, as a result, holding down the wages of workers.

CROWDING OUT
The increased demand for loanable funds by government causes the interest rate to rise, which attracts funds away from business investment.

Human Capital

Recall from the earlier chapter that discussed labor as a factor of production, you can view your decision to attend college in much the same way that a firm decides to use capital in the production process. By investing in education, you are investing in human capital skills that can be used in the future to generate higher levels of production for yourself. This human capital formation is an important aspect of training and an aspect

THE INTERNATIONAL PERSPECTIVE
MULTINATIONAL CORPORATIONS

A multinational corporation can be loosely defined as a corporation with headquarters in one country and plants in one or more foreign countries. The essential element is often defined to be direct ownership rather than simply financial interest in foreign firms.

Why would a firm go abroad with a production facility rather than export to that country or invest in a foreign local firm? After all, it is a hassle to deal with foreign governments and markets that are unfamiliar. It is difficult and costly to get managers to move to foreign countries for long periods of time. Capital theory suggests that the rate of return on investment abroad must be greater by enough to compensate for the additional risks and uncertainty. In fact, if capital markets functioned worldwide as efficiently as they do in the United States, and if worldwide product markets were competitive, there would be no economic rationale for the multinational corporation. Exporting would be one alternative. Portfolio investment, which transfers capital to foreign

local entrepreneurs whose knowledge of the local conditions give them an advantage, would be the second option. The existence of multinationals must therefore be explained by imperfections in product and/or capital markets.

The most obvious explanation is that free trade does not exist, and multinationals operate in part to penetrate high barriers to international trade. Other imperfections in product markets that can be used to explain the existence of multinationals are:

1. The investing firm may have patents and technology that it is unwilling to transfer without a great deal of control.
2. The investing firm may have a highly differentiated product, such as Pepsi Cola, which has some degree of monopoly power. The investing firm can only exploit its brand name capital through direct ownership.
3. The investing firm may have control over a raw material or other input which creates a limited degree of monopoly power.

In all three of these cases, direct ownership would provide the control necessary to exploit any monopoly power that might be present.

Recently, there has been a great deal of direct foreign investment by Japanese automakers in the United States. This investment can be explained by some of the imperfections discussed. First, there has been a great deal of "voluntary restraint" concerning auto exports by the Japanese. This means that they limit their exports because they are afraid the United States will impose even stiffer quotas. It is politically astute to build plants in the United States because this move dilutes the argument that jobs are lost to Japanese producers. In addition, the Japanese have production and management techniques that are unique. They also produce a differentiated product in that consumers view Japanese autos to be of very high quality.

that can be used to explain income differences between individuals. For example, why does a business major receive a higher starting salary than a sociology major? The reason is that the market places a higher value on the tools (human capital) of the business major.

ENTERPRISE AND PROFITS

Profits are a residual. They are what's left for the entrepreneur after the land, labor, and capital have been paid. This is not to say that profits are not important; indeed, as we saw earlier, the quest for profits makes them the prime mover of a market economy. If profits are above normal levels, it will be the signal for firms to enter the industry, and if below-normal profits are earned, firms will leave the industry. In addition, potential profits are the incentive for innovative activity and risk-taking. The entrepreneur takes chances and bets on the future because of potential profits. Henry Ford installed the assembly line because he thought it would increase efficiency and lead to higher profits. The profit motive drove him to be innovative.

The Source of Profits

As you saw when you studied market power, monopoly and restrictions on markets are a source of profit. Entrepreneurs will therefore be very likely to spend a great deal of time trying to monopolize their market. Indeed, much of the teaching that goes on in a business school is training on how to differentiate products, develop unique products, and finance acquisitions. All these actions are aimed at creating market power and generating profits. Any entrepreneur would choose to be a monopolist, rather than a firm in pure competition. There is, of course, nothing wrong with this. It is Adam Smith's invisible hand at work. Most monopolies will be temporary, because entry into markets will erode the success of any successful monopolist.

The entrepreneur engages in risky activities in search of profits. There is a great deal of uncertainty in the economy. The entrepreneur assumes all of the risk and is rewarded with profits for wisdom or luck. It is important to note the difference between uncertainty and risk. Many risks are insurable. You can buy auto insurance or fire insurance to protect yourself against risk because insurance companies are able to predict the average occurrence of auto accidents or fires with a great deal of accuracy. The entrepreneur is not assuming this kind of risk but rather uninsurable risks. These uninsurable risks are the uncertainties surrounding changes in demand and supply. Will a product sell and can it be sold for a price that is higher than the costs of production? If the answer is yes, the entrepreneur has made a profit for assuming the risk of the uncertain outcome. If the answer is yes, and other firms can be kept from entering the market, the entrepreneur now has two sources of profit.

The entrepreneur is also involved in innovation. If the entrepreneur can produce a product faster or more efficiently than any new or existing firm, profits will result. These innovations can be anything, including managerial techniques, that give the firm a cost advantage. If such innovations can't be patented, and they usually can't, they will quickly be copied by competing firms. Competition will force the entrepreneur to make new innovations, if profits are to be maintained. This race after profits gives the market system its vitality.

Are Profits Too High?

To much of the American public, profit is a four-letter word. It is often strung together with adjectives to form words with a distinctly negative connotation such as "windfall profit" or "obscene profit." This attitude about profit comes from a very common misunderstanding about how high profits are for U.S. corporations. A public opinion poll asked consumers how high they thought profits were in U.S. manufacturing.[3] The average consumer thought that after-tax profits were 37 percent of sales in manufacturing and that a 27 percent profit on sales in manufacturing was "reasonable." The profit level in manufacturing at the time of the poll was 3.8 percent of sales.

Profits play a very important role. They are first and foremost the "information signal" of the market system—the reward to entrepreneurs for organizing production, monitoring shirking, and coordinating team production. Profits also generate the incentive to innovate and strive for greater efficiency.

THE DISTRIBUTION OF INCOME

This chapter, in combination with the chapter on labor markets, has developed a theory that explains why the distribution of income is what it is. At its simplest level, the theory says that, given private property and competitive market conditions, a certain distribution of income will be produced. Labor will be paid according to its productivity, and the owners of capital and land will receive payments according to the productivity of the factors they own. Any event that causes the marginal productivity of a factor to increase will increase the remuneration that factor receives.

The theory that productivity determines factor income has received much criticism since it was first developed by John Bates Clark, who was looking for a natural law to explain how the distribution of income was determined. The criticisms of the theory have almost all been on the grounds of **distributive justice**, which involves normative arguments for a particular distribution of income. Critics argue that such a market system of income distribution is unfair because the old, the sick, the young, and the handicapped, among others, will not receive a fair share since they are not as productive as others. Another normative criticism of the theory rests on the premise that economic productivity, rather than social productivity, determines remuneration. A writer of pornographic novels earns more than a writer of poetry. Some critics say this is undesirable. You

DISTRIBUTIVE JUSTICE
Normative arguments for a particular distribution of income.

3. Opinion Research Corporation, "Public Attitudes Toward Corporate Profits," *Public Opinion Index* (August 1983).

should recognize such criticisms for what they are: normative, ethical considerations and not positive criticisms of the theory. Think back to our early discussion of the role of theory. A theory that is valuable provides a good explanation of some aspect of the real world. According to this test, marginal productivity theory stands up quite well.[4]

SUMMARY

1. Land is the factor of production that is in fixed supply. Rent is the return to this fixed factor. Economic rent is a payment above the amount necessary to attract an input into a given use.
2. Henry George proposed a single tax on land. One important economic difficulty with this proposal is that if rents aren't paid, a planning authority would have to decide among competing uses of the land.
3. Capital represents roundabout production.
4. Capital, like the other factors of production, is demanded by firms because it is productive. The payment to capital is interest. As interest rates rise, the quantity of capital that the firm demands will decrease.
5. When an increase in the interest rate is a result of government borrowing, we say that crowding out is taking place in capital markets.
6. Human capital is the skills, training, and education that are embodied in some individuals. It is a form of roundabout production because it is formed by investment.
7. Profits are a residual that entrepreneurs receive. They can come from monopoly power, uncertainty, and innovation. In a market economy, profits serve as the signal for firms to either enter or leave a particular industry.
8. Marginal productivity theory explains how the distribution of income is determined in a market economy. It says nothing about the normative appropriateness of this distribution.

NEW TERMS

demand-determined price
single tax

capitalized value
roundabout production

crowding out
distributive justice

QUESTIONS FOR DISCUSSION

1. What is economic rent? Have you ever earned economic rent? Would taxation of this rent have caused you to behave differently?
2. What does it mean to say profits are a residual?
3. Is there any similarity between the concept of economic rent and economic profit?
4. Why is the interest rate called the price of borrowing money?
5. Third world countries often complain that they are "ripped off" by multinational corporation because these corporations earn excessively high profits in their countries when compared to their profits in home countries? Can you think of any economic explanation for these higher profits?
6. When major airports are built in rural areas it often happens that commercial and residential buildings spring up around them. The housing prices are often lower than comparable houses in other areas. Why? If the residents band together and force planes to follow noise abatement procedures or follow different landing patterns, What is likely to happen? What does this represent to the homeowners?
7. Why does the activity of zoning boards in city and county governments elicit such strong feelings and often stormy meetings?

4. For a review of empirical studies of marginal productivity theory, see David Kamerschen, "A Reaffirmation of the Marginal Productivity Theory," *Rivista Internazionale Di Scienze Economiche e Commerciali* (March 1973).

8. What does an entrepreneur do?

9. If your college raised its tuition by $1, would you drop out of school? If it raised tuition $1000 would

you drop out? How about $10,000?

10. What is meant by distributive justice?

SUGGESTIONS FOR FURTHER READING

Lindholm, Richard W., and Arthur D. Lynn. *Land Value Taxation: The Progress and Poverty Centenary*. Madison: University of Wisconsin Press, 1982. This volume includes papers presented at a symposium commemorating the 100th anniversary of Henry George's *Progress and Poverty*. Many, but not all, of the papers are by present-day economists who support George's view.

Herbert, Robert F., and Albert N. Link. *The Entrepreneur*. New York: Praeger Publishers, 1982. A good source of ideas about what it takes to be a successful entrepreneur.

Aaker, David A., and Robert Jacobson. "The Role of Risk in Explaining Differences in Profitability," *Academy of Management Journal* 30, (June 1987). A recent study that shows that risk, systematic and unsystematic, has significant impacts on return on investment.

CHAPTER 17 ■

■

INCOME DISTRIBUTION: POVERTY, DISCRIMINATION, AND WELFARE

■

INTRODUCTION

No single topic in economics generates more controversy than the distribution of income and government policies to redistribute it. The market generates an unequal distribution of income. The government is a powerful tool for redistribution, although government does not always redistribute from the rich to the poor. This chapter examines the actual distribution of income, the measures of income distribution and poverty, the effects of labor market discrimination, and the role of government in redistributing income.

Income redistribution through government pits one group (taxpayers) against another group (recipients). There is less resistance by taxpayers to income redistribution in a high growth economy. Society can provide for the poor, the elderly, and other groups out of growing income and output. When economic growth is slow, however, redistribution to some means a reduced share for others. Slow economic growth makes the debate over how and how much to redistribute income much more intense. In the last decade, slow growth focused attention on two controversial forms of redistribution: Social Security, which redistributes income primarily from workers to retired persons, and welfare programs, which are a perennial candidate for reform.

INCOME DISTRIBUTION AND THE MARKET

The initial distribution of income in a market economy is determined by prices paid to factors of production, especially to labor. Wages are the largest component of income. However, other sources of income—rent from land, interest on capital, and profit for enterprise—often make the difference between an average income and a prosperous one.

Assume that the market for the factors of production (land, labor, capital, and enterprise) is perfectly competitive. What would determine the *laissez-faire* distribution of income, and is this a just or equitable solution? Economic theory offers an unambiguous and positive answer to the first question, as we discussed in an earlier chapter. The marginal productivity theory of income distribution analyzes how factor incomes change in response to changing market conditions. The second question is a normative one. The distribution of income arising from the market may not be judged satisfactory. Decisions about changing the distribution of income involve value judgments about the "needs" of certain groups, or the "deserving" or "undeserving" poor, as well as some positive considerations about the effects of redistribution on incentives.

The pattern of payments to the factors of production (rent, wages, interest, and profits) is called the **functional distribution of income**. This distribution (shown in Table 17–1) is determined by the supply of and demand for factors of different kinds and qualities. Wages and salaries are the largest single component of income and have increased in relative importance throughout the twentieth century.

FUNCTIONAL DISTRIBUTION OF INCOME
The pattern of payments to the factors of production: rent, wages, interest, and profits.

TABLE 17–1
THE FUNCTIONAL DISTRIBUTION OF INCOME

Average Percent Share for Decade Ending

	Wages and Salaries	Proprietors' Income	Corporate Profits	Interest	Rent
	■	■	■	■	■
1920	60.0	17.5	7.8	6.2	7.7
1940	64.6	17.2	11.9	3.1	3.3
1960	69.9	11.9	11.2	4.0	3.0
1980	75.9	7.1	8.4	6.4	2.2
1987	72.8	9.0	8.4	9.3	0.5

Source: 1920 to 1980 data adapted from Irving Kravis. "Income Distribution: Functional Share." *International Encyclopedia of Social Sciences*, Vol. 7: 1987 data from *Economic Indicators* (Washington D.C.: U.S. Government Printing Office, February, 1988.)

The demand for factors of production is derived from the demand for goods and services that the factors are used to produce. The value of any productive resource depends on the value of what it produces. Differences in factor incomes result from differences in productivity of factors and in the demand for the final products they are used to produce.

Given factor inputs of equal physical productivity, the highest reward will go to those factors employed in the industry whose products are most highly valued in the market. The return to the factor will also be affected by the physical productivity of the other productive inputs with which it is combined. Thus, it is possible that labor (or other factors) of equal quality will receive different earnings when combined with different amounts and qualities of other factors of production.

Examples of productivity-related differences in factor earnings are easy to find. A piece of land near a new interstate highway will be more valuable than a comparable piece of land elsewhere because of its location. An engineer employed in a firm with a highly successful new product might receive a higher salary than an equally skilled engineer in another firm. A quarterback on a winning NFL team might receive a higher salary because he was at the right place at the right time with the right set of teammates.

An important advantage of letting the market determine income distribution is that market rewards are linked to efficiency in resource allocation. *Ceteris paribus*, factors flow to those employments with the highest rewards, that is, those in which their productivity is most highly valued. Such a system rewards and thus encourages higher productivity. In freely operating markets, the return to factors of equal productivity will tend toward equality. Over time, factors will tend to transfer to their highest valued use.

The market-determined distribution of income may be unsatisfactory in other ways, however. Not only is the market income distribution very unequal, but it also involves substantial elements of chance. Most individuals will avoid risk unless they can be compensated for assuming it. An individual's future income is subject to a considerable degree of uncertainty. Most of this uncertainty cannot be shifted or avoided through private market methods. Risk aversion reduces the efficiency of allocation of productive inputs, especially labor. This situation creates a demand for government programs to reduce income uncertainty. Government may respond either by reducing the risk itself or by implementing various types of insurance plans. Reduction in income risk can take the form of education programs, various types of job security, mandating private pension and disability programs to protect workers, or programs to guarantee jobs. Such risk-reducing plans include Social Security, unemployment insurance, and welfare, all of which were instituted in the 1930s and are collectively known as the "social safety net."

Measuring the Distribution of Income

The functional distribution of income is one measure of distribution. Another way of describing income distribution is according to how it is divided, equally or unequally, among individuals or households. This measure is called the **personal distribution of income**. A **Lorenz curve** is a graph showing the cumulative percentage of income that households receive, ranked from the lowest to the highest.

Figure 17–1 shows Lorenz curves for three hypothetical economies. A perfectly egalitarian society would have a Lorenz curve represented by Distribution *A*. If incomes were absolutely uniformly distributed, the lowest 10 percent of the households would have 10 percent of the income, the highest 20 percent would have 20 percent, and so on. When household incomes are not identical, the Lorenz curve diverges from the 45-degree line of perfect equality. Distribution *B* in Figure 17–1 represents a less egalitarian society. The greater the difference between the 45-degree line and the Lorenz curve, the greater the inequality in the income distribution. In terms of Figure 17–1, Distribution *C* represents more inequality than Distribution *B*.

Lorenz curves for different countries can be used to compare levels of income inequality. Sweden's Lorenz curve comes fairly close to

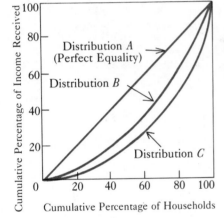

FIGURE 17-1
LORENZ CURVES
A Lorenz curve traces the cumulative percentage of income households receive, ranked from lowest to highest. A perfectly egalitarian society would have a Lorenz curve represented by Distribution *A*. Distributions *B* and *C* represent more unequal distributions of income.

PERSONAL DISTRIBUTION OF INCOME
The distribution of income by person or family.

LORENZ CURVE
A graph showing the cumulative percentages of income that households receive, ranked from the lowest to the highest.

the 45-degree line, while countries in the underdeveloped world tend to be most skewed from the 45-degree line. Lorenz curves can also be used to describe how the distribution of income changes over time. The data in Table 17–2 for 1929 and 1986 are graphed as Lorenz curves in Figure 17–2. Both Table 17–2 and Figure 17–2 indicate that the U.S. income distribution has become more equal since 1929.

TABLE 17-2
INCOME DISTRIBUTION IN THE UNITED STATES, 1929–1986

Income Class	Percentage of Income						
	1929	1947	1960	1972	1979	1983	1986
Lowest Fifth	3.5	5.1	4.8	5.4	5.3	4.7	4.6
Second Fifth	9.0	11.8	12.2	11.9	11.6	11.1	10.9
Middle Fifth	13.8	16.7	17.8	17.5	17.5	17.1	16.9
Fourth Fifth	19.3	23.2	24.0	23.9	24.1	24.4	24.2
Highest Fifth	54.4	43.3	41.3	41.4	41.6	42.7	43.5
Highest 5%	30.0	17.5	15.9	15.9	15.7	15.8	16.7

Source: 1929 to 1983 data, U.S. Department of Commerce, Bureau of the Census, *Statistical Abstract of the United States* (Washington, D.C.: U.S. Government Printing Office, 1987); 1986 data from *Money Income of Households, Families, and Persons in the United States: 1986,* Current Population Reports Series P-50, no. 156 (Washington, D.C.: U.S. Government Printing Office, August 1987).

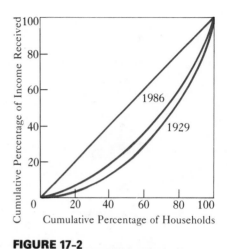

FIGURE 17-2
INCOME DISTRIBUTION IN THE UNITED STATES, 1929 and 1986
Plotting Lorenz curves for the United States for 1929 and 1986 shows that the distribution of income has become more equal.

Information displayed in a Lorenz curve must be interpreted with caution for two reasons. First, Lorenz curves describe the *relative* distribution of income among persons or households. A particular Lorenz curve might indicate that the lowest 20 percent of the households have only 5 percent of the income, but it doesn't say if this amount of income is high or low in an *absolute* sense. This 5 percent could be high enough so that everyone is well fed, well housed, and well clothed. A Lorenz curve only shows the degree of inequality; by itself, it does not measure either wealth or poverty.

Second, Lorenz curves show how income is distributed among households at a given time. If the households that are in the lowest 10 percent change over time, the Lorenz curve will give an unrealistic impression of relative poverty. The typical household income changes in a predictable fashion over time. Income tends to be low when wage earners are young, increases as they reach middle age, and declines in retirement. This life-cycle income pattern means that households will move around in the income distribution over their lifetimes.[1] The Lorenz curve only shows a cross-section at a particular time and therefore may make income inequality appear greater than it actually is over time.

1. Morton Paglin of Portland State University found that when life-cycle changes were taken into account, there was about 50 percent less inequality than would be inferred from simple aggregate income distribution Lorenz curves. Further, Paglin found that adjusting for life-cycle changes revealed a significant trend toward a more equal distribution of income in the United States. See Morton Paglin, "The Measurement and Trend of Inequality: A Basic Revision," *American Economic Review* (September 1975): 598–609.

One useful source of information on the behavior of income distribution over time is the Panel Study on Income Dynamics from the Institute for Social Research at the University of Michigan. This group has followed the income and employment history of 5,000 U.S. families since 1968. Their data show considerable mobility among income levels. For example, of those who were at the top or the bottom of the income scale in 1971, only about half were in the same relative position in 1968. Changes in family composition—births, deaths, divorces, marriages, and children leaving home—had the largest influence on relative economic well-being, lending support to the life-cycle view of income distribution.[2] Their data suggests that the poor may not all be caught in a poverty trap, but rather that many are temporarily rather than permanently poor.

■ Measuring Poverty

Income distribution is not just a relative question. Starvation, malnutrition, and disease suggest that poverty has an absolute meaning as well. Determining the level of income that delineates the border between poverty and nonpoverty is difficult, because poverty is both absolute and relative. People who are relatively poor in one country may be well off by the standards of another country or by the standards of the same country in earlier time periods.

The U.S. government first established an official definition of poverty in 1964. The original poverty income definition was based on the cost of a minimally adequate diet. This figure was then multiplied by three, since the typical fraction of income spent on food was one-third of family income. In 1964, the poverty level for a family of four was $3,000 ($1,000 for food × 3). In 1986, the official poverty income level was defined as income below $5,469 for a single individual and $10,979 for a family of four.

While the poverty threshold has been adjusted each year for inflation, no adjustment has been made for real income growth or for relative poverty. As a consequence, the poverty threshold has fallen from 44 percent of the median family income in 1964 to 33 percent of the median family income in 1986.

Table 17–3 shows that from 1959 to 1979, the fraction of the population below the poverty level decreased. Cuts in social programs and high unemployment rates reversed that trend in the early 1980s, but by 1986 the poverty rate was almost back at the 1980 level.

The poverty measure has been criticized because it only measures poverty after *cash* transfer payments such as Social Security, unemployment compensation, and Aid to Families with Dependent Children. Since 1965, an increasing fraction of programs for the poor have taken the form of *in-kind* transfers. In 1983, the Bureau of the Census reestimated the poverty rate by counting as income the estimate cash equivalent value of three major in-kind programs: food stamps, housing assistance, and

2. Greg Duncan et al., *Years of Poverty, Years of Plenty: The Changing Economic Fortunes of American Workers and Families* (Ann Arbor, MI: Institute for Social Research, 1984).

TABLE 17-3
PERCENTAGE OF POPULATION WITH INCOMES
BELOW THE POVERTY THRESHOLD, 1959-1986

Year	Percent
■	■
1959	22.4%
1970	12.6
1975	12.3
1980	13.0
1983	15.2
1984	14.4
1985	14.0
1986	13.6

Source: U.S. Department of Health, Education, and Welfare, *Social Security Bulletin, Annual Statistical Supplement* (Washington, D.C.: U.S. Government Printing Office, 1987).

Medicare. Their adjustments produced a poverty rate of 6.8 percent in 1979 and 10 percent in 1983.[3]

The poverty rate is a rather crude measure of poverty or changes in poverty because this number gives no indication of *how* poor these people are. A person whose income is $1 below the threshold is counted as poor along with a person who is $3,000 below the threshold. If cash transfers bring the first person's income up by $2, the poverty rate falls; but if transfer payments raise the second person's income by $2,000, the poverty rate is unchanged. Nevertheless, poverty data are some indication of how much poverty exists and how it changes over time.

Who Are the Poor?

The poor come from everywhere and from every age group. However, it may be possible to pinpoint certain social, geographic, and racial characteristics of the poor. Geographically, for example, the poor tend to live in the rural south and in northern cities.

Table 17–4 points out some other important characteristics of people below the poverty line. Almost 12 percent of all persons fell below the poverty line in 1985. However, the poverty rate is above 15 percent for certain segments of the population. Nonwhites are much more likely to be poor. Age is an important variable; children represent a sizable fraction of those below the poverty level. In fact, the problem of poverty has shifted from the elderly to being overwhelmingly a problem of female-headed households with small children.

Nonwhites are more likely to be poor than whites. In addition to discrimination, nonwhites are more likely to be under 17, to have less education, or to live in female-headed households. Whatever the cause of

3. U.S. Department of Commerce, Bureau of the Census, Technical Report no. 51, *Estimates of Poverty Including the Value of Noncash Benefits: 1979 to 1982*; and Technical Report no. 52, *Estimates of Poverty Including the Value of Noncash Benefits: 1983* (Washington, D.C.: U.S. Government Printing Office).

TABLE 17-4
POVERTY INCIDENCE, 1985

Characteristics		Percentage Who Fall Below the Poverty Line
All Persons		11.8%
Adult male in household		8.9%
No adult male (female-headed household)		33.4
Household head under 24 yrs.		30.2
—and black	62.1%	
Household head 65 and over		7.0
—and black	22.0	
Households with children under 18		
One child		10.2
Two children		12.8
Three children		18.0
Four children		25.8
No education		32.8
Less than 8 years schooling		24.1
High school graduate		7.9
Some college		3.1
Employed		5.6
Unemployed		30.6
Not in labor force		16.0

Source: U.S. Department of Commerce, Bureau of the Census, *Money Income and Poverty Status of Families and Persons in the U.S., 1985* (Washington, D.C.: U.S. Government Printing Office, 1987).

race-related poverty, Figure 17–3 shows that the nonwhite-white income differential has shown little improvement for males but remarkable gains for black females (white females, however, only earn about 60 to 65 percent of the annual earnings of white males). After some interim improvement, the black/white income ratio was about the same for males in 1985 as it was in the late 1950s. One encouraging sign is that the educational achievement of nonwhites has been increasing, which should eventually be reflected in higher income levels. Professor Thomas Sowell argues that monetary returns to education are much higher for minority individuals than for nonminority individuals.[4]

DISCRIMINATION AND THE DISTRIBUTION OF INCOME

The poor are overwhelmingly black and female. How big a role does discrimination play in income distribution? Since the Civil Rights

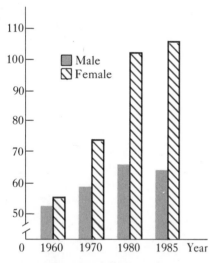

Mean Nonwhite Income as a Percent of Mean White Income

Source: Reynold Farley, "Assessing Black Progress: Employment, Occupation, Earnings, Income, Poverty," *Economic Outlook U.S.A.* (1986)13: 14–19.

FIGURE 17-3
NONWHITE-WHITE INCOME RATIOS

Despite some increases in the 1970s, the nonwhite-white income ratio for males improved only moderately between 1960 and 1985; the improvement for nonwhite females, however, was dramatic.

4. See Thomas Sowell, *Race and Economics* (New York: David McKay Co., 1975).

Act of 1964, discrimination in employment has been illegal. Many companies, in part to show their compliance with federal law, embarked on aggressive affirmative action programs in the 1970s. Yet black-white and male-female wage (and income) differences remain high. These differences, of course, do not prove discrimination. They can be shown to depend at least partly on other factors.

The Demand and Supply of Discrimination

Labor market discrimination today rarely takes the form of setting wages or hiring on the basis of sex or race, which would violate federal laws. Discrimination is usually more subtle, channeling workers by race or sex into occupations that are "more suitable" for females or minorities. As a result of channeling, certain work categories have a greater supply of workers and lower wage rates than they otherwise would. Traditionally, females were directed into nursery, primary, and secondary teaching and secretarial work, while many personal service occupations fit this pattern for certain minority groups. Table 17–5 shows the concentrations of blacks and females in certain occupations. Females account for 45 percent of the labor force, and blacks account for 10 percent. Females are heavily concentrated in sales, clerical, and private household work. However, they have made progress in recent years in some higher paying occupations, doubling their representation in medicine and showing impressive gains in law and management. Blacks, likewise, have broadened their representation in higher paying occupations but are still over represented in low-paying service and blue-collar occupations.

TABLE 17–5
EMPLOYED PERSONS BY SEX, RACE, AND OCCUPATION: 1972 AND 1986

	1972		1986	
	Percent Female	Percent Black	Percent Female	Percent Black
Total Employed	38.0%	9.5%	44.4%	9.9%
Physicians, Dentists, and Related Practitioners	9.3	2.2	15.0	3.3
Lawyers and Judges	3.8	1.6	18.1	3.0
Managers and Administrators	19.0	1.6	43.4	6.0
Sales Workers	41.6	3.0	68.6	8.2
Telephone Operators	96.7	12.4	87.9	17.4
Carpenters	0.5	5.0	1.4	5.3
Textile Operatives	55.2	15.3	79.8	21.4
Cleaning Service Workers	32.8	28.6	41.5	23.8

Source: *Statistical Abstract of the United States*, 1988.

Figure 17–4 illustrates the effects of channeling on wage differences. If a majority of workers in some occupations are able to exclude other workers by sex or race, the supply curve of workers for those protected occupations will be S'_e rather than S_e. Wage rates for workers in these jobs will be higher than they would otherwise be. At the same time, discrimination shifts the supply curve of workers in minority occupations to the right (S'_m). The result of channeling is a lower wage rate (W_m) in designated minority or female occupations than it would have been without discrimination. This wage differential constitutes discrimination only to the extent that it results from workers being excluded from one group of occupations and channeled into another. If there are real productivity differences between the two occupations in Figure 17–4 (reflected in different demand curves), market forces would produce different wage rates even in the absence of racial or sexual discrimination. In the U.S. today, discrimination in employment, housing, and other areas is limited by the 1964 Civil Rights Act and the 1965 Equal Employment Opportunity Act, but wage differences persist. In the real world, both effects—real productivity differences and the effect of exclusion—may coexist in the same markets.

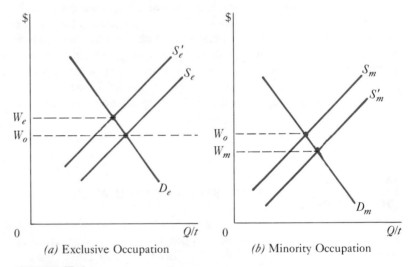

(a) Exclusive Occupation   *(b)* Minority Occupation

FIGURE 17-4
LABOR MARKET DISCRIMINATION
If workers are excluded from certain occupations, the supply curve will shift from S_e to S'_e in panel (*a*). The wage rate will rise to W_e in the excluded occupation. The excluded workers will be channeled into a minority occupation. The supply curve in that occupation in panel (*b*) shifts from S_m to S'_m, and the wage rate falls to W_m.

Does Labor Market Discrimination Exist?

In order to measure labor market discrimination, it is necessary to separate those factors that contribute to differences in productivity and those that contribute to male-female or black-white earnings differentials for reasons other than productivity. The first group of differences is

In one study, Sowell examined the impact of affirmative-action employment plans in higher education. He concluded that such affirmative-action programs did not fulfill the intent of the Civil Rights Act of 1964. That law rejected quotas and placed the burden of proving discrimination on the government. In practice, the burden of proof has been shifted to the employer, increasing costs for higher education. In addition, Sowell questioned whether such programs were necessary; his data indicates that salaries of black academics equaled or surpassed salaries of white academics with comparable training and credentials even before the law was applied in 1971. Sowell's findings also suggest that male-female salary differentials in academic careers are not primarily the result of employer discrimination but are better explained by social mores that place most family responsibilities on females.

In *Ethnic America: A History* (1981), Sowell examined the experience of successive waves of immigrants. He concluded that disciplined hard work and entrepreneurial ability can surmount poverty and bigotry. The impressive record of West Indian Blacks suggests that being black is not a fatal handicap in the United States.

In all of his work, Sowell uses economic theory to examine social policy questions of considerable interest. He does not shy away from very sensitive questions of race and discrimination. To examine Sowell's ideas and arguments, you should read his *Affirmative Action Reconsidered* (1975); *Black Education: Myths and Tragedies* (1970); *Race and Economics* (1975); *Knowledge and Decisions* (1980); *Ethnic America: A History* (1981); and *Markets and Minorities* (1981).

THOMAS SOWELL (1930-   )

Thomas Sowell, an economist at the Hoover Institution at Stanford University, has a B.A. from Harvard, an M.A. from Columbia, and a Ph.D. in economics from the University of Chicago. He uses microeconomic theory to analyze politically explosive problems of race and income distribution in the United States.

called the *productivity gap*, and the second, the *wage gap*. Historically, females and minorities have made less investment in human capital—education, training, and job experience—than white males and thus have lower productivity on the average. Studies suggest that about $3/4$ of the earnings differential can be explained by differences in human capital, by occupational choice, or by other objective factors such as age, health, and geographic location. Do these studies mean that discrimination is not an important explanation—accounting at most for 25 percent of the difference? No! Consider the effect of discrimination on the incentive to invest in human capital and the effect of channeling on occupational choice. The productivity gap is not independent of the wage gap.[5] Thus, it is difficult to determine precisely how much of current wage differentials reflect past and present discrimination and how much of the differentials would persist even in a discrimination-free world.

5. For a discussion of the interaction between the wage gap and the productivity gap, see Thomas D'Amico, "The Conceit of Labor Market Discrimination," *American Economic Review Papers and Proceedings* (May 1987): 310–315.

■ Other Factors in Male-Female Earnings Differences

A number of recent studies have identified other explanations for male-female earnings differences besides discrimination. Contributing factors include career interruptions, role differentiation, hours worked, and geographic mobility.

Career Interruptions

Many working females leave the labor force at least once during their careers. Donald Cox of Washington University in St. Louis examined the effects of such interruptions using data from Social Security records.[6] Cox finds that lifetime earnings of females are significantly reduced by past and anticipated future career interruptions. Income growth is closely linked to job experience which increases human capital; interruptions disrupt the acquisition of experience. His findings suggest that channeling is not entirely based on discrimination, at least for females. Some jobs lend themselves to more career interruptions without loss of skills or continuity. These jobs may be more attractive to females because they blend better with marriage and child-bearing.

Role Differentiation

Stanford University economist Victor Fuchs argues that much of the observed pay inequality between males and females is the result of "role differentiation."[7] Fuchs uses the term *role differentiation* to mean that society has different expectations for males and females. Fuchs contends that role differentiation begins in childhood and influences the decisions females make about schooling, location, occupational choice, and time spent in market work. Role differentiation often encourages a female to choose a job location and job responsibilities that are compatible with her husband's job choice or that lend themselves to career interruptions. Role differentiation is also reflected in hours worked and geographic mobility. Fuchs argues that lower salaries due to role differentiation do not really constitute discrimination in a narrow sense but rather choices made by females based on widely held social values. In the last 15 years more females have chosen to enter nontraditional, previously male-dominated occupations, and wage differences between the sexes have begun to fall.

Hours Worked

Females average fewer hours in paid employment than males. Comparisons of average earnings—such as the popular statistic that females earn 60 percent as much as males—do not always correct for that difference. Even that stubborn 60 percent ratio has begun to change; it is now approaching 65 percent. After correcting for differences in hours worked, the remaining sex differential in earnings is even less.[8]

---

6. Donald Cox, "Panel Estimates of the Effects of Career Interruptions on the Earnings of Women," *Economic Inquiry* (July 1984): 386–403.

7. Victor Fuchs, "Recent Trends and Long-Run Prospects for Female Earnings," *American Economic Review Papers and Proceedings* (May 1984): 235–242.

8. Robert Pear, "Earnings Gap Is Narrowing Slightly for Women," *New York Times*, 3 October 1983.

Geographic Mobility

Immobility increases any monopsony power in local labor markets. Married females often forego attractive job offers because of the geographic choices of their husbands, limiting their job searches to areas close to home. Robert H. Frank of Cornell University has found that such locational restrictions may explain as much as 23 percent of the wage differential between males and females.[9]

One approach to evaluating sex differences in earnings is to compare the earnings of single males and single females. Some studies show that single females, who have the same incentives as males to invest in human capital, to minimize career interruptions, to work longer hours, and to be geographically mobile, earn almost the same wages as males.[10]

■ Discrimination and Market Forces

Many economists argue that racial or sexual discrimination will not persist over time in a market system, because it is costly to entrepreneurs. There would be substantial numbers of minority workers and females who would be earning low salaries but who would have basically the same education and work skills as others who weren't in these "channeled" occupations. A profit-motivated entrepreneur could hire these workers and produce goods and services more cheaply than others who are hiring the more expensive (white male) labor. Thus, the profit motive would work to undermine discrimination.

Some economic historians argue that the Jim Crow laws enacted in the South in the late nineteenth and early twentieth centuries were a response to the threat that market forces would undermine racial discrimination. Jim Crow laws were intended to put the force of law behind segregation and discrimination (these laws were overridden by federal legislation in recent decades). In South Africa, apartheid is needed to maintain a racially segregated system that economic forces would otherwise undermine.

If market forces work to undermine discrimination, and laws penalize discrimination, why do the data show persistent white-black, female-male income differentials? Different sectors of the economy and different occupations adjust to change with different speeds. One would have to conclude that the field of professional athletics has adjusted very quickly to changing laws and customs, while the medical profession has adjusted quite slowly. The presence of monopoly power and licensing, and the length of time that it takes to train for a particular occupation, may influence the speed of adjustment.

Persistence of discrimination also reflects an interaction between discrimination and some of the factors that determine productivity—education, training, experience, and occupational choice. Females or minorities, who expect to be offered lower salaries or to be

9. Robert H. Frank, "Why Women Earn Less: The Theory and Estimate of Differential Overqualification," *American Economic Review* (June 1978): 360–373.
10. See Thomas Sowell, "Affirmative Action Reconsidered," *The Public Interest* (Winter 1976): 47–65; and James Gwartney and Richard Stroup, "Measurement of Employment Discrimination According to Sex," *Southern Economic Journal* (April 1973): 575–587.

excluded from desirable occupations, may invest less in human capital. As it became clear in the 1970s that jobs formerly closed to most females and minorities were now accessible, the distribution of females and minorities—especially females—began to shift. The information on which such decisions are based is disseminated and absorbed slowly.

Discrimination begets poverty, and poverty begets little investment in human capital. While discrimination is not the sole source of poverty, it can be a contributing factor. Government can help with policies that reduce discrimination, including laws against employment discrimination, and equal wages and promotions for government employees regardless of race or sex. These policies are not enough to eliminate poverty. The government may also be called upon to intervene to change the income distribution determined by the market.

INCOME REDISTRIBUTION

INTERDEPENDENT UTILITY FUNCTIONS
Citizens' well-being that is dependent upon the well-being of others.

Why do citizens support income redistribution? First, some people have **interdependent utility functions**, which means that their well-being is dependent upon the well-being of others. These voters would support programs to redistribute income because redistribution would increase their utility. Secondly, some people might view poverty as a noxious externality like air pollution—something that makes the environment less appealing. This group of voters would support redistribution to improve their surroundings. Finally, redistribution can be viewed as an insurance policy. People might support redistribution as a safety net, realizing that they might become poor at some time.

Private Income Redistribution and the Role of Government

Income redistribution responsibilities in the United States, and many other countries, are shared between the private sector and the public sector. Many public goods or goods with substantial public benefits are produced at least partly in the private sector. There are private roads, private schools, private outdoor concerts, and other goods and services that are collectively consumed but privately produced. Income redistribution is another activity with public good characteristics that is produced at least in part by the private sector. The reason for voluntary private redistribution through charity springs from the same kinds of motivations identified for supporting public redistribution.

It is not likely that private redistribution alone will achieve the desired level of income transfers. If the income equality achieved through private charity is a public good, private charity can be expected to produce too little redistribution. Individuals in a large group would recognize that they do not have to contribute since others will. If all followed this strategy, there would be no private redistribution, or at least not enough redistribution. In large groups, there is a tendency to free ride in this way and, in practice, give very little to charity.

The person who gives to others because of the personal satisfaction gained from the act of charity does not experience a free-rider problem. However, if the nature of the benefit to the giver consists in seeing less poverty in the world, then giving by others diminishes the need for any particular individual to give, and the free-rider problem can arise.

An important influence on the amount of private redistribution is the size of the group in which redistribution takes place. In a relatively small, homogeneous group of givers and receivers, there is likely to be relatively more private redistribution. Think about the Mormon church and the Amish sects, for example, or small towns versus large cities. Greater charity in small groups is consistent with the view that the externalities associated with poverty are more significant (i.e., observable) when the group size is smaller. Thus, one might predict that at the national level, a small country with a relatively homogeneous population, such as Sweden, would be likely to practice more redistribution than a large "melting-pot" country like the United States.

While private redistribution has an important role to play, since the 1930s citizens have expected the government to play a major role in redistributing income and alleviating poverty. In both private and public redistribution, there are several important questions to be resolved about what is the best way to redistribute.

Equality of Opportunity or Equality of Results?

One such question concerns the goal of redistribution. Do we want equality of opportunity or equality of results? To the extent that labor market discrimination leads to a more unequal income distribution and poverty, there may be a need for policies that create greater equality of opportunity, specifically government investment in human capital— technical schools, student loans and grants, training programs. Along with penalties for discrimination not based on productivity, such policies should offer the working poor a chance to improve their earnings and escape from poverty.

Government or private programs that reduce unemployment and improve the match between workers and jobs are also indirect forms of poverty relief. Not only do these programs increase total output, but they generally improve job opportunities and earnings of workers at the lower end of the wage scale. Anything that the government does to promote economic growth and reduce cyclical fluctuations will also reduce unemployment for all groups. Since the poor are so often the last hired and first fired, they would benefit more than most from such programs. Even programs that reduce the difficulties of working, such as better public transportation or more day care, can provide significant help for the poor who can work.

Programs to alleviate poverty by creating work opportunities and improving earnings potential result in equality of opportunity. Giving everyone an equal chance at success in the labor market is consistent with the values of freedom, incentives, and individual choice implicit in a market economic system. However, equality of opportunity does nothing to help those poor who are too old, too young, too sick, too disabled, or too unskilled to participate in the marketplace as workers or those with the responsibility for the care of very small children. The only programs that will reach these poor are programs that are aimed directly at equality of results.

The fraction of the poor outside the labor force, or not expected to work, has risen dramatically in the last 50 years. In 1939, less than one-third of poor households were classified as not able to work for one of the reasons listed previously. Today it is closer to two-thirds of poor households that are headed by a person who is elderly, a student, disabled, or a female with one or more preschool children. These people do not benefit from the rising tide of economic growth and job opportunities unless there is a deliberate effort to share those gains through a redistribution program.[11]

In Cash or in Kind?

If the decision is made to alter the market-determined distribution of income, in what form should income be redistributed? Should cash grants, such as a guaranteed income, be given; or should income be redistributed in the form of in-kind transfers of goods and services, such as housing, food, or health care?

Many forms of income redistribution, both private and public, are in-kind transfers of specific commodities or services. In-kind transfers are popular among private charities; examples include soup kitchens, shelters for the homeless, and Meals on Wheels for shut-ins. In-kind transfers are based not on a desire to reduce income inequality but rather a desire by the grantor to ensure the provision of certain basic needs, such as food and shelter. James Tobin of Yale University calls this motivation *specific egalitarianism*. Most economists tend to be *general egalitarians* to the extent they are egalitarian at all. Economists generally argue for giving cash instead of specific goods and services because a transfer of cash allows more options and maximizes the freedom of the recipient. This traditional economic analysis is based solely on the idea of maximizing the utility of welfare recipients.

Tobin argues, however, that the majority of the electorate are specific egalitarians. They are concerned with ill-clothed and ill-fed people, not with inequality *per se*. If this observation is correct, one can expect more transfers to be made in kind rather than in cash. Indeed, for the last 25 years most of the growth in government transfers to the poor has been in-kind.

James Buchanan argues that the preference of the electorate for in-kind rather than cash transfers simply means that voters are maximizing their own utility as donors rather than maximizing the utility of welfare recipients by allowing them freedom of choice. The donor/voter's motive for making an income transfer may not be concern for the welfare of the recipients, as much as a desire to eliminate some objectionable

---

11. Economic growth as a solution to poverty was criticized on this basis by Sheldon Danziger and Peter Gottschalk, "Do Rising Tides Lift All Boats? The Impact of Secular and Cyclical Change on the Poor," *American Economic Review Papers and Proceedings* (May 1986): 405–410.

condition—homeless people on the streets, slum housing, or students who disrupt the learning process in public schools because of illness or hunger. Providing specific goods or services is a more direct way of addressing that concern.

Which Level of Government?

A final issue in structuring an income redistribution program is which level of government should be responsible. In the late 1960s and through the 1970s, strong arguments were made for centralized provision of income support programs. Social Security is a federal program, but other programs are shared between levels of government. States that offered higher welfare benefits attracted low-income migrants from states such as Texas and Louisiana where benefits were lower. Thus, some economists argue, states that would prefer to offer higher benefit levels were deterred from doing so by fear of in-migration. Furthermore, advocates of centralized welfare argue that the level of income support a household receives should depend on its "needs" (ages, family size, or health) rather than the fiscal wealth of the state in which they reside. Redistribution from richer to poorer individuals would also lead to equalization among states, so that even the nonpoor who lived in poor states would benefit from lower state taxes.

After two efforts to centralize welfare in the 1970s (Nixon's Family Assistance Plan and Carter's Program for Better Jobs and Income), it became apparent that such plans were not politically feasible. Several reasons have been suggested for this failure to enact a centralized redistribution scheme. If support for income transfers depends heavily on a desire to eliminate negative externalities (such as crime or blight), then the support for redistribution in one's own area will be stronger because the benefits will be concentrated there. Even if taxpayers are interested in increasing the utility of the recipient rather than their own utility, they will still receive more satisfaction of seeing the poverty relief that results from expenditures made in their own area. Thus, if a substantial part of the benefits of poverty relief are captured at the state or local level, there is reason for a substantial part of the benefits to be financed at that level as well. In addition, the appropriate level and combination of benefits may vary from state to state. If most of the poor live in rural areas in State A, there may be less need for food programs than in State B. A state with a high proportion of elderly residents or a cold climate will opt to offer more medical care or heat assistance benefits than another state. A state with more children might put more resources into day care or remedial education. Tailoring the benefits to the local clientele's needs and the preferences of the local electorate is another reason giving states a major role.

Such reasoning led the Reagan administration to propose sorting out welfare programs and returning more responsibilities to the states in 1982. Like Nixon's centralizing proposal, Reagan's proposal was decisively rejected. Today, income redistribution responsibilities in the U.S. continue to be shared between the federal government, state governments, local governments (in large cities), and private philanthropic organizations.

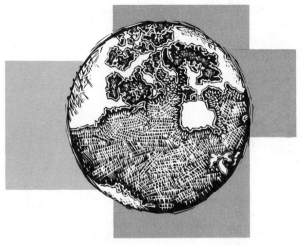

Country	Social Welfare Expenditures (incl. education)	
	as % of Gross Domestic Product	as % of Government Spending
Japan	17.5	46.7
United States	20.8	58.3
Canada	21.5	53.4
United Kingdom	23.7	51.0
France	29.5	61.0
Sweden	33.4	52.2

Source: Rose, Richard, and Rei Shiratori, *The Welfare State East and West* (Oxford, UK: Oxford University Press, 1986).

THE INTERNATIONAL PERSPECTIVE SOCIAL WELFARE SYSTEMS IN OTHER COUNTRIES

Social welfare is a broad term encompassing all of the transfer payments and social services that governments provide to individual citizens. Some of these programs are based on a means (level of income) test while others go to all citizens. Children's allowances in Canada, for example, are provided to all families. Since these grants are taxable income, some of it is recovered from higher income families. Education is traditionally provided to all citizens in industrial countries up to a certain grade level regardless of income. Food stamps and subsidized public housing, however, are subject to an income test.

Despite the hue and cry for welfare reform, social welfare expenditures in the United States are actually low relative to those of most other industrial countries. Only Japan spends a lower percent of Gross Domestic Product on social welfare. Japanese society places much greater responsibility for welfare on the family, especially for the elderly, who are much more likely to live with their grown children than they would be in the United States.

All major industrial countries have some type of publicly funded old age pension system and some provision for unemployment and disability insurance, although the nature of the benefits varies widely. Health care is more likely to be provided at public expense in European nations. Public housing is an important component of social welfare in the United Kingdom, where 28 percent of the population lives in "council houses" (public housing, rented at subsidized rates) but less so in other nations. In Scandinavian countries, the political consensus is that a basic standard of living is a right, and therefore certain basic social services and social insurance guarantees (unemployment, disability, etc.) are provided to everyone without an income test.

The emphasis on individualism and the concern over work incentives that pervade the U.S. welfare debate receive less attention elsewhere, although the conservative Thatcher government in the United Kingdom has shown some interest. Support for the welfare state was at its peak in European countries in the 1960s and 1970s, as it was in the United States. In the 1980s, Japan continued to expand its social insurance programs, but the nations of western Europe as well as the United States have been carefully reconsidering the level of public expenditure on social welfare.

Redistribution to the Nonpoor

Not all redistribution is to the poor or for the poor. Nobel laureate George Stigler of the University of Chicago and Gordon Tullock of the University of Arizona point out that people try to use government programs as a way to redistribute to themselves rather than to others. Stigler theorizes that the government will use its coercive power to extract resources which would not be forthcoming by voluntary agreement in the society. Any group that can gain control of the government can then use this power to its own benefit. Stigler argues that the group that controls government is the middle class; hence, most public expenditures are made for the benefit of the middle class.

Tullock argues that only a small portion of government transfers go to the poor. He argues that in the nature of the voting process, relatively more resources will be taken from the rich in taxes, but it is not entirely clear how they will be distributed. Since the support of middle-income voters will be crucial in obtaining the authority needed to take resources from other members of society, he expects that money will flow from both ends of the income ladder toward the middle.[12]

Both Tullock and Stigler believe that income redistribution tends to be captured by the dominant political group, the middle class, to use for its own benefit. Both Tullock and Stigler present examples, such as farm policy and support for higher education, for which they identify the middle class as the principal beneficiaries. Much redistribution takes the form of special-interest redistribution or redistribution via bureaucracy, and little of it benefits the poor.

GOVERNMENT TRANSFER PROGRAMS IN PRACTICE

Until the 1930s, programs to relieve poverty were small scale, provided mainly by local government and private philanthropy. In the Depression, state and local governments were swamped with demands, and the present system of federal, or federally assisted, income transfer programs was born. These programs include Social Security for workers who are retired or disabled, or for survivors of deceased workers; unemployment compensation for the temporarily unemployed; and welfare programs for those unable to work.

Social Security

Social Security, established in 1935, was initially an old-age pension program. It was later expanded to include survivors' benefits (1939) and disability insurance (1950). Social Security was designed to relieve poverty for several major groups of poor persons—the old, the dependent survivors of prematurely deceased workers, and the disabled. In 1965, a program of health care for the elderly (Medicare) was incorporated into Social Security. Except for Medicare, Social Security is strictly a cash transfer program with no in-kind benefits.

Payments to beneficiaries are financed by taxes on workers and employers, each paying an equal amount. Many workers feel that their employers actually pay the other half of the tax. Microeconomic theory

12. Gordon Tullock, *Economics of Income Redistribution* (Boston: Kluver-Nijhoff Publishing, 1983), Chapter 5.

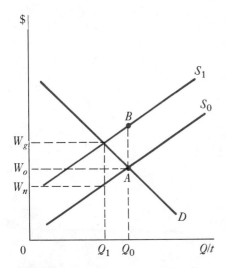

FIGURE 17-5
WHO PAYS SOCIAL SECURITY TAXES?

The higher supply price including Social Security tax reduces the number of workers employed from Q_0 to Q_1. The gross wage, including Social Security taxes, rises from W_0 to W_g, but the worker's net wage falls to W_n.

tells us that at least part of this other half is in fact paid by workers who earn lower wages than they would receive if there were no Social Security tax. Figure 17–5 shows why this is the case. Before the Social Security tax, the supply of labor facing the firm is S_0, and the firm's demand is D. The equilibrium wage is W_0. Adding a Social Security tax in the amount AB shifts the supply curve facing this firm to S_1. If supply is fairly elastic but demand is relatively inelastic, most of the tax falls on the worker. The gross wage (including the tax) rises to W_g, but the net wage taken home by the worker falls to W_n. The precise division of the tax between worker and employer depends, not on the legislation that says half on each, but on the relative elasticities of supply and demand for labor. Economists believe that most of the tax falls on the worker.

Social Security is the United States' largest income redistribution program. It incorporates some aspects of insurance. Workers are required to contribute to the program for a specified minimum period of time in order to be eligible for benefits. Workers do not have a choice about participating; with very few exceptions, everyone who holds a paying job earning more than $50 a quarter must pay Social Security taxes. Self-employed individuals must also pay the tax. Once a worker has become eligible to receive benefits, they are paid regardless of other forms of nonwage income such as interest, dividends, and private pensions. Until recently, Social Security benefits were not subject to federal income tax, and even now, most Social Security benefits are not taxable. As a result, a large share of Social Security benefits goes to people who are not poor. In fact, some of the working poor are paying taxes that are transferred to the rich through Social Security.

When Social Security was established as a compulsory retirement system, many people believed that their payments went into a trust fund. The term *trust fund* is still the label on the account into which workers and employers pay their taxes. Actually, the "trust fund" of Social Security is simply a fund into which current workers pay and from which current beneficiaries receive income. No money is invested and held for workers from which they later will receive income, as is done with private pensions and annuities.

The Social Security system is a tax and transfer mechanism. Individuals are taxed during their working years to pay benefits to those who are retired, disabled, or dependent survivors of covered workers. In the early years of the Social Security system, the funds coming in were more than adequate because there were many workers and few retired people. However, the age distribution of the U.S. population has changed significantly since that time. Table 17–6 shows this dramatic shift in the working versus the retired population. In 1950, an individual worker's payments only had to support 6 percent of one Social Security recipient's benefits. In 1984, each worker had to be taxed enough to support 30 percent of one Social Security recipient's benefits. Coupled with the increasing level of benefits, the changing ratio of workers to beneficiaries has created a heavy burden on workers.

Can today's workers rely on promised future Social Security payments? Many of today's workers are concerned about this aspect of the program and are doubtful of ever receiving the benefits they are being promised. Reforms made in 1985 strengthened the stability of the system.

TABLE 17-6
SUPPORT FOR SOCIAL SECURITY RECIPIENTS

Year	Workers per Social Security Beneficiary
■	■
1950	16.0
1960	5.0
1984	3.3
2010	3.0
2034	2.0

Source: The *1984 Annual Report of Board of Trustees of the Federal Old Age and Survivor's Insurance and Disability Trust Funds* (Washington, D.C.: Social Security Administration, 1984).

These changes were: (1) reducing the growth in benefit levels (including eliminating survivor benefits to college students and delayed retirement ages in the future); (2) broadening the categories of workers required to participate, so that there are more contributors; (3) raising the Social Security payroll tax rate; and (4) raising the income base (the amount of income subject to the payroll tax). Since many beneficiaries are not poor, part of Social Security benefits is now subject to federal income taxes. The real battle over this entitlement program, however, lies ahead, when the large cohort of workers born in 1946 to 1964 retires and must be supported by the smaller generation of workers that follows.

■
Unemployment Compensation

Unemployment compensation is financed by a tax on employers and administered by the states, which set benefit levels and eligibility requirements. Unemployment compensation is intended to be a temporary replacement of lost income while a worker is between jobs or temporarily laid off. The program has been criticized as providing "paid vacations" while workers go through the motions of searching for jobs. It also has been praised as providing a safety net for involuntary unemployment while workers match their skills to the best available jobs, making labor markets more efficient. Of all income-transfer programs, this one is the least criticized because it is financed by a payroll tax paid largely by the workers and also because benefits are of a temporary nature.

■
Welfare

The group of programs lumped together as "welfare" began in the 1930s with Aid to the Aged, Aid to the Disabled, and Aid to Dependent Children (later Aid to Families with Dependent Children, or AFDC). These programs identify categories of people not expected to work. Costs are shared between the federal and state levels of government, with different eligibility requirements and different benefit levels in different states. In the 1960s, these programs were expanded and new ones added as part of President Johnson's War on Poverty. Aid to the Aged, Aid to the Disabled, and several smaller programs were merged into Supplemental Security Income, a federally funded program, in 1972.

In the 1960s, there was a substantial increase in in-kind programs including food stamps, public housing, Medicaid, legal aid, Head Start for preschool children, and job training programs. These efforts to improve the welfare of the poor tried to make sure that they consumed the "right mix" of goods and services, particularly in the areas of health, nutrition, education, and training.

Critics of welfare programs argue that they discourage work. With multiple benefits, it is very likely that a welfare client who takes a job would be worse off. In order to determine the effects of welfare programs on work incentives, the federal government sponsored four large-scale experiments to measure how individuals would respond to various levels of benefits in terms of work effort. Households in New Jersey, Pennsylvania, rural areas of North Carolina and Iowa, Gary, Indiana, Seattle and Detroit were studied at various times from 1969 to 1982. These researchers concluded that higher benefit levels did lead to some modest reductions in work effort, particularly among females.[13]

For these workers and welfare recipients, taking a job means losing not only cash benefits but also medical help, subsidized housing, and other benefits from overlapping programs. The high cost of maintaining the bureaucracy to administer these in-kind programs has led policymakers to search for a solution to the welfare problem. One popular proposal during the 1960s and 1970s was the negative income tax.

A Negative Income Tax?

Milton Friedman first suggested replacing the existing welfare system with a negative income tax in the 1960s.[14] A **negative income tax** is a transfer from the government to the poor based on a formula similar to the present income tax system. A positive income tax is a transfer to the government from citizens. The negative income tax was popular among economists because of its simplicity and positive work incentive.

Under a negative income tax, everyone would be guaranteed at least some minimum income. The first problem is to decide what the minimum income should be. This decision is strictly normative; economic theory offers no clue as to what this level should be. One approach would be to calculate a typical poverty level budget at current prices as a standard for a minimum income.

In addition to the *minimum income guarantee*, a negative income tax also must designate a *negative tax rate*, which is the rate at which transfer payments are reduced per additional dollar of earned income. These two elements determine a third element, the *break-even income*,

NEGATIVE INCOME TAX
A transfer from the government to the poor based on a formula similar to the present income tax system. A negative income tax has two components: an income guarantee and a negative tax rate.

---

13. For a detailed appraisal of the results of the income maintenance program, see *Lessons from the Income Maintenance Experiments*, Alicia H. Munnell (ed.), proceedings of a conference sponsored by the Federal Reserve Bank of Boston and the Brookings Institution, 1986.
14. See Milton Friedman, "The Case for the Negative Income Tax," *Republican Papers*, ed. M.R. Laird (New York: Praeger Publishing, 1968).

which is the level of income at which a household neither pays income taxes nor receives benefits. In Friedman's plan, the basic income guarantee varies with family size. For example, a family of four might have a guaranteed income of $6,000. Assume a negative tax of 50 percent; that is, for each dollar the family earns, it loses 50¢ of welfare payments. When the family earns $12,000, it will lose its last dollar of benefits and live on earned income only. Since the family keeps part of its welfare benefits when it earns a modest income, its work incentive should be stronger than under the present welfare system.

Table 17–7 gives a hypothetical example for four families, assuming a $6,000 income guarantee and a 50 percent negative tax rate. The transfer received by a family is $6,000 minus 50 percent of any income earned that is less than $12,000. The amount of welfare that a family receives can be determined by the formula

$$W = IG - t_n(EI),$$

where W is the welfare payment, IG is the income guarantee, t_n is the negative tax rate, and EI is the earned income.

When the family reaches the break-even income level, at which no more income is transferred, the family starts paying normal, positive taxes. With an income guarantee of $6,000 and a negative tax rate of 50 percent, this break-even point would occur at $12,000. Table 17–7 also shows how another $100 of income would benefit each family.

TABLE 17–7
A NEGATIVE INCOME TAX

Family	A	B	C	D
■	■	■	■	■
Earned Income	$ 0	$2,000	$4,000	$12,000
Welfare Payment	6,000	5,000	4,000	0
Disposable Income	6,000	7,000	8,000	12,000
Increase in Income	100	100	100	100
Earned Income Becomes	100	2,100	4,100	12,100
Tax Rate	(−50%)	(−50%)	(−50%)	(+15%)
Welfare Payment	5,950	4,950	3,950	0
Disposable Income	6,050	7,050	8,050	11,085

The relationship between the three elements—the income guarantee, the negative tax rate, and the break-even income—creates some difficult trade-offs. In order to provide an income guarantee high enough to ensure a minimum standard of living, and a negative tax rate low enough to encourage work, the break-even income would be very high. This combination of choices would raise the cost of the system (requiring higher positive tax rates above the break-even income) and extend welfare benefits much higher up the income scale. The break-even income could be reduced by lowering the minimum income guarantee, but a low minimum would penalize those unable to work and totally dependent on transfers—the aged or blind, for example. Alternatively, the break-even income could be reached more quickly by using a higher negative tax rate, but that higher tax on earnings would discourage work.

A major attraction of the negative income tax is that it would concentrate public funds on the poor rather than on a large welfare bureaucracy through which funds must trickle down to those in need. It would, therefore, cost less for the same amount of redistribution because it is directed specifically at poverty. Such a system would greatly reduce the cost of administering welfare programs, which has grown to a vast array of in-kind transfers.

The negative income tax is also more attractive to recipients. It is an objective and impersonal vehicle, allowing recipients to maintain a sense of dignity and entitlement. Instead of cutting off funds to those whose income is just above the poverty level, the negative income tax provides aid to the nearly poor as well. Perhaps the most important advantage, however, is that the negative income tax does not destroy work incentives as much as the current system, which reduces transfers by 100 percent of any earned income. If a person on welfare earns $1,000, benefits fall by $1,000. A system that allows individuals to keep a portion of what they earn would strengthen work incentives.

A negative income tax that is not merely superimposed on the current system but, instead, replaces all direct public-assistance programs, is considered by many economists to possess decided advantages over other welfare-reform proposals. One major obstacle to its adoption is the self-interests of those presently employed in the welfare bureaucracy. Other obstacles to change include preferences for in-kind programs, concerns about cost, and resistance to centralizing welfare at the federal level.

President Nixon tried to institute a negative income tax (the Family Assistance Plan) in 1971 but succeeded in only two small areas— SSI (Supplemental Security Income) for the aged and the extension of food stamp benefits. President Carter proposed a similar plan in 1978, the Program for Better Jobs and Income, but again it was not enacted. Both plans floundered on three issues: (1) the high cost of a program with an adequate income guarantee and a low enough negative tax rate; (2) the federalization of welfare, which had always been at least partly a state and local responsibility; and (3) the opposition of the "iron triangle" of congressional committees who oversee programs, beneficiaries, and government bureaucracies that administer existing programs.

The Welfare Reform Debate: Workfare?

Welfare reform is, of course, high on the political agenda. The continuing debate throughout the 1980s was precipitated by the 1982 proposal to return the largest welfare program, Aid to Families with Dependent Children, to the states and also by a controversial 1983 book by Charles Murray, *Losing Ground*. In this book, Murray argued that the current welfare system encourages people to do the wrong things; to avoid working, to have more children, and to become welfare dependent. At the same time, the pressures of the budget deficit led to a re-examination of all areas of spending, and some of the most vulnerable programs were social welfare programs. Thus, the 1980s debate on welfare reform centered on three issues; the relative roles of the state and federal governments, work incentives, and cost containment.

The issue of how responsibilities should be shared between state and federal governments was at least temporarily put to rest in 1981 and 1982. Although the federal government reduced grants to state and local governments for social welfare programs, states rejected a proposal that they assume full responsibility for Aid to Families with Dependent Children in 1982. The issues of work incentives and cost containment were joined in 1986 with the development of a variety of experimental programs at the state level. These **workfare** programs encourage or require welfare recipients who are able to work to take jobs, sometimes in the public sector, or to enter training programs that should lead to jobs, as a condition for continuing to receive benefits. A new wrinkle in the workfare program is reconsideration of the point at which mothers of small children are expected to go to work. As more and more nonwelfare mothers have chosen to work outside the home while their children are still small, the age at which mothers are expected to place children in day care in order to work has been reduced from six years to three.

The most celebrated workfare program was established in Massachusetts, where a voluntary program involving training, day care, and help with job search has produced promising results. The initial cost is high, particularly if day care and training programs are involved, but the eventual cost savings from reduced welfare payments could be substantial. In 1988, federal welfare reform legislation incorporated some aspects of experimental state workfare programs.

WORKFARE
Requirement that those receiving welfare, who are able to work, take jobs or participate in training programs in order to be eligible for benefits.

■ SUMMARY

1. Income distribution is determined largely by factor markets. Wages and salaries are by far the largest component of income.

2. The Lorenz curve measures the relative distribution of income in an economy. The Lorenz curve, however, does not reflect life-cycle stages in income and may therefore give a false impression of how much inequality there is.

3. Discrimination in labor markets channels certain groups into certain occupations. Some of what might appear to be discrimination is actually due to differences in productivity or other objective considerations.

4. To the extent that discrimination exists in the labor market, GNP is lower than it could be if all resources were used in the most efficient manner.

5. Market forces will work to break down discrimination, because discrimination is costly and entrepreneurs can be lower cost producers by not discriminating.

6. Income redistribution can be viewed as a public good that is underprovided because of free-riding behavior.

7. Chance plays a role in determining the distribution of income, and people may therefore want to erect safety nets to protect those who suffer bad luck.

8. In-kind transfers, whose use has expanded greatly in the last 25 years, have greatly reduced the incidence of poverty in the United States. Often strings are attached to transfers so as to ensure that funds are used as the donors want them to be.

9. Individuals may support income redistribution programs because they have interdependent utility functions, because of an insurance motive, because they view poverty as an externality, or, finally, because they are seeking to transfer income to themselves through the political process.

10. Social Security is a tax and transfer program. The changing age distribution of the population is putting pressure on the financial viability of the system.

11. The negative income tax has been suggested as a mechanism to ensure some basic level of income while strengthening work incentives. The trade-offs between the minimum income guarantee, the break-even income, and the negative tax rate make it difficult to design a satisfactory negative income

tax system that is adequate, not too costly, and preserves work incentives.

12. The U.S. response to poverty has taken three distinct forms: to provide training and job opportunities, to provide social insurance, and to provide direct assistance to those who are unable to work because of age and health problems.

13. Current welfare reform proposals center on cost control, the federal-state mix in financing and administration, and workfare.

NEW TERMS

functional distribution of income
personal distribution of income

Lorenz curve
interdependent utility functions

negative income tax
workfare

QUESTIONS FOR DISCUSSION

1. What factors determine wages? What causes some people with equal skills to receive different wages? Would a competitive economy reduce or increase these differentials?
2. What is responsible for the fact that some people are poor? What would you do about it if you were in a position to take some action?
3. Do you think a negative income tax would solve the U.S. poverty problem? Why or why not?
4. Should we be concerned with relative or absolute poverty? How would dealing with absolute poverty differ from dealing with relative poverty?
5. Why do many economists feel that markets will work to undermine discriminatory practices?
6. "The social safety net is intended to catch those who fall in, not those who jump in." Discuss the implications of this statement for designing an income-support system.
7. Why are there long-term problems with the financial health of the Social Security system? Identify some possible solutions.
8. Find the missing value in each of these groups of figures for the negative income tax.
   a. Minimum income guarantee, $4,000; break-even income, $12,000; negative tax rate = _____.
   b. Minimum income guarantee, $5,000; negative tax rate, 50 percent; break-even income = _____.
   c. Negative tax rate, 30 percent; break-even income, $9,000; minimum income guarantee = _____.
9. What problems with the welfare system is workfare designed to solve?
10. Why do we redistribute income to the poor? Why is private charity likely to be inadequate?

SUGGESTIONS FOR FURTHER READING

Duncan, Greg J., et al. *Years of Poverty, Years of Plenty: The Changing Economic Fortunes of American Workers and Families.* Ann Arbor, MI: Institute for Social Research, 1984. Summarizes the findings of the Panel Study of Income Dynamics on changes in family incomes over time.

Harrington, Michael. *The New American Poverty.* New York: Holt, Rinehart & Winston, Inc., 1984. A new look at poverty by the intellectual who "discovered" poverty in the early 1960s and persuaded President Kennedy to declare war on poverty. Harrington is critical of past and current policies and believes in much more substantial income redistribution efforts.

Murray, Charles. *Losing Ground: American Social Policy, 1950–1980.* New York: Basic Books, Inc., 1984. A controversial book that argues that the past three decades of well-meaning social programs were a failure.

Tullock, Gordon. *Economics of Income Redistribution.* Boston: Kluwer-Nijhoff Publishing, 1983. This very readable analysis of governmental transfer policy criticizes an array of transfer programs.

PART FIVE

MARKET FAILURE, GOVERNMENT FAILURE, AND THE THEORY OF PUBLIC CHOICE

CHAPTER 18 ■
■
MARKET FAILURE AND GOVERNMENT INTERVENTION

INTRODUCTION

Up to this point, we have spent a great deal of time examining economic outcomes of market forces. Two forms of market failure were identified in earlier chapters: the failure of markets to produce the optimal quantity (and price) of a good when there is monopoly power and the poverty that often is the result of the market distribution of income. Additional instances of market failure exist because of externalities and public goods. In this chapter, we examine the economic arguments for government intervention into resource allocation because of externalities and public goods.[1]

EXTERNALITIES

EXTERNALITY
A cost or benefit associated with consumption or production that is not reflected in market prices and falls on parties other than the buyer or seller.

Externalities are costs or benefits associated with consumption or production that are not reflected in market prices. The cost or benefit is external in that it falls on parties other than the buyer or seller. Externalities represent a form of market failure.

The example of an externality used most often is pollution. Consider a firm producing steel. The firm must purchase iron ore, electricity, labor, and other inputs. The costs of these factors are embodied in the price of the steel. Just as the firm uses electricity in producing steel, it also uses clean air and produces air pollution. Yet, the firm doesn't compensate those individuals who give up the clean air. As a result, the cost of using the air is not embodied in the price of the steel; this cost is external to the production of the steel.

---

1. Recall from Chapter 4 that the functions of government are allocation, stabilization, and redistribution. Stabilization is a topic discussed in macroeconomics. Redistribution was covered in the last chapter. Here, we are giving a closer examination to certain aspects of the allocation question.

Many externality problems result from the fact that property rights to certain resources are not defined. Clean air is a resource that is not owned by anyone. Therefore, the steel mill can use the clean air and not compensate those who give it up, because there is no clearly defined owner to demand payment.

Externalities can be positive or negative. The pollution example just discussed is a negative externality. Another example of a negative externality is the noise resulting from the use of a snowmobile. The cost this noise imposes on other individuals may not be taken into account in the price of snowmobiles or snowmobiling. It is external to their economic calculation.

Positive externalities are not so obvious but do nonetheless exist. Innoculations against contagious diseases or sprays that control mosquitoes are examples of activities that generate positive externalities. Benefits accrue to others if enough people are innoculated or enough mosquito breeding grounds are sprayed, but these benefits are not considered by those deciding on whether or not to incur the cost. Education is another good example. Society benefits from an individual's education. An individual who is educated is a better citizen, is less likely to commit crimes, and is less dependent on others. In addition, that individual will be a more productive person, increasing national income. Yet individuals, in deciding how much education to pursue, do not include these benefits because they are external to the buyer, who is not able to charge those who enjoy the external benefit.

To the extent that externalities exist, the market has failed. Private market decisions will result in too little or too much of certain items being produced. Corrective, collective action may be needed. The government can influence the production or consumption of items subject to externalities by taxes, subsidies, outright prohibitions, or by requiring citizens to consume certain goods, such as innoculations and education.

External Benefits

In order to analyze the economic implications of a positive externality, consider Figure 18-1. Suppose that Figure 18-1 represents the market for automobile tires. D_p represents the private demand for automobile tires, and MC represents the marginal cost. Consumers will purchase Q_1 tires at Price P_1. Assume that line EB represents the external marginal benefits arising from the consumption of new tires. External benefits exist because as people consume more new tires, their cars are safer and the chance of an accident involving others decreases. This greater safety is a social benefit. EB can be viewed as the summation of the demand curves of people other than the immediate consumers of the product. It has a negative slope, as do all demand curves.

We vertically sum EB and D_p to get the "true" demand curve. A vertical summation of the two demand curves is made instead of the horizontal summation we made in earlier chapters, because we are interested in total marginal benefits at various quantities consumed. We are not summing the additional amounts consumers want to purchase but rather

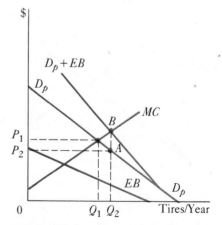

FIGURE 18-1
THE CASE OF EXTERNAL BENEFITS
External benefits cause the "true" demand curve, $D_p + EB$, to lie above the private demand curve, D_p. The market outcome, Q_1, is smaller than the efficient level of consumption, Q_2.

how they value these units. If the external benefits are considered, the combined valuation (D_p + EB) indicates Q_2 rather than Q_1 tires should be consumed. In other words, the existence of the positive externality resulted in this good being underproduced and underconsumed.

It is easy to see how government could correct this market failure. A subsidy to consumers equal to AB on the graph would lower the price consumers pay to P_2 and bring about the "socially beneficial" level of consumption, Q_2. This level is the social optimum because it includes the production demanded by those who are not counted by the market mechanism.

Alternatively, government could require that Q_2 tires be purchased per year. Vehicle inspections, which some states now require, are also attempts (albeit crude ones) to correct for this sort of externality.

External Costs

Earlier, we used air pollution as an example of an external cost. If you live near a steel mill, you are forced to breathe polluted air without being compensated for the fact that the mill is using the air as a place in which to dump its debris. The economic importance of this behavior is that the polluting firm avoids paying part of the costs of production, resulting from the use of air as a "sewer." It is quite simple to determine the theoretical effects of these externalities; it is more difficult to determine how to correct them.

Assume the polluter is in a competitive industry that is generating a negative externality. Smoke causes damage, or what we call social costs, to those in the general area. **Social costs** are costs that are borne by society or some group without compensation. Externalities impose damages, or social costs, on groups in the population. This situation is represented in Figure 18–2. The demand curve is the usual market demand curve for the commodity. The supply curve is the summation of all the individual firms' marginal cost curves (above their average variable cost curves). This supply curve includes all private costs but not marginal social costs. Equilibrium is reached at Price P_1 and Output Q_1. Now suppose we know the value of marginal costs generated by the externality and that these marginal social costs are represented by the curve SC. The social costs are zero when no output is being produced, and we assume that they increase at a constant rate. If we add these marginal social costs to the supply curve, we get the true supply curve, S_t. This curve is the summation of the extra social costs and the private costs embodied in the firms' marginal cost curves. The socially optimal level of production is no longer Q_1 but the smaller Q_2. Likewise, the efficient price is P_2, which is higher than P_1.

In common sense terms, when we include the social costs of production, the good becomes more expensive. It isn't that these costs weren't being borne before but that they weren't being borne by the producers or the consumers of the commodity. Instead, they were being paid by citizens in the area near where production is taking place. In failing to take into account the social costs, the firm is producing too much of the good and charging the consumer too low a price because the firm is not paying some of the costs of production.

SOCIAL COSTS
Costs that are borne by society or some group without compensation. Externalities impose damages, or social costs, on groups in the population.

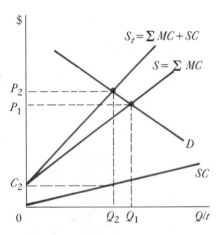

FIGURE 18-2
EXTERNALITIES AND MARKET EQUILIBRIUM
When the social cost of the negative externality (SC) is added to the marginal cost curves of the competitive firms (S), the true supply curve (S_t) is found. This true supply curve indicates that too much of the good is produced at too low a price unless the externality is taken into account.

INTERNATIONAL PERSPECTIVE
CHERNOBYL, A DISASTER FOR THE LAPPS

Externalities not only spill across consumers and producers, but they often spill over national borders. Acid rain, produced by U.S. manufacturers, has destroyed trees in Canada, resulting in political tension between political leaders in the two countries. Perhaps no other recent event has produced as many international externalities as the Soviet nuclear accident at Chernobyl.

The accident itself was staggering: thirty-one people were confirmed as dead, two hundred were seriously injured, and one hundred thirty-five thousand Ukrainians were evacuated from their homes, perhaps never to return. As significant as these costs are, they were far from the only costs of the accident. Some 1,300 hundred miles from Chernobyl the Lapps of Norway, Sweden, and Finland are facing a complete change in their economy and their culture.

The reindeer is the core of the Lapp economy and culture. It provides meat, knife handles, glue, and skin for tents, coats, and shoes. These reindeer eat lichens as their primary food source. These lichens soaked up so much radiation that they may not be a safe food source for more than three decades.

Sweden and Norway averted catastrophe for the Lapps by purchasing all the 1986 meat at 1987 prices. Government officials then destroyed the meat or provided it as food for mink ranchers. It is unclear if this type of program will be continued, as it cost Sweden more than $20 million in 1986. Swedish Government Officials feel that the Soviets are responsible for the radiation damage and they are angered at Soviet refusal to compensate the Lapps for their economic loss.

This incident offers insight into a growing political-economic problem. Environmental externalities will become increasingly significant in the years ahead. Environmental externalities within national boundaries can be solved through the political process. This process is difficult, as anyone who has observed the political fighting over site selection for low level nuclear dumps can attest. What is difficult within a nation becomes nearly impossible internationally. We can therefore expect increasing levels of international tension over international externalities. In some cases, such as acid rain, these issues have the potential of souring very friendly relations. The U.S.-Canadian experience is a case in point.

Source: *U.S. News and World Report*, March 23, 1987, p. 36, and July 20, 1987, p. 14.

In the real world, where production or consumption of a good causes significantly negative externalities, the people who bear the externalities subsidize consumers of the product. The people who live in Gary, Indiana, bear costs that allow consumers of steel to pay lower prices. If steel producers had to pay for the negative externalities they create, less steel would be produced, and it would be sold for a higher price. The general theoretical conclusion is that when negative externalities exist, the amount of production will not be optimal. Too much output will be produced at too low a price.

It is very important to understand that even if the cost of an externality, such as pollution, is placed on the buyer and seller of the product, this does not cause the amount of pollution to fall to zero. In the example in Figure 18–2, the price paid by buyers, including the external-ity, rose from P_1 to P_2, but some pollution and the costs associated with it continued. Only if production of the externality-creating good falls to zero will pollution fall to zero.

Internalizing Externalities

INTERNALIZE
To cause an externality to be incorporated in the market price.

In the jargon of economists, the trick of controlling social costs is to **internalize** the externality. This means that the costs that are borne by society are taken into account in production decisions by the producers. When internalized, the externality is incorporated into the market price. In terms of Figure 18–2, the firms should have to bear the social costs SC, so that S_t becomes the supply curve. How can this be done? It would be a simple matter if we could easily determine what the social costs are. We can draw theoretical cases, as in Figure 18–2, but in the real world it is very difficult to come up with a dollar value. We can determine the dollar value of having to paint your house more often because of air pollution, but what is the cost of a certain number of people dying because of respiratory problems? Or, how much is not being able to picnic in the back yard worth? If government officials could determine these costs, they could place a tax on the industry that would shift the supply curve just the right distance, to S_t (as in Figure 18–2). The market solution then would be the optimal price of P_2 and output of Q_2.

Governmental policymakers could also charge the firms for the amount of externalities they create. Each firm could be monitored and charged for pollution on a monthly basis. It would be possible to put a meter on each smokestack and measure the pollutants. In such a way, firms could be charged for the air they pollute just as for the electricity or labor they use. This pollution charge would cause costs to rise and move production toward the socially optimal level of output. This solution, how-ever, has the same problem as taxation—how to determine the correct charge per unit of pollutant.

These difficulties notwithstanding, there is a legitimate case for government intervention in the market process under these circum-stances. When there are externalities, markets don't produce socially opti-mal results, and it may be appropriate for government to step in to correct for the market imperfection.

The Coase Theorem and Small-Number Externalities

COASE THEOREM
A solution to externality problems which shows that in the case of small numbers of affected parties, a property right assignment is sufficient to internalize any externality that is present.

In an article that has had a significant impact on the field of economics, Ronald Coase of the University of Chicago pointed out that in cases in which the number of affected parties is small, individual maximiz-ing behavior will correct for the externality.[2] The **Coase theorem** states that in the case of small numbers of affected parties, a property right assignment is sufficient to internalize any externality that is present. Coase demonstrated that if property rights are clearly defined, the affected indi-viduals will take action to internalize the externality.

2. See Ronald Coase, "The Problem of Social Cost," *Journal of Law and Economics* 3, (Octo-ber 1960): 1–44.

Consider, as Coase did in his paper, that there are only two parties involved in a particular dispute, a wheat farmer and a cattle rancher. The externality is the damage done by the cattle roaming on unfenced land. As the rancher increases the size of the herd, the damage done by straying cattle will increase. To approach an optimal result, it is necessary to compel the rancher to take these costs into account, much as we discussed earlier and depicted in Figure 18–2. If government intervenes, it is likely to solve the problem by requiring the rancher to pay the farmer for the damage to the farmer's wheat. In this case, the rancher would restrict the number of cattle in the herd until marginal cost equaled marginal revenue (the marginal cost includes the damage to wheat, as we saw in Figure 18–2). Consider Figure 18–3. D and MR represent the demand and marginal revenue curve of raising cattle; MC represents the marginal cost of raising cattle; and SC represents the marginal social cost, or the damage of the externality (the damage to the wheat). Without internalization of the externality, the rancher would raise Q_1 cattle per year, and the farmer would incur a dollar loss to the wheat crop of W_1 for the last (marginal) cow raised. Government intervention would force the rancher to act on the basis of the joint $MC + SC$ curve through some tax scheme or direct regulation. As a result, the rancher would raise only Q_2 cattle.

Now consider a Coase solution. Coase shows that even if government did not intervene, the same solution would result. According to Coase, all that is necessary is that property rights be defined and enforced. First, assume that the farmer's property rights include the right *not* to have the wheat harmed. The rancher will then be forced to pay damages, as shown by the SC curve, and will add these to production costs. The rancher will then raise Q_2 cattle. On the other hand, suppose the rancher has the right to let the cattle roam. The important question then is how much the farmer will be willing to "bribe" the rancher to keep the cattle away. The farmer will be willing to bribe the rancher an amount just slightly less than the cost of the damage done by the cattle because this makes them *both* better off than allowing the cattle to damage the wheat. The farmer would pay W_1 for the last cow not to be raised. The rancher then must include these bribes as opportunity costs because if the cattle are raised, the bribe is foregone. When the foregone bribe is added to the marginal cost curve, the rancher will raise Q_2 cattle.

The result is that Q_2 cattle will be raised regardless of who has the property right, as long as the property right is defined and the number of people involved is small. Small numbers are necessary because the farmer and rancher must get together and work out a solution.

Note that the Coase solution says only that allocative results, or the number of cattle produced, will be the same, whoever has the property rights. It says nothing about the distribution of income. The property right assignment does affect who is better off. In the first case, the farmer's income is higher; in the second, the rancher's income is higher. The assignment of rights might have to be resolved by the law or through the political process since it involves the issue of equity, not economic efficiency. It's not really clear whether the rancher is imposing costs on the farmer (by damaging his crop) or whether the farmer is imposing costs on the rancher (by restricting the grazing range of his herd). Indeed,

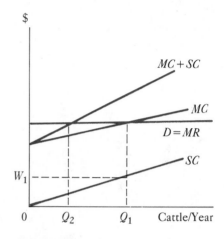

FIGURE 18-3
THE COASE THEOREM
The Coase theorem shows how externalities are internalized by the assignment of property rights. The social cost (SC) is automatically added to the marginal cost curve (MC) to form $MC + SC$, the true cost of raising cattle. The optimal product, Q_2, will result because a bribe or payment equal to the social cost will automatically come about.

that is why there are legislatures to define property rights and courts to define and enforce them.

The importance of the Coase theorem is that it draws attention to the role of property-rights assignment. Many social problems result from ill-defined or nonexistent property-right assignments. Consider, for example, the case of buffalo and cattle in the Old West. Why were buffalo almost wiped out while cattle thrived? The animals are very similar and roamed the same country. The answer is simple. Nobody owned the buffalo, or rather, everyone had a right to shoot them.[3] Consider air pollution as another example. If a copper mine dumped tailings on your yard, you would sue for damages or expect payment for the use of your land as a dump. Yet when this same mine dumps soot into your air, you are helpless because you don't own the air above your land.

Large-Number Externalities
Even if property rights are well defined, there still may be externality problems. If there are large numbers of people sustaining damages or large numbers of firms doing the damage, the Coase theorem may not hold. It may be that the costs of organizing the involved parties are too high to make it worthwhile for the damaged individuals to sue for damages or organize a bribe. The individuals damaged would have to mount a door-to-door campaign, advertise in newspapers, and arouse a group for joint action. If the damaging firms are hard to identify, the problem is even greater. In an area with severe air pollution, it would be necessary to determine how each of many firms contributes to this air pollution and who should be sued (or bribed). Because the information and transaction costs increase rapidly as the number of parties increases, it often is argued that the Coase theorem cannot solve the market failure that externalities create.

Government Intervention Again
We are, in a sense, back to square one, requiring government intervention to correct the externality. Usually government intervention takes the form of direct controls, and such controls often lead to unfairness in their own right. Consider the case of the government requiring that all cars have a pollution control device that costs $300. The salesperson who drives a great deal, and as a result pollutes a great deal, pays very little on a per-unit-of-pollution basis. By contrast, the retired couple who only drive on Sundays must pay the same $300, although they pollute very little. In addition, government intervention affects the distribution of income. For example, as auto prices rise because of pollution equipment, this affects the poor more than the rich because the poor spend a higher proportion of their income on cars.

Since government intervention is not without costs, we need to be sure that the social costs are indeed worth bothering with. Sometimes the government makes mistakes, and these mistakes raise costs of production. Externalities have received much attention in recent years.

3. For a discussion of how to protect eagles by assigning property rights to them, see Ryan C. Amacher, Robert D. Tollison, and Thomas D. Willett, "The Economics of Fatal Mistakes: Fiscal Mechanisms for Preserving Endangered Predators," *Public Policy* 20, no. 1 (Summer 1972): 411–441.

THE FABLE OF THE BEES

For years, apples and bees were used as a classic illustration of the externality problem. It was alleged that markets broke down because the apple grower's orchard provided a positive externality (nectar) for the bee farmer, but the orchard owner received no payment for this nectar. Likewise, the bees provided pol-linating services to the orchard owner, but the beekeeper was not compensated for this necessary service. As a result, it was argued that government intervention was needed to make the orchard owner grow more nectar-yielding apple trees and the beekeeper provide more pollination-supplying bees.

Steven Cheung of the University of Washington refused to take this classic illustration of market failure at its face value.[a] He went into the apple orchards to determine if these two externalities did indeed produce market value. To everyone's surprise, except perhaps Cheung's, he found that the market worked quite well without government intervention. An active market for beehive placement was in operation. Where the honey yield was great, beekeepers paid the orchard owner an "apiary rent" in order to place hives in these production spots. When the honey yield was low, the orchard owner paid a "pollination fee" to induce the beekeeper to place hives in the appropriate place. He even found that bee-keepers move hives to different states to pollinate crops in different seasons.

Cheung's study is important because it shows that markets can adapt well and that market failure may be less widespread than we first might think. The lesson for policymakers is that one should be very careful about determining if market failure exists before proposing political or governmental solutions.

a. See Steven N.S. Cheung, "The Fable of the Bees: An Economic Investigation," *The Journal of Law and Economics* (April 1973).

This attention may cause some to overestimate the real costs. We all have seen gruesome pictures of oil spills and fish kills; yet this damage seems to be of an exceedingly short duration. This is not to say that such damage is insignificant; it is only to suggest that the costs of correcting for an externality may exceed the damage it causes. We need to consider these costs before racing headlong into wholesale government regulation of externalities. We also need to consider what form that intervention should take.

The federal government usually has responded to calls to control noxious externalities with regulations. These regulations impose costs on firms, and the regulatory bodies themselves spend large amounts of money trying to enforce the regulations. The costs imposed on firms are hard to estimate until the required action actually is taken. For example, a regulation to keep copper mines from polluting the air may cause them to close because of increased costs of production. In considering the costs of the legislation, one should examine its impact on the affected industry. Production may move to a state (or country) that has less stringent regulation. Some geographic regions may compete for industrial growth by offering fewer environmental or economic regulations.

Each individual call for externality regulation should be considered carefully. Some of these externalities may have already been corrected by market mechanisms. For example, houses near airports sell for lower prices because of airport noise. The people who buy these houses are freely choosing to do so because the lower price compensates for the noise. To change the law because these people don't like the noise would generate a windfall gain to these people. It is not surprising that these residents should lobby for such a change, but it cannot be justified economically. The problem is complicated, however, by the fact that some residents may have purchased their homes before the noise became bad. These individuals lose twice; they suffer the cost of the noise and also a reduction in the value of their homes. It might make sense to compensate these individuals.

A recent battleground concerning externalities and the need for government intervention has taken place in the area of cigarette smoking and the rights of nonsmokers. The issues involved in this political battle point out once again the property-rights issue that is at the heart of most externality questions. Some states and localities have passed laws prohibiting smoking in some areas (public buildings) and requiring non-smoking areas in restaurants and other such businesses. This could be an arena of increased political action in the future. But, reflect on the need for it. If private demand for either smoke-free or smoking areas were real, some restaurants and other firms would capitalize on the demand without the need for government action. Indeed, some restaurants have done this. The recent opening of a motel chain for nonsmokers gives additional credence to the feasibility of a private solution to some externality problems.

■ Markets for Pollution Rights

More than a century ago, the famous economist John Stuart Mill wrote in his *Principles of Political Economy* (1862) that: "If from any revolution in nature the atmosphere became too scanty for the consumption, . . . air might acquire a very high marketable value." In the 1980s, he is being proven correct as the market is being used to allocate pollution rights. Economists have long argued for such a system over a regulatory approach. In 1970, Congress passed the **Clean Air Act**, which empowered the Environmental Protection Agency (EPA) to set standards for six pollutants and required each state to impose standards that would be met at each emission source. In other words, if emissions were to be reduced by 10 percent, all sources of the pollutant would have to be reduced by 10 percent.

CLEAN AIR ACT
An Act passed in 1970 that empowered the EPA to set emission standards and impose standards on polluters.

Some economists argue that it would be more efficient for the market to solve this problem. Marketing the right to pollute would make it possible to hold pollutants at the desired level and at the same time allocate them to producers who are willing to pay the highest price. Firms that wish to expand production could do so only if the market value of their product enables them to purchase the right to use the scarce commodity, air quality. In addition, if pollution rights had a value, firms would have the incentive to search for alternative ways to produce their product and even to search for alternative ways to control emissions. If they discovered new forms of emission control, they could sell the new technology and their emission rights.

This idea has come into use in the 1980s. In 1979, the EPA endorsed a "bubble" concept. The bubble concept considers a regional grouping of plants and allows these plants to adjust their emissions to achieve regional clear-air standards. The economics of the idea is simple. If the plants in the bubble are all owned by the same company, the company achieves the desired level of pollution by shifting emission control from higher cost to lower cost sources until the marginal cost of control is the same at each source. This minimizes the total cost of pollution abatement. If the plants in the bubble belong to different firms, it is a bit more complicated, but the principle is the same. The plant manager with high costs of pollution control will look for savings by paying neighbor firms in the bubble whose costs are lower to cut their emissions. This approach lowers the total cost of abatement in the bubble.

Such bargaining may seem difficult to achieve, but by 1987 there was evidence that a market was working to solve some of the complexities. In California, several plants financed new technology that saved on emissions by selling their right to pollute to other companies. These other companies found it less expensive to buy pollution rights than to purchase a more costly technology.[4]

PUBLIC GOODS

Public goods have two important characteristics. First, once they are produced, no one can be excluded from consuming them. Second, they are not depleted by consumption. If an individual consumes a public good, this action does not reduce the amount of the good available for other individuals to consume. In the jargon of economists, these two characteristics are referred to as *nonexcludability* and *nonrivalry*. Public goods were discussed in Chapter 4. We review and expand on that discussion here because of their close relationship to externalities and public choice.

Externalities and public goods are not really two separate and distinct arguments for government intervention. The arguments are actually the same. A public good is simply a good that has external benefits that are nonexcludable and nonrivalrous.

Purely Public Goods Versus Purely Private Goods

A purely public good is one that is consumed (automatically) by all members of a community as soon as it is produced. It is impossible to exclude consumption, and the good is perfectly nonrivalrous. This contrasts with a purely private good that has a price equal to the full-

---

4. For more information on the market for pollution rights and the bubble concept see, Bruce Yandle, "The Emerging Market in Air Pollution Rights," *Regulation* (July/August 1978): 21–28; and M.T. Maloney and Bruce Yandle, "Bubbles and Efficiency," *Regulation* (May/June 1980): 49–52.

opportunity cost of production and the consumption of which provides benefits only to that individual (or group) that purchases the good.

It would, of course, be difficult to come up with examples of either a purely public or purely private good. The idea worth noting is that the more private a good is, the easier it is to exclude consumption; and the more any individual consumes, the less there is for others to consume. A bottle of orange soda would be a good example of a private good, while a wilderness park would be an example of a public good. But a theme park, such as Disneyland, can clearly be private, while an empty soda bottle on the side of the road is a public good in a negative sense—a public bad.

No good is purely public because no good can be perfectly nonrivalrous in consumption. Almost any public good, e.g., a road, a park, or a library, gets congested at some point and loses the nonrivalry characteristic.

The Free-Rider Problem

Since nonexcludability is an important characteristic of a public good, it is possible for potential consumers to play the role of strategic holdouts in paying for the good. Economists call this the free-rider problem. Since it is impossible (or at least costly) to exclude you from consumption whether you pay or not, you may choose to hide your demand for the good, let others pay for it, and still consume the good. Thus, free riding makes it difficult for the market to measure actual demand.

The problem for the market is that if benefits from a public good are nonrivalrous and nonexcludable over a large group, it is likely that not enough of the good will be provided or that it will not be provided at all. The free-rider problem increases as the size of the group increases. It is difficult to free ride in a small group where everyone knows how much each person contributes, and social pressure makes it costly for individuals not to participate. This type of social pressure is used in many rural communities as a way of overcoming the free-rider problem. If you don't help rebuild a barn that has been burned, don't expect help if you run into problems.

The free-rider problem can be easily demonstrated by examining Figure 18–4. For simplicity, assume that there are only two demanders of national defense. The demand curve of each individual is derived in the same way we derived demand curves for private goods, reflecting the amount each is willing to pay for a given "quantity" of defense. If MC represents the marginal cost of national defense, the private market will produce Amount Q_1, which will be purchased by Consumer b and consumed by both Consumers a and b. However, the marginal benefits of national defense are determined by a vertical summation of the two individual demand curves. The result is a demand curve, $D_a + D_b$, for the public good, national defense. We can now determine the optimal level of production of national defense. At Price P_1, Q_2 units of national defense represent the efficient level of production. In such an exercise, individuals have every incentive to hide their demand for national defense and consume Amount Q_1.

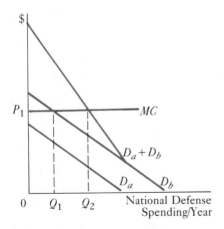

FIGURE 18–4
THE MARKET FOR NATIONAL DEFENSE
Since the benefits of the public good are nonrivalrous, the demand for the public good is found by vertically summing the individual demand curves.

Government financing of a public good overcomes the strategic holdout part of the free-rider problem. Forced tax collection compels the free rider to pay. It does, however, lead to a second problem. In Figure 18–4, we summed individual demand curves to determine the "correct" demand for the public good. In reality, we are talking about the demand of millions of people for a good, such as defense. How could we ever hope to measure all their demand curves? The answer to this difficult problem is that we depend on the political process to reveal the demand for public goods. Voting for Candidate x over Candidate y is, at best, a very imperfect mechanism for determining the "correct" level of public good provision.

PUBLIC GOODS IN PRACTICE

Some economists use the distinction between private and public goods to attempt to determine what projects and activities *should* be undertaken by the government. The idea would be to try to determine which markets might show a more nearly optimal level of output if government intervened in the process. This type of exercise is distinctly different from asking what projects and activities will be undertaken by government. In truth, the economic distinction between public goods and private goods has little to do with what goods and services government actually provides. Many goods that have the characteristics of private goods are supplied by governments. At the same time, many goods that at least partly fit the economic definition of public goods are privately supplied, often by volunteer groups, nonprofit organizations, clubs, and, in some instances, by the market.

Volunteer groups are generally more successful in overcoming the free-rider problem under certain conditions. One is that the group is small—often a small town, where peer pressure and visibility make free riding difficult. While barn raising is not as common as it once was, volunteer fire departments and volunteer recreation programs flourish in small towns. A second condition that alleviates the free-rider problem is the existence of private benefits blended and mixed with social benefits. For example, members of a garden club working for city beautification may derive substantial private benefits from both the companionship of other members and the personal enjoyment of a more beautiful town.

Politicians often incorrectly classify goods as public or private based on who supplies such goods. For example, garbage removal may be considered a local public good even though it might more appropriately be classified in theory as a private good with some external effects. In fact, many goods (food, recreation, education, garbage removal, police protection, etc.) could be classed as both public goods and private goods based on private or collective supply, which may vary from jurisdiction to jurisdiction. The economist then can ask what determines which goods the political unit will choose to supply. An interest-group analysis of the state is developed in the next chapter to address this question.

Income Redistribution as a Public Good

The argument for government redistribution of income is often based on a public-good line of reasoning. If a society decides that the income distribution resulting from the market is unsatisfactory, it can pursue deliberate redistribution. From your study of public goods, you know that if income redistribution is a public good, in the absence of government intervention, less than the optimal amount of redistribution will take place. Free riders will think that there is no need to help the poor because others will give. The electorate, as a result, may decide to redistribute income through government and tax all citizens to achieve a more acceptable outcome than the market-produced outcome.

Support for redistribution comes from the normative conclusion that citizens don't like the distribution of income the market produces. This argument can provide a theoretical basis for the type of income redistribution we saw in the last chapter.

Education as a Public Good

It is easy to see how getting a college degree is an investment in human capital. Your income will be higher because you have developed marketable skills. Economists argue that all schooling is investment in human capital. According to this argument, all schooling, even primary and secondary, increases the productivity of the work force. This claim was supported with a great deal of empirical research that showed the positive effects of education on economic growth. If this is true, much of the return to education does not accrue to the individual being educated; in consequence, individuals will not invest heavily enough in education.

Much of this theory and empirical work was used to support a public goods argument for increased public financing of education. This argument was based on the fact that trained and educated workers cannot directly appropriate all the gain from their education. Some of the benefits spill over to society in general. These externalities are increased economic growth for the nation, a more informed electorate, greater political participation, improved and extended research, and reduction in crime and other antisocial activity. Since these gains cannot be appropriated, individual students will choose to invest too little in education. Government could correct for this market failure by subsidizing the investment in publicly produced education.

MARKET FAILURE	EXAMPLE	GOVERNMENTAL REMEDY
Positive Externality	Tidy Houses	Zoning Fines Subsidies Deed Restrictions
Negative Externality	Pollution	Prohibitions Fines Selling Pollution Rights
Public Goods	National Defense	Provision
Natural Monopoly	Electric Company	Regulation Taxation

WELFARE ECONOMICS

The body of economic theory that concentrated on market failures and that sought remedies for them was developed in the 1930s, 1940s, and 1950s in the United States. This body of theory is part of a larger and older branch of economic theory that deals with normative policy prescriptions called *welfare economics*. The market failures were negative externalities, the underprovision of public goods, inequitable redistribution of income (which was the topic of the last chapter), and economic instability (which is covered in macroeconomics).

The conclusion of these developments in theory led to the policy approach that government *could* and *should* intervene to correct for market failure. Collective choice through the political process would ensure that we would (1) correct the externality, (2) produce the "correct" amount of the public good, (3) create an "equitable" distribution of income, and even (4) "fine tune" the economy to a desired level of employment and price stability. This was a very optimistic theory as it envisioned collective choice and government operating to make the world a much better place through the use of enlightened economic policies. The next chapter will examine some of the problems associated with government intervention to correct market failure.

SUMMARY

1. Externalities distort market outcomes because a cost or a benefit of the production process is not included in the economic decision-making process. This cost (benefit) results in underproduction (overproduction) of the product.
2. The Coase theorem shows that natural market forces can solve small-number externality problems if property rights are well defined.
3. Public goods are underproduced because some individuals will free ride on the production of those goods.
4. Market failure exists because of monopoly power, externalities, and public goods. Market failure often results in a call for political action to correct for the market failure.

NEW TERMS

externality
social costs

internalize
Coase theorem

Clean Air Act

QUESTIONS FOR DISCUSSION

1. Does air or water pollution exist where you live? What should be done about it? Should the pollution be entirely done away with? How much more in taxes or higher prices for goods would you be willing to pay in order to have less pollution?
2. Is education a public good? If not, why should taxes help pay for the college education of some individuals?
3. Why are some tennis courts provided as public goods even though it is relatively easy to exclude free-riding behavior?
4. Does "big time" college football generate any externalities to students that attend these universities?
5. If you happen to live in a dorm or in an apartment populated by students, there is most likely a great deal of noise. Does a Coase solution emerge to deal with this noise externality?

6. Distinguish between public goods as defined by economists and goods that governments publicly provide.
7. What is welfare economics?
8. Why are the demand curves for public goods vertically summed on a graph rather than horizontally summed like a private good?
9. What is free riding behavior? Have you ever practiced free riding? Did it work? How could it have been prevented?
10. Discuss whether the following goods are public goods, private goods, or partial public goods.

National defense   An Apple® computer
A lighthouse   A Buick
Income redistribution   Medical care
Education

SUGGESTIONS FOR FURTHER READING

Browning, Edgar K., and Jacquelene M. Browning. *Microeconomic Theory and Applications*, 2d ed. Boston: Little, Brown, and Company, 1986. This intermediate text contains more advanced material on externalities and public goods.

CHAPTER 19 ■
■

GOVERNMENT FAILURE
AND PUBLIC CHOICE

■

INTRODUCTION

The last chapter examined economic arguments for government intervention into resource allocation to correct for externalities and provide public goods. This chapter analyzes some of the costs of such intervention. Public choice economists have identified ways that government intervention introduces new problems and biases into the economic system. We will examine these biases and how they might affect the growth of government. Finally, we examine some other competing economic theories of the microeconomic role of government.

PUBLIC CHOICE

Public choice theory is not as optimistic about the potential for government intervention to improve the market outcome as the welfare economics discussed in the last chapter. Public choice economists apply the same tools of analysis and simplifying assumptions to the collective choice process that they apply to the market. These economists recognize that there are market failures. They do not ignore externalities, public goods, unequal income distribution, and macroeconomic instability. They do, however, argue that collective choice and the intrusion of government into the economy do not work perfectly either. The weaknesses of the political process mean that government intervention does not work in the ideal fashion suggested by the market-failure school. Public choice analysis begins from the premise that people who are self-interested in making personal economic decisions are the same people who vote, run for office, or are employed in the bureaucracy. They bring this same self-interest to the political process.

Public choice theory is as much political science as it is economics. Public choice analysis seeks to understand how economic incentives and economic self-interest affect political and governmental outcomes. For example, public choice economists expect the voter to be ill-informed because the cost of informed voting is extremely high. They view the politician as a vote maximizer, putting coalitions together to attract a majority of voters. Bureaucrats, who are not profit maximizers, are seen instead as seeking to maximize budgets or ensure the stability of their jobs. The result of such self-interested behavior in the public sector is that the public choice economist sees government as an imperfect intervener in its attempt to correct for market failure. One of the most important insights that emerges from public choice theory is that small groups with concentrated interests will have their way politically because it is irrational (unprofitable) for the majority to oppose them.

William C. Mitchell of the University of Oregon has succinctly summarized the public-sector biases that produce this less-than-optimal intervention into the market. His list provides a good foundation for understanding the thinking of public choice economists. He lists the following ten biases:[1]

1. Proposals with long-delayed benefits are likely to be adopted only if their costs are unknown or can be deferred or concealed.
2. Proposals offering readily apparent short-term benefits and deferred costs stand a good chance of adoption.
3. Proposals that concentrate benefits and diffuse costs stand an excellent chance of adoption. (A direct majority voting system might induce the opposite, depending on the relative sizes of the individual tax share and benefits.)
4. Proposals to abolish programs or reduce public expenditures have a low probability of adoption. Electoral rewards go to politicians who propose new programs or expansions and extensions of existing programs.
5. Packages of reform proposals stand a better chance of adoption than individual reform proposals, even if none of the packages' components would be accepted by a majority of voters if considered separately.
6. Straightforward transfer programs, which clearly designate specific and limited beneficiaries and benefits, stand little chance of adoption.
7. Proposals that rely on inefficient, complex, multiple revenue sources are preferred over those financed by simple, straightforward taxation.
8. Proposals that tax market efficiency stand a better chance of adoption than proposals that reward efficiency.
9. Proposals that limit consumption (e.g., price ceilings and rationing) as a response to product shortages are preferred over proposals that encourage increased production.
10. Policies that protect consumers by restraining producers are preferred over policies that simply improve the information level of consumers.

To the extent that such biases really exist, the implications for policy analysis are striking. Policy problems exist because two imperfect mechanisms are at work. The market fails because of externalities, underproduction of public goods (including unequal income distribution), and business cycles. The collective process fails because the participants in that process are responding to incentives other than those assumed by the

1. William C. Mitchell, *The Anatomy of Public Failure: A Public Choice Perspective*, Original Paper No. 13. (Washington D.C.: International Institute for Economic Research, 1978).

expositors of "perfect intervention." We must, therefore, choose between two imperfect mechanisms in attempting to solve any policy problems. The policymaker must examine the biases inherent in both the market solution and the collective-choice solution. It will not always be clear that the cost of intervention is less than the cost of inactivity. Hence, the public choice approach then may lead to a prescription of no intervention in many cases, on the grounds that the cure could be worse than the disease.

RENT SEEKING

In previous chapters, we introduced the concept of rent. *Economic rent* was defined as the economic return over opportunity cost and was discussed in two different chapters. The chapter concerning rent, interest, and profits introduced economic rent as the payment to any factor of production greater than the amount necessary to bring that factor into productive use. When we studied monopoly, we raised the issue of *monopoly rent seeking*. This was the additional economic cost of monopoly incurred by individuals seeking to establish monopolies. In this argument, monopolists "waste" resources from a societal viewpoint (in addition to the deadweight loss of monopoly) by incurring the costs of certain economic activities aimed at establishing monopoly. If you are uncertain about these two uses of the term *rent*, you should review the relevant sections of these two earlier chapters.

We now want to analyze the concept of rent seeking in a broader sense than just trying to create a monopoly. **Rent seeking** is defined as the commitment of scarce resources to capture artificially (government or quasi-government) created rents. Rent-seeking analysis is used by economists to describe how people compete for artificially contrived transfers. Consider the case in which a government decides to issue a monopoly privilege, for example, to be the sole supplier of food services at a state university. A great deal of effort will be spent to obtain that contract. Lobbyists will work in the legislature, firms will give campaign contributions to legislators, and lawyers will draw up contracts. All these expenditures are used in seeking a rent that has been artificially created by the state, but none of this activity will cause the price of the commodity to fall, as in the case in which rents are competed away by normal competitive methods. This rent seeking is a real cost to society because competition for governmentally created rents, unlike the "real" rents discussed earlier, do not generate increased supply.

RENT SEEKING
The commitment of scarce resources to capture artificially created rents.

The Cost of Rent Seeking

Gordon Tullock of the University of Arizona, in attempting to measure the costs of such contrived rent seeking, was the first to develop the concept.[2] Figure 19–1 shows a Market Demand Curve *D* yielding a

2. Gordon Tullock, "The Welfare Costs of Tariffs, Monopolies, and Theft," *Western Economic Journal* (now *Economic Inquiry*) (June 1967).

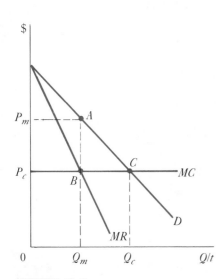

FIGURE 19-1
THE COSTS OF RENT SEEKING
The welfare cost of monopoly is triangle
ABC, but rent seeking could dissipate
rectangle $P_c\,P_m\,AB$, as rent seekers
compete for the monopoly right.

competitive equilibrium (Price P_c and Quantity Q_c) and a monopolistic equilibrium (Price P_m and Quantity Q_m).

As we saw in the chapter on monopoly, the welfare cost of monopoly is traditionally taken to be Triangle *ABC* in Figure 19-1. Area P_cP_mAB is supposed to be the transfer from consumers to monopolists in the form of monopoly profits. But Tullock argues that many of the resources represented by P_cP_mAB do not represent a transfer from consumers to producers. The expenditures to capture these profits turn them into a social cost of monopoly. In fact, if competition for the monopoly were vigorous, the area P_cP_mAB would be exactly dissipated by competition for the monopoly privilege. The dissipation of these rents in the "cost of capture" is unproductive in the sense that it uses scarce resources but does not generate any economic activity that lowers price or increases output.

Legislation and Rent Seeking

We can use this concept of rent seeking to explain governmental action as a form of self-interested behavior by politicians and voters. Many actions of government can be explained by this theory. In fact, it might be argued that an industry of rent seekers exists in most state capitals and most certainly in Washington, D.C.

There are two lines of attack in presenting such an interest-group theory of legislation. The first explains government regulation. George Stigler first presented the explanation in terms of the benefits and associated costs to various interest groups of using the state as a vehicle to increase their own wealth.[3] Some groups, such as agricultural interests, seek income transfers from the state. Other groups, such as automobile producers, use the state to fend off regulation that would have a negative impact on costs and profit. In some cases, management and labor join together to use the state for their mutual benefit against consumers or imports.

The second line of attack is to focus on the economic behavior of legislature itself. In this analysis, the politician is responsible for brokering transfers from one group to another. One can view the politician as an entrepreneur putting together coalitions of rent-seeking groups.

Consider public provision of education as an example. In the United States, education through the 12th grade is primarily produced in the public sector. A public choice economist would argue that even if education is a public good, there is no reason to believe that representative democracy can deliver the optimum subsidy necessary to internalize the external benefits of education. Instead, one would expect that the office holders would broker benefits to certain subsets of the population, including (but not limited to) members of the educational bureaucracy, politicians, and politically articulate student or parent groups. So, what started as a correction of market failure ends in a solution that is quite far removed from the optimal correction for market failure. It might reasonably be called government failure.

3. George Stigler, "The Theory of Economic Regulation," *Bell Journal of Economics and Management Science* (Spring 1971).

Politicians As Rent Extractors

In most of the literature on rent seeking, the politician is viewed as the broker for the private rent seekers. Recently, Fred S. Mc-Chesney of the University of Chicago has focused the analysis on the politician as the rent extractor.[4] He sees the politician as an independent actor making demands and the private sector responding to these demands. The politician first threatens to extract private rents through legislation, which might create special taxes or special regulation. The private sector responds by striking bargains in the form of campaign contributions or other side payments to protect its rent. As long as the cost of protecting the rent is less than the costs imposed in the threatened law, the private incentive to strike such a bargain exists. McChesney reports that this practice is so common that politicians even have a name for it: they refer to such legislation as "milker bills."

The example that McChesney uses to illustrate his argument is the Federal Trade Commission's "used car rule." In 1975, Congress passed a law that ordered the FTC to initiate a procedure to regulate the warranties on used cars. The FTC followed the order of Congress and developed a costly warranty and auto defects disclosure procedure. While the procedure was being written, Congress legislated itself a veto over FTC action. After the FTC formulated its rule, Congress held hearings on the rule. Used car dealers and their trade associations descended on Congress. Congress in turn vetoed the procedure that it had required to be written. What rent was extracted? McChesney reports that 89 percent of those in Congress who supported the veto and ran again in 1982 received contributions from the National Auto Dealers Association (NADA). The average contribution was over $2,300 and was made to 66 members of Congress who previously had not been supported by NADA.

RENT DEFENDING

John T. Wenders of the University of Idaho has extended the analysis of rent seeking by drawing attention to the fact that consumers also spend resources defending their consumer surplus from rent seekers.[5] Wenders recognizes that this activity might more correctly be called consumer surplus defending, but he prefers to label it **rent defending**. Consumers would be willing to pay the area represented by P_cP_mAC in Figure 19-1 to prevent the market from being monopolized. As you saw in an earlier chapter, the area P_cP_mAC represents consumer surplus, the extra utility that consumers gain from the fact that they pay less than they would be willing to pay for the item.

Initially, it appears that this might be double counting because rent seekers and rent defenders are bidding for the same resources. Rent

RENT DEFENDING
Defense of consumer surplus from rent seekers.

---

4. Fred S. McChesney, "Rent Extraction and Rent Creation in the Economic Theory of Regulation," *Journal of Legal Studies* (January 1987): 101–118. For an interesting discussion of the political rent extraction and rent defending that took place in tax reform, see Laura Saunders, "One Man's Problem Is Another's Opportunity," *Forbes* (March 7, 1988): 105–112.
5. John T. Wenders, "On Perfect Rent Dissipation," *American Economic Review* (June 1987): 456–459.

seekers are bidding for the monopoly privilege, while consumers are spending a like amount to prevent them from acquiring a monopoly. Wenders shows that this is not double counting because it is very akin to the prisoner's dilemma; if either party spends less, they will lose to the party spending more. This dilemma ensures that exactly double the amount of area P_cP_mAC will be spent seeking the monopoly and defending the consumer surplus.

The addition of the concept of rent defending expands the analysis of rent seeking. The implication is that in a market where regulation is politically determined, the cost of monopoly is much higher than it is traditionally thought to be.

THE GROWTH OF GOVERNMENT

In the self-interest theory of government, the size of government increases because of rent-seeking activity on the part of individuals and because of the brokering activity of politicians. There are at least two other phenomena related to rent seeking that fit into this general framework. They deserve special mention.

Logrolling

LOGROLLING
Vote trading in a legislative process.

When many issues are before a legislative body at one time, the outcome most preferred by voters may not result. This outcome is due to **logrolling**, which is a form of exchange in which a politician trades support on one issue for support on another issue. Logrolling is the direct exchange of support. The senator from Oklahoma votes for the military base in South Carolina in exchange for the senator from South Carolina voting for the water project that will make Tulsa a seaport.

We don't know much about the properties of logrolling except that it does not necessarily produce "optimal" levels of public output. The size of the budget may be too large and its composition may be altered as a result of logrolling. Any resulting outcome depends on the particular coalitions that surface. It probably is safe to infer that logrolling does not enhance the efficient use of resources.

It often is argued by economists that geographic-based representative democracy and logrolling produce "too much" government spending of a special (pork barrel) nature. This excess spending results from the fact that local citizens see their project cost being shifted to foreigners (i.e., citizens of other states or districts) and reward their elected officials for delivering such projects. With most delegations attempting to be successful at this political "game," logrolling creates larger than desired levels of government spending.

Bureaucrats and Bureaus

Once the governmental unit has decided how much of a public good to produce and how to pay for it, the legislature and the executive branch (president, governor, mayor, etc.) turn the job of supplying the

TO VOTE OR NOT TO VOTE: IS IT AN ECONOMIC DECISION?

When election time rolls around, voters are lambasted with exhortations concerning their civic responsibility to vote. These statements are usually followed with complaints about the low voter turnout levels in U.S. elections.

But think about it rationally for a minute. What are the costs of voting? You must register to vote. You must spend time getting to the polls. You must wait in line at the polls. Most important, you must spend time becoming informed on the issues and the candidates. What are the benefits of voting? It is possible that you might be able to affect the outcome, but the probability of your vote being important is minuscule, at best, especially in national elections. Perhaps you vote because you get a feeling that you have done your duty, or you receive satisfaction from participating in civic affairs. These feelings of civic duty must be important, or we would expect even fewer people to vote.

If we really wanted more people to vote, however, we would work on ways to make it less costly to vote. (One reason that many states make election day a legal holiday is to encourage voting.) If you don't think costs affect turnout, answer this question: Do more people vote when the weather is nice than when it is inclement?

How could the cost of voting be lowered or the benefits increased? Perhaps we could have postcard registration, transportation to the polls, and more voting places so the lines are shorter. Coffee and doughnuts at the polls might lure a few hungry voters, or a rock band at the polling place might bring in younger voters (but turn away older ones!). If you think about it, perhaps you can suggest even more voter-luring techniques to your local election board.

good over to a bureau (a government agency or department) in most cases. In a few cases, governmental units simply purchase privately supplied goods with tax revenue. A classic case of using private suppliers exists in Scottsdale, Arizona, where fire protection is privately supplied and some part of it is purchased by the local government (see Chapter 4). Garbage removal is also often privately supplied. More often, however, a bureau has direct responsibility for production.

Throughout this chapter, we have discussed problems associated with the provision of public goods and the determination of public sector output. Bureaus and bureaucrats further cloud the analysis because they are charged with the delivery of public goods. There are at least two major problems created by the role of bureaus and bureaucracy in supplying public goods. The first problem is that it is exceedingly difficult, if not impossible, to monitor the efficiency of a bureau. Bureaus do not usually produce measurable outputs; instead, they produce activities. For example, a bureau might produce fire protection, education, or defense. These activities usually are monitored by examining expenditures on these activities rather than by measuring outputs. Citizens may be more interested in output levels. Sometimes there is a partial measure of output, such as the number of students educated or length of response time for fire protection. But how do we measure the value of the outputs of the Department of Defense? The value of these outputs usually must be inferred from the activity of the bureau, and the activity of the bureau is most often measured by the size of the expenditure on the activity. Thus, worries over the quality and quantity of education and defense usually are reduced to calls for increased spending on the activity itself.

Monopoly Problems

The monitoring problem of bureaus is further complicated by the fact that bureaus are almost always monopoly suppliers dealing with a single purchaser. This supplier-government relationship makes the monitoring function of the governmental committee charged with oversight difficult at best and usually impossible. The rationale for a monopoly supplier is that it avoids inefficient duplication. This justification may or may not be valid, but it does mean that the legislative committee charged with supervising the monopoly has no competing information by which to judge the efficiency of the supplier.

This very point has surfaced in recent years in debates concerning the public funding of education. Conservative-Libertarian social critics have suggested a voucher system for education as a way to introduce competition into public education. Under a voucher system, each student receives a "chit" that can be used for tuition at any school. They argue that the resulting competition would improve the quality and quantity of publicly produced education.

Budget Maximizing

Still another weakness is created by the way in which bureaucrats are rewarded. As we discussed in a previous chapter, entrepreneurs or hired managers in the private sector generally lay claim to the residual (profit) produced and, therefore, have ample incentive to increase efficiency. In a public bureau, the manager has no such stake in the operation. Indeed, it may even be that the bureau manager's "salary" is inversely related to efficiency. This perverse incentive could happen if salary increases with the size of the budget and budgets grow (in part) because of inefficiency.

There are many possible goals that bureaucrats could substitute for the private manager's goal of profit maximization. Among these substitutes are: salary, perquisites of the office, power, public reputation, patronage, bureau output, ease of management, or investment in future private-sector employment. Government officials should keep these competing motivations in mind when they establish bureaus and when they evaluate bureau managers' behavior. All these motives will give different results from what welfare economists expect to be the results of government intervention.

The Inherent Bias Against Innovation

Government regulation has a built-in bias against new products and new technology. This bias is particularly true in the area of food and drugs, but it holds for any product that faces regulatory approval. The reason is that old products are on the market until they are proven "too harmful," but new products cannot be introduced until they are proven safe. This requirement greatly retards innovation in some areas of the U.S. economy. It is especially apparent in the area of drugs, where many U.S. citizens routinely travel to Europe or Mexico to receive innovative medical treatment.

In the area of drugs, the list of examples is very long. Somatotropin for pituitary deficiency, disopyramide for heart patients, propranolol for blood pressure, and sodium valprote for epilepsy were all available in Europe five to ten years before they could be used in the United States. Similar stories hold for other products and techniques. For six years, Chemical Waste Management has been seeking permission to burn waste 140 miles at sea. The technique has been used in Europe for more than 15 years.

Perhaps the most illuminating story of old versus new relates to sugar substitutes. In 1977, the FDA proposed a ban on saccharin because it had been linked to cancer. Saccharin had been sold on the U.S. market for almost 100 years. The makers of saccharin fought the ban in Congress, and it was overruled. At the same time, it took G.D. Searle eight years and lots of money to win FDA approval of aspartame. The quick approval of aspartame could have saved countless lives lost to cancer if it had been approved in a more timely fashion.

The story is a simple one. Regulation has slowed the introduction of new products. This type of regulation may be having a significant impact on U.S. competitiveness in world markets. As Peter Huber put it:

I strongly suspect that if Henry Ford had to bring out his Model T in today's environment, the courts and the regulators would have stopped him. Darn thing was dangerous; why you could break your arm cranking it. Of course, horses were dangerous, too, but as an established technology, horse transportation would have fared better in the courts and regulatory halls than transportation by new fangled flivver.[6]

WHERE ARE WE LEFT?

Where are we left? What are we to conclude? This chapter leads to disquieting conclusions. We saw in previous chapters, particularly when we studied monopoly, that markets do not always produce beneficial results. The previous chapter added to the list of market failures by introducing externalities and public goods. But this chapter showed that political action designed to correct market failure introduces a whole set of new problems.

The net result is a messy one. Markets may fail, but governments also can fail. Government and government representatives do not

6. Peter Huber, "Who Will Protect Us from Our Protectors," *Forbes* (July 13, 1987): 23.

always work in the "public interest," even if we could define what the public interest is.

This view of government failure as a parallel to market failure has gained much credibility among policymakers and voters. The important point is that economics can identify market failure and government failure and allow policymakers and policy discussions to sort out the least harmful solution to policy problems that affect everyone.

OTHER SCHOOLS OF THOUGHT

In this textbook, we have spent a great deal of time developing microeconomic theory. This theory shows that an economy organized with free markets and decision making by individual units economizes on the need for information to make production and consumption decisions. Changes in relative prices produce all the information that these decision makers need. Markets reward producers and consumers who take the "right" action by increasing their incomes, their profits, or their utility.

After developing this theory, we then looked at some areas where market failure exists, and we examined government activity to correct for these failures. Public choice theory, which was outlined in this chapter, applies microeconomic analysis to the political process. We would now like to draw your attention to two schools of economic thought that usually are ignored in a beginning economics course. Both are schools of thought that offer some useful insights on the role of government and the nature of government failure.

The Austrian School

The Austrian School draws its intellectual roots from Ludwig von Mises and Nobel laureate, F.A. Hayek.[7] Austrian School economists start their analysis from the premise that economic decisions are made in a state of partial ignorance. Individual consumers and producers plan with incomplete and/or incorrect views of the future. Markets play the role of providing feedback, which coordinates actions as individuals adjust their incorrect plans to relative prices. These individuals are frustrated, but by adjusting to relative prices they are better off than they would have been before the adjustment.

The Austrians are in many ways very close to public choice theorists. They stress that political manipulation of the economy is microeconomic in nature, rather than macroeconomic. Politicians do not work to influence the unemployment rate or the inflation rate, but rather work to influence certain markets for their own gain. For example, one politician may work to create subsidies for farmers. Another may work for aid to urban slum dwellers. The result of this action is that the government incurs huge costs, which lead to macroeconomic problems.

7. A very good survey of the Austrian School can be found in Thomas Sowell's, *Knowledge and Decision* (New York: Basic Books, 1981). Austrians in the United States disseminate information through the Ludwig von Mises Institute, which has its academic office at Auburn University.

THE INTERNATIONAL PERSPECTIVE
AGRICULTURE POLICY, EEC STYLE

The European Economic Community (EEC) maintains a common agricultural policy (CAP) for its member nations. The major element in that policy is different from agricultural policy in the United States. Instead of a basic ground rule that says "pay not to produce," the CAP says "pay for everything produced." This system of guaranteed payment has produced huge surpluses that are either stored and are rotting, or are sold to communist countries at bargain basement prices.

The CAP has resulted in what is jokingly referred to as the French wine lake, the European grain mountain and, with the recent admission of Spain and Portugal, the great olive oil sea. Great Britain has 150 storage depots that are stuffed full of grain and butter. John MacGregor, a junior minister in Mrs. Thatcher's government, testified in the House of Commons that the cost of storing and disposing of stocks of cereals, sugar, wine, milk, and beef was about $25 million per day. A "rancher" with three or more cows is entitled to a subsidy from the EEC. In Germany, many people have become cow ranchers. Bavaria is full of cottages on small plots of land that now come with three cows. Margaret Thatcher has herself complained that: "In Europe, believe it or not, the subsidy for every cow is greater than the personal income of half the people in the world." (*U.S. News & World Report* [November 30, 1987]: 9).

Perhaps the biggest recipient (after the farmers) of this largesse from taxpayers in the EEC is the Soviet Union. The Soviet Union has learned that it can play this game well, and use it as a way of supplementing its notoriously poor agricultural output. Great Britain has sold increasingly large amounts of its surplus output to the Soviet Union. In 1984, sales from Great Britain to the USSR equal 125,000 tons of products per week and 35,000 tons per week to other communist countries of eastern europe. The prices were deeply discounted from those paid to farmers. Flour was sold at an 80 percent discount; sugar, 72 percent; butter, 60 percent; beef, 88 percent; and wine 97.5 percent. Maybe the Soviets are better capitalists than we give them credit for being. At least they know how to profit from the central planning of other governments!

Source: Edward Pearce, "Buying the Farm with the EEC," *National Review* (October 18, 1985): 42–44.

Austrian economists take a strong stand against governmental planning. This stand is based on four points made by one of the best known members of the Austrian School, F.A. Hayek. The first is that planning always results in more planning because people will circumvent the rules of the planner. As a result, the planner will devise more rules, which leads to more circumvention, which produces still more rules. Hayek referred to this process as "the road to serfdom." Hayek's second point about planning is that no matter how detailed the plan, it can't cover all the specific cases. A powerful bureaucracy will be needed to implement the plan. This bureaucracy will grow powerful and corrupt. Hayek's third point is that high morale is so important to success in planning that any critics of the plan must be silenced. Hayek's last point about planning is that "the worst get to the top." His point is that planning leads to a dictator. One of the great appeals of Hayek's work is that it so accurately describes the path followed by most countries that have tried central planning. As you will see in a coming chapter, the Soviet Union and The People's Republic of China are trying to address some of these problems. The Austrians would argue that their problems are caused by planning, and reforms in the context of planning are doomed to failure.

■
Radical Economic Thought

Unlike Austrians, radical economists are critical of both the market and government in a capitalistic system. Radical economists in the United States draw on the tradition of Karl Marx and Marxist thought, which we will discuss in a later chapter; but these economists add several new lines of attack on capitalism.[8] The basic difference between radical and orthodox economics, which we have studied in this textbook, is that orthodox economists (including public choice and Austrian) see a basic harmony in the economic system and believe that most problems can be solved by relying on basic market forces. Radicals contend that solutions to the problems of modern capitalism can only be found by a radical restructuring of industrial capitalism. In addition, radical economists regard orthodox economists as being much too narrow in their analyses.

The main themes of radical economics can be summarized as follows:

1. Monopoly Power. Radicals believe that the U.S. economy is dominated by large corporations and that small firms play an insignificant role. These large corporations set arbitrary prices and manipulate consumer wants.
2. State Power. The state is viewed as the protector and fostering agent of the powerful monopolies. The radicals see the federal government as controlled by the big companies. They believe that the state sets economic policy, including defense spending, in the interest of big business.
3. Exploitation. Radicals challenge the marginal productivity theory of income determination developed in an earlier chapter. They argue that monopolistic firms, unequal opportunity, and the unjustifiable private ownership of capital make this theory defective. They base their description of factor incomes on dual or segmented labor markets. **Dual or segmented labor markets** represent the idea that there are artificial barriers in labor markets that keep some workers in artificially low wages. Radicals argue that these two labor markets consist of one in which pay is good and advancements are possible and a second in which pay is low and opportunities for advancement are nonexistent. These dual or segmented labor markets are a result of a conscious effort on the part of capitalists to restrict advancement to certain groups in the labor force. As a result, a large fraction of the labor force will forever be in dead-end jobs, with low pay, little job security, and no opportunities for advancement.

DUAL OR SEGMENTED LABOR MARKETS
The idea that there are artificial barriers in labor markets that keep some workers in artificially low wages.

8. Most radical economists in the United States are members of the Union of Radical Political Economy (URPE). URPE publishes a journal, *The Review of Radical Political Economics*, which you can check if you are interested in learning more about radical economics.

4. Imperialism. Radicals argue that the main obstacle to third-world development is the imperialistic posture of industrial capitalism. Radicals claim (and here they differ from Marx) that industrial capitalists receive capital from the underdeveloped world and that the terms of trade are exploitative of poorer countries. Radicals would support the New International Economic Order, which will be discussed in a later chapter, as a way to change these conditions.

5. Waste and Alienation. Finally, the radicals argue that resources are wasted in a capitalistic system. The "proof" of this waste is the amount of money spent on autos, furs, alcohol, drugs, etc., and by the billions of dollars spent on advertising, which radicals claim is used to manipulate consumer wants. Radicals argue that this waste and the power of monopolies contribute to alienation. Since individuals have little control over their own destiny, they consume high levels of consumer goods and feel alienated from society.

Radical economists have challenged the mainstream to examine more closely some of the weaknesses of capitalism. The response of many orthodox economists to radicals has been, for the most part, not to take radicals too seriously (or to ignore them completely). Radical ideas have, however, led to suggestions for "tinkering" with capitalism in some areas, especially in control of monopoly power. In some cases, they have provided useful insights into the use of government by special-interest groups to serve their own self-interest, not unlike the insights of the public choice school. The most serious weakness in the modern radical critique of capitalism is that it is negative. The radical critique identifies problems but does not present feasible alternative solutions to those problems.

SUMMARY

1. Government often supplies many goods that aren't public goods because there is political demand for these private goods.

2. Public choice theory identifies biases in the political process and applies economic analysis to political processes and outcomes.

3. Rent seeking is the economic description of how individuals use the political process to generate transfers to themselves or to groups they support.

4. Politicians can threaten specific taxes or specific regulation in order to extract rents from private parties.

5. Rent defending is the process by which consumers attempt to defend their consumer surplus from rent seekers.

6. Logrolling in the legislature increases the size of budgets. Legislators agree to vote for a colleague's project in return for a vote on their project.

7. Bureaucracy and bureaucratic decision making are different from firm decision making because bureau managers face a different set of incentives than do private-sector managers.

8. Government regulation of new products introduces a bias that is inherently anti-innovation.

9. Austrian economic thought assumes that decision makers proceed on the basis of incorrect and/or incomplete information. Austrians make a strong case against economic planning by governments.

10. Radical U.S. economic thought, which is related to Marxism, is based on the belief that monopoly capitalism, protected by government, is manipulative and exploitative.

NEW TERMS

rent seeking   logrolling   dual or segmented labor markets
rent defending

QUESTIONS FOR DISCUSSION

1. Should the government intervene in every case in which an externality exists?
2. What is public choice theory?
3. Why do public choice economists argue that straight forward transfer programs that clearly target beneficiaries stand little chance of adoption?
4. Why is it so hard to terminate public programs once they are started?
5. Why do government programs that concentrate benefits and diffuse costs have better chances of being enacted than those that benefit many and impose costs on a few?
6. How might politicians be rent extractors?
7. How might logrolling increase the size of government?
8. Is public choice theory pessimistic? What is its sobering comment on the welfare economics discussed in the previous chapter?
9. According to the Tiebout model (appendix), what would you predict the outcome of a local tax and spending initiative in a metropolitan area composed of many localities, that significantly increased local sales taxes and earmarked all the revenue for spending on primary (grade school) education?
10. How can the basic tool of price elasticity of demand and income elasticity of demand help explain part of the farm problem (appendix)?

SUGGESTIONS FOR FURTHER READING

Buchanan, James M., and Robert D. Tollison. *The Theory of Public Choice-II*. Ann Arbor: The University of Michigan Press, 1984. This book contains a series of articles related to applications of public choice theory.

Frey, Bruno S. *International Political Economics*. New York: Basil Blackwell, Inc., 1984. This book applies some public choice theory in an international setting.

Galston, William A. *A Tough Row to Hoe: The 1985 Farm Bill and Beyond*. New York: Hamilton Press 1985. This book lays out the issues underlying the debate over the 1985 farm bill.

Heilbroner, Robert L. *The Nature and Logic of Capitalism*. New York: Norton, 1985. A critical look at capitalism from a (traditional) liberal perspective.

Heilbrun, James. *Urban Economics and Public Policy*. 3d.ed. New York: St. Martins Press, 1987. A very up-to-date textbook that covers urban economic issues in detail.

Lee, Dwight R., and Richard B. McKenzie. *Regulating Government*. New York: Lexington Books, 1986. This book uses the public choice framework to explain government intervention into the market and why a constitution is needed to restrain government.

Smith, Lee. "How to Cut Farm Spending." *Fortune* (November 10, 1986): 97–103. An essay that argues that the government should stop paying farm subsidies and adopt a straightforward welfare program for farmers.

APPENDIX: MARKET FAILURE AND GOVERNMENT FAILURE: SOME PROBLEMS OF RURAL AND URBAN AMERICA

This appendix applies the theories discussed in the last two chapters to two real-world areas: farm problems and urban problems. We hear and often read in the news about the demise of the family farm and the crisis in agricultural markets. In some areas of the country, traditionally conservative farmers have even borrowed the tactics of protest movements in efforts to draw political attention to their economic problems. Our basic tools can provide many insights into the situation and how it arose. The issues facing urban America are in many instances problems that are not unique to urban areas, but are more severe in the densely populated urban environment. For example, pollution and crime are found in all parts of the world, but pollution and crime are more serious problems in urban areas.

THE FARM PROBLEM

Government involvement in agriculture has a long history in the United States, beginning with the Homestead Act of 1862. During the Great Depression, direct income and price-support programs began. Those who encourage government intervention in agriculture believe that the market has failed in several ways. The structure of farming is very competitive, with a large number of firms. Farmers face unstable prices for farm products producing unstable farm income. Unpredictable weather, international-trading patterns that are subject to governmental influence, and significant technological changes aggravate the market instability.

Problems in agriculture present a case study of the trade-offs involved in well-intentioned government policy as the government becomes part of the problem. Even when it is recognized that this is the case, it is politically very difficult to reduce or eliminate the government's role.

In the short run, the farm problem is simple enough to understand. First, agricultural production takes place in a very competitive market that closely resembles the basic supply and demand model developed in Chapter 3. Second, the demand for these products is price inelastic. Third, weather plays a significant role in determining the size of any particular crop. These conditions taken together mean that the revenue a farmer receives from year to year can be highly variable. The irony for farmers is that in good harvest years, many of them may be in worse shape than in poor harvest years. The situation can be seen by examining Figure 19A-1. Let's say that in the previous year farm output

sold at a price of P_1, so Q_1 units were sold, and farmers received a total revenue of $P_1 \times Q_1$. The next year, the weather is very good and the crop is bountiful, so the supply curve shifts to S_2. Price falls to P_2, and consumers purchase Q_2 units. Since demand is so inelastic, farmers are now making less revenue than they did the year before ($P_1 \times Q_1 > P_2 \times Q_2$); the large fall in price brought only a small increase in sales.

The long-run problem for the farmer is largely the result of huge increases in U.S. farm productivity in the last century. It takes fewer and fewer farmers to produce the same amount of food. In the early 1800s, more than half of the U.S. labor force was engaged in farming, but now less than 5 percent of the work force is in agriculture. In the last few years, the value of farm assets (land and buildings) has declined sharply. This complicates the farm situation because farmers with a high debt load and insufficient income are unable to sell their assets to cover what is owed.

The instability of farm income and the decline of opportunities in agriculture are regarded by some observers as forms of market failure. However, as we saw in this chapter, there are risks of failure associated with government intervention as well. One of the risks is that government will undertake policies that benefit special interests even though the costs to society exceed the benefits.

Many of the political arguments to save the family farm are intended to stop the trend toward fewer and fewer agricultural workers. Even some nonfarmers support maintaining the current number of farmers. They argue that smaller, more numerous farms are more environmentally benign than huge agri-industry. Farmers have political power, so we would expect a governmental response to their calls for action. Among the forms of response have been agricultural price supports and managing production.

Price Supports

Prior to 1973, the **agricultural support program** consisted of attempts to achieve parity for farmers. Parity is an argument for higher relative prices in the agricultural sector. In practice, **parity** creates **support prices** or price floors, which are prices above equilibrium levels. The idea of parity prices is to link farm prices to an index of the purchasing power of farmers as it was in the period selected as the appropriate one, such as 1910–1914. For example, if a bushel of wheat bought five gallons of gasoline or two pairs of

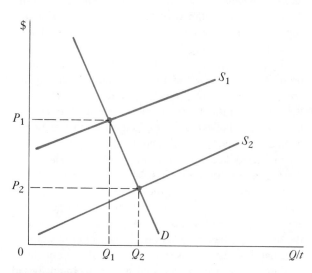

FIGURE 19A-1
THE MARKET FOR FARM OUTPUT
The market for farm output is characterized by erratic supply (due to changes in the weather) and inelastic demand. This means that the total revenue a farmer receives in any one year can be highly variable, and an increase in quantity supplied can reduce total farm income.

shoes in the base period, the price of a bushel of wheat should be kept high enough to permit the same purchases today. Highly respected agricultural economist and Nobel laureate, T.W. Schultz, described parity as "a vulgar economic concept."[a] It is vulgar to Schultz because it does not allow changes in the relative prices of agricultural and nonagricultural products over time.

We saw the effect of price floors in the chapter "Applications of Supply and Demand," so Figure 19A–2 should be familiar. When there is a price floor above the equilibrium price, the quantity supplied exceeds the quantity demanded at the imposed price, and a surplus develops. If the price floor is to be maintained, demand must be increased. A dilemma results: the government can't sell the product on domestic markets or the price will fall back to the equilibrium price.

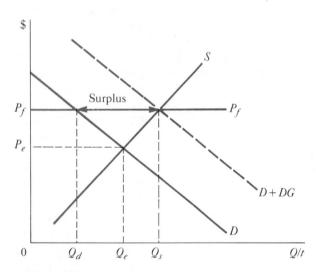

FIGURE 19A–2
PRICE FLOORS IN AGRICULTURE
If the government imposes a price floor or support above the market-clearing price, a surplus will be created.

In the 1950s and early 1960s, the government reacted to this dilemma by building storage bins and storing the farm products. Some of the surplus food was sold to poor countries under the Food for Peace program which accepted local currency in payment, or distributed to the school lunch program and to welfare recipients, but most of it was just stored. At the high point of this storage activity in 1961, the government had 1.3 billion bushels of wheat and 1.7 billion bushels of corn in storage.

There are some other steps that could be taken to dispose of the surplus. The government could destroy the surplus grain, but this action would upset those who consider it wasteful.[b] The government could give the produce away to poor countries, but this might anger other countries who are trying to sell their farm products to those countries. In the 1980s, the Reagan administration distributed large amounts of surplus cheese to people with low incomes to deplete stores. Some of this cheese went to people who were quite well off including retirees with a great deal of accumulated wealth. The government could sell the grain to other countries if customers could be found. Still another alternative would be to hold on to the surplus for future emergency needs. Regardless of the disposal problems, it is absolutely necessary for the government to buy the surplus it has created.

Managing Production

In the mid-1950s, the U.S. government decided that the purchase and storage of surpluses was too costly and that managing production was a better alternative. The idea was that the government could maintain the price floor by keeping the quantity supplied at lower levels than would exist without government intervention. Under this policy, the government is trying to shift the supply curve to the left in order to maintain the higher price without creating a surplus.

The first government attempt to manage production was known as the soil bank program. In the **soil bank program**, which was started by President Eisenhower in the 1950s, farmers were paid to let their land lie idle. Policymakers expected that this reduction in cultivated acreage would reduce the supply. A second attempt to reduce production was the acreage allotment. An **acreage allotment** sets a limit on the number of acres that can be put into production of a particular crop. The government then must determine who gets what acreage allotment. In producing tobacco, for example, the decision is based on historical levels of production. If your parents were tobacco producers and you bought or inherited their farm, you would get an allotment based on their share of past production.

a. T.W. Schultz, "Tensions Between Economics and Politics in Dealing with Agriculture" (Agriculture Economics Paper no. 84:24, Department of Economics, University of Chicago, 10 August 1985), 5.

b. The Canadian government once destroyed 28 million eggs. See Patrick Howe, "Unscrambling the Egg Market: A Lesson in Economics," *Common Sense Economics* 2 (Spring 1977): 42–47. See *Fortune* (November 25, 1985): 149 and (December 9, 1985): 150, for some ludicrous stories of price supports gone amok.

The supplies of many crops that are not directly subsidized by the federal government are controlled by a system called marketing orders. The system of marketing orders dates to 1937 and has as a goal the maintenance of farm income and orderly marketing conditions. **Marketing orders** are producer cartels that control the supply of certain agricultural commodities not subject to price supports. These cartel arrangements are enforced by the federal government through a system of fines for growers. Marketing orders are especially common in the fruit industry. The influence of these cartels on supply can be enormous. For example, in 1983, 20 million cartons of lemons were destroyed to hold them off the market. The amount of lemons destroyed in 1983 actually exceeded the amount sold to consumers.[c]

The transfer to farmers in the case of marketing orders is a bit different from the subsidy in the case of support payments. In support programs, the payment from the government to the farmer represents a transfer from all taxpayers. Under the marketing orders, the subsidy takes the form of a federally enforced artificially high price, and the subsidy is paid by the consumers of the specific products to the growers of those products.

Attempts to manage farm production directly by reducing inputs have not reduced production very effectively because most farmers are good entrepreneurs. Under the soil-bank program, farmers invariably took the least productive land out of production. In the acreage allotment program, farmers had an incentive to cultivate the allowed acres very intensively in an effort to produce larger crops on fewer acres. In both cases, production fell very little. The marketing order system was more effective in reducing quantity supplied because the farmer could not benefit by increasing productivity and output, when the allowed output is specified by the government.

RECENT FARM POLICY

Since 1973, there have been some changes in the system of agricultural support. For *some* products, there no longer are price floors or support prices. Instead, the government sets target prices. **Target prices** are prices the government considers to be fair for farmers. The market is allowed to clear and the equilibrium price is compared to the target price. The govern-

c. See Doug Bandow, "Federal Marketing Orders: Good Food Rots While People Starve," *Business and Society Review* (Spring 1985): 41.

ment then pays each farmer the difference between the target price and the market-clearing price. These target prices are less distortive than support prices because the relative prices of agricultural products are allowed to change. Also the government does not have to purchase and store the surplus product. In addition, the subsidy aspect of target prices is more apparent than is the case with support prices.

The Reagan administration has made some attempts to curtail the price support programs. The first attempt in early 1981 kept a scheduled rise in milk target prices from going into effect. This move did not do away with supports but did prevent an increase at that time.

In 1982, President Reagan initiated a **Payment In Kind (PIK) program**. The idea was to eliminate the current overproduction (caused by the existing support prices) and deal with the huge stocks of farm surpluses. For example, the program gave a farmer 8,000 bushels of stored corn, which the farmer would sell, in exchange for not producing 10,000 bushels. The PIK program was similar to the soil bank program, but the payment was made in surplus commodities rather than in money. The result was the same as for the soil bank program. Farmers idled 47 million acres of land in 1983, but they put aside their least productive land and worked the best land more efficiently. The percentage drop in production was much less than the percentage of land set aside.

The Food Security Act of 1985

In 1985, Congress passed the **Food Security Act.** The bill was intended to make U.S. agricultural products more competitive on world markets and to do away with the price support program that caused the price of U.S. agricultural output to be above world-market prices.

The Food Security Act sets target prices and, to participate in the program, farmers must agree to keep part of their land idle. Thus, it combines elements of both the target price and soil-bank programs. Farmers are then permitted to sell their products at world prices, and the government will pay a deficiency payment equal to the difference between the target price and the world price. The target price is supposed to be related to the costs of production. In 1986, the target price of wheat was $4.38 a bushel while the world-market price of wheat was around $2.75 a bushel. As a result, U.S. taxpayers had to make a payment of $1.63 for every bushel of wheat sold. As you might imagine, the cost of this program is enormous. When Congress debated the bill in early 1985, the cost over its five-year life was estimated at $35 billion. When President Reagan signed the bill in November 1985, his advisers estimated its cost to be $52 billion. In November 1986, the Congressional Budget Office forecast the cost to be $70 billion in the first three years of the program.

Save the Family Farm Act

As it became obvious that the cost of the Food Security Act was so high that it would have to be reconsidered, Senator Tom Harkin of Iowa and Congressman Richard Gephardt of Missouri introduced the Save the Family Farm Act in 1987. The goal of this act is to raise farm prices by drastically decreasing farm output. Farmers would be given the opportunity to control production by voting mandatory limits on the amount of farmland that could be put into production. Farmers would face penalties if they did not limit production; however, the proposed bill did not specify what the penalties would be. *Business Week* commented that the Harkin-Gephardt bill sounded "borrowed from a Soviet economic plan."[d]

The idea behind this bill was to drastically reduce (by more than half) supply so prices paid to farmers would increase. The politicians argued that while prices to consumers would increase, taxpayers would save billions in subsidy payments. One difficulty with this proposal was that, if it were successful in raising U.S. prices, imports would be cheaper and import competition would drive the artificially high U.S. prices down to world-market levels. Thus, the program could only achieve its goal with more restrictive tariffs and quotas on agricultural imports than we have under the present program.

Conflicting Policies

Many of the governmental farm policies work at cross purposes. Consider, for example, the price support program, which guarantees the farmer an unlimited market for grains and dairy products. This policy works to stimulate production, while other programs are intended to decrease production. Farmers expand pro-

duction because they know they have a buyer to generate the cash flow to meet their payments on heavily mortgaged machinery and land.

In 1986, the federal government set out to mop up the milk glut and in the process created a new problem. In a sweeping offensive, called the *Dairy Termination Program*, the government sought to eliminate 12.3 billion pounds of milk from the market by buying up dairy herds and selling the animals for beef. In order to participate in the program, farmers had to agree to stay out of the dairy business for five years. Almost $2 billion was spent on this program aimed at getting 14,000 farmers out of the milk business.

Groups representing cattle farmers were quick to respond. The program designed to increase milk prices by cutting supply had the opposite effect on beef prices. Prices fell as the supply of beef was increased. The California Cattlemen's Association demanded compensation for their losses of from $25 to $60 per head of beef.

In still another program, the **Soil Conservation Service**, grants were given to encourage farmers to conserve land (rather than produce full tilt) by fallowing fields, contour plowing, and other conservation techniques. (These techniques all temporarily reduce crop yields.) The price support and the soil conservation programs, both costing taxpayers' monies, work in opposite directions. One creates incentives to expand production, the other to contract production.

Solutions?

Like many social problems, the farm problem cannot be settled with the tools of economics, but these tools can point out some fundamental truths. There are too many resources in the agricultural industry relative to the demand for its output. The resources are encouraged to stay there by transfers from general tax revenues. Taxpayers' income is being redistributed to farmers, which keeps resources in the farm industry that would otherwise be attracted to other industries. In 1987, the direct budget costs associated with federal agriculture programs were more than $700 for every nonfarm family in the United States.[e] This represents a significant share of federal tax money, and it does not include the off-budget transfers to farmers.

d. Michael A. Pollock, "Farmers Will Reap a Bumper Crop of Supports," *Business Week* (January 12, 1987): 83.

e. Raymond E. Owens, "An Overview of Agricultural Policy . . . Past, Present, and Future," *Economic Review*, Federal Reserve Bank of Richmond (May/June 1987): 48.

The basic tools of economics cannot tell us if this situation is good or bad, nor can they predict if anything will be done to change it. The answer to the first question is a value judgment concerning whether society thinks it is good or bad to maintain the present level of resources in agriculture. The answer to the second question will in part depend on the political strength of farmers and the farm constituency relative to other groups.

URBAN ECONOMICS

The study of urban economics also illustrates the problems of market failure and government failure. The market failure consists of the externalities associated with population density. These negative externalities include crime, traffic congestion, environmental pollution, and noise pollution, to name a few. Provision of public goods in urban areas is complicated by fragmented jurisdictions. Government failure comes when government responds to these market failures in a less than optimal manner. In the 1970s, the growth of population in cities was slower than the population growth in rural areas and in suburbs. This trend was at the time in part attributed to the energy crisis with its high gasoline prices. The 1980s have seen a reversal of this trend, with population growth in metropolitan areas exceeding growth in nonmetropolitan areas. At the same time, the Reagan administration sharply reduced the amount of federal transfers that had previously been going to U.S. cities.

Economies of Scale

Let's review some basic economic concepts as applied to cities. Urban areas spring up because of economies of scale. Urban economists use the more specific term **economies of agglomeration** to describe the cost savings that accrue to individuals when enough of them locate in one city to generate savings for each other. The sources of these lower average costs are similar to the cost savings to a firm when scale economies exist. They result because the size of the city has generated sufficient local demand for highly specialized suppliers. Secondly, large pools of specialized labor exist in urban areas, again because the demand is large enough to create a sufficient pool.

The broadcasting industry is a good example of this principle. Broadcasting is concentrated in New York City and in Los Angeles. This concentration represents demand for writers, actors, musicians, dancers, technicians, directors, and designers, and for firms that specialize in the equipment these individuals use. Start-up costs for new firms are reduced because the suppliers of these services are close at hand. New firms and new artists must set up in these same areas in order to enjoy these cost savings.

Economies of agglomeration usually take the form of production economies, but agglomeration can also provide a wider variety of consumption alternatives. This wider range of consumption alternatives can attract high income residents and lead to further agglomeration.

Just as some costs are lowered as agglomeration takes place, others are increased because of **diseconomies of agglomeration**. There are both negative and positive externalities associated with urban growth. The two most obvious negative externalities are crime and pollution.

Optimum City Size

Since there are economies and diseconomies associated with agglomeration, there should be some optimum city size. The optimum would be the size at which the value of the cost savings exceed the costs of the negative externalities by the greatest amount. In terms of microeconomic theory, the optimum size would be that for which the marginal agglomeration benefits are equal to the marginal agglomeration costs. The optimal size of a city would change as these costs and benefits change. For example, if a technological change would make crime prevention cheaper, the model would predict an increase in city size. Optimal city size would continually change as technology changes. If technology reduced diseconomies of agglomeration, optimum city size would increase. In addition, to the extent that demand for the consumption activities supplied by cities is income elastic, the incomes of residents, and potential residents, of a metropolitan area will affect the optimal size of that metropolitan area. An increase in income would increase the optimal size of urban areas, other things being equal.

Policymakers need not worry about optimal city size. The decision about optimal size will be made by the thousands of individuals that compose the city. Migration out of and into cities will be driven by individual decisions about the value of these positive and negative externalities. Differences in tastes and preferences will ensure a variety of sizes of cities. Most economists would argue that such a decentralized determination is superior to some political decision about how large a city should be. The market determines the optimal size for each city, and the optimum is always in a state of flux.

New Suburbs

The traditional role of the central city is changing. Historically, suburbs grew away from the central city, but most suburban residents commuted to the central city for work, entertainment, and shopping. This pattern has changed significantly, as the information age is decentralizing cities. Since it is no longer necessary to commute to the center to do business, all kinds and types of businesses have moved out of the city and into the suburbs where, among other things, the rents are cheaper. Barbara Boggs Sigmund, the mayor of Princeton, New Jersey, refers to these new suburbs as "urbanoid villages." Sigmund feels that these urbanoid villages breed traffic, fail to deliver services, and hinder rather than promote community.[f]

Public policy to solve the problems created by this change in life and work styles is complicated by the number of political entities involved in these areas. For example, metropolitan Atlanta has 53 separate governments. These governments not only do not always cooperate with one another, but they often are in direct competition for projects and for economic development. This competition adds a new dimension to the concept of government failure. This competition could lessen the potential for government failure by making government more sensitive to voter demand, but it could contribute to government failure by making it harder to overcome the free-rider problem.

■ ■ ■ ■ ■ ■ ■ ■
URBAN PUBLIC GOODS
AND THE SPILLOVER PROBLEM

The problem of supplying public goods is especially complicated by jurisdictional fragmentation. If an urban area consists of many political subdivisions, the external benefits of the provision of a public good would spill over into different jurisdictions, making the political provision of that public good much more difficult. Consider Figure 19A–3, which represents the demand for crime prevention.

f. Betsy Morris, "New Suburbs Tackle City Ills While Lacking a Sense of Community," *The Wall Street Journal*, 26 March 1987, 1.

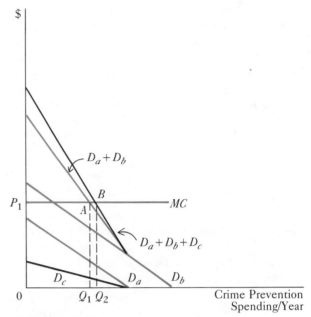

FIGURE 19A–3
THE MARKET FOR CRIME PREVENTION
Crime prevention is a local public good. If D_a and D_b represents the demand of two groups within the jurisdiction, the optimal amount of crime prevention would be Q_1. However, if some of the benefits spill into other jurisdictions and the demand of citizens in other jurisdictions is represented by D_c, the optimum amount of the public good is Q_2.

In Figure 19A–3, two groups of citizens are represented. D_a and D_b represent the demand for crime prevention in the urban area by two groups of citizens in that urban area. Since crime prevention is a public good, it is subject to the free-rider problems discussed earlier. The "true" demand curve is found by vertically summing the two demand curves. The "correct" provision of the public good is Amount Q_1 at Tax Price P_1. Assume for a moment that the free-rider problem can be overcome and that through the political process, the citizens of the urban area vote to tax themselves an amount equal to $0P_1AQ_1$ and supply the optimal amount of crime prevention.

The optimal amount of crime prevention will still not occur if some of the benefits of crime prevention spill into other jurisdictions. D_c represents the demand curve of people who live outside the political subdivision for crime prevention inside the subdivision. They have a demand because they travel to work and shop in the subdivision. In addition, they live close to this subdivision and fear that criminal activity might easily cross into where they live. Since they do not vote and pay taxes in that subdivision, their demand is not incorporated into the political decision to supply Amount Q_1. If it were, the demand curve (again a vertical summation) would be $D_a + D_b + D_c$ and the optimal amount of spending on crime prevention would be Amount $0P_1BQ_2$. The conclusion of this analysis is that, even if it were possible to politically internalize externalities within a political subdivision, internalizing as a solution becomes much more difficult when the externality spills over into other political jurisdictions.

Solving the Spillover Problem

Revenue sharing, or conditional grants from higher to lower levels of government, have been suggested as one way to overcome the problem of interjurisdictional externalities. In this way state government or the federal government can help overcome local urban externality and public goods problems. In the 1970s, this type of grant became very popular. In 1979, 38 percent of the revenue of cities came from higher levels of government, mostly from the federal government. By 1985, this type of grant had been reduced, especially at the federal level, so that it only accounted for 29 percent of local spending.

Fiscal conservatives oppose grants from higher to lower levels of government for two reasons. First, they argue that the federal government should not transfer such funds when the federal budget is facing huge deficits. Second, they argue that if local officials do not have to tax in order to spend, they will be less fiscally responsible than they would be if they had to face taxpayers in order to spend. Proponents of such grants argue that they can redistribute income from richer to poorer jurisdictions and compensate cities for some of the positive externalities they generate for other jurisdictions. The Reagan administration reduced such grants, forcing urban governments to rely increasingly on their own sources of revenue.[g]

One possible way to solve the spillover problem without resorting to intergovernmental grants is through user charges. Some public goods can be financed, or at least partially financed, through user charges. Local governments can charge different fees to residents and nonresidents. This type of payment schedule is particularly applicable for recreational and cultural programs. For example, Greenbelt, Maryland, requires proof of residence in order to pay the lower fee for swimming lessons and tennis classes. If you are attending a state university, it probably has a tuition schedule that differentiates between state residents and out-of-state students.

The Tiebout Solution

Charles Tiebout argued in a now-famous article that the provision of local public goods is best done by small homogeneous jurisdictions[h]. The smaller the jurisdiction, the more responsive the government will be to its citizens. Citizens in an urban area will choose to live in a certain jurisdiction by buying into that package of local public goods and tax prices. For example, residents of the Washington, D.C., area can choose to live in the District or five adjacent counties, two in Maryland and three in Virginia. Each offers different tax levels, transportation services, housing quality, and local public goods. Tiebout argues that a market exists for local public goods and that the price of housing in an area will reflect voter-consumer preferences for these local public goods. This is very close in theory to the privately supplied public goods discussed in the chapter on market failure and government intervention. It forces local governments to seek the desired combination of spending and taxing as individuals migrate to those jurisdictions that produce that combination.

PRIVATIZING: THE CASE OF LOW-INCOME HOUSING

One strategy used by some cities to hold down their tax burdens is privatization. Low-income housing offers an illustration. Federally funded programs to provide public housing in the 1960s and 1970s were notoriously unsuccessful in most cities. It is usually easy to identify "the project" by its boarded-up windows and slum-like appearance. Indeed, in many cities the housing projects built in the late 1960s have already been abandoned; some have even been torn down.

Recently, the Local Initiative Support Corporation (LISC), with financial backing from the Ford Foundation, has reversed this outcome by privatizing the process of supplying low-cost housing. The result is low-income housing that has a blend of public and private financing. LISC works with local community groups to determine what is needed in the area of housing.

g. See Richard P. Nathan and Fred C. Doolittle, "Federal Grants: Giving and Taking Away," *Political Science Quarterly* (Spring 1985): 53–74.

h. Charles M. Tiebout, "A Pure Theory of Public Expenditures," *Journal of Political Economy* (October 1956): 416–424.

These groups blend public money, foundation grants, and loans from private mortgage lenders to rebuild an area. The group then takes ownership of the development and manages the housing units. The result has been impressive. Pride of ownership has meant better maintenance, and these previous problem areas have become models to be emulated. The key has been generating incentives at the tenant level, resulting in tenant associations that maintain and police the areas.[i]

IS MASS TRANSPORTATION A PUBLIC GOOD?[j]

Many cities are expanding or building new mass transportation systems. These systems can cover an entire metropolitan area, in some cases crossing many city or even county jurisdictions, For example, the Metropolitan Atlanta Rapid Transit Authority (MARTA) runs bus and train service from distant suburbs into downtown Atlanta. Perhaps the "snazziest" new entry into urban mass transportation is the Metro in Washington, D.C. Begun more than ten years ago, the system features clean facilities (in contrast to the subway in New York City) with a space-age look to them. In 1987, the Washington Metro was a 47-mile system that will cost more than $6 billion when it is complete. Some critics have joked that it would have been cheaper to buy every citizen of the District of Columbia a new Mercedes automobile.

Are such systems worth the cost? Proponents argue that in essence mass transportation is a public good. Positive externalities are produced by urban bus and subway systems. The low-cost transportation increases population density, which increases the urban tax base. Economic development increases because the dense population increases the flow of business. The transportation network also allows the labor force easier access to work sites. Finally, mass transportation reduces air pollution, congestion on the roads, parking problems. It was argued during the energy crisis that mass transportation networks saved on scarce energy sources. Proponents claim that all these positive externalities are of sufficient value to make the benefits of construction exceed the costs.

Critics disagree. They argue that subsidized public transportation transfers income from taxpayers to users of the system. The systems represent a huge subsidy to riders. The proponents have exaggerated the benefits of the systems and the costs exceed what benefits do occur. For example, critics argue that the benefits of low-cost transportation in allowing the density of the population to increase are overwhelmed by the increase in land prices that the increased density produces. As a result, the main beneficiary of the subsidized transportation are landowners in the urban area. Critics also point to empirical evidence suggesting that road congestion and air pollution do not seem to be much improved by such systems. For example, after the Washington Metro opened, some studies showed that rush-hour auto traffic into the district actually increased.

Transportation, parking, and road congestion problems are vexing questions for urban policymakers. Controversy over mass transportation, like so many other local public-sector problems, hinges on determining a value for positive externalities. Then, the benefits must be weighed against the cost of public-good projects. Conflicting views arise even among economists because it is often very difficult to put an accurate monetary value on what amounts to a speculative, positive externality.

i. See James Cook, "Priming the Urban Pump," *Forbes* (March 23, 1987): 63–64. On the other hand, privatization has taken some of these properties out of the low-income housing supply creating what some view as a "time bomb." See Michel McQueen, "Inadequate Supply of Housing for Poor Could Become Worse, Panel Warns," *Wall Street Journal*, 28 April 1988, 10.

j. See David M. Stewart, "Rolling Nowhere," *Inquiry* (July 1984): 18–23.

PART SIX

THE WORLD

ECONOMY

CHAPTER 20 ■
■

INTERNATIONAL TRADE

■

INTRODUCTION

Except for the international perspective boxes, this textbook has largely neglected the rest of the world in order to concentrate on how the U.S. economic system operates. Yet the world is increasingly an important part of the American economy. You probably ride a Japanese bike, drink coffee from Brazil, eat Mexican tomatoes and Honduran bananas, and take pictures with a German camera. Chances are there is a plant of a foreign-owned multinational corporation close to where you live.

Even for a country as large as the United States, where trade is a relatively small fraction (about 10 to 12 percent) of GNP, international considerations have become increasingly important. The percent of output and sales entering into international trade has doubled in the last 15 years. Foreign competition is important to major industries such as textiles, steel, and autos. Immigration (both legal and illegal), foreign investment in the United States and American investment abroad, and the ups and downs in the value of the dollar have all been controversial issues in the 1980s.

International economics is usually separated into two parts for convenience: international trade and international finance. International trade deals with the largely microeconomic questions of who produces what and who trades with whom and why, as well as multinational firms, tariffs, and quotas. International finance examines the determinants of exchange rates between national currencies, the balance of payments, and the relationship between domestic macroeconomic concerns and the foreign sector.

This chapter covers international trade and the next chapter looks at international finance. You need to recognize, however, that trade and finance are closely related. For example, changes in the price of the dollar affect U.S. imports and foreign demand for U.S. exports. An inflow of investment from abroad can affect U.S. output, employment, and interest rates.

WHY NATIONS TRADE

The reasons for international trade are really no different from the reasons for trade between individuals who live in the same country;

the availability of a better product or a better price, or an opportunity for profit. Exactly what determines the patterns of trade between countries and how much each nation benefits have been important concerns to economists as long as there have been nation states and as long as there have been economists.

Prior to Adam Smith, the dominant view was that government should direct many spheres of economic activity, especially international trade. This view, called *mercantilism*, put heavy emphasis on control of shipping, colonies, discouraging imports, and promoting exports. Two famous economists are responsible for developing the arguments for a policy of free trade. One was Adam Smith, whose *Wealth of Nations* in 1776 made a strong case for freedom in every sphere of economic activity. The other was David Ricardo, a distinguished nineteenth-century British economist and member of Parliament who was very interested in the practical question of what trade policy England should pursue. He developed the principle of comparative advantage in his classic 1814 book, *Principles of Political Economy and Taxation*.

The Benefits of Exchange

It is easier to envision the processes at work in international trade if we first focus on exchange rather than production. Consider Heather and Peter, who are both stamp collectors. Like most stamp collectors, they acquire part of their collection by trading duplicates of stamps they already have. Let's say that Heather has the complete 1938 Presidential series and several extras. Peter has some gaps in that series, but has some extra Canadian stamps that he would like to trade and that Heather would like to have. They work a deal; she trades three spare Presidential stamps for five Canadian stamps. As an outside observer, you might say that the trade was one of "equal values." That may be true in a market sense, but the trades weren't of equal value to Peter and Heather. Heather wanted the Canadian stamps more than she wanted the extra Presidential stamps, and Peter felt just the opposite. They both were better off as a result of the trade.

Economists who look at international trade emphasize the **gains from trade**, or the increase in economic well-being that comes from exchange. The emphasis on exchange is one aspect of international trade theory that makes it different from the rest of microeconomics. Even in international economics, however, we have to back up one step from exchange to production. Rarely do people trade just out of existing stocks of goods. People produce in order to trade. The explanation of how people and nations decide what to produce for trade is based on the concepts of absolute advantage and comparative advantage.

GAINS FROM TRADE
The increase in consumption resulting from specialization and exchange.

Absolute Advantage

Suppose Heather and Peter are sister and brother, and their parents want the 12 windows in the house washed and the 24 square yards of leaves raked. Heather and Peter estimate their output as shown in Table 20-1.

TABLE 20-1
ABSOLUTE ADVANTAGE

	Windows per Hour	Square Yards of Leaves per Hour
	■	■
Heather	4	6
Peter	2	8

If this brother and sister divided the task equally, they would each have to wash half the windows (6 for Heather, which would take her $1^1/_2$ hours, and 6 for Peter, which would take him 3 hours) and rake 12 yards of leaves (which would take Heather 2 hours and Peter $1^1/_2$ hours to complete). At the end of a long afternoon, Heather would have worked $3^1/_2$ hours, and Peter would have worked $4^1/_2$ hours. But if they each were to specialize in what they do better, Heather could have all of the windows washed in just 3 hours and Peter could have all of the leaves raked in 3 hours—a clear gain of a valuable half hour for Heather and an hour and a half for Peter.

Both Heather and Peter are better off if they specialize, because each has an **absolute advantage**. Heather is more efficient than Peter at washing windows, and Peter is more efficient than Heather at raking leaves. It's not difficult to convince anyone of the benefits of specialization and trade when there is a clear absolute advantage for each partner.

ABSOLUTE ADVANTAGE
The ability to produce something with fewer resources than other producers use.

■ **Comparative Advantage**

Suppose, however, that one partner is better at both. Assume that Heather is better at *both* window washing and leaf raking. The new production functions for Heather and Peter are shown in Table 20–2. Is there still an opportunity for specialization and trade?

TABLE 20-2
AN EXAMPLE OF COMPARATIVE ADVANTAGE

	Windows per Hour	Square Yards of Leaves per Hour
	■	■
Heather	4	6
Peter	1	4

If they continue to divide the tasks equally, Heather will spend $1^1/_2$ hours on her six windows and 2 hours on 12 square yards of leaves. She's through in just $3^1/_2$ hours. Poor Peter, however, has to spend 6 hours on windows and 3 hours on leaves for a total of 9 hours of work. Can Heather do something to make Peter better off without spending any more of her own time working?

Suppose they specialize. This time it's not as obvious who should specialize in what. The concept of of opportunity cost provides an answer to this question. When Heather rakes 6 square yards of leaves, she's giving up 4 clean windows she could have "produced" in that time. A clean window costs her $1^{1}/_{2}$ square yards of leaf raking. For Peter, a clean window costs 4 square yards of leaves. Clearly Heather's window washing is cheaper than Peter's in terms of alternatives foregone. Heather has a **comparative advantage** in window washing because her opportunity cost is lower in that activity than in the other one. Peter also has a comparative advantage, even though he has an absolute disadvantage in both. His opportunity cost of raking leaves is only $^{1}/_{4}$ of a clean window per square yard, while Heather's is $^{4}/_{6}$, or $^{2}/_{3}$. So Peter should specialize in that activity in which he has a comparative advantage, i.e., in which his opportunity cost is lower.

Heather and Peter implement a policy of specializing on the basis of comparative advantage. Heather washes all the windows, which takes 3 hours. Peter rakes all 24 square yards of leaves, which takes 6 hours. By specializing on the basis of comparative advantage, both of them are better off! They have produced the same "output" (clean windows and a leaf-free yard) with considerably less input. Heather saved half an hour, while Peter saved 3 hours. Both parties gained from specialization.

From Individuals to Nations

The same principles that determined specialization for Heather and Peter apply to more complex situations—groups, regions, or nations. Trade between nations is also based on comparative advantage. By specializing, both parties can gain from trade. For simplicity, economists usually use a two-country, two-commodity example, but it will work for more countries or more commodities as well.

Assume two countries called Inland and Outland. Before they discover one another they are producing the products shown in Table 20-3. You probably noticed right away that Outland, like Peter, is able to produce less of both commodities. This lack of absolute advantage, or absolute disadvantage, may be because Outland's resources are less efficient, or Outland may just be a smaller or poorer country with fewer resources. The reason for absolute advantage and absolute disadvantage makes no difference for comparative advantage and the gains from trade.

COMPARATIVE ADVANTAGE
The ability to produce something at a lower opportunity cost than other producers face.

TABLE 20-3
PRODUCTION POSSIBILITIES WITHOUT TRADE

	Steel (Tons)	Cloth (Bolts)
Inland	50	75
Outland	20	60
World Total	70	135

The output numbers for Inland and Outland in Table 20-3 represent points on their production possibilities frontiers. (To keep things simple, both production possibilities frontiers are assumed to be straight lines.) One more piece of information is needed in order to draw the straight line production possibilities curve for each country. Assume that each country is devoting two-thirds of its resources to steel and one-third of its resources to cloth. This assumption makes it possible to calculate the end points of their production possibilities frontiers.

If Inland totally specializes in cloth, the country can produce 225 bolts; in steel, 75 tons. If Outland totally specializes in cloth, the country can produce 180 bolts; in steel, 30 tons. These points give the production possibilities curves in Figure 20–1.

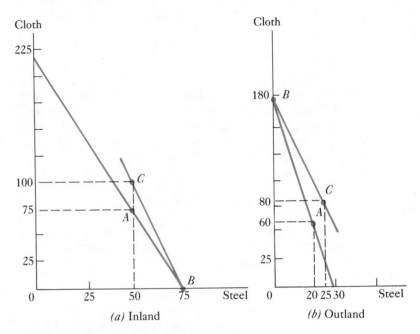

FIGURE 20-1
PRODUCTION POSSIBILITIES CURVES
FOR INLAND AND OUTLAND
The production possibilities curve provides a graphic representation of the gains from specializing on the basis of comparative advantage. Each country moves from pretrade production and consumption (Point *A*), to output with specialization (Point *B*), and to consumption after trade (Point *C*).

Which country should specialize in what product or mix of products? The answer lies in the two countries' opportunity costs. For Inland, the cost of producing 75 tons of steel is 225 bolts of cloth foregone, or 3 bolts of cloth per ton of steel. For Outland, the same calculation says that one ton of steel costs 6 bolts of cloth. Inland's steel is cheaper in terms of cloth foregone. If you flip these numbers upside down, measuring the cost of cloth instead of steel, you should find that one bolt of Inland cloth costs $1/3$ of a ton of steel, and one bolt of Outland cloth costs only $1/6$ of a ton of steel. Measured in terms of opportunity costs, Outland's cloth is cheaper. The result of specialization is shown in Table 20–4.

TABLE 20-4
SPECIALIZATION AND TRADE

	Before Trade		After Specialization	
	Steel ■	Cloth ■	Steel ■	Cloth ■
Inland	50	75	75	0
Outland	20	60	0	180
Total	70	135	75	180

Total world output has increased, with no additional resources, by 5 tons of steel and 45 bolts of cloth. Are the two countries better off?[1] Not yet. After all, they could have been producing those combinations anyway. It is only after trade that they can be better off.

The Terms of Trade

At what rate will Inland and Outland trade steel for cloth? Inland will not accept less than 3 bolts of cloth for a ton of steel, because this country can do that well producing its own cloth. Outland will not offer more than 6 bolts of cloth per ton of steel, because at higher prices it would be cheaper not to specialize and produce its own cloth. Anywhere between 3 and 6 bolts of cloth per ton of steel should be a mutually acceptable trading ratio. Let's make it 4 cloth = 1 steel. This ratio is called the **terms of trade**. The exact terms of trade will lie somewhere between the domestic opportunity cost ratios. Where the terms of trade fall between those limits depends on the relative strength of demand for both products in both countries.

There are numerous after-trade combinations of steel and cloth that could make both countries better off. One possibility is to let Inland take all of its gains from trade in extra cloth, keeping its steel consumption at the original level of 50 tons and trading away the other 25 to Outland for 100 bolts of cloth. That exchange leaves Outland with 25 tons of imported steel and 80 bolts of domestic cloth, a consumption combination that represents more of both goods. These results of trade are summarized in Table 20–5.

TERMS OF TRADE
The rate at which one product is exchanged for another.

TABLE 20-5
GAINS FROM TRADE

	Before Trade		After Specialization		After Trade	
	Steel ■	Cloth ■	Steel ■	Cloth ■	Steel ■	Cloth ■
Inland	50	75	75	0	50	100
Outland	20	60	0	180	25	80
Total	70	135	75	180	75	180

1. To be sure that they are better off, without knowing anything about their tastes and preferences, we need to be sure that each country has at least as much of one commodity as before and more of the other.

These new consumption points are shown in Figure 20–1. Point C in Panel (a) shows Inland consuming 50 steel and 100 cloth, while Point C in Panel (b) represents a consumption combination of 25 steel and 80 cloth for Outland. In each graph, this point lies along a "terms of trade" line or a **consumption possibilities frontier**, beginning from Point B (total production with specialization), with a slope of 1 steel = 4 cloth. Each country is able to get beyond its production possibilities frontier by separating production (at Point B) from consumption (at Point C). The gains from trade are the same kind of improvement in well-being that a country gets from having additional economic resources. Point C in each case represents one of many trade and consumption combinations that make both partners better off.

CONSUMPTION POSSIBILITIES FRONTIER
A line showing the consumption combinations attainable through trade.

The Basis of Comparative Advantage

What makes Inland better at producing steel and Outland better at producing cloth? For some products the reasons are obvious. Climate determines the cheapest place to produce bananas, potatoes, and other agricultural products. Mineral resources determine other production patterns. Some products use a high proportion of unskilled labor relative to capital and other inputs. These products will be produced in countries with relatively large amounts of low-cost, unskilled labor. Other products require relatively more skilled labor, capital, or fertile land. These products will be produced in countries where those resources are most abundant.

Still other products follow what economist Raymond Vernon called the **product cycle**. When the product is introduced it will be exported by the country in which it was developed. But as the product and the production process become standardized, production will eventually migrate to the country with the most suitable resource mix. Automobiles, whose production technology was developed in the United States, are now produced almost everywhere. Textile technology was originally developed in England, but the production of simple cotton textiles (the most standardized part of the industry) has migrated around the globe in search of the inexpensive, low-skill labor that is used heavily in their manufacture.

PRODUCT CYCLE
A series of stages, from development to standardization, through which a new product passes; the country of export may change during this period.

Sometimes the explanation for comparative advantage lies in historical accident. A particular product starts being produced in Country A because that is where it was invented, or because its citizens want such a product. Country A develops the particular skills and resources needed to produce that product, including related industries that supply inputs or use the product in making other goods. If A's resources are at all suited to the production of this good, A is likely to have a comparative advantage that it can retain for some time. If the world market is not large, there may only be room for a few suppliers in the market in order to take advantage of cost savings in large-scale production, and the first producer may enjoy a lasting advantage for that reason.

All these factors contribute to the explanation of comparative advantage. The important point is that it is possible for both partners to increase output and economic well-being by specializing on the basis of comparative advantage, regardless of how that comparative advantage may have originated.

Other Benefits from Trade

There are at least two other important benefits from trade besides the increased output from comparative advantage. One is competition; the other is economies of scale.

Trade increases the number of competing firms from whom consumers can buy, widening their range of choice of goods and suppliers. This benefit of trade can be very important if the domestic industry has only a few firms. For example, U.S. car buyers have a wide range of choice in cars because of international trade, even though there are only a few domestic producers. As a result of foreign competition, domestic producers have responded to demands of some car buyers for smaller, more fuel-efficient cars.

Access to a large world market instead of a smaller domestic one may enable firms to produce at a more efficient scale of operations. Producers of mainframe computers, aircraft, and heavy machinery need a very large market in order to produce at a scale that results in the lowest possible costs per unit.

THE WHY AND HOW OF PROTECTION

With all of these good reasons for free trade, why are some U.S. firms and industries protected from foreign competition? Many arguments are offered by firms that have to compete with imports, but most of the arguments come down to one reason—income distribution. While the country as a whole benefits from free trade, not everyone benefits equally.

To understand how protection works, consider the two primary tools of protection, tariffs and quotas. A **tariff** is a tax on imported goods. The tariff can be specific (based on weight, volume, or number of units; e.g., 10 cents a pound, $5.00 a dozen) or *ad valorem* (a percentage of the price). The average U.S. tariff is now less than 5 percent, but many items bear no tariff at all, while a few items have substantial tariffs. A **quota** is a quantity limit. It specifies the maximum amount that can be imported during a given time period (usually a year). Quotas can be global (e.g., total imports of widgets from all foreign suppliers cannot exceed 1,000 widgets per year) or geographic (assigning quotas to particular countries). Quotas also can be combined with tariffs in a **tariff quota**. In this case, a certain amount of a good from one country is allowed to enter another country without a tariff. For amounts in excess of that limit, a tariff is applied.

TARIFF
A tax on imported goods and services.

QUOTA
A physical limit on the amount of a good or service that can be imported during a given time period.

TARIFF QUOTA
A limit on the amount of a good or service that can be imported without paying a tariff. Amounts in excess of that limit are subject to a tariff.

Effects of a Tariff

Figure 20-2 illustrates the effects of a tariff. In this figure, Inland produces, consumes, and imports cheese. The domestic supply curve is S_d; the domestic demand curve is D_d. Because Inland is a small country, its purchases of imported goods do not affect the world price of those goods. Inland can buy all the cheese it wants at the world price, P_w. At P_w, domestic producers are producing A pounds and consumers are

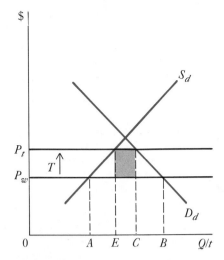

FIGURE 20-2
EFFECTS OF A TARIFF OR QUOTA
A tariff of $P_t - P_w$ or an equivalent quota of EC raises prices for domestic consumers (from P_w to P_t), reduces imports from AB to EC and consumption from OB to OC, and increases domestic output and sales from OA to OE.

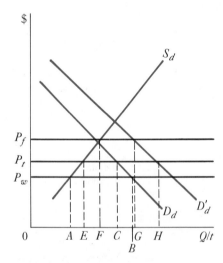

FIGURE 20-3
EFFECTS OF A TARIFF OR QUOTA WHEN DEMAND INCREASES
Under a tariff, an increase in demand increases the quantity of imports (from EC to EH) and consumption (from OC to OH) but leaves the price unchanged at P_t. With a quota, increased demand leads to a rise in price (from P_t to P_f) and domestic production (from OE to OF). Consumption rises slightly, from OB to OG; imports are unchanged at $FG = EC$.

buying B pounds. The difference between production and consumption is imports of AB pounds of cheese.

P_t is the price of imported cheese after Inland imposed a tariff of T. Since the tariff raises the price, consumers buy less. Cheese consumption falls to C. Domestic producers move up along their supply curve to E. They get a bigger share of the smaller market. Imports fall from AB to EC.

Who gains? Domestic producers, including owners, workers, and their suppliers. These firms can charge a higher price and have a larger market share, which benefits everyone connected with that industry. Government also gains some tariff revenue. Who loses? Domestic consumers are paying more and getting less, so they lose. Foreign producers have lost sales. Also, the country imposing the tariff has given up some of the benefits of free trade discussed earlier in this chapter—more output, competition, and economies of scale. Since foreign cheese producers are more efficient than most of Inland's domestic cheese producers, this country is switching from more efficient to less efficient producers.

Effects of a Quota

Quotas are similar to tariffs. In fact, they can be represented by the same diagram. The main difference is that quotas restrict quantity, while tariffs work through prices. If, in Figure 20–2, the government imposed a quota in the amount of EC on cheese, the effects on price, domestic production, consumption, and imports would be the same as those of the tariff of $T = P_t - P_w$. There are a couple of important differences, however.

First, a tariff raises revenue for the government, in the amount of the shaded area in Figure 20–2 ($P_w P_t \times EC$). A quota generates no government revenue.[2] All the benefits of a quota go to protected domestic producers and to those importers who manage to get the scarce and valuable import permits used with quotas. Since permits are limited, permit holders can buy the good at the low foreign price and resell it at the higher domestic price. The difference between the price the importer pays the foreign supplier and the price the importer can charge the domestic consumer ($P_t - P_w$) times the number of units imported is a monopoly profit that comes from having a license to import. Notice that these monopoly profits are precisely equal to the revenue the government would have received under a tariff.

Second, suppose demand increased in this country. With a tariff, the quantity of imports would increase, while with a quota only the price would increase. Originally the tariff $P_t - P_w$ and the quota of EC had the same effect on prices and quantities. But when demand shifts from D_d to D'_d under a tariff (Figure 20–3), imports rise to EH and consumption to H. With a quota, price rises to P_f. Imports remain the same ($EC = FG$), while domestic production rises to F and consumption rises slightly to G.

2. Proposals in the 1980s surfaced that would require the government to auction the right to import under a quota to the highest bidder. If this policy were adopted, then quotas could also be used to raise revenue for the government.

TARIFFS AND QUOTAS COMPARED

A tariff	A quota
• Raises prices	• Raises prices
• Reduces imports and consumption	• Reduces imports and consumption
• Increases domestic output	• Increases domestic output
• Produces government revenue	• Creates monopoly profits for those with import licenses
• Lets imports rise when demand increases	• Makes prices rise when demand increases

Most economists prefer free trade to either tariffs or quotas. If they have to choose, a tariff usually is considered less harmful than an equivalent quota. A tariff does allow imports to increase in response to increases in demand, and at least some of the tariff revenue accrues to the

THE INTERNATIONAL PERSPECTIVE
DO QUOTAS REALLY RAISE PRICES?

In 1981, the United States imposed "voluntary" quotas limiting Japanese auto exports to this country. According to the theoretical model of tariffs in this chapter, these quotas should have raised prices of both imported and domestic cars. More elaborate explanations of tariffs suggest increases in wages and profits in the quota-protected industry. How does the theory square with U.S. real-world experience?

According to *Newsweek* magazine,[a] the textbook model accurately described the experiences of U.S. car buyers in 1983 and 1984. Buyers saw an average price increase of $2,600 from April, 1981, to early 1984, during a period in which the overall consumer price index was rising very slowly. Prices rose sharply on imported Japanese cars as well, reflecting additional "dealer markups" of $1,000 to $2,000. The article also cited a study by Robert Crandall of the Brookings Institution, who calculated that the prices of domestic cars rose 8 to 9 percent in the 12 months ending in early 1984, compared to cost-of-production increases on the order of 4 to 5 percent during the same period. This price increase reflects not only higher sticker prices but also elimination of rebates, as well as charges for features that were formerly standard but became optional extras.

Where did these quota-created profits go? General Motors put large sums into executive bonuses. Chrysler's profits helped it to recover from difficult past years. These record profits reflected price, not quantity, increases, exactly as the quota model predicts. While sales rose in 1983 and 1984, compared to the recession years of 1981 and 1982, Chrysler found that its record profit of $701 million in 1983 was achieved while selling 2 million fewer cars than in 1977.

a. "Carving Up the Car Buyer," *Newsweek* (March 5, 1984): 72–73.

government, which will presumably use it to further the general welfare. Also, a tariff is more visible and therefore easier to get rid of, while a quota is less obvious and more likely to remain in place indefinitely.

Nontariff Barriers to Trade

In addition to tariffs and quotas, there are other kinds of government barriers to trade. Domestic laws other than tariffs and quotas that interfere with the free exchange of goods and services across national borders are called **nontariff barriers**. Some of these barriers are intentional, such as domestic preference laws requiring the government to give preference to domestic suppliers in making purchases for government agencies and programs. Other nontariff barriers consist of laws or regulations enacted for domestic reasons but make it more difficult for foreign suppliers to compete. For example, it may be difficult for a foreign supplier to comply with U.S. safety standards and labeling requirements. A common form of nontariff barrier is excessive paperwork on imports that adds to costs and reduces profits for foreign suppliers and domestic importing firms. In France, a shortage of customs inspectors creates delays for long periods and thus discourages imports.

Sometimes nontariff barriers work the other way, and American laws and regulations make it more difficult for U.S. firms to sell abroad. If American products must meet higher safety standards, for example, the American firm may not be able to compete with foreign producers who do not have to incur those costs.

A special case of nontariff barriers is dumping and antidumping codes. Dumping consists of selling a good at a lower price in the foreign country than in the home country. Firms may dump abroad to get rid of surpluses, to take advantage of differences in elasticity of demand (price discrimination), or to establish a foothold in a competitive market. Most countries, including the United States, have antidumping regulations that forbid this practice as unfair competition. If a foreign firm is accused of dumping (usually by a competing firm in the importing country), the International Trade Commission will hear the case and may impose countervailing duties. Often competing American firms claim dumping in order to make selling in the United States more difficult for foreign competitors.

U.S. Commercial Policy

The set of actions that a country undertakes to deliberately influence trade in goods and services is its **commercial policy**. For most of its history, the United States has had high tariffs and other trade restrictions. The highest U.S. tariff ever was the Smoot-Hawley Tariff of 1930, with an average tariff of 53 percent.

Since 1934, the United States has reduced tariffs and other trade barriers dramatically by negotiating treaties with other countries. Trade liberalization was accomplished under a series of Congressional acts, beginning with the Reciprocal Trade Agreements Act of 1934. Regular trade negotiations led to reductions in tariffs by the United States and U.S.

NONTARIFF BARRIER
A trade restriction other than tariffs and quotas.

COMMERCIAL POLICY
The total of actions that a country undertakes to deliberately influence trade in goods and services.

major trading partners. The latest complete series of trade negotiations, which took place from 1974 to 1979, was called the *Tokyo Round*. Now that the tariff cuts agreed to in that round have finally been implemented, the average U.S. tariff is only about 4.2 percent. The Tokyo Round also involved some agreements on reducing nontariff barriers. At present a new round of negotiations is taking place, called the Uruguay Round.

Lower tariffs are not free trade. Quotas still protect autos, steel, textiles, and other industries. Nontariff barriers are still an important impediment to free trade. As the value of the dollar rose from 1981 to 1985, making imports cheap and U.S. exports expensive, pressures for protection rose. These pressures fell, however, as the dollar declined in 1986 and 1987. Critics of free trade point to the successes of Japan and Korea which experienced economic growth behind very restrictive trade barriers. The battle between free trade and protectionism is an ongoing one.

THE POLITICS OF PROTECTION

Most demands for protection come from industries that once had a comparative advantage but lost it when other industries developed in which U.S. relative efficiency was even greater; or from industries where domestic monopoly or oligopoly conditions allowed them to ignore the need to improve technology and productivity. Shoes, clothing, steel, and, most recently, automobiles are industries that have asked for protection because they have lost their comparative advantage. Part of the problem with steel and automobiles is that they have been slow to modernize and to respond to changes in what buyers wanted.

It is easy to identify gainers and losers from tariffs and quotas. Consumers lose. Foreign producers lose sales. Domestic competitors gain. One loser who does not show up in Figures 20–2 and 20–3 is the U.S. exporter. When one country raises tariffs, other countries are likely to retaliate, and the first country's exports fall. Thus, political support for free trade should come from a coalition between exporting firms and consumers, with help from wholesalers and retailers of imported goods. However, such a diverse coalition is not easy to organize and hold together.

Firms that gain from protection spend large sums of money in lobbying to get or keep that tariff or quota. Consider a shoe tariff. As a consumer, you may find that the tariff only costs you a few more dollars a year for shoes, so it's hardly worth your while to lobby to fight the tariff. But if you are a worker whose present job in a shoe factory depends on protection, or a shoe manufacturer losing sales to imports, you will work much harder to get and keep protection. Even if the total benefits of free trade exceed the costs, complaints from a few big losers tend to generate far more noise and attention than the lobbying for free trade. If the losers are geographically concentrated, the American system of representation by states and districts makes it easier for them to develop "client" relationships with members of Congress from their states or districts.

When workers and owners from import-competing firms go to Washington to lobby for protection, they cast their arguments in terms of some tried and true arguments for protection. Some of these arguments have some economic validity. Others have strong political or emotional appeal, but weak economic foundations.

Infant Industry Protection

One theoretically valid argument for protection is the infant industry argument. An infant industry is a new industry that is not yet ready to compete with established foreign producers. Given some time (and sheltered circumstances) to master the technology, establish a reputation, train the workers, and reach economies of scale, the infant industry may eventually be competitive. Comparative advantage changes over time. Temporary protection could give this fledgling industry an opportunity to acquire a comparative advantage and "catch up" with established foreign firms.

This argument has to be used with care. There is no reason to protect industries that will never be competitive, wasting scarce resources that could be better used elsewhere. There should be no need to protect industries that will quickly become competitive, because entrepreneurs (and lenders) should be able to see past early losses to eventual profits. The only industries that really qualify are those that generate some kinds of external benefits to society that they can't recoup in the early years. Thus, deserving infant industries are those few that are not profitable on the basis of private cost and revenue calculations, but are nevertheless worth establishing because they meet two tests:

1. They will eventually be able to compete in the market without protection.
2. They generate benefits to society that are worth the cost of a tariff.

What kind of external benefits might this firm create? Examples include development of roads and power sources that are then available to other industries, training a labor force that may migrate to other firms, or developing a low-cost input that other industries can use. Benefits such as these are likely to exist in less-developed countries. It's difficult to create a plausible infant industry case for protecting a firm or industry in a developed country such as the United States. Even in less-developed countries, a complicated argument such as this one is easily abused by overstating external benefits and underestimating how long it will take for the industry to be competitive.

National Defense

Another argument for protection with economic validity is national defense. This product may be needed in wartime, the argument goes, but the domestic producer can't compete with cheaper foreign producers. Without protection during peacetime, the firm may not be here when war comes and foreign supplies are cut off. This argument had considerable merit during the War of 1812, when England was initially the United States's main trading partner and then became an enemy who successfully blockaded the U.S. coast. Even in World War II, German interference with shipping created problems in obtaining some needed supplies.

However, this argument make less sense for the United States today. The government stockpiles strategic raw materials, and most products needed in wartime are those in which the United States has a comparative advantage, such as heavy machinery, sophisticated electronics, and aircraft. Economists Leland Yeager and David Tuerck argue that the national defense argument really applies to another World War II—what they describe as a "prolonged nonnuclear war of attrition." But, they argue, the more likely kinds of wars—the kind the Pentagon seems to be preparing for—are either "brush fire" wars, such as Nicaragua, Lebanon, and other localized battles, which do not affect U.S. supplies, or else all-out nuclear war, in which case there would be no time to resupply.[3]

Balance of Payments

Most other arguments for protection have more emotional or political appeal than economic logic. Proponents of protection argue that a balance of payments deficit (or at least that part of the deficit that is accounted for by exports and imports) could be reduced by imposing a tariff and by importing less. Up to a point, this argument is correct, but only in the short run. Over time, tariffs encourage the development of industries producing import substitutes, usually products in which that nation has a comparative disadvantage. This policy encourages inefficient use of scarce resources. Furthermore, such tariffs usually lead to retaliatory tariffs on the exports of the country imposing the tariff.

Employment

The employment argument suggests that reducing imports can create jobs producing import substitutes. That's true, but the cost of doing so is high. Protectionism encourages misallocation of resources and tends to lead to retaliation; the tariff-imposing country may gain jobs in import-competing industries and lose them in efficient, competitive export industries.

Cheap Foreign Labor

Cheap foreign labor argument is a popular catch phrase of protectionists. The argument goes something like this: "We're just as efficient as U.S. foreign competition—we use the same machinery and technology and produce at least as high a quality product. However, U.S. labor costs are at least $7.00 an hour, and some foreign countries have to pay only $1.00 an hour. How can we possibly compete?"

There are several possible answers. One is that cheap labor often means lower productivity. Another is that while labor, especially

3. Yeager, Leland B., and David G. Tuerck. *Foreign Trade and U.S. Policy*. New York: Praeger Publishers, 1976.

unskilled labor, may be cheap in some countries, other inputs such as capital and unskilled labor are relatively expensive. A country such as the United States should concentrate on producing those products that use relatively more of its abundant (and, therefore, relatively less expensive) resources of capital and skilled labor.

■ Fair Trade and Maintenance of the U.S. Market

If there are so few valid economic arguments for protection, why does protection exist? There is a group of politically appealing arguments labelled **fair trade**. The concept of fair trade is often described as a "level playing field." If foreign countries erect tariff barriers, nontariff barriers, or quotas that prohibit U.S. firms from exporting to those countries, protectionists feel that the United States should do likewise. For example, if the Japanese make it very difficult or expensive for their citizens to buy U.S. automobiles or beef, protectionists argue that Americans should treat Japanese exporters the same way.

One version of the fair trade argument is called "maintenance of markets." Some protectionists argue that the U.S. market is more costly to operate in than other markets. U.S. firms pay high corporate taxes, face stiff environmental and safety standards, and have to follow such employment regulations as affirmative action, minimum wage, and overtime pay. Many foreign producers, particularly in less developed countries, do not incur similar costs. They can participate in the U.S. market without incurring the costs of maintaining it.

These fair trade arguments are usually put forward by organized lobbies for industries that are losing sales to foreign competitors. The appeal makes sense to the average voter, because it is couched in terms of fair play and equal treatment. Coupled with political arguments against trading with communist countries and other political enemies, the case for "fair trade" looks even more appealing. International trade differs from domestic trade in that the political dimension carries much more weight. Political concerns help to explain why the economically sound case for free trade is rarely put into practice.

To the extent that government-created cost differences or foreign trade restrictions affect all industries equally, they will not affect comparative costs and distort the efficient pattern of specialization and trade. It is only when these factors affect different industries differently that there may be a distortion of relative prices that justifies some kind of protection. For example, the minimum wage has more impact on costs in those industries using large amounts of unskilled labor than on other industries that use primarily highly skilled labor and capital. Thus, the minimum wage would raise the costs of the first type of industry more than the second.

Advocates of protection on the basis of fair trade, or the costs of maintaining the U.S. market, offer two policy solutions. The more traditional solution is a tariff on foreign goods. This tariff would be equivalent to the restrictions placed on U.S. exports to those countries, or to the excess cost of maintaining the U.S. market. Computing the appropriate tariff in each case would be a difficult task. In the case of some European nations, with larger government sectors and more restrictive laws governing employment, the appropriate tariff might actually be negative.

FAIR TRADE
The argument that the U.S. should impose trade barriers equivalent to those that U.S. trading partners place on U.S. exports.

An alternative approach has been suggested by Senator Phil Gramm of Texas (an economist by training) and Representative Jack Kemp of New York. Both Gramm and Kemp are basically in favor of free trade, but are also responsive to political pressures for protection based on these two arguments. They propose trading with each country on the same basis

THE INTERNATIONAL PERSPECTIVE
TRADE POLICY IN JAPAN

American advocates of free trade have a hard time explaining why one of the most prosperous, fast-growing nations in the noncommunist world does not practice anything close to free trade. This nation is Japan, a major U.S. trading partner. Japan subsidizes at least some of its exports, directly or indirectly, and severely restricts imports.

The theory behind Japan's commercial policy is partly infant industry, partly industrial policy. After World War II, Japan set out to rebuild its economy by identifying promising industries and encouraging their development. Japan recognized that it would always be dependent on foreign suppliers for raw materials, energy, and some part of its food supply because of limited domestic resource endowments and scarce land. In order to pay for those imports, it was necessary to develop industries both to supply other domestic needs and to earn foreign exchange through exporting. Part of that strategy called for protection. As those industries became competitive, most of the direct Japanese barriers to imports were reduced. However, it was still difficult

for foreign producers to sell in Japan because of tightly controlled networks of suppliers and distributors.

Even in agriculture, where scarce land puts Japan at a comparative disadvantage, political forces have created protection. U.S. agricultural exports to Japan face severe trade restrictions. Protection has driven the price of beef to $25 a pound in Tokyo.

Much of the hostility toward Japan is centered on its export strategies rather than its import protection. Many Japanese firms have been accused of dumping, or selling abroad below the price at home. A minor trade war between the United States and Japan was set off in 1987 by the dumping of Japanese computer chips. The United States reacted with retaliatory tariffs. Both Japanese firms and the Japanese government also actively promote exports with trade fairs and other export subsidies and export promotions.

The result of this commercial policy has not been entirely beneficial for Japan. First, the export surplus led to a rise in the price of the Japanese currency, the yen, which has made it difficult to continue to sell even their best products—cars and electronic equipment—in the United States and Europe. Second, in order to dispose of the surplus revenue from exporting more than they import, the Japanese have invested in other countries, especially the United States. Hondas and Toyotas made in the United States have begun to displace exports. Finally, strong demand for Japanese goods has put upward pressure on Japanese prices. As Japanese goods become more expensive, their less competitive industries, such as steel and textiles, are feeling pressure from firms in Taiwan, Korea, and the Philippines. The Japanese commercial policy has resulted in high prices and limited supplies of goods for domestic consumers. The standard of living of the average Japanese consumer is not as high as economic growth rates would lead us to expect.

The Japanese illustrate the point that no nation can—or should—continue to export more than it imports indefinitely. Comparative advantage suggests very strongly that exports and imports should pay for each other. The best way to bring that about, with the most efficient use of resources, is still free trade based on comparative advantage.

that they trade with the United States. They believe that this policy would result in freer trade because the U.S. market is so important to other countries that they will lower their barriers rather than see barriers raised in the United States. The appeal of this proposal is that it responds to the fair trade and maintenance of market arguments with economic incentives to promote free trade and specialization based on comparative advantage.

MOVEMENT OF RESOURCES

If both countries benefit from the flow of goods and services, what about benefits from the flow of inputs? Labor, capital, and raw materials also move between countries. When they do, objections are sometimes raised by those who are threatened by competition from abroad. Foreign competition is unpopular with owners of factors of production, whether the competition is in product markets or in factor markets. Consequently, restrictions are sought on the movement of factors as well as on the movement of goods.

Labor, for example, opposes an inflow of immigrants but also opposes building plants abroad. Newly arrived workers compete for jobs and depress wages, while an offshore plant of a U.S. firm means more jobs for foreign workers and fewer jobs for American workers. Competing domestic firms oppose having foreign competitors locate inside the country with no tariff wall for protection. Canada is cautious about letting U.S. firms build new plants in that country, and countries such as Kuwait and Japan have even tighter restrictions. Emotional and political arguments are sometimes more important than economic concerns. Many U.S. citizens are unhappy about the purchase of U.S. banks, farmland, and resort islands by foreign firms and individuals, even when there are no obvious adverse consequences.

The United States puts fewer restrictions on the inflow or outflow of capital than most countries. Except for strategic raw materials (those needed for defense), there are no restrictions on the flow of natural resources. Exports of natural resources are often restricted by countries with some market power over raw materials, such as oil and copper. Often these countries use controls on resource exports to generate revenue for the government or to attract industries that use natural resources in manufacturing. Cartels are designed to take advantage of market power in natural resources when that power is shared among a small number of countries.

Immigration policy has been a source of much controversy in the United States. After several previous attempts, a new immigration bill was finally passed in 1986. The most controversial provisions of that bill center on illegal aliens, who have come to the United States in large numbers in the last 15 years. The bill makes it possible for illegal aliens who resided in the United States prior to 1982 to become citizens but also imposes stiff penalties on employers for hiring illegal aliens in the future. The large number of illegal aliens in the United States reflects past restrictive immigration quotas. Organized labor generally opposes liberalizing immigration quotas because they want to protect jobs for U.S. citizens.

In general, the movement of inputs between countries can substitute for free movement of goods. If a country is poor in raw materials, capital, or skilled labor, it has two choices. It can import goods that incorporate large quantities of those inputs, or it can import those inputs and produce its own final products. Both kinds of trade should be beneficial. In the absence of artificial barriers, market considerations would determine which choice was more efficient—to move the final product or to move the input.

MULTINATIONAL CORPORATIONS

Another important influence on patterns of trade and factor movements is the multinational firm. A **multinational corporation** is a company with headquarters in one country and plants or majority-owned foreign affiliates in one or more other countries. Many large and well-known multinationals are headquartered in the United States—Ford, General Motors, IBM, and AT&T. (So are many of the smaller and less known ones.) Other large multinationals are headquartered in foreign countries, particularly in Japan (Honda and Mitsubishi) or Europe (Shell Oil, Nestle, Michelin, and BASF). While multinationals have been around for a long time, most of their growth has come since World War II.

MULTINATIONAL CORPORATION
A firm with headquarters in one country and a majority-owned subsidiary in at least one other country.

Why Firms Go Abroad

Why do firms build plants in foreign countries? Why not just export or invest in a local firm producing the same product? Exporting may not be the best alternative because of trade barriers, perishability, or a need to produce a product tailored to the local market. Investing in a firm by purchasing stock or making loans is sometimes a solution; but often the firm wants more control over management, product quality, and patented processes. Sometimes the only way to get access to needed local resources, especially raw materials, is to build a local plant.

U.S. labor unions oppose letting firms go abroad, arguing that they are in search of cheap foreign labor. They would rather see plants built in the United States, from which the firm could export. However, trade barriers or the needs of the local (foreign) market are much more common reasons for building foreign plants than the attraction of cheap labor. Furthermore, U.S. workers have found jobs in the many foreign multinational plants in the United States. The rapid influx of Japanese-owned firms in the 1980s, bringing with them lower wages and a very different, cooperative management style, has brought adjustments not only for their American employees but also for their American competitors.

Effects of Multinationals

Multinationals are accused by their critics of stifling competition in the countries in which they locate, creating balance of payments problems, and leading to undue concentration of economic and political power at home and abroad. Advocates argue that they often increase competition, speed up the transfer of capital and technology, and help trade find its way around artificial barriers.

Competition

In some cases, the multinational "shakes up" sleepy domestic competitors, forcing them to try harder when they can no longer hide behind a protective tariff wall. On the other hand, multinationals often simply buy out local competitors or keep local competition from developing. Sometimes multinationals increase competition, and other times they reduce it. Japanese and other multinationals have generally been regarded as beneficial in the United States, where they compete for resources and markets with established American firms that must adjust or decline.

Transfer of Technology

Multinationals speed up flows of technology between countries. They use processes and methods that the firm wouldn't share with a competitor but will make available to its own subsidiaries. Less-developed countries sometimes argue, however, that this transfer doesn't spill over to other industries for maximum benefit. They also argue that multinationals, which are generally from developed industrial countries, don't try very hard to adapt technology to the local mix of available resources.

Large Multinationals and Small Countries

Probably the most serious concern is that small countries are at a disadvantage in dealing with large multinationals. That large firm may have an annual revenue much larger than the small country's GNP. The multinational may be the largest employer, landowner, and taxpayer in a small country. That can threaten the sovereignty of the host country in dealing with a firm that is larger and more powerful than the government.

Despite these problems, there are real benefits to having multinationals. They offer a way around trade and cultural barriers for a flow of resources and technology, which has been very beneficial to the world economy. In most cases, they promote the same free-trade goals of more output with less effort that were the concern of classical economists two centuries ago when they formulated the theory of comparative advantage.

SUMMARY

1. Trade takes place because both parties benefit. Trade is based on the principle of comparative advantage, which means that each country produces that product in which its opportunity cost is lower in terms of other production foregone.

2. Specialization increases total output, and trade allows that increase to be shared. Trade also increases competition and allows countries to take advantage of economies of scale in some products.

3. Tariffs, quotas, and nontariff barriers interfere with free trade. A tariff or quota will raise the price, reduce imports, reduce consumption, and increase domestic production.

4. The United States has had high tariffs for most of its history but has led efforts to reduce tariffs and other trade barriers since 1934.

5. Arguments for protection include infant industry, national defense, balance of payments, employment, and cheap foreign labor. The first two have some validity but must be used with caution. Most arguments for protection are really thinly disguised requests for income redistribution.

6. Movements of resources can substitute for trade in goods and services.
7. Multinational corporations may increase competition in some cases and decrease it in others. They increase the transfer of technology between countries and may represent a threat of concentrated power in small, less-developed countries.

NEW TERMS

gains from trade
absolute advantage
comparative advantage
terms of trade
consumption possibilities frontier

product cycle
tariff
quota
tariff quota
nontariff barrier

commercial policy
fair trade
multinational corporation

QUESTIONS FOR DISCUSSION

1. Consider the following situation for Upland and Downland. Each country uses half of its resources in bananas and half in apples, and the figures given are what they produce in the absence of trade.

	Apples	Bananas
Upland	40	80
Downland	60	60

Do these figures represent absolute advantage, comparative advantage, or both? What is the opportunity cost of apples for each country? By how much will total output rise when they specialize? Can you find a better consumption combination for each country through trade?

2. Represent the information in Question 1 on a graph with a pair of production possibilities frontiers.
3. Who gains and who loses from a tariff? How do the effects of tariffs differ from the effects of quotas?
4. If you were running a small country, why might you have mixed feelings about the possible benefits of having a big multinational build a plant in your country?
5. Among the industries that have received tariff protection in recent years are textiles and autos. Using one or more of the arguments in this chapter, present a case for protection in one of those two industries.
6. Write a criticism of the argument you presented in Question 5, citing the benefits of free trade.
7. A tariff is proposed on imported pineapple. Economists calculate that one million pineapple buyers will incur additional costs for their purchases of $2 each. Five thousand pineapple workers will earn an additional $100 a year. One hundred unemployed workers will find jobs at an average salary of $10,000. Owners of pineapple packing firms (100 owners) will experience an average income increase of $5,000. What are the gains to the gainers? the losses to the losers? Are there other losses not counted in these figures? Do you think the tariff is likely to be enacted?
8. Why do multinational firms go abroad?
9. Why do economists generally prefer tariffs to quotas?
10. Why is the consumption possibilities frontier different from the production possibilities frontier? How does this concept help explain the benefits of trade as being similar to the benefits of economic growth?

SUGGESTIONS FOR FURTHER READING

Adams, John, ed. *The Contemporary International Economy: A Reader.* 2d ed. New York: St. Martin's Press, Inc., 1984. Articles on commercial policy, multinationals, and other trade issues for the general reader.

Ulbrich, Holley. *International Trade and Finance; Theory and Policy.* Englewood Cliffs, N.J.: Prentice-Hall, Inc., 1983. An intermediate-level textbook covering both international trade and international finance.

Yeager, Leland B., and David G. Tuerck. *Foreign Trade and U.S. Policy.* New York: Praeger Publishers, 1976. The case of free trade and a criticism of protectionism in theory and practice; many examples and illustrations from congressional hearings.

CHAPTER 21 ■

INTERNATIONAL FINANCE

INTRODUCTION

International finance addresses some exotic questions—foreign exchange markets, hedgers and speculators, floating rates and gold hoarders, balance of payments deficits and surpluses, the ups and downs of the U.S. dollar, and dealing under the table by international banks to affect currency prices. In fact, the foreign exchange market is really very similar to other markets.

The previous chapter described international trade in goods and services, but not exchange of currencies or financial assets. One important difference between trade within nations and trade between nations is that people in different countries use different currencies. In order to pay for goods purchased abroad, the buyer must acquire foreign currency. While it is relatively easy for U.S. citizens to purchase foreign currency, in many other countries citizens can only import if the government allows them to buy the needed foreign currency.

This chapter looks at the market for foreign currencies and what determines the price of one currency in terms of another (the exchange rate). We also will discuss the accounting statement for the foreign sector—the balance of payments—and its links to the domestic economy. Finally, we will examine different kinds of international monetary systems to see how they work and how they affect trade between countries.

THE MARKET FOR FOREIGN EXCHANGE

The network of banks and financial institutions through which national currencies are exchanged for one another is called the **foreign exchange market**. The foreign exchange market works much like markets for wheat, apples, or skateboards. There is a supply curve, a demand curve, and an equilibrium price and quantity. There are also conditions that are held constant (*ceteris paribus*). When these conditions change, the curves shift and the equilibrium price and quantity change.

FOREIGN EXCHANGE MARKET
The network of banks and financial institutions through which national currencies are exchanged for one another.

436

Supply and Demand for Foreign Exchange

Figure 21-1 represents the foreign exchange market as it appears to U.S. buyers and sellers. In this market, foreign currencies or foreign exchange is represented by the German mark (*DM*). The price of foreign exchange is measured in dollars. (This market could also be drawn as the supply and demand for U.S. dollars, but for the sake of simplicity we will focus on the U.S. market for other countries' currencies.)

Citizens of other countries supply foreign exchange in order to buy U.S. exports, to travel or invest in the United States, or to purchase U.S. services or assets. U.S. citizens demand foreign exchange in order to import foreign goods and services (including traveling abroad) and to invest in foreign assets.

In Figure 21-1, the equilibrium price of the mark is 50 cents, and the equilibrium quantity is 100 million. At a price of 70 cents per mark (equivalent to 1.4 marks per dollar), there would be a surplus of foreign exchange of 60 million marks. Quantity supplied is 130 million marks, and quantity demanded is only 70 million. At 30 cents per mark (equivalent to 3.3 marks per dollar), there would be a shortage of foreign exchange of 60 million marks (130 million marks demanded less 70 million marks supplied).

Shifts in Supply and Demand

Demand for foreign exchange will increase if something causes U.S. citizens to want to import more foreign goods and services or to invest more abroad. The supply of foreign exchange will increase if foreigners want to buy more U.S. goods and services or invest in the United States. Recall from Chapter 3 some of the factors that shift demand curves—the *ceteris paribus* conditions. Some of those demand shifters apply here, including changes in tastes, population, or income. Others show up a little differently because the foreign exchange market is a macroeconomic market.

A particular commodity's price is affected by changes in the prices of related goods. For example, demand for coffee is affected by the price of tea. In the foreign exchange market, it is aggregate rather than individual prices—changes in the price level in the United States relative to the price level abroad, or at least changes in the prices of U.S. exports in general relative to prices of foreign goods. Note that the price on the vertical axis is the price of foreign exchange. Changes in other prices, including the domestic price level, can shift the supply and demand curves for foreign exchange. If the U.S. price level rises more than foreign price levels, imports become cheaper relative to domestic goods, and Americans will want to buy more. Rising domestic prices shift the U.S. demand curve for foreign exchange outward. U.S. citizens demand more foreign exchange to buy more imported goods. At the same time, the supply of foreign exchange shifts to the left because foreigners want to buy fewer American exports at higher prices. In fact, economists who forecast changes in ex-

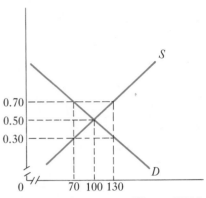

Price of DM in U.S. $

Foreign Exchange (millions of DM)

FIGURE 21-1
THE FOREIGN EXCHANGE MARKET
The foreign exchange market shows the supply of foreign exchange from abroad, the demand for foreign exchange by U.S. citizens, and the equilibrium price (50 cents per mark) and quantity (100 million marks).

change rates find that changes in relative price levels are the most significant determinant.[1]

Changes in relative interest rates also shift demand for foreign exchange. If interest rates are higher abroad, Americans will demand more foreign exchange to buy foreign financial assets, such as bonds or bank deposits. From 1981 to 1985, interest rates in the United States were higher than in most other countries, attracting an inflow of foreign capital. This increased supply of foreign exchange drove the price of foreign currencies down, or the price of the dollar up. As U.S. interest rates fell after 1985, the price of the dollar began to fall (i.e., the prices of marks, yen, and pounds began to rise).

Another source of shifts in demand for foreign exchange is changes in government restrictions on trade in goods and services in the form of tariffs, quotas, or nontariff barriers. Often these commercial policy tools are used specifically in order to shift the demand for foreign exchange, either to change the currency price or to "cure" a shortage of foreign exchange (balance of payments deficit). Export subsidies and promotions, likewise, will encourage foreign purchases and shift the supply of foreign exchange to the right. Finally, demand for foreign exchange shifts when there are changes in technology or input costs, which can change demand for foreign inputs or foreign products.

The same kinds of factors that shift one nation's demand for foreign exchange also operate abroad to shift other countries' supply of foreign exchange. Changes in relative price levels or incomes, foreign tastes, population, technology, interest rates, and foreign tariffs and quotas all affect the supply of foreign exchange from other countries.

SOURCES OF SHIFTS IN SUPPLY AND DEMAND FOR FOREIGN EXCHANGE

Changes in:

- Relative price levels
- Relative incomes
- Relative interest rates
- Tastes and preferences
- Population
- Technology
- Input cost and availability
- Tariffs, quotas, and nontariff barriers
- Export subsidies

---

1. The explanation of changes in exchange rates due to changes in price levels in different countries is called purchasing power parity. Much attention was given to using price level changes to predict exchange rates in the 1970s and the 1980s under floating exchange rates. Most studies indicate that purchasing power parity as an explanation of exchange rate changes works well in the long run, but doesn't explain short-run variations in exchange rates very well.

Unique Features of the Foreign Exchange Market

The foreign exchange market possesses unique characteristics. First, the operations of this market have important macroeconomic implications. What happens in the market for foreign exchange affects (and is affected by) interest rates, output, and price levels. Second, governments are often heavily involved in price setting, especially when trying to limit fluctuations in the currency price. Third, a well-developed **forward market** exists for foreign exchange, where people make contracts for future deliveries of currency at a fixed price. Finally, the foreign exchange market sometimes suffers from persistent disequilibrium.

Macroeconomic Implications

Exports and imports, which are heavily influenced by changes in exchange rates, each constitute about 10 to 11 percent of GNP. In addition, the foreign exchange market supports some large transactions in financial assets, such as stocks and bonds. Exports, imports, and capital transactions affect the domestic economy in many ways. A rise in exports can increase output but will also put upward pressure on prices as output expands. Rising imports can reduce domestic output but will also reduce inflationary pressures. An inflow of foreign capital can drive up interest rates, the money supply, and prices. The opposite is true for a capital outflow. Thus, any macroeconomic model of the U.S. economy must incorporate the foreign sector if it is to predict output, employment, prices, and interest rates accurately.

Domestic events in turn affect exports, imports, and trade in capital assets. Changes in output, prices, and interest rates spill over into the foreign sector. Rising output means rising income, some of which will be spent on more imports. A fall in output and income will reduce imports, as it did in the 1982 recession. Rising U.S. prices (relative to foreign prices) encourage both U.S. citizens and foreigners to substitute cheaper foreign goods for more expensive American products. When the price level rises faster in the United States than abroad, exports fall and imports rise. Falling prices, or prices rising more slowly than in the rest of the world, stimulate exports and discourage imports. Higher interest rates attract capital from abroad, while lower rates encourage U.S. capital owners to try to earn a higher return in other countries. All these changes shift the supply and demand for foreign exchange, and thus change currency prices under the present floating exchange rate system.

Government Intervention

Governments have always been heavily involved in the market for their own currencies. A government may want to keep the price of its currency from falling because of national pride, or because of the effect on the terms of trade.[2] Alternatively, government officials may want to keep the price of the currency from rising too high, because such an increase would make it more difficult for their exporters to compete and easier for imports to undersell domestic goods. Monetary authorities, particularly in

---

2. If the price of U.S. currency falls, then Americans have to pay more U.S. dollars for foreign goods. That translates into giving up more U.S. goods per unit of foreign good, which makes U.S. consumers worse off. The ratio of U.S. goods exchanged to foreign goods received is called the *gross barter terms of trade*.

small countries where foreign trade is a substantial part of total economic activity, may be concerned about the effects of changes in the currency's price on the volume of their monetary reserves and the money supply. Finally, officials may just want to keep the price of their currency stable in order to encourage trade and foreign investment by reducing risk and uncertainty.

Governments set and maintain prices in other markets, including minimum wages, farm price supports, and rent controls. In these markets, the government usually sets either a floor price or a ceiling price. In the market for foreign exchange, governments historically have set both a floor and a ceiling. Even under floating rates, governments don't always allow the market to set the prices of their currencies.

The Forward Market

FORWARD MARKET
The market in which transactions are made for future delivery of currency; e.g., 1,000 francs in 90 days at a price set today.

Another special feature of the foreign exchange market is a well-developed **forward market**, in which contracts are made for future delivery of a currency at a particular price. Forward (or futures) markets also exist in other goods and services. Probably the best-known forward market is the commodities market, where contracts for the future delivery of corn, wheat, pork bellies, copper, tin, gold, and other metals and agricultural goods are traded.

HEDGERS
People who try to reduce their risk by buying or selling currency for future delivery in the forward market.

Traders who try to reduce their risk by buying or selling contracts for future delivery are called **hedgers**. Those who are willing to assume risk in return for the chance of a profit are called **speculators**. Let's look at a simple illustration of how hedgers and speculators interact in the foreign exchange market.

Suppose a Honda dealer in the United States receives a shipment of Hondas on six months' credit from Japan. The dollar cost of the shipment is $100,000, but the contract calls for payment in yen. Right now the yen is trading for 150 yen per U.S. dollar, so the dealer owes 15 million yen. What the dealer really needs in six months is not $100,000, but however many dollars it takes at that time to buy 15 million yen.

SPECULATORS
People who assume risk in the forward market by guaranteeing a price to a hedger.

Suppose the Honda dealer thinks the price of a dollar in six months will fall to 120 yen. Then 30 million yen would cost more dollars—125,000, to be precise. There goes the profit! If the Honda dealer can find someone right now who will guarantee a reasonably attractive price, say 145 yen to the dollar, that will eliminate the exchange risk worry and the dealer can go back to the main business of selling cars and motorcycles.

What about the opposite situation—that of the speculator? Chances are the speculator is a large commercial bank, with forward transactions going in many directions. There is probably some Japanese firm in need of dollars who can be matched with this need for yen. Other speculators are gambling on changes in currency prices. Perhaps the dealer who offered 145 yen per dollar expects the price of yen to go the other way, say to 160 yen per dollar. If the dealer can buy dollars at 145 yen per dollar and sell them at 160, there will be a 15 yen profit on each dollar bought and sold.

The forward market has been around for a long time. Since 1973, when most countries adopted floating exchange rates, the forward market has played an important role in reducing foreign exchange risk.

Persistent Disequilibrium

If the price of currency is set by the government, it may not be a market-clearing price. If it isn't, there will be a persistent disequilibrium, i.e., surpluses or shortages of foreign exchange. This situation is shown for the United States in Figure 21–2. The market shows a shortage of foreign exchange because the price of 40 cents per mark is too low for equilibrium. The quantity of deutsch marks demanded exceeds the quantity supplied by 50 million marks.

One way to deal with this problem is to change the price of foreign exchange. Another way is to try to shift supply or demand in order to get the curves to intersect at the official price. A third possibility is for the government to ration foreign exchange. Finally, if the government has some accumulated foreign exchange reserves, it may just draw on those reserves to meet the shortage, hoping that the shortage will disappear of its own accord.

A shortage of foreign exchange is equivalent to a balance of payments deficit. A **balance of payments deficit** is an excess of a country's foreign exchange spending over its foreign exchange earnings in a particular year. In Figure 21–2, that difference or deficit amounts to 50 million marks. (At 2 marks per dollar, that translates into $25 million.) A nation could also have a balance of payments surplus (foreign exchange earnings exceed foreign exchange spending) or be in equilibrium if the foreign exchange inflows and outflows are equal. Before exploring the various ways of dealing with disequilibrium, it would be helpful to know a little more about how such surpluses and deficits are measured. That source of information is the balance of payments.

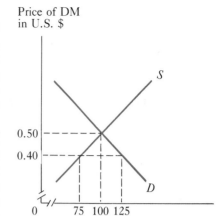

**FIGURE 21-2
EXCHANGE MARKET
DISEQUILIBRIUM**
At 40 cents per mark, the quantity of foreign exchange demanded exceeds the quantity of foreign exchange supplied by 50 million marks. This gap between supply and demand corresponds to a balance of payments deficit.

BALANCE OF PAYMENTS DEFICIT
An excess of a country's foreign exchange spending over its foreign exchange earnings in a particular year.

THE BALANCE OF PAYMENTS

The statistical summary of the transactions between residents of one country and residents of the rest of the world is called the balance of payments. The **balance of payments** is an income statement—a summary of the flows of goods, services, and assets in and out of a country in a particular year.

The balance of payments was a matter of great concern to the United States during the years 1945 to 1973 when there was a fixed rate of exchange, or a currency price set and maintained by the government. Every time the U.S. balance of payments was in deficit (which was most of the time), U.S. reserves fell, putting greater downward pressure on the price of the dollar. Since 1973, the balance of payments accounts have been less important. However, they still provide several kinds of useful information. Table 21–1 presents a summary of the U.S. balance of payments for 1987 in a simplified form.

A word about the pluses and minuses: A transaction that gives rise to a payment to this country, or a claim to future payment, is entered with a " + " sign. A transaction resulting in a payment from this country, or a claim to future payment, is entered as a "–" sign.

BALANCE OF PAYMENTS
A statistical summary (usually annual) of the transactions between residents of one country and residents of the rest of the world.

TABLE 21-1
U.S. BALANCE OF PAYMENTS, 1987 (millions of dollars)

CURRENT ACCOUNT
■

Merchandise Exports	+250,814	
Service Exports	+ 57,651	
Merchandise Imports		−410,015
Service Imports		− 58,069
Investment Income (Net)	+ 14,484	
Unilateral Transfers		− 13,467
Miscellaneous		− 2,079
Balance on Current Account		− 160,681

CAPITAL ACCOUNT
■

Changes in Foreign Private Assets in the United States	+158,297	
Changes in U.S. Private Assets Abroad		− 74,166
Changes in Government Assets Other Than Reserves (Net)		− 2,008
Balance on Capital Account		+82,123

STATISTICAL DISCREPANCY   +21,893
■

Overall Balance   − 56,667

SETTLEMENT ACCOUNT
■

Changes in U.S. Reserve Assets	+ 9,151	
Changes in Foreign Official Holdings of Dollars	+ 47,516	
Balance in Settlement Account		+56,667

Source: Adapted from U.S. Department of Commerce, *Survey of Current Business* (Washington, D.C.: U.S. Government Printing Office, March, 1988).

■
Component Accounts

The balance of payments provides much useful information. The sum of merchandise and service exports and imports (the *balance of trade*) describes how competitive U.S. exports are compared to earlier years. The deficit in the balance of trade for the United States in the last decade has been a matter of great concern to policymakers. The buzzword "competitiveness" reflects concern for the big gap between U.S. exports and imports of goods and services.

The current account, which adds investment income and a few other items to the balance of trade, is roughly equivalent to that part of the national income accounts called net foreign investment. The **current account** groups together that part of the balance of payments account

CURRENT ACCOUNT
That part of the balance of payments account which summarizes transactions in currently produced goods and services, including merchandise, services, investment income, etc.

which summarizes transactions in currently produced goods and services, including merchandise, services, investment income, and several smaller items. Note that in 1987, the United States had a large deficit on this account, reflecting an excess of imports over exports. From 1960 to 1971, the United States regularly had a surplus on this account. Prior to the 1980s, the largest deficits on current account were in 1977 and 1978, at $14 billion and $15 billion. After some small surpluses in 1980 and 1981, the deficit in current account reappeared and grew rapidly from $9 billion in 1982 to $46 billion in 1983, $117 billion in 1985, and $161 billion in 1987. These figures set off a wave of alarm about loss of U.S. competitiveness with foreign products. Part of the reason for the current account deficit, however, was the high price of the dollar. The price of the dollar was bid up in the foreign exchange market by a demand for dollars to invest in the United States. The value of the dollar began to fall and, with a lag, there has finally been some decline in the deficit on current account in early 1988. The current account is linked to the capital account through changes in the market for the U.S. dollar.

The **capital account** summarizes purchases and sales of financial assets, such as bonds, short-term debts, bank deposits, stocks, and direct purchase of foreign plants. This category showed a large surplus in 1987, although it was less than a few years earlier when high U.S. interest rates attracted foreign capital. The figure of $158 billion in foreign private investment in the United States is enormous compared to past experience, while the outflow of private U.S. investment of $74 billion is small compared to levels of investment abroad in previous years. This pattern of a large net inflow of foreign private capital has only existed in the last few years.

The category labeled statistical discrepancy is rather large. The **statistical discrepancy** reflects imperfect information or unrecorded transactions such as workers' remittances, smuggling and other illegal activities, and inaccurate estimates of spending by U.S. tourists abroad or foreign tourists in the United States. If you've taken accounting, there were probably times when you wished you could give up trying to make accounts balance and just throw in a statistical discrepancy. However, there is a good reason for this entry. Balance of payments accountants do not have perfect information. When the discrepancy is large, as it has been in the 1980s, it is believed to consist mainly of unrecorded bank deposits. Thus, in addition to other forms of capital flowing into the United States, the surplus in statistical discrepancy suggests additional unrecorded capital inflows.

CAPITAL ACCOUNT
That part of the balance of payments account that summarizes purchases and sales of financial assets, such as stocks, bonds, short-term debts, bank deposits, and direct purchases of foreign plants or businesses.

STATISTICAL DISCREPANCY
That part of the balance of payments account that reflects imperfect information or unrecorded transactions.

■
Surpluses, Deficits, and Settlement Account

The sum of the three categories—current account, capital account, and statistical discrepancy—is the surplus or deficit in the balance of payments. In 1987, there was a deficit of about $56 billion. If you drew the supply and demand curves for the dollar, you would find that at the 1987 exchange rate, the demand for foreign exchange in the United States exceeded the supply of foreign exchange by about $56 billion. That figure is not large relative to the other sums in the individual accounts. A moderate balance in the settlement account and a corresponding moderate surplus or deficit in the other three accounts is normal even under a floating exchange rate. When price is allowed to adjust to clear the foreign exchange market, the small surplus or deficit at the end of the year reflects the fact that the market is moving toward equilibrium but hasn't arrived there. Under a fixed exchange rate, surpluses or deficits would be larger, reflecting the fact that when price is not allowed to adjust, a disequilibrium (surplus or deficit) can be large and persistent.

SETTLEMENT ACCOUNT
That part of the balance of payments account that explains how the deficit or surplus was financed, including gold and foreign exchange flows and government acquisition of currency.

The **settlement account** explains how the deficit or surplus was financed. In 1985, the deficit was settled by selling foreign exchange in the amount of about $9 billion, plus foreign central banks' increase in their dollar holdings of over $47 billion. The Federal Reserve watches changes in foreign exchange reserves closely because they are a component of the monetary base and can affect the size of the U.S. money supply.

Under the present system of floating exchange rates, persistent surpluses or deficits suggest whether the price of a country's currency is likely to rise or fall. Under floating rates, a market-determined rise in the price is called **appreciation**, and a market-determined fall is called **depreciation**.

APPRECIATION
A rise in the market price of a currency due to market forces.

DEPRECIATION
A fall in the market price of a currency due to market forces.

Although the United States and most major industrial countries are on a floating rate exchange system, many other countries maintain a fixed price for their currencies. Even within the category of a floating rate, the float can be "clean"—no government intervention to influence the currency's price—or, more commonly, dirty. A dirty float implies some government involvement in the market to limit fluctuations, which is a common practice in recent years.

There are four different kinds of international monetary arrangements that have been tried in the past, and two of them, exchange control and floating rates, continue to coexist in the present. Some economists and policymakers advocate a return to one of the other systems, the gold standard or the Bretton Woods system. Thus, no discussion of international finance would be complete without considering the four alternative international monetary systems.

INTERNATIONAL MONETARY SYSTEMS

Consider what goals an international monetary system might be designed to achieve. Many traders and bankers would like to have fixed or at least stable exchange rates. Fixed or stable rates would reduce much of the uncertainty and the need for hedging in international transactions, making foreign trade more like domestic trade. Another goal that has widespread support is freedom of trade and capital movements, so that nations can enjoy the benefits of specialization and trade.

Still another goal is that many countries would like to have more freedom in domestic monetary and fiscal policy. If the government feels a need to fight recession or contain inflation, it should be free to do so without having to worry about the effects of its policies on the balance of payments or international transactions.

Finally, a satisfactory system would ensure balance of payments equilibrium. The system should have some way of correcting deficits and surpluses. Alternative international monetary systems address these goals with different degrees of success.

The Gold Standard

From the late 1800s until the 1930s, most industrial countries were on the gold standard. The **gold standard** was an international monetary system in which currencies were defined in terms of gold, money supplies were tied to gold, and balance of payment deficits were settled in gold. Gold has served as money in most of the world for centuries. Thus, gold was a logical choice for settling accounts between countries with different national currencies. A country on the gold standard was supposed to observe three rules:

1. To define the value of its currency in terms of its gold content. Under the gold standard, the dollar price of an ounce of gold was $20.67 from 1837 to 1934, while the price of gold in British pounds was £4.25. The price of each currency in gold automatically determined the exchange rates between the two countries. The British pound was worth $4.86 ($20.67 divided by £4.25).
2. To have its money supply consist of gold, or be tied to the gold stock in some fixed ratio. For example, the ratio of gold to money in the United States was 1:4 in the nineteenth century. The nation's supply of currency could not exceed four times the U.S. monetary gold stock, although it could be less than the maximum.
3. To require the central bank or monetary authority to buy gold from anyone or to sell gold to anyone at the official price.

Correcting Deficits and Surpluses

These rules, if followed, automatically corrected deficits and surpluses. When there was a deficit in the balance of payments (surplus of U.S. dollars offered for foreign exchange), the price of foreign exchange would tend to rise. As the dollar price of foreign exchange started to rise, U.S. citizens would find that they could get more pounds or francs for a dollar by exchanging their dollars for gold, shipping it abroad, and exchanging it there for pounds or francs.

As gold flowed out of the country, the U.S. money supply would shrink and prices and output would fall. When prices fall in the United States, exports rise and imports fall; there is a shift in demand and supply for foreign exchange. Foreigners supply more of their currencies to buy more of relatively cheaper U.S. exports, while U.S. citizens demand less foreign exchange because they want to buy less of other countries' relatively more expensive products. Also, as U.S. output and national income falls, Americans buy less of everything, including imports.

Figure 21–3 shows these effects. German marks again represent all foreign currencies. The official price of the mark is 40 cents, and the cost of shipping gold is 5 cents. In a free market, the equilibrium price of the mark would be 50 cents, but because this country is on the gold standard, the price of foreign exchange cannot rise above the official price

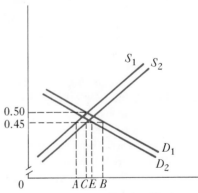

**FIGURE 21-3
AUTOMATIC ADJUSTMENT
UNDER THE GOLD STANDARD**
At 45 cents per mark, gold flows out of the country to cover the deficit *AB*. The gold outflow shrinks the money supply, reducing income and prices. Lower income and prices reduce demand for imports (to D_2) and increase foreign currency supply to buy U.S. exports (to S_2). The deficit falls from *AB* to *CE*.

THE GOLD BUFFS

The idea of returning to the gold standard has never died. It just went underground, surfacing as regularly as the Punxsutawney (Pa.) groundhog every February. Although the Reagan administration never officially endorsed returning to the gold standard, some financial advisers were very much inclined in that direction. Jude Wanniski, in a popular book on supply-side economics, *The Way the World Works* (New York: Basic Books, Inc., 1981), argued very strongly for a return to the gold standard.

Why does this idea keep returning? In part, it is because gold seems to offer a degree of certainty that paper money does not. When governments have gone down in revolutionary flames, the new government has usually restored faith in the currency by tying it to gold. When refugees leave countries in turmoil, the safest way to transport their wealth is in the form of gold. Fifty years after abandoning the gold standard, some people still think of gold as money—the only universal money.

Gold buffs, however, are not sentimental; most of them are hardheaded profit seekers. Many of them invested in gold when it made its dramatic rise from $35 an ounce in 1967 (the official price, maintained by central banks) to over $1,000 an ounce in the mid-1970s in a free market. (Some also had the foresight to get out of gold before it dropped sharply to under $400 an ounce in the early 1980s.) They didn't invest because of the demand for gold to use for jewelry and dental work. They invested because gold was, is, and probably always will be considered money by a substantial part of the world. The gold buffs would like to see gold return to being *the* money of the world in the same way that it was in earlier centuries.

Gold buffs usually want to return to gold because they do not trust the government to control the money supply. They would rather have the money supply determined by an arbitrary, impersonal force, namely the marketplace and the supply of monetary gold. Give governments the freedom to print money, they argue, and political pressures will sooner or later run up the money supply and the price level.

One argument offered against the gold buffs is that the chief advantage of gold is also its chief disadvantage. No one can control the supply of gold. Big discoveries can cause inflation and have done so in the past. Very slow growth of the gold supply compared to growth of output and population can lead to deflation, which can be very painful. Gold buffs would argue that at $400 an ounce, the supply is much greater than 50 years ago, both because an ounce now represents much more money and because there is an incentive to mine gold at higher prices. They admit, however, that it would be necessary to fix the price of gold. Over time, that fixed rate would fail to encourage gold mining as the additional cost of finding and retrieving gold gets higher.

The main reason, however, that the gold buffs are unlikely to get their way is that governments don't like to tie their own hands. Returning to the gold standard would mean giving up any sort of stabilization policy. No elected government is going to be willing to give up that option. The argument will go on, but as nations adapt to floating rates, the likelihood of going back on the gold standard gets smaller and smaller each year.

plus the cost of shipping the gold to Germany. Thus, at the maximum price of 45 cents, *AB* of gold flows out of the United States. That outflow shrinks the U.S. money supply, lowering national income and the price level and shifting supply and demand to S_2 and D_2. The deficit falls to *CE*.

This process of gold flows and shifts in supply and demand continues until the official price is restored and the deficit is eliminated.

The effects of the gold flow are reinforced by events in the other country (West Germany) into which gold is flowing. West Germany's money supply expands, raising income and prices and further shifting supply and demand in the correct direction. This automatic correction of deficits and surpluses, recognized in the early eighteenth century by David Hume, is called the **specie flow mechanism**. (*Specie* refers to money with a commodity value, such as gold or silver.)

Historical Experience

The gold standard worked satisfactorily in the late nineteenth and early twentieth centuries. Numerous discoveries of gold in California, Colorado, Alaska, Canada, and South Africa provided ample new gold. The gold standard meant that governments could not control their money supplies, but nineteenth-century governments didn't pursue an active monetary policy anyway. There were few major disturbances, such as wars and revolutions, that might have caused shifts in supply and demand so great that they would have been difficult and painful to correct.

World War I marked the end of the gold standard, although some countries (including the United States) remained on gold until the 1930s. Gold's main attractions were fixed exchange rates and automatic correction. However, the slow growth in the supply of gold in the twentieth century and restrictions on monetary policy were problems that could not be handled within the rigid requirements of the gold standard.

The gold standard supports three of the four goals of an international monetary system: stable exchange rates, freedom of trade and capital movements, and balance of payments equilibrium. It sacrifices independent monetary and fiscal policy. If the money supply is controlled by gold flows, there is little discretion left to the monetary authority to use the money supply to change the levels of output, employment, and prices. This drawback, combined with the problem of ensuring an adequate gold supply, makes a return to the gold standard very unlikely.

SPECIE FLOW MECHANISM
The automatic correction of deficits and surpluses through the effects of gold flows on money supplies.

Bretton Woods

From 1945 to 1973 international monetary arrangements were governed by the Bretton Woods system, named for the small New Hampshire town where delegates from major countries met to create a new international monetary system. Bretton Woods had some of the characteristics of a gold standard and some of the advantages of floating rates.

Operating Rules

Under the **Bretton Woods system**, a country defined a par value for its currency in terms of gold. The government was then obliged to keep its currency price within one percent of that par value.[3] Central

BRETTON WOODS SYSTEM
The international monetary system in effect from 1945 to 1973, based on infrequent changes in currency prices, ample reserves, and the dollar as key currency.

3. The Bretton Woods system, like the gold standard, had both a floor and a ceiling price for each currency. Under the gold standard, the floor and ceiling prices were determined by the cost of shipping gold. Under the Bretton Woods system, the floor and ceiling prices were arbitrarily set at 1 percent above and below the official price.

banks bought and sold their own currencies in trade for gold, dollars, or other foreign currencies in order to maintain the currency price.

Thus far this system sounds much like the gold standard. The difference, however, was that there was no connection between gold, deficits, and the money supply. Countries could pursue independent monetary policies. Since there was no automatic correction for deficits and surpluses, a balance of payments disequilibrium might last indefinitely. Because of this problem, the designers of the Bretton Woods system created a pool of **international monetary reserves**, or funds that members could borrow to settle deficits and would repay when they ran surpluses. Reserves consisted of gold, dollars, and a pool of other currencies contributed by members. These reserves were kept at a newly created institution, the International Monetary Fund (IMF). The **International Monetary Fund (IMF)** was the agency that supervised the operation of the Bretton Woods system by recording par values, consulting on devaluations/revaluations, and providing a pool of reserves for countries with deficits.

What happened if a country kept running deficits and borrowing from the IMF? The system was not intended to sustain deficits forever—just long enough for the situation to get back to normal. If a disequilibrium continued, the Bretton Woods system had a second method for coping with deficits (or surpluses): changing the currency's price, or the exchange rate. Thus, the Bretton Woods system gave up a central feature of the gold standard: unchangeable currency prices. In this respect, this system was more like floating rates, except that currency prices changed infrequently by large amounts instead of frequently by small amounts.

Why Bretton Woods Failed

The key to the failure of Bretton Woods lay in the difficulty of finding enough reserves in a satisfactory form. Since there was not enough gold, the next choice was the U.S. dollar, for two reasons. First, at the end of World War II, the United States had $2/3$ of the monetary gold stock and was the only nation willing to redeem its currency in gold. Second, the United States dominated world trade as the biggest supplier and the biggest customer. Because dollars were so popular and so useful, they were even used to make payments when no U.S. citizens or firms were involved. A currency which serves as a major reserve asset and is used to settle transactions between third party nations is called a **key currency**. The dollar, as the most popular key currency, joined gold as the second major form of international reserves.

Unfortunately, with no built-in corrections in the system, deficits grew large and persistent for many countries. Demand for reserves grew rapidly; the United States obliged by creating reserves. To create reserves, the United States ran deficits. The bigger and more frequent the United States' deficits were, the more reserves were created. But the more dollars there were outstanding, the less likely it became that the United States would be able to redeem them from its dwindling gold stock, and the more likely it became that a devaluation of the dollar would be needed to correct persistent deficits. No one wanted to be holding dollars when they were devalued, because of the financial loss. The pending crisis came to a head in 1971, when foreigners started turning in dollars for gold. The U.S. was forced to suspend the gold convertibility of the dollar in August,

RESERVES
The international media of exchange. Under the Bretton Woods system, reserves included gold, the U.S. dollar, and other major currencies.

INTERNATIONAL MONETARY FUND (IMF)
The agency that supervised the operation of the Bretton Woods system by recording par values, consulting on devaluations/revaluations, and providing a pool of reserves for countries with deficits.

KEY CURRENCY
A currency used for foreign exchange reserves and for settling transactions between other countries.

1971—an event known as the "closing of the gold window." In December, 1971, the dollar was devalued by about 8 percent, raising the dollar price of gold from $35 to $38. In February, 1973, the dollar was devalued again, raising the dollar price of gold to $42. After that, the United States and its major trading partners all switched to floating rates.

Bretton Woods was an attempt to have the best of all possible worlds. Nations wanted stable exchange rates, independent monetary policy, and free trade. The system sacrificed balance of payments equilibrium. The failure of Bretton Woods reminded policymakers that there must be some mechanism to deal with deficits. When the nations of the world finally came to recognize that problem, Bretton Woods could not survive.

Floating Rates

A system of floating exchange rates represents a pure market approach, in which any shift in supply or demand will change the price. This system had been tried by some individual countries, such as Canada, but was not widely adopted until 1973. Since 1973, most major industrial countries have had floating exchange rates. Figure 21–4 shows what has happened to the price of the U.S. dollar under floating exchange rates.

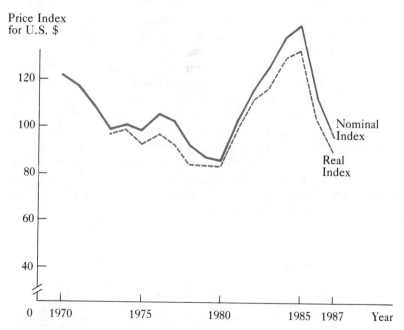

FIGURE 21-4
THE RISE AND FALL OF THE U.S. DOLLAR
The dollar was devalued in 1971 and again in early 1973. Beginning in 1973, the dollar was floated. Its value has fluctuated in both nominal terms (solid line) and real terms (dashed line, corrected for price level changes) against a market basket of other currencies of the U.S.'s major trading partners.

Floating exchange rates work on the basic principles of supply and demand. Floating rates support all of the suggested goals except stable exchange rates. If exchange rate adjustments clear the market, then the balance of payments should always be at or near equilibrium, and there is no need to shift the curves back to intersect at a fixed price or to use restrictions in order to get international payments to balance.

When countries first began to use floating exchange rates, there was widespread fear that the volume of trade would shrink because exchange rates would be very unstable. While exchange rates have indeed been very unstable, well-developed forward markets have limited the impact of exchange rate instability on trade. One serious problem has been that when a currency's exchange rate falls, it often falls below its ultimate equilibrium before finding its way back up to equilibrium. In the interim between equilibria, the exchange rate is still wrong, but in the opposite direction from before. During this time, price signals to importers, exporters, consumers, and producers are distorted. Decisions are made that would not be profit-maximizing decisions at the correct exchange rate.

Floating rates have not resulted in balance of payments equilibrium. Why? Part of the problem is measurement, but another part of the problem reflects a basic truth about market equilibrium. Equilibrium is never where the market is, but rather the direction in which it is headed. If supply and demand shift often, the market may always be in the process of moving from one equilibrium to another. However, deficits and surpluses generally have been much smaller under floating rates than they were under fixed rates.[4] In fact, the floating-rate system has coped fairly successfully with severe shocks (major supply and demand shifts), such as the OPEC oil price hike that created large deficits and surpluses and the 1980–1982 recession.

The floating-rate system of the 1970s and 1980s does not work exactly like the textbook model. Governments continue to intervene in the market, buying and selling their own currency and foreign exchange to limit swings in the price. While countries have not allowed the market to determine exchange rates, they are closer to doing so than they have ever been in the past. While there is still some unhappiness with floating rates, there is little pressure right now to return to a fixed-rate system. Many government officials are reluctant to go back on a gold standard because it limits their flexibility of action, or to return to the Bretton Woods system of 1945 through 1973.

Exchange Control

EXCHANGE CONTROL
A foreign exchange arrangement in which the government purchases all incoming foreign exchange and is the only source from which foreign exchange can be purchased legally.

The last method of dealing with deficits and surpluses is the one used by all Communist countries, by most less developed countries, and even occasionally by the major industrial nations. When the government requires that all earnings of foreign exchange be turned in to it and then sells foreign exchange to those who want to import, travel abroad, or invest in other countries, that country has opted for a system of **exchange control**.

4. The United States has had large deficits in the balance of trade in recent years, but those have been offset by inflows of foreign capital in most years.

	Currency Units per U.S. Dollar		
	March, 1977	December, 1987	% Change
French Franc	4.97800	5.7524	+15.6%
Japanese Yen	282.70000	135.5400	−52.1%
SDRs	.8639	.7230	

devaluation (in December, 1971), the dollar was worth .92105 SDRs. After the second devaluation (in February, 1973), the dollar dropped to .82895 SDRs. During the ups and downs that followed, the dollar hit a low of .74141 SDRs—more than 25 percent below its predevaluation price. Since then it rebounded sharply to a high of 1.035 SDRs in 1985 before dropping back to .723 SDRs at the end of 1987.

Other currencies have seen equally dramatic shifts in prices. In the table below, for example, are the high and low values since 1975 for five major currencies:

THE INTERNATIONAL PERSPECTIVE WATCHING CURRENCIES UNDER FLOATING RATES

One problem of a floating rate system is trying to measure changes in the price of one currency when others are moving around at the same time. If the price of the dollar is measured in French francs instead of Japanese yen, the picture of what is happening to the dollar may look very different.

One way to obtain a consistent measure of a currency's price is to use SDRs. SDRs (special drawing rights) are issued by the International Monetary Fund and are only exchanged among central banks. One SDR = one U.S. dollar before the 1971 devaluation. This international currency provides a constant measuring rod. In the table below, for example, are the prices of the dollar in March, 1977, and March, 1986, measured in francs, yen, and SDRs. The SDR measure is the most accurate reflection of changes in the price of dollars because it is the only constant measuring rod. While the dollar rose relative to the franc, and fell sharply with respect to the yen, there was less change measured in SDRs. (Note from Figure 21–4, however, that there were some sharp ups and downs in the interim.)

Measured in SDRs, the dollar and most other currencies have had a lively market since 1973. After the first

	Currency Units per SDR		
Currency	1971	Low Value (date)	High Value (date)
U.K. Pound Sterling	.4250	.8476 (1984)	.4250 (1975)
French Franc	5.6718	9.4022 (1984)	5.2510 (1984)
Canadian Dollar	1.0809	1.5451 (1983)	1.1725 (1975)
German Mark	3.5481	3.0857 (1984)	2.2810 (1976)
Japanese Yen	341.7800	368.4700 (1974)	175.2000 (1987)

What's a currency watcher to do? Daily rates (including forward prices) are published in most major newspapers, but long-term trends can be followed in *International Financial Statistics*, a monthly publication of the International Monetary Fund (and the source of these exchange rate figures). Importers, exporters, foreign exchange dealers, lenders, and multinational corporations all follow these figures carefully to make decisions about what to trade, when to trade, and at what price to trade.

Usually, exchange control is adopted because a currency price is too high and the country doesn't want to change it. Without exchange control, the country would run deficits. Typically the country has limited reserves and little international credit. By insisting that exporters turn in their foreign exchange to the government, which then sells it to importers, the country can make the balance of payments accounts balance.

Exchange control does accomplish three goals—stable exchange rates, independent monetary and fiscal policy, and no apparent deficit in the balance of payments. However, free trade is sacrificed. In addition, black markets almost always exist. People make side deals in foreign exchange in order to bypass the government. Bribery, smuggling, and misrepresentation of earnings from exports and cost of imports are regular events in countries with exchange control.

However, exchange control can accomplish other objectives. Often there are multiple exchange rates—different rates for buying and selling, and different rates for different uses. Suppose the government wants to encourage factory construction and discourage luxuries. It can charge a low price for foreign exchange to people who want to import machinery and a high price for foreign exchange to those who want to buy air conditioners and yachts. Thus, the government can promote particular consumption and production goals. Also, the government can raise revenue for public purposes when it can buy at a low price and sell at a higher price.

In some communist countries, such as China, exchange control involves two different kinds of currency. One that is used solely by foreigners, such as tourists and approved traders, and a second type that is used by ordinary citizens. Some stores and service institutions, such as hotels, accept only the first type. In this way the government can closely control the use of foreign exchange, deciding who buys imports and who gets the currency that foreigners spend in the country. With this type of exchange control, the risk of creating black markets is lower, because a country's own citizens are not allowed to hold exchangeable currency.

Some degree of exchange control is practiced by all but a few industrialized countries. Total or partial exchange control can coexist with either a fixed rate or a managed float, although fixed rates are more common. While floating rates have been adopted by the major industrial countries, the majority of countries do not have floating currencies, regardless of whether they practice exchange control. Most countries still maintain fixed exchange rates or "peg" them to a major currency. For example, many former French colonies in Africa keep a fixed relationship between the prices of their currencies and the French franc. Since France is still their major trading partner, this link creates a fixed exchange rate for most of their transactions. If the price of the franc falls 10 percent relative to the dollar, the price of a currency pegged to the franc will also fall by 10 percent relative to the dollar, but it would have the same relationship to the franc as before. Various combinations of floating rates, managed floats, exchange control, fixed rates, and pegged rates make up the hodgepodge international monetary system of the 1980s.

SUMMARY

1. Special features of foreign exchange markets are the forward market, government price-setting, and links to important macroeconomic variables.

2. U.S. demand for foreign exchange reflects demand for foreign goods, services, and financial assets. The supply of foreign exchange reflects foreign desire to buy U.S. exports of goods and services and/or U.S. financial assets.

3. Surpluses and shortages in the market for foreign exchange are equivalent to surpluses and deficits in the balance of payments.

4. Shifts in supply and demand for foreign exchange result from changes in relative prices, incomes, and interest rates and from changes in tastes, population, technology, and input cost and availability.

5. The forward market is a way to deal with the risk of changing currency prices.

6. Disequilibrium often persists in the foreign exchange market. Ways of dealing with disequilibrium, besides changing the price, include shifting the supply and demand curves, rationing, and drawing on reserves.

7. The balance of payments is a summary of transactions between U.S. residents and foreigners. It is divided into four accounts—the current account, the capital account, the statistical discrepancy, and the settlement account. The sum of the first three is the deficit or surplus. The settlement account explains how the deficit or surplus was financed.

8. The gold standard relied on movements of gold to settle deficits. Gold flows changed money supplies, affecting prices and income and shifting supply and demand for currency back to equilibrium at the official price.

9. The Bretton Woods system (1945–1973) tried to provide some stability in exchange rates and relied on reserves to settle deficits. It broke down because it was too dependent on a single currency—the dollar—which had to run deficits to provide reserves and which could not be devalued.

10. Floating rates, in which the market determines the exchange rate, have been widely used since 1973.

11. Under exchange control, all sales and purchases of foreign exchange pass through the government. Many less-developed countries use exchange control. Usually, black markets in foreign exchange develop under this system.

NEW TERMS

foreign exchange market
forward market
hedgers
speculators
balance of payments deficit
balance of payments
current account

capital account
statistical discrepancy
settlement account
appreciation
depreciation
gold standard
specie flow mechanism

Bretton Woods system
reserves
International Monetary Fund (IMF)
key currency
exchange control

QUESTIONS FOR DISCUSSION

1. Look up the balance of payments for the United States in the last two years in the *Federal Reserve Bulletin*. See if you can put it into the simplified format used in the chapter and calculate the surplus or deficit. How has it changed in the last few years?

2. What might shift a country from equilibrium into deficit in its balance of payments? How would the deficit be dealt with under the gold standard? Bretton Woods? floating rates? exchange control?

3. Why is the forward market particularly important under floating rates?

4. How do changes in prices and incomes in one country affect the supply and demand for its currency? What about changes in prices and incomes in other countries?

5. Why do some people want to return to the gold standard? What drawbacks does the gold standard have?

6. If interest rates rise in the United States, what happens to the supply, demand, and price of the dollar? Why? How might this affect U.S. exports and imports of goods and services?

7. Where would each of the following items appear on a balance of payments?
   a. Sale of tractors to Poland.
   b. Gift of tractors to Mexico.
   c. You buy a restaurant meal in Canada.
   d. A British resident buys U.S. government bonds.

8. How does a recession in one country affect economic conditions in another country?

9. The ways of dealing with a disequilibrium (shortage or surplus of foreign currency at a given price) are to change the price, ration, shift the curves into equilibrium at that price, or draw on or accumulate reserves. Identify the international monetary system that uses each of those as its primary way to deal with disequilibrium.

10. Why is there a statistical discrepancy in the balance of payments?

■ SUGGESTIONS FOR FURTHER READING

Adams, John ed. *The Contemporary International Economy: A Reader*. 2nd ed. New York: St. Martin's Press, Inc., 1985. About a dozen of the readings in this book deal with balance of payments accounting and international monetary systems. Not highly technical.

Aliber, Robert Z. *The International Money Game*. 5th ed. New York: Basic Books, Inc., 1984. A delightful reader on a variety of current international monetary issues.

Chrystal, K. Alec. "A Guide to Foreign Exchange markets." *Review* (St. Louis: Federal Reserve Bank of St. Louis, May, 1984), 5–18. A nontechnical explanation of how foreign exchange markets work.

Ulbrich, Holley H. *International Trade and Finance: Theory and Policy*. Englewood Cliffs, NJ: Prentice-Hall, Inc., 1983, Chapters 11–19. An intermediate text with emphasis on alternative monetary arrangements.

Pool, John Charles, and Steve Samos. *The ABCS of International Finance*. Lexington, MA: Lexington Books, 1987. A simple, nontechnical discussion of current international finance issues, emphasizing the evolution of the international monetary system and the problems of debtor nations, including the United States.

CHAPTER 22 ■ ■
■
ECONOMIC DEVELOPMENT AND THE THIRD WORLD
■

■
INTRODUCTION

This chapter uses the economic principles discussed in earlier chapters to compare relative rates of development among countries and to examine some of the reasons for differences in the levels of development. Most of development economics is based on statistical evidence and case studies rather than on theoretical models. Development economists spend a great deal of time trying to solve practical problems in less developed countries (LDCs) and trying to design and implement programs that will aid in the economic development of particular economies. We will discuss the major problems faced by poor countries and outline the current debate over the role developed countries should play in assisting the LDCs.

■ ■ ■ ■ ■ ■ ■
COMMON CHARACTERISTICS OF LDCs

Almost 30 years ago, the general manager of the United Nations Special Fund, a program to fund development projects, painted a concise, yet very illuminating, picture of what was, at that time, referred to as an underdeveloped country.[1] The picture is still valid:

Everyone knows what an underdeveloped country looks like; it is a country characterized by poverty, with beggars in the cities and villagers eking out a bare subsistence in the rural areas. It is a country lacking in factories of its own, usually

1. In the jargon of development economists, the name for the less developed countries has changed frequently, in part reflecting the increased political power of these countries. In the 1950s and 1960s, the term "underdeveloped countries" was most commonly used. (Before that, they often were called "backward" countries.) In the late 1960s and early 1970s, the term "less developed countries" (LDCs) emerged. In the late 1970s, the term "Third World" was in vogue. In the early 1980s, United Nations publications used the term "low-income countries," "middle-income countries," and "industrialized countries" to designate the level of development. In most recent UN publications, the term "developing countries" is used. These countries often refer to themselves as the Group of 77.

with inadequate supplies of power and light. It usually has insufficient roads and railroads, insufficient government services, and poor communication. It has few hospitals and few institutions of higher learning. Most of its people cannot read or write. In spite of the generally prevailing poverty of the people, it may have isolated islands of wealth, with a few persons living in luxury. Its banking system is poor; small loans have to be obtained through money lenders who are often little better than extortionists. Another striking characteristic of an underdeveloped country is that its exports to other countries usually consist almost entirely of raw materials, ores, fruits, or some staple product with possibly a small admixture of luxury handicrafts. Often the extraction or cultivation of these raw material exports is in the hands of foreign companies.[2]

Low Per Capita Income Levels

The United Nations considers any country with a GNP of less than $400 per capita (in 1984 U.S. dollars) as a low-income country. There were 36 countries categorized as low-income countries in 1987. Per capita income or per capita GNP is not a very precise indication because of the problems associated with statistical measures of income and production. These problems apply with even greater force in LDCs, since these countries do not have very sophisticated methods of gathering and processing data, and much of the output does not pass through the market, so it doesn't enter the statistics. For example, the food a family grows for itself is not included.

Table 22–1 presents the latest World Bank data for selected, representative countries at various income levels. The most obvious measure of low levels of development is low-income levels per capita. Table 22–1 sorts countries into groups on the basis of per capita income. The first three categories are low income, middle income, and industrial market economies. The fourth category, high-income oil exporters, includes three rich countries whose wealth is based on oil resources rather than on development. They export more than they import. The East European communist countries are also listed separately as "East European Nonmarket Economies." Since they rely less on the market system than most other countries, the quality of their statistics is often poor compared to other countries at similar levels of development. We will discuss the centrally planned economies in much greater detail in the next chapter.

Agriculture

Agriculture is usually the largest sector of economic activity in LDCs. It is basically subsistence agriculture, designed to provide food for the individual family rather than crops sold for cash. Rural overcrowding, small land holdings that prevent modern economical cultivation, and low agricultural yields per acre predominate. An examination of Tables 22–2 and 22–3 on page 458 confirms this dependence on agriculture. In the

2. Paul G. Hoffman, *One Hundred Countries—One and One Quarter Billion People* (Washington, D.C.: Committee for International Economic Growth, 1960), 14.

TABLE 22-1
BASIC INDICATORS OF ECONOMIC DEVELOPMENT

	Population Mid-1985 (Millions)	Area (Thousand Square Kilometers)	Gross National Product per Capita In Current U.S. Dollars 1985	Average Annual Growth (Percent) 1965–1984	Average Annual Rate of Inflation (Percent) 1965–1973	1973–1984
Low-Income Countries	**2,389.5**	**31,795**	**260**	**2.8**	**1.6**	**5.9**
Bangladesh	98.1	144	130	0.6	7.3	9.9
India	749.2	3,288	260	1.6	6.3	7.8
Uganda	15.0	236	230	2.9	5.6	64.5
Sierra Leone	3.7	72	310	0.6	1.9	15.4
Middle-Income Countries	**1,187.6**	**40,927**	**1,250**	**3.1**	**5.5**	**38.0**
Egypt	45.9	1,001	720	4.3	2.6	13.1
Philippines	53.4	300	660	2.6	8.8	12.9
Paraguay	3.3	407	1,240	4.4	4.3	12.9
Chile	11.8	757	1,700	−0.1	50.3	75.4
Mexico	76.8	1,973	2,040	2.9	4.8	31.5
Portugal	10.2	92	1,970	3.5	4.9	20.5
Industrial Market Economies	**733.4**	**30,935**	**11,430**	**2.4**	**5.2**	**7.9**
United Kingdom	56.4	245	8,570	1.6	6.2	13.8
Japan	120.0	372	10,630	4.7	6.0	4.5
France	54.9	547	9,760	3.0	5.3	10.7
Federal Republic of Germany (West)	61.2	249	11,130	2.7	4.7	4.1
United States	237.0	9,363	15,390	1.7	4.7	7.4
High-Income Oil Exporters	**18.6**	**4,312**	**11,250**	**3.2**	**6.1**	**11.8**
Saudi Arabia	11.1	2,150	10,530	5.9	5.1	14.1
Libya	3.5	1,760	8,520	−1.1	9.4	10.8
Kuwait	1.7	18	16,720	−0.1	4.6	9.2
East European Nonmarket Economies	**389.3**	**23,421**	—	—	—	—
Hungary	10.7	93	2,100	6.2	2.6	4.3
Soviet Union	275.0	22,402	2,100	1.5	—	—
Poland	36.9	313	—	—	—	—
German Democratic Republic (East)	16.7	108	—	—	—	—

Source: Adapted from *World Development Report, 1987* (New York: Oxford University Press, 1987). Copyright © 1987 by the International Bank for Reconstruction and Development/The World Bank.

low- and middle-income countries, more than half the labor force is engaged in agriculture, more than a third of the Gross Domestic Product (GDP) is attributed to agriculture, and the growth in the agricultural sector is slower than in other sectors of the economy in these countries. To a large degree, the extent to which a country devotes itself to agriculture indicates its level of poverty. No country is poor if it can easily feed itself by producing its own food, or by exporting nonfood items and importing food, and still have ample resources left for other kinds of production. Today, only 2 percent of the U.S. labor force can produce enough to feed the entire United States well, with a surplus left for export. In low-income countries, an average of 70 percent of the population was in agriculture in 1985, compared to 44 percent in middle-income countries, and 7 percent in industrialized countries.

TABLE 22-2
AVERAGE ANNUAL GROWTH RATES OF PRODUCTION (Percent)

	GDP* 1965–1973	1973–1984	Agriculture 1965–1973	1973–1984	Industry 1965–1973	1973–1984	Manufacturing 1965–1973	1973–1984	Services 1965–1973	1973–1984
Low-Income Countries	5.6	5.3	3.0	3.6	8.9	7.4	—	—	6.8	5.0
Middle-Income Countries	7.4	4.4	3.6	2.7	9.1	4.4	9.2	5.5	7.8	5.1
Industrial Market Economies	4.7	2.4	1.8	1.1	5.1	1.8	5.3	2.1	4.8	2.1

*GDP is a concept very close to GNP. We will use the terms interchangeably.

Source: Adapted from *World Development Report, 1987* (New York: Oxford University Press, 1987). Copyright © 1987 by the International Bank for Reconstruction and Development/The World Bank.

TABLE 22-3
STRUCTURE OF POPULATION

	Percentage of Population In Urban Areas 1965	1985	Of Working Age (15–64 years) 1965	1985	Percentage of Labor Force in Agriculture 1965	1985
Low-Income Countries	17	23	53	59	78	70
Middle-Income Countries	36	49	53	56	57	44
Industrial Market Economies	72	77	63	67	14	7

Source: Adapted from *World Development Report, 1987* (New York: Oxford University Press, 1987). Copyright © 1987 by the International Bank for Reconstruction and Development/The World Bank.

As a producing sector, agriculture faces problems in both developed and less developed countries. We discussed the problems of U.S. agriculture in an earlier chapter. In both developed and less developed countries, supply is unpredictable, depending on the weather. Demand is not very responsive to price changes. Thus, a bumper crop will lead to a big price drop; a poor harvest will command high prices, but high prices are little comfort when you have little or nothing to sell. For this reason, reducing dependence on agriculture is a goal of every development program.

TABLE 22-4
DISTRIBUTION OF GROSS DOMESTIC PRODUCT (Percent)

	Agriculture		Industry		Manufacturing		Services	
	1965	1985	1965	1985	1965	1985	1965	1985
Low-Income Countries	42	36	28	35	14	15	30	29
Middle-Income Countries	21	14	31	37	20	22	48	49
Industrial Market Economies	5	3	39	35	29	25	56	62

Source: Adapted from *World Development Report, 1987* (New York: Oxford University Press, 1987). Copyright © 1987 by the International Bank for Reconstruction and Development/The World Bank.

Climate

Almost all the poorest of the low-income countries are in tropical climates. Conversely, all the industrialized countries are in temperate climes. Even the pockets of lower development in the industrialized countries tend to be in their southern regions; for example, southern Italy and the southern United States. This relationship between climate and development is so strong that it seems to many people that it could hardly be a coincidence. It is sometimes referred to by development economists as the *North-South problem*. Some development economists have suggested that warmer climates produce lower human effort, more diseases, and unfavorable agricultural conditions. On the other hand, Hong Kong, Singapore, and Saudi Arabia, all in very warm climates, are doing rather well.

Population

Perhaps the most striking features of LDCs are their demographic characteristics. (*Demography* is the study of populations.) Tables 22-3 and 22-4 show some striking differences in urbanization and in the dependency ratio, or the percentage of the population not of working age. Low-income countries are significantly more rural and have higher dependency ratios.

Higher dependency ratios result from high birth rates. The **crude birth rate** is demographics jargon for the number of births per thousand of population. As Table 22-5 shows, there is a significant difference between the crude birth rates in poor and industrialized countries. The median crude birth rate in the low-income countries is 29 per thousand; in the middle-income countries, 33 per thousand; and in the industrialized countries, 14 per thousand. (The median is the middle value in a distribution arranged from highest to lowest.)

There are many reasons for these high birth rates. Perhaps the most obvious is that women marry soon after puberty in many poor regions. In economic terms, they marry early because they have few economic alternatives except marriage, and they may produce children early

CRUDE BIRTH RATE
Number of births per one thousand of population.

TABLE 22-5
DEMOGRAPHIC INDICATORS

	Crude Birth Rate		Crude Death Rate		Percent Change in Crude Birth Rate	Crude Death Rate
	1965 ■	1985	1965 ■	1985	1965–1985 ■	1965–1985 ■
Low-Income Countries	43	29	17	11	−31.2	−39.3
Middle-Income Countries	42	33	15	10	−19.5	−35.3
Industrial Market Economies	19	14	10	9	−28.6	− 7.3

Source: Adapted from *World Development Report, 1987* (New York: Oxford University Press, 1987). Copyright © 1987 by the International Bank for Reconstruction and Development/The World Bank.

because children, especially sons, are useful as labor and as old-age insurance. On the cultural side, they may marry and have children early because of social stigmas that may result if they don't. In most poor countries, for example, there are few worse social stigmas for a woman than to be childless, and a man's prestige is often measured by the number of children and grandchildren he has.

The most important consequence of this high birth rate is that a very large proportion of the population is unproductive. As Table 22–3 indicates, almost half of the population of low-income countries is not of working age, compared to less than 33 percent in the industrial economies. These children and older people have to be fed and clothed but produce very little output. Additionally, people in poorer countries have a shorter life expectancy, as Table 22–6 indicates. The median life expectancy at birth is 60 years in the low-income countries compared to 73 years in the industrialized world. This means that the productive work life of any adult is shorter in the LDCs. The consequences of the short life expectancy and the high birth rate are large numbers of children with relatively few adults to support them. This is a very inefficient age distribution from the point of view of the society's ability to increase economic output.

Recent health techniques have substantially lowered the death rate in most poorer countries, while it remained almost constant in the industrialized countries. As Table 22–6 indicates, the crude death rate fell significantly from 1965 to 1985 in the low- and middle-income countries. The **crude death rate** is the absolute number of deaths per one thousand of population. The consequence of the declining death rate and the high and stable birth rate has been a population explosion in low-income countries. The population growth means that these countries must grow rapidly in productive capacity just to stay *even* in per capita income.

The effect of the population explosion on per capita income is easily seen by comparing Tables 22–1 and 22–2. Table 22–2 shows that the average annual growth rates of production in the low-income and middle-income countries were in some cases higher than the rates in the industrialized countries. Even the median growth rates for the middle-

CRUDE DEATH RATE
Number of deaths per one thousand of population.

TABLE 22-6
HEALTH-RELATED INDICATORS

	Life Expectancy at Birth		Mortality Rates per Thousand Infants		Children Aged 1–4		Median Population per: Physician		Nursing Person		Calorie Supply As a Percent of Daily Requirement
	1965 ■	1985	1965 ■	1985	1965 ■	1985	1965 ■	1981	1965 ■	1981	1985 ■
Low-Income Countries	49	60	125	72	19	9	8,357	5,375	5,037	3,920	102
Middle-Income Countries	51	59	115	72	22	11	11,192	4,764	3,526	1,474	110
Industrial Market Economies	68	73	24	9	1	1	867	554	425	177	130

Source: Adapted from *World Development Report, 1987* (New York: Oxford University Press, 1987). Copyright © 1987 by the International Bank for Reconstruction and Development/The World Bank.

income countries are higher in all four sectors than the rates in the industrial countries. But the picture changes when we examine per capita GNP growth in Table 22–1. The high rates of population growth have meant that poor countries have fallen further behind on a per capita basis, even though their growth has been more rapid in terms of aggregate GNP. This population time bomb will be discussed in detail in a later section of this chapter.

Investment in Human Capital

Most low-income countries invest very little in human capital, or the health, education, and skills of their citizens. Labor that is healthy and well-educated is more productive, so investment in humans can be as productive as investment in machines, bridges, and tractors. Of course, one reason that low-income countries invest little in human capital is that they have little to invest, and one of the reasons they have little to invest is that they have had such low levels of investment in human capital and other kinds of capital. This is called the **vicious circle of poverty**. There is little investment because there is a low level of income, and there is a low level of income because there has been little investment.

The very low level of investment in human capital is easily seen in Tables 22–6 and 22–7. Table 22–6 lists median population per physician and per nursing person. There are many more persons per physician in low-income countries and middle-income countries, compared to the industrialized countries. The relationship with nursing persons per population has improved greatly since 1960, but it is still a problem. These data indicate the very important point that the population in the low-income countries is less healthy, less vigorous, and, as a result, less productive.

VICIOUS CIRCLE OF POVERTY
Little investment because of a low level of income, and a low level of income because of little investment.

Illiteracy in low-income countries tends to be quite high. The reasons for this can easily be found by examining the data in Table 22–7, which presents school enrollment data. The reasons for the low enrollments in the low- and middle-income countries are easy to understand. In a subsistence economy, everyone must work to support the family. Education is a luxury that the family cannot afford. The effects are obvious; an uneducated work force is a less productive work force.

TABLE 22-7
SCHOOL ENROLLMENT (AS A PERCENT OF RELEVANT AGE GROUP)

	Primary School Total		Female		Secondary School		Higher Education	
	1965	1984	1965	1984	1965	1984	1965	1984
Low-Income Countries	80	91	46	76	23	31	2	4
Middle-Income Countries	84	105	77	100	20	47	4	12
Industrial Market Economies*	106	102	106	101	63	85	21	37

*For countries with universal primary education, the gross enrollment ratios exceed 100 percent, since some pupils are below or above the official primary school age.

Source: Adapted from *World Development Report, 1987* (New York: Oxford University Press, 1987). Copyright © 1987 by the International Bank for Reconstruction and Development/The World Bank.

Culture

Another characteristic of the LDCs is that they typically have what might be termed "uneconomic" cultures. Many of these countries cling to ways of life that are in conflict with industrialization and economic development. This is not to say that these cultural traits are bad in any normative or moral sense but only that they hinder economic development. Economic development may not be a society's primary goal.

In many LDCs, these values manifest themselves in an acceptance of the status quo. In some countries, particularly in Asia, consumption and wealth are considered vulgar, and Hinduism and Buddhism both consider self-denial virtuous. Even begging, which flourishes in these poor countries, is not considered undesirable. These social attitudes are in stark contrast to western values and particularly to the so-called "Protestant work ethic," which holds that economic success and its trappings are positive accomplishments.

In many low-income countries, superstition plays a key role. Success in business or in agriculture is thought to depend heavily on benevolent spirits. Even in Latin America, where most of the population is Catholic, people in many areas solicit the help of pre-Christian deities.

All this activity works against the development of modern industrial and agricultural techniques and, as a result, slows the course of economic development.

Lack of upward mobility is also a common characteristic of low-income countries. The intelligent, vigorous individual is often blocked from advancement by a rigid social system or suspicions or sanctions against such advancement. As a result, entrepreneurial talents are often given an opportunity only in the military or government service. The private sector and manufacturing suffer. Many talented individuals emigrate from LDCs to countries that offer greater opportunities.

The grip of custom strangles many less developed economies. Much is done in a prescribed manner because it is dictated by custom. Economic growth and development require the acceptance of technological changes and innovations. Custom works against such change. A number of writers have argued that, in part, the success of the Industrial Revolution was the result of radical changes that took place during this period that touched and challenged the basic customs of the population. Indeed, industrial revolutions have often occurred after social upheavals that changed and challenged entrenched power structures.

THEORIES AND MODELS OF DEVELOPMENT

The study of economic development is not characterized by elegant economic theories; indeed, the field of economic development has attracted practitioners and field economists rather than theorists. There are, however, several models or theories (using theory in a loose sense) of various aspects of the development process. These models have, at times, been the basis of policies aimed at helping the development process along.

Historical Theories of Development

There are two basic theories of development that are historical in nature in that they try to examine history and draw from it guidelines for development. The first is the theory of Karl Marx as expressed in *Das Kapital*. The second is the theory of W.W. Rostow, presently a professor at the University of Texas and formerly an adviser to President Lyndon Johnson.

Marx: Das Kapital

While Karl Marx is best known as the intellectual founder of communism (discussed in detail in the next chapter), he also has a clearly laid-out theory of economic development. Marx saw all society passing through a sequence of historical stages: (1) primitive society (tribal communism); (2) slavery; (3) feudalism; (4) capitalism; (5) socialism; and, finally, (6) communism. At this final stage, Marx argued, scarcity would not exist, and workers would produce without material incentives. To Marx, the important step was the decay of capitalism and the transition to socialism. Marx felt that the transition would come about because of fundamental weaknesses inherent in capitalism. One of the major weaknesses in capitalism that Marx saw was based on the **labor theory of value** and

LABOR THEORY OF VALUE
A central element in the theory of Karl Marx. All commodities were reduced to a common denominator of the labor time embodied in the product.

on the class struggle that would emerge between the proletariat and the capitalists. To Marx, as to many nineteenth century economists, all value in produced goods was derived from labor. The machines that were used in the production process were simply embodied or congealed labor from earlier production. All commodities were valued in terms of the common denominator of the labor time embodied in them. The relative prices of goods were thus determined by the labor time embodied in them. If a wagon took five times longer to produce than a harness, it would sell for five times the price of the harness.

The labor theory of value was widely held by mainstream economists in the early part of the nineteenth century but was discarded later in the century by most of them. However, the early followers of Marx adhered to this theory. The labor theory of value led to predictions of a struggle based on Marx's observation that capitalists pay workers only the amount necessary to survive. He argued that wages always tend toward the subsistence level because capitalists, seeking profits, pay only the lowest amount necessary. Marx labeled the difference between the labor value of the goods produced and the subsistence wage the workers received **surplus value**. This surplus value represented capitalistic exploitation of workers.

Marx also believed that there would be an eventual decline of profits as capitalists accumulated more and more capital. The private economy would become very monopolized, and business cycles would increase in severity. As a result of all these forces, a large group of unemployed laborers, called the **reserve army of the unemployed**, would emerge. These unemployed workers would unite in protest, and socialism would ultimately develop from their overthrow of capitalism.

The labor theory of value, on which Marx's model of development is based, is not a particularly good theory. As we saw earlier, price is determined by the interaction of supply and demand. It is true that labor costs play a large role in determining price, but other costs of production also play a role, as does demand. Thus, even among radical and socialist economists today, the labor theory of value plays a much more minor role than it did to Marx. Marx's economics was quite simplistic, even in its own day.

Marx's prognosis for the future course of economic and political development did not fare much better than his economics. It is true that industrialization spread throughout the world in the aftermath of the Industrial Revolution, particularly throughout the Western world; but the Industrial Revolution did not result in just a few capitalists acquiring all the wealth at the expense of the working masses. In fact, the material well-being of workers increased rapidly with spreading industrialization.

Rostow: A Non-Communist Manifesto

W.W. Rostow, in a book entitled *Stages of Economic Growth*, responded to Marx's theory with an alternative development theory in the same historical tradition.[3] Rostow, in fact, subtitled his book *A Non-Communist Manifesto*, making clear that it was intended as an anti-Marxist statement.

SURPLUS VALUE
The difference between the labor value of goods produced and the subsistence wages received by workers.

RESERVE ARMY OF THE UNEMPLOYED
The large group of unemployed laborers that Marx predicted would unite, ultimately developing socialism.

3. W.W. Rostow, *Stages of Economic Growth*, 2d ed. (New York: Cambridge University Press, 1971).

Rostow argues that all countries go through five stages of economic growth. He believes that it is possible to classify countries according to the stage they are in and that we can then investigate why some countries have not advanced into the next stage in their development process.

The first stage is the traditional society. A **traditional society** is a society largely governed by tradition in which economic decisions are made on the basis of custom and obligation. Rostow characterizes this stage as *pre-Newtonian*. By pre-Newtonian, he means that the scientific age and advanced technology have not yet arrived. Countries in this stage would exhibit the characteristics of underdevelopment we discussed earlier, including the noneconomic culture. The second stage develops the **preconditions for takeoff**. In this stage, the uneconomic culture is overcome, advances in agriculture take place, and an entrepreneurial class of risk takers begins to emerge. **Takeoff**, the third stage, follows. During takeoff into sustained growth, there is a significant increase in the rate of saving, and leading sectors develop. Increased saving finances investment in capital goods in the leading sectors. These leading sectors grow rapidly, and their growth pulls other sectors along. The takeoff is, of course, the key to emerging as an industrialized country. The Industrial Revolution in Western Europe and the United States would mark the takeoff in these countries. Some of the countries in the middle-income range in Table 22–1 might presently be in the takeoff stage.

The final two stages are the drive to maturity and high mass consumption. The **drive to maturity** is the stage when lagging sectors of the economy catch up to the leading sectors, and the industrial revolution is consolidated into sustained growth. The fifth stage, **high mass consumption**, describes the level of development in the United States and Western Europe at the present time. It is the stage in which growth settles into a high level of consumption for most members of the society.

Rostow's stage theory implies that all countries follow a (roughly) similar path to development. Critics of the theory have pointed out that while the stages might usefully categorize how the present industrialized nations have developed, the present LDCs will not necessarily follow the same sequence. The pre-Newtonian stage, while perhaps characteristic of pre-Industrial Revolution England, does not describe today's LDCs, in which very modern technology exists next to urban squalor. Simon Kuznets, a Nobel prize-winning economist, has pointed out that there are significant differences between today's LDCs and the preindustrial phase of developed countries.[4] Among the most important of these is the fact that per capita agricultural production in today's LDCs is about one-fourth the level it was in preindustrial stages of the present developed countries. Social and political obstacles are more formidable in today's less developed world. Indeed, it can be argued that pre-Industrial Revolution England was not an underdeveloped country at all compared to today's LDCs.

TRADITIONAL SOCIETY
A society largely governed by tradition in which economic decisions are made on the basis of custom and obligation.

PRECONDITIONS FOR TAKEOFF
The stage of development in which "uneconomic" culture is overcome, advances in agriculture take place, and an entrepreneurial class of risk takers begins to emerge.

TAKEOFF
The stage of development in which there is a significant increase in the rate of saving. Leading sectors develop and pull others along, and sustained growth is achieved.

DRIVE TO MATURITY
The stage of development in which the lagging sectors of the economy catch up, and the industrial revolution is consolidated into sustained growth.

HIGH MASS CONSUMPTION
The stage of development in which growth settles into a high level of consumption for most members of the society.

4. See Simon Kuznets, *Economic Growth and Structure* (New York: W.W. Norton & Co., Inc., 1965).

Big Push Versus Leading Sector Strategies

Other approaches to development look for specific workable strategies rather than grand historical designs. A number of strategies have been devised to try to break the cycle of poverty and cause a spurt in economic growth. Two basic strategic approaches are the big push and leading sectors approach.

BIG PUSH
The development strategy calling for one major thrust on all fronts in the economy by government or induced by government through private enterprise.

The **big push** calls for one major thrust on all fronts in the economy by government or induced by government through private enterprise. This idea is based on the classical notion that growth in the output of an industry is limited by the extent of the market. At low levels of economic development, it is futile for any one industry to expand its output to a larger scale because it would be unable to sell its product. But if all industries expand in a big push, the inputs needed for the production of one commodity become the demands for other industries' output, and the incomes generated will create a demand for the final products. This push must be orchestrated by the government, the proponents of the big push argue, because no single entrepreneur or group of entrepreneurs has the incentive to expand production without the simultaneous expansion in other industries.

The argument calls for government action to stimulate the growth process. One challenge to this approach rests on the fact that the industrialized countries, the developed world, did not usually have such a government-sponsored big push. A second concern is that the big push calls for a large role for government in planning. This concern will be addressed in detail in the next chapter.

LEADING SECTORS
The development theory calling for concentration on a number of leading sectors that will pull along other sectors in the development process.

Albert O. Hirschman, a development economist with a great deal of field experience, of the Institute for Advanced Studies in Princeton, New Jersey, takes a different tack from the big push strategy.[5] Hirschman supports Rostow's **leading sectors** strategy for economic growth and feels that a country does not need a big push on all fronts or in all sectors of the economy. Instead, Hirschman argues, a country should concentrate on developing backward and forward linkages from and to successful industries. In development economics, the idea of concentrating on the encouragement of a particular sector that will then influence other sectors in the chain of production is called **linkage**. For example, if there is a successful sardine-fishing industry, it could be linked forward to a canning operation, which in turn could be linked forward to a packing and shipping industry. Backward linkages could develop effective demand for cans, stimulating a mining industry for metal for cans and a paper industry for shipping cartons. In this view, if the government is to be involved in the development process, it should concentrate its efforts on certain sectors or industries that maximize the number of potential linkages. Private entrepreneurs would then take over in response to the demand created through the linkages. The role of the government would be smaller, and the power of the market would be used to allocate productive resources efficiently.

LINKAGE
In development economics, the idea of concentrating on the encouragement of a particular sector that will then influence other sectors in the chain of production.

5. Albert O. Hirschman, *The Strategy of Economic Development* (New Haven: Yale University Press, 1958).

■
Laissez-Faire Versus
Government-Directed Development

No single comprehensive theory of development has emerged that has superseded the original work by Adam Smith in 1776. The complete title of Smith's *Wealth of Nations* was *An Inquiry into the Nature and Causes of the Wealth of Nations*. In this book, Smith set forth the classical principles of economic development. These principles rested on a governmental policy of *laissez-faire*—nonintervention—toward private industry and commerce. The division of labor and the increased productivity brought on by the division of labor were limited only by the size of the market. As a result, free trade was advocated as a way to promote this division of labor by exploiting each nation's comparative advantage in production.

Development policies of some LDCs and policies advocated by some development economists are often at odds with this *laissez-faire* approach. They argue that government must direct the development process. Many of these views grew out of the experience of the 1930s and 1940s, when the Soviet Union was able to grow very rapidly by applying severe authoritarian development techniques.[6] As a result of the Soviet development success, some economists began to argue that:

No policy of economic development can be carried out unless the government has the capacity to adhere to it. . . . Quite often, however, democratic governments lose equanimity and determination in the face of opposition. . . . This is the dilemma of most democratic governments. It is here that socialist countries . . . have an immense advantage: their totalitarian structure shields the government from the rigorous and reactionary judgments of the electorate. . . . Another advantage of the socialist countries is their passionate conviction and dedication to the objective of economic growth—which contrasts visibly with the halting and hesitant beliefs and actions of most democracies. The firm and purposive sense of direction . . . is in pointed contrast to the extensive revisions and changes in policies and methods which are prompted by minor setbacks in most democratic governments and which produce a sense of drift and helplessness. The political economy of development poses, in this respect, a cruel choice between rapid (self-sustained) expansion and democratic processes.[7]

This idea that development requires authoritarian leadership has been challenged in an empirical study by G. William Dick, an economist with the U.S. government.[8] He divided the independent LDCs into three classifications: authoritarian, semicompetitive, and competitive. An authoritarian government is headed by one political party, and a competitive government has two or more political parties competing for power with free elections at regular intervals. A semicompetitive government has one majority party and several minority parties or one political party that conducts legitimizing elections. In any case, there is no extensive control

6. This drastic approach to development is sometimes called the *Stalinist model*. For a more complete discussion, see the next chapter.

7. Jagdish Bhagwati, *The Economies of Underdeveloped Countries* (New York: McGraw-Hill Book Co., 1966), 203–204.

8. G. William Dick, "Authoritarian Versus Nonauthoritarian Approaches to Economic Development," *Journal of Political Economy* (July/August 1974).

of the population in a semicompetitive country. Dick then examined the growth rates of real gross domestic product per capita in each of the LDCs. He found that countries with authoritarian governments generally have lower growth rates than those with competitive governments. The main lesson of this empirical study is that rapid growth and democracy are not necessarily incompatible.

Most approaches to development are at neither the totalitarian nor the *laissez-faire* extreme. Government usually is expected to play some role, particularly in the development of human capital through health and education and in the provision of social overhead capital such as roads, schools, and hospitals.

Property Rights and Development

Although there are no definitive theories of development, there is ample evidence that certain institutions associated with private enterprise and open competition can play an important role. The critical institution seems to be private property. (We discussed the importance of private property in Chapter 2 when the stage was being set for the study of economics.) Private property, the ability to buy and sell and exchange the products of one's labor, is necessary if individual incentives are to be maintained. When government regulation and control restrict property rights to the extent of reducing work and investment incentives, economic growth is retarded.

In many African countries formerly under British rule, another problem of poor incentives resulted from colonial policies. British colonial policies promoted government monopoly of many export industries, licensing of government activities, and state enterprises that spawned huge bureaucracies. Independence from British rule often meant that even more state intervention was used to create jobs for political reasons. Many of the most talented and enterprising individuals turned their attention to rent seeking rather than entrepreneurial activity.

The most remarkable evidence on the importance of market forces is gained from comparing pairs of countries that have similar resources, cultures, and climates, but have adopted different attitudes toward private property and exchange. Hong Kong-The Peoples' Republic of China, South Korea-North Korea, and Brazil-Peru offer excellent case studies. The first country in each of these pairs is a successful developing country. The most significant difference between it and its mate is that it has made extensive use of market forces to generate the private incentives necessary to unleash the entrepreneurial drive of its population. As you will see in the next chapter, The Peoples' Republic of China is attempting some similar experiments within its own borders, beginning with the privatization of agriculture.

The Role of Development Assistance

Still another approach to development is for the already developed countries to provide assistance. The United States and Canada received substantial aid, both public and private, in their earliest days. Israel often is cited as a modern-day developmental miracle with massive infusion of foreign capital of all kinds—physical, financial, and human. Japan and the Soviet Union, on the other hand, developed almost in isolation.

The United States concentrates its official development assistance through the **Agency for International Development (AID)**, which is part of the State Department and which is in charge of U.S. aid to foreign countries. A publication of AID states:

Programs to assist these people reflect an American tradition of sharing and helping the needy as well as enlightened national self-interest. In part, foreign aid is an expression of the American people's sense of justice and compassion. It also plays an important role in the continuing effort to achieve an enduring structure of world peace. This role is essential to the quest for global tranquility, freedom and progress. There are some things, however, that foreign aid cannot do. Experience has shown that it cannot right all social wrongs or solve every economic problem in a developing country. It cannot bring about instant progress. Nor is it designed to accomplish alone what diplomacy cannot. It must be considered as a complement to other elements of foreign policy.[9]

The United States is a major contributor to the development programs of low-income countries. In 1987, the latest year for which figures are available, the United States contributed almost 20 percent of all the aid funds given by western industrialized countries and gave far more than any one of these countries. However, if we look at that giving as a percentage of GNP, the figures tell another story. Some countries gave a much larger share of their GNP to low-income countries than did the United States; on this basis, for example, France gave more than three times as much, and Norway more than five times as much, as the United States. In addition to foreign development, assistance of a government-to-government variety, many countries are aided by direct foreign investment, which supplies scarce capital. Both private loans and multinational corporations transfer capital to these countries. The private loans can present other problems, which we will discuss later in this chapter.

TIME BOMBS IN THE DEVELOPMENT PATH

There are two major problems that developing countries must address. The first is the control of population growth. The second is the huge international debt that many of the LDCs have compiled in recent years.

The Population Bomb

As we saw earlier in this chapter, one way to measure the economic well-being of a country is to examine its per capita income or GNP. Even countries experiencing economic growth can see their per capita incomes decline if their population is growing at a faster rate than

AGENCY FOR INTERNATIONAL DEVELOPMENT (AID)
The U.S. agency that is part of the State Department and which is in charge of U.S. aid to foreign countries.

9. Agency for International Development, *AID's Challenge in an Interdependent World* [AID, DN-RIA-119, 90/78] (Washington D.C.: Office of Public Affairs, 1978), 3.

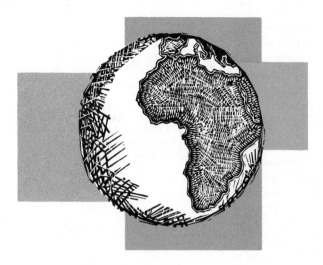

THE INTERNATIONAL PERSPECTIVE
HOW DO AMERICANS FEEL
ABOUT THE THIRD WORLD?

A report published in 1987 by The Overseas Development Council documents the attitudes of U.S. citizens toward economic development and U.S. development assistance. This very comprehensive survey carried out by the Strategic Information Research Corporation made the following 16 conclusions:

1. Americans are aware of the problems of poverty and underdevelopment that face the Third World and do not believe that much progress has been made in improving Third World living conditions over the past decade.
2. Americans have strong negative perceptions of Third World *governments*, but not of the *people* of these countries.
3. A majority of Americans favor U.S. efforts to assist Third World countries with development.
4. Policymakers perceive American public support for U.S. economic assistance to be weak and fluctuating.
5. Most Americans are poorly informed about U.S. foreign policy in general, about the Third World, development issues, and U.S. relations with developing countries.
6. Most Americans are aware in very general terms of the existence of economic relationships between the United States and the Third World and believe such relationships to hold potential mutual benefits.
7. The perceived trade-off between promoting *domestic* well-being and helping those *overseas* limits public support for specific U.S. trade, aid, and financial policies to promote Third World growth or alleviate poverty.
8. Most Americans recognize that the United States has political or strategic interests in the Third World, but many are concerned about U.S. over-involvement in developing country affairs.
9. The major reason for public support for economic assistance is a humanitarian concern or a sense of responsibility; economic or political self-interest rationales are generally less compelling.
10. Americans consider economic assistance a legitimate tool to use in pursuing U.S. political or strategic objectives, but they are concerned that this result is not always achieved.
11. On some U.S.-Third World issues, public preferences about the U.S. aid program appear to be at odds with official U.S. policy.
12. Americans express a strong preference for those types of U.S. economic aid programs that most recognizably aim to deliver help directly to poor people.
13. Economic aid is widely perceived to be ineffective or wasted; however, this opinion does not dissuade many Americans from supporting assistance efforts.
14. The American public makes little distinction between private and official aid efforts.
15. Only a small—but not insignificant—proportion of Americans have been personally involved in efforts to eliminate poverty and stimulate development in the Third World; a larger active constituency may, however, exist.
16. Personal experience or personal approaches are most likely to motivate Americans to become actively involved in efforts to promote development or to alleviate poverty in Third World countries.

Source: Christine Contee, *What Americans Think: Views on Development and U.S.-Third World Relations* (New York: InterAction and The Overseas Development Council, 1987).

their income. Yet discussions of managing population growth are very sensitive. Many countries regard foreign advice concerning birth rates as inappropriate. Such responses as "cultural imperialism" or even "genocide" are common.

In 1800, the world's population is estimated to have been about 1 billion; in 1988 it was 5.1 billion, and by the year 2000, it will have swelled to 6 billion. That means that the world's population is growing by 250,000 people per day or 90 million people per year. The problem for development is that more than 90 percent of that projected growth will occur in the LDCs.

Table 22–8 shows the world's most populous countries and estimates their populations and population growth rates. It is important to note that no developed country can be found in the column of fastest growing nations. The problem is easy to identify but difficult to solve.

TABLE 22-8
POPULATION GROWTH RATES OF NATIONS WITH POPULATIONS OF 5 MILLION OR MORE

Fastest Growing Nations	Population in 2000 (millions)	Average Annual Growth Rate 1988–2000	Slowest Growing Nations	Population in 2000 (millions)	Average Growth 1988–20
Kenya	20	4.4%	West Germany	60	−0.1
Zimbabwe	16	4.4	Denmark	5	0.1
Ghana	24	3.9	Hungary	11	0.1
Saudi Arabia	19	3.7	Sweden	9	0.1
Ivory Coast	17	3.7	Britain	57	0.1
Algeria	39	3.7	Austria	8	0.1
Rwanda	11	3.6	Belgium	10	0.1
Zambia	11	3.6	Italy	58	0.1
Syria	17	3.5	Switzerland	6	0.1
Nigeria	169	3.5	East Germany	17	0.2
Tanzania	36	3.5	Czechoslovakia	17	0.4
Iraq	26	3.4	Netherlands	15	0.4
Malawi	17	3.4	France	55	0.4
Uganda	25	3.4	Japan	128	0.4
Zaire	55	3.3	Greece	11	0.4
Niger	11	3.3	Portugal	11	0.6
Senegal	10	3.1	Yugoslavia	25	0.6
Iran	70	3.1	Spain	43	0.7
Bangladesh	157	2.9	Romania	25	0.7
Sudan	34	2.9	Soviet Union	306	0.7
Pakistan	140	2.7	Poland	41	0.7
Ecuador	13	2.6	United States	259	0.7
Venezuela	26	2.6	Canada	33	1.0
Morocco	31	2.5			
Egypt	63	2.0			
WORLD AVERAGE		1.4			

Source: Adapted from *World Development Report, 1984* (New York: Oxford University Press, 1984). Copyright © 1984 by the International Bank for Reconstruction and Development/The World Bank.

Escaping the Population Bomb

Understanding why populations grow provides a clue to a solution. During the industrial revolutions in Western Europe and the United States, populations grew rapidly but not at the explosive rates in today's LDCs. As the standard of living began to rise, the birth rate increased, but it took an improving standard of living for the death rates to start to decline. In addition, after incomes increased to higher levels, the birth rate declined. This pattern of declining birth rates appeared to be a general phenomenon. Today, medical advances, innoculations, and many life-lengthening techniques have spread throughout the world. This means that poor countries have high birth rates and declining death rates and, therefore, an exploding population.

The only solution for the LDCs is to try to influence their birth rates even though income levels are still low. (Remember, birth rates didn't decline in the developed world until relatively high levels of per capita income occurred.) This solution appears to be easy, but acceptable solutions are hard to find. Highly organized and publicized birth control plans have not worked. In China, the communist authorities have instituted a get-tough campaign that denies many state-supplied benefits to couples with more than one child. This "planned" approach has slowed China's population growth but has had many unintended side effects, including claims of female infanticide and a high number of late-term abortions.

Population and Poverty

Economists must be careful in their analysis of the problems of overpopulation. After all, the existence of large numbers of people has little to do with poverty. Most stories of famine and the problems of the population explosion start with a visit, most likely on film, to a sector of the world, such as Africa, in the middle of the most densely populated city, in one of the poorest countries in the world. A reporter will ask the pregnant mother of ten how many children she wants and she will giggle and say ten more. The implication will be that development is stifled by the growth of the population. The report will probably be produced and certainly broadcast from New York City or Washington, D.C., two of the richest *and* most densely populated places on earth. The point that is lost in such reports is that people aren't starving because of dense population and rapid population growth; they are starving because they are poor. As we saw above, population growth and slow economic growth may be interrelated, but the relationship is not causal. If LDCs developed and poverty lessened, franchisers would be bidding for prime spots to sell food!

The Debt Bomb

One of the elements of the vicious circle of poverty that we discussed earlier was a low level of investment. It seems logical, then, that one way to break this circle would be to borrow from the developed world.

For many years, the World Bank operated with this very goal in mind.[10] The World Bank would make project loans to LDCs at low rates of interest. The modest amount of borrowing that was done from private-sector financial institutions was mainly short-term commercial credit and was not viewed as a serious developmental problem.

All this changed in 1973 and 1974 as a consequence of the success of the Organization of Oil Exporting Countries (OPEC). The OPEC cartel quadrupled the price of oil and began running huge current account (balance of payments) surpluses in the oil-rich countries. The oil-rich countries deposited this money in accounts in private banks in the developed countries (mostly in the United States). While the oil-rich countries were earning these huge surpluses, the developing countries (without oil) were running huge deficits to pay for their oil imports.

In order to match up these surpluses and deficits, banks in the United States and Europe recycled OPEC surpluses to developing countries by granting them loans. Senator Bill Bradley of New Jersey put it succinctly in a speech on the Senate floor (August 3, 1982): "The formula for a new financing cycle was obvious: OPEC had pools of dollars which it could not spend; Western banks turned them into lending capital . . . developing countries had . . . appetites for credit. . . ."

By 1982, problems began to surface. Not all of the loans were being used for capital investment that would generate income to make repayment. Many of the loans went to finance current consumption (especially oil imports) or ill-conceived investment projects. Loans to Mexico were singled out as being used particularly unwisely, often for lining the pockets of corrupt politicians.

By mid-1982, the crisis was obvious in the U.S. banking community. Some banks had risky loans to developing countries in excess of their capital. In addition, some nations were unable to service their debts; i.e., to meet scheduled payment of interest and/or principal. As a result, banks were increasingly reluctant to extend or renew existing loans to those countries (to say nothing about making new loans). Although it seemed unlikely that any country would entirely default on these loans, Henry Kissinger, former Secretary of State, warned that they might:

Because the debtors can never escape their plight unless they receive additional loans, the comforting view has developed that no debtor country would dare default and wreck its creditworthiness. Unfortunately, political leaders march to a different drummer than financial experts. They see the political interests of their country through a prism of their own survival. If pushed into a corner, a political leader may well seek to rally populist resentment against foreign "exploiters." This will surely occur if the so-called rescue operation concentrates primarily on the repayment of interest. A blow-up is certain sooner or later if debtor countries are asked to accept prolonged austerity simply to protect the balance sheets of foreign banks.[11]

10. The proper name for the World Bank is the International Bank for Reconstruction and Development. The World Bank was created after World War II to aid in the recovery of Europe from the war and to assist countries newly liberated from colonialism with economic development projects.

11. Henry A. Kissinger, "Saving the World Economy," *Newsweek* (January 24, 1983): 48.

Solutions

By 1987, the total debt of Third World countries exceeded $437 billion. Brazil topped the list, owing U.S. banks $22.4 billion and other creditors $78.6 billion. There really is only one long-term solution to the Third World debt problem, although it may have several aspects. The solution is that of any debtor: consumption must be cut, and income must be generated to repay the debts. In this instance, debtor nations must improve their trade balances to earn income to repay or refinance the loans. This can be done by decreasing imports, allowing more foreign investment, and setting realistic exchange rates.

In addition to domestic growth, economic growth in the developed world will aid this process. As developed nations grow, they demand more imports from the LDCs. These imports allow the LDCs to earn foreign currency needed to repay their debt.

The debtor countries in the past have often threatened default in order to renegotiate their loans. Recognition of the possibility of default and preparation for default lowers the value of this type of threat. On May 19, 1987, the president of Citicorp, John Reed, announced that Citicorp was adding $3 billion to its reserves to protect itself against loan losses to developing countries. Reed's announcement caused other U.S. banks to follow suit. Within a week, Norwest Corporation of Minneapolis added $200 million, and Chase Manhattan added $1.6 billion. The major result of this announcement is that it lessened the hold of some of the debtor nations on the banks. Reed's move was hailed as a bold and smart move by most financial experts. Reed indicated that any future loans to developing countries would be made only on the condition that . . . "there has to be some reasonable prospect that the money is going to get paid back."[12]

THE NEW INTERNATIONAL ECONOMIC ORDER

NEW INTERNATIONAL ECONOMIC ORDER (NIEO)
A proposal for a fundamental change in international economic institutions to redistribute income from richer nations to poorer nations.

Economic aid and Third World debt are two of a number of issues underlying the call by many Third World countries for a **New International Economic Order (NIEO)**. This program is an international political call for a fundamental change in the international economic institutions discussed in the preceding two chapters. NIEO proponents seek to alter market outcomes to redistribute income from richer nations to poorer nations.

The NIEO really represents an attempt to use international commerce for redistribution of income between nations. Not surprisingly, the demand for an NIEO has coincided with dramatic growth in the membership of the United Nations (UN). In 1955, the UN had 59 members; by 1975, it had 141 members (125 were in attendance at that year's session); 110 of these members belong to the group of nonaligned, LDCs that are referred to as the Group of 77. The Group of 77 has voiced increasing dissatisfaction with the existing economic order and has been calling for a "better deal" for the developing world.

12. Jaclyn Fierman, "John Reed's Bold Stroke," *Fortune* (June 22, 1987): 29.

There has been more heat than light shed on the NIEO in most discussions. The Group of 77 hails the NIEO as a major new order that will greatly increase global welfare, while many of the developed countries have reacted with suspicion and confusion over what the NIEO means. The NIEO is a set of demands and proposals for a restructured world economy, which embodies the Group of 77's conception of international equity and justice. In other words, the NIEO is aimed primarily at income and wealth redistribution and only secondarily at economic growth.[13] To this point, the international political success of the NIEO has been small.

ECONOMIC DEVELOPMENT IN THE UNITED STATES

The United States, like most industrialized countries, has areas that are less developed. Many of the characteristics that have been described fit these less developed regions very well. In the United States, these areas usually have high birth rates, high infant mortality, low levels of human capital formation, and they often have cultural impediments to development. President John F. Kennedy was one of the first national politicians to draw attention to these pockets of poverty when he campaigned for the presidency in West Virginia in 1960. In the last decade, most state governors have pursued economic development as a major political goal. This goal has been particularly important in the southern states that have been historically less developed than the rest of the United States.

The pursuit of economic development by policymakers in state government often clearly demonstrates the conflict between the governmental approach to development and the *laissez-faire* approach to development. The *laissez-faire* approach to development says the state government should have low taxes, provide minimum services, and not interfere with economic activity. Firms would then be attracted because of the favorable business climate. The governmental or planning approach says that government has to "do things" to promote economic development. It has to build better schools, it has to develop recreational opportunities, it has to have a state development board to recruit industry, and so on. An idea currently in vogue is that government has to promote the arts because executives aren't going to relocate to a state that doesn't have theaters, museums, and art galleries. Many economists dispute these arguments for development and believe that low taxes and a good nonunionized work force are the primary reasons for state economic development.

Perhaps the most interesting consequence of industrial mobility in the United States is that no state can get too far out of line with competing states in terms of its tax or regulating policies, or its industry will move to another state. The U.S. Constitution prohibits state govern-

13. The real issue that should concern us is economic growth, not the inequality of income distribution among trading countries. An examination of pairs of countries with similar cultural and geographic characteristics shows that those countries that have chosen to use market-based international trade as an engine of growth have enjoyed significant economic success.

THE INTERNATIONAL PERSPECTIVE
NEGATIVE DEVELOPMENT:
THE DECLINE OF ARGENTINA

Argentina was once one of the richest countries in the world. In 1900, New Zealand and Argentina, in part fueled by agricultural exports to Europe, had the two highest GNPs in the world. Wage rates in Argentina in 1910 were 25 percent higher than in Paris and 80 percent higher than in Marseilles. Europeans were migrating to Argentina in large numbers. Over the 50-year period before 1914, Argentina's economy grew by an average rate of 5 percent per year, ranking as one of the highest and longest periods of long-term economic growth in all of economic history. In fact, at the turn of the century the Argentinean rancher played much the same role in the famous French farces of the era as the vulgar Texas oil tycoon does in *Dynasty*.

In 1987, Argentina had a per capita GNP of $2,520, while that of New Zealand was $7,920. New Zealand was labeled (by the World Bank) as an industrialized market economy, while Argentina was labeled a middle-income country.

What happened? Argentina taxed its exports heavily. Very little was invested. Argentines spent—Buenos Aires became the center of high living. Elvio Baldinelli, an Argentine trade expert, explained it well, "Argentina despised its export industries and taxed them very heavily, yet lived off them very well until markets closed and prices fell." Norman Gall writes in *Forbes* magazine that Baldinelli's lament and the explanation for the decline of Argentina can be summed up in one sentence: "To succeed in the modern world, a country needs economic policies that encourage, not hamper, economic initiative."[a]

Economic development is not something that is achieved and then enjoyed forever. The decline of the Roman Empire, the decline of Britain in the 1960s and 1970s, and the rapid rise and fall of some of the oil-rich countries suggests that attention to the causes of economic growth are important for even the most developed of countries.

a. Norman Gall, "The Four Horsemen Ride Again," *Forbes* (July 28, 1986): 96.

ments from interfering in interstate commerce. As a result, if state policymakers in some state, say Minnesota, tax or regulate a company too much, it will move to another state, say Texas. This mobility greatly reduces the monopoly-monopsony power of any state government and may be the single most important check on the growth of state government.

IS ECONOMIC DEVELOPMENT GOOD OR BAD?

Of course, development is neither wholly good nor wholly bad. Economic development raises the standard of living, but it changes lifestyles and even affects culture. The appropriate question is, What policies can be adopted to minimize the undesirable aspects of economic growth and encourage the beneficial aspects?

In the 1940s, Los Angeles was surrounded by orange groves. Now its suburbs stretch for more than 60 miles inland from the Pacific Ocean. In the 1950s, smog was not a problem in Phoenix, but population and economic growth have made smog a serious problem. Some of these problems and their causes can be remedied, at least in part. Antipollution regulations have improved the air quality in Arizona and in Southern California, in spite of continued high growth.

Economic growth is condemned by some and praised by others. It is clear that there are costs to growth. However, it is also clear that growth is virtually the only way for standards of living to rise. This is true for the average family and also true for poorer families. It simply isn't true that redistributing existing wealth would do much to improve the lot of the poor. When we see the vast gulfs of wealth between the very rich and the very poor in LDCs, we have to realize that only a small segment of the population is rich. Even if all wealth were distributed equally in a poor country, everyone would still be poor. The only hope for improving the economic welfare of poor people everywhere is economic development.

SUMMARY

1. Development economics is concerned with specific, detailed policies for improving the development of a particular country rather than with general theoretical models.

2. LDCs have similar characteristics that can be easily recognized when countries are grouped by level of income. Subsistence agriculture dominates in LDCs. Many of these same countries lie in tropical and subtropical climates. A poor harvest means disaster for the countries' populations.

3. The demographic characteristics of LDCs also exhibit a common structure. Birth rates are high, which means that a significant share of the population consumes but doesn't produce. The crude death rate in low-income countries is falling. This, coupled with the high birth rates, produces the population explosion, which causes per capita income either to fall or to rise at a slow rate.

4. Low-income countries invest little in human capital, that is, in the health, vigor, and education of the population. An unhealthy and uneducated labor force is relatively unproductive.

5. Cultural factors play a significant role in the development process. Economic growth requires a progressive economic attitude. This attitude is slow to develop in some cultural environments.

6. There are two basic historical models of economic development. The first is Marx's theory, in which countries advance through stages from primitive society to communism. This transition comes about because of a fundamental weakness in capitalism that forces all workers to a subsistence level of income. Many workers would be thrown out of work as the economy becomes more monopolized and business cycles become increasingly severe. These unemployed workers, the reserve army of the unemployed, would unite, and socialism, the stage before communism, would develop. Marx's prognosis has not fared well. As industrialization spread in the world, the standard of living of the work force improved dramatically.

7. W.W. Rostow has also developed a theory based on stages of growth, but it is quite distinct from Marx's. In Rostow's theory, each country proceeds in stages from traditional to high mass consumption. Rostow argues that every country proceeds through a similar growth path.

8. The big push strategy suggests that government can speed the process of economic development through a major coordinated thrust on all fronts of the economy.

9. The leading sectors strategy strongly suggests that if growth is concentrated on some key sectors and if linkages are developed, these sectors will create demand on other sectors to grow.

10. Both strategies suggest an active role for government in the development process. A key question is the extent to which government should play a role. Some economists argue that government should play an active role, even at the expense of demo-

cratic policy. Others argue that development does not require authoritarian leadership.

11. Evidence from paired countries suggests that private property and market forces are powerful engines of economic growth.

12. The United States has traditionally aided LDCs. Much of U.S. aid is channeled through the Agency for International Development. U.S. aid is large in an absolute sense, but other Western nations contribute a larger share of GNP than does the United States.

13. Population growth is a serious threat to development, but addressing the problem often has unintended consequences.

14. The debt of developing countries is an increasingly serious problem for those countries and for the banks that have been granting development loans. Recently, private U.S. banks have taken steps to protect themselves against default.

15. The New International Economic Order (NIEO) is a call for a new international economic system. It is primarily a demand for income and wealth redistribution.

16. The problems of regional underdevelopment in the United States are very similar to those of world economic development. Even the issue of planned versus *laissez-faire* development is part of the domestic debate.

◼ NEW TERMS

crude birth rate	traditional society	leading sectors
crude death rate	preconditions for takeoff	linkages
vicious circle of poverty	takeoff	Agency for International Development (AID)
labor theory of value	drive to maturity	New International Economic Order (NIEO)
surplus value	high mass consumption	
reserve army of the unemployed	big push	

◼ QUESTIONS FOR DISCUSSION

1. Does development change the cultural environment or does the cultural environment cause economic development?

2. What role do you think the United States should play in world development?

3. What effect do "no growth" policies have on different economic levels of society?

4. Should the U.S. government bail out banks that have made "bad" loans to LDCs? What would happen if it didn't?

5. In recent years, there has been a great deal of television coverage concerning drought and famine in Africa. Is this an agricultural problem or an economic development problem?

6. Why is the study of demographic trends so important in the study of economic development?

7. What is the New International Economic Order?

8. What do development economists have in mind when they speak of linkages?

9. What is the vicious circle of poverty?

10. What constitutes Rostow's preconditions for takeoff?

◼ SUGGESTIONS FOR FURTHER READING

Bianchi, Andres, Robert Devlin, and Joseph Ramos. *External Debt in Latin America: Adjustment Policies and Renegotiation*. Boulder, Co.: The United Nations Economic Commission for Latin America and the Caribbean, 1985. A description of the magnitude of the debt problem with some calm and reasoned solutions.

Gillis, Malcolm, Dwight Perkins, Michael Roemer, and Donald Snodgrass. *Economics of Development*. New York: W.W. Norton & Co., 1983. An unusual development text that includes case studies done by development economists with field experience.

McCord, William, and Arline McCord. *Paths to Progress.* New York: W.W. Norton & Co., 1986. The McCords, who are field sociologists, argue that Third World countries must make profound cultural, political, and social changes if they are to experience economic development.

Reynolds, Lloyd G. *Economic Growth in the Third World*. New Haven: Yale University Press, 1985. A book that contains good statistical surveys on 40 countries.

Schumacher, Ernest Friedrich. *Small Is Beautiful: Economics As If People Mattered*. New York: Harper & Row Publishers, Inc., 1976. A somewhat dated, but still popular book that questions the value of economic growth.

CHAPTER 23 ■
■

COMPARATIVE ECONOMIC SYSTEMS IN THEORY AND PRACTICE

■

INTRODUCTION

People often talk about and refer to other economic systems without really knowing how to define such terms as *capitalism, socialism*, and *communism*. What are the key differences among these systems, and to what degree do these differences affect economic outcomes? Chapter 2 began the study of economics by stating that all economic systems are mixed systems and that the material covered in the intervening chapters would allow you to analyze any economic system. That statement was valid because the concepts of opportunity cost, the law of demand, the principle of diminishing returns, and the concepts of specialization, exchange, efficiency, and self-interest do not differ from country to country. Competing ideologies may respond to these concepts differently, but no ideology can escape its impact on economic life.

You might ask, If the economics we have already learned is good for all systems, why include a chapter on alternative systems? The answer is that politics and ideology mix with economics to create widely differing economic-political systems. It is enlightening to examine the way economics works in different political, economic, and historical settings.

To introduce the subject of comparative economics, we will begin with an attempt to define ideological systems. We will then examine some of the different forms of communism as well as recent changes in Great Britain. We will next present a decision-making approach to the analysis of differing systems and discuss advantages and disadvantages of economic planning. Finally, we will examine reform movements in China and the Soviet Union, and outline the unique features of the Japanese form of capitalism.

IDEOLOGIES

Chapter 2 divided economic systems into three major groups, which we labeled *traditional*, *planned*, and *market* economies. The field of comparative economic systems breaks this categorization into smaller parts so classification of economies can be made more easily. A very common approach, and perhaps the oldest, is to classify systems according to two criteria: the underlying political philosophy and ownership of the factors of production. This might be called the *isms* approach because it concentrates on four major *isms*: capitalism, socialism, communism, and fascism.

This approach oversimplifies the diversity that exists in alternative economic systems. There is a myriad of economic systems in the world. The term capitalism is often applied to the economic systems found in western democracies, but the differences among economic institutions in the United States, Great Britain, France, and Sweden are significant. Likewise, the economic organizations in Eastern Europe and the Soviet Union are considered communism, but there are significant differences among the institutions in the Soviet Union, Yugoslavia, and Rumania. In this complexity lies the difficulty of separating the critical elements of variety between and among various economic systems. We must identify the differences in institutions and then determine if these differences cause economic behavior to be different among the systems. The most important factor distinguishing among the *isms* lies in the ownership of the factors of production.

Capitalism

Capitalism is a system characterized by the private ownership of the factors of production by individuals (or groups of individuals). In pure capitalism, these individuals are free to use the property as they see fit. Any limitations on the use of the property diminishes its value. These private property holders are at the center of the decision-making process in capitalism.

A system based on private ownership is one in which individuals maximize their own well-being, whether in terms of profit or utility. The term *capitalism* can be and is viewed very broadly to allow for a great deal of government intervention, as long as the primacy of private ownership is retained. It thus is possible for systems as divergent as the U.S. economy and the British economy to be labeled as capitalism.

CAPITALISM
An economic system based on the idea of private ownership of the factors of production by individuals or groups of individuals.

Socialism

Under a system of **socialism**, the nonhuman means of production are owned by society or the state. Socialism shifts the decision-making authority from individual entrepreneurs to a central authority. This central authority then makes the major economic decisions. Utopian socialists see this central authority as promoting the "common good," usually greater equality and/or economic development. Writers who are critical of

SOCIALISM
An economic system in which the nonhuman means of production are owned by society or the state.

socialism point out that this authority may develop into a centralist, personal dictatorship, as in the cases of Stalin in the Soviet Union and by Rumania's President Nicolae Ceausescu in present-day Eastern Europe.

As with capitalism, there are many types of socialism. There is utopian socialism, such as the Fourier movement, that was practiced in the United States in the early to mid-1900s. Utopian socialists established communes with shared possessions and cooperative labor. Other variations, particularly those espoused by the Social Democrats in Western Europe, have become forceful political movements. For instance, Francois Mitterand, a socialist, was elected president of France in 1981 and 1988. Because of the great variety of people and ideas that the term *socialism* is used to describe, it is almost meaningless to label someone as a socialist or a set of institutions as being socialistic.

Communism

COMMUNISM
The final stage in the theory of Karl Marx, in which the state has withered away and economic goods are equally distributed.

To Karl Marx, **communism** was the final stage of the progression from capitalism, with socialism representing the middle stage of the transition. Under communism, Marx foresaw the end of scarcity, the end of conflict among the classes, and the creation of a new social order. An ideal member of this new order would be the antithesis of the self-interested individual on which we based much of the preceding analysis. In the final stage, individuals would receive goods and services according to their needs, and the state would wither away to a point at which all it would do is administer the economy. The organizational structure that Marx foresaw under communism is not at all clear. Presumably everyone would contribute labor in exchange for goods and services needed. One major problem is the definition and determination of needs. A second problem is the motivation driving the system and creating incentives; in the absence of self-interested economic incentives, the motivation would have to lie in the development of this new economic order.

Fascism

FASCISM
An economic system that combines monopoly, capitalism, private property, and a strong authoritarian central government.

In the countries in which Fascism has been practiced (which include Spain, Portugal, Germany, and Italy), it combines monopoly capitalism, private property, and a strong authoritarian central government personified by a dictator. **Fascism** is an economic system that combines monopoly, capitalism, private property, and a strong authoritarian central government. This unusual permutation promotes monopoly and then imposes "national interests" on that monopoly structure. This lacks both the large degree of personal freedom that is a characteristic of free-enterprise capitalism and the egalitarian ideals of socialism and communism.

Weaknesses of the *Isms* Approach

The problem of the *isms* approach to comparing economic systems is that it is often too simplistic and does not include many of the keys to determining control over resources. The *isms* approach tends to equate ownership with control and control with decision-making power over the factors of production. This distinction is becoming less clear over time. Consider a few examples. In the Soviet Union, the leaders of the government do not own much of anything, yet they unmistakably control the system. In the United States, many people own land, but they cannot use it as they please because of local zoning regulations, state land-use planning, or federal environmental regulations. All economies are mixed in varying degrees; that is, they contain elements of socialism (or planning) and elements of capitalism (or markets). So, all in all, the *isms* approach, while often used in political-economic classification schemes (and political rhetoric), is not very useful. In fact, to apply this classification scheme across countries would likely produce just two sets of systems, capitalism and socialism. Yet no serious analyst would consider a scheme that places the United States, France, and Great Britain in one classification significant. However, capitalism and socialism, like pure competition and monopoly, offer some polar cases to aid in understanding real-world mixed systems.

■ Contrasting Capitalism and Socialism

Recognizing that there is no such thing as a pure system, we can construct a continuum and attempt to place countries on this continuum. Figure 23–1 presents the end points of such a continuum. On one end, we have pure, market-directed capitalism, and on the other end, we have pure, centrally planned socialism. Since capitalism and socialism represent the two polar ends of this continuum, it is worthwhile to contrast the distinguishing features or essential characteristics of each type of economic system.

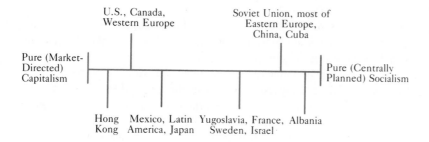

FIGURE 23–1
A CONTINUUM OF ECONOMIC SYSTEMS
No country represents a pure type of economic system. All countries mix market and planning to some degree, but it is possible to locate countries along a continuum on the basis of their relative reliance on the market or on a plan.

Property rights are important because they create incentives and make exchange possible. In capitalism, the property rights to resources and factors of production, including labor, is vested with the individual. In socialism, the state is vested with property rights, including

THE INTERNATIONAL PERSPECTIVE
CHINA, HONG KONG, AND TAIWAN

The political-legal developments concerning China, Hong Kong, and Taiwan and the economic comparisons among them demonstrate much about capitalism and socialism. The levels of economic development invite comparison because the areas are similar in many ways. The essential differences are political and economic.

In 1997, the 100-year lease that the British have for Hong Kong expires, and Hong Kong reverts to Chinese rule. This change is expected to have a profound effect on Hong Kong. There are, at present, virtually no government impediments to doing business in Hong Kong. A corporation can be started for a fee of only $250 and no reporting requirements exist. There are no currency exchange controls, and there are no tariffs or quotas. The entrepreneurs in this prosperous capitalist state are casting a wary eye on 1997 and the arrival of the Communist Chinese. In 1997, the country will go from almost pure *laissez-faire* capitalism to communist rule.

Taiwan is another interesting contrast to mainland China. The Chinese nationalists who fled mainland China during the communist revolution of 1949 fled to Taiwan, where they dominated the native Taiwanese majority and established a market-directed economy. The People's Republic of China insists that Taiwan is not a country but rather that it is a province of China with which reunification is inevitable. Yet the Taiwanese insist that they must remain independent. A comparison of China and Taiwan is perhaps an interesting experiment in development under capitalism and socialism. In 1950, the socialist People's Republic and the capitalistic Taiwan had basically the same level of development. Today, the average income in Taiwan is about $2,600 per year, more than ten times the per capita income in China. Perhaps this fact is understood in China, where elements of market capitalism are being introduced in the disguise of economic reform.

property rights to the individual's labor. In socialism, people are often assigned jobs in certain geographic locations and do not enjoy the right to switch occupations or geographic location.

Workers under capitalism are vested with the property rights to their own labor. They are free to move about, but they are not guaranteed a job. Under socialism, it is often the case that workers are assigned jobs, and these jobs cannot be altered. The method of job assignment in the military is analogous to job assignment in most socialistic states. Workers have greater job security but less freedom to choose jobs.

Investment decisions follow a similar pattern. In socialism, the level and composition of investment is determined by the central plan. Actual coordination and implementation of the central plan are carried out by the state.

Production decisions and those decisions that affect the distribution of income are also determined by the central plan under socialism. These are the *what* and the *for whom* questions of Chapter 2. To better understand the variants of socialism, one must first understand its theoretical roots in Marx and its real-world roots in the various revolutions and their leaders.

THE ESSENTIAL CONTRAST BETWEEN CAPITALISM AND SOCIALISM

	Capitalism	Socialism
PROPERTY RIGHTS	Resources are owned by individuals or groups of individuals.	Resources are owned by the state.
LABOR	Workers have a property right to their own labor. They are self-employed or work for private firms.	Workers are employed by the government and most often are not allowed to change jobs.
INVESTMENT	Determined and undertaken by entrepreneurs.	Determined and undertaken by government.
PRODUCTION MIX	Determined by market forces.	Determined by central plan.
DISTRIBUTION OF INCOME	Determined by market, productivity, and ownership patterns.	Determined by central plan.
INCENTIVES	Labor, management, and entrepreneurs respond to wages, prices, and profits.	Often many nonmaterial incentives are used.

MARX, MARXISTS, AND MARXISM

Perhaps no other economist has had more effect on the political shaping of the world than Karl Marx, who with Friedrich Engels, published the *Communist Manifesto* in 1848. This book, along with Marx's magnum opus, *Das Kapital*, published in three volumes in 1867, 1885, and 1894, form the philosophical basis for a widely divergent group of socialistic-communistic, economic-political systems. Today, almost all communist governments claim to be Marxist. Since such a diversity of communists all lay claim to being the true Marxists, it is necessary to distinguish between Marx and Marxism (or Marxists).

The central ideas of Marx's economic theory were outlined in the previous chapter. He believed that every society would evolve through the historical stages of tribal communism, slavery, feudalism, capitalism, socialism, and, finally, communism. The most important transition came when capitalism decayed because of internal contradictions and was succeeded by socialism. In particular, the regular cyclical ups and downs of a capitalist society (the business cycle) would become more and more severe until capitalism finally collapsed. Marx saw the empire building of European countries in the nineteenth century as an attempt to postpone the inevitable failure of capitalism. Under communism, scarcity would disappear and workers would produce without material incentives. It is curious that the countries to which communism has spread have been those in which the level of industrialization was very low. This pattern is inconsistent with what Marx predicted.

What, then, is the significance of Marx's writings? The significance of Marx and his writings is not in the historical accuracy of his predictions but rather in the theoretical, philosophical movement his work has spawned. A widely divergent group of communist parties in many countries consider themselves Marxists and appeal to the writings of Marx to justify their views on various issues. In some respects, they have similar roots. They all condemn the exploitation of workers by monopoly capitalism and eschew the use of the term *profit*. Countries in which the communists are in power all claim to have full-employment economies and to have overcome the problem of the capitalistic army of unemployed workers. But there are also wide differences among communist countries. Countries as diverse as China, Yugoslavia, the Soviet Union, Albania, Rumania, and Cuba all claim to be the true Marxists. The significance of Marx is that he is the father of a political, as well as an economic, movement.

LEADER-*ISMS*

Socialism was Marx's intermediate stage between capitalism and communism. Under a system of socialism, the decision-making authority is shifted from individual entrepreneurs to a central authority. These central authorities historically have almost always been personified by strong, dominant individuals. It is thus possible to view many of the offshoots of Marxism as the products of the interaction of Marxist ideas with the personalities of these strong-willed leaders.

Leninism

Vladimir Lenin (1870–1924) was active in developing the Communist Party in Russia and led that country's successful Bolshevik Revolution in 1917–1918. He claimed to be a follower of Marx but developed new directions for the achievement of communism. Lenin refused to wait for the maturation of capitalism and instead developed a different model for revolution based on four essential ingredients: (1) a small, revolutionary elite; (2) economic underdevelopment (the opposite of Marx's industrialization); (3) an estranged peasantry; and (4) war against an outside force. Lenin's formula worked in Russia and has worked in Yugoslavia, China, Vietnam, and Cuba. In fact, Lenin's formula is the way communism has almost always taken root. The exceptions are those countries of Eastern Europe in which communism was imposed by the Soviet Union following World War II.

Lenin became the first communist to be faced with the task of setting up an economic system after the political system was secure. **War Communism** was the economic system that was imposed by Lenin in Russia immediately after the Bolshevik Revolution. This system substituted rigid administrative control of the economy for the previous market economy in an attempt to marshal the requisite resources to engage in a civil war with noncommunist white Russians. Widespread nationalization took place throughout this period, and all private trading was outlawed. All labor mobility was rigidly controlled, and money as an exchange mechanism virtually disappeared. This period is difficult to evaluate, and some

WAR COMMUNISM
An economic system that was imposed by Lenin in Russia immediately after the Bolshevik Revolution. It is called War Communism because there was a continuing civil war at the time.

economic historians claim that Lenin instituted War Communism only because of the pragmatic demands of carrying out a civil war.[1]

In 1921, Lenin abandoned War Communism and instituted a program referred to as the **New Economic Policy (NEP)**. This policy was an attempt at *market* socialism with rigid plans for only the key industries in the economy. The remainder of the economy was to be organized under basic market principles. There was very rapid economic growth during this period, and the Soviet economy quickly recovered from the protracted civil war. Lenin died in 1924, and in 1926 the NEP came to an end for a variety of reasons. A major cause was that the remarketization of the economy during NEP greatly reduced the power of the Communist Party to channel and direct the course of economic development.

NEW ECONOMIC POLICY (NEP)
An attempt at market socialism from 1921 to 1926 in the Soviet Union.

Stalinism

After Lenin's death, open controversy over the direction of development took place in the Soviet Communist party. The **Great Industrialization Debate** was an open debate that took place in the Soviet Union from 1924 to 1928 concerning the correct way to industrialize the economy.[2] The left wing, led by economist E.A. Preobrazhensky, argued that the country should make a concerted effort to pursue rapid industrialization of key sectors of the economy. This policy would be carried out by the central allocation of investment expenditures. N.I. Bukharin, who was the spokesperson for the right wing, disagreed with this position and stressed balanced growth of the economy. Bukharin argued that all sectors of the economy must grow together because they all support and feed one another.

GREAT INDUSTRIALIZATION DEBATE
An open debate that took place in the Soviet Union from 1924 to 1928 concerning the correct way to industrialize the economy.

Joseph Stalin (1879–1953) was both an observer and a participant in the debate. Stalin played one side against the other while consolidating his own power base. At the time of Lenin's death, Stalin allied himself with the right wing of the party in order to counteract the power of Leon Trotsky and the left wing of the party. This alliance allowed him to discredit and weaken the left wing, a task he accomplished by 1927. He then turned on the right wing and, by 1928, had the leaders of the right wing denounced by the party. Stalin was then in complete control, since he had purged all dissidents.[3]

The planning system that Stalin adopted was centrally directed and was set up in five-year increments. The five-year time increment was chosen since most investment projects can be completed in such a period. Stalin's first five-year plan was an extreme version of the left-wing super-industrialization plan. Its achievement required very centralized planning, investment in heavy industry, and forced collectivization in the agricultural sector, which was expected to supply food and raw materials. Industrialization was very rapid, but the costs of this policy were great in human terms. Millions of people were purged, and many others starved to death.

1. Others claim Lenin instituted War Communism out of a desire to see such a system evolve as the economic application of communism. For this view, see Paul Craig Roberts, *Alienation and the Soviet Economy* (Albuquerque: University of New Mexico Press, 1971).

2. See Alexander Erlich, *Soviet Industrialization Debate, 1924–1928* (Cambridge: Harvard University Press, 1960).

3. For an excellent economic history of the Soviet Union, including this period, see Alec Nove, *An Economic History of the USSR* (London: Penguin, 1975).

The Soviet Union's rigid system of central planning is the legacy of Stalin. Today, the term Stalinism is associated with a ruthless dictatorship as well as with a highly centralized planning structure. However, Stalinism is not openly practiced in any communist country today. Rumania perhaps comes the closest by combining the rigid, very centralized planning of Stalinism with a strong leader in the person of its president, Nicolae Ceausescu. Ceausescu has not, however, demonstrated the bloody ruthlessness that characterized the Stalin era in the Soviet Union.

Titoism

Josip Broz Tito (1892–1980), president of Yugoslavia, broke with Stalin in 1948 over Soviet interference in Yugoslavia's internal affairs. Tito was not a puppet of Stalin's, since he had carried out his own revolution in Yugoslavia. In the other Eastern European communist countries in the post-World War II period, communism and the leadership had been installed by the Soviets. Tito formulated his own "road to socialism," which began as a Stalinist-prototype centrally planned economy but evolved into a partly market, partly planned economy with less central control than some western market economies (France, for example). A key element, and one that is unique in the world, is the Yugoslav concept of **workers' self-management**. The concept calls for all the workers, including blue-collar and white-collar workers as well as managers, to help direct the firm for which they work. Workers have a financial stake in the firm's performance. Such a system could only have economic meaning if the firm were autonomous; as a result, a great deal of central authority has withered away in Yugoslavia. Yugoslav communists claim that such self-management by the workers is the true Marxist ideal because it removes the alienation of the worker.

Titoism owes much to the strength and personality of one man, Tito. In planning for his own death, Tito fashioned an elaborate, collective leadership, consisting of a 23-member presidium with rotating membership. After his death in the spring of 1980, the collective leadership promised to continue Tito's policies. After almost a decade, it appears that this collective leadership is working smoothly, but one would expect that the situation is not likely to persist in the long term.

Maoism

In China, the Communist Party came to full power in October, 1949, after decades of struggle. Mao Zedong was the revolutionary leader who had taken command, just as Lenin's formula for communist revolutionaries had dictated. In the early years of Chinese communism, the goal was industrialization, much as it had been in the Soviet Union; but this policy was formulated without the help of Moscow. The Chinese Communist party, from the very beginning, was fiercely independent of the Soviet Union.

In 1958, the Great Leap Forward took place. The **Great Leap Forward** was an impossibly overambitious modernization plan to

WORKERS' SELF-MANAGEMENT
The system in Yugoslavia in which workers direct and have a financial stake in the firm in which they work.

GREAT LEAP FORWARD
Communist China's highly overambitious modernization plan that was launched in 1958 to increase per capita income in China by 25 percent in five years.

increase per capita income in China by 25 percent in five years. Many of the programs were ill-conceived, such as the production of steel on a small scale in backyard furnaces. The result was a worthless product.

The Great Leap significantly increased the collectivization of Chinese agriculture. Mao sought to mobilize the huge underemployed population of China in collectivized agriculture. The result was disastrous. In two years, agricultural production fell by 20 percent. Mao was ousted from control, and a pragmatic leadership took over. With the aid of revolutionary youth, Mao was able to return to power in 1966 with a massive political coup.

The period 1966 through 1969, called the Cultural Revolution, represented the high point in the adulation of Mao. The **Cultural Revolution** embraced revolutionary values. Mao envisioned a completely classless society, organized as a collective operation rather than as a state enterprise, as in the Soviet Union. The motivation for the society was to be completely altruistic, embracing the concept of the "new man" who responds to social rather than to material incentives.

The Cultural Revolution was particularly devastating to the educational system. Professors were sent to work in communes and in factories. Education came to a standstill during this period. The Cultural Revolution was also an economic disaster, and, as a result, in 1969, Mao turned more authority over to Chou En-Lai, who tempered some of its more drastic policies.

The Chinese economy has changed often and in radically different directions. There is at present not enough information to get any real feel for the success of Maoism relative to economic development. Several economists have traveled to China and give strikingly different reports. For example, John Gurley of Stanford argues that China has made great strides and has eradicated poverty, while James Tobin of Yale University argues that there was not much economic progress under Mao.[4]

Interesting developments in China have occurred since Mao's death in 1976. The new leaders have pursued a very pragmatic development strategy that often seems openly hostile to Mao's ideas. They openly attacked the "Gang of Four," consisting of Mao's widow and three other radicals. In attacking the Gang of Four, the leaders attacked the ideas of the Cultural Revolution and, in fact, Mao himself, although they have been very careful not to attack Mao by name. *Newsweek* reported that Chinese officials argued that "Chairman Mao was deceived by the Gang of Four."[5] The attack on the Gang of Four culminated in their trials in 1981. Later in this chapter, we will review the latest reforms and the effects they are having on the Chinese economy.

Castroism

Fidel Castro, who overthrew the Batista government in Cuba in 1958, learned the lesson of Lenin's formula for revolution very well. He

CULTURAL REVOLUTION
The revolutionary reevaluation of the Chinese economy that took place from 1966 through 1969. This period represents the high point in the adulation of Mao.

4. John Gurley, "Maoist Economic Development," and James Tobin, "The Economy of China: A Tourist's View" in Edwin Mansfield, *Economics: Readings, Issues, and Cases* (New York: W. W. Norton and Co., Inc., 1977).
5. *Newsweek* (October 30, 1978): 50.

led a small group of committed revolutionaries in an economy with a large, estranged peasant class and an underdeveloped economy. The United States offered an outside enemy that he used to unify the diverse elements within Cuba. In many ways, the Cuban system is most like Chinese communism in that Castro has placed heavy emphasis on a "new man."[6] The goal is to remove all social inequities and motivate workers with moral incentives rather than with material incentives. This is very close to Marx's view of the final stage of communism. In Cuba, this policy was in large part the work of Che Guevara; it was received skeptically by the Soviets, who were financially underwriting the Cuban economy and, therefore, had a large economic interest in Cuba.

Rather than attempt to industrialize the Cuban economy rapidly, Castro concentrated on agriculture and sought to exploit the export potential of the sugar cane industry. This policy required the transfer of labor from cities to rural areas, the exact opposite of the experience of the European communist regimes. Planning in Cuba is carried out in the System of Budgetary Finance, an extreme centralized planning system that views the economy as a single firm to be rigidly controlled by the central authority. The Cuban economy remains heavily reliant on agriculture.

As in many other communist countries, Cuban communism is uniquely the product of one man, Castro. Like Stalin in the Soviet Union, Tito in Yugoslavia, and Mao in China, Castro is a strong leader. The true face of communism in Cuba may not emerge during his lifetime. That is why it is perhaps most correct to refer to communism in Cuba as Castroism, at least for the present.

Retreat from Socialism: Thatcherism

As just discussed, the movement to socialism through revolution has been significantly influenced by strong leaders. In the one instance of a significant retreat from socialism through significant reprivatization of the economy, this is also the case. The re-election of Margaret Thatcher in June, 1987, makes her the western world's longest serving political figure. It also makes her the longest continuously serving British prime minister of the twentieth century. Thatcher has often been linked with former President Reagan as a proponent of supply-side economics and privatization. However, her program aimed at decreasing the size of government has been far more successful than was Reagan's. Thatcher has significantly reduced taxes, reversing the "talent drain" of singers and other highly paid individuals from the country. She convinced the Parliament to pass legislation that greatly reduces the power of labor unions by requiring that they poll their members before they call a strike.

Perhaps the main and most important element of Thatcherism has been the privatization of the economy. When she became prime minister in 1979, the economy was best described as one in which large governmental enterprises were deadlocked with large labor unions. (This situation was referred to as the "British Disease.") During her tenure, she

6. For a good review of Castro's Cuba, see Carmelo Mesa-Lago, ed., *Revolutionary Change in Cuba* (Pittsburgh: University of Pittsburgh Press, 1971).

has reversed the trend by selling off more than $31 billion in state-owned industries to private investors. These sales included the government's share in British Gas, Rolls-Royce, British Airways, and British Petroleum. Her action and the effect it has had on the economy (productivity increases have averaged over 3 percent) have inspired similar privatization strategies in Italy and France.

ORGANIZATION AND DECISION-MAKING APPROACH TO THE STUDY OF SYSTEMS

We have been looking at alternative economic systems in terms of how the underlying ideology affects the organization of each system. In many cases, this led to a consideration of how a dominant personality's interpretation of that ideology shaped an entire system. Some of you may have found this an exciting and useful way to categorize the world. Others may have found it frustrating to examine each individual system or country, rather than developing general principles of how differing systems are organized and how they affect behavior. The first approach has been the dominant way economists have historically examined alternative economic systems. In recent years, however, a new approach has developed. This new approach, instead of looking at individual countries, attempts to formulate organizational principles using economic theory as a coherent analytical framework.[7]

The System

To understand an economic system, it is necessary to examine both the organizational setting for the production of goods and services *and* the institutional setting for the distribution of those goods and services. The important questions concern the structure of decision making in production and distribution. Perhaps the most important question concerns which individuals, and at which levels, make the important decisions concerning production and distribution. In the United States, production decisions would be made at the entrepreneurial level; in the Soviet Union, these same decisions would be made at the planning level.

Once the assignment of decision-making responsibility is determined, the next question is the motivation for those responsible for decision making. How do the decision makers bear the costs of wrong decisions or reap the rewards of correct decisions? Additionally, it is necessary to determine how one person's participation in the decision-making process influences another's. This process may differ from individual rewards and punishments to the extent that it is possible to change another individual's internal values. In other words, do institutions affect individuals' value systems?

Once these two aspects of the decision-making structure are determined, we can turn to the informational structure in the system. This

7. For a comprehensive development of this path-breaking approach, see Egon Neuberger and William J. Duffy, *Comparative Economic Systems: A Decision-Making Approach* (Boston: Allyn & Bacon, Inc., 1976).

concerns the way in which individuals learn about their options so they can act on these options. In the U.S. economy, prices are an important source of information; in the Soviet economy, the plan plays this role. As decision making becomes centralized, more and better information is critical because the costs of wrong decisions are so much higher. System questions are predominantly microeconomic in nature.

The Environment

After examining the system, we turn to a country's environment, that is, its social structure, physical conditions, and international situation. Some of the more critical aspects of the environment in terms of possible impact on the system are: the level of economic development; the size of the country in area and population; the availability of natural resources from within and from safe allies; the values of the people (religious, cultural, and so on); the political system; the size of the country relative to its near neighbors; the level of development relative to the rest of the world and relative to near neighbors; and the sphere of influence the country is in (American, Soviet, or Chinese, for example). These are only a few of the considerations that can influence an economic system, but they are representative of the concept of environmental influence.

Performance

The way in which an economy performs is an important evaluation measure. Economists usually focus on the performance of the Gross National Product and examine per capita growth in production, stability of production (business cycles can be socially destabilizing), and equity in the distribution of this production. These are predominantly macroeconomic measures of performance.

Policy

Policy changes can be made within a system without changing the underlying fabric of the system. Policy refers to marginal changes in the system and its environment in order to affect performance. Policy changes can influence the system in a positive or negative way. A "good" system might develop "bad" policies that produce "bad" performance and in turn result in a negative change in the "good" system. For example, a central planning policy decision to consolidate farms into larger units, or to shift from corn to wheat, can increase (or reduce) productivity and efficiency.

Interaction of Systems, Environment, Performance, and Policy

Of course, all these organizational elements interact in a simultaneous fashion. But using this terminology can help in understanding the slippery concept of why economic systems differ and why they are similar. For example, consider a small country having the Soviet Union or the United States as a close neighbor. How would this affect the development of the system? It has had a profound effect on the communist countries of Eastern Europe. Likewise, being close to the United States has affected the trade pattern, the output mix, and the level of development in Canada, Mexico, and Cuba. What environmental factors caused the Industrial Revolution to spread from England to the United States but not to Russia?

How might performance influence an economic system? Performance is part of Lenin's formula: If things get bad enough, there might be a revolution. On the other hand, after the revolution if economic conditions stagnate in communist countries, there might be a move toward capitalism or market socialism. We can't begin to answer all these complex questions, but this approach may give you a start in finding the answers and in organizing your thoughts. Certainly the organization and decision-making approach gives some insight into the many and varied expressions of capitalism and socialism we have encountered thus far.

PLANNING

Throughout this chapter, whether we were using the *isms* approach to systems or a more structured organizational approach, we continually encountered the question of planning. Such questions as who directs production, who makes decisions, and who bears the costs for wrong decisions or receives the rewards for correct decisions kept coming to the forefront. This is the essence of the problem of understanding systems. The question is not whether planning should take place but rather who should do the planning. General Motors plans, homebuilders plan, wheat farmers plan—and so do you. The question is the degree of centralization of planning and control. At extremes, the market position would be that only individual consumers and entrepreneurs should plan, and at the command end of the spectrum, the position would be that only the central authority should plan.

The Socialist Controversy[8]

Marx had little to say about the actual workings of the economic system under socialism. Instead, Marx criticized capitalism and left the development of the economics of socialism to his followers. In 1922, a professor at the University of Vienna, Ludwig von Mises, wrote a famous article, "Economic Calculation in the Socialist Commonwealth."[9] This article purported to show that rational economic calculations were impossible under socialism. Von Mises based his argument on a number of factors,

8. For a thorough discussion of the socialist controversy, see Paul R. Gregory and Robert C. Stuart, *Soviet Economic Structure and Performance* (New York: Harper & Row Publishers, Inc., 1974).
9. Ludwig von Mises, "Economic Calculation in the Socialist Commonwealth," in F.A. Hayek, ed., *Collectivist Economic Planning* (Clifton, N.J.: Augustus M. Kelley Publishers, 1967): 103.

but the essence of the argument was quite simple. If the state owned the factors of production (other than labor), it would have to allocate them between competing uses. Without a market to determine prices, this would be an impossible task. A simulated market with shadow prices could not supply correct prices because of the absence of the profit motive. **Shadow prices** are simulated market prices used by economic planners.

The **socialist controversy** was a debate started by von Mises and Oskar Lange concerning the feasibility of planning without markets. Von Mises argued that "the most serious menace to socialist economic organization" was the lack of reward for correct managerial decisions and penalty for incorrect managerial decisions. Lange, a famous Polish economist who at the time was on the faculty at the University of Chicago, responded to von Mises by developing a model sometimes referred to as the **competitive solution**. In the model, Lange tried to prove that a socialist economy with a combination of central *and* local decision making can arrive at the same efficiency standards as the model of pure competition we developed earlier. Prices are arbitrarily set by the central authority. Local managers are told to maximize profits, although they cannot keep these profits. They are solely accounting profits. If shortages or surpluses develop, the price is changed, and in this way an equilibrium price is finally reached. One of the most telling criticisms of Lange's solution is that much of the power of profits lies not as a measure of success but as an *incentive* to succeed.[10]

The debate has never been resolved as to the technical feasibility of centralized planning. Is it possible for a central authority to make the necessary calculations to produce efficiently? In an article that might be considered a continuation of this debate, Nobel laureate F.A. Hayek says no.[11] Hayek argues that information is the friction in the system that causes economic models to diverge from the textbook ideal of either von Mises or Lange. Information is costly to develop and disseminate, taking scarce resources away from other uses. Hayek argued that market systems are superior because they need less information than do centrally planned systems.

Consider a situation in which an earthquake destroys a copper mine in the United States and a copper mine in the Soviet Union. In both countries, copper is now more scarce and needs to be used more sparingly. What happens in each economy? In the United States, the price of copper will rise, reflecting its decrease in supply. Profit-minded entrepreneurs will substitute cheaper metals to minimize costs. The entrepreneur does not need any information other than the fact that the price of copper has risen.

In the Soviet Union, the planner must first be informed of the disaster. The planner must then make some estimate of the severity of the scarcity. Each user of copper must be informed that in the future less copper will be supplied and that other metals should be substituted. Producers of other metals also will need to be contacted and will be told to ship to the enterprises that had been using copper. Additionally, the plan-

---

SHADOW PRICES
Simulated market prices used by economic planners.

SOCIALIST CONTROVERSY
A debate started by Ludwig von Mises and Oskar Lange concerning the feasibility of planning without markets.

COMPETITIVE SOLUTION
The name given to the model developed by Oskar Lange to show that a planned economy could theoretically reach the same efficiency solutions as a market economy.

---

10. Paul Craig Roberts, "Oskar Lange's Theory of Socialist Planning," *Journal of Political Economy* (May–June 1971): 562–568.

11. F.A. Hayek, "The Use of Knowledge in Society," *American Economic Review* (September 1945): 519–528.

ner will have to set priorities as to how the available copper is to be utilized. In the market system, this priority setting was done by the increase in price. Hayek's position is quite simple; central planning can never be as efficient as a market system because it requires so many resources to be used in transmission of information. The market system, on the other hand, economizes on the amount of information needed.

■ How to Plan

Whether or not central planning is efficient does not change the fact that it is undertaken. Most socialist countries rely heavily on central planning to move production in the desired direction. We should, therefore, examine how planning takes place in the Soviet Union, the command economy with the longest experience in planning.

First, priorities must be established; the decision has to be made as to what to produce. In the early years of Soviet planning, this decision was only made at the aggregate level. The first plan was, in fact, called the State Plan for the Electrification of Russia. Today planning is done in the state planning commission, commonly called the **Gosplan**. At the aggregate level, the decision can be made as to whether to produce consumer or investment goods. This was one of the early uses of planning in the Soviet Union. Since the goal of the leaders was rapid economic growth, they made the decision to produce investment goods at the expense of consumer goods. As a result, very few consumer goods were available, and consumers were forced to save. This permitted heavy investment and very rapid rates of economic growth. There were, and still are, significant shortages of consumer goods in the Soviet Union. Tourists traveling in the Soviet Union are well aware of these shortages and are familiar with Soviet citizens' attempts to buy items from them.

GOSPLAN
The state planning commission in the Soviet Union.

Once the decision of what to produce is made, the planners must turn their attention to how much to produce. This is a difficult planning problem because the amount depends on the productive capacity of the existing industry and on the resources that will be available during the period. Production uses up resources; therefore, the planners must plan for the production of the resources that will be used for the final output. At this stage of planning, the various industries are brought into the picture and the ministries, one for each major industry, make their plans ahead of the overall plan. Once these plans are finalized, they must be communicated to all the productive enterprises so they can take the necessary action to put the plan into operation. Planning is an ongoing process, and even though the planning period is usually expressed in five-year increments, it is a continuous exercise in revision and implementation.

This process in itself uses up a great deal of time and productive resources. The individuals engaged in this planning are highly trained engineers and economists, people who are taken out of other productive activities in order to plan. It is not, therefore, difficult to understand the burden that planning places on the economy. Many of the poorest countries, where most communist revolutions have taken place, are the very ones that can least afford to plan because of the opportunity cost of the resources used in the planning process.

Input-Output Analysis

The complexity of planning can easily be seen by examining an input-output table for a small, fictitious economy in which there are only a few industries to control. Input-output analysis, developed by Nobel prize-winning economist Wassily Leontief, shows that everything depends on everything else. These interrelationships are what make planning so difficult because specific plans must be made as to how much of each good is to be produced, by whom, and for whom. **Input-output analysis** is an attempt to quantify the flows between different sectors of the economy. Input-output analysis is useful in economic planning.

To begin, we look at an aggregate economy in Table 23–1 that has only three industries—electricity, trucks, and steel. We also show a labor sector and a corresponding category of consumption. The input to labor is consumption. Reading across the rows of Table 23–1 gives us the output of each industry and the labor sector and shows how that output is distributed. One of the reasons that input-output tables are especially useful in the communist economies is that the units are expressed in physical units, and prices of these outputs and inputs are not needed for the analysis. The fact that prices are not needed is important in a system where market prices are not available, and the prices that exist do not necessarily reflect relative scarcity.

TABLE 23-1
INPUT-OUTPUT TABLE
FOR A SIMPLE THREE-INDUSTRY ECONOMY

	Output				
Input	Electricity	Trucks	Steel	Consumption	Total Output
Electricity	1,000	1,500	5,000	1,500	9,000 Kilowatts
Trucks	1,000	1,500	2,000	1,000	5,500 Trucks
Steel	4,000	3,000	8,500	3,500	19,000 Tons
Labor	2,000	500	3,000	0	5,500 Worker-days

To interpret this input-output table, read across the rows. For example, the steel industry had an output of 19,000 tons, which was sold or allocated by the central authority to the following sectors: 4,000 tons to the electricity industry, 3,000 tons to the truck industry, 8,500 tons to the steel industry, and 3,500 tons to the labor sector. Reading down a column shows the inputs that were needed to produce the output. Take steel as an example again. In order to produce the 19,000 tons of steel, the steel industry used inputs. These inputs were: 5,000 kilowatts of electricity, 2,000 trucks, 8,500 tons of steel, and 3,000 person-days of labor. Once we understand the simple arithmetic of input-output, we can use it to plan future output.

The key assumption used in input-output analysis is that production takes place in all industries at *constant* costs. There are no economies or diseconomies of scale, so that if planners want to double the production of the steel industry, all they need to do is double the inputs.

Regardless of the level of output planned, the amount of inputs required per unit of output remains the same. However, for large increases in output, this assumption is very unrealistic.

Table 23–2 can be used to calculate the input needed to produce additional units of output. The numbers calculated are referred to as input coefficients in the jargon of input-output analysis. An **input coefficient** shows the ratio of a particular input to the total outputs in that industry. Each input coefficient in Table 23–1 can be calculated by dividing each cell in a column by the total output of that industry. For example, the input coefficient of electricity in the truck industry is 0.27 kilowatts/truck ($^{1,500}/_{5,500}$). Table 23–2 reproduces a part of Table 23–1 with input coefficients instead of physical units. Each input coefficient represents the amount of input needed per unit of output.

INPUT COEFFICIENT
In input-output analysis, the ratio of a particular input to the total outputs in that industry.

TABLE 23-2
INPUT COEFFICIENTS

Input	Output Electricity	Trucks	Steel
Electricity	0.11	0.27	0.26
Trucks	0.11	0.27	0.11
Steel	0.44	0.55	0.47
Labor	0.22	0.09	0.16

The input coefficients can be used to plan increases in output. Reading Table 23–2 gives a clue to the use of the input-output technique. Examine the column for trucks. The input coefficient tells what increase is needed from each supplying industry in order to get a given increase in output in the truck industry.

The input-output system in Tables 23–1 and 23–2 can be used to plan for this fictitious economy. Suppose planners want to expand the output of the electricity industry by 2,000 kilowatts. A 2,000-kilowatt expansion in output would require 220 kilowatts of electricity, 220 trucks, 880 tons of steel, and 440 person-days of labor. These needed inputs are found by multiplying the input coefficient by the desired increase in output. Planners would, therefore, know how to direct these industries to deliver the required inputs to produce the planned output.

You should note that there are feedback effects in this simultaneous system. In order to produce more electricity, more electricity must be consumed in the production of the additional steel and trucks used to produce electricity. Feedback happens throughout this interdependent system. The example assumes that there are no bottlenecks in the capacity of any sector of the economy. In fact, however, this may not be the case. In order to produce more electricity, it may be necessary to build new power generators. Generators may require time and, as a result, may disrupt the plan.

The problems encountered in actually using input-output analysis for planning stem from the fact that the coefficients are constant and are calculated on the basis of historical experience. In other words, the required inputs are calculated on the assumption that the input mix is the same as that used in the time period for which the table of input coefficients were compiled.

Problems of Central Planning

The technique of planning is conceptually simple. The actual calculations for a realistic economy can soon become overwhelming, however. Consider an input-output table for an economy with 100 industries, 1,000 industries, or maybe 5,000 industries. The interdependencies between the industries become mind boggling, not to mention computer boggling.

Perhaps more significantly, the problems of planning really begin after the plan has been created. These are the problems of implementing the plan, as well as the problems of creating and maintaining incentives that get workers and managers to support the plan. It is not surprising that plans often are announced with a great deal of publicity and fanfare, while the unsatisfactory results are often played down.

The more an economy grows, the more sophisticated it becomes, and the more difficult it is to control the complexity of the interrelationships between the sectors. This increased complexity explains, in part, the trend in several of the communist countries to introduce market forces to replace some aspects of the plans.

REFORMS: ECONOMIC FREEDOM AND POLITICAL FREEDOM

Socialist countries have found through experience that the application of more stringent planning has not necessarily improved economic performance. This was evident during the Great Leap Forward and the Cultural Revolution in China and is also represented by the declining rate of economic growth in the Soviet Union. Because of poor economic performance, both the Peoples' Republic of China and the Soviet Union have entered into a series of reforms that are aimed at freeing the economy by introducing market forces. The difficulty with such reform is that the economic freedom of markets always produces pressure for other types of freedom, and these reforms reduce the power and prestige of the central authorities. The trade-off is a simple one. In order to stimulate economic growth, incentives are needed. Markets are freed up to produce these incentives. Markets diminish the control of the party and the large and powerful party bureaucracy. The dilemma is made more sharp when the economic reforms produce the inevitable demands for other freedoms. Bureaucrats can seize on the demands for political freedom as a way of beating back the economic reforms and, by so doing, restore their diminished power. To understand how each of these socialist countries is coping with the conflicting goals of economic growth and tight administrative control, it is helpful to examine the reform movements in greater detail in the two countries.

China

Since Mao's death in 1976, there has been rapid reform in China. Almost every aspect of the economy has been affected. Much of this reform is the responsibility of Deng Xiaoping, Party General Secretary, who rose to preeminence in December, 1978.

Political—Social—Intellectual Reforms

Many of the holdovers of Maoism have disappeared from China. In the old days, class labels from before the 1949 revolution were used. These labels (e.g., peasant, landlord, and intellectual) stuck with people and determined how they were treated by the courts and if they were allowed into schools, for example. These labels have now been eliminated, and the holdovers have been "rehabilitated." Intellectuals have witnessed a great liberalization since the days of the Cultural Revolution. They are encouraged to debate and exchange ideas with western scholars. One economist has remarked, "The chains are now off me."

A system of laws is evolving along similar lines. Mao removed all laws because they interfered with the "dictatorship of the proletariat." This system replaces the arbitrary role of party secretaries and is bringing some local stability to the country.

Economic Reform

The first stage of the economic reforms championed by Deng has required the "readjustment" of some priorities. The first is the shift in output priorities in China. If one is to establish economic incentives, it is necessary to increase wages *and*, equally important, to produce consumer goods for people to buy with those higher wages. This priority shift has been accomplished through the establishment of lower planned targets for heavy industries and more investment into light, consumer-oriented industry.

Most noticeable has been the change in the Maoist principle of self-reliance, i.e., independence from other countries. Trade with the rest of the world has been greatly expanded. In the ten years between 1975 and 1985, China's international trade increased from 3.5 percent of GDP to 16 percent of GDP.

The basic reforms of the economic system have had profound effects. In agriculture, the "household responsibility system" assigned land that had been held in communes to individual farm families. In exchange, these farmers have contractual obligations to provide a certain amount of food to the state. Production in excess of contracted amounts can be sold on the markets. The response has been dramatic, with production increasing significantly, and the peasant farmers rising to rank among the wealthy in China.

The industrial sector also is being radically reformed along similar lines. Once production goals have been met, the industrial enterprises can sell any surplus on the open market, or they can barter it for other goods. Profits and losses are being used to reward or penalize managers. In some instances, factories that had been making losses have been turned over to workers in the same fashion that communal agricultural land was assigned to households.

In addition, the state is now charging industrial enterprises for the investment capital it supplies. In some cases, these "loans" are made with assigned payment schedules and interest charges, just as they are in capitalist countries.

The changes brought about by Deng Xiaoping are thus fundamental and profound. They have injected a great deal of market influence into the Chinese economy. With the market influence and foreign trade, there is an observable change in the economy.

Western dress, music, and ideas about democracy have crept in with economic reform. Herein lies the danger. Deng has been responsible for these reforms that are not universally popular with party leaders. Their frustration is understandable, since the freeing of the economy greatly reduces the power and influence of party functionaries. As a result, a political movement to reverse the reforms surfaced. In 1985, some party leaders began to complain about the "excesses" of the reforms and the "spiritual pollution" that had been created. In January 1987, the conservatives in the party finally acted when students demonstrated demanding democratic reforms including freedom of expression. The student demonstrations united the police and military elements in the party leadership. The result was that Hu Yaobang, party leader, reform advocate, and likely heir to Deng's power, made a "self-criticism" and was forced to step down. He was replaced by Zhao Ziyang whose first act was to fire the top security official for lenient treatment of the student demonstrators. Zhao has been described in the press as a cautious reformer.

The Chinese reform movement is thus at a crossroads. The economic reform produced economic gains, which in turn led to political demands. These demands led to the firing of Hu and a campaign against "bourgeois liberalization." Increasingly the party leaders are stressing central planning, thrift, and reduced consumption. Factory managers are lying low while party leaders are reasserting their political control of the factory. The political backlash now seems to be restricting the economic reforms. Some western firms that had been investing in China fear that the political crackdown will reverse the economic gains. Others contend that the economic reforms have gone so far that it would be impossible to reverse them. The answer to this important question will depend largely on high-stakes politics being played out in Beijing.

The Soviet Union

Planning in the Soviet Union is carried out today much as it was 30 years ago. Gosplan supervises the planning and the implementation of the plan through approximately 50 ministries. Each ministry has a responsibility for a segment of the Soviet economy.

The Soviet Union's economic performance has been lackluster since Stalin's time, when growth rates were high. Brezhnev, Andropov, Chernenko, and now Mikhail Gorbachev, the new general secretary, have all acknowledged the poor economic performance in their speeches.

Concern focuses on several areas. First and foremost, economic growth has been slow. Coupled with this slow growth are "imbalances" (shortages) in consumer areas. Wages have increased, but the

THE INTERNATIONAL PERSPECTIVE
MINORITY PROBLEMS IN THE
SOVIET UNION

Americans tend to think of the USSR, the Union of Soviet Socialist Republics, or the Soviet Union, as equivalent to Russia. Nothing could be further from the facts. In 1987, Russians made up 50 percent of the population, but if present birth rates continue the Russian population will be 48 percent of the population in 2000 and 40 percent of the population in 2050. The Soviet Union encompasses 130 ethnic groups that speak dozens of different languages and live within 15 national republics comprised of 38 smaller jurisdictions. After the Bolshevik Revolution, the party cemented its domination by sending millions of Russians (and other Slavs) into non-Russian areas to dominate the regions. Much of the non-Russian population seethes under the political, cultural, and economic domination of the Russians. As one Rand Corporation expert put it: "The Soviet Union for all practical purposes is the last colonial empire. It

won't survive in the long term unless minorities are given a sense of belonging."[a] At present, 9 of the 12-member Politburo are Russians, and minorities are becoming more restless.

The most violent outburst of minorities occurred around Christmas in 1986 when Gorbachev replaced Dinmukhamed Kunayer, the leader of the Communist Party in the Kazakh Republic, with a Russian. A ten-hour riot broke out in Alma-Ata, the capital of the Kazakh Republic (near the Chinese border). Kazakhs stormed the streets, looted stores, burned cars, and attacked Russians and their property. Thirty police officers were reportedly killed.

The Kazakh Republic is not the only problem area. The most persistent area of nationalism is the Ukraine, where a distinct language, literature, and broad heritage have helped Ukrainians withstand an onslaught of "Russification" that began in the 1930s. Forty percent of the political prisoners in the Soviet Union are Ukrainians, double their representation in the population. Soviet Sunni Moslems in the east and southeast are joining fundamentalist secret brotherhoods. These Moslems feel that they are second-class citizens in their own country. In the Republic of Lithuania, the Roman Catholic Church, which is as powerful as the church in Poland, operates as a state in itself despite Soviet efforts to undermine it. In the Republics of Estonia and Latvia, Protestant churches are centers of political activism. In May, 1988, party leaders in the two republics were dismissed for their inability to deal with such political activism.

These ethnic and religious minorities all present obstacles to economic reform. As you saw in this chapter, economic reform requires decentralization, which invariably produces social-political freedoms. Freedom and dissent in turn will lead to greater ethnic demands that will have to be solved.

a. *U.S. News & World Report* (February 2, 1987): 41.

production of consumer goods has not. As a result, production incentives of workers are weak. In addition, shortages and surpluses abound as the plan does not adjust supply and demand. As consumers have become gradually relatively better off in the Soviet Union, they have resisted purchasing shoddy merchandise, and surpluses have resulted in some products.

The reasons for the poor performance are not hard to pinpoint. The centralization of economic decision making, which rests upon detailed, explicit plans at the most central level, leads to mistakes. There is no good mechanism for channeling input from consumers into the plans. Ultimately, the managers of enterprises are only concerned with satisfying the central planners in the relevant ministry. This concentrated central planning, coupled with enterprise security (the enterprises face no competition) and employment security (workers face no job-loss threat), creates a system that offers few incentives to increase productivity and to be more responsive to consumer preferences.

Prospects for Reform

There are three basic paths that could be followed. The first would be to do nothing. The second would be to tinker with incentive systems in an attempt to spur productivity. This has been done with varying degrees of success since the days of Lenin and the New Economic Order. The third possibility would be to alter the system radically to introduce market pressures into the economy. Under such reform, enterprises would control their daily operations, purchase their own inputs, and sell their own products. This type of reform would be similar to the reforms pursued by Deng in China.

In March 1985, Mikhail Gorbachev was made general secretary of the Soviet Communist Party following the death of Konstantin Chernenko. Gorbachev, who is in his 50s, represents a significant change from rule by elderly men. His first steps in the direction of economic reform began to surface in early 1987. The economic reforms are referred to as *perestroika*. These reforms are part of a policy known as *glasnost*, or openness.

Perestroika represents the first steps toward economic reform. It will not be easy to accomplish because every step toward markets and efficiency represents a step away from central planning. *Glasnost* and *perestroika* are dramatic changes from earlier periods when the Soviet Union intervened first in Hungary, then in Czechoslovakia, and finally in Poland to make sure that economic reform did not mean a slide toward capitalism. Time will tell if Gorbachev has the power and savvy to reform the system.

JAPAN

To conclude our look at comparative systems, lets examine Japan, where great strides were experienced in a modified capitalistic structure. The Japanese "miracle" is of great interest to developing countries and industrial managers in the United States. The interest stems in part from wanting to borrow those elements of the Japanese success that can be transplanted into other economies.

In 1950, Japan was starting to recover from the devastation of World War II. The U.S. Commerce Department reports that Japanese per capita income in 1950 was only about $1/8$ that in the United States. Thirty-five years later, in 1985, the per capita level of income was $4/5$ that of the United States. In the 1950s, the phrase "Made in Japan" implied cheap, shoddy copies of U.S. products. In the 1980s, "Made in Japan" implies the finest of automotive and high-tech production. All this economic growth occurred in a country smaller than the state of California with few natural resources (Japan imports almost all its oil) and a population about half that of the United States.

To some extent, Japan's success is rooted in the devastation of World War II. The war destroyed so much capital that most factories in Japan are of postwar vintage. Compare that with the aging steel plants of Gary, Indiana, or the auto plants of Detroit. Second, the war changed the social structure of the economy. A highly ordered society was turned on its head by the war. This type of turmoil often allows entrepreneurial energies to be released. But there are other unique elements to be found in the Japanese model.

Taxes

When compared to Western Europe and the United States, Japan's taxes are very low. For example, Japan's taxes are around 25 percent of national income, compared to 30 percent in the United States, 35 percent in the United Kingdom, and almost 40 percent in West Germany.

Supply-siders in the United States would point to this tax structure as an important reason for growth. They would particularly note that the tax structure in Japan is not used to redistribute income. Until very recently, there was no social insurance system, and even now it is very limited. The pretax distribution of income is about the same as the post-tax distribution. As a result, there are powerful incentives to engage in risky, entrepreneurial activity.

Investment and Saving

The Japanese people save about 20 percent of their annual incomes. These savings find their way into capital investment, which creates future income. The high rate of Japanese saving is the result of two powerful influences. The first has already been mentioned. Since only a very limited social insurance system exists in Japan, workers must save for their retirement. Second, the tax system is structured in such a way that tax credits are given for saving. Contrast this to the United States, where dividends and interest—the returns to saving—are taxed, and where social security reduces saving for retirement.

Labor-Management Relations

Perhaps the aspect of the Japanese economy that has generated the most interest in the U.S. business community is the labor-management relationship. Great firm loyalty exists in Japan. Many workers in the manufacturing sector receive lifetime employment to age 55, when mandatory retirement occurs. These workers belong to company unions that cooperate with management in setting goals, work schedules, and plans for the company.

THEORY Z
A management idea that workers are motivated to perform if they are made part of the management process.

QUALITY CIRCLES
Groups of workers organized to discuss production problems and to suggest solutions.

There are aspects of this labor-management relationship that are being tried by U.S. businesses. **Theory Z** is the concept that employees are not motivated by negative incentives, such as threats, or by monetary incentives, such as raises and promotions but are motivated instead by being included as active participants in the management process. The use of quality circles is one of the tools of a Theory Z management style. In **quality circles**, workers organize themselves into units that try to improve quality by discussing work problems and making suggestions. A quality circle is a kind of activist, organized, suggestion box.

Has Japan Peaked?

Many observers feel that the Japanese economy may have peaked in the mid-1980s[12]. They point to the fact that Japanese exports have dropped and industrial production has fallen. The Japanese Ministry of International Trade predicts that Japan will lose 560,000 manufacturing jobs by the year 2000. This job loss in part is caused by the increasing tendency for the Japanese to produce in foreign countries rather than to produce in Japan and export. Approximately 20 percent of Japanese manufacturing is expected to be "offshore" in the year 2000 as compared to 5 percent in 1987. Declining exports and shifting to foreign production both reflect the very high price of the Japanese yen in international financial markets.

The Japanese response to this changing economic position will be important. If Japan opens its market to foreign trade it will be able to live off its investments rather than its production. This openness will be a challenge because changing the pattern of economic development has been disturbing to Japanese leaders. These same leaders have demonstrated a propensity to seek protectionist policies in the past. In the face of rising production costs at home, a rise in protectionist policies may follow. These trends could represent a cloud on the Japanese horizon.

SUMMARY

1. The study of comparative systems allows the economist to analyze different institutions to determine how they can affect economic outcomes.

2. The most common approach to this study of systems is to classify the systems according to the dominant ideology. This approach is not very useful because almost all systems can be labeled as either capitalism or socialism. Since systems can differ considerably within these general labels, the approach is limited.

3. Marx's writings form the basic political framework on which all the communist countries are based. The economic systems of these countries are, however, widely divergent.

4. The development of the varying systems has been, in many cases, the result of very significant and dominant political leaders. As a result, it is possible to distinguish among Leninism, Stalinism, Titoism, Castroism, and Maoism as separate variants of communism.

5. Another way to analyze different systems is to examine their organizational and decision-making differences. This approach looks at the levels at which decisions are made as well as the informational requirements and motivation of the decision-making units. This approach also examines the interaction of systems, environment, performance, and policy to determine how each affects the other.

12. See "Fear and Trembling in the Colossus," *Fortune* (March 30, 1987): 32–52.

6. Planning is carried out in all economies; the key difference between systems is the level at which the planning is carried out. The higher the level of planning, the greater the informational requirements of the system.

7. Central planning requires the determination of what to produce. In the Soviet Union, such planning resulted in rapid growth because the central authority decided not to produce many consumer goods. This forced the population to save and generated high rates of investment.

8. The planning technique is exemplified in input-output analysis. Input-output analysis presents the historical experience of the inputs necessary to produce a given output. The experience then can be used to determine what inputs are necessary to produce a desired output. Input-output analysis assumes that this historical production record will hold in the next period.

9. After all the technical problems of planning are worked out, it is necessary to put the plan into operation. Implementation requires transmitting the plan to the production units and creating the proper incentives to bring about the desired production.

10. China and the Soviet Union face reform movements in their own countries. The course of economic growth in each will depend on these reform movements.

11. The Japanese "miracle" is based on low tax rates, high saving rates, and labor-management harmony.

NEW TERMS

capitalism	Great Industrialization Debate	competitive solution
socialism	workers' self-management	Gosplan
communism	Great Leap Forward	input-output analysis
fascism	Cultural Revolution	input coefficients
War Communism	shadow prices	Theory Z
New Economic Policy (NEP)	socialist controversy	quality circles

QUESTIONS FOR DISCUSSION

1. How does a union, such as Solidarity in Poland, threaten the Communist Party? Why is the Soviet Union so interested in developments in Poland?

2. How did Lenin change the theories of Marx? Which of the two appears to be more important as the inspiration of communist revolutions?

3. Is planning an important function in all economies? Is it more important in market or command economies?

4. How would allowing the input coefficient to vary complicate input-output analysis? Is the assumption of fixed coefficients a damaging one?

5. Try to list as many problems of maintaining proper incentives under a central planning system as you can. Do these problems exist only in centrally planned economies?

6. How do you evaluate the performance of the Japanese economy? Are there lessons for the U.S. economy?

7. What is fascism?

8. What was the period of the New Economic Policy in the Soviet Union?

9. What is the socialist controversy?

10. What is the connection between economic freedom and political freedom?

SUGGESTIONS FOR FURTHER READING

Cheung, Steven N.S. "China in Transition: Where Is She Headed Now?" *Contemporary Policy Issues* (October 1986): 1–12. A prediction that the reforms will continue, but at a slower pace, based on the argument that they have gone too far to be reversed.

Doder, Dusko. *Shadows and Whispers: Power Politics Inside the Kremlin from Brezhnev to Gorbachev*. New York: Random House, 1986. An excellent description of politics in a system that lacks a formal mechanism for political change.

Galbraith, John Kenneth. *Economics in Perspective*. New York: Houghton Mifflin Co., 1987. A fast paced economic history that has a little bit of everything about economics from Adam and Eve to the present.

Lindbeck, Assar. *The Political Economy of the New Left: An Outsider's View*. 2d ed. New York: Harper and Row Publishers, Inc., 1977. Presents a critical review of the radical economics movement.

Perkins, Dwight Heald. "Reforming China's Economic System" *The Journal of Economic Literature* (June 1988): 601–645. A review of reforms and an analysis of their success from 1977–1987.

Pryor, Frederic L. *A Guidebook to the Comparative Study of Economic Systems*. Englewood Cliffs, N.J.: Prentice Hall, 1985. An examination of how countries from different systems respond to different economic issues.

Szulc, Tad. *Fidel: A Critical Portrait*. New York: Morrow, 1987. An argument that Castro embraced communism early on and intended from the very beginning to turn Cuba into a Marxist-Leninist state.

Yoshino, M.T., and Thomas B. Lifson. *The Invisible Link: Japan's Sogo Shosha*. Boston: MIT Press, 1986. Examines how the Japanese general trading houses coordinate trade and production.

PART SEVEN

BEING AN

ECONOMIST

CHAPTER 24 ■
■

BEING AN ECONOMIST:
A CHEERFUL LOOK
AT THE DISMAL SCIENCE

■

■ **INTRODUCTION**

Nineteenth century historian Thomas Carlyle gave economics the nickname "the dismal science." Perhaps economics acquired its reputation as a dismal science because economists emphasize costs, or because they focus on the negative aspects of each phase of the business cycle—inflation during expansion and unemployment during recessions. Economics is really a very optimistic subject in many ways. Economists have more faith in the rationality of people than psychologists, more optimism about the possibility of progress than historians, and in general a remarkable trust in the ability of the market to solve a whole host of problems if just left to itself. All that faith, trust, and optimism hardly sounds typical of a dismal science!

Now that you have completed your first course in economics, it is time to consider how to use what you have learned, whether to take other economics courses, and perhaps whether to consider economics as a major field of study. This chapter discusses majoring in economics, career opportunities for economists, and graduate study in economics. We will also present a guide to material that can help you stay current in economics, whether or not you take any additional economics courses.[1]

THE STRUCTURE OF ECONOMICS

Where does economics go after the basic principles course? The topics covered in this principles course gives you some idea of the content of intermediate and advanced courses. The core of undergraduate

1. Parts of this chapter draw heavily from a handbook prepared by Dr. Laurence E. Leamer and the Center for Economic Education and Public Policy of the State University of New York at Binghamton. Dr. Leamer graciously permitted us to use his ideas, his format, and in some cases his exact words.

508

economics, after principles, is intermediate macroeconomic theory and intermediate microeconomic theory. Each of these courses reviews and expands on the theoretical topics in microeconomics and macroeconomics studied on the principles level.

If you are interested in where economic ideas came from and how they developed, you should take a course in the history of economic thought. Traditionally, undergraduate economics majors or minors take at least one applied course in the microeconomic areas, such as labor economics, government and business, or industrial organization; and one applied macroeconomics course, almost always money and banking. These courses are a blend of theory, institutions, and policy questions. Students who are interested in applying economics to data problems will want to take a course in econometrics (application of statistical methods to economic questions) and perhaps mathematical economics.

Economics majors can round out their curricula with courses in specialized areas involving applications of both microeconomics and macroeconomics, such as public finance, international economics, economic development, economic history, and comparative economic systems. If the economics department is in the business college, it is very likely that the student will complement the economics curriculum with related business courses in finance, accounting, marketing, or management. If the economics department is in the liberal arts college, related courses will come from the other social sciences—sociology, political science, psychology, and history. In either case, a good dose of mathematics and statistics is not only helpful in undergraduate economics courses but also good preparation for careers in government or business or for graduate study.

MAJORING IN ECONOMICS

British economist Alfred Marshall (see Chapter 3 for a biographical sketch) wrote that, "Economics is a study of mankind in the ordinary business of life."[2] You will find that an economics major prepares you for many professional careers, because economics offers a way of thinking about the ordinary business of life that is clear, concise, and rigorous. Job recruiters and graduate admissions committees are favorably inclined toward economics majors as candidates for jobs or graduate work in a variety of fields. It is for this reason that 20,711 students chose to earn their bachelor's degrees in economics in 1985—a 47 percent increase over 1975.[3]

In choosing a major, you should consider several important and related questions. First, what profession(s) do you have in mind? Second, does the major offer flexibility, so that if your originally chosen occupation becomes unattractive, you have sufficient opportunities within the field without switching majors? Third, if your chosen profession can be approached through several different avenues, are there any advantages in

2. Alfred Marshall, *Principles of Economics*, 8th ed. (Don Mills, Ontario: The Macmillan Co. of Canada, Ltd., 1920), 332.
3. Elizabeth M. Fowler, "Economics Still a Road to Jobs," *The New York Times* (January 20, 1987): 34.

choosing one major over another? Fourth, will the major be useful for everyday life as well as for training for your life's work? Finally, is it enjoyable? Remember, your major is with you forever; why not pick a major that makes work pleasant and interesting? With these questions in mind, why choose economics?

One enduring strength of economics is its logical, ordered way of looking at problems and issues. Economics is at the same time the most applied, most quantitative, and most scientific of the social sciences, and the most theoretical of business degrees. It draws on history, philosophy, and mathematics to confront topics ranging from how households or businesses can make sound decisions, to societal issues such as unemployment, inflation, crime, and environmental decay.

An undergraduate major in economics can be ideal preparation for work on a Master of Business Administration (MBA) degree at a graduate business school, leading to a career in business management. Most business graduate schools encourage students to take at least some economics courses before starting graduate school. In fact, many of the best business graduate schools prefer students with a broad liberal arts background, which an economics major provides.

A large part of the content of an MBA program is based on economics. Economics provides the theoretical background for business courses. In the competition for top grades in the program, there is an advantage in already being familiar with the central ideas of economics. Furthermore, an MBA program emphasizes making good business policy decisions. One important approach to those decisions is through economic reasoning. It is certainly helpful to have acquired some skill at this sort of thinking as an undergraduate.

If you plan to be a lawyer, an economics major offers excellent preparation. Many law schools believe that economics represents one of the best backgrounds for the study of law because economics takes a logical ordered approach to problems. Specific courses recommended for prelaw students include intermediate economic theory, government and business, public finance, industrial organization, and law and economics.

Graduate training in public policy or public administration, as a preparation for a governmental career in policy analysis, also requires a strong economics background. Virtually every public policy issue has a substantial economic dimension, so economics majors would have a head start in such a program.

Job opportunities are also good for economics majors who don't go on to graduate school. Governments—federal, state, and local—employ economists in many roles. Private business firms, particularly banks and other financial institutions, also employ economists. Business firms employ economics graduates to analyze economic conditions, forecast sales, and also to do nonspecialized work in sales and management. Students with a strong background in both economics and at least one foreign language may have some exciting opportunities available with multinational corporations.

Many economists are employed in colleges and universities, both as professors and administrators. In general, graduate degrees are required for such positions—a master's degree for two-year colleges, and a Ph.D. for four-year institutions. Numerous economists are employed in international agencies in development planning and policy studies by the Agency for International Development, the United Nations, and the U.S. State Department. Finally, many economists do private research, working as consultants to corporations and government agencies.

An economics major, like other majors, may lead to graduate study and, therefore, possibly to becoming a professional scholar or teacher. For the nation as a whole, approximately 10 percent of economics majors complete an M.A. in the subject, and 10 percent of these complete a Ph.D.

THE BENEFITS AND COSTS OF STUDYING ECONOMICS

Your college education is only the beginning of a long road that will have countless twists and turns. There is ample time to change jobs and careers. It is for precisely this reason that economics is a good major. You need to prepare yourself to take advantage of whatever opportunities become available. Economics provides a good foundation for such changes because it teaches a disciplined way to analyze and to make choices.

Reasons for Studying More Economics

Pay attention to the economics majors who are juniors and seniors. They enjoy what they are learning because it is challenging and relevant. It is fun to understand subjects that baffle other students and the general public—maybe even your parents. It is also fun to major in a subject that enjoys prestige. You can wear your economics major with pride.

Keynes tried to capture what was unique about the competent economist in these words: ". . . the master economist must possess a rare combination of gifts. . . . He must be a mathematician, historian, statesman, philosopher—in some degree. He must understand symbols and speak in words. He must contemplate the particular in terms of the general, and touch abstract and concrete in the same flight of thought. He must study the present in the light of the past for purposes of the future. No part of man's nature or his institutions must lie entirely outside his regard." If that sounds like the kind of thinking that challenges your skills, economics may be where you belong.

You are already aware, from your study of introductory economics, of some reasons why many students find economics a challenging area for undergraduate study, while others choose to avoid it. Here are some good reasons for studying economics.

Economics Deals with Vital Current Problems

Inflation, unemployment, monopoly, economic growth, pollution, free markets versus central planning, poverty, productivity, and other headline issues are all covered in the study of economics. Economics is a problem-based social science, and the problems with which it is especially concerned are among the central issues of our times. These issues fill newspapers and pervade politics. Economics is relevant not only to the big problems of society, but also to personal problems, such as one's job, wages, unemployment, the cost of living, taxes, and voting.

Economics Is a Successful and Prestigious Social Science

The accomplishments of economics have established it as perhaps the most successful social science. No other social science has had equivalent impact in applying reason and science to the shaping of the nation's social destiny. No other social science has a Nobel Prize. The Council of Economic Advisers is unique; no such permanent agency exists for any other social science. Indeed, few scientists of any kind enjoy so much prestige as the economists John Kenneth Galbraith, Paul Samuelson, Lester Thurow, or Milton Friedman.

Economics Uses Theoretical Models and the Scientific Method

Some students become impatient with the seemingly endless array of conjecture and descriptive material which characterizes much of the social sciences. Economics offers a social science with models for organizing facts and for thinking about policy alternatives. Because economics deals with prices and numbers and because so many of its magnitudes are objectively measurable, economic theory is more fully developed than most other kinds of social theory. Many students find this rigor and completeness one of the attractive aspects of studying economics.

Sometimes students view math as a fascinating game or language but are impatient at not being able to use it for human problems. While mathematics is increasingly used by all the social sciences, economics has long been in the forefront in this respect. A student with a background in algebra, geometry, calculus, and statistics finds many places to use these skills in economics.

Economics Majors Have Many Career Options

As noted earlier, economics, unlike some majors, leads to a diversity of career opportunities. These include careers in business, law, journalism, teaching, educational administration, politics, finance and banking, government service, public and private overseas service, labor leadership, or graduate study in a related professional area, such as law, business, or public administration.

Employers, particularly business firms, looking for liberal arts graduates often favor economics majors because these students are a preferred employment risk. According to a *New York Times* article in 1987, economics is still a road to good jobs, particularly if the candidate has a bachelor's degree.[4] The demands of the economics major itself tend to drive away the less ambitious, while many better minds are attracted to it. Thus, a degree in economics may prove to be a valuable credential. A good grade point average in economics courses speaks for itself. The payoff goes beyond getting a job; the salaries of economists, both academic and nonacademic, tend to be higher than those of other social scientists. In a 1984 survey by the Bureau of the Census, the average monthly salary for persons with a bachelor's degree in economics was $2,846, compared to an average of $1,841 in all fields.

4. Fowler, "Economics Still a Road to Jobs," 34.

An Economics Major Prepares Students for Community Leadership

A knowledge of economics and an understanding of current economic institutions and problems are not only essential for certain occupations, but for leadership roles as well. Economics can serve as an avocation as well as a career foundation. As a person knowledgeable about economics, you may play a leading role in a local or national political party, a civic club or organization concerned with the local economy, a union or teacher's association, or be an informed commentator on current issues in any setting. Few disciplines are equal to economics in preparing one to be an interested, interesting, and understanding observer of passing events, and a leader in making decisions that require understanding economics.

Reasons for Avoiding Courses in Economics

There are reasons why students avoid studying economics. Other disciplines may simply be more attractive; something else may interest students more. Here are some reasons for avoiding economics.

Economics Is a Quantitative Social Science

Some students find that mathematical thinking is difficult, or simply lack a mathematical background or interest. While it is true that much of economics (probably most of undergraduate economics) is presented in a narrative-descriptive form, mathematics is still frequently employed as a way to understand economic phenomena because of its greater precision and clarity. It is possible, however, for a student who has only a basic knowledge of algebra, geometry, and introductory calculus to major successfully in economics. Lack of interest and ability in mathematics, however, would make it unlikely that such a student would do well in graduate studies in economics.

Science, even social science, is a bore to some students and a threat to others. They are unwilling to employ a method that begins with careful observation and proceeds to hypotheses, then to testing and possible verification, and finally to a tentative conclusion. If you are unwilling to accept the constraint of scientific methodology, perhaps you should look elsewhere for a major.

Economics Involves Abstract Thinking and Theory

Some students have an aversion to theoretical thinking. They defend their aversion by saying that theory is impractical or irrelevant. Their minds thrive on the concrete, the real, but they are turned off by theory. Underlying this attitude is a valid complaint. Teachers of a science, such as economics, that has developed an extensive theoretical system sometimes make mastery of theory the primary goal of their teaching, rather than using theory as a tool for understanding real problems. Thus, students may legitimately complain that while economics is potentially the most relevant of the social sciences, it is sometimes taught as if it hardly related to the real world. You can overcome this problem by mixing theory courses with applied, policy-oriented courses, or by challenging your professors to offer more concrete examples and applications of theory.

Economics Is a Narrowly Focused Discipline

Other social sciences often study society or societies as a whole, including their economic aspects among others (for example, anthropology, history, or sociology). Economics tends to exclude many very important aspects of society. It usually takes as given the tastes and preferences, the family relationships, the political structures, and the goals of society, and leaves those questions to other fields of study.

If social science or social philosophy are what you really want to study, then you should consider another major. On the other hand, if the economic side of life really fascinates you, and you want put what you learn in your economics courses in the context of social institutions and social philosophy, you could major in economics and use electives outside of economics to broaden this sometimes narrowly focused discipline.

Economic Reasoning Can Be Stifling

Economists are always considering costs; that is, they are constantly reminding people that choices usually are made at the cost of other things. Economics is a conservative science. It tends to instill in its audience a fear of possible costs of change. The economic way of thinking may lead to an obsession with efficiency, i.e., with improving the organizations of society with the purpose of attaining whatever society values. In its defense, Alfred Marshall said that economics is a science concerned with the "material means to a refined and noble life." Before it is possible to be creative, it is first necessary to be productive.

If you are a creative person, you might want to combine a major in economics with some complementary discipline, perhaps from the creative arts. Such a combination might enable you to become an intellectual leader in the effort to broaden the scope and perspective of economics, or to develop new applications of old methods to achieve new purposes. Economics is an evolving social science, and you could play a role in its evolution.

CAREER OPPORTUNITIES FOR ECONOMISTS

Jacob Viner, the teacher of many great economists, once described the nature of the discipline as, "Economics is what economists do." What is it that an economist does? According to the National Science Foundation, an economist is someone who has had professional training in economics at the graduate level and is a member of a professional group, such as the American Economic Association or the National Association of Business Economists.

The economist's job title may or may not include the word economics or economist, particularly if his or her background is limited to an undergraduate major in economics. Instead, a B.A. economist is likely to have a job that makes use of training in economics as a basis for a position in personnel, management, marketing, education, or some other field.[5] If you want to be an *economist* as such—to pursue one of the three traditional career paths of academia, government, or business—you will usually need graduate training.

5. Very few undergraduate degrees lead to jobs in which the job classification is the same as the student's major. Accounting and engineering are two exceptions to this rule.

The Academic Economist

Almost half of all professional economists are college teachers. A Ph.D. degree is essential to teach at a four-year college. Junior college instructors usually have a master's degree in economics, but a Ph.D. or work toward a Ph.D. may be required.

A new Ph.D. generally begins an academic career as an assistant professor. Starting salaries in 1988 ranged from $28,000 to $38,000 for the academic year. Salaries vary widely with the type of school and the area of the country, as well as the particular skills and area of specialization that the new faculty member has to offer. Responsibilities usually include teaching from two to four courses a term. Promotion to associate professor and tenure (permanent employment) typically takes from five to seven years. At more prestigious schools, the rule for promotion and tenure is "publish or perish." Faculty members must publish articles (and increasingly, obtain research grants) in order to be promoted. Promotion to the full professor rank usually occurs from five to fifteen years after the promotion to associate professor, depending on the candidate's research record, publications, and teaching ability.

Academic economists often supplement their incomes by writing textbooks and other educational materials and by consulting. In recent years, economists have provided consulting services for a variety of clients in such diverse areas as environmental quality, health care, public education, the value of human life in lawsuits, rural development, and industrial location.

The Business Economist

The rapidly growing professional field of business economics reflects the increased use of economics as a business tool. For many years the business community disdained academic training and expressed a preference for practical experience. Early business schools were largely training grounds for middle managers, founded to teach accounting and practical management skills. Any contact that these early business students had with economics was accidental and usually unsatisfactory; economists were considered theoretical ivory-tower dreamers. Bernard Baruch, the famous industrialist, was reported to have defined an economist as a man with a Phi Beta Kappa key on his watch chain, but no watch!

Today economics courses play a major role in the general business curriculum. The increased interest in the uses of economics in business is also reflected in the increasing number of graduate-trained economists in the business community and on the faculty of business schools. Economists today are found throughout the business community from top management positions down through the company hierarchy.

It is most likely that an economist would begin a business career in a firm's economics department. These organizational divisions undertake a variety of tasks, including forecasting the general business environment and how it might affect markets in which the particular firm operates, interpreting the effects of governmental policy on the firm, and gathering and processing economic data. From this beginning, the economist may move into the management side of the business organization. In this manner, the economist is following the same career path often pursued by engineers, accountants, and lawyers who work for private business firms. Business economists receive excellent salaries and are in great demand. The largest employers of economists, according to the National Association of Business Economists (NABE), are firms engaged in manufacturing, banking, business services, and securities and investments.

The Government Economist

Since the New Deal era in the 1930s, economists have moved into the forefront of governmental policy analysis. In recent years, economists have begun to displace political scientists and lawyers in top government administrative posts. Recent presidential cabinets have included a high proportion of economists.[6]

There are positions for economists in every federal governmental agency, primarily as policy analysts. A few positions are available at junior grades for economists with undergraduate degrees, but most government economists must possess a master's or a doctoral degree in economics. There are jobs for labor economists, international economists, agricultural economists, development economists, public finance economists, and population economists, as well as macro- and microeconomists. The duties of a governmental economist are very diverse and in large part depend on the particular governmental agency. For example, in the State Department or the CIA an economist might become an expert on the economy of a particular country; in the Office of Management and Budget, an expert in a program area such as welfare or health care; and at the Treasury, a specialist in tax policy.

Until the 1970s, except for the Joint Economic Committee, very few congressional committees or individual congressional staffs hired economists. Since 1974, the Congressional Budget Office has become an important research arm of Congress. It serves the same research role as the Office of Management and Budget does for the President. Legislation and issues facing Congress are becoming increasingly complex and economic in nature. As a result, Congress is turning to economists for expert advice on these issues. The career of Paul Craig Roberts illustrates some of these possibilities. Roberts, who writes a column for *Business Week*, started as an academic economist, then became a congressional staff member. From there he became an assistant secretary of the Treasury before returning to academia and journalism.

Salaries for government economists are attractive. In 1988, an individual with a B.A. or B.S. degree and at least 21 semester hours in economics could get a job at the GS5 or GS7 level, which paid a starting salary of $14,390 and $17,824, respectively. An M.A. degree in economics qualified one to start work at the GS9 level at $21,804 per year, and a Ph.D. qualified an individual to start work at the GS13 level at $37,599 per year.

6. For an interesting view of the economist as a policy adviser from a professional economist with extensive high-level government experience, see George P. Shultz and Kenneth W. Dam, *Economic Policy Beyond the Headlines* (New York: W.W. Norton and Co., Inc., 1978).

Another area of employment for economists is in state and local government. State government economists play a wide variety of roles, just as they do in the federal government, but there are a few differences. State economists are more likely to be involved with microeconomic problems and issues because states do not carry out independent monetary and fiscal policy. They are also likely to be less narrowly specialized, working on a variety of problems and issues. Developing strategies for state economic development, compiling state economic indicators, interpreting the impact of changes in federal policy on state agencies and programs, and developing good state and regional data bases are all important responsibilities for state government economists. Almost all state governors now have the services of at least one economist in a high administrative position.

At the state and local level, the primary areas of research by economists are labor market analysis, school finance issues, state and local taxation and tax reform, natural resource and environmental issues, and budget expenditure analysis. Economists are also moving into important administrative responsibilities in state and local government.

CAREERS IN ECONOMICS

- ACADEMIC: Teaching, research and writing, and/or administration at a
      major university
      graduate school
      state college
      small private college
      junior college
      technical school
      secondary school
- RESEARCH: In a private or public economic research organization
- BUSINESS: Forecasting, planning, and other economic tasks for
      banks and financial institutions
      manufacturing
      wholesale and retail trade
      multinational firms
   Consulting for private firms and public agencies
   Economic journalism
- SPECIAL   Economic adviser, interpreter, defender, speech writer
   INTEREST   for
   GROUPS   lobbying/research organizations
      political party or candidate
- GOVERNMENT: Policy analysis or statistical work for
      international agencies
      federal, state, or local governments

GRADUATE STUDY IN ECONOMICS

Many career possibilities require graduate training. If you think you may need graduate work in economics for your chosen career, you should begin planning now. You might start by reading an article about current experiences of graduate students in economics by David Colander and Arjo Klamer, "The Making of an Economist."[7] They report on a survey taken of graduate students enrolled in six top-ranking graduate programs in economics, covering their areas of interest, perceptions of how to succeed, and different views on policy issues and theoretical controversies at different institutions.

Graduate schools in economics currently award about 800 Ph.D. degrees and about 2,000 master's degrees annually. There are over 100 graduate schools in the United States offering the Ph.D. degree in economics and a number of others offering only a master's degree. Which ones would you like to attend? To which ones should you apply? What should you do as an undergraduate to prepare for graduate school and to increase the likelihood of being admitted to the schools of your choice?

Undergraduate Preparation

If you aspire to graduate study in economics (or if you are unsure but want to keep that possibility open), there are certain guidelines you should keep in mind when choosing your undergraduate courses.

Mathematics

Most graduate departments require a background in mathematics including at least introductory calculus and statistics. Matrix algebra is also helpful. Some schools offer a course called Mathematical Analysis for Economists, in which students learn mathematics in a context of economic applications. Some graduate departments allow you to make up deficiencies in mathematics after entrance, but you will be better prepared if you acquire some of the needed mathematics as an undergraduate.

Theory

Macro and micro theory are the basic foundations for graduate study. Your first graduate courses will probably be in micro and macro theory, but the professor will assume a firm foundation in basic theory at both the introductory and intermediate levels. Economics is a science based on theory; there is no more important part of your undergraduate economics study than theory courses as preparation for graduate study.

Grades

If you are to go on to graduate school, your undergraduate grades really matter. An *A* average or at least a *B*+ is essential. An upward-moving grade point average as you progress through your undergraduate studies may indicate blooming promise; a grade point average that falls as commencement approaches makes admission much less likely.

Related Skills and Interests

Graduate study in economics usually is very specialized. Your area of specialization may depend in part on the kinds of courses you took other than in economics and the interests you developed in undergraduate school. Knowledge of a foreign language may be a major determinant of

7. David C. Colander and Arjo Klamer, "The Making of an Economist," *Journal of Economic Perspectives* (Fall 1987): 95–112.

how you later use your economics. A working knowledge of Chinese, Russian, or Arabic may provide a highly marketable skill (for research, for government service, for work in a multinational corporation or other international entities). Likewise, an economist with a strong foundation in accounting, in law, or in politics has a combination of talents of unusual value. An economist who is skilled in communication—in listening and understanding, in writing and speaking—has one of the scarcest talents in the profession. With the expansion of knowledge and the consequent alienation of economics from the average citizen by reason of its use of a specialized vocabulary and language, the synthesizer or communicator of knowledge is becoming indispensable.

The foundations of all these skills (languages, related disciplines, communication skills) must be laid in undergraduate school. Indeed, your undergraduate education is likely to be more important than your graduate training for determining whether you become any more than a technically competent economist. Give some thought to development of other skills and interests that expand or complement your skills as an economist.

Determining Your Goals

Before trying to select a school, review and possibly revise your goals, for they should influence your choice of the right school for you. You may need a year of some other kind of experience between undergraduate and graduate work to help you to define and reconsider those goals. A year of work, or an internship in business or government, can be invaluable.

What kinds of professional roles do you find appealing? You may have identified some aspect of economics that you would like to develop as a specialty. There may also be some particular personal skills that you already possess or hope to develop to a very high level of proficiency. For example, you may have a particular talent for the application of mathematical methods in economics; for teaching, clear writing, oral explanation, or argument; for interpreting economic ideas, synthesizing and clarifying professional and/or political issues. These interests and skills will help you to identify a field of specialization (shown in Table 24–1) and some possible career choices.

TABLE 24-1
FIELDS OF SPECIALIZATION IN ECONOMICS

Macroeconomic theory	Comparative economic systems
Microeconomic theory	Economic development
Labor economics	Government and business regulation
Public finance	Environmental economics
Agricultural economics	Industrial organization
Urban and regional economics	Political economy and public choice
History of economic thought, methodology	Economic planning
	Policy analysis
Statistics, econometrics, mathematical economics	Law and economics
	Health care
Money and banking, monetary theory	Social welfare policy

Constraints on Your Choice

Before looking at graduate schools, you need to identify what constraints are likely to limit or influence your choice. Here are several that may apply.

Money

Do you have the financial resources to attend school—$7,000 to $20,000 a year for room, board, and tuition for two years for a master's program, and three to five years for a Ph.D.? If not, are you able and willing to work? What about fellowships, assistantships, loans, and so forth? Most graduate programs offer some form of financial assistance, but the fraction of costs that financial aid will cover is highly variable, and more difficult to obtain at the more prestigious institutions. Financial assistance will depend on your undergraduate record. Most Ph.D. programs offer advanced students the opportunity to teach undergraduate courses to enable them both to develop teaching skills and to earn an income.

Status

How important is the prestige of the institution from which you are to receive your degree in terms of your career opportunities? The status of the graduate school is more important for academic positions than for business or government. In state and local government, it is often helpful to attend a school in the region in which you ultimately would like to work.

Your Academic Qualifications

The most important qualifications are your undergraduate grades and courses. A minimum 3.0 GPA is required for almost any graduate program, and considerably higher in the more prestigious programs. The Graduate Record Examination (GRE) is often required; sometimes an excellent score on the GRE will make up for some deficiencies in your undergraduate record. The status of your undergraduate school and the quality of your references can also make a difference. You will be competing with graduates of other, perhaps better known, colleges and universities. Finally, while it is possible to be accepted for graduate work in economics with a background other than an undergraduate economic degree, you should at least have had the essential training in mathematics and economic theory.

Geographic Location

Are there important reasons—family or personal preferences—that would incline you to study in one part of the country as opposed to another? Where would you like to be employed upon graduation? Some graduate schools have a national reputation and hence a national placement market. Others are regional; if you are interested in a particular geographic area, you may be better off going to school in that area, particularly for a career in business or state government.

Schools Offering the Ph.D. Degree in Economics

Table 24–2 presents a list of the top ten universities offering the Ph.D. in economics. The top ten ranking is based upon publications by professors on each school's graduate faculty and on citations of their works by other economists.[8] This method of ranking has gained popularity because it is more objective than rankings based on opinion surveys. Using publications and citations favors the larger departments, however, because they are more likely to have long-established senior faculty with many publications. This method shortchanges newer programs, those with few graduates, those serving primarily a regional area, and those whose primary aim has been something other than educating academic and research economists. (Programs whose goal is to train teachers, public servants, and business economists are likely to be ignored.) Also, the table does not list departments offering only a master's degree. A recent study in the *American Economic Review* used a similar ranking method for schools with only a master's program.[9] Table 24–3 provides a list of all schools offering the Ph.D. in economics listed by geographic region.

TABLE 24-2
TOP TEN ECONOMICS DEPARTMENTS OFFERING PH.D.'s
(by Rated Quality of Graduate Faculty)

1–2	University of Chicago, Harvard University
3	Massachusetts Institute of Technology
4	Stanford University
5	Princeton University
6	Yale University
7	University of Pennsylvania
8	University of Wisconsin-Madison
9	Columbia University
10	University of California-Berkeley

TABLE 24-3
SCHOOLS OFFERING PH.D.'S IN ECONOMICS
(by Geographic Region)

Northeast	South
■	■
Boston College	Alabama, University of
Boston University	American University
Brown University	Arkansas, University of
Bryn Mawr College	Auburn University
Carnegie-Mellon University	Catholic University of America
Clark University	Clemson University
Columbia University	Duke University
Connecticut, University of	Florida, University of
Cornell University	Florida State University
Fordham University	George Mason University
Harvard University	Georgia, University of
Johns Hopkins University	Georgia State University
Lehigh University	Georgia Institute of Technology

8. Davis, Paul, and Gustav Papenak, "Faculty Ratings of Major Economics Departments by Citations," *American Economic Review* (March 1984): 225–230.
9. Blair, Dudley, Rex Cottle, and Myles Wallace, "Faculty Ratings of Major Economics Departments by Citations: An Extension," *American Economic Review* (March 1986): 264–67. This article extends the citation method to evaluating the quality of master's-only programs.

University of Massachusetts
  at Amherst and at Boston
Massachusetts Institute of
  Technology
New Hampshire, University of
New School for Social Research
New York University
Northeastern University
Pennsylvania State University
Pennsylvania, University of
Pittsburgh, University of
Princeton University
Rensselaer Polytechnic Institute
Rochester, University of
Rutgers The State University
  of New Jersey
State University of New York
  at Albany
  at Binghamton
  at Buffalo
  at Stoney Brook
Syracuse University
Temple University
Tufts University
Yale University

Houston, University of
Howard University
Kentucky, University of
Louisiana State University
Maryland, University of
Miami, University of
Mississippi, University of
Mississippi State University
North Carolina at Chapel Hill,
  University of
North Carolina State University
North Texas State University
Oklahoma, University of
Oklahoma State University
Rice University
South Carolina, University of
Southern Methodist University
Tennessee, University of
Texas, University of
Texas A&M University
Texas Tech University
Tulane University of Louisiana
Vanderbilt University
Virginia, University of
Virginia Polytechnic Institute
West Virginia University

Mid-West
■

Case Western Reserve University
Chicago, University of
Cincinnati, University of
Illinois, University of
  at Urbana-Champagne
  at Chicago
Indiana University
Iowa, University of
Iowa State University
Kansas, University of
Kansas State University
Kent State University
Michigan, University of
Michigan State University
Minnesota, University of
Missouri, University of
Nebraska, University of
Northern Illinois University
Northwestern University
Notre Dame, University of
Ohio University

West
■

Arizona, University of
Arizona State University
California, University of
  —Berkeley
  —Davis
  —Irvine
  —Los Angeles
  —Riverside
  —San Diego
  —Santa Barbara
Claremont Graduate School
Colorado, University of
Colorado State University
Hawaii, University of
New Mexico, University of
Montana State University
Oregon, University of
Southern California, University of
Stanford University
Utah, University of
Utah State University

Ohio State University
Purdue University
St. Louis University
Southern Illinois University
Washington University at St. Louis
Wayne State University
Wisconsin, University of
  —Madison
  —Milwaukee

Washington, University of
Washington State University
Wyoming, University of

Armed with this list, how should you identify possible departments for further study? Following is a list of criteria which you may want to employ in evaluating departments. Individual criteria are not listed in order of their importance; you must determine what is important.

Professional Status of the Department

Would you prefer to attend one of the more prestigious departments (and do you have the qualifications)? If so, then the top ten rankings in Table 24–1 are your guide. Keep in mind that in the past, the academic economic community has been very stratified. A graduate of one prestigious school may be employed by another prestigious school and may be avidly sought after by the lower-rated ones, while a graduate of a little-known department is likely to move on to another little-known one, or possibly into government or business, or into some employment in which one is judged more by what one can do than by the prestige of the school from which one graduated. Of course, with the recent increase in non-academic employment opportunities for new Ph.D.s, it is possible that this situation will change in the future.

Location of the School

If you have a preference as to the part of the country in which you want to study, Table 24–1 should assist you in identifying schools in your preferred region. If your graduate school professors are willing to help in your future job search, their contacts are likely to be local with the exception of the top-rated institutions, and thus they can be most helpful in the immediate region.

Maturity of the Doctoral Program

You may prefer one of the more mature departments or one of the newer programs. Newer departments may try harder. Being smaller, and knowing that the reputation they have yet to build will be through their products, they may invest more time in the development of individual students. Or, being insecure, they may be more conservative and traditional: They may seek to copy the prestigious programs rather than trying to be innovative.

Information from Descriptive Brochures

You should select a few economics departments from this list for a more thorough investigation. Most departments publish descriptive brochures which they will mail to prospective students, or which may be posted in your undergraduate economics department. Program descriptions can also be found in the latest *Peterson's Annual Guides to Graduate Study—Economics*, or the American Economic Association's *Graduate Study in Economics*. These two resources offer brief summaries of each department and its program. While you should perhaps focus on your selected schools, browsing is a good idea, for you may discover possibilities you had not previously considered. What are some of the criteria to keep in mind?

Curriculum Design

Largely prescribed or elective? Narrow in focus or broad? Confined to economics courses or permitting some from other fields? Prerequisites? Math requirements? Traditional in design, innovative, or experimental? Adequate course alternatives? Adequate areas of specialization? Enough course offerings and faculty members actively doing research in your area of special interest?

Departmental Specialization

Is there any evidence that the department is trying to make anything special of itself? Beware of the unfocussed aim of general or all-around excellence. Are the specialties of the department of real interest to you? Are they marketable?

The Department's Real Values

Watch for clues as to what the department really values. What kind of information is stressed about its faculty members or its graduates—scholarship, teaching, status, number of publications? What is stressed in its view of economics—rigor, relevance, the place of applied or institutional economics? In the description of the goals of the department's Ph.D. program, what seems to be most important? How does the department seem to value teaching, research, and public service?

Department Size

A class of around 50 graduate students has been suggested as an optimum size, large enough to permit a reasonable variety of courses and to foster an effective intellectual community of students. You will learn a great deal with and from your fellow students. In very large departments, one's choices and contacts may be increased, but possibly at the expense of impersonalization. The reverse may occur in very small departments.

Costs, Assistantships, and Student Aid

If these considerations are important to you, contact the university's graduate office or the department and request information. Usually, there is considerable financial assistance available for graduate study.

Student Body

Are most of the students full-time? Is there a large component of the program that is taught in the evening for part-time students? Is a large part of the student body from foreign countries? What percentage of the students are supported by assistantships?

Interpreting Graduate Catalogs and Materials

From your survey of department brochures and national guides to graduate economics departments, you should be able to narrow your

THE INTERNATIONAL PERSPECTIVE MASTER OF INTERNATIONAL BUSINESS

One of the newest kinds of graduate programs in economics and business is the Master of International Business degree, offered at about a dozen schools. One of the first MIB programs to develop was the Thunderbird school in Arizona, now called the American Graduate School of International Management. This program prepares people to work for the growing number of multinational corporations combining training in economics, management, accounting, and other business skills with development of language skills and appreciation for the cultural differences that affect the workings of markets and business relationships. Some programs include an internship experience in a foreign country; different programs will have links to different multinational corporations or different countries. The Master of International Business program at the University of South Carolina, for example, specializes in internships in Central America and the Caribbean.

Universities that offer master's degrees in business with the word international in the title, such as MIBS (Master of International Business Studies) or MIM (Mas-

ter of International Management) are few in number. In 1986, Peterson's Guide listed only nine. In alphabetical order, they are:

American Graduate School of International Management
Baylor University
Columbia University
Florida International University
Monterey Institute of International Studies
Roosevelt University
Saint Mary's College of California
United States International University
University of South Carolina

More programs are being planned, and many MBA programs offer an international focus. It is possible to supplement a traditional MBA program with language training and/or an international exchange or internship to accomplish the same career goal.

A Master of International Business program, or an MBA with an international focus, has exciting career possibilities for those who combine an interest in business and economics with a skill for learning languages and an interest in travel and other cultures. International financial firms, such as banks and insurance companies, need persons with this combination of skills and interests. Multinational corporations of all kinds also need this specialized mix of skills for managing international operations ranging from manufacturing to retailing imports, handling international currency transactions, dealing with import licensing and export procedures, and providing service to foreign customers.

If you are interested in a graduate program in international business, a foreign language—or even two—is an essential part of your undergraduate program. If you lack the aptitude or discipline to become fluent in a foreign language, this program is not for you. A course in international economics is a must, and it would be helpful to take any other international courses that are available. Check the political science department for offerings in international relations, and the business school for offerings in international business, international marketing, and international finance. The opportunities in multinational firms are numerous and growing for people with the right combination of skills and training.

choice to several which appear to meet your goals and fit your constraints. Write to those departments for catalogs and application blanks, or inspect the catalogs found in your school library. Your professors may have suggestions, although you may want to discount recommendations that you attend their alma maters. In addition to the above criteria, here are other kinds of information that the catalog may contain, or that you can search out from other sources.

Departmental Efficiency, Courtesy, and Imaginativeness

A department may reveal itself to you by the way it responds to your interest. Has it been prompt, imaginative, and helpful in designing materials to aid your choice?

Teaching

How seriously does the department take its teaching? For example, are new graduate students just out of undergraduate school immediately assigned to teaching? This may be a clue that the department really does not take teaching seriously and exploits cheap student labor in order to free faculty time for research. Is there a teaching seminar for graduate students who are being trained to teach? Is there a carefully planned teaching apprenticeship as part of the Ph.D. program? Or does the department leave students to learn these skills for themselves?

Quality of Faculty

The list of faculty or perhaps brief biographies the department may provide should indicate where faculty members received their degrees, what their scholarly interests are, and where and how recently they have had books or articles published. How many faculty members really seem to have a currently vital professional specialty?

Employment Market

Where are its graduates placed? Does it have contacts with markets for the kind of employment you want? This test is particularly important because it provides a market evaluation of the quality of the program.

Special Facilities and Programs

What is the quality of the school's library, computers, and data banks? What does it offer in the way of lecture programs, seminars, workshops, and visiting professors? How successful are its faculty in obtaining outside funding and grants?

CALENDAR FOR GRADUATE SCHOOL APPLICANTS

- Sophomore and Junior Years—Prepare; choose your curriculum carefully, consider your career goals and possible areas of specialization.
- Early in your Senior Year—Review your goals and constraints, put together your list of potential schools, take the Graduate Record exam. The GRE is similar to the SAT or ACT, only more difficult. Many schools require this test in order for you to be considered.
- Late fall semester, Senior Year—Survey flyers, write for information, make application to three or more schools, including a sure one.
- January to April—Await results, make plans to relocate and enjoy commencement.

ECONOMICS AS AN AVOCATION

After all this discussion of economics careers and graduate schools, the truth of the matter is that most of you who are finishing this course will not major in economics. Even those majoring in economics are likely to be employed in some occupation other than that of economist. For the majority of you, economics will be, at most, an avocation that makes you a more informed citizen. Some of the economics you have learned in this course will be superseded by new theories, new institutions, and even new problems. Ten years ago economics textbooks devoted much less space to international economic issues and the linkages between national economies that are now of such great concern. You have, however, learned principles that will allow you to sort through new problems if you continue to be informed. The course you have just finished and this book will have been successful if they opened your eyes to how the economy works and activated your interest in it!

Recurring Economic Events

The following calendar of recurring economic events should aid you in your continued study of economics. These events usually set off reactions in the form of interpretive news articles, editorials, comments by columnists, and television reporting and commentary. This calendar lists the monthly cycle and yearly patterns of recurring economic events and the release of important information.

Monthly (or more frequently)

Every Thursday: Money supply figures.

First Week: Unemployment for prior month, both actual rate and seasonally corrected rate.

Second Week: Producer prices (wholesale price index) for prior month, both actual and seasonally corrected index. (Either first or second Friday of month.)

Third Week: Industrial production index for prior month. Personal income for prior month. This is the only monthly national income figure and, thus, a monthly indicator of changes in aggregate output.

Fourth Week: Index of leading indicators for prior month. This is an index of variables that tends to lead real output; that is, tends to indicate when booms or recessions are likely to be coming. Consumer price index for prior month, both actual and seasonally corrected index.

Annually

January: Early in month—Annual economic review of the prior year and forecasts for current year abound in newspapers and periodicals; for example, the *New York Times.* After mid-month—Gross National Product for the October–December quarter. Revised figures are often issued one month later. Last week—President's annual economic message and annual *Economic Report of the President.*

February: Hearings by the Joint Committee on the Economic Report. Prominent economists usually appear. Their views are reported in the press. Budget is submitted.

March: Final Report of the Joint Committee on the Economic Report. Around the 20th—Balance of payments for the prior year.

April: Fourth week—Balance of payments for the first quarter. After mid-month—First quarter Gross National Product; personal income figures by state for the previous year, final figures on preceding year for balance of payments and gross national product.

June: Late in month—Mid-year report of Council of Economic Advisers. Most state governments end their fiscal year on June 30th and begin the next one on July 1st.

July: After mid-month—Second quarter Gross National Product and state personal income.

September: Congress is supposed to complete the budget; if not, passes continuing resolution to keep federal government operating until budget is ready. Third week—Second quarter balance of payments.

October: First of the month—Beginning of new federal budget year. After mid-month—Third quarter Gross National Product.

December: Last week—American Economic Association annual meeting. Many organizations also sponsor forecast luncheons at this time of year to try to anticipate economic conditions in the coming year.

Regular Reading for the Armchair Economist

While professional economists read journals such as *The American Economic Review* or *The Journal of Political Economy*, there is considerable reading material available for the armchair economist who wishes to keep abreast of new developments and economic events. Here are some suggestions for daily, weekly, monthly, or occasional reading:

Daily: A good local newspaper, and the *Wall Street Journal*.

Weekly: Any good newsmagazine carries business and economics news, including *Newsweek, Time*, and *U.S. News & World Report*. If you are interested in international news with a strong economic flavor, the British weekly *The Economist* is an excellent resource. Weekly business magazines include *Business Week, Fortune*, and *Forbes*.

Monthly or Quarterly: The Brookings Institution publishes the *Brookings Review* each quarter, with policy analyses; its more conservative counterparts also have regular publications. The American Enterprise Institute publishes *Contemporary Policy Issues* and the Heritage Foundation, *Policy Review*. For interesting data sources and analyses of trends in particular areas, try *Monthly Labor Review* (employment, earnings, and consumer prices); *Survey of Current Business* (output, GNP, interest rates, international trade); *The Federal Reserve Bulletin* and/or the *Review* published by your regional Federal Reserve Bank (money, banking, prices, and regional economic conditions). These quarterly *Reviews* are usually available free of charge. There are a number of issues-oriented magazines for popular consumption such as *Challenge: The Magazine of Economic Affairs*.

Annually: Both the Brookings Institution and the American Enterprise Institute publish an annual volume that examines public policy in various areas. The current titles are *Economic Issues 19--* for Brookings and *Contemporary Economic Issues 19--* for the American Enterprise Institute.

This list is far from exhaustive. In addition to the regular flow of periodicals listed above, there are many good books on economic subjects written for popular consumption, such as those by Thomas Schelling, John Kenneth Galbraith, Milton Friedman, Lester Thurow, and Thomas Sowell. Many of these books are listed in the suggested readings at the ends of chapters. There is no shortage of materials to keep your economics fresh, lively, and up-to-date. Happy reading!

SUMMARY

1. This chapter provided basic information for those interested in economics as a career or as an avocation.
2. An undergraduate major in economics can open the door to a wide range of professional careers.
3. Economist as a job classification usually calls for graduate training in economics. Economists are employed in academia, business, and government.
4. Graduate study in economics requires careful planning of your undergraduate program, clarification of your professional goals, and an informed search for the graduate program that is right for you.
5. Economics can be an enjoyable avocation. A wealth of interesting material is available to help you keep your economics up-to-date.

SUGGESTIONS FOR FURTHER READING

Boulding, Kenneth. *Economics As a Science*. New York: McGraw Hill, 1970. A classic book on the relationship of economics to other disciplines.

Norton, Hugh S. *The World of the Economist*. Columbia: University of South Carolina Press, 1973. Gives a readable account of the things economists do and the way they think.

Peterson's Annual Guides to Graduate Study: Humanities and Social Sciences. Edited by Phyllis Marsteller. Princeton, NJ: Peterson's Guides, Inc., annual. This annual volume gives up-to-date information on graduate programs in economics. It includes costs, financial aid available, and information on facilities and faculty.

Buchanan, James. *What Should Economists Do?* Indianapolis IN: Liberty Press, 1979. Discusses what economists do, how they do it, and how economics relates to other social science disciplines.

Nelson, Robert H. "The Economics Profession and the Making of Public Policy." *Journal of Economic Literature* (March 1987): 49–91. A readable and lively account of what economists do in policy-making positions in the federal government.

GLOSSARY

ABILITY-TO-PAY PRINCIPLE The concept that people should pay taxes in relation to their capacity to pay as indicated by income, assets, or spending.

ABSOLUTE ADVANTAGE The ability to produce something with fewer resources than other producers use.

ACCOUNTING PROFIT The difference between explicit costs and total sales.

ACREAGE ALLOTMENT A farm program that sets a limit on the total number of acres that can be placed in production.

ADMINISTERED PRICES A term coined by Gardiner Means to describe price inflexibility in concentrated industries. Means labeled prices that were relatively rigid, or changed only infrequently, as administered prices.

AFL-CIO The merged American Federation of Labor and Congress of Industrial Organizations. The merger took place in 1955 and gave labor a more unified political stance.

AGENCY FOR INTERNATIONAL DEVELOPMENT (AID) The U.S. agency that is part of the State Department and which is in charge of U.S. aid to foreign countries.

AGRICULTURAL SUPPORT PROGRAM A group of programs designed to maintain farm incomes. Most programs in agricultural support are aimed at decreasing supply or increasing demand for raw agricultural production.

ALLOCATION Any activities of government that affect the allocation of resources and the combination of goods and services produced.

ALLOCATIVE EFFICIENCY The allocation of resources to produce the goods most desired by society. Free markets produce allocative efficiency.

AMERICAN FEDERATION OF LABOR (AFL) Founded by Samuel Gompers in 1886, the AFL was the first business union. The AFL was an exclusive union organized for skilled workers.

AMERICAN FEDERATION OF STATE, COUNTY, AND MUNICIPAL EMPLOYEES (AFSCME) One of the few unions that grew in the 1970s. A union of public employees.

APPRECIATION A rise in the market price of a currency due to market forces.

ARBITRATION A third party hears the arguments of both management and labor in a labor dispute, studies their positions, and renders a decision. In binding arbitration, the sides must abide by the decision.

ARC ELASTICITY Average elasticity over the space between two points.

ASSOCIATION-CAUSATION FALLACY The false notion that association implies causality.

AVERAGE FIXED COST (AFC) Total fixed costs of production divided by output. Average fixed costs decline as production is increased.

AVERAGE PHYSICAL PRODUCT (APP) The total physical product (output) divided by the number of units of a factor used.

AVERAGE REVENUE Total revenue divided by the quantity sold. A demand curve is an average revenue curve.

AVERAGE TOTAL COST (AC) Total costs of production divided by the number of units of output.

AVERAGE VARIABLE COST (AVC) Total variable cost divided by the number of units of output.

BALANCE OF PAYMENTS A statistical summary (usually annual) of the transactions between residents of one country and residents of the rest of the world.

BALANCE OF PAYMENTS DEFICIT An excess of a country's foreign exchange spending over its foreign exchange earnings in a particular year.

BAR CHART A graphic representation of data as the heights of columns; useful for comparing data for different time periods or different countries.

BARRIERS TO ENTRY Natural or artificial obstacles that keep new firms from entering an industry.

BENEFIT PRINCIPLE The concept that people should pay taxes in relation to the benefits they receive from government programs.

BIG PUSH The development strategy calling for one major thrust on all fronts in the economy by government or induced by government through private enterprise.

BILATERAL MONOPOLY Monopolies dealing with each other as buyers and sellers, such as when a monopoly labor union sells labor to a monopsonistic firm.

531

BLACK MARKETS Markets in which people illegally buy and sell goods and services at prices above imposed price ceilings.

BLOCK GRANT Transfer of funds from the federal government to state and local governments for use in a general spending category, such as health care or public education.

BOARD OF DIRECTORS The individuals elected by the stockholders of a corporation to select the managers and oversee the management of the corporation.

BONDS Interest-earning certificates issued by governments or corporations as a method of borrowing money.

BRACKET CREEP A situation in which inflation moves people into higher income tax brackets, even though their real incomes haven't increased.

BRETTON WOODS SYSTEM The international monetary system in effect from 1945 to 1973, based on infrequent changes in currency prices, ample reserves, and the dollar as key currency.

BUDGET CONSTRAINT A given level of income that determines the maximum amount of goods that may be purchased by an individual.

BUDGET LINE The graphing of the budget constraint, indicating achievable levels of consumption given the prices of goods and the consumer's income.

BUSINESS FIRM An organization formed by an entrepreneur to transform inputs into marketable outputs.

BUSINESS UNION Samuel Gompers's description of a union that worked for economic goals without wanting to change or destroy the business organization or the political environment in which it worked.

CAPITAL The durable, but depreciable, man-made inputs into the production process. Machines, tools, and buildings are examples of capital.

CAPITAL ACCOUNT That part of the balance of payments account that summarizes purchases and sales of financial assets, such as stocks, bonds, short-term debts, bank deposits, and direct purchases of foreign plants or businesses.

CAPITALISM An economic system based on the idea of private ownership of the factors of production by individuals or groups of individuals.

CAPITALIZED VALUE The present value of the stream of future rent payments.

CARTEL A group of independent firms that agree not to compete but rather to determine prices and quantity jointly. Perfect cartels are shared monopolies.

CATEGORICAL GRANT Transfer of funds from the federal government to state and local governments for specific purposes.

CELLER-KEFAUVER ANTIMERGER ACT A 1950 act that made it illegal in certain circumstances for a firm to merge with another by purchasing its assets. This act strengthened the Clayton Act.

CETERIS PARIBUS A Latin term that means "holding everything else constant."

CETERIS PARIBUS FALLACY The false notion that arises when an observer fails to recognize that other variables have changed.

CHISELING Cheating on a cartel arrangement by lowering prices in an attempt to capture more of the market.

CIRCULAR FLOW MODEL A visual representation of the relationships between factor markets that generate income and product markets in which income is used to purchase goods and services.

CLAYTON ACT Passed in 1914, it prohibited the acquisition of the stock of a competing company if such an acquisition would "substantially lessen competition."

CLEAN AIR ACT An act passed in 1970 that empowered the EPA to set emmision standards and impose standards on polluters.

CLOSED SHOPS Firms where workers must be union members before employment.

COASE THEOREM A solution to externality problems which shows that in the case of small numbers of affected parties, a property right assignment is sufficient to internalize any externality that is present.

COEFFICIENT OF PRICE ELASTICITY OF DEMAND (E_d) The numerical measure of price elasticity of demand. The percentage change in quantity demanded divided by the percentage change in price.

COEFFICIENT OF PRICE ELASTICITY OF SUPPLY (E_s) The numerical measure of price elasticity of supply. The percentage change in quantity supplied divided by the percentage change in price.

COLLUSION Agreements between firms in an industry to set certain prices or to share markets in certain ways.

COMMAND (PLANNED) ECONOMY An economy in which the fundamental questions are answered through central command and control.

COMMERCIAL POLICY The total of actions that a country undertakes to deliberately influence trade in goods and services.

COMMODITY CREDIT CORPORATION (CCC) A government agency that makes loans to farmers as part of the price support programs.

COMMUNICATION Firms' ability to signal their intentions to each other.

COMMUNISM The final stage in the theory of Karl Marx, in which the state has withered away and economic goods are equally distributed.

COMPARABLE WORTH The idea that there should be equal

pay for jobs that require similar levels of training, responsibility, and other characteristics of "worth."

COMPARATIVE ADVANTAGE The ability to produce something at a lower opportunity cost than other producers face.

COMPARATIVE STATICS A technique of comparing different equilibrium positions to determine the character of changing relationships between variables.

COMPETITIVE FRINGE The sometimes substantial number of small competitors in markets with one large, dominant firm.

COMPETITIVE SOLUTION The name given to the model developed by Oskar Lange to show that a planned economy could theoretically reach the same efficiency solutions as a market economy.

COMPLEMENTARY GOODS Those goods that are jointly consumed. The consumption of one good enhances the consumption of the other good.

CONCENTRATION RATIO An index of the relative degree of concentration in an oligopolistic market.

CONGLOMERATE The combination of many unrelated operations in a single firm.

CONGRESS OF INDUSTRIAL ORGANIZATIONS (CIO) An affiliation of industrial unions that was organized when the AFL decided not to promote unions in the mass-production industries.

CONSTANT COST INDUSTRY An industry in which expansion of output does not cause average costs to rise. The long-run supply curve is perfectly elastic.

CONSTRAINED SALES MAXIMIZATION Occurs when a manager's primary goal is to increase the sales of the firm because managers are rewarded by stockholders for increasing the firm's relative share of the market.

CONSUMER SURPLUS The benefit derived from a purchase in excess of the market-determined price.

CONSUMPTION POSSIBILITIES FRONTIER A line showing the consumption combinations attainable through trade.

CONTESTABLE MARKETS Markets that may be comprised of large firms, but these firms are efficient because easily reversible entry is possible.

CONTRACT LAW Law that deals with the enforcement of voluntary exchanges.

COORDINATES The values of x and y that define the location of a point in a coordinate system.

COORDINATION Firms' ability to relate their production decisions to those made by other firms in an industry.

CORPORATION The form of business enterprise in which stockholders are the legal owners of the firm. The legal liability of the stockholders is limited.

COST-PLUS PRICING The practice in price regulation of allowing firms a markup on average costs of production. This is the most common form of price regulation.

COUNTERVAILING POWER The notion put forward by Galbraith that monopoly sellers and monopoly purchasers offset each other's power in bargaining with one another.

CRAFT UNIONS Unions composed of skilled workers, such as plumbers and carpenters.

CROSS ELASTICITY OF DEMAND A measure of the responsiveness of changes in quantity demanded for one product to changes in the price of another product.

CROWDING OUT The increased demand for loanable funds by government causes the interest rate to rise, which attracts funds away from business investment.

CRUDE BIRTH RATE The number of births per one thousand of population.

CRUDE DEATH RATE The number of deaths per one thousand of population.

CULTURAL REVOLUTION The revolutionary reevaluation of the Chinese economy that took place from 1966 through 1969. This period represents the high point in the adulation of Mao.

CURRENT ACCOUNT That part of the balance of payments account which summarizes transactions in currently produced goods and services, including merchandise, services, investment income, etc.

DEADWEIGHT LOSS The lost gains from trade due to monopoly restriction of output.

DECISION SCIENCE A discipline that deals with the processes by which decisions are made.

DECREASE IN DEMAND A shift in the demand curve indicating that at every price, consumers demand a smaller quantity than before.

DECREASE IN SUPPLY A shift in the supply curve indicating that at every price, suppliers will supply a smaller quantity than before.

DECREASING COST INDUSTRY An industry in which an expansion of output causes average costs to fall in the long run. The long-run supply curve has a negative slope.

DEMAND The desire and ability to consume certain quantities of goods at certain prices over a period of time.

DEMAND CURVE A graphical representation of a demand schedule showing the quantity demanded at various prices over a particular time period.

DEMAND-DETERMINED PRICE If supply is perfectly inelastic, the price is determined by changes in demand only.

DEMAND SCHEDULE A tabular listing that shows the quantity demanded at various prices over a particular time period.

DEPENDENT VARIABLE The variable, normally measured on the vertical axis in a coordinate system, in which value is determined by the other (independent) variable or variables.

DEPRECIATION A fall in the market price of a currency due to market forces.

DERIVED DEMAND A demand that is the result of the demand for another product. For example, the demand for labor is derived from the demand for the good that the labor produces.

DIAMOND-WATER PARADOX The problem that classical economists faced when they argued that value in use could not determine price (demand) because diamonds, while less useful than water, are more expensive than water.

DIFFERENTIATED OLIGOPOLY An oligopoly that produces a heterogeneous or differentiated product.

DIFFERENTIATED PRODUCT A good that has real or imagined identifiable characteristics that are different from other goods.

DIMINISHING MARGINAL UTILITY For a given time period, the greater the level of consumption of a particular commodity, the lower the marginal utility. Less satisfaction is obtained per additional unit as more units are consumed.

DISCOUNTING The technique of calculating present values by adjusting for interest that would be earned between now and some specific future time.

DISECONOMIES OF AGGLOMERATION Cost that are imposed on firms and individuals when a large number is located in one area.

DISECONOMIES OF SCALE Increases in long-run average cost that are due to increased plant size.

DISEQUILIBRIUM A state in which variables are moving toward equilibrium but are not yet at equilibrium—an unstable position.

DISTRIBUTIVE JUSTICE Normative arguments for a particular distribution of income.

DOMINANT FIRM The most influential firm in an industry, usually the price leader.

DRIVE TO MATURITY The stage of development in which the lagging sectors of the economy catch up, and the industrial revolution is consolidated into sustained growth.

DUAL OR SEGMENTED LABOR MARKETS The idea that there are artificial barriers in labor markets that keep some workers in artificially low wages.

DUMPING The practice of selling in foreign markets at lower prices than in domestic markets. This is a form of price discrimination.

ECONOMIC EFFICIENCY The least-cost method of production.

ECONOMIC PROFIT The difference between total sales and the total of explicit and implicit costs of production.

ECONOMIC RENT A payment to a factor of production in excess of the opportunity cost of that factor of production.

ECONOMICS The scientific study of how people and institutions make decisions about producing and consuming goods and services and how they face the problem of scarcity.

ECONOMIES OF AGGLOMERATION Savings that accrue to firms and consumers when a large number locate in one area.

ECONOMIES OF SCALE Declines in long-run average cost that are due to increased plant size.

ELASTICITY A measure of the sensitivity or responsiveness of quantity demanded or quantity supplied to changes in price (or other factors).

EMINENT DOMAIN A doctrine that gives government the right to buy property at "fair market value" if it is in the public interest.

ENDOGENOUS VARIABLES Variables that are explained or determined within a theory or system.

ENTERPRISE This is the input to the production process that involves organizing production, innovation, and risk taking.

EQUILIBRIUM A position that a system or model is at rest or when it is moving at a constant rate in a steady direction.

EQUITY A normative measure of fairness.

EXCESS CAPACITY Underutilization of existing plant size. In monopolistic competition, the firm produces less than the efficient capacity of the plant.

EXCHANGE CONTROL A foreign exchange arrangement in which the government purchases all incoming foreign exchange and is the only source from which foreign exchange can be purchased legally.

EXCISE TAX A tax that is placed on the sale of a particular item, such as liquor, cigarettes, or electricity.

EXCLUSIVE UNION A union that restricts supply and maintains a higher-than-competitive wage by excluding workers from the profession. Craft unions are exclusive unions.

EXOGENOUS VARIABLES Variables that are determined outside a theory or system.

EXPANSION PATH A curve that shows how the firm's choice of inputs changes as the price of one of the inputs changes.

EXPECTATIONS Individual forecasts for the state of the future.

EXPLICIT COST Accounting cost or money outlay.

EXTERNALITY A cost or benefit associated with consumption or production that is not reflected in market prices and falls on parties other than the buyer or seller.

FACTOR MARKET Markets in which owners of factors of production sell these factors' services to producers

FACTORS OF PRODUCTION The inputs of land, labor, capital, and enterprise that a firm uses to produce outputs.

FAIR RATE OF RETURN The idea that a regulated industry must earn a normal profit, or it will go out of business.

FAIR TRADE The argument that the U.S. should impose trade barriers equivalent to those that U.S. trading partners place on U.S. exports.

FALLACY OF COMPOSITION The false notion that what holds for the parts holds for the whole.

FASCISM An economic system that combines monopoly, capitalism, private property, and a strong authoritarian central government.

FEATHERBEDDING The maintenance of jobs that management claims are unnecessary or redundant. Unions often insist on featherbedding in industries that are declining.

FEDERAL TRADE COMMISSION ACT A 1914 act establishing the Federal Trade Commission to police unfair and deceptive business practices.

FISCAL FEDERALISM A division of responsibilities and revenue sources between the three levels of government in the United States—federal, state, and local.

FIXED FACTORS The factors of production that cannot be varied in the short run, such as the size of the plant.

FLOW VARIABLE A variable that is defined over a period of time.

FOOD SECURITY ACT A bill passed by Congress in 1985 that attempts to do away with loan supports by establishing a system of target prices.

FOREIGN EXCHANGE MARKET The network of banks and financial institutions through which national currencies are exchanged for one another.

45° LINE A line in the first quadrant, passing through the origin, with a slope of 1, which divides the quadrant in half. Along the 45° line, the value of the x-variable is equal to the value of the y-variable.

FORWARD MARKET The market in which transactions are made for future delivery of currency; e.g., 1,000 francs in 90 days at a price set today.

FREE RIDERS People who consume collective goods without contributing to the cost of their production.

FUNCTIONAL DISTRIBUTION OF INCOME The pattern of payments to the factors of production: rent, wages, interest, and profits.

GAINS FROM TRADE The increase in consumption resulting from specialization and exchange.

GAME THEORY A mathematical technique that can provide insight into oligopolistic behavior. "Players" try to reach an optimal position through strategic behavior that takes into account the anticipated moves of other players.

GOLD STANDARD An international monetary system in which currencies were defined in terms of gold, money supplies were tied to gold, and balance of payment deficits were settled in gold.

GOSPLAN The state planning commission in the Soviet Union.

GREAT INDUSTRIALIZATION DEBATE An open debate that took place in the Soviet Union from 1924 to 1928 concerning the correct way to industrialize the economy.

GREAT LEAP FORWARD Communist China's highly overambitious modernization plan that was launched in 1958 to increase per capita income in China by 25 percent in five years.

HART-SCOTT-RODINO ANTITRUST IMPROVEMENT ACT A 1970 act amending the FTC Act to require firms to report mergers or acquisitions to the FTC and Department of Justice prior to their consummation.

HEDGERS People who try to reduce their risk by buying or selling currency for future delivery in the forward market.

HERFINDAHL INDEX An index of concentration that takes into account all the firms in an industry.

HIGH MASS CONSUMPTION The stage of development in which growth settles into a high level of consumption for most members of the society.

HOLDING COMPANIES Firms set up for the sole purpose of owning and controlling other firms.

HORIZONTAL EQUITY A situation that is achieved when all taxpayers in a certain economic category pay the same tax.

HORIZONTAL INTEGRATION The combination of many production operations in the same industry.

HUMAN CAPITAL The investment in human beings to improve the quality of labor skills with education, training, health care, and so on

HUMPHREY-HAWKINS ACT A 1978 amendment to the Employment Act of 1946 that set specific targets for output, employment, and prices.

IMPLICIT COST Cost measured by the value of alternatives given up.

INCLUSIVE UNION A union that attempts to organize all the workers in an industry and maintain a strong bargaining position vis-á-vis management.

INCOME EFFECT When the price of a good or service falls, *ceteris paribus*, the household's real income rises, and the consumer buys more of all normal goods.

INCOME ELASTICITY OF DEMAND A measure of the way in which quantity demanded responds to changes in income.

INCOME-CONSUMPTION CURVE A curve that shows how the consumption of two goods changes as income changes.

INCREASE IN DEMAND A shift in the demand curve indicating that at every price, consumers demand a larger quantity than before.

INCREASE IN SUPPLY A shift in the supply curve indicating that at every price, a larger quantity will be supplied than before.

INCREASING COST INDUSTRY An industry in which expansion of output causes average costs to rise in the long run. The long-run supply curve has a positive slope.

INDEPENDENT VARIABLE The variable, normally measured on the horizontal axis in a coordinate system, in which value is determined outside the system and which determines the value of the dependent variable.

INDIFFERENCE CURVE A graphing of an indifference set. An indifference curve shows all combinations of two commodities which give equal satisfaction.

INDIFFERENCE CURVE ANALYSIS A technique of analyzing consumer behavior that does not require the concept of measurable utility.

INDIFFERENCE MAP A series of indifference curves representing different levels of satisfaction for the consumer.

INDIFFERENCE SET Bundles of goods among which a consumer is indifferent. The bundles yield equal satisfaction.

INDUSTRIAL UNIONS Inclusive unions such as the Steelworkers, Autoworkers, and Teamsters that gain power by organizing all (or a large share) of the workers in an industry.

INDUSTRIAL WORKERS OF THE WORLD (IWW) An international union that organized U.S. steelworkers after World War I. The IWW was viewed as a socialistic organization in the United States, and this contributed to its demise.

INDUSTRY A group of firms producing similar or related products.

INDUSTRY STUDIES Investigations of particular industries to determine the degree of competitive behavior in the industry.

INFERIOR GOOD A good for which demand decreases as income increases.

INJUNCTIONS Court orders in labor union-management disputes to order labor to stop some activity or return to work.

INPUT COEFFICIENT In input-output analysis, the ratio of a particular input to the total outputs in that industry.

INPUT-OUTPUT ANALYSIS An attempt to quantify the flows between different sectors of the economy. Input-output analysis is useful in economic planning.

INSATIABLE WANTS The fact that there can never be enough of everything to satisfy everyone's wants for all goods and services.

INTERDEPENDENT DEMAND The demand for a factor of production depends on the amount of other factors that the firm plans to use.

INTERDEPENDENT UTILITY FUNCTIONS Citizens' well-being that is dependent upon the well-being of others.

INTEREST The return to the capital factor of production.

INTERNALIZE To cause an externality to be incorporated in the market price.

INTERNATIONAL MONETARY FUND (IMF) The agency that supervised the operation of the Bretton Woods system by recording par values, consulting on devaluations/revaluations, and providing a pool of reserves for countries with deficits.

INTERPERSONAL UTILITY COMPARISONS Attempts to compare amounts of utility between consumers.

INVESTMENT Purchases of real, tangible assets, such as machines, factories, or stocks of inventories that are used to produce goods and services.

INVISIBLE HAND The idea advanced by Adam Smith that individuals pursuing their own self-interest produce socially desirable outcomes.

ISOCOST LINE A curve that shows all equal-cost input combinations. It is in effect the firm's budget constraint.

ISOQUANT CURVE A curve that shows all combinations of input quantities that produce a given quantity of output.

KEY CURRENCY A currency used for foreign exchange reserves and for settling transactions between other countries.

KINKED DEMAND CURVE A model used to explain price rigidity under oligopoly. The kink comes from pricing behavior in which other firms' price cuts, but not price increases, are matched.

KNIGHTS OF LABOR Organized by Uriah Stevens in 1869, the Knights of Labor was a secret organization. It won the first major strike in the United States against the railroad industry. The organization had political reformist goals, which led to its demise.

LABOR The physical and intellectual exertion of human beings in the production process.

LABOR THEORY OF VALUE A central element in the theory of Karl Marx. All commodities were reduced to a common denominator of the labor time embodied in the product.

LAND Natural resources that can be used as inputs to production.

LANDRUM-GRIFFIN ACT The act, passed in 1959, aimed at curbing union power; it made unions more democratic, restricted Communist party members and convicted felons from union leadership, and made picketing illegal under certain circumstances.

LAW OF DEMAND The quantity demanded of a good or service is negatively related to its price, *ceteris paribus*.

LEADING SECTORS The development theory calling for concentration on a number of leading sectors that will pull along other sectors in the development process.

LERNER INDEX OF MONOPOLY OF POWER (LMP) An index that measures the gap between price and marginal cost as a proxy for monopoly power.

LIMITED LIABILITY The fact that the stockholders of a corporation cannot be sued for failure of the corporation to pay its debts; only the corporation itself can be sued.

LINKAGE In development economics, the idea of concentrating on the encouragement of a particular sector that will then influence other sectors in the chain of production.

LOCAL MONOPOLY A firm that has monopoly power in a geographic region. Even though close substitutes exist, the distance between sources of supply creates monopolies.

LOGROLLING Vote trading in a legislative process.

LONG RUN The period of time in which all inputs, including plant and equipment, can be varied.

LONG-RUN AVERAGE COST CURVE (LRAC) The lowest attainable average cost of producing any given output. A curve tangent to all the possible short-run cost curves.

LONG-RUN PROFIT MAXIMIZATION The argument that even if managers follow satisficing behavior or constrained sales maximization, they do so only because it leads to higher profits in the long run.

LORENZ CURVE A graph showing the cumulative percentages of income that households receive, ranked from the lowest to the highest.

MACROECONOMICS The study of the economy as a whole, or economic aggregates, such as the level of employment and the growth of total output.

MARGINAL ANALYSIS A technique used to analyze problems in which the results of small changes are examined.

MARGINAL COST The change in total cost from producing one more (or one less) unit of output.

MARGINAL COST PRICING A theoretical technique for forcing a monopoly to behave more like a competitive firm by regulating the monopoly price so that it is equal to marginal cost.

MARGINAL PHYSICAL PRODUCT (MPP) The change in physical output that is produced by a unit change in a factor of production.

MARGINAL PRODUCTIVITY THEORY A theory originally developed by John Bates Clark that explains how the distribution of income comes about. Each factor is paid according to its contribution, or its marginal productivity.

MARGINAL RATE OF SUBSTITUTION The consumer's trade-off between two goods represented on an indifference curve. The slope of the indifference curve represents this trade-off.

MARGINAL RESOURCE COST (MRC) The cost of each additional unit of a productive resource.

MARGINAL REVENUE (MR) The change in total revenue from selling one more (or one less) unit.

MARGINAL REVENUE PRODUCT (MRP) The amount that an additional unit of the variable factor of production adds to a firm's total revenue.

MARGINAL UTILITY The amount of satisfaction provided by one more or one less unit of consumption.

MARKET CLEARING PRICE The equilibrium price. It is market clearing because there are no frustrated purchasers or suppliers.

MARKET CONCENTRATION DOCTRINE A hypothesis that holds that the degree of concentration in an industry is a reliable index of monopoly behavior and performance in that industry.

MARKET DEMAND The summation of all of the individual consumer demand curves. A market demand curve shows what quantity will be demanded over a particular time period by all consumers in a certain market at various prices.

MARKET ECONOMY An economy in which the fundamental questions are answered through the market, relying on self-interested behavior and incentives.

MARKET EQUILIBRIUM The price at which quantity demanded by consumers is equal to quantity supplied by producers; also called market-clearing price.

MARKET POWER The ability of firms or buyers to affect price. Large numbers of buyers and sellers ensure that no one buyer or seller affects price.

MARKET SUPPLY The summation of all of the individual firm supply curves. A market supply curve shows what quantity will be supplied by all firms over a particular time period at various prices.

MARKETING ORDERS A farm program which creates producer cartels that specify how much output a grower can bring to market.

MAXIMUM The point on a graph at which the y, or dependent, variable reaches its highest value.

MEDIATION Third-party intervention in a strike. The mediator attempts to keep the parties together and talking by offering suggestions and clarifying issues.

MERIT GOODS Goods that consumers will not buy in sufficient quantities if they are not compelled to do so by government.

MICROECONOMICS The study of individual market interactions. Microeconomics concentrates on production and consumption by the individual consumer, the firm, and the industry.

MINIMUM The point on the graph at which the y, or dependent, variable reaches its lowest value.

MINIMUM WAGE A price floor imposed by a governmental unit in the labor market.

MIXED CAPITALISM An economy in which most decisions are made individually in the market, with a substantial number made collectively through government.

MIXED ECONOMY An economy in which the fundamental questions are answered partly by market forces and partly by government.

MODEL A set of assumptions and hypotheses that is a simplified description of reality.

MONOPOLY The market structure in which there is a single seller of a product that has no close substitutes.

MONOPOLY POWER The ability to exercise some of the economic effects predicted in the model of pure monopoly.

MONOPOLY RENT SEEKING The efforts and resources expended by those attempting to establish monopolies to earn monopoly profits.

MONOPSONISTIC COMPETITION The market situation that arises when there are relatively large numbers of buyers of a factor of production.

MONOPSONISTIC EXPLOITATION The reduction in wages due to monopsony power. Labor receives less than it would receive in competitive markets.

MONOPSONY A single purchaser of a factor of production.

MULTINATIONAL CORPORATION A firm with headquarters in one country and a majority-owned subsidiary in at least one other country.

NATIONAL LABOR RELATIONS BOARD (NLRB) Established by the Wagner Act (1935), the NLRB was empowered to investigate employer unfair labor practices and to determine legitimate bargaining agents for labor when there were competing unions.

NATIONAL LABOR UNION The first successful union in the United States that had a national scope. Founded in 1867 by William Sylvis, the union quickly grew to 600,000 members but fell apart rapidly after Sylvis' death in 1869.

NATIONAL RECOVERY ADMINISTRATION (NRA) A major New Deal program aimed at business recovery. The NRA was anticompetitive since it allowed and encouraged agreements between firms and was eventually declared unconstitutional.

NATURAL MONOPOLY A monopoly that emerges because of economies of scale. The size of the market is such that there is room for only one optimal-size firm.

NEGATIVE INCOME TAX A transfer from the government to the poor based on a formula similar to the present income tax system. A negative income tax has two components: an income guarantee and a negative tax rate.

NEGATIVE RELATIONSHIP A relationship between two variables in which an increase in the value of one is associated with a decrease in the value of the other.

NEUTRAL TAX A tax that causes no distortion in economic activity.

NEW ECONOMIC POLICY (NEP) An attempt at market socialism from 1921 to 1926 in the Soviet Union.

NEW INTERNATIONAL ECONOMIC ORDER (NIEO) A proposal for a fundamental change in international economic institutions to redistribute income from richer nations to poorer nations.

NONPRICE COMPETITION Competing through advertising, style changes, color changes, and techniques other than lowering price.

NONTARIFF BARRIER A trade restriction other than tariffs and quotas.

NORMAL GOOD A good for which demand increases as income increases.

NORMAL PROFIT The opportunity cost of capital and enterprise. This is the level of profit that is necessary for a firm to remain in a competitive industry.

NORMATIVE ECONOMICS A set of propositions about what ought to be; value judgments about the world.

NORRIS-LA GUARDIA ACT A law passed in 1932 that vastly strengthened the power of labor unions by limiting the court's use of injunctions in labor-management disputes.

(NOT QUITE) LAW OF SUPPLY The *quantity supplied* of a good or service is *usually* a positive function of price, *ceteris paribus*.

NUMBER EQUIVALENT The reciprocal of the Herfindahl Index used as a measure of the theoretical number of equal-sized firms that should be found in an industry.

OLIGOPOLY The market structure in which there are few firms. This causes firms to recognize their interdependence.

OLIGOPSONY The market situation in which there are few buyers of a factor of production.

OPPORTUNITY COST The value of the next best opportunity given up in order to enjoy a particular good or service.

OPTIMAL-SIZE PLANT The plant represented by the short-run average cost curve with the lowest attainable per-unit costs.

ORDINAL UTILITY A utility comparison that only requires that choices be ranked, rather than assigned numerical values.

ORIGIN The intersection of the vertical and horizontal axes of a coordinate system, at which the values of both the x and y variables are zero.

PARITY An attempt to define fair prices for farm products relative to nonfarm products by establishing prices of farm products so as to maintain agricultural purchasing power at some past level.

PARTNERSHIP The form of business enterprise in which there is more than one owner, and the firm does not have a legal existence separate from the owners.

PAYMENT IN KIND (PIK) PROGRAM A program that distributed surplus grain to farmers in exchange for planting less.

PERFECTLY ELASTIC A price elasticity of demand coefficient of infinity. The quantity demanded responds in an infinite way to a change in price. The demand curve is a horizontal line.

PERFECTLY INELASTIC A price elasticity of demand coefficient of zero. There is no response in quantity demanded to changes in price. The demand curve is vertical.

PERSONAL DISTRIBUTION OF INCOME The distribution of income by person or family.

PIE CHART A graphic representation of actual economic data that is expressed as percentage components of a whole, drawn in the shape of a pie. The slices of the pie correspond to the percentage shares of the components.

PLANNING CURVE The long-run average cost curve. In the planning stage, a short-run curve tangent to the long-run curve can be selected.

POINT ELASTICITY The responsiveness of quantity demanded to price at a particular point on a curve.

POSITIVE ECONOMICS A set of propositions about what is, rather than what ought to be.

POSITIVE RELATIONSHIP A relationship between two variables in which an increase in one is associated with an increase in the other, and a decrease in one is associated with a decrease in the other.

PRECONDITIONS FOR TAKEOFF The stage of development in which "uneconomic" culture is overcome, advances in agriculture take place, and an entrepreneurial class of risk takers begins to emerge.

PREDATORY PRICING The act of selling below cost to destroy competitors.

PRESENT VALUE The capitalized value of an item to be paid for or sold in the future. A future value discounted to the present.

PRICE CEILINGS Prices imposed by a governmental unit that are set as a limit. The ceiling is a price that cannot be exceeded.

PRICE CLUSTERS Groupings of prices for similar, but not homogeneous, products.

PRICE DISCRIMINATION The practice of charging different consumers different prices, or a particular consumer different prices, for different quantities purchased.

PRICE ELASTICITY OF DEMAND A measure of the responsiveness of the quantity demanded to changes in price.

PRICE ELASTICITY OF SUPPLY A measure of the responsiveness of the quantity supplied to changes in the price.

PRICE FLOORS Prices established as minimum prices. A governmental unit sets a price that cannot be undercut.

PRICE LEADERSHIP The practice of industry pricing in which other firms follow the pricing initiatives of a particular firm, the price leader.

PRICE SEARCHER A firm that sets price in order to maximize profits. A price-searching firm has monopoly power.

PRICE TAKER A firm in pure competition is a price taker because the firm views itself as having no influence on price. It can sell any amount at the market-clearing price.

PRICE-CONSUMPTION CURVE A curve that shows how the consumption of two goods changes as the price of one of the goods changes.

PRIMARY EFFECT The immediate effect of a change in an economic variable.

PRINCIPLE OF COMPARATIVE ADVANTAGE The idea that output will be maximized if people specialize in those goods in which their opportunity costs are lowest and engage in exchange to obtain the other goods they want.

PRINCIPLE OF DIMINISHING MARGINAL RATE OF SUBSTITUTION As a consumer receives more and more of a particular good, its value in terms of other goods declines. This is represented by the changing slope of the indifference curve.

PRINCIPLE OF DIMINISHING RETURNS As more and more units of a variable factor are added to a set of fixed factors, the resulting additions to output eventually will become increasingly smaller.

PRIVATIZATION The transfer of governmental activities and/or assets to the private sector.

PRODUCT CYCLE A series of stages, from development to standardization, through which a new product passes; the country of export may change during this period.

PRODUCT GROUP A classification for a set of goods that is differentiated but has a large number of close substitutes.

PRODUCT MARKET Markets in which goods and services produced by firms are sold.

PRODUCTION The transformation of inputs into marketable outputs.

PRODUCTION FUNCTION A description of the amounts of output expected from various combinations of input usage.

PRODUCTION POSSIBILITIES CURVE A graph that depicts the various combinations of two goods that can be produced with available resources in an economy.

PROFIT The return to enterprise as a reward for organizing production, innovation, and risk taking. Profit is the residual after all other factors have been paid.

PROGRESSIVE TAX A tax that takes a greater percentage of income as income rises.

PROPERTY LAW Law that concerns the enforcement of property rights.

PROPERTY RIGHTS The legal right to a specific property, including the rights to own, buy, sell, or use in specific ways. Markets and exchanges can occur only if individuals have property rights to goods, services, and productive resources.

PROPORTIONAL TAX A tax that takes a constant percentage of income as income rises.

PUBLIC "BADS" Goods for which it is possible to pass some costs along to other people (negative external effect).

PUBLIC GOODS Goods that are nonrival in consumption and not subject to exclusion.

PURE COMPETITION The market structure in which there are many sellers and buyers. The firms produce an homogeneous product, and there is free entry and exit of these firms to and from the industry.

PURE OLIGOPOLY An oligopoly that produces a homogeneous product.

QUALITY CIRCLES Groups of workers organized to discuss production problems and to suggest solutions.

QUOTA A physical limit on the amount of a good or service that can be imported during a given time period.

REDISTRIBUTION Actions by government that transfer income from one group to another group.

REGRESSIVE TAX A tax that takes a lower percentage of income as income rises.

RENT The return to the land factor of production.

RENT CONTROL Price ceilings that are imposed by governmental units on apartment rentals.

RENT DEFENDING Defense of consumer surplus from rent seekers.

RENT SEEKING The commitment of scarce resources to capture artificially created rents.

REPRESENTATIVE FIRM A typical or "average" firm in pure competition.

RESERVE ARMY OF THE UNEMPLOYED The large group of unemployed laborers that Marx predicted would unite, ultimately developing socialism.

RESERVES The international media of exchange. Under the Bretton Woods system, reserves included gold, the U.S. dollar, and other major currencies.

RESIDUAL CLAIMANTS Individuals, or groups of individuals, who share profits.

REVOLUTIONARY UNIO Unions that sought changes in the social order.

RIGHT-TO-WORK LAWS State laws that allow people to hold jobs without belonging to unions.

ROBINSON-PATMAN ACT A 1936 act that amended the Clayton Act to make predatory pricing illegal.

ROUNDABOUT PRODUCTION The production of capital goods (tools) that enhance productive capacity and ultimately allow increased output.

RULE OF REASON Indicated that monopolies that behaved well did not violate the Sherman Antitrust Act. The court held that the existence of competitors was sufficient to demonstrate "reasonable behavior."

SATISFICING Management does not seek to maximize profits but rather seeks target levels of output and profits that are satisfactory to the ownership interests.

SCARCITY The central economic problem that there are not sufficient resources to produce everything that individuals want.

SCATTER DIAGRAM A graph that plots actual pairs of values of two related variables to determine whether there is any apparent, consistent relationship between them.

SECONDARY BOYCOTTS Union actions to stop one employer from doing business with another employer. This involves action to create pressures on third parties.

SECONDARY EFFECT An effect indirectly related to the immediate effect that is often smaller and only felt with the passage of time.

SELF-INTERESTED BEHAVIOR A basic assumption of economic theory that individual decision makers do what is best for themselves.

SEPARATION OF OWNERSHIP AND CONTROL Corporations are run by hired managers, not owners. These managers might operate by some principle other than profit maximization. This behavior results if managers have goals different than the owners' and if the owners cannot control the managers.

SETTLEMENT ACCOUNT That part of the balance of payments account that explains how the deficit or surplus was financed, including gold and foreign exchange flows and government acquisition of currency.

SHADOW PRICES Simulated market prices used by economic planners.

SHARED MONOPOLY The idea that oligopolists coordinate and share markets to act as a monopoly.

SHERMAN ANTITRUST ACT Passed in 1890, the first antitrust law. Section 1 of the act declared every contract, combination, or conspiracy in restraint of trade to be illegal. Section 2 made it illegal to monopolize or attempt to monopolize.

SHIRKING Not putting forth agreed-to effort.

SHORT RUN The period of time too short to vary all the factors of production. Short-run decisions are those concerned with using the existing plant more or less extensively.

SHORTAGE The amount that consumers wish to purchase at some price exceeds the amount suppliers wish to supply. A shortage can occur only on a lasting basis when a price ceiling is in effect.

SHORT-RUN SUPPLY CURVE The supply curve in the short run—the period in which the size of the plant cannot be varied. In pure competition, the short-run marginal cost curve is the short-run supply curve.

SHUTDOWN POINT The level of output at which the firm minimizes its losses by ceasing operation.

SINGLE TAX A tax on land proposed by Henry George to capture the economic rent on land.

SLOPE The ratio of the change in the dependent (y) variable to the change in the independent (x) variable.

SOCIAL COSTS Costs that are borne by society or some group without compensation. Externalities impose damages, or social costs, on groups in the population.

SOCIAL SCIENCE A discipline that studies the behavior of human beings, individually and in groups, and examines their interactions.

SOCIALISM An economic system in which the nonhuman means of production are owned by society or the state.

SOCIALIST CONTROVERSY A debate started by Ludwig von Mises and Oskar Lange concerning the feasibility of planning without markets.

SOIL BANK PROGRAM A program which attempts to raise farm income by paying farmers to allow their land to lie idle.

SOIL CONSERVATION SERVICE A federal agency chartered to aid farmers in the conservation of land as a scarce natural resource.

SOLE PROPRIETORSHIP The form of business enterprise in which no legal distinction is made between the firm and its owner.

SPECIALIZATION Limiting production activities to one of a small number of goods and services that one produces best in order to exchange for other goods

SPECIE FLOW MECHANISM The automatic correction of deficits and surpluses through the effects of gold flows on money supplies.

SPECULATORS People who assume risk in the forward market by guaranteeing a price to a hedger.

STABILIZATION Actions by government to reduce fluctuations in output, employment, and prices.

STANDARD INDUSTRIAL CLASSIFICATION (SIC) SYSTEM A system devised by the U.S. Census Bureau for classifying industries. The SIC system divides the economy into about 400 four-digit industries.

STATISTICAL DISCREPANCY That part of the balance of payments account that reflects imperfect information or unrecorded transactions.

STOCK VARIABLE A variable that is defined at a point in time.

STOCKHOLDERS The owners of a corporation.

STOCKS Certificates of ownership in a corporation.

SUBSTITUTE GOODS Goods that replace the consumption of other goods.

SUBSTITUTION EFFECT When the price of a good falls, it becomes less expensive relative to all other goods and more of it is consumed, substituting for other goods.

SUPPLY The quantity of goods offered for sale over a particular time period at various prices.

SUPPLY CURVE A graphical representation of a supply schedule showing the quantity supplied over a particular time period at various prices.

SUPPLY SCHEDULE A tabular listing that shows quantity supplied over a particular time period at various prices.

SUPPORT PRICES Price floors in agriculture.

SURPLUS The amount that suppliers wish to supply at some price exceeds the amount that consumers wish to purchase. A surplus can only occur on a lasting basis when a price floor is in effect.

SURPLUS VALUE The difference between the labor value of goods produced and the subsistence wages received by workers.

TACIT COLLUSION Unorganized and unstated attempts to practice joint action.

TAFT-HARTLEY ACT Passed in 1947 over President Truman's veto, the act was designed to reverse some of the labor excesses created by the Wagner Act. The Taft-Hartley Act shifted some legal rights back to the employers.

TAKEOFF The stage of development in which there is a significant increase in the rate of saving. Leading sectors develop and pull others along, and sustained growth is achieved.

TANGENT LINE A line just touching a curve (nonlinear graphic relationship) at a point, used to measure the slope. The slope of the tangent line at that point is equal to the slope of the curve at that point.

TARGET PRICES Prices that the government determines are fair to farmers. After the market clearing price is determined, the government pays each farmer the difference between the target price and the market price.

TARIFF A tax on imported goods and services.

TARIFF QUOTA A limit on the amount of a good or service that can be imported without paying a tariff. Amounts in excess of that limit are subject to a tariff.

TAX EFFICIENCY A measure of how a tax affects economic activity.

TAX INCIDENCE The place where the tax burden of any tax actually rests; those who pay the tax after all shifting has occurred.

TEAMS Groups of employees that work together to produce something.

TECHNICAL EFFICIENCY A method of production that minimizes physical usage of inputs according to some specific rule.

TECHNOLOGICALLY DETERMINED DEMAND The demand for a factor of production is determined by the techniques of production and the level of technology used.

TERMS OF TRADE The rate at which one product is exchanged for another.

TESTABLE HYPOTHESIS An inference from economic theory that can be subjected to empirical testing.

THEORY A set of principles that can be used to make inferences about the world.

THEORY Z A management idea that workers are motivated to perform if they are made part of the management process.

TORT A wrongful action (or failure to act) that causes damage to the property of another individual.

TORT LAW Law that deals with intentional and unintentional wrongs inflicted by one party on another.

TOTAL COST (*TC*) The sum of all the costs of production for a given level of output.

TOTAL FIXED COST (*TFC*) The cost of the fixed factors of production. Total fixed cost does not vary in the short run.

TOTAL PHYSICAL PRODUCT (*TPP*) The amount that a firm produces in physical units.

TOTAL REVENUE (*TR*) The quantity of a good or service that a firm sells, multiplied by its price.

TOTAL VARIABLE COST (*TVC*) The total of costs that vary directly with output, increasing as more output is produced.

TRADITIONAL ECONOMY An economy in which the fundamental questions are answered by custom or long-standing rules of behavior.

TRADITIONAL SOCIETY A society largely governed by tradition in which economic decisions are made on the basis of custom and obligation.

TRANSACTION COSTS Costs associated with gathering information about markets (prices and availabilities) for consuming or producing.

TRANSFER PAYMENTS Income payments to individuals who do not have to provide any goods or services in exchange.

TREBLE DAMAGES A provision under the Sherman Antitrust Act that victims of monopoly can recover three times the damages they have sustained.

TRUSTS Legal organizations set up to control the stock of other companies through boards of trustees.

TYING CONTRACTS Agreements between producers and retailers whereby a retailer must agree to handle certain items as a prerequisite to being allowed to handle other items.

UNINTENDED EFFECTS Effects of policy that are unanticipated by policymakers but which become evident through careful economic analysis.

UNION SHOPS Firms where union membership is necessary for a worker to remain employed.

UNIT ELASTIC A price elasticity of demand coefficient of one. The change in quantity demanded responds at the same rate as any change in price. The demand curve is a rectangular hyperbola.

UNITED MINE WORKERS (UMW) The industrial union for mine workers.

USER CHARGE A fee charged to consumers by governments for the provision of certain goods and services.

UTIL An arbitrary unit used to measure utility.

UTILITY The satisfaction that an individual receives from consuming a good or service.

UTILITY FUNCTION A preference function ordering a consumer's desire to consume differing amounts of goods.

UTILITY MAXIMIZATION The way a consumer adjusts consumption, given a budget constraint and a set of prices, in order to attain the highest total amount of satisfaction.

VALUE OF THE MARGINAL PRODUCT (*VMP*) The value of the marginal product is found by multiplying the marginal physical product by the price at which the firm can sell the product.

VARIABLE FACTORS The factors of production that can be increased or decreased in the short run.

VERTICAL EQUITY A situation in which individuals of different economic categories pay suitably different taxes.

VERTICAL INTEGRATION The combination of many steps in the production process.

VICIOUS CIRCLE OF POVERTY Little investment because of a low level of income, and a low level of income because of little investment.

WAGES The return to the labor factor of production.

WAGNER ACT A law passed in 1935 that gave employees the right to organize and bargain collectively and outlawed certain employer unfair labor practices.

WAR COMMUNISM An economic system that was imposed by Lenin in Russia immediately after the Bolshevik Revolution. It is called War Communism because there was a continuing civil war at the time.

WELFARE UNIONS Unions that had lofty ideals of social welfare and sought to establish worker cooperatives.

WHEELER-LEA ACT A 1938 act amending the FTC Act to make unfair or deceptive acts or practices in commerce illegal.

WILDCAT STRIKES Local strikes that are unauthorized by the national union.

WORKERS' SELF-MANAGEMENT The system in Yugoslavia in which workers direct and have a financial stake in the firm in which they work.

WORKFARE Requirement that those receiving welfare, who are able to work, take jobs or participate in training programs in order to be eligible for benefits.

X-AXIS The horizontal line in a coordinate system that measures the values of the independent variable; horizontal axis.

X-INEFFICIENCY The inefficiency associated with the "slack" management of monopoly. The monopoly escapes the market discipline and is therefore less conscious of management efficiencies.

Y-AXIS The upright line in a coordinate system that measures the values of the dependent variable; vertical axis.

YELLOW-DOG CONTRACTS Contracts in which an employee must agree to refrain from union activity as a precondition for employment.

INDEX